American Economic History

Essays in Interpretation

THE LIPPINCOTT AMERICAN HISTORY SERIES

Under the Editorship of

Robert F. Byrnes, Indiana University

Robert D. Cross, Columbia University

J. B. Lippincott Company

American Economic History

Essays in Interpretation

Edited by

STANLEY COBEN *Princeton University*

and FOREST G. HILL *University of Texas*

Philadelphia and New York

Preface

As editors we faced many problems in making our final selections for this volume of interpretive essays on American economic history. Although we have not tried to impose a central theme, we have sought essays which highlight the fundamental forces, problems, and achievements which characterize this country's economic development. We therefore have selected interpretive analyses—typically representing recent scholarly work on leading issues—provocative of further discussion and inquiry.

Individual selections stress the role, for example, of such varied influences as religious or ethical values, political institutions, and technological and organizational advances. As a whole, these essays reveal the extent to which our economic development has been affected by values peculiar to Western society, and in some respects especially powerful in the United States. They also make it clear that beginning early in our history agricultural production for the market, urban-commercial development, and transportation improvements advance together almost of necessity. Sometimes this expansion proceeded at a more rapid pace than the ability of world markets to absorb our goods. In addition, the selections point to unresolved problems such as farm surpluses, erratic economic growth, recurring unemployment, and poverty. Some of the most stimulating recent research in American economic history demonstrates that government has always assumed a heavy responsibility for dealing with problems and for ensuring economic growth.

As we survey these selections, we are forcefully reminded that American economic history is no separate compartment or narrow aspect of this nation's historical development. Quite the contrary: we continually rediscover the relevance that political, social, scientific, and intellectual history, and of course business history, necessarily have for the interpretation of American economic history. Sharing this belief, we hope that our experiment in co-operation between a historian and an economist has enabled us to combine our perspectives and experience in a way that will be helpful to other instructors and students of economic history.

This book's origins lie in our classroom experience. We are convinced that some of the most illustrative, as well as challenging, material for the study of American economic history is to be found in journal articles or as chapters in specialized books. These can hardly be assigned as reading for students when the libraries of even the most affluent universities often contain only one copy. All too frequently, fine articles appear in journals to which college libraries do not subscribe, or did not in the past.

Furthermore, increasing concern with worldwide problems of economic development has recently given rise to a wealth of excellent articles reinterpreting important aspects of the American experience. With few exceptions, textbook authors have been slow to adopt the new research and to assess the new interpretations. Finally, it seems to us that students, especially those in advanced courses in economic history, can gain much from studying the thinking and the methods of some of the best minds at work on the subject. Such wide contact cannot be achieved through the assignment of a handful of books, and short selections from monographs pose many problems for both teacher and students. For these reasons, we have initiated this experiment in interdisciplinary cooperation.

The editors are grateful to Robert A. Lively, of Princeton University, for his careful analysis of the entire volume and to Alex Fraser of J. B. Lippincott Company, whose enthusiasm and sound advice helped us to overcome many obstacles.

December 15, 1965   *Stanley Cohen*
                                                                     Forest G. Hill

Contents

PART ONE

Emergence of a Secular Society

Economic development and social change seem to be inextricably connected. While the history of western Europe and the United States provides evidence enough of that relationship, analysts of economic growth have found additional proof while puzzling over the experience of nations still attempting to industrialize.[1]

In *Selection One*, R. H. Tawney presents a classic analysis of dramatic changes in what he calls "the system of valuations, preferences and ideals—the social environment within which individual character functions"—which prepared the way for the great burst of industrial activity in western Europe and the United States in the nineteenth century. It is one of Tawney's theses that the effort to establish Calvinist social discipline in the New World was a last-gasp effort to maintain the fading influence of religious ideals on economic life. The England of Bacon and Shakespeare, although still largely feudal, was being transformed into a commercial civilization. In the American colonies the changes in "social environment" and in "individual character" proceeded at a different pace than in England, probably slower at first and then more rapidly. Without an understanding of these changes, it is difficult to account for the social ferment which stimulated industrialization in the colonies, providing a necessary foundation for the stupendous economic accomplishments of nineteenth-century Americans.

[1] See for example, Thomas C. Cochran, "Cultural Factors in Economic Growth," *Journal of Economic History*, XX (December, 1960), 515–530; Thomas W. Shea, Jr., "Barriers to Economic Development in Traditional Societies: Malabar, A Case Study," *Journal of Economic History*, XIX (December, 1959), 504–522.

1

If the settlers of America did not set out immediately to make full use of the boundless riches that surrounded them, it was not altogether because of the handicaps frequently mentioned: lack of capital and of skilled workers, competition from European goods, and the difficulties of conquering the wilderness. Early Americans placed a much larger premium than their descendants did on religious salvation and on communal rather than individual welfare. Although this country was settled just as the pace of economic activity in Europe accelerated noticeably, most Europeans as well as the European settlers in America remained somewhat medieval in economic outlook. These attitudes posed an obstacle to the accumulation of capital and to the achievement of industrial and mercantile skills. Richard B. Morris and Jonathan Grossman (*Selection Two*) describe some of the limitations imposed by Calvinist morality upon economic behavior, particularly government attempts to set "fair" prices and wages, which minimized earnings for craftsmen and merchants. Obviously, Christian ethics and business practices were not yet separated in the American mind. That unrestricted exploitation of all available resources which encouraged rapid growth in the nineteenth century was not yet a part of the American creed.

There were groups within the colonies, however, whose economic experiences led them first to act counter to the prevailing ethics, then to question the ethical code itself. In *Selection Three* Thomas J. Wertenbaker shows how New England merchants—and to a lesser extent land-owners and fishermen—found that commercial practices of pricing and profit-making conflicted with accepted morality. At first the merchants suffered at the hands of civil authorities. Gradually, as a new generation replaced the original settlers and new merchants came from the more secular atmosphere of the British port cities, a large portion of the mercantile class separated itself from the established religion, repudiated old standards of economic behavior, and displayed a more uninhibited entrepreneurial spirit.[2]

In the southern colonies also, a well-to-do group of planters,

---

[2] For a superb description of these changes among Massachusetts merchants, see Bernard Bailyn, *The New England Merchants in the Seventeenth Century* (Cambridge, Mass.: Harvard University Press, 1955); also available in a paperback edition published by Harper & Row, 1964.

lawyers, and merchants was susceptible to the pragmatic ideals of post-Restoration England. The planters, along with the merchants and lawyers who depended on the plantation economy for their economic well-being, soon found themselves tied to an international trading system, dominated by credit, and subject to manipulation.

The career of Daniel Dulany of Maryland reveals a good deal about the accumulation of wealth in the American colonies and about the changing value system as well. A poor boy, almost auctioned off as an indentured servant to pay his passage from England, Dulany rose from clerk in a law office to become one of the most successful attorneys in eighteenth-century Maryland, as well as a large-scale land speculator, money lender, and investor in promising industrial enterprises. Typically, in a land where the government controlled huge areas of unsettled territory and could issue paper money almost at whim, this successful businessman served also in the highest colonial political offices. In *Selection Four* Aubrey C. Land describes Dulany's career, pointing out that the originator of the Dulany family fortunes made money any way that he could, including trade in slaves. In one venture, he bought the notes of a local planter, foreclosed, and thereby obtained control over land, slaves, and goods worth far more than the face value of the notes.

Among Dulany's successful ventures was his investment in the Baltimore Company, one of the largest iron-producing firms in the colonies. Keach Johnson (*Selection Five*) finds that the mercantile experiences of the founders was a key factor in the company's success. Faced with a small domestic market for their output, the Baltimore Company was obliged to seek markets abroad. Only the partners' capital, trading experience, and contacts with British merchants enabled them to explore the potential markets until customers could be found for a large annual production. Experience gained in the tobacco trade—which also involved sale of raw or semifinished materials—was an essential ingredient in the commercial success of these Chesapeake area industrialists. For similar reasons manufacturers in the northern colonies found mercantile experience an important asset.[3]

Another disadvantage under which colonial entrepreneurs

[3] See James B. Hedges, *The Browns of Providence Plantation—Colonial Years* (Cambridge, Mass.: Harvard University Press, 1952).

labored was a general shortage of currency. To some extent this can be attributed to British restrictions on the minting of coins in America and to the unfavorable balance of trade, especially with Great Britain. Until 1764, however, the colonies could and did issue paper money. E. James Ferguson suggests in *Selection Six* that, contrary to the views of earlier historians, the quantities of currency issued were not large in comparison to the volume of trade and were preferable to the paralyzing effects of an insufficient medium of exchange. Perhaps the most important questions to be asked about colonial money are why so little was issued and why the British government, experienced since the early eighteenth century in using notes of the Bank of England, did not help the colonies establish a sounder financial system.

Curtis P. Nettels (*Selection Seven*) cites evidence that British imperial regulation brought the colonists benefits as well as handicaps. Not only were certain American products given protection in the most lucrative market of the world—Great Britain—but England poured money into the colonies during the wars with France. American-built ships and American tobacco, indigo, naval stores, and bar iron found their primary market in the mother country. Partly as a result of encouragement from England, the colonial merchants, planters, and their legal advisors accumulated the wealth and experience which enabled them to promote a successful revolution when British trade restrictions tightened intolerably after 1763.

Despite the advantages of colonial status, the Revolution seems to have had a liberating effect upon the American economy. Clarence L. Ver Steeg points out in *Selection Eight* that while the British market for indigo was lost to southern planters, cotton production was thereby stimulated. Northern merchants lost much of their West Indian trade and turned instead to Asia. Businessmen widened their contacts among fellow colonists, partnerships expanded, and new products were manufactured and distributed here in larger quantities to meet wartime needs. Use of paper money far exceeded pre-war levels. Able minds such as those of Alexander Hamilton and Robert Morris explored problems of national development. Ver Steeg points to this and other evidence supporting his conclusion that the American Revolution had far-reaching economic, as well as social and political, consequences.

More specific evidence about the economic effects of the Revolution is offered by Robert K. Lamb (*Selection Nine*). Lamb contends that in the New England commercial towns groups of leading families dominated both economic and political life even before the Revolution. Members of these families who sided with the rebels emerged from the war wealthier than ever and in a position to exploit the new technology which already was the basis of rapid industrialization in England. He believes that the banking, currency, and tariff policies of the new government were determined by the leading families and their political representatives. Lamb may exaggerate the effect on national politics of family or even of class influence. Nevertheless, government policies did encourage the accumulation of large reservoirs of capital. These, when invested in successful commercial and manufacturing enterprises, created numerous opportunities for ambitious Americans with and without illustrious family connections.

By the time the French aristocrat Alexis de Tocqueville visited the United States in 1831–32, he found a people vastly different in important respects from the settlers who had left Europe in the seventeenth century. The intertwined religious and secular values of the early colonist had been trampled in the furious rush of the later American for "this vast booty that fortune offers him." Analyzing the "basic democrat" revealed by our most perceptive visitor, Marvin Meyers (*Selection Ten*) finds that Tocqueville's "eager and apprehensive men of small property" believed that "money and goods alone [were] legitimate counters for the social competition of dissociated equals." Nineteenth-century Americans as described by Tocqueville may remind the reader of Tawney's observation (*Selection One*) that "From a spiritual being, who, in order to survive, must devote a reasonable attention to economic interest, man seems sometimes to have become an economic animal, who will be prudent, nevertheless, if he takes due precautions to assure his spiritual well-being." But it was these same enterprising "democrats" who, in their unleashed greed as well as their ingenuity, created an economy of hitherto undreamed-of wealth.

The Protestant Ethic in America

1. From Religion and the Rise of Capitalism

R. H. Tawney

Of English-speaking communities, that in which the social discipline of the Calvinist Church-State was carried to the furthest extreme was the Puritan theocracy of New England. Its practice had more affinity with the iron rule of Calvin's Geneva than with the individualistic tendencies of contemporary English Puritanism. In that happy, bishopless Eden, where men desired only to worship God "according to the simplicitie of the gospel and to be ruled by the laws of God's word,"[1] not only were "tobacco and immodest fashions and costly apparel," and "that vain custom of drinking to one another," forbidden to true professors, but the Fathers adopted towards that "notorious evil . . . whereby most men walked in all their commerce—to buy as cheap and sell as dear as they can,"[2] an attitude which possibly would not be wholly congenial to their more businesslike descendants. At an early date in the history of Massachusetts a minister had called attention to the recrudescence of the old Adam—"profit being the chief aim and not the propagation of religion"—and Governor Bradford, observing uneasily how men grew "in their outward estates," remarked that the increase in material prosperity "will be the ruin of New England, at least of the Churches of God there."[3] Sometimes Providence smote the exploiter. The immigrant who organized the first American Trust—he owned the only milch cow on board and sold the milk at 2*d.* a quart "being after at a sermon wherein oppression was complained of . . . fell distracted."[4] Those who escaped the judgment of Heaven had to face the civil authorities and the Church, which, in the infancy of the colony, were the same thing.

Naturally the authorities regulated prices, limited the rate of interest, fixed a maximum wage, and whipped incorrigible idlers; for these things had been done even in the house of bondage from which they fled. What

[1] W. B. Weeden, *Economic and Social History of New England,* 1890, vol. i, p. 11. The words are Governor Bradford's.
[2] *Winthrop's Journal "History of New England,"* 1630–49, ed. J. K. Hosmer, 1908, vol. i, pp. 134, 325; vol. ii, p. 20.
[3] Weeden, *op. cit.,* vol. i, pp. 125, 158.
[4] Winthrop, *op. cit.,* vol. ii, p. 20.

was more distinctive of the children of light was their attempt to apply the same wholesome discipline to the elusive category of business profits. The price of cattle, the Massachusetts authorities decreed, was to be determined, not by the needs of the buyer, but so as to yield no more than a reasonable return to the seller.[5] Against those who charged more, their wrath was that of Moses descending to find the chosen people worshipping a golden calf. What little emotion they had to spare from their rage against religious freedom, they turned against economic license. Roger Williams touched a real affinity when, in his moving plea for tolerance, he argued that, though extortion was an evil, it was an evil the treatment of which should be left to the discretion of the civil authorities.[6]

Consider the case of Mr. Robert Keane. His offense, by general consent, was black. He kept a shop in Boston, in which he took "in some . . . above 6d. in the shilling profit; in some above 8d.; and in some small things above two for one"; and this, though he was "an ancient professor of the gospel, a man of eminent parts, wealthy and having but one child, having come over for conscience' sake and for the advancement of the gospel." The scandal was terrible. Profiteers were unpopular—"the cry of the country was great against oppression"—and the grave elders reflected that a reputation for greed would injure the infant community, lying as it did "under the curious observation of all Churches and civil States in the world." In spite of all, the magistrates were disposed to be lenient. There was no positive law in force limiting profits; it was not easy to determine what profits were fair; the sin of charging what the market could stand was not peculiar to Mr. Keane; and, after all, the law of God required no more than double restitution. So they treated him mercifully, and fined him only £200.

Here, if he had been wise, Mr. Keane would have let the matter drop. But, like some others in a similar position, he damned himself irretrievably by his excuses. Summoned before the church of Boston, he first of all "did with tears acknowledge and bewail his covetous and corrupt heart," and then was rash enough to venture on an explanation, in which he argued that the tradesman must live, and how could he live, if he might not make up for a loss on one article by additional profit on another? Here was a text on which no faithful pastor could refrain from enlarging. The minister of Boston pounced on the opportunity, and took occasion "in his public exercise the next lecture day to lay open the error of such false principles, and to give some rules of direction in the case. Some false principles were these:—

"1. That a man might sell as dear as he can, and buy as cheap as he can.

---

[5] J. A. Doyle, *The English in America*, vol. ii, 1887, p. 57; the price of cattle "must not be judged by urgent necessity, but by resonable profit."
[6] Roger Williams, *The Bloudy Tenent of Persecution*, 1644, chap. lv.

"2. If a man lose by casualty of sea, etc., in some of his commodities, he may raise the price of the rest.

"3. That he may sell as he bought, though he paid too dear, and though the commodity be fallen, etc.

"4. That, as a man may take the advantage of his own skill or ability, so he may of another's ignorance or necessity.

"5. Where one gives time for payment, he is to take like recompense of one as of another."

The rules for trading were not less explicit:—

"1. A man may not sell above the current price, i.e., such a price as is usual in the time and place, and as another (who knows the worth of the commodity) would give for it if he had occasion to use it; as that is called current money which every man will take, etc.

"2. When a man loseth in his commodity for want of skill, etc., he must look at it as his own fault or cross, and therefore must not lay it upon another.

"3. Where a man loseth by casualty of sea, etc., it is a loss cast upon himself by Providence, and he may not ease himself of it by casting it upon another; for so a man should seem to provide against all providences, etc., that he should never lose; but where there is a scarcity of the commodity, there men may raise their price; for now it is a hand of God upon the commodity, and not the person.

"4. A man may not ask any more for his commodity than his selling price, as Ephron to Abraham: the land is worth thus much."

It is unfortunate that the example of Ephron was not remembered in the case of transactions affecting the lands of Indians, to which it might have appeared peculiarly appropriate. In negotiating with these children of the devil, however, the saints of God considered the dealings of Israel with Gibeon a more appropriate precedent.

The sermon was followed by an animated debate within the Church. It was moved, amid quotations from I Cor. v. II, that Mr. Keane should be excommunicated. That he might be excommunicated, if he were a covetous person within the meaning of the text, was doubted as little as that he had recently given a pitiable exhibition of covetousness. The question was only whether he had erred through ignorance or carelessness, or whether he had acted "against his conscience or the very light of nature"—whether, in short, his sin was accidental or a trade. In the end he escaped with his fine and admonition.[7]

If the only Christian documents which survived were the New Testament and the records of the Calvinist Churches in the age of the Reformation, to suggest a connection between them more intimate than a

---

[7] Winthrop, *op. cit.*, vol. i, pp. 315–18. A similar set of rules as to the conduct of the Christian in trade are given by Bunyan in *The Life and Death of Mr. Badman*, 1905 ed., pp. 118–22.

coincidence of phraseology would appear, in all probability, a daring extravagance. Legalistic, mechanical, without imagination or compassion, the work of a jurist and organizer of genius, Calvin's system was more Roman than Christian, and more Jewish than either. That it should be as much more tyrannical than the medieval Church, as the Jacobin Club was than the *ancien régime,* was inevitable. Its meshes were finer, its zeal and its efficiency greater. And its enemies were not merely actions and writings, but thoughts.

The tyranny with which it is reproached by posterity would have been regarded by its champions as a compliment. In the struggle between liberty and authority, Calvinism sacrificed liberty, not with reluctance, but with enthusiasm. For the Calvinist Church was an army marching back to Canaan, under orders delivered once for all from Sinai, and the aim of its leaders was the conquest of the Promised Land, not the consolation of stragglers or the encouragement of laggards. In war the classical expedient is a dictatorship. The dictatorship of the ministry appeared as inevitable to the whole-hearted Calvinist as the Committee of Public Safety to the men of 1793, or the dictatorship of the proletariat to an enthusiastic Bolshevik. If it reached its zenith where Calvin's discipline was accepted without Calvin's culture and intellectual range, in the orgies of devil worship with which a Cotton and an Endicott shocked at last even the savage superstition of New England, that result was only to be expected.

The best that can be said of the social theory and practice of early Calvinism is that they were consistent. Most tyrannies have contented themselves with tormenting the poor. Calvinism had little pity for poverty; but it distrusted wealth, as it distrusted all influences that distract the aim or relax the fibers of the soul, and, in the first flush of its youthful austerity, it did its best to make life unbearable for the rich. Before the Paradise of earthly comfort it hung a flaming brand, waved by the implacable shades of Moses and Aaron.[8]

The England of Shakespeare and Bacon was still largely medieval in its economic organization and social outlook, more interested in maintaining customary standards of consumption than in accumulating capital for future production, with an aristocracy contemptuous of the economic virtues, a peasantry farming for subsistence amid the organized confusion of the open-field village, and a small, if growing, body of jealously conservative craftsmen. In such a society Puritanism worked like the yeast which sets the whole mass fermenting. It went through its slack and loosely knit texture like a troop of Cromwell's Ironsides through the

[8] I owe this phrase to the excellent book of J. T. Adams, *The Founding of New England.*

disorderly cavalry of Rupert. Where, as in Ireland, the elements were so alien that assimilation was out of the question, the result was a wound that festered for three centuries. In England the effect was that at once of an irritant and of a tonic. Puritanism had its own standards of social conduct, derived partly from the obvious interests of the commercial classes, partly from its conception of the nature of God and the destiny of man. These standards were in sharp antithesis, both to the considerable surviving elements of feudalism in English society, and to the policy of the authoritarian State, with its ideal of an ordered and graded society, whose different members were to be maintained in their traditional status by the pressure and protection of a paternal monarchy. Sapping the former by its influence and overthrowing the latter by direct attack, Puritanism became a potent force in preparing the way for the commercial civilization which finally triumphed at the Revolution.

The complaint that religious radicalism, which aimed at upsetting the government of the Church, went hand in hand with an economic radicalism, which resented the restraints on individual self-interest imposed in the name of religion or of social policy, was being made by the stricter school of religious opinion quite early in the reign of Elizabeth.[9] Seventeenth-century writers repeated the charge that the Puritan conscience lost its delicacy where matters of business were concerned, and some of them were sufficiently struck by the phenomenon to attempt an historical explanation of it. The example on which they usually seized—the symbol of a supposed general disposition to laxity—was the indulgence shown by Puritan divines in the particular matter of moderate interest. It was the effect, so the picturesque story ran,[10] of the Marian persecution. The refugees who fled the continent could not start business in a foreign country. If, driven by necessity, they invested their capital and lived on the proceeds, who could quarrel with so venial a lapse in so good a cause? Subsequent writers embellished the picture. The redistribution of property at the time of the Dissolution, and the expansion of trade in the middle of the century, had led, one of them argued, to a great increase in the volume of credit transactions. The opprobrium which attached to loans at interest—"a sly and forbid practice"—not only among Romanists and Anglicans, but among honest Puritans, played into the hands of the less scrupulous members of "the faction." Disappointed in

---

[9] See, e.g., Thos. Wilson, A Discourse upon Usury, Preface, 1925 ed., p. 178: "There bee two sortes of men that are alwayes to bee looked upon very narroly, the one is the dissembling gospeller, and the other is the wilfull and indurate papiste. The first under colour of religion overthroweth all religion, and bearing good men in hande that he loveth playnesse, useth covertelie all deceypte that maye bee, and for pryvate gayne undoeth the common welfare of man. And touching thys sinne of usurie, none doe more openly offende in thys behalfe than do these counterfeite professours of thys pure religion."

[10] Fenton, A Treatise of Usurie, 1612, pp. 60–1.

politics, they took to money-lending, and, without venturing to justify usury in theory, defended it in practice. "Without the scandal of a recantation, they contrived an expedient, by maintaining that, though usury for the name were stark naught, yet for widows, orphans and other impotents (therein principally comprising the saints under persecution) it was very tolerable, because profitable, and in a manner necessary." Naturally, Calvin's doctrine as to the legitimacy of moderate interest was hailed by these hypocrites with a shout of glee. "It took with the brethren like polygamy with the Turks, recommended by the example of divers zealous ministers, who themselves desired to pass for orphans of the first rank." [11] Nor was it only as the apologist of moderate interest that Puritanism was alleged to reveal the cloven hoof. Puritans themselves complained of a mercilessness in driving hard bargains, and of a harshness to the poor, which contrasted unfavorably with the practice of followers of the unreformed religion. "The Papists," wrote a Puritan in 1653, "may rise up against many of this generation. It is a sad thing that they should be more forward upon a bad principle than a Christian upon a good one." [12]

Such, in all ages, is history as seen by the political pamphleteer. The real story was less dramatic, but more significant. From the very beginning, Calvinism had comprised two elements, which Calvin himself had fused, but which contained the seeds of future discord. It had at once given a whole-hearted *imprimatur* to the life of business enterprise, which most earlier moralists had regarded with suspicion, and had laid upon it the restraining hand of an inquisitorial discipline. At Geneva, where Calvinism was the creed of a small and homogeneous city, the second aspect had predominated; in the many-sided life of England, where there were numerous conflicting interests to balance it, and where it was long politically weak, the first. Then, in the late sixteenth and early seventeenth centuries, had come the wave of commercial and financial expansion— companies, colonies, capitalism in textiles, capitalism in mining, capitalism in finance—on the crest of which the English commercial classes, in Calvin's day still held in leading-strings by conservative statesmen, had climbed to a position of dignity and affluence.

Naturally, as the Puritan movement came to its own, these two elements flew apart. The collectivist, half-communistic aspect, which had never been acclimatized in England, quietly dropped out of notice, to crop up once more, and for the last time, to the disgust and terror of merchant and landowner, in the popular agitation under the Commonwealth. The

[11] *Brief Survey of the Growth of Usury in England,* 1673.
[12] S. Richardson, *The Cause of the Poor Pleaded,* 1653, Thomason Tracts, E. 703 (9), p. 14. For other references, see note 72 below. For extortionate prices, see Thomason Tracts, E. 399 (6), *The Worth of a Penny, or a Caution to keep Money,* 1647. I am indebted for this and subsequent references to the Thomason Tracts to Miss P. James.

individualism congenial to the world of business became the distinctive characteristic of a Puritanism which had arrived, and which, in becoming a political force, was at once secularized and committed to a career of compromise. Its note was not the attempt to establish on earth a "Kingdom of Christ," but an ideal of personal character and conduct, to be realized by the punctual discharge both of public and private duties. Its theory had been discipline; its practical result was liberty.

Given the social and political conditions of England, the transformation was inevitable. The incompatibility of Presbyterianism with the stratified arrangement of English society had been remarked by Hooker.[13] If the City Fathers of Geneva had thrown off by the beginning of the seventeenth century the religious collectivism of Calvin's régime, it was not to be expected that the landowners and *bourgeoisie* of an aristocratic and increasingly commercial nation, however much Calvinist theology might appeal to them, would view with favor the social doctrines implied in Calvinist discipline. In the reign of the first two Stuarts, both economic interests and political theory pulled them hard in the opposite direction. "Merchants' doings," the man of business in Wilson's *Discourse upon Usury* had observed, "must not thus be overthwarted by preachers and others that cannot skill of their dealings." [14] Behind the elaborate façade of Tudor State control, which has attracted the attention of historians, an individualist movement had been steadily developing, which found expression in opposition to the traditional policy of stereotyping economic relations by checking enclosure, controlling food supplies and prices, interfering with the money-market, and regulating the conditions of the wage contract and of apprenticeship. In the first forty years of the seventeenth century, on grounds both of expediency and of principle, the commercial and propertied classes were becoming increasingly restive under the whole system, at once ambitious and inefficient, of economic paternalism. It was in the same sections of the community that both religious and economic dissatisfaction were most acute. Puritanism, with its idealization of the spiritual energies which found expression in the activities of business and industry, drew the isolated rivulets of discontent together, and swept them forward with the dignity and momentum of a religious and a social philosophy.

It would be misleading to dwell on the limitations of Puritan ethics without emphasizing the enormous contribution of Puritanism to political freedom and social progress. The foundation of democracy is the sense of spiritual independence which nerves the individual to stand alone against the powers of this world, and in England, where squire and parson, lifting arrogant eyebrows at the insolence of the lower orders, combined to crush

---

[13] Hooker, Preface to *The Laws of Ecclesiastical Polity*, Everyman ed., 1907, vol i, p. 128.
[14] Wilson, *op. cit.*, p. 250.

popular agitation, as a menace at once to society and to the Church, it is probable that democracy owes more to Nonconformity than to any other single movement. The virtues of enterprise, diligence and thrift are the indispensable foundation of any complex and vigorous civilization. It was Puritanism which, by investing them with a supernatural sanction, turned them from an unsocial eccentricity into a habit and a religion. Nor would it be difficult to find notable representatives of the Puritan spirit in whom the personal authority, which was the noblest aspect of the new ideal, was combined with a profound consciousness of social solidarity, which was the noblest aspect of that which it displaced. Firmin the philanthropist, and Bellers the Quaker, whom Owen more than a century later hailed as the father of his doctrines, were pioneers of Poor Law reform. The Society of Friends, in an age when the divorce between religion and social ethics was almost complete, met the prevalent doctrine, that it was permissible to take such gain as the market offered, by insisting on the obligation of good conscience and forbearance in economic transactions, and on the duty to make the honorable maintenance of the brother in distress a common charge.[15]

The general climate and character of a country are not altered, however, by the fact that here and there it has peaks which rise into an ampler air. The distinctive note of Puritan teaching was different. It was individual responsibility, not social obligation. Training its pupils to the mastery of others through the mastery of self, it prized as a crown of glory the qualities which arm the spiritual athlete for his solitary contest with a hostile world, and dismissed concern with the social order as the prop of weaklings and the Capua of the soul. Both the excellences and the defects of that attitude were momentous for the future. It is sometimes suggested that the astonishing outburst of industrial activity which took place after 1760 created a new type of economic character, as well as a new system of economic organization. In reality, the ideal which was later to carry all before it, in the person of the inventor and engineer and captain of industry, was well established among Englishmen before the end of the seventeenth century. Among the numerous forces which had gone to form it, some not inconsiderable part may reasonably be ascribed to the emphasis on the life of business enterprise as the appropriate field for Christian endeavor, and on the qualities needed for success in it, which was characteristic of Puritanism. These qualities, and the admiration of them, remained, when the religious reference, and the restraints which it imposed, had weakened or disappeared.

[15] W. C. Braithwaite, *The Second Period of Quakerism*, 1919, pp. 560–2. Defoe comments on the strict business standards of the Quakers in *Letter xvii* (*Of Honesty in Dealing*) in *The Complete English Tradesman*. Mr. Ashton (*Iron and Steel in the Industrial Revolution*, p. 219) remarks, "The eighteenth century Friend no less than the medieval Catholic held firmly to some doctrine of Just Price," and quotes examples from the conduct of Quaker iron-masters.

Societies, like individuals, have their moral crises and their spiritual revolutions. The student can observe the results which these cataclysms produce, but he can hardly without presumption attempt to appraise them, for it is at the fire which they kindled that his own small taper has been lit. The rise of a naturalistic science of society, with all its magnificent promise of fruitful action and of intellectual light; the abdication of the Christian Churches from departments of economic conduct and social theory long claimed as their province; the general acceptance by thinkers of a scale of ethical values, which turned the desire for pecuniary gain from a perilous, if natural, frailty into the idol of philosophers and the mainspring of society—such movements are written large over the history of the tempestuous age which lies between the Reformation and the full light of the eighteenth century. Their consequences have been worked into the very tissue of modern civilization. Posterity still stands too near their source to discern the ocean into which these streams will flow.

In an historical age the relativity of political doctrines is the tritest of commonplaces. But social psychology continues too often to be discussed in serene indifference to the categories of time and place, and economic interests are still popularly treated as though they formed a kingdom over which the *Zeitgeist* bears no sway. In reality, though inherited dispositions may be constant from generation to generation, the system of valuations, preferences and ideals—the social environment within which individual character functions—is in process of continuous change, and it is in the conception of the place to be assigned to economic interests in the life of society that change has in recent centuries been most comprehensive in its scope, and most sensational in its consequences. The isolation of economic aims as a specialized object of concentrated and systematic effort, the erection of economic criteria into an independent and authoritative standard of social expediency, are phenomena which, though familiar enough in classical antiquity, appear, at least on a grand scale, only at a comparatively recent date in the history of later civilizations. The conflict between the economic outlook of East and West, which impresses the traveller today, finds a parallel in the contrast between medieval and modern economic ideas, which strikes the historian.

The elements which combined to produce that revolution are too numerous to be summarized in any neat formula. But, side by side with the expansion of trade and the rise of new classes to political power, there was a further cause, which, if not the most conspicuous, was not the least fundamental. It was the contraction of the territory within which the spirit of religion was conceived to run. The criticism which dismisses the concern of Churches with economic relations and social organization as a modern innovation finds little support in past history. What requires explanation is not the view that these matters are part of the province of religion, but the view that they are not. When the age of the Reformation begins, economics is still a branch of ethics, and ethics of theology; all human activities are treated as falling within a single scheme, whose character is determined by the spiritual destiny of mankind; the appeal of theorists is to natural law, not to utility; the legitimacy of economic transactions is tried by reference, less to the movements of the market, than to moral standards derived from the traditional teaching of the Christian Church; the Church itself is regarded as a society wielding theoretical, and sometimes practical, authority in social affairs. The secularization of political thought, which was to be the work of the next two centuries, had profound reactions on social speculation, and by the Restoration the whole perspective, at least in England, has been revolutionized. Religion has been converted from the keystone which holds together the social edifice into one department within it, and the idea of a rule of right is replaced by economic expediency as the arbiter of policy and the criterion of conduct. From a spiritual being, who, in order to survive, must devote a reasonable attention to economic interest, man seems sometimes to have become an economic animal, who will be prudent, nevertheless, if he takes due precautions to assure his spiritual well-being.

The result is an attitude which forms so fundamental a part of modern political thought, that both its precarious philosophical basis, and the contrast which it offers with the conceptions of earlier generations, are commonly forgotten. Its essence is a dualism which regards the secular and the religious aspects of life, not as successive stages within a larger unity, but as parallel and independent provinces, governed by different laws, judged by different standards, and amenable to different authorities. To the most representative minds of the Reformation, as of the Middle Ages, a philosophy which treated the transactions of commerce and the institutions of society as indifferent to religion would have appeared, not merely morally reprehensible, but intellectually absurd. Holding as their first assumption that the ultimate social authority is the will of God, and that temporal interests are a transitory episode in the life of spirits which are eternal, they state the rules to which the social conduct of the Christian must conform, and, when circumstances allow, organize the discipline by which those rules may be enforced. By their successors in the eighteenth century the philosophy of Indifferentism, though rarely formulated as a matter of theory, is held in practice as a truism which it is irrational, if not actually immoral, to question, since it is in the heart of the individual that religion has its throne, and to externalize it in rules and instructions is to tarnish its purity and to degrade its appeal. Naturally, therefore, they formulate the ethical principles of Christianity in terms of a comfortable ambiguity, and rarely indicate with any precision their application to commerce, finance, and the ownership of property. Thus the conflict between religion and those natural economic ambitions which the thought of an earlier age had regarded with suspicion is suspended by a truce which divides the life of mankind between them. The former takes as its province the individual soul, the latter the intercourse of man with his fellows in the activities of business and the affairs of society. Provided that each keeps to his own territory, peace is assured. They cannot collide, for they can never meet.

History is a stage where forces which are within human control contend and coöperate with forces which are not. The change of opinion described in these pages drew nourishment from both. The storm and fury of the Puritan revolution had been followed by a dazzling outburst of economic enterprise, and the transformation of the material environment prepared an atmosphere in which a judicious moderation seemed the voice at once of the truest wisdom and the sincerest piety. But the inner world was in motion as well as the outer. The march of external progress woke sympathetic echoes in hearts already attuned to applaud its triumph, and there was no consciousness of an acute tension between the claims of religion and the glittering allurements of a commercial civilization, such as had tormented the age of the Reformation.

It was partly the natural, and not unreasonable, diffidence of men who were conscious that traditional doctrines of social ethics, with their impracticable distrust of economic motives, belonged to the conditions of a vanished age, but who lacked the creative energy to state them anew, in a form applicable to the needs of a more complex and mobile social order. It was partly that political changes had gone far to identify the Church of England with the ruling aristocracy, so that, while in France, when the crash came, many of the lower clergy threw in their lot with the *tiers état*, in England it was rarely that the officers of the Church did not echo the views of society which commended themselves to the rulers of the State. It was partly that, to one important body of opinion, the very heart of religion was a spirit which made indifference to the gross world of external circumstances appear, not a defect, but an ornament of the soul. Untrammelled by the silken chains which bound the Establishment, and with a great tradition of discipline behind them, the Nonconformist Churches might seem to have possessed opportunities of reasserting the social obligations of religion with a vigor denied to the Church of England. What impeded their utterance was less a weakness than the most essential and distinctive of their virtues. Founded on the repudiation of the idea that human effort could avail to win salvation, or human aid to assist the pilgrim in his lonely quest, they saw the world of business and society as a battlefield, across which character could march triumphant to its goal, not as crude materials waiting the architect's hand to set them in their place as the foundations of the Kingdom of Heaven. It did not occur to them that character is social, and society, since it is the expression of character, spiritual. Thus the eye is sometimes blinded by light itself.

The certainties of one age are the problems of the next. Few will refuse their admiration to the magnificent conception of a community penetrated from apex to foundation by the moral law, which was the inspiration of the great reformers, not less than of the better minds of the Middle Ages. But, in order to subdue the tough world of material interests, it is necessary to have at least so much sympathy with its tortuous ways as is needed to understand them. The Prince of Darkness has a right to a courteous hearing and a fair trial, and those who will not give him his due are wont to find that, in the long run, he turns the tables by taking his due and something over. Common sense and a respect for realities are not less graces of the spirit than moral zeal. The paroxysms of virtuous fury, with which the children of light denounced each new victory of economic enterprise as yet another stratagem of Mammon, disabled them for the staff-work of their campaign, which needs a cool head as well as a stout heart. Their obstinate refusal to revise old formulae in the light of new facts exposed them helpless to a counter-attack, in which the whole fabric of their philosophy, truth and fantasy alike, was overwhelmed together. They despised knowledge, and knowledge destroyed them.

Few can contemplate without a sense of exhilaration the splendid achievements of practical energy and technical skill, which, from the latter part of the seventeenth century, were transforming the face of material civilization, and of which England was the daring, if not too scrupulous, pioneer. If, however, economic ambitions are good servants, they are bad masters. Harnessed to a social purpose, they will turn the mill and grind the corn. But the question, to what end the wheels revolve, still remains; and on that question the naïve and uncritical worship of economic power, which is the mood of unreason too often engendered in those whom that new Leviathan has hypnotized by its spell, throws no light. Its result is not seldom a world in which men command a mechanism that they cannot fully use, and an organization which has every perfection except that of motion.

Puritan Economic Control

2.   The Regulation of Wages in Early Massachusetts

Richard B. Morris and Jonathan Grossman

The impact of external mercantilist regulation upon the life of the American colonists has been studied time and again by historians, although their conclusions still reveal a sharp division of opinion. Far less attention has been paid to mercantilism operating within the colonies for purposes of internal economic control. Scholars have been content to relegate wage and price controls to the scrap-heap of abortive experiments of a collective or community nature, with the result that they have not received the attention they deserve. In point of fact, wages and prices were regulated in a number of the colonies, at various times in the seventeenth century perhaps most significantly in Massachusetts Bay, the happy hunting ground for paternalistic controls over religion, morals, and business. It is generally known that, in the first decade of the colony's history, ambitious legislation was launched to establish maximum wages, but it is commonly thought that these laws were not enforced and were quickly discarded. The most recent writer maintains that "by 1640 . . . the trend of thought was away from the fixation of prices" and "men of affairs" had discredited price and wage controls.[1] For this impression the early writers are largely responsible. Hubbard looked back with high favor upon that first decade as the "golden age of New England, when vice was crushed . . . especially oppression and extortion in prices and wages." [2] Winthrop admitted as early as 1640 that the General Court

> having found by experience, that it would not avail by any law to redress the excessive rates of labourers' and workmen's wages, etc. (for being restrained, they would either remove to other places where they might have more, or else being able to live by planting and other employments of their own, they would not be hired at all[ )], it was therefore referred to the several towns to set down rates among themselves. This took better effect, so that in a voluntary way, by the counsel and persuasion of the elders, and example of some who led the way, they

[1] E. A. J. Johnson, *American Economic Thought in the Seventeenth Century* (London, 1932), 129–130 and 210–212.
[2] William Hubbard, *A General History of New England from the Discoverie to 1680* (Reprinted Boston, 1848), 248.

"Wage Regulation in Massachusetts," by Richard B. Morris and Jonathan Grossman, is reprinted by permission from *New England Quarterly*, XI (March, 1938), 470–500.

were brought to more moderation than they could be by compulsion. But it held not long.[3]

In reality, the rulers of the Bay Colony and the early settlers in her towns, possessed of unusual powers of supervision over strangers, vagrants, and the idle, authority to establish compulsory labor, and the right to impress men to pursue fugitive servants on land and over water, appear to have experimented in the matter of maximum wages with some measure of persistence for several generations. Their efforts did not fully cease until the last quarter of the century. As late as 1670 the Assistants proposed a sweeping regulatory measure, and although defeated in that year and again two years later, when they presented the bill in revised form, they retrieved some measure of victory in the passage of extensive legislation during King Philip's War. The consequences of introducing maximum wage legislation in a country where land was reasonably plentiful and labor scarce would seem to us gifted with opportunities of hindsight, fairly obvious. These comparative bounties of nature offset in large part the absence from the Massachusetts labor system of certain safeguards found, at least on paper, in the Tudor labor code, such a general or local regulations preventing dismissals [4] and the rare occasions when wage minima were prescribed by law.[5]

That the colonists borrowed heavily from medieval economic thought and current mercantilist ideology is now well established.[6] The mercantilists gave concrete enforcement to the medieval aim to prevent the engrossing of indispensable necessaries, of which labor, like food and raw materials, was a basic element.[7] The program which the Massachusetts authorities launched, of placing the regulation of wages and prices in the hands of the central authorities, had been first seriously attempted in England in the medieval Ordinance of Labourers and the Statute of Labourers, enacted in 1349 and 1351, respectively. Statutes of 1351 and 1388 established specific maximum wage scales, but this policy was dropped in 1390, when the justices of the peace were authorized to impose

[3] John Winthrop, *History of New England* (or *Journal*), edited by James Savage (Boston, 1853), II, 25 and 26.

[4] W. S. Cunningham, *Growth of English Industry and Commerce* (London, 1912), II, 50; W. S. Holdsworth, *A History of English Law* (Boston, 1923), II, 463 and 464. Holdsworth regards the early English labor codes as reasonable and fair to servant as well as master.

[5] E. Lipson, *The Economic History of England* (London, 1931), III, 239–254 and 259. In fairness to the Bay Colony it should be pointed out that the four general laws relating to servants in the Body of Liberties were more humane than those prevailing at common law. *Colonial Laws of Massachusetts, reprinted from the edition of 1660* (hereinafter *Laws, 1660*), edited by W. H. Whitmore (Boston, 1889), 51–53; R. B. Morris, "Massachusetts and the Common Law," *American Historical Review*, xxxi, 450.

[6] See Note 1, above.

[7] The regulatory background in England and the continent has been treated in the studies of Tawney, Hauser, Heckscher, Lipson, Bertha H. Putnam, Estelle Waterman, and Knoop and Jones, among others.

wages "according to the dearth of victuals." Between 1445 and 1515 maximum wage scales were once more set by statute, but the great Statute of Artificers of 1563, which laid down principles determining the legal relations of master and servant for more than a century and a half, threw specific maximum scales overboard and authorized the justices of the peace to fix wages according "to the plenty or scarcity of the time." [8]

This fluctuation in policy was also reflected in Massachusetts, where the authorities were torn between the desire to establish maximum wage scales by legislative fiat and to confer upon administrative officials discretionary authority to levy assessments. The settlers of the Bay Colony had come in considerable part from East Anglia and its neighborhood, including Norfolk, Suffolk, Essex, and southern Lincolnshire, and considerable evidence is at hand of wage assessments in these centers of the manufacture of woollen cloth on the eve of the great Puritan migration.[9] Some of the leaders doubtless had had first-hand experience with such regulation at home and an acquaintance with the legal technicalities of the prevailing labor code. Such were John Winthrop, who had served as a justice of the peace in the mother country; Richard Bellingham, who had been recorder of the borough of Boston in Lincolnshire; and Nathaniel Ward, who had enjoyed the advantages of legal education in England. Aside from their probable acquaintance with the English statutes and practices of the country justices, the American Puritan leaders, in legislation and public utterance, mirrored the prevailing views of the mercantilists as to "the lower orders," who were enjoined to obedience and honest carriage.[10] Maximum wage regulation was thoroughly consistent with that social attitude.

In England the regulation of wages and prices originated in the towns and was adopted as a general policy by the central government; in Massachusetts, on the other hand, it was first launched by the central government and subsequently handed over to the local authorities. Therefore, the course of this legislation will be pursued herein, first in the General Court, and then in the towns, after which the sporadic evidences of enforcement in the law courts will be examined.

Owing to the scarcity of skilled craftsmen in the early days, the first series of enactments, launched in 1630, was directed toward regulating wages in the building trades. Carpenters, joiners, bricklayers, sawyers, and thatchers were limited to two shillings a day. Both giver and taker of higher rates were subject to a fine of ten shillings. For piece work, the wages for sawyers were established at 4s. 6d. per hundred for boards at six score to the hundred if they had their wood felled and squared for

---

[8] See Richard Burn, *The Justice of the Peace* (London, 1800), IV, 206 f.

[9] See Lipson, *Economic History*, III, 259.

[10] *Records of the Governor and Company of Massachusetts Bay in New England* (hereinafter *Massachusetts Bay Records*), edited by N. B. Shurtleff (Boston, 1853–1854), I, 397. See also E. S. Furniss, *The Position of the Laborer in a System of Nationalism* (Boston, 1920); and Johnson, *American Economic Thought*, 31.

them, and not above 5s. 6d. if they did these extra tasks themselves. Hardly a month elapsed before the rates of master carpenters, masons, joiners, and bricklayers were levelled down to 16d. a day with meat and drink, and assistants or journeymen were restricted to 12d. a day, with a similar fine in both categories for violations. Shortly thereafter it was enacted that sawyers should not take more than 12d. a score for sawing oak boards, and 10d. for pine boards, if they had their wood felled and squared for them.[11]

After slightly more than six months' experience with these regulations, the General Court abolished them in 1631, without even providing posterity with a good rationalizing preamble, and ordered that "the wages of carpenters, joyners, and other artificers and workmen . . . shall nowe be lefte free and att libertie as men shall reasonably agree." [12] This did not involve any repudiation of the general program of wage-fixing, for very shortly thereafter the rates of sawyers were reestablished at twelve pence a score for boards, and if they did their own felling and squaring, at not above seven shillings the hundred, five score to the hundred.[13] Massachusetts Bay was now embarked upon a building program of some magnitude, and the scarcity of labor and the relatively high wage scale obtaining spurred the magistrates to new legislative restrictions. Writing in the fall of 1633, Governor Winthrop reported that carpenters were demanding three shillings a day and laborers two shillings, sixpence. As they could make enough in four days to keep them a week, he reported that they spent the remainder of their time in idleness and their surplus money in tobacco and strong waters.[14]

Following the Governor's observations, which reflected the hostility shared by Puritan and mercantilist both toward leisure and toward expenditures above mere subsistence on the part of the laboring class, the General Court, alleging "great extortion used by divers persons of little conscience" and great disorder resulting from "vain and idle waste of much precious time" for which "immoderate gains" were responsible, enacted the most comprehensive of its first series of wage statutes. Carpenters, sawyers, masons, clapboard rivers, bricklayers, thatchers, joiners, wheelwrights, and mowers were limited to two shillings a day without board and to fourteen pence a day with refreshment. "The best sorte of labourers" were forbidden to accept more than eighteen pence a day without board and eight pence with diet. The wages of tailors were limited to twelve pence for the master and eight pence for the journeyman, with diet in each case. A constable and two others were given authority under the act to regulate the wages of inferior laborers. It was also ordered "that all workemen shall worke the whole day, alloweing

[11] For these successive enactments, see Massachusetts Bay Records, i, 74, 76, and 79, respectively.
[12] Massachusetts Bay Records, i, 84.
[13] Massachusetts Bay Records, i, 91.
[14] Journal, i, 116.

convenient tyme for foode and rest." The constable was given authority to summon idlers before two assistants to deal with as they thought meet.[15] This regulation was followed by one forbidding the sale of commodities at prices higher than one-third above those prevailing in England, with the exception of cheese, liquors, oil, and vinegar, for which the hazard of transportation and dangers of leakage justified maintaining a free market. In the absence of such hazards, as with linen goods, the General Court ordered the settlers "not to exceede the bounds of moderation" under threat of severe punishment.[16] In connection with public works projects, the Court in the following year empowered the overseer of the works, in conjunction with an assistant, to award "such extraordinary wages as they shall judge the worke to disserve," and provided them with the authority to issue warrants to constables of adjacent locations for laborers and artificers as need arose.[17]

If maximum wages were to be successfully enforced in time of scarcity, it was quite clear that a system of forced labor had also to be implicit in the regulatory scheme,[18] the unemployed or idle summarily dealt with, servants restrained from leaving their masters, and strangers generally restricted in their movements.[19] Still, a fixed wage basis and a runaway price scale would have thrown the labor system out of equilibrium and thus the early statutes included elaborate regulations of the prices of basic commodities, for in a general way, such leaders of early American Puritan thought as Winthrop and Cotton accepted the medieval doctrine of the "just price." [20] The General Court in 1641 conferred on the towns power over the regulation of the prices of commodities as well as wages. The assize of bread was the most persistent regulatory measure, but other price, quantity, and quality regulations include the assizes of casks, leather, wood, and bricks. Oppression in price was punished by the Court on numerous occasions. Michael Wigglesworth, in *The Day of Doom*, placed those who acquired wealth by "oppression" in the same category with adulterers and whoremongers.

[15] *Massachusetts Bay Records*, I, 109.

[16] *Massachusetts Bay Records*, I, 111.

[17] *Massachusetts Bay Records*, I, 124.

[18] For instances of coercion, see *Massachusetts Bay Records*, I, 74, 124, 137, 148, and 157; II, 180–181; and III, 102–103; and *The Laws and Liberties of Massachusetts* (hereinafter *Laws*), 1648, 55. Numerous instances are also found in town records.

[19] From the beginning the authorities were anxious that "no drone be permitted to live among us." (*Massachusetts Bay Records*, I, Appendix.) For coercive and restrictive legislation, see *ibid.*, I, 109; II, 180; IV, 394; and V, 375. *Acts and Resolves, Public and Private, of the Province of the Massachusetts Bay* (hereinafter *Acts and Resolves*), (Boston, 1869–1924), I, 67, 378–381, and 538–539; II, 42; and VIII, 232–234; *Journal of the House of Representatives* (Boston, 1919–), VIII, 99, 104, and 106; *Laws, 1684*, 38 and 49; and *Laws, 1660*, 174 and 193.

[20] See *Massachusetts Bay Records*, I, 115; Winthrop, *Journal*, 313 and 317, *Records and Files of the Quarterly Courts of Essex County* (hereinafter *Essex Court*), (Salem, 1911–1918), I, 34 and 49; II, 69, 100, and 117–119; and VI, 71, "Suffolk County Court Records," *Publications*, Colonial Society of Massachusetts, XXIX–XXX (hereinafter "Suffolk Court"), 632.

As time went on, the founding Fathers wrestled continually with the problem of scarcity and high wages. It is quite clear that the wage law of 1633 was generally ineffective and that current wages exceeded the levels laid down by fifty per cent.[21] The entering wedge to broad class discrimination was contained in the act of September, 1634, which abolished the penalty against employers for giving wages in excess of the law, but left untouched the penalties against workers. As a matter of fact, no employer was ever penalized under this act. In line with this effort to counteract labor scarcity, the statute attempted to restrict the trend of workers toward agriculture by the provision that no servant could be allotted land until he had "approved his faithfullnes to his master during his time of service." [22] Later regulation by the towns is foreshadowed in the provision that where a wage contract proved inequitable to either party, three men appointed by the town should be empowered to set a new rate.

The trend of legislation was now definitely turning toward discretionary rates and to the decentralization of the administrative system. In 1636 John Cotton, member of a committee appointed "to make a draught of laws agreeable to the word of God, which may be the Fundamentals of this Commonwealth," [23] presented to the General Court a copy of his proposed code, "Moses his Judicialls," largely based upon Biblical precedents.[24] Cotton proposed specifically a plan which was in substance embodied in the act of 1636. Dealing with the subject of commerce, his code provides:

> To the intent that all oppression in buying and selling may be avoided, it shall be lawful for the judges in every town, with the consent of the free burgesses, to appoint certain selectmen, to set reasonable rates upon all commodities, and proportionably to limit the wages of workmen and labourers; and the rates agreed upon by them, and ratified by the judges, to bind all the inhabitants of the town. The like course to be taken by the governor and assistants, for the rating of prizes throughout the country, and all to be confirmed, if need be, by the general court.[25]

Along the lines of Cotton's proposal, the magistrates, in October, 1636, turned the regulation of wages over to the freemen of the towns, with discretionary punishment to be vested in the court "according to the

[21] United States Bureau of Labor Statistics *Bulletin*, Number 449 (1929), 9–10.

[22] *Massachusetts Bay Records*, I, 127. Workmen boarding themselves were to be allowed 2d. extra day in wages, according to the same act.

[23] *Massachusetts Bay Records*, I, 147; Winthrop, *Journal*, I, 191.

[24] Insufficient weight has been given by historians to the non-common law elements in Cotton's code, for example by Charles M. Andrews, *The Colonial Period of American History* (New Haven, 1936), II, 156–157.

[25] *Collections*, Massachusetts Historical Society, First Series, v, 180. W. B. Weeden (*Economic and Social History of New England*, I, 167, note) quite carelessly attributes this reference to the Body of Liberties, the official code of 1641, which, as a matter of fact, is silent on this point. Probably his mistakes arose from the fact that in 1641 Cotton's proposed, but unadopted, code was published in London under the misleading title *An Abstract of the Laws of New-England, as they are now established.*

quality and measure of the offence." Anticipating possible competition of town against town for the services of badly needed workers, the General Court made provision that the Court or the Governor and Assistants might hear complaints against towns "For alowing greater rates or wages then themselves." [26] This attempt at local regulation, according to the admission of the Court in 1638, resulted in "divers complaints made concerning oppression in wages" and in prices, particularly in the wages of smiths and the rates of cartage and teams, "to the great dishonour of God, the scandoll of the gosple, and the greife of divers of Gods people, both heare in this land and in the land of our nativity." A distinguished committee headed by Endecott, Bellingham, Saltonstall, and John Winthrop, Jr., was appointed to propose remedies,[27] but no report of their findings is found in the records.

For all practical purposes the General Court had turned wage regulation over to the towns; yet there was no offical renunciation of authority. Because of crop conditions in 1640 and 1641, the General Court in the latter year, pointing to the lower commodity prices then prevailing, enacted that laborers should be "content to abate their wages according to the fall of the commodities wherein their labors are bestowed." The Court announced its firm intention of proceeding against those laborers who acted contrary to this order, although no specific penalties are provided. Workers were to be paid in commodities, and according to a subsequent act of the same year, in corn, the price, where agreement could not be reached, to be set by two "indifferent freemen," one chosen by the master, the other by the workman.[28] The codes of 1648 and 1660, and the supplement of 1672 continued substantially the basic law of 1636 against oppression in wages and prices. The specific provisions of that act permitting discretionary fines or imprisonment to be imposed and turning regulation over to the towns, were retained, and county courts were authorized to punish violations at their discretion.[29] The emphasis upon discretionary rather than fixed penalties accorded both with experience and with the legal philosophy of the leading magistrates, who opposed definite penalties except in capital cases in order to strengthen their own authority at a time when it was being challenged on many sides, and also out of deference to theories of individualizing punishment. Thus, John Winthrop pointed to the case in which a penalty "hits a rich man" and "pains him not; but if it lights upon a poor man, it breaks his back." [30]

The experiment in wage-fixing was imitated in the neighboring colonies of Plymouth and Connecticut at this time.[31] The commissioners of the

[26] *Massachusetts Bay Records*, I, 182.
[27] *Massachusetts Bay Records*, I, 223.
[28] *Massachusetts Bay Records*, I, 326 and 340.
[29] *Laws, 1648*, 38, 39, and 43; *Laws, 1660*, 174 and 187.
[30] "Arbitrary Government Described," 1644, in *Life and Letters* (Boston, 1869), II, 445 ff.
[31] *Records of the Colony of New Plymouth, 1620–1692*, edited by N. B. Shurtleff and David Pulsifer (Boston, 1855–1861), II, 60; and XI, 30; and *Public Records of the Col-*

New England Confederation recommended to their respective governments in 1646 that "some serious provision be speedily made against
oppression" in wages.[32]

In the years ensuing before King Philip's War, the authorities continued
to be greatly exercised over the need for wage-fixing, but the problem was
left in large measure to the localities. In the seventies, however, there was
a revival of activity on the part of the central government. On May 15,
1672, the General Court passed an act which, while specifically prohibiting the giving of wine or strong liquors to workmen, was only in part a
sumptuary measure; from its phraseology it appears to have been motivated by a desire to curtail the demands of the workers:

> Whereas there have binn sundry and frequent complaints preferred
> to this Court of oppression by excessive wages of worke men and
> labourers, which, notw[th]standing the endeavours of this Court to re-
> dress such oppressions, continue, and further increase, by a dangerous
> imposition of such persons on those they worke and labour for, by
> demanding an allowance of licquors or wine every day, over and above
> their wages, w[th]out which it is found, by too sad experience, many
> refuse to worke. Now, forasmuch as such a practize of drincking lic-
> quors and wine tends much to the rooting young persons in an evill
> practise, and by degrees to trayne them vp to an habitt of excesse, it
> is therefore ordered by this Court and by the authority thereof, and
> be it hereby enacted, that if any person or persons, after the publication
> hereof, shall give wine or strong liquers to any workmen or boyes that
> worke wth them, except in cases of necessity, shall pay twenty shillings
> for every such offence.[33]

The town of Ipswich drew up a regulation in similar tenor.[34] Elsewhere,
however, the act of 1672 was not enforced. In Watertown, only one year
after its passage, the town granted Isaac Micktur the sum of five shillings
in lieu of a gallon of liquor owing for work on a bridge.[35] Again, in 1679,
the town allowed 9s. 2d. for liquors for labor at the mill bridge; and in
1681, to push forward work on the bridge, the selectmen gave Caleb
Church, the miller, fourteen shillings to procure good liquor as cheaply as
possible to be disbursed in such manner as would best aid the work. It is
clearly apparent that the exception in the statute for cases of necessity was
generously interpreted.[36]

---

ony of Connecticut, 1636–1776, compiled by J. H. Trumbull and C. J. Hoadly (Hartford, 1857), I, 11, 52, 61, and 65.

[32] *Records of Plymouth,* IX, 81.

[33] *Massachusetts Bay Records,* IV, Part ii, 510.

[34] J. B. Felt, *History of Ipswich, Essex, and Hamilton* (Boston, 1934), 105.

[35] *Watertown Records,* I, 116 and 132, and II, 10.

[36] For a discussion of the temperance movement in Massachusetts in this period, see
J. A. Krout, *The Origins of Prohibition* (New York, 1925), 51–53. In 1674 Increase
Mather delivered two sermons, published as *Wo to Drunkards* (Cambridge, 1673), in
which he enjoined his listeners to "Kill this Serpent before it be grown too big for you"
(Page 29). See also K. B. Murdock, *Increase Mather* (Cambridge, 1925), 103–104.

Two years earlier, on May 17, 1670, there had been introduced in the General Court a bill which went to the heart of wage and hour regulation. This proposed legislation is included in the Massachusetts Archives, but was omitted from the published record of the colony's proceedings. Because of the sweeping character of these proposals, the complete text is herewith given: [37]

This Court considering the great difficultie and discouragem', that at p'sent lyes pressing vpon many inhabitants of this jurisdiction especially vpon Such, as whose callings are in husbandry, not onely by reason of the afflicting hand of God vpon them severall yeares in blasting thier principall grayne and abating their increase in other Corne, and Slowenes of market and exceeding low price for that the husbandman can raise; vnto whose afflicting hand all ought to Submitt and humble themselves and yet with the prophet confesse, Thou, Lord, hast afflicted vs lesse then we deserve, but also Difficultie and discouragem' is yet heaped and increasing vpon them and others by reason of the excessive deerenes of labour by artifficers, Labourers, and Servants, contrary to reason and equitie, to the great prejudice of many householders and their Familyes, and tending to their vtter ruein and vndoeing, and the produce thereof is by many Spent to mayntayne Such bravery in Apparell which is altogether vnbecomeing thier place and ranck, and in Idleness of life, and a great part spent viciously in Tavernes and alehouses and other Sinful practices much to the dishonour of God, Scandall of Religion, and great offence and griefe to Sober and Godly people amongst vs. All which timely to prevent, this Court account it their duty carefully by all good meanes to provide, and therefore doe order as followeth,

It is therefore ordered by this Court and the Authoritie thereof that no person within this Jurisdiction, directly or indirectly, shall hereafter either paye or receave for worke, labour or comoditie, more or aboue, then is in this present order appointed, and that vpon the penalties therein heere after expressed.

s   d

Imprimis. Labourers by the daye from the end of September to the end of March dyeting themselves .... 1—3 per day
From the end of March to the end of June. 1—8

The editors of the Bureau of Labor Statistics *Bulletin*, Number 499, reprinted in the appendix Felt's version of this bill, and then added quite unwarrantably the curious statement that the bill was "introduced into the Court of Essex County, Massachusetts, in 1670 and again in 1672." As a matter of fact, both bills were proposed in the General Court. This error is repeated in the revised bulletin, Number 604 (1934).

[37] Volume cxix, Folios 28–29. Joseph B. Felt published this bill with certain editorial emendations in his *Historical Account of Massachusetts Currency* (Boston, 1839), 243–245. Felt listed nine sections, but the original has ten, of which the fifth, providing restrictions on the tanning of hides, was deleted.

From the end of June to the end of Sept^{ember}
they workeing 10 houres in the daye besides
repast .... 2—0

2. Takes worke. One Acre of salt marsh, and one
Acre of English grasse well mowen .... 2—0 per acre
one Acre of wheat well reapeing .... 4—0
one Acre of Rye well reapeing .... 3—0
one Acre of Barly, and one Acre of oats, each
well moweing .... 1—0
one Acre of peas, cutting .... 3—0
one Coarde of woode, cutting, and well Coarding 1—3
This wages is [sic] allowed as above to workemen
Dyeting themselues.

3. Carpenters and Masons and Stonelayers, from
1 March to 10 of October .... 2—0 per day
and all worke taken by the great or peice by
Carpenters, masons, joyners, or shinglers, is to be
apportioned according to the equitie of the value
of Daye's worke as above they dyeting themselves.

4. Master Taylors, and Such as are fully workmen of
that Trade for one daye's worke of 12 hours .... 1—8
Apprentices to that trade the first 4 yeares, the
like daye .... 1—0
And all weavers for thier worke at 12 hours per
day, are to have the like wages as Taylors.

6. All men and women Servants shall in their respective wages be moderated according to the proportion of labour above limitted.

7. No person shall pay, neither shall any Shoemaker
receave, more than 5^s for men's Shoes of elevens
or twelves, nor for women's Shoes of Seavens or
Eights more than 3^s–8^d. And all bootes and shoes
of other Sizes proportionable to the rates above-
saide.

8. Cowpers shall not receave nor any person paye for
a thight barrel of 32 gallons above 2–8, and other
Cowper's worke proportionable in price to barrels.

9. Smythes Shall not take nor any person paye for
great worke, as for Ships, Mills, plough Irones, all
Irones for Cart wheeles well layd vpon the
wheeles, and other the like great worke, about
5^d per lb. For smaller worke as Chaynes and other
the like Solde by weight, not aboue 6^d per lb. For
the largest horse shoe well set with 7 nayles, not
above 6^d per shoe. For removeing a horse shoe,
2^d. For an ordinary felling axe, 3^s 6^d. For one
broade axe, 5^s 6^d, one broade hough 3^s, all being
good and well steeled, and all other Smithe's

worke not named to be proportioned according
to the prices aboueSaid.

10. And whereas it apears that Glovers, Sadlers, Hatters,
and Seuerall other artifficers doe at present greatly
exceed the rules of equitie in their prizes, they
are all required to moderate the Same according
to the rules prescribed to others, or know that in
neglect thereof they are lyeable to presentment,
and proceeded against according to the Lawe,—
Title, opression.

Inkeepers and ordinary keepers are required to attend the dutie of
them expected according to Lawe—Title Inkeepers, Sect. 11,[38] which
order ought more carefully and strictly to be executed for the prevention of oppression in Selling of wine, and as for Selling beere they
are to attend the Lawe that orders what quantitie of malte is to be putt
into each hogshead of beere, and that when malt is vnder 4^s per bushell
then to Sell no lesse than one quarte for 1^s–½^d, and for entertaynm^t of
horses in *Summer* not to take more then 4^d for one daye and night, and
in *winter* not to exceed 6^d for the like time.

All these paym^{ts} are to be made in merchantible Corne at the price
from yeare to yeare, set by the Generall Courte, prouided that when
the materials are brought from the market by the artifficer, as shoemakers, Smythes, and the like, allowance my be made for that Charge
by the buyer according to what the transportation may be.

If any person shall paye or receave more then according to the rates
aboue expressed, he or they, both buyer and Seller, shall forfeit the
full treble value of what Shall be payed or receaved, one-halfe to the
enformer and the other halfe to the Treasurer of the Seuerall Countie
Courts.

The President of euery Countie Courte shall at euery such Court
giue in charge to the Grand Jury to enquire into the breach of this
order in euery particular thereof.

And all Grand Jurymen are required vpon their oath to present all
offences against this Lawe, and if it shall apeere to the Court of the
Countie at any time within one yeare after the offence is comitted, that
any Juryman have knoweingly neglected his duties heerein, he shall
vpon conuiction before the Courte be fined Tenn times So much as the
offenders should have payed whome he ought to have p^{r}sented.

The division of opinion between the upper and lower houses in the
Court is represented in the ensuing record:

The Deputyes having Considered of this Bill regulating workmen's

---

[38] The law referred to provides that "no Taverner, seller of wine by retaile, Licensed
as aforesayd, shall take above *nine pound profit*, by the Butt or Pipe of wine (and
proportionably for all other Vessels) towards his wast and drawing, and otherwise, out
of which allowance, every such Taverner or Vintner, shall pay *fifty shillings* by the Butt
or Pipe, and proportionably for all other Vessels to the Country, for which they shall account with the Treasurer or his Deputy every six months, and discharge the same, all
which they may do by selling *six-pence a quart* in retaile (which they shall no time exceed) more then it cost by the Butt." *Laws, 1660,* 165.

wages, doe think it meete to Referre the same to consideration vntill the next Court of election, o' hono^{red} magistrates Consenting.

Wm. Torrey, Cleric

May 17, 70. The Magistrates haue passed this Bill for an order of this Court, desiring the consent of o' brethren the deputyes.

John Pynchon, per order.

The Deputyes Consent not hereto.

William Torrey, Cleric.

When the proposals in this bill are compared with corresponding assessments set only the year before in East Yorkshire, both husbandman and skilled worker in Massachusetts appear at a decided advantage.[39] Carpenters by the day, for example, were allowed 1s. in the English county as against the rate of 2s. proposed in Massachusetts, and agricultural laborers in the Bay Colony were to be permitted wages from three to four times greater than those prevailing under the English assessment.

The wage proposals of 1670 were reintroduced, but with several important changes, in 1672.[40] The preambles of the two bills are similar, but there are a number of differences in detail, and with one exception when rates were changed, they were revised downward.[41] Again the bill

[39] See R. K. Kelsall, "Two East Yorkshire Wage Assessments, 1669, 1679," *English Historical Review,* LII, 283–289. The assessments were somewhat higher in Hertford around this time. *Session Books of Hertford County,* C. E. Longmore, editor, VI, 400–405.

[40] Massachusetts Archives, CXIX, Folios 32–33. Felt completely ignored the differences between the two proposals and treated the 1672 bill as a mere duplicate of the 1670 measure, an error into which the editors of the Bureau of Labor Statistics *Bulletins,* Numbers 499 and 604, likewise fall.

	1670		1672	
	s	d	s	d
[41] One acre of wheat "well reapt"	4—0		5—0	
One acre of peas, cutting	3—0		2—6	
Shoemakers, for shoes of elevens or twelves	5—0		4—0	
for women's shoes of sevens and eights	3—8		3—0	
Smiths, for iron work	5—0	per lb.	4—½	per lb.
for smaller work such as chains	6—0		5—½	
for the largest horseshoe	6—0		5—½	
for removing a horseshoe	2—0		1—½	
for an ordinary felling axe	3—6		3—0	
for a broad axe	5—6		4—6	
for a broad hoe	3—0		2—6	

In Sections 1 and 3, changes are also made in the dates of the working season. In Section 4 the following additional provision regulating tailors is inserted: "and to regulate work on making garments or weaving by the sq. yard to the same rate proportably." Among the artificers specified in Section 10 who were not to exceed the rules of equity in setting prices are included in addition, brickmakers and limeburners. The innkeepers' law referred to in Section 11 of the 1670 bill includes also a citation of Section 8, referring to drunkenness. There is the further provision that, when malt is under 4s. a bushel, beer is to be sold for no more than 1d. a quart instead of 1½d. as in the earlier proposal. Oats were not to be sold "aboue 8^d per peck." The 1672 bill provides for payments in merchantable corn at the price set by the General Court from year to year "according to our valluation in money." The later bill omits the earlier provision allowing the seller transportation charges.

failed of passage in the lower house. According to the entry, dated August 11, 1672:

The magist⁸ haue past this wᵗ the payne affixt as an order of the Court. Their brethren the deputyes hereto Consenting.

Edward Rawson Secret.

The Deputyes Consent not hereto

William Torrey Cleric.

In the absence of a record of debates, some obvious questions cannot be answered definitively. Was the 1670 proposal altered in minor details to meet the objections of the deputies? Did the veto of the lower house rest on any fundamental opposition to wage regulation? Thus much is clear in the light of the legislative record of the General Court in this period: neither deputies nor assistants opposed wage regulation in principle.

As a matter of fact, in the very same year, 1672, the whole question of wage, price, and sumptuary controls was brought to a head when the General Court investigated labor and commodity costs of tanners, glovers, and shoemakers. The shoemakers pointed out that the current French styles involved the use of more leather than previous fashions; that long credits were customarily extended in the trade; that curriers were paid 4s. a hide, whereas in England the cost was only 2s. 8d.; and that thread was also much dearer than in England. The glovers pointed out that alum and lime were much higher, and likewise silk, but that to a large degree excessive costs were due to "the bad flayeing the skinnes by gashes and holes whereby they must Sell the tanned skinnes that are good and well flayed at Such a price as may make good for the loss by them that are full of holes." They complained further that "labour is very deere and help hard to attayne." The tanners suggested that none but skilled men be permitted to tan and that no raw hides be dried before tanning. They also charged that labor costs comprised a heavy item, some workers receiving £30 per annum, "some more."

In regard to the quality and condition of hides and skins used in these three occupations, the General Court acted at once, specifically ordering that searchers be appointed by the selectmen of the towns to inspect hides and skins before they left the butchers' hands. The Committee of Nine which investigated these industries, in summing up its findings, reported that tanners, glovers, and shoemakers were all oppressed by the high wages demanded by journeymen, and took occasion further to criticize "the excess of pride of meane people that will weare no other shoes generally but of the newest fashion and highest price." Hence such people would not work "but for Such wages wᵗ will mayntaine them in this profuse expensive manner." They concluded these mercantilist lamentations with a specific recommendation that a law be enacted providing a maximum sales price for shoes of elevens or twelves at 5s. a pair and other sizes in proportion, "upon penaltie of forfeiting the value of the whole price of those Solde aboue those values." This was similar to the recommendations embodied in the proposed bill of 1670 and somewhat higher than the scale fixed in the 1672 proposal, neither of which was adopted. The committee further proposed "that Some effectuall meanes be used to Suppresse the groweing excesse in Aparrell in this Countrey, pride and Idleness beginning to be the prevayling evills and shames of the people especially of the younger and meaner Sorte, and it is feared they are Some of the provoking Sinnes that procure the Frownes of our God upon us." [42]

This recommendation was incorporated by both houses in a compromise plan adopted to meet the labor scarcity, during the Indian War of 1675, when the Court passed a series of laws for the reformation of "Provoking Evils," with the express purpose of enforcing virtue and avoiding God's wrath. Its numerous provisions embraced wage-fixing, price regulation, and sumptuary legislation. Article XI of the "Provoking Evils" authorized selectmen to hear complaints against takers of excessive wages, and empowered such officials not only to require the offending laborers to make double restitution to their employers, but also to pay double the excess value of their work as a fine.[43] This compares with the treble damages assessed in the 1670 bill, which were to be shared by infomer and county court. No penalties were exacted of masters who competed for the labor of artisans by offering excessive wages. Under this act a new machinery for price regulation was set up; complaints were to be directed to the grand jurors. The "Provoking Evils" denounced "the evil pride in Apparel, both for Costliness in the poorer sort, and vain, new strange Fashions both in poor and rich." Of all sections of the statute, these sumptuary provisions were the most widely enforced.[44] It is a fair

---

[42] The General Court had been concerned with the regulation of quality, price, and wages in the leather industry at least as far back as 1648, when the shoemakers' guild had been chartered. See *Massachusetts Bay Records*, III 132; Massachusetts Archives, LIX, Folios 29–32, 125, 126, 227–233, and 413. Johnson testified early to the high prices prevailing in this trade. *Wonder Working Providence* (London, 1664; reprinted Andover, 1867), 207–209.

[43] *Massachusetts Bay Records*, v, 62–63; *Laws, 1660*, 236.

[44] The English authorities had already found it impossible to enforce an extensive system of sumptuary legislation. See F. E. Baldwin, *Sumptuary Legislation and Personal Regulation in England* (Baltimore, 1926).

For sumptuary legislation in Massachusetts against extravagance in dress, see *Massachusetts Bay Records*, I, 126, 183, and 274; II, 84; III, 243; and IV, 41, 42 and 60. See also *Records of Plymouth*, IX, 81. Numerous instances of enforcement are found in the records of the Quarterly Court of Essex County shortly after enactment (See *Essex Court*, I, 257 and 271–275, *passim*), but no convictions are found between 1663 and 1675. For the enforcement of the provision of the "Provoking Evils" against excess in dress, see *Suffolk Court*, 698, 751, and 752; *Essex Court*, VI, 26, 73, and 135; and VII, 291. For enforcement in Hampshire County, see Sylvester Judd, *History of Hadley*, 90–92. By 1690 enforcement seems to have become ineffective and was no longer seriously attempted.

inference from the broad mercantilist controls set up under the act of 1675 that the objections in 1670 and again in 1672 by the deputies, representing the more democratic elements in the colony, were not to the principle of wage regulation, but rather to the specific wage provisions of the proposed code. As late as 1675 there was clearly no expressed objection to a flexible system of control to be administered in the localities.[45]

While the central government on numerous occasions between 1630 and 1675 regulated the wages of workers and the prices of commodities, the same function was also being performed by the towns of the Bay Colony. Almost a year before the General Court authorized the towns to regulate wages, Boston, probably exceeding its authority at the time, appointed in November, 1635, a committee which, among other things, was to set "prices upon . . . laborer's and workingmen's wages." [46] Dorchester was one of the first towns to take advantage of the authority granted by the act of 1636, and in May of the following year, used the Pequot War as a pretext, ordering

> that any of the members or house keep[rs] wh[ch] shal be Chosen to goe fo[r] a Souldier and have a Charge of busenesse to leaue behind him, he may commend the Care of his busenesse to some friend which he shall nominate, who, if he cannot of himself or p'cure others to doe it at the same wages that is giuen to the souldiers it shall be lawful fo[r] Henery Withington, M[r] Brankard, M[r] Bates and Nathan duncan or any of them to enjoyne any one they shall thinke fitt to worke in this k[ind] fo[r] the helpe of such as [shall] need, and if any being so joyned shall refuse to worke he shall pay five shill. fo[r] Such refusall, to be levied by distresse.
>
> It is ordered, also, that any that haue servants or any other which goe in the Sevices shall haue the Benfitt of this order.[47]

This order illustrates the practice of labor impressment combined with that of wage regulation, but it is surpassed in scope by the regulation of 1642, in which the town set a specific wage scale for common laborers, in which category were included hoers, reapers, and tailors. The prevailing wages of 2s. per day for the period from March 25 to October 25 were reduced to 28d., and other seasonal variations were taken into account in the following manner:

[45] Other events in the year 1675 indicate that the "Provoking Evils" was merely one phase of a broad program to keep down wages and maintain a large labor market by discouraging idleness and labor monopoly. In that year the selectmen were ordered to check on idlers (*Massachusetts Bay Records,* 12, 62); and a group of ship carpenters who had ridden an interloper out of Boston on a rail because he had worked in the yard without having served his full seven years' apprenticeship were fined five shillings apiece payable to the government and a like amount to the victim. *Suffolk Court,* 603.

[46] *Boston Records,* II, 5.

[47] *Early Records of the Town of Dorchester,* W. B. Trask, editor (Boston, 1867), 32; *Boston Records,* IV, 23 and 24.

                                                          Rate per diem

Oct. 25–Dec. 1 .... 15*d*
Dec. 1–Feb. 1 .... 12*d*
Feb. 1–March 15 .... 25*d*

By the same order these proportionate wage reductions were extended to "those that doe other mens worke at thire owne houses." Finally, the order provided that "al men Com in due tyme to thire labor uppon such penalty as the Court uppon iust Complaint made shal be pleased to inflyct." [48] There was good precedent in the Elizabethan statute for combining maximum wage regulations with an hours schedule.

Hingham in 1641 ordered "by a joint consent" that "the prices of labourer's wages and commodities . . . should be abated 3 pence upon the shilling of what has been formerly taken." Wages of common labor were fixed at 1*s*. 6*d*. per diem, of mowers and wheelwrights, 2*s*., and of carpenters 1*s*. 10*d*. Specific rates were also established for work of field teams of men and oxen. The flat percentage reduction was also held to apply to tailors and shoemakers. The interesting provision is also found that "they are to work eight hours a day," but this probably referred to the field teams rather than to the craftsmen generally, who were customarily required to work much longer hours.[49] The phraseology of the ordinance is indicative of previous wage-fixing activity by the town. Salem acted in specific cases when necessary. In 1643 that town set the wages of one Tom Tuck, ironworker, and in the following year ruled that the wages of two carriage-makers conform to the prevailing Boston scale.[50] Rowley, a leading town in the manufacture of cloth, settled by Yorkshire families quite familiar with wage regulation at home, established the wages of various categories of workers in 1651. The town mowers were limited to 20*d*. a day; laborers to 18*d*. in summer, 13*d*. in the months of October and November, and 12*d*. in the three winter months; and "Reapers and other tradsmen, excepting Taylors, to have the same wages." [51] As late as 1668 the town of Ipswich was moved to set the maximum wage for laying a thousand shingles at 7*s*. 6*d*.[52]

For several generations the Puritans were in dead earnest about their wage codes. Both the Court of Assistants and the inferior county courts enforced on occasion the specific penalties of the law or drew upon their discretionary authority to discipline refractory workers. The first case on the records of the central courts occurred four years after the earliest wage statute. At a session of the court held at Boston on March 4, 1634,

---

[48] *Boston Records*, IV, 51.
[49] Solomon Lincoln, Jr., *History of the Town of Hingham* (Hingham: 1827), 52, Note.
[50] *Salem Records*, I, 134.
[51] *The Early Records of the Town of Rowley, 1639–1672* (Rowley, 1894), I, 72.
[52] Felt, *Ipswich*, 104.

John Chapman was fined twenty shillings for charging the rate of eight shillings per hundred for boards. Upon his promise to contribute three hundred feet of four-inch plank toward the building of the "sea fort," one of several charter violations charged up to Massachusetts by her overseas enemies—the fine was remitted.[53] As this case indicates, where the rates in question were those charged by masters, the borderline between price and wage regulation was extremely shadowy. On August 5 of the same year, Francis Godson was haled before the Court of Assistants and compelled to give bond for his appearance at the October session "to answer for breach of an order of Court in takeing to greate wages." [54] No further entry dealing with this case is found.

After the General Court abolished the penalty against employers who gave excessive wages but retained the fine against workers, a master named Hutchinson brought charges in the Court of Assistants on August 4, 1635, against four workmen for taking wages of 2s. 6d. per diem for their services. James Hawkins was accused of receiving this exorbitant wage for thirty-six days, and Arthur Hilbridge, Thomas Munt, and Richard Bulgar, for thirty, nine, and six days, respectively. Another employer named Cogan also appeared on the scene and denounced Hawkins for having taken similarly oppressive rates of wages from him for fourteen days' labor. The Court fined each violator, in accord with the law, five shillings per diem. These were grossly excessive penalties, as Hawkins was required to pay more than twelve pounds and Holbridge close to eight, as much as they could be expected to earn under the legal wage scale during an entire season. Not being able to pay the fines, Holbridge and Hawkins were imprisoned, but on September 1 the Court ruled that all four could pay the marshal three shillings weekly until the fines were discharged.[55] Whether or not these tremendous fines shocked the Puritan conscience will probably never be known, but shortly thereafter the law restraining "workingmen's wages to a certainty" was repealed, and discretionary penalties were substituted.[56]

In 1639 the General Court fined Edward Palmer five pounds for charging an excessive price for the plank and woodwork on the Boston stocks, and with grim Puritan humor sentenced him, in addition, to sit in the stocks he himself had made. Through his lawyer, the outspoken Thomas Lechford, Palmer petitioned the Court for remission of the fine, setting forth that he was "poor and no wayes able to pay the said fine having a wife and six children all or some of which he expects to come forth of England shortly." Having forced the culprit to eat humble pie, the Puritan magistrates, who preferred exemplary or humiliating punishments

[53] *Records of the Court of Assistants* (hereinafter *Assistants*), (Boston, 1901–1928), II, 40 and 42.
[54] *Assistants*, II, 48.
[55] *Massachusetts Bay Records*, I, 153–154; *Assistants*, II, 56–57.
[56] *Massachusetts Bay Records*, I, 159–160.

to any other sort, reduced the fine to a mere ten shillings.[57] Hubbard, the Puritan historian, appears to have derived much satisfaction from this case. He thoroughly approved the severity of the punishment on the ground that "oppression and extortion in prices and wages" were an "injustice to the public."[58] In 1642 William Shepheard was fined two pounds "for covenanting for £15 wages per annum," and Laurence Copeland similarly for an identical contract of wages, in both cases their employer having agreed to release them half of their working time.[59] In 1643 Anker Ainsworth was presented for taking excessive wages, and at the same session one Stodder for selling cloth at an excessive price; but the oppression was proved in neither case, and both were discharged.[60] Later in the year six persons, including a man and wife, were presented for "taking too much wages,"[61] but the final action of the court is not found in the record. These were the last cases to come before the central authorities.

For thirty-five years longer the inferior courts and local authorities prosecuted violators of the wage code, the principal prosecutions occurring in the Quarterly Court of Essex County between 1635 and 1676. Under the act of 1635 setting discretionary penalties,[62] the Quarterly Court at Salem at a single session fined William Dixie, John Stone, and Jonathan Sibley three shillings apiece for taking the oppressive wages of three shillings a day, while James Smith, for taking "too great wages," did not get off so lightly, but was fined twenty shillings.[63] In a case in 1651 in which Mark Symonds was fined £1 5s. for lying and 5s. for "railing" against the magistrates, depositions were made that the culprit had lied about the wages he was paid for the use of his boy and cattle by one Kimball, by implication to secure a similar rate from Goodman Beals, who felt that "it was too much and that none in the town would give it." This is not a prosecution under the wage code, but it is doubtful whether the authorities would have concerned themselves with the deceit if they did not feel that Symonds had set a bad example by his oppressive demands.[64]

Under the authority of the act of 1636, John Alderman in 1652 charged Thomas Trusler before the magistrates at Salem with taking excessive wages from him.[65] No further action is recorded. In 1653 Humphrey Wilson prosecuted James Wall for taking excessive wages in building a

[57] *Massachusetts Bay Records,* 260 and 291; *Note-Book kept by Thomas Lechford, Esq., Lawyer* (Cambridge, 1885), 242.
[58] Hubbard, *General History,* 248.
[59] *Assistants,* ii, 128.
[60] *Assistants,* ii, 131.
[61] *Assistants,* ii, 135, Cases of Loranson, Callwell, Danford, Gill *et, uxor,* and Pope.
[62] *Massachusetts Bay Records,* i, 160; *Laws, 1660,* 120.
[63] *Essex Court,* i, 3.
[64] *Essex Court,* 226–227.
[65] *Essex Court,* 247.

sawmill. It is not clear from the record whether this is an action of contract, as the work was alleged to be "insufficient," or a criminal prosecution, and the action was withdrawn.[66] In 1658 the Ipswich court discharged William Godhue of the complaint that he took excessive wages for his son [67] and the next year the court admonished John Applefourd for taking excessive wages.[68] Somewhat analogous was the case of the attorney and deputy marshal who, in 1669, was given the choice of a whipping or a fine of £10 with costs.[69] In 1672 the Ipswich court dismissed the several charges against Lawrence Clenton, among which was the accusation that he took the high wage of sixteen shillings and his dinners for three and a half days' work in painting a room. The charge was not proved.[70] In 1676, shortly after the passage of the sweeping general wage code enacted during King Philip's War, one Richard Scammon was presented for charging too much for repairing a pistol lock, among other work. According to the evidence, he took five hundred feet of boards for his labor—for work which by his own statement was "not worth more than 6s. 6d.,"—and as a punishment was ordered to return two hundred and fifty feet to his employer and fined the remaining two hundred and fifty.[71] In 1679 John Wilkinson was prosecuted in the Salem court for "entertaining other men's servants" without their master's knowledge. According to one deponent, Wilkinson, a barber, started to shave him and then refused to finish unless he gave him one shilling, which he was thus forced to do or "he would have had to go away in that condition to another barber." [72] While the case does not appear to have turned on this point in the testimony, it bears evidence that at this late date such acts of oppression were still looked upon as contrary to the public welfare. Curiously enough, no case under the wage acts was reported in the early records of the Suffolk County Court, although as late as 1675 there is a prosecution for oppression in the price of cloth.[73] Occasionally the selectmen of the towns were moved to act, as in Woburn in 1676, when the selectmen fined Hopestill Forester for oppression in making boards, nails, and other carpentry work, a portion of the fine being assigned by the court to the two injured complainants.[74]

The act of 1675 for the reformation of "Provoking Evils" marked the culmination of wage regulation in the pre-Revolutionary period. Only four years later a synod held in Boston considered the need for a

---

[66] *Essex Court,* 281.
[67] *Essex Court,* II, 119. At the same session William Bartholomew was fined 10 shillings "for selling dear."
[68] *Essex Court,* 152.
[69] *Essex Court,* IV, 178 and 198; Godfrey *versus* Ela (1669).
[70] *Essex Court,* V, 37.
[71] *Essex Court,* VI, 142.
[72] *Essex Court,* VII, 326 and 327, note.
[73] Batt's Case, *Suffolk Court,* II, 632.
[74] Samuel Sewall, *History of Woburn* (Woburn, 1868), 58.

reformation of social and moral conditions in the community and wrestled with two great questions: "1. What are the evils that have provoked the Lord to bring his Judgements on New England? 2. What is to be done so that these Evils may be Reformed?" In answer to the first, the elders found that sabbath-breaking, intemperance, gaming, and "mixed dancing" were provocative of God's wrath, manifest in plagues, fire, and war. In addition, they pointed to "Inordinate affection of the World," as evidenced in the "oppression which the land groaneth under," owing, among other things, to the fact that "Day Labourers and Mechanics are unreasonable in their demands." [75] As a program of action, the synod recommended adherence to the laws which had been passed a few years earlier "for Reformation of Provoking Evils," not mentioning the regulation of wages specifically, but singling out for emphasis the act of 1672 which aimed to curb immoderate drinking in order to check the demands of workers. Thereafter the church, according to Cotton Mather,[76] took it upon itself to see that such "evils" were eliminated. As late as 1690 Mather justifiably complained that the good old laws for the reformation of "provoking evils" had been indifferently enforced.[77]

Typical of the regulatory measures passed by the towns of Massachusetts in the latter part of the century for the control of commerce and industry was the provision of the town of Suffield in 1685 regulating the price of boards at the sawmill and the rate for grinding corn at gristmills.[78] Again in 1697 the town set the wages of townsmen engaged in clearing the minister's meadow at 2s. 6d. per diem, all above sixteen being required to appear and cut wood for that dignitary. Down to the Revolution, porters, carmen, millers, grave-diggers, chimney-sweepers, and others who might be considered to fall in the category of quasi-public utilities were generally licensed and their fees were regulated either by the central, or more commonly, the local authorities.[79] Massachusetts towns still set the wages for those who labored on the public roads in order to work off taxes.[80] But all signs point to the disintegration in the eighteenth century of the general scheme of wage-fixing in Massachusetts, despite the fact that the basic system embodied in the Codes of 1648 and 1660 remained on the law books unrepealed. The absence of extensive regulatory codes, considered in conjunction with other factors, is evidence of

[75] The Necessity of Reformation . . . Synod at Boston (Boston, 1679).
[76] Magnalia Christi Americana, II, 287–289.
[77] Cotton Mather, The Present State of New-England (Boston, 1690).
[78] H. S. Sheldon, Documentary History of Suffield (Springfield, 1879), III, 104 and 129.
[79] For regulation of the wages of porters in the eighteenth century, see Acts and Resolves, II, 830, 831, 1067, and 1068; and V, 1121; of chimney sweepers, Boston Records, VIII, 58, 63, 82, 83, 295, and 296; XI, 196 and 197; XIII, 51; and XIV, 310, 311, 321, and 322.
[80] Muddy River and Brookline Records, 90–361 passim; Lee Records, 20 and 107; and Watertown Records, III, 219; and IV, 50, 67, 121, 136, and passim.

the breakdown of mercantilism as a system of internal regulation and of the rise of laissez-faire practices in industry and commerce considerably before the Revolution.[81]

In England, although wage assessments continued in one branch or another of industry down to the third decade of the nineteenth century, as early as the latter part of the seventeenth century the system had become largely ineffective. The scale set by the justices is believed to have lagged behind the amounts actually paid. Considering the cloth-manufacturing areas from which the bulk of the Puritan emigrants came, it is interesting to note that in the West Riding of Yorkshire the textile groups disappeared as early as 1671 from the list of industries in which wages were assessed, although statutes regulating wages in the woollen industry were enacted in the century following.[82] There is little doubt that in England the system was not in general operation in the eighteenth century. In Middlesex, for instance, after 1725 there was not "the faintest sign of the most perfunctory action." The passing of the "sleeping law," as one writer called it late in the century, brought cheer to Adam Smith, who felt that the law never could regulate wages properly, though it often pretended to do so.[83]

During the American Revolution, as a result of the rapid depreciation of paper money, the various state governments, including Massachusetts, once more resorted to the type of controls which had been attempted in the seventeenth century for preventing rapid increase in prices and wages.[84] Since this experiment has no logical connection with the early colonial efforts, it is deserving of separate study. The regulations were drawn up by the state legislature and by regional conventions, and relied for sanctions primarily upon the boycott and social ostracism. This later experiment marks a dramatic, though short-lived, chapter in the legal history of Massachusetts.

Not alone from the point of view of economic regulation, but also from the angle of our constitutional history, the early colonial tendency to confer upon administrative or court officers broad discretionary powers in

[81] E. A. J. Johnson, emphasizing colonial industrial self-sufficiency, regards the second decade of the eighteenth century as marking "the highest point of development of the Massachusetts mercantilistic ideas," and sees a gradual breakdown thereafter to the sixties. "Some Evidence of Mercantilism in the Massachusetts-Bay," *New England Quarterly*, I, 395.

[82] H. Heaton, "The Assessment of Wages," *Economics Journal*, XXIV, 228; and *The Yorkshire Woollen and Worsted Industries* (Oxford, 1920), 313 ff. In numerous counties, however, assessments were continued down to the middle of the eighteenth century.

[83] Adam Smith is corroborated in this view by such recent investigators as Lipson, Heckscher, and Dowdell, among others.

[84] Space limitations do not permit full documentation on the subject of wage regulation during Revolutionary times, but the *Acts and Resolves* and such Massachusetts newspapers as the *Continental Journal, Independent Chronicle, Boston Gazette, Evening Post,* and *Massachusetts Spy* testify to the social sanctions behind these regulations, and the eventual collapse of these efforts.

matters of wages and prices has unquestioned significance. In point of time these administrative powers were initiated prior to the external imposition upon the colonies of a broad administrative system to enforce the Acts of Trade. Students of the current expansion of administrative justice, as evidenced particularly in the labor sections of the defunct National Industrial Recovery Act and recent federal labor legislation, as well as framers of public policy, might find it profitable to explore in operation and consequences the colonial experiments in economic administration, including crop restriction and moratory legislation, strikingly analogous to contemporary trends, as well as wage and price controls in which Massachusetts pioneered.

The Secular Rebellion

3.   More of the World, Less of Heaven

Thomas Jefferson Wertenbaker

The Puritan fathers in founding New England were but dimly aware of the effect of local conditions upon their great venture. Yet, as they looked out from the decks of their little vessels upon the safe harbors in which they cast anchor, or noted the great schools of cod and herring which swarmed offshore, or explored every nook of Massachusetts Bay, Buzzards Bay and Narragansett Bay or peeped into the mouths of the Thames, the Connecticut and other rivers; as they examined the sandy soil of southeast Massachusetts, the boulder-covered uplands of the interior and the ancient mountain ranges to the north and west; as they viewed the vast reaches of the forests, they must have realized that these things would have a profound influence, not only upon their lives, but upon the future of the theocratic society it was their purpose to found.

If so, they were comforted by the thought that it was God Himself who had selected this region as the future home of His people, so that it must be in every way suitable. The abounding fish of the ocean had been placed there for their use, the noble harbors had been especially fashioned for their ships, the forests had been planted so that they might have wood for building houses and vessels, the soil had purposely been made rather infertile so that they would not forget religion for the quest of wealth. The Lord had led the Children of Israel into a land flowing with milk and honey, and it was to be expected that in the new Canaan He wished His people to enjoy the good things He had provided for them.

The ideal Puritan State was a very delicate plant, requiring not only constant care, but the most favorable conditions of soil and climate. It demanded isolation from the rest of the world lest it wither under the impact of new ideas, new discoveries and new ideals; the concentration of the people in centers of population so that they would not escape the ministrations and admonitions of the preachers and elders; an even distribution of wealth that there might be no influential group whose authority did not have its roots in religion; political sovereignty, so that no outside power might reach across the Atlantic to overthrow its laws and break down its safeguards against heresy. Exacting demands these, so exacting that Massachusetts and her sister Commonwealths were to find it impossible to meet them.

The town with its agricultural village was the ideal economic and social unit for the Puritan State, and had it continued unchanged the forces of disintegration would have been greatly retarded. But when thousands turned from agriculture to commerce, shipbuilding and fishing, when many villages grew into thriving cities, and when the farm began to replace the common field, the effect upon the established order was decidedly unfavorable. The "fathers," as we have seen, showed remarkable foresight in making the agricultural village the center of life in every community, but their vision did not extend beyond the first generation, for the typical town contained from the first the germ of disintegration.

It was land-hunger which proved the undoing of the original scheme. In England where great areas were held by the aristocracy and where tenantry was so widespread, the ownership of land in fee-simple was the ambition of every agricultural worker. It was the promise of land, not an acre or two, but scores, perhaps hundreds, of acres, which brought many of the first settlers to America and which later drove thousands of pioneers westward until the frontier had been wiped out. Had the founders of New England so restricted the size of each town that no point within its bounds lay more than two or at most three miles from its center, the course of New England history might have been different. But with each group of newcomers clamoring for land, and pointing eagerly to the vast unoccupied reaches, it seemed unreasonable for the government to be niggardly. So they usually set out for their new home bearing with them a charter for a tract far larger than they or their sons after them could hope to put under cultivation.

This was not a matter of serious concern during the first generation, for the town committee, after laying out the village and dividing the land adjacent to it, left the outlying tracts as common property to be held by the proprietors for future use. But its effects became apparent when the sons of the original settlers came of age, married and demanded land of their own, for the setting off of new divisions three, four or perhaps five miles from the village, made it imperative that the owners should organize their holdings as farms and erect on them dwellings and barns. The most conservative of selectmen, the most earnest minister, could not insist that a young proprietor reside in the old "center," when it would force him to go so great a distance to and from work, taking his farm implements with him and perhaps driving his ox team.

Consequently the more distant parts of the town were usually divided, not into strips of land within a field, but into farms. This all-important development may be traced in the records of scores of towns in Massachusetts, Connecticut, New Jersey and other colonies. The case of Enfield was typical. The original grant, embracing as it did a wide expanse of land in north-central Connecticut, was far too large for the first settlers to put under cultivation, and many square miles of good land were left in common. But in 1697 it was decided to make a new division, allotting each proprietor extensive holdings east of a north-south line four miles from the village.[1] Most of these new lots lay idle for years, but gradually the owners' sons, as they grew to manhood, cleared away the trees from limited areas and put them under cultivation. It is probable that in some cases these young men continued to live in the village, making the trip to the fields only when plowing or harvesting, and erecting crude shacks in which from time to time they could spend the night. The first settler in what is now Somers, one Benjamin Jones, lived on his land only during the summer. But in time many proprietors moved out permanently, built houses and established themselves as farmers.

Thus was the original plan of the founders undermined. While the village of Enfield, with its system of fields and lots continued for many more decades, it had ceased to be the place of residence for an ever-increasing part of the people. In 1729 the number of families in the eastern part of the town had become so numerous that they were permitted to have their own school. The establishing two decades later of a school system for the entire town, with buildings in the northern, southern, northeastern and southeastern parts, shows how widespread the farm system had then become.

The Enfield ministers must have viewed with dismay the dispersal of their congregation over so wide an area. No longer was it possible for them, as in the old days when their entire flock lived within the village, to catechize the children, visit all the sick, watch over the wavering and

[1] Francis O. Allen, *History of Enfield, Conn.*, I, pp. 289–308.

admonish the wayward. When the roads were blocked by snow or washed by heavy rains, they knew that there would be many vacant seats during the Sunday sermon. Even though they did their best to hold the congregation together, riding out to the outlying farms to catechize the children and visit the sick, the effort was a severe one and the results unsatisfactory. So they made no serious objection when, in 1723, the farmers in the most distant part of the town set themselves off as the East Precinct, or when, four years later, they drew up their covenant as a separate Church, or when, in 1734, they broke off completely from Enfield and established their own town.[2]

The experience of Enfield was repeated by town after town. In Woodbury, when a new community was formed known as the Upper Farms, the good people living there retained their membership in the parent Church for years, trudging from four to seven miles every Sunday in winter and summer to the village meeting-house, carrying with them their fire-arms as protection against the Indians. But at last, when they begged the Assembly to have mercy on their souls by permitting them to establish a Church of their own, that body, after long delays, constituted them into the parish of Roxbury. Still later another group, living in what was known as the North Purchase, "near ten miles distant from the first society," established a third Church.[3]

Even more instructive is the story of the Church of South Hadley. When the people south of Mount Holyoke, tired of walking eight miles over mountain paths to attend Sabbath services, gained permission to have their own ecclesiastical society, they began plans to erect the meeting-house. But now a bitter controversy arose over its location. If it were placed in the east part of the precinct, the farmers in the west would still have to cover miles of bad road to reach it; if in the west part, the eastern farmers would suffer. When at last the western group won and actually began construction, some of the others under the cover of night cut off the plates and pushed over one end of the frame. After this act of vandalism, so inconsistent with the "brotherly sweetness" urged by the ministers, the two parts of South Hadley were divided into separate Churches, so that each could have its own meeting-house.[4]

It was perhaps inevitable that the first village to be founded in New England was also the first to suffer from the transition to rural life. The Pilgrim fathers, toiling upon their infertile soil, found it difficult to supply themselves with the bare necessities of life. But with the Great Migration came a decided change, for the demand for grain and cattle, which sent prices soaring, brought sudden and unexpected prosperity. This in turn

[2] *Ibid.*, I, p. 344. The new town was named Somers.
[3] William Cothren, *The History of Ancient Woodbury, Conn.*, pp. 239–257, 273–276.
[4] Sylvester Judd, *History of Hadley*, pp. 289 n., 395–401.

influenced the people to make new clearings for pastures and cornfields, which, in many cases, were at such a distance from the village that the owners were forced to reside upon them. "There was no longer any holding them together," complained Governor Bradford, "but now they must of necessity go to their great lots. And no man now thought he could live except he had cattle and a great deal of ground to keep them, all striving to increase their stocks. By which means they were scattered all over the bay quickly and the town, in which they had lived compactly till now, was left very thin, and in a short time almost desolate." [5]

The Governor did not begrudge the people their sudden prosperity, but he bewailed the effect of this dispersal upon religion, which turned benefit into hurt and "accession of strength to their weakness." For the scattering of the settlers was followed by the dividing of the Church so that "those that had lived so long together in Christian and comfortable fellowship must now part and suffer many divisions. First, those that lived on their lots on the other side of the bay (called Duxbury) they could not long bring their wives and children to the public worship and Church meetings here, but with such burden as, growing to some competent number, they sued to be dismissed and become a body of themselves, and so they were dismissed . . . though very unwillingly." [6]

Warned by this experience, the town tried an experiment which it was hoped would prevent the further disintegration of the village. Some especially desirable land at Green Harbor, which had remained in common, was now laid out in farms and granted to certain persons who were "likely to be helpful to the Church and commonwealth," on the express condition that they reside in Plymouth, leaving their cattle and cornfields under the supervision of servants. In this way the land was to be "tied" to the village. "But alas! this remedy proved worse than the disease, for within a few years those that had thus got footing there rent themselves away, partly by force, and partly wearing the rest with importunity and pleas of necessity . . . and others still, as they conceived themselves straitened . . . break away under one pretence or other." [7]

When the Indians, in King Philip's War, laid waste town after town and brought sorrow to hundreds of New England families, the Reverend William Hubbard placed the blame in part upon this movement. "The first that came over hither for the Gospel could not tell what to do with more land than a small number of acres, yet now men more easily swallow down so many hundreds and are not satisfied," he said in the election sermon of 1676. If they were but a "little straitened," they thought it necessary to move, even though by so doing they parted with "a good

[5] William Bradford's *History of Plymoth Plantation* (Boston, 1899), pp. 361–362.
[6] *Ibid.*, p. 362.
[7] *Ibid.*, pp. 362, 363.

neighborhood and the beautiful heritage of Church communion, or Gospel worship, to pitch with Lot in the confines of Sodom. . . . Is it a wonder then that we find war at our gates? God is knocking the hands of New England people off from the world and from new plantations, till they get them new hearts resolved to reform this great evil." [8]

As late as 1705 the Reverend Joseph Easterbrooks was bewailing the fact that men were no longer living together in compact communities where they could enjoy the religious instruction of learned clergymen, but were going out to remote places "for worldly conveniences." "By that means [they] have seemed to bid defiance, not only to religion, but to civility itself, and such places thereby have become nurseries of ignorance, profaneness and atheism." [9]

In Massachusetts Bay when the movement from the villages to the farms began to gain headway, the founders attempted to put a stop to it by law. In September, 1635, the General Court ruled that thereafter no dwelling should be built more than half a mile from the meeting-house without especial leave, "in any new plantation granted at this Court." The order applied to "Ipswich, Hingham, Newbury and Weymouth, as well as to all towns to be established in the future," [10] and the next year it was extended "to all the towns in the jurisdiction." But the General Court was no match for economic law, and the pressure from those who had experienced the inconvenience of dwelling at one place and conducting a farm at another was so great that in 1640 they rescinded the order. [11] Four decades later Increase Mather complained: "People are ready to run wild into the woods again and to be as heathenish as ever, if you do not prevent it." [12]

The change from the unified economy of the agricultural village to the farm system constituted a revolution which was not the less profound because usually so gradual. No longer was it possible for the minister and the elders to know their parishioners with the old intimacy so that they could admonish them for every breach of the Sabbath or for every exchange of gossip. If there were vacant seats at the Sunday's sermon, the absentees might reasonably plead the great distance of their farms from the meeting-house and the badness of the roads. And in winter, when heavy snows blocked the roads, the farmer was practically cut off from the rest of the world despite his sled or his snowshoes.

The ecclesiastical character of the town meeting, so vital in the old scheme of things, might have survived the transition to farm life, had the splitting off of territory from an old town to form a new one preceded and

---

[8] William Hubbard, *The Happiness of a People*, pp. 58, 59.

[9] Perry Miller and Thomas H. Johnson, *The Puritans*, p. 17.

[10] Nathaniel B. Shurtleff, ed., *Records of Massachusetts Bay*, p. 157.

[11] *Ibid.*, p. 291.

[12] Increase Mather, *A Discourse Concerning the Danger of Apostasy*, second edition, 1685, p. 104.

not followed the organization of the new Church. There would then have been but one "society" in each of the separated territories, so that the old meeting could have retained its ecclesiastical functions and the meeting of the new town assumed them the moment the new Church was organized. As it was, the pleas for Gospel preaching were so urgent and so reasonable that Church dismembership almost invariably antedated civil dismemberment, and when the voters of the new town assembled for the first time, their ecclesiastical society had already been in existence for years, perhaps for decades.

The old unity within the town which had resulted from the singleness of purpose of the people was weakened, also, by the gradual breakdown of the laws against the admission of strangers. When Master Dawson, the blacksmith, or Goodman Calkins, the tanner, or Parke, the cooper, needed an apprentice, it seemed a hard case if the Selectmen refused to permit them to look beyond the town limits in case the sons of the original settlers were busy with their own affairs—opening new fields, building barns, planting orchards, caring for their livestock. Moreover, when after years of hard labor, a degree of prosperity had come to some of the families, so that they could afford to employ a servant or a field hand, the community was not inclined to balk them. Nor did it seem reasonable to exclude a "foreigner" from some other part of New England or even from old England when he presented letters from well-known Puritans, attesting to his orthodoxy and his good conduct.

In time, as the number of newcomers increased, a sharp division was drawn between them and the families of the original settlers. Since it was the founders who had endured the hardships of frontier life, who had taken the risks, who had purchased the land from the Indians, they and their descendants contended that all undivided land belonged to them rather than to the town as a whole. On the other hand, the newcomers protested violently against being excluded, so that the little meeting-houses resounded to the speeches of the contending factions. In the end the old planters usually won the day. In Milford, for instance, the town-meeting decided in 1713 to give over the proprietorship of all common land "to those persons and their heirs forever which are in the present public list of estates to be proportioned to or by the said list." [13]

Enfield had taken similar action two years before, when the proprietors of the common lands met in Sergeant James Pease's house "to regulate some things that may be just grounds of dissatisfaction respecting commonage and undivided lands." Hereafter it was this group, meeting as a distinct body having their own moderator and records, and not the town-meeting, which had the authority to grant and sequester land, to lay out grants for "foreigners," orphans and others, to confirm grants formerly

[13] Leonard W. Labaree, "Milford, Conn.," Tercentenary Commission, *Historical Publications,* Nos. 1–10.

made by the town and to employ persons to defend their rights in the courts.[14]

In some of the towns the victory did not rest entirely with the original planters, since many late comers were included in the lists of proprietors. Milford, for example, decided to draw the line at 1688, excluding all who had been admitted to the town since that date save those whom their committee should deem it reasonable to except. Since the completed list contained 197 names as compared with 134 in the division of 1687, it is evident that a large proportion of newcomers had been added.[15]

The proprietors were more active in safeguarding their rights and conserving the commons than had been the town-meeting. It had become the custom for the inhabitants to cut timber, gather stones for building, and to pasture their cattle in undivided tracts, but with wood becoming scarce and land more valuable, the proprietors took steps to exclude trespassers. They also kept a vigilant eye on squatters.

In Milford the situation was complicated by the purchase from the Indians of two large tracts which extended the northern boundary of the town to Waterbury, twenty miles from the village. In each case the money was raised by selling shares, so that one tract was known as the "Two Bit Purchase" and the other the "One Bit Purchase." In each case the shareholders constituted themselves into a body of proprietors to hold the tract in common and to make divisions and grants. Although the two groups were interlocking, they were quite distinct from each other, one comprising 195 names, the other 178 names. Since a proprietary body had been created for sequestered lands as early as 1688, there now existed in Milford no less than four separate bodies each distinct from the town-meeting and each exercising certain functions which in a democratic community should have belonged to the government.

Thus did local forces change the character of the original New England town. It must have saddened the founders as they saw the beginnings of this transformation; it would have caused them deep apprehension had they lived to witness its later stages. Unity had been the key word in the organization of the old town, a unity marked by the identity of Church members and freemen, of town and proprietors, a unity sealed by the agricultural village embracing as it did within its narrow bounds the entire population. Now all was quite different. For an increasingly large part of the people farm life superseded life in the village; the town had surrendered its function as an ecclesiastical society so that no longer did all the people belong to one single congregation; to the village school had been added other schools in different parts of the town; the common land

---

[14] Francis O. Allen, *History of Enfield, Conn.,* I, pp. 315, 680–685.
[15] Leonard W. Labaree, "Milford, Conn.," Tercentenary Commission, *Historical Publications,* Nos. 1–10.

belonged not to the people of the town but to a single privileged group.

This revolution within the town should not be overemphasized in explaining the ultimate failure of the experiment of the Bible Common-wealth. A farmer might, despite the remoteness of the meeting-house and the badness of the roads, be as ardently religious as his father who had lived in the village. But when Cotton Mather, Increase Mather, Urian Oakes and other leading preachers bemoaned the decay of religion and pointed out the growth of levity, immorality, drunkenness, skepticism, indifference, profanity, Sabbath breaking, vanity in dress, pride, etc., they had every right to lay the blame in part upon changed conditions within those foundation stones of the religious-political states—the towns.

The spread of farm economy was accompanied by the transformation of many coastal villages into commercial cities, and the development of trade as the mainstay of the entire region. It was a change not wholly unwelcome to the founders, since it brought prosperity and wealth to New England and gave them evidence that God was showering favors upon His chosen people, yet it loosened new influences which many feared would in the end undermine the structure of Church and State. Edward Johnson gave vigorous voice to both points of view. He gloried that the Lord had in so brief a time converted that "remote, rocky, barren, bushy, wild-woody wilderness, a receptacle for lions, wolves, bears, foxes . . . and all kind of wild creatures," into a world mart, "Holland, France, Spain and Portugal coming hither for trade, shipping going on gallantly." But he was no less emphatic in expressing his disapproval of those who were "so taken up with the income of a large profit that they would willingly have had the commonwealth tolerate divers kinds of sinful opinions to entice men to come and sit down with us, that their purses might be filled with coin, the civil government with contention and the Churches of our Lord Christ with errors." [16]

It had been the hope of the fathers of New England that the region would afford some staple product for which there would be a ready market in England and which would place their venture upon a solid economic basis. Some even went so far as to predict what that staple would be. "How serviceable this country must needs be for provisions for shipping, is sufficiently known already," wrote John White in *The Planters Plea*. "At present it may yield planks, masts, oars, pitch, tar and iron, and hereafter, by the aptness of the soil for hemp, if the colony increase, sails and cordage." With this opinion, Thomas Morton, however much his religious views differed from those of the pious White, was in full accord. The forests of New England would produce many needed products, he pointed out, chief among which were "resin, pitch, and tar," commodities

[16] J. Franklin Jameson, ed., *Johnson's Wonder-Working Providence*, p. 254.

so essential to England that were they not imported from foreign countries, England's navigation would decline.[17]

Unfortunately, this expectation was disappointed. The great forests, extending hundreds of miles inland, stood ready to yield their products, the English merchants were eager to buy, but the toil expended in felling trees, splitting and sawing timbers, producing tar was so heavy and the cost of labor so high that the profits did not justify the venture. So the settlers began to look elsewhere for the promised staple, some of them hopefully, others with skepticism. Edward Johnson tells us that for a long time the great fear of many, "and those who were endued with grace from above also," was that New England "would be no place of continued habitation for want of a staple commodity." [18]

Eventually they found what they were looking for, not in the soil, nor in the mines, but in the waters which washed New England's shores. It was Captain John Smith who had predicted that fish would become the staple of the region. "Let not the meanness of the word fish distaste you," he said, "for it will afford as good gold as the mines of Guiana and Potassie with less hazard and charge, and more certainty and facility." [19] King Charles, in the Massachusetts Bay Company's charter, had promised that nothing should "hinder our loving subjects whatsoever to use and exercise the trade of fishing upon that coast of New England" nor to erect stages and houses "necessary for the salting, drying and packing their fish."

It was the Dorchester men, many of them from Dorset and Devon, who were "the first to set upon the trade of fishing in the bay," but Marblehead, Gloucester and other places were quick to follow. Before the end of the third decade of the seventeenth century scores of little sloops and ketches, each manned by a crew of three, could be seen offshore from Cape Cod to Maine, their sails furled and lines cast out. Later, as the fishermen grew bolder, they ventured out to the dangerous waters off Sable Island, and then to the Grand Banks.[20]

With the advent of longer and more dangerous voyages, the open boat gave way to the pinkie, of ten to twenty tons, decked over and carrying two fore-and-aft sails, a foresail and a mainsail. The men wore a hat of canvas laid over with tar, a thick knitted jersey, heavy cowhide boots and a leather apron. Voyages to the Grand Banks lasted from ten to twelve days, but the catch, which usually was excellent, was ample compensation provided the vessel was not wrecked in the perilous shoal water. It was no unusual thing to return so heavily laden with cod that the seas swept over the decks. These early fishermen set out their lines chiefly for cod,

---

[17] Thomas Morton, "New England Canaan," Peter Force, *Tracts and Other Papers,* II, No. 5, p. 44.

[18] J. Franklin Jameson, ed., *Johnson's Wonder-Working Providence,* p. 246.

[19] John Smith, *Works* (Edward Arber, ed.), p. 784.

[20] Wm. B. Weeden, *Economic and Social History of New England,* I, p. 132.

although they also valued bass and alewives. Mackerel, in colonial times, served mainly for bait.[21]

The life of the fisherman was not necessarily unfavorable for religion, since he lived usually in the village within easy reach of the meeting-house. In fact, many were sincerely devout, and it was the practice for the skipper to take his Bible with him so that, when the weather was rough or the fish were not biting, he could read passages from it to the crew. Nor would he permit fishing on Sunday, even when the run was at its best and delay might mean failure for the entire voyage. Some, however, were not scrupulous, and it was with a touch of envy as well as stern disapproval that the Bible-reading skipper watched on a Sabbath morning his rivals haul in cod after cod while his own lines were idle.[22] Cotton Mather states that when a Massachusetts minister was exhorting the congregation of a certain fishing village to remain steadfast for religion, since it had been the main end of their coming to America, "a well-known person there in the assembly cried out, 'Sir, you are mistaken—our main end was to catch fish.' " [23]

The New Englanders were not long in discovering that in fish they had a commodity greatly desired by other peoples. Portugal and Spain wanted fish, the Canaries wanted fish, Barbados wanted fish, southern France wanted fish. So the fishermen doubled and tripled their catch, split and salted the cod on shipboard, rinsed them in salt water on shore, spread them to dry on stages or hurdles, packed them in barrels and shipped them off to market. In 1641 no less than 300,000 were exported and the number grew with the years. The best grade was sold to the countries of southern Europe; the middling grade of dried codfish, because it was easy to keep, was sold in large quantities to the colonial farmers, while the lowest-grade fish and pickled bass, mackerel and alewives fed the slave populations of the West Indies.[24]

The merchants, when their vessels came to anchor in the ports of southern Europe or of the Caribbean islands, were quick to discover that their customers had many valuable products stored in their warehouses ready for exchange. So when they turned their prows back toward New England their holds were usually filled.

The trade thus started, with fish as its original incentive, received new impetus with the advent of the English Civil War and the consequent falling off in immigration. For more than a decade there had been a constant stream of vessels from English ports bringing large supplies of manufactured goods, together with hundreds of newcomers, all eager purchasers of corn, wheat, cattle and whatever else they had been unable

[21] James B. Connolly, *The Port of Gloucester*, p. 11.
[22] *Ibid.*, p. 14.
[23] Cotton Mather, *Magnalia* (Hartford, 1820), I, p. 62.
[24] Samuel E. Morrison, *The Maritime History of Massachusetts*, pp. 13, 14.

to bring with them. But when the flow of settlers was cut off hard times followed. "All foreign commodities grew scarce and our own of no price," wrote Governor Winthrop. "Corn would buy nothing; a cow which cost last year £20 might now be bought for 4 or £5. . . . These straits set our people on work to provide fish, clapboards, plank, etc. . . . and to look out to the West Indies for trade."

The traders did not turn to the mother country as a market for their goods because they had very little to offer which she stood in need of. Fish she had in plenty, brought by her own bold fishermen from the waters off Iceland, Greenland and Newfoundland; she considered it unwise to import grain and meat to the discouragement of her own farmers; American naval stores and timber, after transportation costs had been paid, proved too costly.

On the other hand, England eagerly purchased all the furs which the colonists could send over. The Plymouth settlers discovered the value of the fur trade several years before the coming of the main body of Puritans, and by keeping a constant supply of wampum on hand, secured large quantities of beaver from the Kennebec region for export to England. Nor were other towns long in following their example. Trading posts were established on the more important rivers, to which the Indians brought their beaver and other furs in exchange for wampum, knives, blankets and, only too often, for firearms. From these posts the peltry found its way to the commercial centers, where it was brought up by the exporters. John Hull, the Boston merchant, was a constant dealers in furs and more than once tells us of his losses, when his cargoes were taken by enemy warships or went down in a shipwreck.[25]

Yet New England was not destined to be a great fur-trading region comparable to Canada or New Netherlands. The supply within her own territory was limited, and dwindled rapidly with the advance of the frontier and with the Indian wars. At the same time she lacked any great waterway comparable to the St. Lawrence, or the Hudson and the Mohawk, leading to the vast fur-bearing regions around the Great Lakes. No doubt the clergy were well satisfied that the number of New Englanders who were exposed to the debauchery of life at the trading posts was small, but the Boston and Salem merchants regretted deeply the scarcity of furs to throw into the balance of trade with England.

A glimpse at the lading of the *America*, a 300-ton vessel sailing in 1692 from Portsmouth, shows that by that date the emphasis for exports to the mother country had shifted from furs to naval stores and barrel staves, for it included 18 masts, 9 bowsprits, 13 yards, 11,400 feet of oars, 2,900 feet of wood, 25,000 staves, 46 spars and but 84 pounds of beaver and 130 small furs.[26] John Hull was especially active in the trade with England.

[25] "Diary of John Hull," American Antiquarian Society *Transactions and Collections*, III, p. 148.

[26] *Provincial Papers of New Hampshire*, II, p. 80.

In contrast to the English trade the interchange of goods with the West Indies became more and more extensive.[27] The keen New England merchants, once they cast anchor in the ports of Antigua, or Jamaica, or Barbados, were not long in noting that fish was not the only commodity which they could supply for which there was a lively demand. Before long they were back again with a part of their cargo space filled with dried beef, pork, wheat and pease, or perhaps with staves for sugar or molasses barrels or for wine pipes; perhaps with horses for the sugar mills, or with timber for the framing of houses.[28] Edward Johnson could boast that the Lord, "whose promises are large to his Sion," had turned everything in the country into a staple—"wheat, rye, oats, pease, barley, beef, pork, fish, butter, cheese, timber, mast, tar, soap, plankboard, frames of houses, clapboard and pipestaves." [29]

Having discharged their cargoes at the wharves of Bridgetown, or Kingston, or St. John, the New England masters loaded their holds with West Indian products—barrels of molasses, barrels of sugar, packages of cotton or tobacco or indigo, perhaps a few Negro slaves. Back in New England they could dispose of these goods to advantage, for what could not be consumed there was re-exported and brought excellent returns. The sugar and molasses were welcome on every table, while the rum into which much was converted was welcomed not only by lumbermen and fishermen, but by the mass of the people. Newport had twenty-two "still-houses" at one time and it was estimated that the Massachusetts stills consumed 15,000 hogsheads of molasses yearly. However, the larger part of the fiery liquor went, not down the throats of the New Englanders, but to Africa as an important item of exchange. The tobacco, too, was in part sold in the local markets, for, if we may judge from the number of pipes imported, the people must have been inveterate smokers. Nor were the slaves left on the hands of the merchants, since servants were always in demand and even the clergy looked upon it as no sin to purchase them. When some of the members of Cotton Mather's congregation presented him with a slave he rejoiced at Heaven's smile,[30] while Reverend Ebenezer Bridge considered it a "sore providence," when his "negro servant Venus died of the throat distemper." [31]

The vessels which left New England with cargoes of fish and staves for La Rochelle, Bordeaux, Marseilles, Bilboa, Lisbon, Malaga, Barcelona, Leghorn and other southern European ports brought back pipes and butts full of wine to grace the tables of the well-to-do; salt, so essential to the fishing industry; fruits, oil, soap, raisins and many other products.[32] This

[27] William B. Weeden, *Economic and Social History of New England,* I, p. 56.
[28] Charles M. Andrews, *Colonial Period of American History,* I, p. 516.
[29] J. Franklin Jameson, ed., *Johnson's Wonder-Working Providence,* p. 247.
[30] "Diary of Cotton Mather," Massachusetts Historical Society *Collections,* Seventh Series, VII, p. 579.
[31] *Diary of Ebenezer Bridge,* MSS. II, p. 265.
[32] Charles M. Andrews, *Colonial Period of American History,* I, p. 517.

trade, which yielded so much profit to the merchants and such luxuries to the people, was, however, subject to losses from shipwreck in the long voyage across the Atlantic or from capture by hostile raiders in time of war. "The Lord brought all the vessels I was concerned in this year in safety," wrote John Hull in 1671. "But, upon 23d of 9th, John Harris, with his ketch, being gone out to sea . . . came back . . . but could not reach the harbor and was put on shore. . . . One half of the vessel and cargo was mine."

Not content with their European and West Indian trade, the New Englanders made themselves at home in every port of the American North Atlantic. As early as 1634 we find them in Virginia waters and we know from Winthrop that both Plymouth and Massachusetts Bay "had oft trade" with the Dutch in the Hudson River. In the Chesapeake Bay region the Yankee skippers became unpopular when they sent rowboats up the creeks at night to trade with the slaves for stolen goods. Yet they found the planters and storekeepers quite ready to trade tobacco, corn, beans and meat for West Indian sugar and molasses. The voyage of the *Orataro*, of Rhode Island, from Barbados to Virginia with a cargo of rum, molasses and brown sugar for exchange for wheat, corn, beeswax, leather, pork, beef and staves, although made in 1740, was typical, even for the mid-seventeenth century.[33]

Nor did the New Englanders scruple to take on a cargo of Virginia or Maryland tobacco, bring it to Boston or Newport or Salem and then sail with it directly to the continent of Europe in defiance of the Acts of Navigation. In 1679 Robert Holden, a British collector of customs, reported that six Boston merchants received regularly the larger part of the Albemarle Sound tobacco crop and shipped it to Ireland, Holland, France and Spain "under the notion of fish and such goods." English merchants complained that "New England men did carry much tobacco and other commodities of the growth of the plantations to New England and from thence did carry them to foreign nations, whereby they could undersell them."[34] Parliament responded with the Navigation Act of 1673, placing a duty on the shipment of tobacco and other commodities from one colony to another, but the traders found various ways of evading it.

Edward Randolph, writing in 1676, gives an instructive account of the commerce of New England. The native products suitable for exportation he lists as "all things necessary for shipping and naval furniture," especially the trunks of pines "for masts the best in the world," but also pitch, tar, hemp, and iron; various kinds of timber products, such as "clapboards, pipestaves, planks and deal boards"; "horses, beeves, sheep, hogs and goats"; the furs or skins of "beaver, otter, moose, deer, stags, foxes," etc.;

[33] T. J. Wertenbaker, *Norfolk—Historic Southern Port*, p. 38.
[34] George L. Beer, *The Old Colonial System*, I, p. 80.

"also plenty of wheat, rye, barley, oats, and peas"; several kinds of fish, "especially cod, mackerel and herring, which are very large and fat."

To Virginia, Maryland and Jamaica, the merchants sent "beef and pork salted, pease, flour, biscuit and malt, codfish and salt mackerel"; to Barbados, Nevis and St. Christopher the same commodities together with horses, dealboards, pipestaves and "houses ready framed"; to Spain, Portugal, Madeira and the Canaries "fish, timber, pipestaves and dealboards"; to England "masts and yards for ships, fir and oak planks, with all sorts of peltry." The exports to Europe were not confined to the products of New England, but included those of other colonies, while the return cargoes were made up of goods "vendible either in New England or in any other of his Majesty's dominions in America—as brandy, Canary, Spanish and French wines, bullion, salt, fruits, oils, silks, laces, linnen of all sorts, cloth, serges, bays, kersies, stockings and many other commodities." It was the great care of the merchants to keep their ships in constant employ, which made them "try all ports to force a trade." [35]

Among the trading centers of New England Boston early took the lead, partly because of her fine harbor, in which several hundred vessels could lie at anchor in good depth of water, partly because of the enterprise and ability of her merchants. As early as 1640 we find the town government encouraging the building of wharves and supervising storage. Along the irregular water front of the Boston peninsula one might see long lines of wagons and, tied up to the jetties, scores of small vessels all laden with country produce, while the countinghouses and storage houses were crowded with busy traders. At the larger wharves were sloops, ketches and ships, their sailors heaving at barrels and crates as they unloaded their cargoes of sugar, molasses, or European goods, or took on fish, meat, breadstuffs and tobacco. Conspicuous was the dock at the foot of Dock Square, and the market place, which was famous for its great hoisting crane. [36]

Boston, in 1664, was reported to have 14,300 souls, and its growth continued throughout the colonial period. Its merchant fleet, numbering in less than 300 vessels, plied back and forth from the West Indies, the Chesapeake, Madeira, etc., while its numerous fishing craft brought in tons of cod and mackerel from Cape Sable waters. [37] "Boston may be esteemed the mart town of the West Indies," stated Edward Randolph. [38] The interchange of goods was carried on almost exclusively in New England-built vessels, many of them Boston built, for from a very early date the banks of the Back Bay and the Mystic were dotted with the frames of ketches, sloops and ships. In 1700 Bellomont, after going

[35] "Hutchinson Papers," II, *Publications of Prince Society*, pp. 230, 231.
[36] Charles M. Andrews, *Colonial Period of American History*, I, p. 514.
[37] *Calendar of State Papers, Colonial, America and West Indies*, 1665–68, p. 532.
[38] "Hutchinson Papers," II, *Publications of Prince Society*, p. 231.

through the registers, sent word to the British government that the town could boast of 25 ships of from 100 tons to 300, 39 of about 100 tons or under, 50 brigantines, 13 ketches, and 67 sloops.

Edward Johnson gloried in the prosperity of Boston as a signal evidence of God's indulgence to His chosen people. "The chief edifice of this city-like town is crowded on the sea-banks and wharfed out with great industry and cost, the buildings beautiful and large, some fairly set forth with brick, tile, stone and slate and orderly placed with comely streets, whose continual enlargement presages some sumptuous city. . . . But now behold the admirable acts of Christ; at this His people's landing the hideous thickets in this place were such that wolves and bears nursed up their young from the eyes of all beholders, in those very places where the streets are full of girls and boys sporting up and down, with a continuous concourse of people. Good store of shipping is here yearly built, and some very fair ones. . . . This town is the very mart of the land; French, Portugals and Dutch come hither for traffic." [39]

But the ministers and elders were not quite so positive as Johnson that the growth of commerce in New England was entirely the Lord's doing. They feared that all this bustle and stir in the ports, this constant attention to business affairs, this eager desire for profits, this discussion of markets and prices, this bringing in of a rough seafaring element, most of them frequenters of the taverns rather than of the meeting-houses, this creation of a wealthy merchant class, would turn the face of the people away from religion. Like Jefferson they considered agriculture the ideal vocation, not because, like Jefferson, they were concerned with its influence upon democracy, but because they thought it the best foundation for a religious commonwealth. And, like Jefferson, they were powerless to prevent the growth of another form of economic life, when the force of natural conditions dictated it. Had they declared an embargo on trade as a kind of "peaceful coercion" against irreligion, it would have failed just as, a century later, Jefferson's embargo failed to keep the United States out of the Napoleonic wars.

But though the religious leaders accepted the growth of commerce as inevitable, they battled fiercely against the evils which followed in its wake. In the election sermons and in every local pulpit the ministers warned the people that they must not substitute Mammon for the true God. "It concerneth New England always to remember that originally they are a plantation religious, not a plantation of trade," pleaded John Norton in the election sermon of 1657.[40] Four years later John Higginson echoed his words. "My fathers and brethren, this is never to be forgotten that New England is originally a plantation of religion, not a plantation of trade. Let merchants and such as are increasing cent per cent remember

[39] J. Franklin Jameson, ed., *Johnson's Wonder-Working Providence*, p. 71.
[40] John Norton, *The Heart of New England Rent*, p. 58.

this, that worldly gain was not the end and design of the people of New England, but religion." [41] Eleazer Mather, pastor of the Northampton Church, asked whether in the first years of settlement, when there had been "less of the world," there had not been more of Heaven. "Less trading, buying, selling, but more praying, more watching over our hearts, more close walking, less plenty and less inequity?" [42]

The ministers were especially concerned at the development of the merchant aristocracy, for they realized that it would inevitably become a rival of the aristocracy of religion. In the train of successful sea ventures came wealth, and wealth brought power. The merchants of Boston, Salem, New Haven and other New England ports built handsome residences and filled them with fine furniture and silver, became the acknowledged leaders in social life, frequently played important roles as selectmen, deputies, judges and commanders of the militia, contributed generously to charity or to public works, added a touch of rationalism to an atmosphere supercharged with religion.

Their absorption in acquiring worldly riches rather than heavenly riches was especially displeasing to the clergy. The founders of New England had come into the wilderness, not in search of great estates, they reiterated, but to enjoy the pure worship of God after the apostolic manner. But now their descendants were deserting the good old ways, were forgetting that they were God's chosen people, in their eager search of profits. "Some there are, and not a few, that are so engaged in their own interests that, let the cause of God and his people sink or swim, they care not, so their own ends be compassed," complained John Wilson and Samuel Whiting. "We have been changing in our main fundamental interests," Samuel Torrey warned; "we have been deserting our own religious interest and espousing another, a worldly interest; we are turning from God after the world; the world is becoming the main interest of New England." "When men have property, outward riches, and know not what to do with them besides making gods of them, this is a sign that God's gracious presence is not among a people, when men lose religion in the world, and what they get in temporals they lose in spirituals," pointed out Eleazer Mather. "Outward prosperity is a worm at the root of godliness, so that religion dies when the world thrives." [43]

Yet many of the merchants were men of religious lives and ardent supporters of the established order in Church and State. Typical was John Hull, who reveals himself in his *Diary* as an interesting amalgam of the astute businessman and the religious devotee. When a ketch was cast ashore on Cape Cod and lost with part of her cargo, he jotted down: "One half the vessel and cargo was mine. The Lord give me spiritual and

[41] John Higginson, *The Cause of God and His People in New England*, p. 11.
[42] Eleazer Mather, *A Serious Exhortation.*
[43] Eleazer Mather, *A Serious Exhortation.*

heavenly treasure when he taketh from me earthly, and that will be a good exchange." On June 17, 1672, he wrote: "This winter the ships that went home to London were many of them taken by the Dutch capers. I lost in Master Hilton, Master Jonas Clark and Thomas Moore six hundred and forty pounds. God mixeth His mercies and chastisements." [44]

At times Hull seems to have had misgivings as to the effect of his success in business upon the welfare of his soul. On one occasion he wrote that he would "more and more affect and embrace opportunity of getting out rather than running into the business of this world, specially foreign traffic, as desirous to be more thoughtful of launching into that vast ocean of eternity whither we must all shortly be carried that so I might be in a prepared posture for my Lord's coming." [45]

Edward Johnson found it difficult to explain why pious merchants and masters were permitted to perish with the sinful. "The Lord was pleased to command the wind and seas to give us a jog on the elbow by sinking the very chief of our shipping in the deep and splitting them in shivers against the shore; a very goodly ship, called the *Seaforce*, was cast away and many New England people put to hard shifts for their lives, and some drowned, as the godly and dearly beloved servant of Christ, Mr. Thomas Cortmire, a very able seaman and a good scholar, one who had spent both his labor and estate for the helping on of this wilderness work. As also another ship set forth by the merchants of New Haven, of which the godly Mr. Lamberton was master, neither ship, person nor goods ever heard of. . . . This seemed the sorer affliction to these New England people, because many godly men lost their lives." [46]

Prominent among the seventeenth-century merchants was Philip English of Salem. Coming to the colony from the Isle of Jersey, he rose in the world until he became one of the richest men in New England. Out from his wharf and warehouses went goods in his own vessels for Bilboa, Barbados, St. Christopher's and elsewhere. His mansion on Essex Street, known as English's Great House, a large frame structure whose overhanging second story and steep roof proclaimed it a typical example of East Anglian architecture, stood for a century and a half as a reminder of his wealth and influence. Like Hull a man of piety, English constantly interlined his business records with references to God and the Bible. "Shipped by the Grace of God . . . in the good sloop called *Mayflower* whereof is master under God for the present voyage John Swazey . . . and by God's grace bound for Virginia or Maryland . . .

[44] "Diary of John Hull," American Antiquarian Society *Transactions and Collections,* III, p. 160.
[45] *John Hull Letter Book,* quoted by W. B. Weeden, *Economic and Social History of New England,* I, p. 249.
[46] J. Franklin Jameson, ed., *Johnson's Wonder-Working Providence,* p. 253.

twenty hogsheads of salt. . . . And so God sent the good sloop to her desired port in safety. Amen." [47]

English's power, influence and religious life did not suffice to save him and his wife from being "cried out upon" as witches in the "epidemic" of 1690. Mrs. English, a woman of education and piety and a loving wife and mother, was accused first, when the High Sheriff, deputy and other officers came at night to arrest her. When six weeks later her husband, also, was taken into custody, they were both removed to Boston. They would no doubt have perished on the gallows had not two ministers, more practical than some of their fellows, urged them to flee. Finding a safe refuge in New York, they waited there until the witchcraft craze had run its course, and then quietly returned to Salem. [48]

Prominent among the Salem merchants was Captain George Corwin. Merchant and shipbuilder, the owner of wharves, warehouses, ships and farms; honest, shrewd and energetic, though inclined to be cold and unrelenting; devoting much time to the public service as selectman, captain in the militia and deputy to the General Court, he was little inferior in wealth and influence to English. Of similar stamp, but of a kinder and more charitable disposition was William Browne, Sr., a successful merchant and shipbuilder. Devoutly religious and interested in the advancement of education, he made large gifts to Harvard, to the Salem school, to the poor and to the Salem meeting-house. [49]

It must have been with perplexity and perhaps alarm that men of the type of John Hull, Philip English and William Browne, as they sat in their prominent seats in the meeting-house, listened to the ministers' warnings of the evil influence of wealth. Ardent supporters of the established order in Church and State, they gladly devoted their influence, their time and their money to its support, and were convinced that in return the way to salvation would be opened to them. True, the Bible stated that it was easier for a camel to pass through the eye of a needle than for a rich man to enter Heaven, but they would not admit to themselves that their property, valued perhaps at £10,000, perhaps at £8,000 or £6,000 would exclude them. After all, was not their prosperity the result of God's will and a clear evidence of His favor to His chosen people?

Nor was it to be expected that these men should realize the broadening influence which contact with the outside world was having upon them. The ministers might reiterate that God had led his people into the wilderness to protect them from contamination, but the effects of isolation were in part lost when the Yankee traders sailed their little vessels into every port along the Atlantic seaboard and swarmed in West Indian,

[47] R. D. Paine, *The Ships and Sailors of Old Salem*, pp. 23, 24.
[48] *Ibid.*, pp. 26, 28.
[49] James D. Phillips, *Salem in the Seventeenth Century*, pp. 261–62.

Spanish, Portuguese and British waters. When they learned to their surprise that the Roman Catholic Spaniard, the Anglican Marylander or Virginian, the Quaker Pennsylvanian had many good qualities, were often honest, kindhearted, industrious, they weakened in their belief that they were all headed for damnation. Nor was it unusual for outsiders, no doubt because of their friendship for individual merchants, to make protracted visits to New England. "Mr. Tho. Smith from Barbados brings the Honorable Francis Bond, one of his Majesty's Council for that island, and of great estate, also one Middleton: former comes to recover his health," wrote Samuel Sewall in his *Diary* in 1685. A few months later he added: "This day Mr. Morgan, his lady and family arrived from Barbados intending to dwell here some time." [50]

Of the merchants themselves, a large proportion had migrated to New England decades after the first founding, many of them from foreign countries. The Devereux, Delano, Faneuil and Bowdoin families came from France; Patrick Tracy from Ireland, Casper Crowninshield from Germany, John Wendell from Holland.[51] Some came for religion's sake, to escape persecution in their native lands, or because they were in sympathy with the reformed Church established in Massachusetts; but others migrated to take advantage of the opportunities for lucrative trade. However sincerely they tried to adjust themselves to the Puritan State, they could not fail to become an element of disunity. John Hull was surprised and outraged when, in 1662, "sundry young merchants and others, being non-freemen, boldly offered their votes to the freemen, when they were together for nomination of magistrates." [52] Even more significant was the petition of the Boston merchants in 1645 against the law restricting the entertaining of strangers and the statute for banishing Anabaptists.[53] And later, during the Salem witchcraft delusion, it was the merchant Robert Calef who had the common sense to see the folly of the inquisition and the hardihood to ridicule the great Cotton Mather for his share in it.

The theory of economic determinism, which has led so many writers to overemphasize commerce, industry and agriculture in interpreting the great movements of history, is quite inadequate as a full explanation of either the rise or the fall of the New England Zion. Unless we weigh also the forces of religious zeal, of political developments, of the advance of science, of the growth of rationalism, we secure an incomplete picture with a distorted perspective. Yet it would be equally incorrect to minimize

---

[50] "Diary of Samuel Sewall," Massachusetts Historical Society *Collections,* Fifth Series, V, pp. 71, 97.

[51] Samuel E. Morison, *The Maritime History of Massachusetts,* p. 21.

[52] "Diary of John Hull," American Antiquarian Society *Transactions and Collections,* III, p. 207.

[53] William B. Weeden, *Economic and Social History of New England,* I, p. 80.

the importance of the decline of the agricultural village, the growth of the farm, the development of a wealthy merchant class and the multiplying of the number of seafaring men in hastening the "decay" of the old order.

The Accumulation of Capital

4.   Genesis of a Colonial Fortune: Daniel Dulany of Maryland

Aubrey C. Land

The career of Daniel Dulany the Elder (1685–1753) coincides with the beginnings of a transition in Maryland from a purely agrarian economy to the combination of planting, commerce, and industry which formed the groundwork of a flourishing prosperity in the nineteenth century. Outside New England, with its lively commerce and ancillary occupations, agriculture had supported an overwhelmingly predominant proportion of the population in the American continental colonies during the seventeenth century. Not until the 1700's did New York and Philadelphia, then belatedly Baltimore, give signs of the promise they were to fulfill after the Revolution. The name of Dulany, directly linked with the beginnings of Baltimore as the commercial center of the Chesapeake, includes in its larger connotation changes in the structure of colonial economy—those changes basic to the diversification which characterized the later state of Maryland.

Alongside the colorful episodes of the last colonial wars and the wrangling over imperial trade restrictions, the growth of colonial fortunes lacks dramatic appeal. But these accumulations of wealth, representing a sturdy growth of capitalism, nourished a self-reliant attitude among colonial entrepreneurs and created vested interests with important political and social implications. In this context the builders of fortunes become significant as agents maturing an economy which survived when striking its own course after independence.

Aside from the leavening effect on the economy of the important personal fortune Dulany amassed during fifty years residence in the

"Genesis of a Colonial Fortune: Daniel Dulany of Maryland," by Aubrey C. Land, is reprinted by permission from *William and Mary Quarterly*, third series, XXVII (April, 1950), 255–268, published by Institute of Early American History and Culture, Williamsburg, Virginia.

colony of Maryland, his career is an early and striking example of a type, the self-made man, especially celebrated by Americans and held up as models for youth by Horatio Alger. Arriving penniless in the colony in 1704 at the age of eighteen, Dulany found a place as clerk in the law office of George Plater, a wealthy planter and prominent provincial official, who according to family tradition paid the young immigrant's passage to prevent his sale as an indentured servant.[1] From this clerkship Dulany went into legal practice for himself, entered the ranks of the provincial gentry, and advanced through a succession of minor posts to several of the highest proprietary offices, steadily increasing his personal wealth by land speculation, money lending, and investment in industrial undertakings. After educating his sons, setting them up in business, and providing his daughters with handsome dowries, he died in 1753 leaving for his heirs large holdings in unimproved lands, plantations, slaves, and money at interest.[2] Although success stories from the time of Dick Whittington are common enough in western culture to preclude an American monopoly on the rags to riches theme, the examples of men climbing to wealth and position from Dulany and Franklin to Rockefeller and Carnegie have animated the view of America as the land of opportunity.

Among the poorer immigrants to Maryland in the early eighteenth century, men with educational backgrounds sufficient to enable them to qualify for professional work were rare. Plater secured a scarce and valuable servant in Dulany; at the same time he made possible a legal apprenticeship equally valuable to his protegé who turned this training to good account. For the planter—which Dulany was to become—with his multiplicity of cares from securing his land titles to marketing his crops, a firm grasp of the law and legal procedure was necessary. Planters appeared frequently *in propria persona* to conduct their own law suits. Legal knowledge served the planter both as a useful tool and as a badge of his class. As a citizen of local distinction, he was called upon, as was his English counterpart the country squire, to serve as justice in the inferior courts. A further benefit accruing from legal training was not lost on Dulany. In the first decades of the eighteenth century a class of lawyers was beginning to emerge, not yet consciously professional by virtue of education and occupation, but already emphatically concentrating on consultation and representation of clients at court. Rewards for these services were high.

[1] Richard Henry Spencer, "Hon. Daniel Dulany, 1685–1753, The Elder," *Maryland Historical Magazine*, XII (1917), 20.

[2] Inventories, Vol. 84, folios 45, 46, 67, 70. When his second son, Walter, entered business as a merchant Dulany turned over to him among other goods two warehouses in Annapolis and 5621 acres of land in Baltimore county. Deeds, Anne Arundel County, Liber RB No. 3, folios 23–24; Provincial Court Deeds, Liber EI No. 8, folios 462–465, 486–488. The official records cited in this paper are housed at the Hall of Records, Annapolis, unless otherwise noted.

When Dulany, aged twenty-four, qualified for admission to practice in Charles County at the August court in 1709, provincial attorneys still vividly recalled investigations of a few years back by both the governor, John Seymour, and the provincial assembly.[3] Without established professional traditions and standards of practice to guide them, the Maryland courts had admitted to the bar several poorly prepared persons of questionable character who had created bad general impressions of attorneys and had called forth charges of malpractice and extortion of undue fees from clients. Feeling ran high enough against one Thomas Macnemara, a practitioner particularly obnoxious to clients and officials, that Governor Seymour issued a proclamation in 1707 restricting admission to those persons who could present evidence of training at the Inns of Court or Chancery or who could demonstrate their fitness in an examination before the governor and council.[4] Despite opposition of the lawyers, the assembly passed an act in 1708 establishing maximum fees attorneys could accept in the various courts of the province. These prescribed fees seem modest enough as payment for conducting a law suit, but they actually amounted to a considerable total for an attorney who often appeared for many clients at one session of court.[5]

From evidence scattered through the court records, it is possible to indicate the extent of Dulany's practice and his returns from this source of income. Between 1709 and 1711 he was admitted to plead at the bar of four courts in southern Maryland counties: St. Mary's, Charles, Calvert, and Prince George's. These four courts met on successive Tuesdays in each court month, March, June, August, and November, enabling attorneys to attend the sessions in all four counties.[6] For those attorneys who made the circuit of all four, court months became the busiest seasons of the year. In a typical session, March, 1713, Dulany acted as counsel for either plaintiff or defendant in twenty-one cases brought to trial in Prince George's County.[7] According to the table of fees established by the Act of 1708 he could demand one hundred pounds of tobacco "and no more" for each action prosecuted to a conclusion. Exact conversion of these tobacco fees into terms of sterling money is complicated by uncertainty in tobacco

[3] Charles County Court Records, Liber B No. 2, folio 608. Dulany may have been admitted as attorney in St. Mary's County before 1709. Exact dates for this county are difficult to establish without the court records which perished in a disastrous fire in the nineteenth century. "Recognizance of William Roach to Joshua Guibert," dated May, 1707, in St. Mary's County and witnessed by Dulany and Andrew Hamilton, suggests that he was active as a lawyer at this earlier date. Black Book, III, No. 36.

[4] Carroll T. Bond, ed., *Proceedings of the Maryland Court of Appeals* (Washington, 1933), xxvii. Judge Bond erroneously calls this proclamation the "Act of 1707." The admission of attorneys to practice was regulated by law the following year in a clause added to an act establishing lawyer's fees. *Archives of Maryland*, XXVII, 360–362.

[5] *Archives*, XXVII, 360–362.

[6] Act of 1708, Chapter 12. Citations of legislation refer to Thomas Bacon, *Laws of Maryland* (Annapolis, 1765).

[7] Prince George's County Court Records, Liber G, folios 300–340.

prices which fluctuated from season to season, but for rough estimation
the figure of ten shillings per hundred pounds represents an acceptable
approximation over the whole period. At this rate Dulany's fees for the
twenty-one cases at March term in Prince George's County amounted to
£10–10–0 sterling. His practice in Charles County was similarly large.
While no accurate check of the number of his cases can be made for
Calvert and St. Mary's Counties, since the court proceedings of both
counties for this period are no longer extant, scattered transcripts from
these two courts in other legal records indicate that Dulany practiced
extensively in both counties during this part of his career.[8]

Following a successful beginning in the county courts, Dulany moved
up into the higher ones. In 1711 he began pleading before the Provincial
Court which exercised original jurisdiction in cases involving sums of
money beyond the realm of the county courts and which heard cases on
appeal from the county.[9] The fees, permitting an attorney in the Provincial
Court four hundred pounds of tobacco for each suit, attracted relatively
greater legal talent in keeping with the larger stakes. In 1713 Dulany
conducted his first chancery case and the following year acted as attorney
in the highest court of the colony, the Court of Appeals.[10] In both these
courts fees of six hundred pounds of tobacco were permitted. Within a
year after his admission to the Provincial Court Dulany had accumulated
a modest practice with ten cases on the docket at the July session in 1712.
In fees these cases were worth four thousand pounds of tobacco or £20
sterling when judgment was rendered.[11] At the July court in 1718 over
sixty of his cases are listed.[12]

Dulany maintained his extensive legal practice until his brilliant son,
Daniel Dulany the Younger, returned from his studies at Cambridge and
the Inns of Court to enter the law in Maryland. The gift of this practice
was a part of the valuable endowment bestowed on the son who in the
quarter century before the Revolution became a legal oracle in Maryland.

Besides provincial practice Maryland attorneys had important clients
outside the colony. After the elder Dulany had established himself as one
of the foremost lawyers in the colony he was retained as local representative by several English merchant firms, including Samuel Hyde and
Company, Jonathan Forward, Thomas Colmore, and William Hunt.
Ordinarily the work of American representatives consisted of sending

[8] Such transcripts appear in the Anne Arundel County Court Judgments, Liber
RC, folios 523–526, and in the Provincial Court Judgments, Liber WG No. 1, folio 296.
[9] Provincial Court Judgments, Liber PL No. 3, folios 412–413. His first case,
Frogg v. Miller, is continued in Liber TP No. 2, folios 98–100.
[10] Chancery Record, Maryland Land Office, Annapolis, Liber PL, folios 8–9. Bond,
Proceedings of the Maryland Court of Appeals, 192–195.
[11] Provincial Court Judgments, Liber TP No. 2, folios 519, 538–539, 543.
[12] Provincial Court Judgments, Liber PL No. 4, folios 9–12, 14 ff.

immediate notices to the merchants of customers who died, in order that
accounts due could be forwarded for filing claims in the probate court.
Occasionally, however, special situations demanded more than this sort of
routine operation and consequently greater acumen in legal matters. The
complicated litigation growing out of the case, *Powlson v. Forward,*
extended over ten years and entailed five appeals from the colony to the
King in Council before Dulany's client emerged the victor.[13] Dulany
maintained for thirty years not only the position of legal representative
but also an intimate connection with the firm of Samuel Hyde, a London
merchant active in the Maryland tobacco trade, delivering to this firm a
major share of the tobacco raised on his plantations or received in fees
until the great bankruptcy of 1746 finally terminated Hyde's mercantile
business.[14] The English merchant was of central importance in the
economic structure. He acted as broker of tobacco, banker of funds
received from sales, and purchasing agent for provincial customers. Thus
advantageous connections and favorable credit ratings with English
merchants enhanced the position of the colonist whose bills of exchange
were drawn on them and passed through the hands of successive endors-
ers, taking the place of specie which was chronically in short supply.

The Maryland lawyer Dulany was in a peculiarly favorable position for
gathering the money lender's rewards in a colony poor in specie and other
forms of ready money. The financing of agricultural operations and small
business enterprises created a demand for funds which offered tempting
returns to persons who could make loans either in cash or bills of exchange
on English merchants. Early in his career Dulany began making loans
which provided a lucrative source of profit throughout his life. Though
the bulk of these loans was absorbed by planters and small farmers for
purchasing land or for defraying the expenses of tobacco culture, a
significant part fertilized other pursuits in the slowly diversifying economy. Tanners, brewers, shipwrights, printers, tailors, blacksmiths, gla-
ziers, merchants, and mariners borrowed sums of varying sizes from
Dulany. A typical example of a small account submitted by Dulany in a
suit against one Clagett shows the amounts involved in many such
loans:

To cash lent him July 17, 1729	— 7.11.8½
To note allowed Clagett of same day	—13.16.7
To Money paid Robt Alexander by your order February 4, 1729/30	— 4.13.6
To money paid Mr. Woodward by your order	—23.0.0
To do John Jordan	— 3.0.0

[13] Bond, *Proceedings of the Maryland Court of Appeals,* xlii.
[14] Dulany to Samuel Hyde, June 7, 1747, Dulany Papers, Maryland Historical
Society, Baltimore.

This amounted to £52–1–9½ current money.[15] The extent of Dulany's secured loans during the last decade of his life is indicated by suits in the Provincial Court where in 1744 he recovered £1016–15–7 currency and in 1747 the larger sum of £1488–0–0 currency.[16] What percentage of his loans were repaid without recourse to court action is not indicated by these figures. Other money lenders varied enough in their experience with debtors that establishment of a ratio between loans returned with and without court action would be hazardous. Generally only a fraction of well-secured loans required legal action for collection. Charles Carroll of Annapolis, who sued for sums only slightly larger than those involved in the Dulany suits, calculated his total money outstanding at interest in 1762 to be £24,230–9–7 sterling.[17]

Interest rates on loans of all sizes were strictly regulated by legislation passed in 1704, "An Act against excessive usury," which set a maximum rate of six per cent for loans to be repaid in money.[18] This rate of return, which seems surprisingly small in a colony hungry for money, led to strenuous efforts by money lenders to prevent the accumulation of funds lying idle in their hands. The unceasing search for profitable yet safe investment gives a highly individualistic aspect to eighteenth-century finance and raises difficulties to full description of the pattern of capital accumulation and investment.

Some of the problems of the colonial capitalist, especially those of inadequate funds and undue risks, were solved by temporary partnerships, although such arrangements frequently brought embarrassments of their own. Often each of the partners in a particular project had in progress several concurrent financial undertakings involving mutually conflicting aims; bickering among partners over these conflicts was common. During his fifty years in Maryland Dulany entered into many partnerships with one or several persons to carry on some profitable undertaking. In 1729 he engaged in slave merchandising with Richard Snowden and Peter Hume as co-partners handling a cargo of two hundred choice Negroes worth £4000 sterling by a conservative estimate.[19] Later, when John Galloway, one of the larger Maryland merchants, assumed debts of a local planter to the amount of £1267–5–2 sterling, Dulany and Dr. Charles Carroll, surgeon and merchant, pooled their resources to take

[15] The value of "current money" and currency in terms of sterling was subject to exchange rates and varied greatly. Very roughly they may be assessed at about two-thirds sterling. C. P. Gould, *Money and Transportation in Maryland, 1720–1765* (Baltimore, 1915), 67, 87, 98.

[16] Provincial Court Judgments, Liber El No. 9, folios 136–137, 140–147, 170–171; Liber El No. 10, Vol. I, folios 556–557, 572–573, 580–581, 801–803.

[17] Kate Mason Rowland, *Life and Correspondence of Charles Carroll of Carrollton* (New York, 1889), I, 60.

[18] Act of 1704, chapter 69. On loans to be repaid in tobacco eight per cent was permitted.

[19] *Maryland Gazette*, May 20, 1729.

over these debts from him. They paid Galloway £376 sterling for the opportunity to acquire title to the security pledged for them by foreclosure. The partners had a distinct bargain in the transaction. On foreclosing the notes they acquired the securities, including 660 acres of plantations, three lots in London Town (Anne Arundel County), two lots in Beale Town (Prince George's County), one lot in Chester Town (Kent County), thirty-seven slaves, the ship *Frederick,* the scow *Londontown,* the four sloops *Benedict, Swan, Swallow,* and *Bachelor's Hall,* all the tobacco raised during the year, the cargoes of the six vessels, a parcel of livestock, and a quantity of silverplate.[20] Proceeds from the sale of this property add up to a handsome profit for the partners, even if each article is assessed at lowest values then obtaining for the commodities in question.[21]

Although most of these partnerships were ephemeral, disappearing with the accomplishment of a specific objective, a few solidified into permanent arrangements cemented by the nature of operations which required large amounts of capital goods. Exploitation of natural resources, particularly minerals, made heavy capital demands for blast furnaces, forges, buildings, and property in slaves or indentured servants to provide the unskilled labor about the works. The area of the upper Chesapeake around Baltimore had by 1725 already attracted the attention of iron masters who made small quantities of pig iron at forges built along the wooded "falls" in Baltimore and Cecil counties at the head of the bay. Several gentlemen of Annapolis, among them Dulany, became interested in the possibilities of a joint enterprise to work the rich beds of white iron or siderite deposited along the coastal plain in clays near the surface or actually exposed.[22] In 1732, after careful investigation, articles of agreement were signed by five wealthy citizens creating a partnership under the name, the Baltimore Company.

The initial capital stock of the Baltimore Company, £3500 sterling, was subscribed in equal shares of £700 by each of the partners, Daniel Dulany, Benjamin Tasker, Dr. Charles Carroll, Daniel Carroll of Duddington Manor, and Charles Carroll of Annapolis. At intervals the part-

[20] Deeds, Anne Arundel County, Liber RD No. 2, folios 515–517. The partner's share of the cargoes included 800 bushels of wheat worth about £140 sterling, 1000 bushels of Indian corn worth about £80 sterling, 700 bushels of beans worth about £120 sterling. The livestock comprised 68 cows, 58 steers, 50 sheep, 100 hogs, 19 horses, and 4 mares.

[21] Land sales are comparatively easy to locate but only a part of the other sales can be traced in the records. Some 520 acres of the land sold for £535 sterling and four of the six lots for £184 sterling. Deeds, Anne Arundel County, Liber RO No. 3, folios 32–33, 95–96, 131–132, 237–238; Provincial Court Deeds, Liber EI No. 3, folios 156–157. Six of the slaves sold for £20 each. Deeds, Anne Arundel County, Liber RD No. 2, folio 518. For the remaining items I have used the lowest prices current as shown in the Inventories.

[22] William B. Clark and Edward B. Matthews, "Maryland Mineral Industries," *Maryland Geological Survey,* VIII (1909), 154.

ners made additional contributions in money or more frequently in land, slaves, or goods needed in carrying on the work. The double effect of enlargements in capital stock and appreciation of assets raised the value of each share to above £6000 sterling over a period of thirty years.[23] The diversity of interests among members of the company brought frequent quarrels over policy questions and details of the business yet at the same time gave a broad base in provincial life beneficial to the position of the company. Dulany, long a leader in the popularly elected lower house of the colonial assembly, had often been in political opposition to Benjamin Tasker, a senior member of the Lord Proprietor's Council which sat as the upper house of the legislature during session time. Daniel Carroll and his cousin, Charles Carroll of Annapolis, both men of wealth and talent, though barred from political life because of their Catholic faith, brought important mercantile and financial connections as assets to the company. Dr. Charles Carroll's recent conversion from the Roman church to the Anglican faith opened for him the door to political affairs and gave him the opportunity to rise in the lower house to a position of leadership in the "country party" when Dulany was seduced into the smaller "court party," supporters of the Lords Baltimore.

Warned by the experience and advice of Pennsylvania entrepreneurs in iron production of the hazards resulting from mismanagement, the partners attempted at first to run the Baltimore Company directly by issuing orders to Stephen Onion, their supervisor at the works. Uncoordinated interference by individual partners eventually necessitated a change of procedure to an arrangement whereby the owners acted as a board of directors deciding major questions of policy and production but allowing greater discretion to the manager in the details of operation.[24] During this schooling in business management, iron production, limited initially by the lack of technical sophistication, rose rapidly to eighteen tons for a good week by 1734.[25] Onion informed the partners that he counted fourteen tons a normal week, but added in his clipped style, "The furnace will if had a mind to work her at highest rate, make well towards 20 Tons per week but fear shall want Ore to proceed at nigh that rate." [26]

Each partner sold iron when possible to local consumers and to their correspondents in England or other colonies, a merchandising technique that lasted for many years. When the company met on December 20, 1733,

[23] Rowland, *Charles Carroll*, I, 60.

[24] Clement Plumsted to Charles Carroll, April 20, 1731; Dulany and Partners to Alexander Lawson, 1739, Carroll-Maccubbin Papers, Maryland Historical Society. A. C. Bining, *Pennsylvania Iron Manufacture in the Eighteenth Century* (Harrisburg, 1938), gives an excellent account of the early iron industry in a neighboring colony showing the limitations and difficulties faced by the entrepreneurs who attempted to establish and operate works.

[25] Stephen Onion to Charles Carroll, February 9, 1734, Carroll-Maccubbin Papers.

[26] Onion to Carroll, December 16, 1734.

to settle accounts, Dulany reported sales of £913–19–7 sterling and £526–10–7½ currency. Benjamin Tasker had disposed of a quantity which returned £636–15–6 sterling and £731–8–4 currency. Daniel and Charles Carroll operating jointly had sold smaller portions amounting to £218–11–4½ sterling and £313–9–9 currency.[27] While these figures illustrate the size of the Baltimore Company's affairs they say nothing of net profits which are difficult to determine because of the paucity of information on costs of production. Only occasionally and for short periods can profits be calculated. After deducting operating expenses for the four good months April to August, 1741, each partner received a dividend of £203–8–7 sterling, rather more than a normal return in those years.[28] Charles Carroll estimated the annual net profit on one share of the iron works at £400 sterling during the 1750's.[29]

Uncertainty of labor and scarcity of technicians capable of building furnaces or other capital goods discouraged investment in enterprises of the magnitude of the Baltimore Company in the colonies south of Pennsylvania. Furthermore, temptation to take the necessary risks in the face of these difficulties was not great in a society where planting offered the conventional approach to social and political preferment. Men of position usually achieved their status in the customary manner as tobacco planters, measuring their relative rank according to plantations, slaves, and other tangible forms of wealth.

Along with their planting, however, several of the wealthiest provincials did engage in land speculation, a socially approved and highly lucrative pursuit. In addition to his other kinds of capitalist ventures, Dulany also invested in this type of enterprise. Extensive land holdings insured the individual planter against soil depletion by the greedy tobacco plant which demanded new ground after very few crops.[30] Excess land, particularly near convenient shipping points, always found ready sale to new immigrants at prices well above original cost. A large part of the Dulany fortune was in land, either areas cleared for planting or tracts yet unexploited. The elder Dulany began acquiring real property in 1713 when he purchased for £50 sterling and 2000 pounds of tobacco a plantation of moderate size, Brooke's Reserve, one hundred and seventy-eight acres with houses and improvements.[31] Within a few months his designation in the court records was changed from Mr. Daniel Dulany to

[27] Miscellaneous Accounts, Baltimore Company, Carroll-Maccubbin Papers. Sterling accounts generally represented sales outside the colony, either in England or in another colony. Local consumers ordinarily paid for their iron in Maryland currency.
[28] Baltimore Company Iron Account Ending 10 September 1741, Carroll-Maccubbin Papers.
[29] Rowland, *Charles Carroll*, I, 60.
[30] Planters seldom counted on more than three or four tobacco crops before lands were turned into corn fields. Avery O. Craven, *Soil Exhaustion as a Factor in the Agricultural History of Virginia and Maryland, 1606–1860* (Urbana, 1926), 32.
[31] Prince George's County Land Records, Liber E, folios 164–165.

"Daniell Dullany of Prince George's County, gentleman," following the firm custom of indicating both station and habitat in the Maryland legal proceedings. Later in the same year he bought two additional tracts, Chance, a plantation of one hundred seven acres in Calvert County, and another piece of property of four hundred acres.[32] Two years later he added further to his holdings by the purchase of Bodkin's Quarter, an improved tract of two hundred sixty-four acres near his seat in Prince George's County.[33] Some portions of these holdings were leased to tenants who could furnish their own labor, but a large part of the land already cleared was put under cultivation with his own slaves or white indentured servants, who numbered at least nineteen by the end of the decade.[34] During these three years Dulany had acquired nine hundred sixty-nine acres of land principally with funds derived from his legal practice and had attained a new status as a member of the provincial squirearchy of Prince George's County.

In 1720, when he was thirty-five years old, Dulany moved from his country home to the center of the province's official life, Annapolis. The city was already beginning to show signs of social and commercial activity as the important state officials put up town houses as places of residence or entertainment to be used during sessions of the legislature and the superior courts. In the capital city Dulany found a broader field for exercising his social and political talents. He was a member of either the lower or the upper house of the assembly for all but four of the thirty remaining years of his life. In addition he held the important offices of attorney general, receiver general, commissary general, and judge of the court of vice-admiralty, sometimes presiding over two or more at once. The fat fees attached to these offices swelled his income while his position as an important personage enhanced his success as a speculator in land.[35] Shortly before his move to Annapolis, Dulany had stepped up into the top bracket of landlords with the purchase of two large tracts, Charles Bounty, one thousand acres located in Baltimore County, and Remains of My Lords Gracious Grant, five thousand acres in Kent County on the Eastern Shore.[36]

Dulany's embarkation on a career of land speculation was not without

<hr/>

[32] Provincial Court Deeds, Liber TP, No. 4, folios 176–180. For the two he paid £150 sterling.

[33] Prince George's County Land Records, Liber B, folios 383–385.

[34] Black Book, X, No. 10.

[35] An example of the favor accorded men of rank appears in a note of Dulany to a clerk of the land office: "Mr: Geist Be pleased to let the bearer have a wart. [warrant] in my name for five thousand acres of land to be laid out in any part of the province and I'll pay his Lordship the Caucon for the same within Twelve months from this date Witness my hand. D:Dulany." Warrant Records, Maryland Land Office, Liber BB, folio 325. A warrant for the desired amount immediately issued.

[36] Provincial Court Deeds, Liber TP No. 4, folios 518–519; Liber PL No. 5, folios 101–105.

careful forethought, as an analysis of his strategy during the decade preceding the move to Annapolis clearly shows. Between the years 1713 and 1715 when he was acquiring the several plantations which established him as a country squire, a prerequisite to easy intercourse with the official class, he was also building up a backlog of land warrants against the day when he could turn them to profitable use.

In the land system instituted for their province, the Lords Baltimore had attempted to keep the process of acquiring land as simple as possible with the idea of attracting settlers who would swell the proprietary revenues by purchases and quit rents. The warrant was the first of three steps in obtaining secure title to vacant land. On payment of caution money at the uniform rate of forty shillings sterling per hundred acres, the land office issued a warrant which gave the purchaser the right to take up any vacant land within the province. Common warrants contained a provision for initiating the second step of the process in the form of a directive to the surveyor to lay off the prescribed amount of land and return a certificate describing the exact location of the plot with metes and bounds. A patent under the Lord Proprietor's seal, the final document, granted in fee simple the tract described in the surveyor's return, subject to an annual quit rent payable to his Lordship's receivers.[37] Land warrants, the stock in trade of the Maryland land speculator, represented a considerable initial investment in the form of caution money. By 1715 Dulany had purchased warrants to take up 13,500 acres at a cost of £300 sterling.[38]

Returns on investment in land warrants were often delayed for a decade or longer but were relatively great when finally realized. From a warrant issued in 1739 for 1,450 acres costing £29 sterling, Dulany had surveys run for several plantations, varying in size from thirty to two hundred and fifty acres, for individual purchasers who paid a total of £249–10–4 sterling.[39] Against this gross profit of eight hundred and sixty per cent his

[37] The wealth of detail overlaying this essentially simple system is fully discussed in C. P. Gould, *The Land System of Maryland, 1720–1765* (Baltimore, 1913), and in Beverley W. Bond, *The Quit-Rent System in the American Colonies* (New Haven, 1919).

[38] The following tabulation gives a more detailed picture of Dulany's investment in land warrants:

Before 1715—11,500 acres	1730–34— 1,300 acres
1715–19 — 7,500 "	1735–39—11,302 "
1720–24 — 5,000 "	1740–44— 7,000 "
1725–29 — 1 escheat warrant of	1745–49— 8,290 "
undetermined size.	1750–53— 1,800 "

[39] If all the data were available, Dulany's return would appear even larger. I have been able to trace only 1311 acres of land sold from this warrant, leaving 139 unaccounted for. Furthermore in the conveyance for one small tract of 30 acres no price consideration is given, though probably Dulany did not give this piece away.

cost was the compound interest on the original outlay of £29 for four years. During his lifetime Dulany bought some 55,000 acres of land warrants, mainly for speculative purposes.[40]

The traffic in land warrants does not account for the whole of Dulany's income as a landlord. When choice lands came to the market he acquired large and small tracts already patented, usually in the sparsely settled areas or beyond the line of settlement. The country around Remains of My Lords Gracious Grant in Kent County was far from developed in 1720 when he bought the tract. In 1724 he acquired 1,750 acres, half of Valley of Jehosephat and Addition to the Valley of Jehosephat. Altogether by direct purchase of patented tracts Dulany amassed a total of 30,000 acres. A major part of these lands remained in the family as part of the endowment bestowed on his sons as they became of age. In the intervening years Dulany leased portions to farmers without land or to planters with insufficient acreage.[41]

Dulany made a most fortunate purchase in 1745 when he took over a rectangular tract of seven thousand acres, Tasker's Chance, stretching from the Monocacy River to the edge of the valley at the foot of the Catoctin range in present-day Frederick County. The double advantage of location along the path of inland migration from Pennsylvania to the western areas of Virginia and a rich loamy surface soil assisted Dulany in attracting settlers to develop this frontier region of western Maryland. Immediately he began exploiting the new property by settling a score of German farmers on plantations carved out of Tasker's Chance. To the first settlers he sold a total of 4,895¼ acres, more than two-thirds of the whole tract, for £427 currency, suggesting that he took a serious loss since he had paid £2000 currency for the seven-thousand-acre block.[42] Such a view fails to take into account the history of the two thousand acres remaining in his hands. Settlement greatly enhanced the value of these lands which by 1750 had advanced in price to £1–10–0 currency per acre and continued to rise during the following years as Dulany disposed of successive portions.[43] Thus by 1750 the value of the remaining two-sevenths was greater by fifty per cent than the purchase price of the whole, a striking commentary on the wisdom of Dulany's policy of selling at an initial loss to enhance profits in the long run.

Besides the value of farm land included within the bounds of Tasker's

[40] The figures do not include twelve special warrants issued to take up vacancies adjacent to land he already possessed.

[41] *Maryland Gazette*, March 10, 1747; Conveyances, Kent County, Liber JS No. 22, folios 277–278, 132–134.

[42] Indenture between Benjamin Tasker and Daniel Dulany, January 20, 1745; Prince George's County Land Records, Liber BB No. 1, folios 250–251. Dulany sold a plantation of 473 acres to Stephen Ramsberger for £15 currency or about 7½ d. per acre. Average cost of the land in Tasker's Chance to Dulany was 5/8¼ per acre.

[43] Land Records, Frederick County, Liber B, folios 274–275.

Chance, Dulany realized further returns from the town he laid out in the southeast corner of the tract along Carroll Creek. Frederick Town, named in honor of the Lord Proprietor, provided a trading center for the west country, a seat for the county court, and an urban life for those German artisans who were not yet accustomed to the plantation life prevalent in other parts of Maryland. Dulany laid out Frederick Town in September of 1745, offering half-acre lots for sale at £2–10–0 currency, subject to an annual ground rent that became characteristic of some Maryland urban communities. Ground rents on the first lots sold were at the rate of one shilling annually for the first twenty-one years and two shillings a year thereafter, payable to Dulany or his heirs and assigns, thus assuring them a permanent return after the land had passed out of the family's hands. As the town grew prices of lots advanced and ground rents rose. In 1752 Joseph Hardman, an innkeeper, paid £6 currency for a lot which was subject to a ground rent of three shillings a year for the first twenty-one years and six shillings a year thereafter.[44]

The author of Dulany's fulsome obituary credits his success to his application to the law as a young immigrant to Maryland.[45] William Eddis, author of the *Letters from America,* remarks that the Dulany fortune derived principally from land dealings, especially in western Maryland.[46] Between these two pursuits, one representing an early phase and the other a later development, lie a long series of successful ventures in manufacturing, merchandising, planting, and money lending, elements in the creation of a notable fortune and stepping stones to a career of public service which further enhanced this rise to wealth and achievement.

[44] *Ibid.,* folio 757. Dulany's sons developed the ground rent system still further, enlarging the perpetual rent but selling the lots at a nominal price. In 1764 John Cary, a merchant, paid five shillings for one choice lot which was subject to an annual rent of £5–2–0 currency. Land Records, Frederick County, Liber J, folio 333. One of these lots had increased enough in price that it was deemed sufficient security for a loan of £200 currency in 1756. Land Records, Frederick County, Liber F, folios 47–48.

[45] *Maryland Gazette,* December 6, 1753.

[46] William Eddis, *Letters from America, Historical and Descriptive* (London, 1792), 83.

Origins of Manufacturing in America

5.　The Baltimore Company Seeks English Markets: A Study of the Anglo-American Iron Trade, 1731–1755

Keach Johnson

The American iron industry originated in the seventeenth century but did not become well established until after the close of Queen Anne's War when it entered a period of rapid growth that led to the construction of ironworks in most of the thirteen colonies. In the forefront of this expansion was the Baltimore Company, which built the second major ironworks to be established in Maryland and the first of consequence to be locally owned and operated. Preceded only by the Principio Company, an English enterprise that was organized about 1715 and operated in Virginia as well as in Maryland, the Baltimore Company was formed as a partnership in 1731 by Daniel Dulany, Dr. Charles Carroll, Benjamin Tasker, Charles Carroll of Annapolis, and his brother, Daniel Carroll.[1] Beginning modestly with the construction of a furnace on the Patapsco River,[2] the partners began to ship pig iron to England in 1734, their exports to the mother country averaging about five hundred tons annually during the next few years.

The Baltimore Ironworks was the largest and most ambitious industrial enterprise yet undertaken by anyone in Maryland.[3] The construction and operation of a furnace required a large amount of capital for the purchase of land, slaves, equipment, and supplies. Beginning with a capitalization of £3500 sterling, the partners put additional capital into the works during the next few years; by 1737 their investments amounted to

[1] See Keach Johnson, "The Genesis of the Baltimore Ironworks," *Journal of Southern History*, XIX (May 1953), 157–179. Unless otherwise noted, the following summary of the company's growth is based on this article.

[2] See Jefferson and Fry, "A Map of the Most Inhabited Part of Virginia Containing the Whole Province of Maryland," in Lawrence Henry Gipson, *The British Empire before the American Revolution* (Caldwell, Idaho and New York, 1936–1956), II, Map No. 1, p. 347. The Patapsco area had water power, seemingly inexhaustible woodlands for charcoal, an abundance of ore lying on or near the surface of the ground, and convenient transportation.

[3] Aubrey C. Land, *The Dulanys of Maryland: A Biographical Study of Daniel Dulany, the Elder (1685–1753) and Daniel Dulany, the Younger (1722–1797)*, Studies in Maryland History, No. 3 (Baltimore, 1955), p. 108.

"The Baltimore Company Seeks English Markets: A Study of Anglo-American Iron Trade, 1731–1755," by Keach Johnson, is reprinted by permission from *William and Mary Quarterly*, XVI (January, 1959) 37–60, published by Institute of Early American History and Culture, Williamsburg, Virginia.

£14,835 sterling and £2873 provincial currency. The next year they completed the construction of a forge to convert part of their pig iron into bar iron.

Gradually expanding the scope of their operations, the associates became one of the largest producers of pig and bar iron in the thirteen colonies. The Baltimore Ironworks eventually included several furnaces, three forges, 150 slaves, and 30,000 acres of land. Charles Carroll valued his fifth share at £10,000 in 1764, while Daniel Dulany estimated at the close of the Revolution that a tenth share was worth, "at a moderate Estimate," £7000 sterling.[4] Probably overstatements—Tasker's share sold for £5200 following his death in 1768 [5]—these valuations suggest, nevertheless, the size and scope of the company's operations. It was a notable exception to the rule that most of the large ironworks in the colonies were financed with British capital.[6]

Except for the fabrication of a few items, such as backs for fireplaces, the operations of the Baltimore Ironworks were confined to primary production: the making of pig and bar iron. The secondary phases of the colonial iron industry were located mainly in the northern colonies, notably in Massachusetts and Pennsylvania. The ironmasters of Massachusetts, using pig iron imported from other colonies, manufactured kettles, nails, pots, and implements. Pennsylvania exported rod and bar iron, stoves, tools, and agricultural implements to the other colonies and made sugar machinery for the West Indian planters.[7] In Maryland, however, the centrifugal forces of the tobacco culture prevented the growth of towns and the development of a class of skilled artisans whose workshops formed the basis of manufacturing in the eighteenth century. The Baltimore Company did not make "potts skilletts or such kind," Dr. Carroll explained to a Boston merchant: "we have neither the Industry or number of People to Create it which you have in your Colony." [8] Dr. Carroll and his colleagues, like the tobacco planters, were engaged essentially in preparing raw materials for manufacture and sale in distant markets.

Finding profitable outlets for several hundred tons of crude iron

[4] Daniel Dulany to George Fitzhugh, Nov. 11, 1783, in "Extracts from the Dulany Papers," *Maryland Historical Magazine*, XVI (1921), 47.

[5] Charles A. Barker, *The Background of the Revolution in Maryland* (New Haven, 1940), pp. 37, 108.

[6] The Principio Company, Governor Spotswood's furnaces in Virginia, and the ironworks established in New Jersey and New York by Peter Hasenclever—the most ambitious colonial industrial undertaking—were financed wholly or partly by British investors. Victor S. Clark, *History of Manufactures in the United States* . . . (New York, 1929), I, 146–147, 173–174.

[7] *Ibid.*, I, 114–115. Arthur C. Bining, *British Regulation of the Colonial Iron Industry* (Philadelphia, 1933), pp. 18–20.

[8] Dr. Carroll to Edmond Quincy, July 9, 1748, in "Extracts from Account and Letter Books of Dr. Charles Carroll . . . ," (hereafter cited as "Extracts"), *Md. Hist. Mag.*, XVII–XXVII (1923–32), XXII, 374–375.

annually was a formidable task, since the demand in Maryland was limited. The partners were forced to seek markets in other colonies and in Great Britain, making the factors of slow communication and transportation of major importance. Moreover, the company was pioneering a branch of colonial trade still in its infancy, and there were few to whom the associates could turn for instruction.[9] Lacking reliable and up-to-date information regarding demand and prices, they were compelled to gamble, shipping their iron wherever they thought it might sell at a profit. Only by a slow process of trial and error, in which they explored markets from Massachusetts to the West Indies and from London to Liverpool, were the partners able to discover the best outlets for their iron.

Marketing problems were further complicated by the modes of production. Pig and bar iron were produced mainly in furnaces and forges which utilized power-driven machinery, thus foreshadowing modern industry in organization and technology;[10] but the manufacture of iron and steel into finished articles remained a handicraft carried on in homes or shops by artisans working independently or as wage earners under the putting-out system.[11] This ultimate market for pig and bar iron was dispersed among a number of small craftsmen; consequently, individual sales were small and turnover was slow—ordinarily months, even years, elapsed before the iron shipped to England by the partners was finally sold.

Finding a purchaser did not end the marketing operations of the associates; it was merely the first in a series of transactions characteristic of eighteenth-century commerce. Iron was generally sold on credit, the agents of the Baltimore Company allowing the purchaser from three to eight months to complete payment. Moreover: "Iron it Self is Such a commodity," observed a London merchant, "as does not Sell for Cash but for goods in Barter."[12] The partners were generally forced, therefore, to

[9] Pig and bar iron did not become important items in colonial trade until the 1720's. Exports of these commodities from the colonies—chiefly Maryland and Virginia—to the mother country rose from 3.7 tons in 1718 to almost 900 tons in 1728, jumped to more than 2,000 tons in 1731, and then remained fairly constant until the 1760's when they rose again, reaching a maximum of 5,303 tons of pig iron and 2,222 tons of bar iron in 1771. In 1772, however, shipments fell to 3,724 and 965 tons of pig and bar iron, respectively, and remained at approximately those levels until the outbreak of the Revolution. Bining, *Iron Industry*, Appendices B, C, and D, pp. 128–133.

[10] For an excellent example, see E. N. Hartley, *Ironworks on the Saugus: The Lynn and Braintree Ventures of the Company of Undertakers of the Ironworks in New England* (Norman, Okla., 1957), pp. 3–20, and passim.

[11] The remarkable growth of the hardware industry in the West Midlands, for example, was based on thousands of small craftsmen. Abraham Spooner, ironmonger, estimated in 1738 that at least 135,000 people living in or near Birmingham depended on the iron industry for their livelihood. Another contemporary estimated that craftsmen in the vicinity of Birmingham used no less than 9,000 tons of bar iron annually in making various wares, particularly nails. Gipson, *British Empire*, III, 205–206. Thomas S. Ashton, *Iron and Steel in the Industrial Revolution* (Manchester, 1924), p. 19.

[12] James Buchanan to the Baltimore Company, London, Apr. 4, 1741, Carroll-Maccubbin Papers, Maryland Historical Society, Baltimore.

accept partial payment in ironware, a fact which made further exchanges and sales necessary before a return on a shipment could be realized. Much of their capital, consequently, was always tied up in trade. These conditions point up the fact that relatively more operating funds were needed to produce iron in the eighteenth century than is true at present, and they illustrate the necessity for British and European capital in developing the iron industry in America.

To meet the difficulties involved in selling iron, the partners were able to mobilize a number of resources. They were men of wealth and influence, with extensive experience in business, public life, and the professions. Alert to the opportunities for investment that were opening up with the growth of population and wealth, they typified the Southern planter-merchants who combined tobacco culture with a number of other pursuits, including land speculation and moneylending as well as trade and industry. Dr. Carroll, for instance, valued his estate at £10,000 sterling and £5000 provincial currency—some 30,000 acres of land in western Maryland, loans totaling £818 sterling, and £4000 provincial currency—in 1754.[13] Charles Carroll owned 40,000 acres of land, houses and lots in Annapolis, 285 slaves, and held loans amounting to £24,230 in 1762, a total of £88,380.[14] Daniel Dulany became the leading lawyer in Maryland, held most of the important offices in the provincial government at various times, lent money on a large scale, and speculated extensively in western land.[15] Equally prominent was Benjamin Tasker, who belonged to one of the leading Maryland families, enjoyed the favor of Lord Baltimore, and became one of the wealthiest and most influential men in the province.[16]

All of the partners were experienced merchants with well-established connections in London and the outports as well as in the West Indies and the mainland colonies. These far-flung ties enabled them to gather information about potential markets and placed them in as favorable a position to sell iron as the time and circumstances permitted. They were, in short, well qualified to cope with the hazards their project involved. Enterprising and resourceful, they combined the ability and means to organize business on a large scale with a willingness to risk their capital in new ventures. In the expressive phrase of the time, they were "undertakers": the colonial counterparts of the European entrepreneurs, who were

[13] Dr. Carroll to William Black, May 8, 1754, and to his son, May 8, 1754, in "Extracts," *Md. Hist. Mag.*, XXVII, 218, 221. R. Bruce Harley, "Dr. Charles Carroll —Land Speculator, 1730–1755," *ibid.*, XLVI (June 1951), 106.

[14] Charles Carroll to his son, Jan. 9, 1764, in "Extracts from the Carroll Papers," *ibid.*, X–XVI (1915–21), XII, 27.

[15] Land, *The Dulanys*, pp. 53–57, 59, 63, 66–69, and passim. Dulany's interest in land speculation led him to pioneer the settlement of western Maryland where he acquired extensive tracts along the Monocacy River, established the town of Frederick, and brought in German immigrants to colonize his holdings.

[16] *Ibid.*, pp. 52, 128, 131–132, and passim.

becoming increasingly prominent in the eighteenth century and who had already emerged as the leading figures in English commerce and industry.[17]

England was the principal outlet for Baltimore iron from the outset. The associates, in fact, probably built the works mainly for the purpose of supplying the English market. They were undoubtedly aware that colonial markets were too localized and dispersed to offer adequate outlets for the large-scale production of pig and bar iron. The growth of colonial agriculture and commerce, it is true, enabled them to dispose of part of their output locally and through the coastwise trade. Their sales in Maryland were generally small, however, frequently consisting of a ton or less, while their consignments to the other colonies ordinarily did not exceed twenty tons per shipment.[18]

In England, on the other hand, the inability of the furnace and forgemasters to meet the needs of the fabricators created a ready market for pig and bar iron. During the seventeenth and eighteenth centuries the manufacture of ironware in England increased steadily, whereas the production of pig and bar iron remained stationary if it did not actually decline.[19] An important cause of this imbalance was the fact that the craftsmen were able to use coal as fuel, whereas the producers of pig and bar iron relied mainly on charcoal until coke came into general use during the latter part of the eighteenth century.[20] Since the furnaces and forges consumed large quantities of charcoal, the exhaustion of timber and the resulting shortage of fuel became an increasingly difficult problem in the traditional centers of production, such as the Weald in Sussex and the Forest of Dean in Gloucester.[21] This led to a gradual migration of the

[17] See Ephraim Lipson, *The Growth of English Society: A Short Economic History* (New York, 1950), pp. 75–120.

[18] The partners' extant correspondence deals primarily with transactions in England. Judging from scattered references, however, the Eastern Shore was their best local market, while Massachusetts and Virginia were their principal outlets in the other colonies. They also explored the possibilities of the West Indian trade, for Dr. Carroll shipped iron to Barbados in the early 1740's. His iron brought less there than at home, and he discontinued the trade after the outbreak of King George's War and apparently made no further effort in the West Indies. (See Dr. Carroll to Coddrington Carrington, Oct. 25, 1742, Mar. 12, 1743, Feb. 6, 1744, in "Extracts," *Md. Hist. Mag.*, XX, 174–175, XXI, 56, 209.) Typical transactions were Charles Carroll's shipment of several tons of bar iron to Alexander McKenzie of Hampton, Va., Tasker's consignment of 209 bars of iron to Robert Tucker of Norfolk, and Dr. Carroll's shipment of 20 tons of bar iron to Paul Binney of Boston. See accounts of sales, Alexander McKenzie to Charles Carroll, June 20, 1740, Mar. 15, 1741; account of sales, Robert Tucker to Benjamin Tasker, Aug. 5, 1741; bill of lading, Dr. Carroll to Paul Binney, Apr. 18, 1747; all in Carroll-Maccubbin Papers.

[19] Bining, *Iron Industry*, pp. 24–31, and passim. Bining points out that there were more furnaces and forges—and greater production of pig and bar iron—in the colonies on the eve of the American Revolution than there were in Great Britain.

[20] *Ibid.*, pp. 25 26, 32, 122.

[21] As early as the sixteenth century, Parliament enacted a series of laws limiting iron production in the southeastern counties and the Forest of Dean. One motive for

industry to the north and west—as ironmasters sought areas where timber and other raw materials were more plentiful—and to the increasing concentration of smelting, refining, and manufacturing in the West Midlands, Wales, and the northern counties.[22]

Dispersion failed to relieve the over-all shortage of pig and bar iron, however, for even in the newer regions the furnaces and forges did not keep pace with the manufacture of finished products. The West Midlands, for example, produced more bar iron than any other section of Great Britain, turning out almost one half of the national output.[23] Yet even here the rapid growth of the hardware industry forced the craftsmen of Birmingham and other manufacturing centers to import iron.[24] For the kingdom as a whole, the annual production of bar iron met about one half of the manufacturers' needs, and the resulting deficit was made up by importations from Sweden and, to a lesser extent, from Russia and Spain.[25] Such dependence was dangerous to the national welfare, according to the mercantilists, and led to a movement to encourage the production of pig and bar iron in America. This movement had the full support of colonial agents and ironmasters, including the members of the Baltimore Company who took an active part in it.[26] The possibility that Parliament might be

---

colonizing America was the belief that the New World would provide fuel for industries such as iron and glass, thereby conserving England's dwindling supply. (Lipson, *English Society*, pp. 100–101. Gipson, *British Empire*, III, 207–213. Clark, *History of Manufactures*, I, 9–11.) Some writers believe that the depletion of timber has been overemphasized, that the major problem of the iron industry was the cost of labor— the principal expense in making charcoal. In their estimation, this is why the cost of producing iron in England was greater than in Sweden or Russia but less than in America where labor was "Extream Dear," to use Dr. Carroll's phrase. See Michael W. Flinn's review of Hartley, *Ironworks on the Saugus*, in *William and Mary Quarterly*, 3d Ser., XV (Apr. 1958), 279–280. Dr. Carroll to Charles Carroll, Jan. 1, 1733, Carroll-Maccubbin Papers.

[22] Ashton, *Iron and Steel*, pp. 13–23. William H. B. Court, *The Rise of the Midland Industries, 1600–1838* (London, 1938), pp. 78–81, 170–172. See also Wilfred Smith, *An Economic Geography of Great Britain* (New York, 1948), Table VII, p. 89, which lists the number of furnaces and forges in each region about 1720. South Wales and the Forest of Dean led in the output of pig iron and the West Midlands led in bar iron.

[23] Ashton, *Iron and Steel*, Appendix B, pp. 235–238. Court, *Midland Industries*, pp. 170–172.

[24] See note 11, above, for the growth of the hardware industry in Birmingham and its environs.

[25] Smith, *Economic Geography*, p. 90. Bining, *Iron Industry*, pp. 30, 33, 35, 55, 56, and passim. Statements regarding the disparity between British production and consumption of bar iron are only approximations, since there is much variation in contemporary figures. According to some estimates, British production of bar iron declined from 18,000 tons in 1718 to as low as 12,000 tons in 1738, the latter figure constituting only about one third of the kingdom's needs. Gipson, *British Empire*, III, 212–213.

[26] The question of what policy to adopt with regard to the colonial iron industry arose shortly after the close of Queen Anne's War and became a leading issue in Great Britain during the next half-century. Bining describes how the conflicting interests of the numerous groups involved complicated the question and emphasizes that British policy, as embodied in the acts of 1750 and 1757, was designed to encourage the production and importation of colonial pig and bar iron while restricting the manu-

induced to subsidize the colonial iron industry and, more important, the favorable opportunity presented by the shortage of pig and bar iron in England were undoubtedly uppermost in the minds of the partners when they decided to launch their enterprise.

The tobacco trade also drew the partners to England, since it largely determined the conditions under which the ironmasters of Maryland and Virginia shipped and sold their product. The iron of the two colonies was sent to the mother country aboard the tobacco ships, the pigs and bars being stowed among the tobacco hogsheads in the hold. This method of shipment limited the size of consignments but also made freight inexpensive, since the rate for iron was based on cargo space rather than weight.[27] The rate paid by the partners was only one sixteenth that for tobacco: 10s. a ton as against £8.[28] Their consignments generally ranged from 15 to 70 tons, occasionally rising to 80 and once falling to only 5.[29]

In seeking English outlets for their iron, the partners turned first to London. Since the metropolis dominated the tobacco trade,[30] the partners dealt much more with her merchants than with those of the outports, developing ties that extended far beyond the immediate requirements of trade. The complex nature of these relationships can be seen in Dulany's varied activities as the local representative of several London mercantile houses with extensive interests in Maryland. Dulany advised their local factors, handled their litigation and collected their debts, entered into partnership with them to buy land, watched over their traffic in British convicts sold in Maryland as indentured servants, and otherwise super-

---

facture of colonial ironware. He concludes that British policy was a decided failure, for colonial shipments of iron never supplied more than a fraction of Great Britain's needs and her attempts to limit the manufacture of ironware in the colonies were ineffectual. For the American side see Keach Johnson, "The Baltimore Company Seeks English Subsidies for the Colonial Iron Industry," *Md. Hist. Mag.*, XLVI (Mar. 1951), 27–43.

[27] Arthur Pierce Middleton, *Tobacco Coast: A Maritime History of Chesapeake Bay in the Colonial Era* (Newport News, Va., 1953), pp. 170–171.

[28] Undated memoranda, "The Charge on a Ton of Mettell," and "Charges on Pigg Mettall"; John Price's Account, "Charges on Baltimore Pigg Iron the Property of Charles Carroll Esq. in Maryland," Feb. 1754; all in Carroll-Maccubbin Papers. Middleton, *Tobacco Coast*, pp. 211, 298, 300. The cost of freight fluctuated of course, particularly during war, but 10s. a ton seems to have been the rate usually paid by the partners in time of peace.

[29] Charles Daniell to Charles Carroll, Baltimore Ironworks, Oct. 23, 1734, Carroll-Maccubbin Papers. Memoranda of Iron Shipped, 1736, 1737, 1741, and 1743, *ibid.* In 1734, for example, the 292 tons shipped by the partners comprised eight consignments of 30, 40, 20, 80, 45, 20, 30, and 27 tons. The 538 tons exported in 1736 included twelve shipments of 26, 25, 18, 50, 34, 28, 82, 46, 67, 56, 41, and 65 tons.

[30] Merchants of such outports as Bristol, Bideford, Liverpool, and Plymouth were active in the Maryland tobacco trade, but their influence was secondary to that of the London merchants who owned most of the ships engaged in the trade, bought the greatest part of the annual crop, and generally dominated the traffic. See Margaret S. Morriss, *Colonial Trade of Maryland, 1689–1715* in Johns Hopkins *Studies*, XXXII (Baltimore, 1914), No. 3, pp. 87–88, 95 ff.

vised their numerous interests in the province.[31] In shipping iron to London, therefore, the associates were utilizing well-established connections. As experienced merchants, they were well aware that their success depended very largely on the honesty and skill of their English correspondents. "I perceive that let our care and Industery for a liveing be never so well exerted and aplyed here," Dr. Carroll observed to a London merchant, "our good or ill fate in the consequence depends Intirely on your Management for us there." [32]

Although the migration of the industry to the north and west had left the craftsmen of the metropolis remote from the principal English centers of production and thereby dependent on foreign sources for their supply of iron, London continued to be a leading center for its manufacture and sale. Along with Newcastle, the capital received most of the bar iron imported from Sweden and Russia, while it was also one of the chief centers importing American pig and bar iron, which were beginning to enter England. Much of this iron was made into manufactured goods locally, but part of it was sent inland or transshipped to such outports as Bristol. Conversely, London was an important market for ironware manufactured in other parts of Great Britain, particularly the northeast.[33]

Among the ironmasters who utilized the London market, none were more important than the Crowley family, who carried on extensive operations near Newcastle and dominated the iron industry in northeastern England.[34] Typical of the large-scale, capitalistic enterprise that was taking form in England at this time, the Crowley Ironworks resembled a modern factory in organization and scope of operations. Carrying on all of the processes involved in the production and manufacture of iron and iron goods except that of smelting, the Crowleys maintained their own warehouses in London where they engaged in both the retail and wholesale trade. The only element lacking in this highly integrated organization was an adequate supply of bar iron, which had to be imported from Sweden. Consequently the Crowley firm evinced an early interest in the potentialities of the colonial iron industry and became one of the Baltimore Company's most important customers.[35]

[31] Land, The Dulanys, pp. 86–87.
[32] Dr. Carroll to Samuel Hyde, Dec. 17, 1733, in "Extracts," Md. Hist. Mag., XX, 59–60.
[33] Ashton, Iron and Steel, pp. 13–23, 119–120, Appendix C, 239–242.
[34] The head of the family was Sir Ambrose Crowley, who started out as a blacksmith, became one of the wealthiest and most influential ironmasters in England, was knighted in 1707, and left an estate worth £200,000 when he died in 1713. Lipson, English Society, pp. 79 and note, 191. Bining, Iron Industry, p. 35 and note.
[35] Ashton, Iron and Steel, pp. 20–21, 195–197. Lipson, English Society, pp. 97, 99. See also the discussion of the Crowley Ironworks in A History of the County of Durham, ed. William Page, The Victoria History of the Counties of England (London, 1905–28), II, 281–287.

The connection between the two concerns was established in 1735 while Dr. Carroll was making a firsthand investigation of English markets on behalf of the Baltimore Company. Carroll learned that the Crowleys bought most of the Maryland iron sent to England by the Principio Company. While in London, therefore, he had several talks with John Banister, an official of the Crowley firm, who offered to contract with the Baltimore Company for four or five hundred tons of iron annually at £6 5s. per ton or at the market price whenever it was higher. The partners were to deliver the iron to the Crowley wharf at Greenwich and to take one half payment in ironware, which Banister promised to barter at the "Ready Money Price." [36]

Carroll sought to keep Banister "in Expectation" until he had consulted his colleagues. He put him off, telling him that his price was too low and that his terms included a disproportionate amount of ironware. Actually, however, he was favorably impressed by Banister, who appeared to be a "Man of Integrity," although "tenacious in Points relating to his business." He felt that the terms were by no means unfavorable and included several fringe advantages that ought to be taken into account. Delivering the iron directly from shipboard to the Crowley wharf at Greenwich would save the cost of wharfage, while the "Ready Money Price," which Banister offered to charge for ironware, was 5 per cent less than the price which the partners paid the London merchants. Carroll decided, therefore, to instruct Philip Smith, a tobacco merchant who received a consignment of Baltimore iron at this time, to sell it to Banister (if he could not get more than £6 5s. per ton elsewhere) and to direct the company's other factors in London not to sell for less than Banister offered. [37]

Despite Dr. Carroll's favorable impression, the partners evidently decided they could do better by dealing with their agents than with the ironmongers and manufacturers. This proved not to be the case as far as the Crowley terms were concerned, for the factors were unable to improve on Banister's offer. In 1735, for instance, Samuel Hyde, one of the company's principal agents in London, sold Banister about two hundred tons of Baltimore pig iron at £6 5s. a ton, agreeing to accept one half of the payment in ironware and the remainder in cash, which was to be paid "in four, Six and eight Months" from the time the iron was delivered to the Crowley wharf at Greenwich. [38] Two years later, Hyde contracted to sell Banister between 340 and 400 tons of Baltimore iron at the same price. This time, however, Banister stipulated that two thirds of the payment was to be made "in Wrot Iron of such Sorts as are usually sold by the Said

[36] Dr. Carroll to Charles Carroll, London, Mar. 3, 1735, and to Samuel Hyde, Sept. 2, 1735, Carroll-Maccubbin Papers.

[37] Dr. Carroll to Charles Carroll, London, Mar. 3, 1735, *ibid.*

[38] Agreement signed by John Banister, Dec. 2, 1735 (copy), enclosed in Samuel Hyde's letter to Benjamin Tasker and Company, London, Feb. 28, 1736, *ibid.*

Mr Theo Crowley." The remaining one third was to be paid in cash within eight months after March 1, 1738, subject to the customary 2½ per cent discount.[39]

The large amounts of Baltimore iron purchased by the Crowley firm attest its worth. Indeed, Banister had not offered Dr. Carroll a contract until samples of Baltimore pig iron were tested and reported as equal in quality to that made by the Principio Company. These trials, Carroll declared, showed that Baltimore iron could be made into wire and was even better than Oregrund iron, the best Swedish bar iron, then topping the English market at £18 a ton.[40] Similar tests conducted by the Admiralty also, proved, according to Carroll, that Baltimore iron was as good as the best Swedish iron.[41]

At this time the Crowley firm probably bought more Baltimore iron than anyone else in England, a fact which helps to explain why the partners shipped most of their iron to London during the 1730's. Unwilling to rely entirely on the metropolis, however, they also sent several shipments to Bristol. Endowed with a fine harbor on the Avon River not far from where it entered the Severn, Bristol had long been a center for trade and industry and was the most important port in England outside of London. It led all of the outports in the importation of tobacco from Maryland and Virginia and was also important as a market and distributing center in the iron trade. Much of the iron produced in South Wales and the Forest of Dean was sent there for sale or forwarding to other markets, while American and Swedish iron was unloaded at Bristol and carried in barges up the Severn to the forges, mills, and smithies of the West Midlands. The hardware of this region in turn passed down the river to Bristol for transshipment.[42]

It is quite possible that Dr. Carroll included the West Midlands in his investigation of English markets, for he wrote from London that he intended to go "into the Country" soon in order to "try all the Forges and

[39] Agreement signed by John Banister, n.d. (copy), enclosed in Samuel Hyde's letter to Benjamin Tasker and Company, London, Dec. 30, 1737, *ibid.*

[40] Memorandum, "To Doctr Cha: Carroll att Mr Woodwards att the blackmooreshead Ten Church Street," n.n., Feb. 25, 1735, enclosed in Dr. Carroll's letter to Charles Carroll, London, Mar. 3, 1735, *ibid.* This note announcing the results of the tests made by the Crowley forges was undoubtedly written by John Banister. Dr. Carroll's comments on the results of the trials appear on the memorandum.

[41] Dr. Carroll to Samuel Hyde, Oct. 27, 1740, *ibid.* Dr. Carroll's statements constitute the only evidence available regarding the relative merits of Baltimore and Swedish iron. However, Edward Knight of Worcestershire, one of the leading ironmasters of Great Britain, declared that bar iron made from Baltimore pig was equal in quality to the best tough English iron and could be used for the same purposes. *Journals of the House of Commons* [1738–41], XXIII (1762), 109–110.

[42] Gipson, *British Empire*, I, 39, II, 121 *n.* Ashton, *Iron and Steel*, Appendix C, pp. 242–244. A. H. John, "Iron and Coal on a Glamorgan Estate, 1700–1740," *Economic History Review*, XIII (1943), 98–99. B. L. C. Johnson, "The Foley Partnerships: The Iron Industry at the End of the Charcoal Era," *ibid.*, 2nd Ser., IV (1952), 331–335.

places" where there might be a market for iron.[43] Whether he actually visited the area is uncertain, but it is clear that he was in close touch with Lyde and Cooper, the partners' agents in Bristol. The agents wrote to Carroll in London on March 8, 1735, that they had received about forty tons of Baltimore pig iron. Since this was the first shipment to arrive in Bristol and its quality was unknown, they had sent ten tons of the iron for testing to Edward Kendall of Stourbridge, "a man of undoubted Probity," and they also intended to submit five tons to a Mr. Humphray in whose skill and integrity they had great confidence. "One Furnace cannot be a president for the value of another," they stated, and they would not price the iron until its worth was ascertained. They added that they had sold iron in London and Liverpool but had found Bristol to be the best of the three markets. They were confident, therefore, that if the Baltimore iron proved to be of good quality, it would always have a quick sale in Bristol notwithstanding the fact that "great Quantitys of Ordinary Pigs lye on hand." [44]

While the partners were testing the market in Bristol, they also sent two consignments to Bideford, a nearby port in Devon active in the tobacco trade. They soon discovered, however, that Bideford was little more than a satellite of Bristol. "Bristol is to us," explained George Buck, their correspondent in Bideford, "as London is to the Ports the other Side of the Land, tho I observe the Pigg Iron from London: is also Sent up the Thames, for them Ports, the charge, whereon is much more than the charge from this Port." Everyone agreed that Baltimore iron was of the best quality, but there was no demand for it in Bideford. Buck thought, however, that he could get £6 5s. for it in Bristol by accepting nails in return. Since he had occasion to buy nails "for the Shipping," he was inclined to accept these terms in order to complete the sale of the iron and settle his account with the company.[45]

Baltimore iron brought no more in Bristol at this time than it did in London. Since the associates had not sold any of their iron in London for less than £6 5s. a ton, they set this as their minimum figure in Bristol, insisting that even £6 5s. was a low price in view of the fact that no iron equaled theirs in toughness or was better suited to be used with "ordinary Pigg" in making bar iron. Lyde and Cooper were able to get £6 5s. and alleged that they could have obtained more if the Baltimore iron which Buck sent to Bristol had not been sold at that figure.[46] Another mercantile house reported that £6 10s. was the most that was given for American iron in Bristol. They had recently sold some Philadelphia iron at a "Top Price" but the market had declined since then.[47] When the partners informed

[43] Dr. Carroll to Charles Carroll, London, Mar. 3, 1735, Carroll-Maccubbin Papers.
[44] Lyonel Lyde and Cooper to Dr. Carroll, Bristol, Mar. 8, 1735, *ibid.*
[45] George Buck to Benjamin Tasker, Bideford, Sept. 27, 1736, *ibid.*
[46] Charles Carroll to George Buck, July 21, 1736, *ibid.*
[47] Devonsheir and Reeves to Benjamin Tasker, Bristol, Dec. 4, 1736, *ibid.*

Buck that Principio iron commanded six shillings a hundredweight (approximately £6 14s. per ton) in Bristol, Buck was skeptical. He had sold a great deal of Principio iron in Bristol, he said, but never at that price. Large quantities of iron "of Divers Sorte" had been received recently in Bristol, but the sale of most of it had been postponed, although some had been sold for five shillings per hundredweight (approximately £5 12s. per ton). Barring an unusual demand, Buck thought, there was little chance that iron would ever bring more than £6 5s. in Bristol.[48]

Bristol eventually became one of the Baltimore Company's most important markets, but in the 1730's it was overshadowed by London. Of the 1,977 tons of pig iron shipped to England by the partners during the period 1734–37, only 121 tons went to Bristol, 81 to Bideford, the rest going to London.[49] Although the figures are incomplete, London probably continued as the chief market throughout the 1740's. There is no evidence that the associates shipped appreciable quantities of iron to any other British port until after the close of King's George's War. During the years 1741–43, for example, all recorded shipments to England—some 767 tons—were consigned to London merchants.[50]

Trade was disrupted seriously during King George's War. The partners continued to send iron to England, but, as Dr. Carroll observed in 1745, the times were "Very precarious," and many ships had been captured. Two years later, he wrote that the company's losses at the hands of the enemy had been "very considerable" since the beginning of the war. "These are very difficult times with us," he said, "haveing nothing but what go's and comes thro the fire and attended with great charges in freight and Insurance."[51]

The spiraling freight rates led the partners to protest that the ironmasters of Maryland "must suffer Extremely" unless the price of iron rose proportionately. Dr. Carroll warned the London merchants that if they failed to sell his iron "at some advanced price adequate to the charges neither I nor my Famely can subsist." Continuing to complain of losses at sea, hard times, and the consequent difficulty of collecting debts, Carroll

[48] George Buck to Benjamin Tasker, Bideford, Sept. 27, 1736, ibid.

[49] The Carroll accounts in John Digges's Account Book, 1720–49, Division of Manuscripts, Library of Congress. The Carroll accounts fall into two parts: (1) Charles and Daniel Carroll's joint account with the Baltimore Company, which covers the period 1730–37 and consists of twenty-eight folios in the back of the Account Book, and (2) Charles Carroll's accounts with various English merchants, which appear on four unnumbered folios following the joint account. The above figures are based partly on the joint account, folios 11, 28, and partly on Charles Carroll's accounts.

[50] Memoranda, "1741 Iron Shiped," and "1743 Iron Shiped," Carroll-Maccubbin Papers. Dr. Carroll to William Black, June 29, July 22, 1742 (copies), and to Hyde, June 29, 1742 (copy), ibid. Dr. Carroll to Hyde, Sept. 27, 1742, in "Extracts," Md. Hist. Mag., XX, 167–168. The memoranda list the various shipments which the partners made to England in 1741 and 1743, the number of tons per shipment, and the name of each consignee.

[51] Dr. Carroll to John Hanburry, Oct. 1745, to William Black, Nov. 24, 1747, and to William Woodward, Nov. 18, 1747, ibid., XXI, 259–260, XXII, 363, 360.

was compelled to retrench and to call on his English factors to carry him until business improved. "I am too old to run away nor do I know well where to Run to," he lamented, "The Rice trade is as bad as ours and I shall want more Cloaths if I go Northward therefore I hope you will contribute to keep me here a little longer till better times." [52] Perhaps Carroll exaggerated his plight, but he and his colleagues were undoubtedly forced to curtail their operations because of the stagnation of trade and the general economic distress which prevailed in Maryland as a result of the war.

The end of King George's War brought little immediate relief: it was followed by a slump in English markets which the partners' agents attributed to an oversupply of iron. "The Late Scarcity of Iron this way," explained Daniel Cheston, a Bristol merchant, "Engaged all the Works that Possibly Could Get into Blast to Doe all they Could to Supply the Demand." Also contributing to the surplus, according to Cheston, was the fact that English shipmasters, unable to fill their vessels with tobacco, had brought home more iron than usual.[53]

The decline in prices resulting from overproduction and colonial competition created much discontent and suffering among English ironmasters and workers. The conditions which prevailed in the Forest of Dean, Monmouth, and Wales were described by Cheston: "Labour at the works is drove as Low as possible," he reported, "and the people Get Bread and the Masters say (How True I am Not A Judge) that Except they Could Buy wood for Coaling Cheaper they Cannot possibly afford their Barr Iron Cheaper Than the present price which is £15 per Ton and the Landed Gentlemen Say that rather than Lower the price of their Woods theyl Throw Them Open to their Young Stock which utterly prevents their Growth." [54]

London too felt the pinch. The partners complained frequently about the sluggishness of the market, where their iron sold for as little as £5 10s. during the postwar period. Protesting against the low prices and slow turnover in London at this time, Dr. Carroll accused the ironmongers of attempting to "run down" the price of pig iron and predicted that some of the Maryland furnaces would inevitably fail during the next few years unless the trade improved. "Our Mother Country will Ruin her Children in the Plantations nor suffer them to Live," he warned one of his London agents. When the London market failed to recover during the next few years, Carroll suspended his shipments there, declaring that nothing was

---

[52] Dr. Carroll to William Black, Mar. 25, Jan. 1, 1747, Sept. 1, 1746; to John Addison, Jan. 21, 1747; to Black, Dec. 4, 1746; *ibid.*, XXII, 286, 365, XXI, 377–378, XXII, 367–368, 191.

[53] Daniel Cheston to Charles Carroll, Bristol, Feb. 26, 1750, Carroll-Maccubbin Papers.

[54] *Ibid.*

to be gained by "Glutting" the market with "an unsaleable Commodity." [55]

Equally pessimistic regarding the condition of the London market were the letters of John Price, a member of the Principio Company and Charles Carroll's principal London agent at this time.[56] Of the 130 tons which the latter consigned to him in 1750, Price reported on July 4, 1751, that he had been able to sell only 15 tons, 7 at £6 each and 8 at £6 5s. A few months later he wrote that five tons was the largest individual sale made by the Principio Company in London during the past year. Price attributed the slow movement of Baltimore and Principio iron to the fact that there was little demand in London for tough pig iron. He also thought that the practice of bartering pig iron for hardware tended to depress prices, as the ironmongers often sold pig iron below cost.[57]

In Bristol, by contrast, the postwar slump proved to be short-lived. The partners were well aware that prices were higher in Bristol and the West Midlands than in London, but they hesitated to transfer much of their iron because of the expense and risk involved in reshipment.[58] Although the cost of shipping iron from London to Bristol fluctuated considerably during this period, it was frequently prohibitively high. During the summer of 1751, it amounted to 13s. 6d. a ton. Early in 1752, it totaled 10s. 5d. a ton (freight being 8s. 6d., insurance 5d., and wharfage and related charges 1s. 6d.). As long as these high rates prevailed, the London merchants argued that it was more profitable to accept £6 or even slightly less locally than to sell in Bristol for £6 5s.[59]

It was not until 1752 that the costs of the coastal trade fell to the point where the London merchants thought it profitable to reship Baltimore iron to Bristol. During that year, John Price sent a large part of Charles

[55] Dr. Carroll to William Black, Oct. 16, 1751; to Charles Carnan, July 15, 1751; to Black, Oct. 9, Nov. 18, 1753, May 8, 1754; "Extracts," *Md. Hist. Mag.*, XXIV, 261–262, 192, XXVI, 196, 236, XXVII, 218–219. Carroll did not ship any iron to London in 1753, declaring that it was more profitable to sell it in Maryland or Bristol.

[56] It should be noted that the partners no longer sold their iron in common but followed a policy of apportionment and separate sales in which they dealt with factors individually rather than collectively. Their original policy was to sell jointly, but they decided in 1742 to divide their iron into fifths and allow each member to sell his portion independently. Thereafter, the partners disposed of their respective shares individually. See Charles Carroll @ Benjamin Tasker, Charles Carroll, Barrister, Charles Carroll, son of Daniel, and Daniel and Walter Dulany, Chancery Records, 1791, 145, Maryland Land Office, Annapolis.

[57] John Price to Charles Carroll, London, July 4, 1751, Feb. 1, 1752, Mar. 2, 1751, Carroll-Maccubbin Papers.

[58] When Charles Carnan, one of Dr. Carroll's London agents, sold some of his iron in the West Midlands, agreeing to deliver it at £6 12s. 6d. a ton, Carroll feared that freight and insurance would "Eat deep" and wished that Carnan had sold the iron in London rather than incur the costs and hazards of reshipment. Dr. Carroll to Charles Carnan, July 15, 1751, in "Extracts," *Md. Hist. Mag.*, XXIV, 191–192.

[59] John Price to Charles Carroll, London, July 4, 1751, Feb. 1, 1752, Carroll-Maccubbin Papers.

Carroll's iron to the outport at 5s. 8d. a ton. He thought it would sell for the same prices Principio iron commanded, namely, £6 to £6 5s. in Bristol and £6 10s. in Bewdley (an important market in Worcester located near the junction of the Stour River with the Severn).[60] Price declared that these were the highest prices to be had in England, and that all of the Principio iron consigned to London had been reshipped to Bristol.[61] Charles Carroll's iron sold for more in Bristol and Bewdley than Price had anticipated, much of it bringing from five to fifteen shillings a ton more in those two markets than in London.[62]

Baltimore iron continued to command good prices in Bristol and Bewdley. Since the latter was located in the heart of the West Midlands and was closer to the principal manufacturing centers, prices were higher there than in Bristol. In 1753, for instance, Cheston, Sedgley, and Hilhouse, who handled most of the partners' consignments to Bristol at this time, sent one of their employees to the West Midlands to make a firsthand investigation of markets and prices. He visited the works along the Stour and Trent Rivers and talked with most of the important ironmasters of Birmingham, Stourbridge, and Wolverhampton. The highest price offered was £6 10s. a ton delivered at Bewdley, payable in three months.[63] Despite the higher price, however, this survey confirmed the belief of the Bristol firm that they had been justified in selling Baltimore iron locally at £6 7s. 6d. a ton: freight to Bewdley was five shillings a ton, wharfage there came to eight pence a ton, and the risk of "Embezzlement" was "not Inconsiderable." They concluded that Bristol was the better of the two markets. "Few Men in this City have it in their power to serve you in the Disposal of Iron, on equal Terms with us," they wrote, "as most in this Town who buy, have yearly large Sums from us, so that we almost sell it at our own prices."[64]

Most of the iron which the Baltimore Company partners sold in Bristol was reshipped from London, since their direct consignments were limited

---

[60] Bewdley was one of the most important entrepôts in the West Midlands at this time: ironware from Manchester, Stourbridge, Dudley, and the numerous works along the Stour River was brought there to be shipped to market, while American, English, and foreign iron was unloaded at Bewdley for sale to the forgemasters and manufacturers of Shropshire, Stafford, and Worcester. Ashton, *Iron and Steel*, Appendix C, pp. 242–244.

[61] John Price to Charles Carroll, London, Jan. 22, 1753, Carroll-Maccubbin Papers.

[62] In Bristol, Carroll received from £6 to £6 15s. a ton, 97 tons selling at £6, 31 at £6 5s., 57 at £6 10s., and 8 at £6 15s. In Bewdley all of his iron sold for £6 15s. In London, on the other hand, his average price during this period was about £6. See account, "General Imports of Baltimore Pigg Iron from Charles Carroll Esqr. . . . of Maryland," n.n., n.d., prepared by Price and probably received by Carroll in Feb. 1754; John Price's Account of Sales, 1754; William Perkins's Account of Sales, Dec. 1754; *ibid.* Perkins was a London merchant to whom Price transferred part of Charles Carroll's iron for sale.

[63] Cheston, Sedgley, and Hilhouse to Charles Carroll, Bristol, June 30, 1753, *ibid.*

[64] *Ibid.* Sedgley, Hilhouse, and Berry to Charles Carroll, Bristol, May 1, 1754, *ibid.* Berry became a member of the firm when Cheston died sometime in 1753–54.

by a lack of shipping. Their exports to Cheston, Sedgley, and Hilhouse were restricted by the fact that the Bristol firm dealt primarily with the merchants and planters of the Eastern Shore, and they were sometimes prevented by their commitments in this area from accepting shipments of Baltimore iron. Dr. Carroll wrote in 1754, for instance, that he would "gladly" have sent them iron during the year if the Bristol firm's ships had not been engaged by previous contracts.[65] As it was, the partners' direct consignments to the outport were small and infrequent. Of the 245 tons exported by Dr. Carroll in 1750–52, for example, only 53 tons were shipped to Bristol as against 192 to London.[66]

While the associates were turning from London to the West Midlands, they were also probing other English markets. Dr. Carroll investigated the potentialities of Whitehaven, offering to barter pig iron for the copper and brassware manufactured there.[67] Charles Carroll sent two consignments directly to Liverpool and also considered the possibility of transferring there some of his London shipments. He abandoned the latter idea, however, on the advice of his agent in Liverpool, James Gildart, a prominent tobacco merchant active in the Maryland trade. Noting that reshipment would cost ten shillings a ton and that the local ironmasters imported large quantities of iron from New England and Virginia, Gildart stated that no pig iron had ever been brought from London to Liverpool as far as he could remember. He predicted, nevertheless, that Carroll would find Liverpool to be as good a market as London for direct shipments, adding that he was asking £6 10s. a ton for Carroll's iron.[68]

Liverpool proved to be a poor outlet despite Gildart's prediction. The forgemasters of the city found fault with the quality of Carroll's iron, complaining that when they broke a pig there was a black spot in the center which they declared was dross and an indication of poor workmanship. Consequently, they refused to give more than £5 or £5 5s. for it. Gildart then sold the first of Carroll's two consignments for £5 5s. a ton and, after holding the second for more than a year, reshipped it to Bristol where it brought £6 12s. 6d. a ton.[69]

[65] Dr. Carroll to Sedgley and Cheston, Sept. 27, 1751, to William Black, Oct. 24, 1752, and to Sedgley, Hilhouse, and Berry, Sept. 6, 1754, in "Extracts," *Md. Hist. Mag.*, XXIV, 258, XXV, 55, XXVII, 315.

[66] Dr. Carroll's consignments to Bristol and London during this period were 12 tons and 60 tons respectively in 1750, 13 and 45 in 1751, and 28 and 87 in 1752. Dr. Carroll to Sedgley and Cheston, May 29, 1750, Sept. 27, 1751, Mar. 30, Oct. 31, 1752, *ibid.*, XXIII, 260, XXIV, 258–259, 276–277, XXV, 55–56; to Charles Carnan, Aug. 10, 1750, *ibid.*, XXIII, 380–381; to William Black, Nov. 15, 1750, Aug. 17, 1751, Aug. 13, Sept. 22, 1752, *ibid.*, XXIV, 35, 248, 372–373, 373–374.

[67] Dr. Carroll to Captain Richard Parker, May 15, 1748, and to John Philpott and Company, June 5, 1748, *ibid.*, XXII, 371–372, 373.

[68] James Gildart to Charles Carroll, Liverpool, Apr. 12, 1751, Apr. 18, 1752, Carroll-Maccubbin Papers.

[69] When Carroll insisted that the black spots were marks of excellence rather than flaws, Gildart replied that he had shown the iron to a number of forgemasters and that

The fact that Charles Carroll received £1 7s. 6d. more per ton for his iron in Bristol than in Liverpool is a further indication that the partners obtained higher prices in Bristol and Bewdley than elsewhere in England during the period 1752–55. There was an increasing demand for pig iron in Bristol during these years, and its value rose accordingly. During the latter part of 1753, the price varied from £6 12s. to £6 15s. a ton. The market remained strong in 1754 and in 1755, when it reached a price of £7 10s. per ton, with indication it would probably go higher, according to the partners' agents.[70] They did not explain why the market was so lively, but the growing tension in Anglo-French relations, the outbreak of fighting in America, and the approach of the Seven Years' War were probably responsible.

The amount of iron sold by the associates in England in the early 1750's was probably the same as in 1734–37, when their shipments totaled 1,977 tons and comprised one fifth of the pig iron exported to the mother country by the thirteen colonies.[71] Charles Carroll's consignments to John Price and James Gildart—376 and 60 tons respectively—averaged over two hundred tons a year in 1750–51. Dr. Carroll's exports in 1750–52, as noted above, totaled 245 tons.[72] Assuming that the shipments of Dulany and Tasker equaled those of the Carrolls, the partners maintained the pace which they had set in 1734–37 and continued to ship about five hundred tons a year to the mother country. That they ranked among the major colonial exporters in the 1750's is also indicated by John Price's observation in 1751 that Baltimore and Principio iron constituted "the Chief body" of the pig iron imported from the colonies.[73]

To what extent did the partners profit from the sale of their iron, and what were the relative strengths of London, Bristol, and Bewdley as

---

they had all agreed the spots represented defects. James Gildart to Charles Carroll, Liverpool, June 6, 1751, Apr. 18, 1752, May 24, 1753; Sedgley, Hilhouse, and Berry to Carroll, Bristol, May 1, 1754; *ibid.*

[70] Cheston, Sedgley, and Hilhouse to Charles Carroll, Bristol, Sept. 20, 1753; Sedgley, Hilhouse, and Berry to Charles Carroll, Bristol, May 1, 1754, May 1, 1755; *ibid.*

[71] Colonial shipments of pig iron to Great Britain during this period totaled approximately 9,798 tons. Bining, *Iron Industry*, Appendix B, pp. 129–130.

[72] His shipments during this period may have exceeded 245 tons. On September 29, 1752, after shipping 87 tons to William Black of London, Dr. Carroll wrote that he hoped his consignments to Black would total 200 tons by the end of the year. It is probable, however, that his estimate included some iron produced by the Lancashire furnace in Baltimore County in which he owned an interest (subsequently sold to the Principio Company for £2675). Dr. Carroll to William Black, Sept. 29, 1752, in "Extracts," *Md. Hist. Mag.*, XXV, 53–54. William G. Whitely, "The Principio Company," *Pennsylvania Magazine of History and Biography*, XI (1887), 196.

[73] John Price to Charles Carroll, London, Mar. 2, 1751, Carroll-Maccubbin Papers. As Price's statement implies, Maryland and Virginia furnished most of the iron which Great Britain imported from the American colonies. For 1734–37 and 1750–52, exports of the two colonies constituted about 90 per cent of the whole. See Bining, *Iron Industry*, Appendices B and C, pp. 128–137.

markets by the 1750's? These questions can best be answered by analyzing the sales of Charles Carroll's consignments to John Price in 1750–51, 341 tons shipped directly to London and 35 to Bristol, totaling 376 tons. Price sold 108 tons in London—57 himself and 51 through William Perkins, another of Carroll's agents—for £640 7s. 1½d. Of the remaining 268 tons, he sold 193 in Bristol for £1182 6s. 7¾d. and 75 in Bewdley for £501 15s. 7d.[74] Thus Carroll's gross receipts were £2324 10s. 2d. From this amount must be substracted shipping, selling, and production costs.

The cost of shipping and selling the 376 tons was £545 1s. 9d.[75] The shipment of 341 tons to London came to £246 12s. 9d., the principal items consisting of freight at 10s. per ton, lighterage at 12d., and wharfage at 2s. 6d.[76] Carroll's shipment of 35 tons to Bristol proved costly when the *Charming Molly*, which carried the consignment, was driven ashore in Wales and damaged so badly that vessel and cargo were sold for salvage at an ultimate cost to Carroll of £106 10s. 3d.[77] Reshipment from London to the West Midlands was another major expense. Price reshipped 233 tons to Bristol at a cost of £95 14s. 8d. Included in this sum were freight at 5s. 8d. per ton, landing at 6d., weighing at 6d., the commissions of the Bristol merchants at 12d., and such other expenses as insurance. Transporting 75 tons to Bewdley—the 35 from the *Charming Molly* plus 40 from Bristol—imposed an additional cost of £21 3s.[78]

[74] "Rough state of My Acct with Mr Perkins & Mr Price," in Charles Carroll's handwriting, Nov. 15, 1755; John Price's Account, "General Imports of Baltimore Pigg Iron from Charles Carroll Esqr. . . of Maryland" (cited hereafter as Account of Imports), Feb. 1754; John Price's Account of Sales, 1754 (probably received by Carroll in Feb.); William Perkins's Account of Sales, Dec. 1754; all in Carroll-Maccubbin Papers.

[75] John Price's Account, "Charges on Baltimore Pigg Iron the Property of Charles Carroll Esq. in Maryland" (cited hereafter as Account of Charges), Feb. 1754; John Price's Account of Sales, 1754; William Perkins's Account of Sales, Dec. 1754; *ibid.* The account of charges deals with the cost of shipment, including reshipment to Bristol and Bewdley, while the sales accounts include, respectively, Price's commissions and Perkins's small charge for weighing and sufferance.

[76] John Price's Account of Charges, Feb. 1754, *ibid.*

[77] The iron was taken to Bristol and sold at £5 12s. 6d. a ton, the 35 tons totaling £196 17s. 6d. Price thought this was too low, however, and decided to redeem the iron by paying the general average: the percentage of the loss borne by the owners of the *Charming Molly* and the shippers in proportion to their stakes in the voyage. Since the general average was estimated as 50 per cent of the sales value of ship and cargo, Price paid the London Assurance House which adjusted the losses and computed the general average, £98 8s. 6d. Added to this figure was the expense of landing and selling the iron which raised the cost of salvage to £106 10s. 3d. John Price to Charles Carroll, London, May 6, 1752, Jan. 22, 1753; Edward Wilcox's Account, "Charges on 35 Ton Pig Iron p the Charmg Molly Jam Creagh Mar: [from] Maryland," n.d. (Feb. or Mar. 1752); Copy of a bill of exchange drawn by Edward Wilcox on John Price payable to Peter Fearon, Bristol, Mar. 12, 1752, accepted by Price, Mar. 23, 1752; Memorandum signed by Peter Fearon, Mar. 21, 1752 (copy); Peter Fearon's Account of Settlement, "General average on the Charming Molly Stranded in Wales," n.d.; and John Price's Account of Charges, Feb. 1754; *ibid.*

[78] John Price's Account of Imports, Feb. 1754; John Price's Account of Charges, Feb. 1754; John Price's Account, "Sundrys Accounts of Baltimore Pigg Iron The Property of Charles Carroll Esqr," received by Carroll Feb. 15, 1754; *ibid.*

With the addition of miscellaneous expenses, Price's charges against Carroll at this point stood at £478 15s. 8d. In addition, Perkins charged Carroll £2 6s. 3d. for weighing and sufferance; his commission, however—£2 10s.—was included in Price's charges. There remained, consequently, only Price's commissions of £63 19s. 10d., bringing the grand total for shipping and selling to £545 1s. 9d.[79]

How much Carroll spent in producing 376 tons is not shown but can be computed at £1170 6s., since the cost of making a ton of Baltimore pig iron was £3 2s. 3d.[80] In all probability, therefore, his total cost—shipping, selling, and production—was £1715 7s. 9d., leaving a balance of £609 2s. 5d.

Computation of Carroll's net profit in each of the three markets discloses that his greatest return per ton was in London.[81]

	London 108 tons	Bristol 193 tons	Bewdley 75 tons
Sales	£640 7s. 11d.	£1182 6s. 8d.	£501 15s. 7d.
Cost	£437 10s. 7d.	£ 852 8s. 2d.	£425 9s. 2d.
	£202 17s. 4d.	£ 329 18s. 6d.	£ 76 6s. 5d.
Net profit per ton	£ 1 17s. 7d.	£ 1 14s. 2d.	£ 1 4d.

Two adjustments should probably be made in Carroll's cost and profit at Bewdley in order to get more representative figures. Both concern the 35 tons on the *Charming Molly* which were sold there. Since Price's charges do not include freight from Maryland to Bristol, this expense

---

[79] John Price's Account of Charges, Feb. 1754; William Perkins's Account of Sales, Dec. 1754; John Price's Account of Sales, 1754; *ibid.* (Price's commissions were as follows: 1 per cent of his charges, £4 15s. 9d.; 2½ per cent of his sales, £50 12s. 1d.; and 1 per cent of £859 6s. 6d. which he deposited with Perkins for Carroll's account, £8 12s.)

[80] Memorandum, "The Charge on a Ton of Mettell," n.d., n.n., *ibid.* The memorandum itemizes cost per ton as follows: two loads of charcoal, £2; three tons of ore, £1 2s. 6d.; wages of founder and assistant 8s.; lime and "charge to ye furnace," 12s. 6d. Total £4 3s. currency or £3 2s. 3d. sterling.

[81] The allocation of cost in the following table is based on the tonnage sold in each market; for example, London:

Production (108 tons at £3 2s. 3d.)	£336	3s.	
Shipment to London (108 of 341 tons = .317 of £246 12s. 9d.)	78	4	
Price's commissions (108 of 376 tons = .287 of £63 19s. 10d.)	18	7	4
Perkins's commission and charges	4	16	3
	£437	10s.	7d.

The only available information concerning the profit of the other members consists of a few passing and inconclusive references in Dr. Carroll's correspondence. For example, see Dr. Carroll to Charles Carnan, July 15, 1751, and to William Black, Nov. 18, 1753, in "Extracts," *Md. Hist. Mag.*, XXIV, 191, XXVI, 236.

should be added to the cost at Bewdley.[82] On the other hand, the cost allocated to Bewdley in the above table includes salvage, making the expenses there disproportionately higher than they were in Bristol or London. If salvage is deducted to obtain a more accurate comparison of the three markets, Carroll's net profit at Bewdley becomes £165 6s. 8d. or £2 4s. 1d. per ton. These figures are probably a better indication of Bewdley's relative strength as a market than are those given in the above table.

Also important in determining the relative merit of the three markets was the rate of turnover. Here Bristol and Bewdley enjoyed a decided advantage over London. Almost four years were required to sell 108 tons in London, only seven to eight months for the 268 tons marketed in Bristol and Bewdley. Sales in London extended from February 1751 to December 10, 1754, comprising thirteen transactions varying in amount from 2 to 15 tons.[83] In Bristol, on the other hand, the sale of 193 tons was completed in seven months: July 15, 1752, to February 8, 1753. Since one firm, Daniel and Reynolds, bought 80 per cent of the total, individual sales were larger in Bristol than in London or Bewdley, the nine transactions there ranging from 8 to 55 tons.[84] The 75 tons in Bewdley were disposed of in nine sales of from 5 to 10 tons between May 11, 1752, and January 10, 1753.[85]

Judging by Carroll's experience, the members of the Baltimore Company made a substantial profit and found Bristol and Bewdley to be better markets than London from 1752 to 1755.[86] Carroll's net profit per ton, it is true, was less in Bristol and Bewdley than in London because of the expense of salvage and reshipment. Salvage of course was not a fixed charge, but reshipment imposed an additional cost that largely offset the higher prices of the West Midlands. The expense of reshipping Carroll's iron to Bristol and on to Bewdley was almost as great as the cost of shipment from Maryland to London: 13s. 10d. per ton as against 14s. 6d.[87] Consequently, the partners' net profit per ton was probably no greater in

[82] No figures are available to show how much freight the partners paid on their shipments to Bristol, but there was evidently little difference between London and the outports. See Clark, *History of Manufactures*, I, 89, and George Buck to Benjamin Tasker, Bideford, Sept. 27, 1736, Carroll-Maccubbin Papers. At 10s. a ton, then, freight for 35 tons was £17 10s., thereby reducing Carroll's balance to £58 16s. 5d. or 15s. 8d. per ton.

[83] John Price's Account of Sales, 1754; John Price's Account of Imports, Feb. 1754; and William Perkins's Account of Sales, Dec. 1754; *ibid.*

[84] John Price's Account of Imports, Feb. 1754; John Price's Account of Sales, 1754; *ibid.*

[85] John Price's Account of Imports, Feb. 1754, *ibid.*

[86] Sales in all three markets were frequently based on credit. When Price submitted a sales account in 1754, £443 14s. 6¾d.—one-fifth of the whole—was outstanding. A year later, Carroll estimated that the amount of £315 15s. 4d. was still due. "Rough state of My Acct with Mr Perkins & Mr Price," in Charles Carroll's handwriting, Nov. 15, 1755, *ibid.*

[87] These figures are based on the expenses discussed above, p. 57.

Bristol and Bewdley than in London except when they shipped their iron directly to the outport.

But the success of the Baltimore Company depended on volume of sales as well as net profit per ton. And it was at this point, of course, that Bristol and Bewdley, with their greater demand and quicker turnover, surpassed London. This was particularly true of Bristol where Carroll's iron moved twice as rapidly as in Bewdley. All things considered, therefore, Bristol was probably the best market for Baltimore iron during the years immediately preceding the outbreak of the French and Indian War, just as London had been back in the 1730's when their search for markets began.

The Currency Problem

6. Currency Finance: An Interpretation of Colonial Monetary Practices

E. James Ferguson

The accepted view of the financial and monetary history of the American colonies needs revision. It owes too much to the influence of nineteenth-century scholars who were themselves partisans in currency disputes. In their own day, William G. Sumner, Albert S. Bolles, Charles J. Bullock, and Andrew M. Davis stood for "sound money" against inflationist movements. One of their chief aims was to show the disastrous effects of wandering off the straight line of a sound-money policy.[1] Hence, they studied those colonies whose money depreciated and relied on the opinions of such eighteenth-century controversialists as Dr. William Douglass, Thomas Hutchinson, and others in whose views they con-

---

[1] See a review by Curtis Nettels of Richard A. Lester, *Monetary Experiments, Early American and Recent Scandinavian* (Princeton, 1939), in *English Historical Review,* LVI (1941), 333.

"Currency Finance: An Interpretation of Colonial Monetary Practices," by E. James Ferguson, is reprinted by permission from *William and Mary Quarterly,* X (April, 1953), 153–180, published by Institute of Early American History and Culture, Williamsburg, Virginia.

curred.[2] With the notable exception of Andrew M. Davis, who did a scholarly work on Massachusetts,[3] they were interested in the colonies chiefly as background to the financial history of the Revolution. Their works in the latter field incorporated study in primary sources and were generally accepted as authoritative.[4]

[2] The treatment of the colonies in William Graham Sumner, *A History of American Currency* (New York, 1874) is hardly a serious effort, and the same can be said of the earlier work of William M. Gouge, *A Short History of Paper Money and Banking in the United States, Including an Account of Provincial and Continental Paper Money,* 2nd ed. (New York, 1835). Of considerably greater merit are two studies of particular colonies: Joseph B. Felt, *An Historical Account of Massachusetts Currency* (Boston, 1839) and Henry Bronson, "An Historical Account of Connecticut Currency, Continental Money, and the Finances of the Revolution," New Haven Historical Society, *Papers,* I (1865), 1–192 (separate pagination following page 170). Early works displaying another bias are Henry Phillips, *Historical Sketches of the Paper Currency of the American Colonies, Prior to the adoption of the Federal Constitution* (Roxbury, Mass., 1865–1866) and John H. Hickcox, *A History of the Bills of Credit or Paper Money Issued by New York from 1709 to 1789* (Albany, 1866). The book by Phillips includes surveys of several colonies, written by different authors.

The case against paper money as drawn by nineteenth-century historians rested heavily on the data and opinions supplied by William Douglass, *A Discourse Concerning the Currencies of the British Plantations in America* (Boston, 1740). This treatise came out of a bitter controversy and was highly partisan. A careful reading shows how deeply the local situation in New England colored Douglass's attitudes and his judgment of the situation in other colonies. Even in the case of New England, he correctly attributed depreciation to the uncontrolled emissions of one province, Rhode Island. His observations on other colonies are not reliable.

[3] Andrew M. Davis, *Currency and Banking in the Province of the Massachusetts-Bay,* American Economic Association, *Publications,* 3rd ser., I (1900), no. 4. Davis was a careful and honest scholar, but his main concern was to expose the evils of fiat money. He relied, for example, on the testimony of Thomas Hutchinson and Douglass, although his chapter on sources listed without comment works by Franklin and Thomas Pownall, as well as secondary accounts, which gave quite another view of colonial currency. It must be said, however, that these sources related to provinces outside New England and therefore lay beyond the immediate scope of his study. See *ibid.,* I, 413–435.

The same year that Davis's essay came out, Charles J. Bullock published *Essays in the Monetary History of the United States* (New York, 1900), which included a general survey of colonial currency and more detailed treatment of North Carolina and New Hampshire. The latter studies were based on research in primary sources and are of value.

[4] Charles J. Bullock, *The Finances of the United States from 1775 to 1789, with Especial Reference to the Budget* (Madison, 1895), University of Wisconsin, *Bulletin, Economics, Political Science and History Series,* I (1895), No. 2; William Graham Sumner, *The Financier and the Finances of the American Revolution* (New York, 1891); Albert S. Bolles, *Financial History of the United States from 1774 to 1789* (New York, 1879). None of these works gives much space to the colonies. Bolles dismisses their financial history as a "dark and disgraceful picture" and, in another place, writes: "nowhere had the experiment [paper money] worked satisfactorily except in Pennsylvania." *Ibid.,* 29, 56–57. It is interesting that Bolles made an exception of Pennsylvania. His later book, *Pennsylvania, Province and State* (Philadelphia, 1899), praises the paper money system of that province. See *ibid.,* I, 243–251, 262–265, 396–398. Had he studied other colonies at first hand, he might have altered his general conclusions.

Another influential work published at the turn of the nineteenth century was Davis R. Dewey, *Financial History of the United States* (New York, 1903). Dewey

The pattern they stamped on historical interpretation still survives in its major outlines. Recent books sometimes modify their harsher judgments and bring in new material, but the interpretation rests largely on the story they told of paper money in Massachusetts, Rhode Island, and the Carolinas. These were the provinces where depreciation created a major problem. Neglect of other colonies whose experiments were more fortunate conveys the impression that paper money typically depreciated and was harmful to the community.

A correlated idea is that paper money was significant mainly as a ground of conflict between colonial debtors and creditors. No doubt this view is more readily accepted because it fits in with the Turner hypothesis. Here again, Massachusetts furnishes the prime example. The land bank controversy of 1740 is portrayed as a struggle of creditors against debtors, coastal merchants against back-country farmers. Other instances can be found in the early history of South Carolina.

While the debtor-creditor thesis has logical probability and a foundation in fact, it is nonetheless inadequate when viewed in a perspective embracing the whole development of the American colonies. Historians generally concede, for example, that in most provinces, a propertied aristocracy dominated the government. The debtor-creditor thesis, broadly considered, affords no sufficient explanation for the fact that in the half century before the Revolution, these aristocratic bodies regularly and persistently issued paper money.[5] The thesis is also at odds with the fact that in the middle provinces, at least, mercantile groups strongly opposed the act of Parliament which prevented the colonies from making paper money a legal tender in private transactions. On the assumption that serious internal conflict existed between debtor and creditor, the stand taken by merchants would be inexplicable.

Several accounts of individual provinces appearing in the last few decades appraise the fiat money methods of the colonies in their setting. As the authors have stayed close to primary sources and have extended their range beyond New England, they depict a more successful use of paper money.[6] The collective influence of these works has not been as

---

was circumspect, avoiding gross errors of fact or judgment in his treatment of colonial and Revolutionary finance. His reliance on existing secondary works molded his interpretation into the customary formula.

[5] Conflict between colonial debtors and British creditors may explain the interest of wealthy planters and merchants in currency expansion, but even this proposition needs careful investigation. The extent to which British merchants as a whole favored restriction of colonial currency varied with conditions in the colonies to which they traded.

[6] Cf. Kathryn L. Behrens, *Paper Money in Maryland* (Baltimore, 1923), in Johns Hopkins University, *Studies in Historical and Political Science*, 41, no. 1; Clarence P. Gould, *Money and Transportation in Maryland, 1720–1765* (Baltimore, 1915), in Johns Hopkins University, *Studies in Historical and Political Science*, 33, no. 1; Carl Lotus Becker, *History of Political Parties in the Province of New York, 1760–1776*

great as one might suppose. Curtis P. Nettels has added a general study of monetary affairs; unfortunately, it covers only the period before 1720, when the colonies were just beginning to employ paper currency.[7]

There are signs, however, that the dogmas which have prejudiced research are giving way. Fiat money is now the rule, and most economists have ceased to believe that currency must be convertible into gold or silver. Governments freely manipulate currency, as a means of economic control. In this frame of reference, the ways of the American colonies acquire new significance. An economist, Richard A. Lester, explores their use of paper money in the attempt to curb economic depression.[8] He finds that their tactics were analogous to those of the New Deal and bore some ancestral relationship to present-day Keynesian doctrine. The most promising effort, however, is an unpublished doctoral dissertation by Leslie Van Horn Brock,[9] which displays a grasp of colonial usages and attitudes seldom found in older studies. When such works as these attract more notice, other scholars may be persuaded to explore a field which is rich in implications for social and economic history.

Until more evidence is brought together, any general conclusions must be tentative. The formulations attempted in this paper are, therefore,

(Madison, 1909), in University of Wisconsin, *Bulletin, History Series,* II, no. 1. Historians of Pennsylvania all praise the colony's paper money. Winfred T. Root, *The Relations of Pennsylvania with the British Government, 1696–1765* (New York, 1912), is not enthusiastic, but see Bolles, *Pennsylvania, Province and State,* and Isaac Sharpless, *Two Centuries of Pennsylvania History* (Philadelphia, 1900). Isaac S. Harrell, *Loyalism in Virginia* (Durham, 1926), is the best discussion of that province yet in print, though it is very brief. William Roy Smith, *South Carolina as a Royal Province, 1719–1776* (New York, 1903), is most extensive. Historians of North Carolina have left the subject very vague. Except for the early study included in Bullock's *Essays in the Monetary History of the United States,* which is somewhat lacking in coherence, there is no satisfactory treatment published. For an abbreviated pamphlet see Mattie Erma Parker, *Money Problems of Early Tar Heels,* issued by the North Carolina Historical Commission (Raleigh, 1942). Herbert L. Osgood, *The American Colonies in the Eighteenth Century* (New York, 1924), gives money and finance far less attention than they merit, although his brief treatment is well-considered. The other multi-volumed histories leave the subject virtually untouched. Other works will be cited in discussing particular colonies.

[7] Curtis P. Nettels, *The Money Supply of the American Colonies Before 1720* (Madison, 1934), in University of Wisconsin, *Studies in the Social Sciences and History,* no. 20.

[8] Lester makes the colonies appear more self-conscious in attempting to regulate prices by currency manipulation than they probably were, but his provocative essays, though based on limited research, have nevertheless opened a new approach to colonial economic history. Richard A. Lester, "Currency Issues to Overcome Depressions in Pennsylvania, 1723 and 1729," *Journal of Political Economy,* XLVI (1938), 324–375; and "Currency Issues to Overcome Depressions in Delaware, New Jersey, New York and Maryland, 1715–1737," *ibid.,* XLVII (1939), 182–217. Lester recapitulates this material in *Monetary Experiments, Early American and Recent Scandinavian.*

[9] *The Currency of the American Colonies, 1700 to 1764* (Doctoral Dissertation, University of Michigan, 1941). Brock's conclusions fully support those advanced in this paper. See *ibid.,* 528–563.

exploratory and subject to correction. It seems possible, however, to qualify older interpretations and point out the tendency of future research. An effort will be made to show that in the middle colonies, from New York to Maryland, paper money was successful. Secondly, it will be argued that except in New England and the Carolinas, paper money did not engender any great conflict between broad classes of the population. Finally, the system of paper money will be described in general terms and an attempt made to define the essential features of "currency finance."

In judging the success of paper money, the first question is whether it depreciated. The answer cannot always be explicit. Different authors do not mean exactly the same thing by the word *depreciation*. Older historians were inclined to go by the rate of exchange. If currency passed below its legal rate [10] in trade for hard money or in the purchase of bills of exchange, they considered that it had depreciated and inferred that too much had been issued or that people lacked confidence in fiat money. This was certainly true in colonies like Rhode Island, Massachusetts, and the Carolinas, where currency sank to low levels. In colonies where fluctuations in the value of money were only moderate, however, a discount on currency in exchange for specie or sterling bills did not necessarily imply that the currency was unsound. Historians of such provinces refer to paper money as stable, even though its value sometimes sank in relationship to specie.

It was normal to discount currency somewhat in exchange for hard money. First of all, the colonies sought to attract foreign coin by giving it a high level value. They fixed such rates that hard money equivalent to £100 British sterling was legally worth from £133 to around £175 in the currency of different provinces.[11] This was the legal rate. But hard money ordinarily commanded a premium beyond this, for it had more uses than

[10] Colonial accounts were kept in terms of pounds and shillings. In the seventeenth century, provincial governments began enacting laws which placed a higher value on Spanish and other coins than these coins were worth in British sterling. In an effort to attract hard money, the colonies vied with one another in raising the legal value of foreign coin. To preserve some kind of uniformity, the Board of Trade prepared a royal proclamation, issued in 1704, which allowed the colonies to fix a value of up to £133 on coins worth £100 in sterling. The crown thus sanctioned a double standard, by which the pound in America might be valued less, in terms of silver, than the British pound. At the so-called proclamation rate, £100 sterling was worth £133 in colonial proclamation money. Evading royal and Parliamentary restrictions, however, the colonies raised the legal value of coin even higher.

When they came to issue paper currency, the colonies placed different values on their bills (in terms of coin or silver). In some colonies the proclamation rate was maintained and colonial "current money" passed legally at £133 to £100 sterling. In other colonies the legal ratio was as high as £178 to £100 sterling. For a discussion of this matter, see Nettels, *Money Supply*, 162–181, 229–249.

[11] It should be understood that the term *specie* was used in a double sense in the eighteenth century. It denoted a standard of value, legally established by the colonies. Thus, at the proclamation rate, £133 specie would equal £100 sterling, or an equivalent amount of silver. But the term also meant actual silver or gold, i.e., hard money. When the latter meaning is intended, the phrase "in specie" will be used, or the sense otherwise clarified by the context.

paper. It was more negotiable in payments to foreigners and in inter-colonial transactions.

Besides a general preference for hard money, other factors sometimes worked to bring about a further discount on paper money. Detailed information on the processes of colonial trade is lacking, but it appears that most payments to Britain were made in bills of exchange, that is, drafts payable in Britain which the colonists procured largely by shipments of cargoes. The availability of sterling bills in America depended on the condition of trade. When British purchases fell off and the colonies shipped less than would pay for their imports, sterling bills became scarce and expensive, and people sought hard money to make payments abroad. Specie and bills of exchange rose in value relative to paper money. On the other hand, there were times during the French and Indian War when the colonies enormously increased the volume of their domestic currency, yet the exchange with specie remained constant or even improved because large British expenditures, decreased importations, and a greater supply of specie at hand reduced the need for hard money.[12] Circumstances beyond the control of colonial governments affected the rate of exchange, regardless of how scrupulously the colonies managed their paper money or how good its credit was at home.

The most accurate test of the stability of paper money would be its value in exchange for commodities sold in colonial markets. An adequate price study exists for Pennsylvania, and there is some information for a few other colonies.[13] Unfortunately, this kind of data is fragmentary, and historians usually have to depend on scattered figures and the casual remarks found in contemporary letters.

The weight of evidence suggests, however, that in the middle colonies fluctuations were not great enough to impair the credit or utility of paper money. Historians agree that Pennsylvania "maintained the system without fear of repudiation and to the manifest benefit of the province."[14] It appears that for the half century before the Revolution, the domestic price level was more uniform than in any succeeding period of equal length.[15]

[12] Exchange rates are discussed in Anne Bezanson, Robert D. Gray, Miriam Hussey, *Prices in Colonial Pennsylvania* (Philadelphia, 1935), 314–336. A contemporary analysis may be found in the valuable public letters of Robert Carter Nicholas, provincial treasurer of Virginia, "Paper Money in Colonial Virginia," *William and Mary Quarterly*, 1st ser., XX (1911–1912), 254–256. See also Jerman Baker to Duncan Rose, February 15, 1764, *ibid.*, 1st ser., XII (1903–1904), 241.

[13] Arthur H. Cole, *Wholesale Commodity Prices in the United States, 1700–1861* (Cambridge, 1938), has price studies for Boston, New York, Philadelphia and Charleston.

[14] Sharpless, *Two Centuries of Pennsylvania History*, 115–116, 119, 134–136; Bolles, *Pennsylvania, Province and State*, I, 243–251, 262–265, 396–398. Favorable testimony can be found in nearly all commentators, modern or contemporary. See Adam Smith's famous observations on the subject in *Wealth of Nations*, Modern Library ed. (New York, 1937), 311.

[15] According to Lester, "Currency Issues in Pennsylvania," 373. See the concluding chapter in Bezanson, *Prices in Colonial Pennsylvania*.

The emissions of New Jersey and Delaware are said to have been stable and to have passed usually at par with that of Pennsylvania.[16] New York's currency was highly regarded, and the colony's ability to keep its bills at par was a "subject for special commendation." [17]

Maryland's first emission of 1753 depreciated, even though well-secured, apparently because tobacco remained the primary medium of exchange. Later her bills rose in value and by 1764 were reported "locked up in the Chests of the Wealthy" for the sake of the interest falling due on them.[18] Thereafter, in spite of heavy additions, the bills held their value. "As a colony," writes a modern scholar, "Maryland had solved the problem of a paper currency." [19]

The provinces further south had trouble with their currency. Until 1755, Virginia supplemented the hard money in circulation with tobacco notes, which passed in local exchange and payment of taxes. But the coming of the French and Indian War forced the colony to emit paper money. The bills held their value until 1760, when a sharp break in tobacco prices marked the onset of a long and severe depression. For the next several years, planters could hardly sell their crops, and prices stayed very low. A shortage of the planter balances ordinarily arising from tobacco sales in

[16] Richard P. McCormick, *Experiment in Independence, New Jersey in the Critical Period, 1781–1789* (New Brunswick, 1950), 190–191, 233–234; Brock, Currency of the American Colonies, 93–99, 391–409; Lester, "Currency Issues in Delaware, New York and Maryland," 185–186, 192, 199, 216; Phillips, *Historical Sketches of Paper Currency,* I, 67–76; Richard S. Rodney, *Colonial Finances in Delaware* (Wilmington, 1928), 23.

[17] Becker, *Political Parties in New York,* 66–67; Lester, "Currency Issues in Delaware, New Jersey, New York and Maryland," 207, 216; Brock, Currency of the American Colonies, 66–74, 336–353. Nettels, *Money Supply,* 273–274, refers to New York's early bills as depreciated. His statement appears to rest on a decline in the rate of exchange occurring about 1717. The general opinion in colonial times, however, was that New York had a very sound currency. Even A. M. Davis admitted that New York as well as Pennsylvania were "partially immune from the severe penalties paid by the New England colonies for their infatuation." Davis, *Currency and Banking in Massachusetts-Bay,* 427. See Edmund B. O'Callaghan, ed., *Documents Relative to the Colonial History of the State of New York* (Albany, 1853–1887), VII, 884–885. Clarence W. Loke, The Currency Question in the Province of New York, 1764–1771 (Master's thesis, University of Wisconsin, 1941), Appendix D, surveys newspaper price quotations for tea, pork, wheat, sugar, and molasses, finding them stable from 1760 to 1775. Writing generally of the middle colonies, Lester says: "In all, except Maryland for the first few years, the exchange value of the currency seems not to have fallen more than about 30 per cent in terms of gold and silver for any year during the period of fifty or sixty years that these colonies were on a paper standard prior to the Revolutionary War." "Currency Issues in Pennsylvania," 325.

[18] Jerome Baker to Duncan Rose, February 15, 1764, *William and Mary Quarterly,* 1st ser., XII (1903–1904), 240.

[19] Behrens, *Paper Money in Maryland,* 9–58; Gould, *Money and Transportation in Maryland,* 87–105. The Maryland legislature reported in 1787 that more than £238,000 in colonial currency and above £200,000 issued by the Revolutionary convention passed at par with specie until August, 1776. Address of the Maryland House of Delegates to their Constituents [1787], Broadsides, Portfolio 28, no. 24, Rare Books Division, Library of Congress.

Britain caused bills of exchange and specie to grow scarce, and their value rose in terms of the currency offered by planters obliged to make payments to British creditors. Virginia currency was discounted as much as 50 per cent to 60 per cent in purchase of bills of exchange. Although specie was extremely scarce, the colony did not put aside its plans to retire wartime paper emissions, and it probably contributed to the easement of conditions that the treasurer of the province, John Robinson, restored some £100,000 to circulation through secret loans to hard-pressed planters. Robinson's defalcations probably occurred in 1765 and 1766. It appears, however, that the decline in Virginia's currency in these and preceding years owed little to Robinson's private emissions, but was rather the result of trade depression. In the last years of the decade, the value rose, and by 1771 it was reported that the British merchants who had formerly complained of paper money were among its warmest advocates.[20]

In the Carolinas, depreciation was severe, though it occurred for the most part early in the eighteenth century, when these colonies were thinly populated and undeveloped. Clearly, however, the legislature of North Carolina did little to sustain its first emissions, and the bills steadily depreciated. In 1748, they were called in to be exchanged for new bills at the rate of 7½ to 1. The new bills fluctuated thereafter around a point considerably below their nominal value, but were rising towards the end of the colonial period, when the British government kept the legislature under close rein.[21]

A different situation prevailed in South Carolina, where all the depreciation occurred before 1731. The infant colony was then under heavy financial strain resulting from war. Debtor elements found the depreciation to their liking, however, and tried to maintain the downward trend. They were overcome after a bitter struggle. The currency was stabilized in 1731 at the rate of 7 to 1 of sterling, which remained unchanged until the

[20] There is no good modern account of Virginia's financial history. Two published contemporary sources are "Paper Money in Colonial Virginia" and letters to the assembly's English agent, "Proceedings of the Virginia Committee of Correspondence, 1759–67," *The Virginia Magazine of History and Biography*, X (1902–1903), 337–356; XI (1903–1904), 1–25, 131–143, 345–357; XII (1904–1905), 1–14, 225–240, 353–364. The recent biography by David John Mays, *Edmund Pendleton, 1721–1803* (Cambridge, 1952) has a vivid story of these years of depression, told as an incident of the long-term decline of the tobacco planters. Mays has a full account of the Robinson affair. *Edmund Pendleton*, I, 142–149, 174–188. See also Brock, Currency of the American Colonies, 467–497; George Louis Beer, *British Colonial Policy, 1754–1765* (New York, 1907), 179–188.

[21] The most coherent account of North Carolina's finances is in Brock, Currency of the American Colonies, 106–113, 428–446, Table 22. Brock draws from Bullock, *Essays on Monetary History*, 125–183.

North Carolina's paper money suffered, among other things, from the fact that commodities were employed as a tender in all transactions and "in the public mind were the 'money' of the province." Parker, *Money Problems of Early Tar Heels*, 7–8. Also, like Virginia and Maryland, North Carolina established public warehouses, whose receipts for deposits of tobacco constituted another medium of exchange.

Revolution. During its maturity, the province had a stable currency and a record of successful management.[22]

Constancy of value was not, in many minds, the sole test of a currency. Another criterion is suggested by the remark of Thomas Pownall, that in spite of the depreciation in New England, "it was never yet objected that it injured them in trade." [23] Thomas Hancock, one of the greatest merchants in America, seems at one time not to have been altogether convinced that paper money was an unmitigated evil, though he had dealt in a depreciated medium all his life. Of the legislation which placed Massachusetts on a sound money basis, he said: "This d——d Act has turn'd all Trade out of doors and it's Impossible to get debts in, either in Dollars or Province Bills." [24] No study has been made of the economic effects of depreciation in the provinces where it occurred. It is possible that a steady and continuing inflation was not wholly injurious to an expanding country whose people seldom had fixed incomes or large stores of liquid capital.

Even if stability is taken as the sole rule in judging the success of colonial currency, the record is not entirely black. The depreciation in New England was mainly the fault of Rhode Island, whose emissions flooded the unitary economy of that area and undermined the currency of her neighbors. Elsewhere, North Carolina was the leading offender. The colonies, it must be said, did not have complete freedom to act. Each of them felt, in varying degree, the weight of British authority, which was always cast on the side of moderation in the use of currency. Nevertheless, the predominating fact was not the failure of paper money but its success and good credit—in the colonies from New York to Maryland, and in Virginia, as well as in South Carolina during its later development.

Serious conflicts between debtors and creditors did not arise when paper money stayed near par value. Ideally, perhaps, men of property would have preferred a circulation of coin or a currency backed by

[22] About £ 106,500 in legal tender bills circulated without any provision for redemption. The government met annual expenses by issuing "public orders" and "tax certificates" which, although not legal tender in private transactions, functioned as a supplemental currency. This additional paper passed at par with the legal tender bills. Smith, *South Carolina as a Royal Province*, 228–279; Robert L. Meriwether, *The Expansion of South Carolina, 1729–1765* (Kingsport, Tenn., 1940), 8–9; Brock, Currency of the American Colonies, 115–127, 446–462; Alexander Hewatt, *An Historical Account of the Rise and Progress of the Colonies of South Carolina and Georgia* (London, 1779), II, 58; Cole, *Wholesale Commodity Prices*, 52–53; Osgood, *American Colonies in the Eighteenth Century*, 371–383.

Georgia was undeveloped as a colony, and her monetary affairs will not be discussed.

[23] Pownall also observed that the trade of North and South Carolina went on as usual, in spite of depreciation. Thomas Pownall, *The Administration of the Colonies*, 4th ed. (London, 1768), 220, 221.

[24] Quoted by William T. Baxter, *The House of Hancock* (Cambridge, 1945), 112. This book is a valuable addition to economic history.

precious metals. Practically, however, most of them shared the popular belief that there was no alternative to the existing system. "Contrary to the traditions that historians have perpetuated," writes a modern student of economic thought, "a critical analysis of the contemporary literature indicates that the proponents as well as the critics were not poor debtors or agrarians, but for the most part officials, ministers, merchants, and men of substance and learning in general." [25]

Pennsylvania's currency was esteemed by all classes and regarded as having contributed to the growth and prosperity of the colony. In his widely read work on colonial affairs, Thomas Pownall wrote that there "never was a wiser or a better measure, never one better calculated to serve the uses of an encreasing country . . . never a measure more steadily pursued, nor more faithfully executed for forty years together." [26] Merchants and traders of Philadelphia formally opposed the restraining act of 1764 which prevented the colonies from making paper money legal tender. [27] As colonial agent in England, Benjamin Franklin fought the enactment of the law and afterward wrote pamphlets urging its repeal. [28] Franklin joined other colonial representatives and English merchants to argue the case for repeal before British ministers and members of Parliament. By 1767, the American agents planned to secure the introduction of a repealing act into Parliament. They gave up the idea only when it became known that Parliament would very likely insist that the price of such a concession must be the surrender by the colonies of permanent revenues to the crown. [29]

[25] Joseph Dorfman, The Economic Mind in American Civilization (New York, 1948–1949), I, 142. Dorfman's comment must be given additional weight in view of the fact that most of the spokesmen he considers were from New England.

[26] Pownall, Administration of the Colonies, 185. Pownall referred to Pennsylvania's land bank.

[27] See a merchant petition in Samuel Hazard, The Register of Pennsylvania (Philadelphia, 1828–1835), II, 222–223. John Dickinson wrote against the restraining act, giving high praise to Pennsylvania's paper money system. [John Dickinson], "The Late Regulations Respecting the British Colonies on the Continent of America, Considered . . . ," The Political Writings of John Dickinson (Wilmington, 1801), I, 54–58.

[28] Franklin's views are well known. He had long been an advocate of paper money, though he did not favor making it legal tender in private transactions. See Albert H. Smyth, ed., The Writings of Benjamin Franklin (New York, 1905–1907), II, 133–155; Carl Van Doren, ed., Letters and Papers of Benjamin Franklin and Richard Jackson, 1753–1785 (Philadelphia, 1947), 125–135. Franklin's opinions, as well as his effort to get the restraining act repealed, are treated in Lewis James Carey, Franklin's Economic Views (New York, 1928), 1–24.

[29] Carey, Franklin's Economic Views, 19–24; Van Doren, Letters of Franklin and Jackson, 196–197; Verner Crane, "Benjamin Franklin and the Stamp Act," Colonial Society of Massachusetts, Transactions, 1933–1937 (1937), 57–58; Franklin to Joseph Galloway, June 13, 1767, Smythe, Works of Franklin, V, 25–28; Osgood Hanbury and Capel Hanbury (London commissioners for the Maryland Bank of England stock) to Charles Hammond, George Steuart, and John Price, May 6 and May 21, 1767, Black Books, V, 19, 20, Maryland Hall of Records, Annapolis.

Franklin told the House of Commons that restrictions on paper money were among the leading reasons why the American provinces had become alienated from the mother country.[30] In 1774, the First Continental Congress cited the restraining act among the violations of colonial rights.[31]

New York merchants also protested the restraining act. The assembly appointed a committee of New York county members, whose duties included corresponding with other provinces and the colonial agent with respect to the act.[32] Governor Moore espoused the cause and repeatedly asked the Board of Trade to sanction an emission on the terms desired by the province.[33] The assembly refused aid to British troops unless the crown approved a currency bill, and, according to Carl Becker, opposition to the Townshend Acts had one of its sources in this grievance. Popular unrest was stilled not only by the repeal of the duties, but also by a special act of Parliament which allowed the colony to issue paper money.[34]

Public opinion in Maryland, according to historians of the province, was nearly unanimous in favor of paper money. Among the beneficiaries of the currency system were many of the most prominent men of the colony, who received loans from the government. The list included a "surprising number" of merchants. After Parliamentary restrictions were laid down in 1764, all classes concurred in the need for further emissions, and Maryland's agents in London tried to get the act repealed.[35]

In spite of the notorious depreciation which afflicted North Carolina's emissions, paper money does not seem to have been a major factor in the sectional antagonisms of that colony. Both houses of a legislature presumably dominated by the "court house ring" petitioned the crown in 1768 to approve paper money legislation. At a time when the Regulator Movement in the backcountry had begun to split the colony into warring factions, Governor Tryon added his pleas to those of the legislature. His letters to the Board of Trade repeated familiar arguments, which, coming from less responsible sources, have often been dismissed as the pretence of

[30] John Bigelow, ed., *The Complete Works of Benjamin Franklin* (New York, 1887–1888), III, 418.

[31] Worthington C. Ford and others, eds., *Journals of the Continental Congress, 1774–1789* (Washington, 1904–1937), I, 71.

[32] Becker, *Political Parties in New York*, 26–27; Hickcox, *Bills of Credit Issued by New York*, 43–46. Two memorials of the legislature are printed in *Journals of the Votes and Proceedings of the General Assembly of the Colony of New York, 1743–1765* (New York, 1766), II, 779, 799. Mercantile objection to the restraining act is noted by Arthur M. Schlesinger, *Colonial Merchants and the American Revolution, 1763–1776* (New York, 1918), 55–56.

[33] O'Callaghan, *New York Colonial Documents*, VII, 820–821, 878, 884–885, VIII, 1, 72, 169–170. Lieutenant-Governor Colden also pressed the legislature's demands. *Ibid.*, VIII, 189, 206.

[34] *Ibid.*, VIII, 189; Becker, *Political Parties in New York*, 26, 69–80, 88.

[35] Gould, *Money and Transportation in Maryland*, 105, 109; Behrens, *Paper Money in Maryland*, 45, 47–48.

debtors trying to evade their obligations. He said a larger circulating medium was necessary and that much distress arose from the lack of it.[36]

In South Carolina, the early struggle between debtors and creditors was never quite forgotten, but in time the memory grew so dim that the contemporary historian, David Ramsay, could write: "From New-York to Georgia there had never been in matters relating to money, an instance of a breach of public faith." [37] On the basis of his personal recollection, no doubt, he wrote that the use of paper money "had been similar from the first settlement of the colonies, and under proper restrictions had been found highly advantageous." [38] Another historian of the province, Alexander Hewatt, an extreme foe of paper money at the time he wrote, acknowledged the benefit of currency emissions to a "growing colony" like South Carolina, provided they were kept within bounds.[39]

Virginia's treasurer, Robert Carter Nicholas, expressed the view of a conservative planter. In a public defense of the government's conduct in emitting paper money, he declared that the outbreak of the French and Indian War had made it absolutely necessary. Sufficient funds could be obtained in no other way, and, though hesitant at first, the assembly found no other course open. Nicholas himself knew well the dangers of a paper medium and was conversant with the arguments against it, including the pamphlet of William Douglass, its ardent foe in New England. But Nicholas believed that the evils discovered in some places did not arise from paper money as such. "They have been chiefly, if not totally owing," he wrote, "either to these Bills of Credit not being established upon proper Funds, or to a Superabundance of them or to some Mismanagement." Granting a risk was involved, Nicholas believed that many countries had derived great benefit from paper money. He thought it had been helpful to Virginia.[40]

Nicholas's opinion was much like that of a conservative New York merchant, John Watts, who was highly critical of the restraining act of 1764. Like many others, Watts thought the act would virtually put an end to paper money. "The use of paper money is abolished as an evil," he complained, "when, properly treated, it is the only medium we have left of

[36] William L. Saunders, ed., *The State [and Colonial] Records of North Carolina* (Goldsboro, 1886–1907), VII, 679, 680, 681, 682, VIII, 11–12.

[37] David Ramsay, *The History of the American Revolution* (Dublin, 1793), 437.

[38] *Ibid.*, 432. A modern historian remarks that the crown had so long protected Charleston merchants against inflation they had become "oblivious of danger." Smith, *South Carolina as a Royal Province*, 279. See *ibid.*, 234–235.

[39] Writing after the inflation of the Revolution, Hewatt said the colonies would have been better off if they had never known paper money. But elsewhere in his history, he acknowledged that South Carolina's first emissions were "absolutely necessary" to pay war expenses and that paper money supplied a circulating medium which the colony's economic growth required. Hewatt, *An Historical Account of South Carolina and Georgia*, I, 155–156, 205–206, II, 54–58.

[40] "Paper Money in Colonial Virginia," 232–233, 244–247, 251, 254.

commerce and the only expedient in an exigency. Every man of estate here abominates the abuse of paper money, because the consequences fall upon himself, but there is just the same difference in the use and abuse of it as there is in food itself . . ." [41]

The writings of the post-Revolutionary era contain many allusions to the success of paper money in colonial times and the esteem in which it was then held. In 1786, a correspondent to a New York newspaper recalled how easily the provinces had maintained their paper money systems: [42]

> Before the commencement of the late war, when public faith was still in possession of vestal chastity, divers of the states, then provinces, had large sums in circulation at full value, depending on funds calculated to redeem only five to ten per centum per annum of the amount issued; consequently it must be from ten to twenty years before the whole would be redeemed; and yet, tho' the money drew no interest . . . it circulated freely and at its full nominal value on a perfect equality with specie . . .

As this article appeared, the New York Chamber of Commerce made the same point in declaring its opposition to a paper money issue contemplated by the legislature. The Chamber of Commerce acknowledged that paper money had worked well in colonial times, but argued that this should not be taken as evidence that it would succeed under changed conditions.[43]

An observation frequently made in these times was put down by David Ramsay in his *History of the American Revolution*. Noting that Continental currency held its value during the first year or two of the war, even though it had no security behind it, Ramsay explained: "This was in some degree owing to a previous confidence, which had been begotten by honesty and fidelity, in discharging the engagements of government." [44] Alluding to the same fact, Financier Robert Morris observed: "There was a time when public confidence was higher in America than in any other country." [45]

The inflation of the Revolution destroyed that confidence, at least among propertied men, for they believed that paper money could never be a reliable instrument in an era when the whims of the people dictated, as they said, the policy of the government. A great proportion of the

[41] Quoted in Leonard Woods Labaree, *Conservatism in Early American History* (New York, 1948), 51. See also pp. 48–55. In discussing conservative opinion on paper money, Labaree, like so many historians, draws heavily on New Englanders for expressions of hostility.

[42] "Thoughts on Banks and Paper Money," *Daily Advertiser*, February 2, 1786.

[43] *Ibid.*, March 3, 1786.

[44] Ramsay, *History of the American Revolution*, 437. Ramsay's opinion of the trustworthiness of state governments was entirely different. See *ibid.*, 439–441.

[45] Francis Wharton, ed., *The Revolutionary Diplomatic Correspondence of the United States* (Washington, 1889), IV, 607.

people, however, never lost the old affection for paper money. "From the earliest settlement of America," declared a petition composed in 1785 for presentation to the Pennsylvania legislature, "most of our improvements have been aided by the medium of paper currency . . . and your petitioners are persuaded that . . . public faith might be restored, and the ancient system revived, to the great ease of the inhabitants and emolument of the community." [46] Such an appeal invoked common knowledge.

It becomes clear that paper money occupied an important place in colonial affairs not because it embodied the aims of a particular class, but because it rendered important services to the community.

The circumstances which led to the adoption of paper money are well known. There was not enough hard money to provide a medium of trade for domestic transactions. Gold and silver coins flowed outward in purchase of British commodities and while in the colonies circulated mainly among merchants. Much business was done on the basis of book credits and debits, [47] but specie was nearly always in short supply. Economic depression intensified the problem, for when cargoes did not raise enough to meet debts owed abroad, specie had to be shipped. Domestic trade became almost wholly barter. People who had specie could get an exorbitant premium, and those forced to make payments in hard money faced difficulty. Provincial governments could not collect taxes. The inhabitants felt the need of a medium of exchange which, unlike specie, would not "make unto itself wings and fly away." [48]

The colonies, therefore, adopted paper money. It was issued by two different processes. The first method, in point of time, was the direct emission of fiat money by the government to pay expenses, particularly the costs of war. The other method, which we shall consider immediately, was the emission of money through a loan-office or "land bank."

The land bank was the primary social legislation of colonial America. It was a method of putting currency into circulation and at the same time affording loans to farmers which they could scarcely obtain from other sources. Provincial governments set up loan offices which advanced

[46] *Pennsylvania Packet*, March 4, 1785.

[47] Baxter, *House of Hancock*, affords a valuable discussion of business practices.

[48] The quotation is from a circular printed (1779) in *Journals of the Continental Congress*, XV, 1057. The circular continues: "It [paper money] remains with us, it will not forsake us, it is always ready at hand for the purpose of commerce or taxes and every industrious man can find it."
The general problem of the currency is treated in many places. For a brief discussion, see Nettels, *Money Supply*, 202–203. Among contemporary sources, the preambles to money acts sometimes furnish an elaborate justification for the emission. Much testimony of the same kind is reproduced in the two articles by Richard A. Lester already cited. Pownall, *Administration of the Colonies*, 177–187 analyzes the problem at length. For comment on Britain's failure to appreciate the legitimate needs of the colonies, see Oliver M. Dickerson, *American Colonial Government* (Cleveland, 1912), 320; Phillips, *Historical Sketches of Paper Money*, I, 75; Charles M. Andrews, *The Colonial Period of American History* (New Haven, 1938), IV, 350–352.

currency to farmers at low rates of interest, taking mortgages on real property as security. An individual could usually get only a limited sum. He repaid the loan in annual installments over a period of years. Frequently, though not always, the bills were legal tender in private transactions; in any case, they were almost always accepted in payments to the government for taxes, land, etc. As the annual installments due on the principal came back into the loan office, the bills were cancelled and retired, though they were often reissued, or successive banks established to keep up a continuous flow of loans. The colonies thus developed a medium of exchange out of "*solid* or *real* property . . . melted down and made to circulate in paper money or bills of credit." [49]

The land banks of the middle colonies were, from all accounts, markedly successful. Pennsylvania managed one almost continuously after 1723 without mishap. For more than twenty-five years before the French and Indian War, the interest received by the government from money out on loan supported the costs of provincial administration, without the necessity of direct taxes. Relative freedom from taxation probably contributed to Pennsylvania's remarkable growth.[50]

Other middle colonies also obtained good results. New Jersey enacted three separate loans up to 1735, and the interest enabled the government to exist without direct taxation for sixteen years before 1751. Delaware issued land bank notes from 1723 to 1746, with apparent benefit to the province.[51] New York extended its land bank of 1737 until the last installment of the principal fell due in 1768, at which time all classes demanded its renewal. The bank was reinstituted in 1771 by virtue of the

[49] The quotation is from Address of the Maryland House of Delegates to their Constituents [1787], Broadsides, Portfolio 28, no. 24, Rare Books Division, Library of Congress.

[50] Robert Morris wrote, in 1782, of the "notorious" fact that farmers made 12 per cent on borrowed capital, which he said equalled profits in trade or the professions. It is not clear whether he spoke generally or merely alluded to the exceptional conditions which prevailed during the Revolution. *Journals of the Continental Congress*, XXII, 430.

On Pennsylvania's land bank, see above, notes 14 and 15; also, Lester, "Currency Issues in Pennsylvania," 357, 369; Brock, Currency of the American Colonies, 74–84; Pownall, *Administration of the Colonies*, 185–186; Van Doren, *Letters of Franklin and Jackson*, 81.

A search of the Pennsylvania statutes confirms the fact that the province long existed without direct taxes and even without substantial duties on imports. A property tax was passed in 1717 and no other enacted until after the outbreak of the French and Indian War (1755). See James T. Mitchell and Henry Flanders, comps., *The Statutes at Large of Pennsylvania, 1782–1801* (Harrisburg, 1896–1911), III, 128–138, 408–417, V, 201–212, 352–361.

[51] McCormick, *Experiment in Independence*, 190–191; Brock, Currency of the Colonies, 93–99, 391–409; Phillips, *Historical Sketches of Paper Currency*, 67–76; Lester, "Currency Issues to Overcome Depressions in Delaware, New Jersey, New York and Maryland," 183–199.

Donald L. Kemmerer, *Path to Freedom, the Struggle for Self Government in Colonial New Jersey, 1703–1776* (Princeton, 1940), is not sympathetic with the popular passion for paper money, though he leaves no doubt that New Jersey's experiments were successful.

special act of Parliament, of which mention has already been made. Governor Tryon's report in 1774 showed that the interest from loans comprised about half the revenue of the province, an amount which nearly matched expenses in time of peace.[52]

The notes which Maryland issued on loan in 1733 fell considerably below par, but later rose to nominal value. A modern historian writes: [53]

> Considering the peculiar benefits to grain and tobacco culture, the conveniences offered to trade, the exceptionally high exchange that the bills maintained throughout most of their life, and the faithful redemption of every shilling at face value, it is hardly too much to say that this was the most successful paper money issued by any of the colonies.

A new bank was instituted in 1769, and the notes stayed at par until the Revolution.[54]

Virginia never adopted a land bank. In North and South Carolina, land banks figured in the early depreciation of paper money, and it became the settled policy of the British government to disallow acts for their establishment. Similarly, as is well known, the land banks of the New England colonies, particularly those of Rhode Island, contributed to the decline of currency in that area and brought on the first statutory regulation of paper money by Parliament.

This system of agricultural credit so widely practiced in the colonies would seem to be a subject of considerable importance for social and economic history, yet it has not received the attention it deserves. The economist, Richard A. Lester, offers a general view of the use of land bank emissions to curb depressions, and it may be added that such a background of experience explains why even after the financial chaos of the Revolution, the common people still looked to paper money for relief from hard times. But the subject has further ramifications. Agriculture's need for credit facilities has been a constant factor in American history and a source of political unrest. Banks have served commerce and industry; until lately, agriculture remained at a disadvantage. It should be an interesting fact that colonial governments loaned money to farmers at low rates of interest. But no analysis has been made of the effects of land bank loans in the domestic economy, nor has anyone yet approached the general subject with sufficient breadth of view to place it in its relationship to the main currents of American development.[55]

[52] *The Colonial Laws of New York from the Year 1664 to the Revolution* (Albany, 1894), II, 1015–1040, IV, 708–710; O'Callaghan, *New York Colonial Documents*, VIII, 452–454.

[53] Gould, *Money and Transportation in Maryland*, III.

[54] *Laws of Maryland made since M,DCC,LXIII* . . . (Annapolis, 1787), November sess., 1769, Chapter XIV; Behrens, *Paper Money in Maryland*, 46–58.

[55] Earl Sylvester Sparks attempts it in the first chapter of his *History and Theory of Agricultural Credit in the United States* (New York, 1932), 1–19, but falls short of a contribution because the accounts upon which he relies are so few and one-sided.

The revenue problems of colonial governments were lessened by land bank emissions; taxes were more easily collected when citizens had access to money. During the frequent wars of the eighteenth century, however, the provinces developed another use of paper money. They emitted it to pay governmental expenses. The procedure became a rationalized system of public finance.

Provincial revenues were normally small and inflexible. Officials drew fees rather than salaries, and the few public services were performed mainly by local government. Such provinces as Pennsylvania and New York spent no more than £5,000 a year apart from war expenses.[56] Taxation was adjusted to limited needs. Imposts and excise taxes usually afforded a maintaining fund, while direct levies on polls and property raised what else was needed. None of these revenues could be freely expanded. Heavy duties on imports tended to drive off trade or cause smuggling. Direct taxes were often hard to collect and slow coming in.[57]

Colonial governments found it difficult or impossible to borrow money from their own citizens. Private capital was tied up in lands or commodities.[58] No banks or business corporations existed with liquid capital which could be enlisted in the public service.[59] When a war or other emergency required large outlays, colonial governments knew no alternative but to issue paper money.[60] Massachusetts hit upon this device in 1690, and

[56] A State of the annual Expense of the several Establishments of the British Colonies in North America . . . C.O., 323/19, f. 13, Public Record Office (London), photostats, Library of Congress. Massachusetts had the highest costs, about £18,000 in 1760. South Carolina's peace-time expenditures the same year were £8,000. The other colonies spent less than £5,000. Bolles, *Pennsylvania, Province and State*, I, 376, reports a statement of William Penn in 1775 that Pennsylvania's ordinary expenditures were £3,000. £5,000 was the cost of government in New York, exclusive of expenses originating in war, as late as 1774. O'Callaghan, *New York Colonial Documents*, VIII, 453–454.

[57] Two informative tax studies on provinces with contrasting economies are: Charles H. J. Douglas, *Financial History of Massachusetts from the Organization of the Massachusetts Bay Colony to the American Revolution* (New York, 1892), in Columbia University, *Studies in History, Economics and Public Law*, I, no. 4, and Percy Scott Flippin, *The Financial Administration of the Colony of Virginia* (Baltimore, 1915), Johns Hopkins University, *Studies in Historical and Political Science*, 33, no. 2.

[58] Robert Morris wrote in 1781: "To expect loans within the United States presupposes an Ability to lend, which does not exist in any considerable number of the inhabitants. The personal property, not immediately engaged either in commerce or the improvement of lands, was never very considerable." Wharton, *Revolutionary Diplomatic Correspondence*, IV, 532–533.

[59] The absence of commercial or banking corporations is emphasized by Joseph Stancliffe Davis, *Essays in the Earlier History of American Corporations* (Cambridge, 1917). See the chart of early corporations and their types, *ibid.*, II, 22–23.

[60] Brock, for example, writes of the methods by which the colonies financed their participation in the French and Indian War: ". . . the colonies' only means of timely and adequate exertion was the issuance of bills of credit. No colony succeeded in supplying the funds by any other method. This was obvious to men in all classes at the time, but has been lost sight of since, because later writers, filled with the enthusiasm of those embarked on a sacred crusade for 'sound' money, have found it more convenient to write the history of colonial currency everywhere from the well-publicized

eventually all the colonies took it up. "Currency finance" became the regular mode of financing government during war and often, as well, in time of peace.

Practice varied in details, but over the period in which the colonies experimented, they regularized their procedure in something like a system conducted on the basis of known principles. The one exception was Massachusetts, which went on a sound money basis in the 1750's.[61] Elsewhere, methods fall into a pattern that can be described in general terms.

The essential feature of the system was that it avoided dealing in hard money. During a war, for instance, colonial legislatures printed, from time to time, the money needed to pay their expenses. Usually, the act which authorized the emission also appropriated sufficient taxes to withdraw the money from circulation. If expenses were large, the taxes for several years ahead might be pledged to the redemption of money issued during a single year.[62]

The credit of the bills depended on several interrelated factors. Regardless of any promise on the face of the notes, the basic security was the fund assigned to withdraw the money. The holder had to be certain that all taxes and payments to the government taken together would be enough to create a general use for the bills and ensure a demand for them. He must rest easy in the knowledge that withdrawals would be continuous and that future governments would have the ability and the will to collect taxes. As this money was created and upheld by political acts, confidence in government was essential to its value.[63]

---

happenings at certain periods in New England, and more particularly in Rhode Island, than to examine the facts elsewhere." Currency of the American Colonies, 466–467.

[61] Massachusetts anticipated future revenue mainly by issuing treasury notes, which bore interest in specie. It is difficult to tell from accounts now available just how far in practice her methods resembled or differed from those of other colonies. Massachusetts, however, was probably better able than any other province to deal in specie. In an earlier period, at least, Boston was the "coin center" of North America. Curtis P. Nettels, "The Economic Relations of Boston, Philadelphia and New York, 1680–1715," *Journal of Economic and Business History*, III (1930–1931), 201–202. See also Nettels, *Money Supply*, Chapter IV. Massachusetts's finances after 1749 are treated in Davis, *Currency and Banking in Massachusetts-Bay*, 233–252. A contemporary analysis is to be found in a letter of Governor Bernard to the Board of Trade, Aug. 1, 1764, C.O. 323/19, f. 33–35, Public Record Office.

[62] The currency legislation in the Pennsylvania statutes gives a good picture of the uses and adaptations of currency finance, as well as the operation of a land bank. See Mitchell and Flanders, *Statutes at Large of Pennsylvania*, III, 324–338, 389–407; IV, 38–51, 98–116, 150–152, 322–326, 344–359; V, 7–15, 45–49, 201–212, 243–261, 294–302, 303–308, 337–352, 379–396, 427–443, 456–462; VI, 7–22, 226–229, 311–319, 344–367.

[63] An enlightening discussion of the theory of currency finance may be found in "Thoughts on Banks and Paper Money," New York *Daily Advertiser*, February 2, 1786. Dorfman, *Economic Mind in America*, I, 141–178, samples formal theorizing on the subject of money.

Certain exceptions to the system here outlined, besides that of Massachusetts, may

Meanwhile, the value of the money was sustained by its current usages, as in paying fees, buying land from the province, or use in ordinary trade. So long as there was no great reason to question it, the people accepted currency in day-to-day transactions because it was the recognized medium of exchange. Colonial legislators, however, knew something about the quantity theory of money and understood that the amount must not exceed too far the requirements of trade at existing price levels, else depreciation would occur regardless of guarantees.

The system appears to have worked against the accumulation of public debt. The debt at any particular time consisted of bills of credit in circulation; to retire it, the government levied taxes payable in the certificates of indebtedness themselves. If the debt was large, paper money was apt to be correspondingly plentiful and widely distributed. The people were taxed in a medium readily accessible to them.[64] As withdrawals reduced the supply of currency and it became concentrated into fewer hands, the debt was by that token rendered less onerous, until at some point the taxes imposed to cancel it could be discontinued and the remaining currency left in circulation.[65] Under the benign operation of currency finance, the facility with which the public debt could be retired was in rough proportion to its size.

Other means than currency were used to anticipate future income. Colonial governments, and to a much greater extent the state governments of the Revolution, issued various kinds of warrants and certificates which, though often given an extensive circulation, did not serve as a medium of exchange to the same degree as paper money. With certain exceptions, however, these notes were issued and redeemed on the same terms as currency. In spite of variations, therefore, it is possible to trace a basic pattern in the financial methods employed by the colonies. They met

---

be noted. Part of Maryland's direct emissions, as well as her first land bank notes, were backed by Bank of England stock, purchased with the income from a permanent export duty on tobacco. See Behrens, *Paper Money in Maryland*, 20–21, 46–58. Although the facts are not clear, Connecticut appears to have paid interest in specie on some of her notes. Henry Bronson, "An Historical Account of Connecticut Currency," 66–84. North and South Carolina paid annual administrative expenses by issuing various kinds of warrants instead of paper money.

[64] A circular issued by Congress in 1779 well expressed the distinction which contemporaries made between the ease of paying public debts by withdrawals of a paper medium and the hardship imposed on the taxpayer by having to redeem them in specie. The circular contrasts the happy circumstances of the United States with the difficult situation which Britain must face when the war is over and debts must be paid. America's debt, it is said, may be cancelled by withdrawals of paper money that is within the country and available to the people; whereas Britain "will find her national debt in a very different situation . . . she must provide for the discharge of her immense debt by taxes to be paid in specie, in gold or silver perhaps now buried in the mines of Mexico or Peru, or still concealed in the brooks and rivulets of Africa or Indostan." *Journals of the Continental Congress*, XV, 1057.

[65] A growing economy would absorb ever larger quantities of unredeemed paper.

expenses by issuing a paper medium, whether currency or certificates, directly to individuals in payment for goods and services. They redeemed this paper not by giving specie to those who held it, but by accepting it for taxes or other payments to the government. This was the system of currency finance.

It was not a system which would stand the strain of a prolonged and expensive war. Nonetheless, it sufficed for the wars in which the colonies engaged. During the French and Indian War, for example, New York emitted £535,000. Pennsylvania, whose currency normally stood at £80,000, issued £540,000. Virginia authorized £440,000.[66] Other colonies made extraordinary contributions. The Board of Trade estimated that the North American provinces spent £2,500,000 sterling beyond their ordinary costs of government. About £800,000 of this represented expenditures of Massachusetts, the sound money colony. The remainder of £1,700,000 sterling consisted almost entirely of currency or certificates issued in the expectation that they would be retired only by acceptance for taxes and other payments to the government.[67] In spite of the volume of this paper, little or no depreciation appears to have resulted in most provinces.[68] The colonies benefited from expenditures of the home government, and from large British subsidies which put specie in their hands.[69]

Debt retirement was rapid after the war. Virginia's currency was down to £206,000 by 1767, according to the treasurer's report, and though two small post-war emissions restored some money to circulation, only £54,391 was afloat in 1773.[70] Pennsylvania, no longer tax free, made regular withdrawals until the Revolution. In New York, an acute shortage of currency existed by 1768.[71] Elsewhere, the provinces quickly freed themselves of their debts. A speaker in the House of Commons observed

[66] Brock, Currency of the American Colonies, Tables XV, XVIII, XXVIII; An Account of the Tender and Amount of the Bills of credit . . . in . . . Pennsylvania since . . . 1749, C.O. 323/19, f. 85, Public Record Office; "Proceedings of the Virginia Committee of Correspondence," Virginia Magazine of History and Biography, XI (1903–1904), 355–357.

[67] A State of the Debts incurred by the British Colonies in North America for the extraordinary Expences of the last War . . . C.O. 323/19, f. 19, Public Record Office. Massachusetts issued non-interest-bearing notes to soldiers, which seem to have had a considerable circulation. Ibid., f. 33–35. See also cancellations listed in regular reports in The Acts and Resolves of the Province of Massachusetts Bay (Boston, 1869–1922), XV–XVIII.

[68] The total amount did not circulate at any one time, as withdrawals were continuous even during the war. Serious depreciation occurred in New Hampshire and North Carolina. See C.O. 323/19, f. 29, Public Record Office; Brock, Currency of the American Colonies, 437, 476–477.

[69] See Beer, British Colonial Policy, 52–57.

[70] "Paper Money in Colonial Virginia," 228, 234.

[71] Journal of the Votes and Proceedings of the General Assembly of New York . . . , 799; O'Callaghan, New York Colonial Documents, VII, 820–821, 843–845.

in 1766 that they had already retired £1,755,000, and that most of the remaining debt of £760,000 could be written off within two years.[72]

How much this happy situation was due to British subsidies is hard to know. During the war, Parliament granted over £1,150,000 sterling for distribution among the American colonies, a sum which was nearly half of the £2,500,000 estimated as their war expenses. Even so, when one compares their real expenditures during the war with the sums involved in their ordinary fiscal operations, it appears that they made what was for them a most unusual effort, and the ease with which they retired their debts must in some measure be attributed to the peculiar facility offered by the methods of currency finance.[73]

British policy on matters pertaining to colonial currency is a subject which has scarcely been touched. No doubt it was a factor of greater importance in imperial relations than is commonly understood. From the one considerable treatment available,[74] it appears that most of the time the British government acknowledged the necessity of colonial emissions. Before 1740, the Board of Trade was "reluctantly sympathetic and essentially reasonable" in sanctioning both land bank loans and direct emissions. The Board, however, always opposed making currency a legal tender in private transactions, even though it approved laws for this purpose. Generally speaking, the Board tried to regulate colonial issues by ensuring that the amounts were reasonable, that funds for redemption were adequate, and that emissions were withdrawn within a limited period of time. Control was exerted largely through instructions to governors, who were ordered to refuse assent to laws which did not have a clause suspending their execution until approved by the crown.[75]

Supervision was not effective and lapsed almost completely during frequent periods of war. As currency emissions were the only way the provinces could furnish aid, governors were permitted to approve acts without a suspending clause, provided the Board's other stipulations were satisfied. The colonies took advantage of their bargaining position, however, to procure the governors' assent to laws which did not comply with the Board's requirements. Neither governors nor the crown could afford to scrutinize too closely the modes by which assistance was rendered.

---

[72] T. C. Hansard, publisher, *Parliamentary History of England* (London, 1806–1820), XVI, 204; C.O. 323/19, f. 19, Public Record Office.

[73] Lawrence H. Gipson, "Connecticut Taxation and Parliamentary Aid Preceding the Revolutionary War," *American Historical Review*, XXXVI (1931), 731. Though Gipson overstates the case, he argues forcefully that British subsidies enabled Connecticut to remain solvent during the war and pay her debts afterwards with ease. Unfortunately, there is no complete account of the British subsidies to individual colonies, nor the way in which these subsidies were used.

[74] Brock, Currency of the American Colonies, 168–243, 476–508, 520–527, 558–563.

[75] Examples of the Board's instructions may be found in Leonard W. Labaree, *Royal Instructions to British Governors, 1670–1776* (New York, 1935), I, 218–238; O'Callaghan, *New York Colonial Documents*, VI, 949; VII, 463–464.

War still hindered the enforcement of policy, but British control tightened after 1740. Rhode Island's emissions were a flagrant abuse. The Board also appears to have been more susceptible to complaints of British merchants, some of whom claimed injury from legal tender laws. The same mercantile and creditor interests carried their appeals to Parliament, with the result that after 1750 the standing instructions of the Board of Trade were given statutory effect.[76]

The act of 1751 applied only to New England. It did not abolish the paper money system even in that area, as is sometimes supposed, but merely established rules for carrying it on. Bills already in circulation were to be retired in strict accord with the terms of the issuing acts. When these were withdrawn, no paper money was to be legal tender. The provinces were allowed to emit bills from year to year to pay governmental expenses, provided they committed taxes sufficient to redeem them within two years. This clause was flexible enough to accommodate a moderate expansion of currency. In event of war or other emergency, all curbs were relaxed as to the amount which could be issued, provided enough taxes were appropriated to redeem the bills within five years. The act of 1751 left the colonies outside New England undistrubed. Within New England, its major effect was to prohibit legal tender laws and to rule out land banks.[77]

The restraining act of 1764 came at the end of the French and Indian War, when the colonies had large sums outstanding. As first drafted, it would have placed all the provinces under the curbs imposed on New England. In its final form, it merely prohibited legal tender laws and required that existing legal tender currencies be sunk at their expiration dates.[78] Many colonies protested, in the belief that the legal tender feature was an essential prop to their money. Experience was to show, however, that the restriction did not materially impair the workings of the currency system.

There is more than a hint that by this time Britain's policy as to paper money was subordinated to the larger purpose of securing a permanent civil list, and that attempts were being made to trade approval of colonial emissions for the grant of a fixed revenue to the crown.[79] Even so, the colonies made headway against British restraints, though they could not again pass legal tender laws. New York was permitted to renew its land

[76] Besides the work by Brock already cited, see Dickerson, *American Colonial Government*, 314–319.

[77] 24 Geo II, C-53, Danby Pickering, comp., *The Statutes at Large from Magna Charta to the End of the Eleventh Parliament of Great Britain, Anno 1761* (London, 1762–1807), XX, 306–309.

[78] 4 Geo III, C-34, *ibid.*, XXVI, 103–105; Van Doren, *Letters of Franklin and Jackson*, 116, 139, 169.

[79] Brock makes the most of this point, although he covers in detail only the period to 1764. *Currency of the American Colonies*, 409–411. See also Phillips, *Historical Sketches of Paper Currency*, I, 69–71; Dickerson, *American Colonial Government*, 316.

bank in 1771. After a long struggle, New Jersey exacted consent for the establishment of a land bank in 1774. Pennsylvania continued to emit currency and in 1773 renewed its land bank. Maryland issued £173,733 to pay war debts and over half a million dollars to finance improvements and to establish a land bank.[80] Virginia's council annulled two land bank acts passed by the lower house, but the province emitted £40,000 for other purposes. North Carolina, closely confined by the British government, issued treasury notes and debenture bills, while South Carolina emitted "public orders" and "tax certificates," which were in effect a non-legal tender currency.[81]

Parliament in 1773 legalized colonial monetary practices as carried on under the restrictive acts of 1751 and 1764. A question had arisen as to how far the prohibition of legal tender applied. To clarify the matter, Parliament passed an explanatory act which declared that the prohibition ruled out only those laws which made currency legal tender in private transactions. The colonies were allowed to make it legal tender in payments to the government. In stating the latitude permitted by existing law, Parliament defined the essential workings of the currency finance system. The act is worth quoting because it verifies the general survey given above: [82]

> Whereas the want of gold and silver currency is several of his Majesty's colonies and plantations in America may make it necessary, as well for the publick advantage as in justice to those persons who may have demands upon the publick treasuries in the said colonies for services performed, that such publick creditors should be secured in the payment of their just debts and demands, by certificates, notes, bills, or debentures, to be created and issued by the authority of the general assemblies . . . on the securities of any taxes or duties given and granted to his Majesty—for and towards defraying expences incurred for publick services; and that such certificates, notes, bills or debentures, should be made chargeable on the public treasurers of the said colonies and received and taken by them as a legal tender in discharge of any such duties or taxes, or of any debts whatsoever, due to the publick treasuries . . . be it enacted . . . That . . . any cer-

---

[80] 10 Geo III, C-35, Pickering, *Statutes at Large of Great Britain*, XXVIII, 306. *Colonial Laws of New York*, V, 149–170; *Acts of the General Assembly of the Province of New Jersey* . . . (Burlington, 1776), 419–441 (act of March 11, 1774); Mitchell and Flanders, *Statutes at Large of Pennsylvania*, VII, 100–107, 204–211; VIII, 15–22, 204–220, 264–283, 284–300, 417–423, 447–455; *Laws of Maryland made since M,DCC,LXIII*, November sess., 1766, Chapter XXVI; November sess., 1769, Chapter XIV; November sess., 1773, Chapter XXVI.

[81] "Paper Money in Colonial Virginia," 236–237, 262; Phillips, *Historical Sketches of Paper Currency*, I, 206–208; Parker, *Money Problems of Early Tar Heels*, 13; Smith, *South Carolina as a Royal Province*, 275–279; Brock, Currency of the American Colonies, Tables XXIV, XXVI, XXVII.

[82] 13 Geo III, C-57, Pickering, *Statutes at Large of Great Britain*, XXX, 113–114. See also Brock, Currency of the American Colonies, 525–527.

tificates, notes, bills or debentures which shall . . . be voluntarily
accepted by the creditors of the publick . . . may be made . . . to
be a legal tender for the publick treasurers . . . for the discharge of
any duties, taxes, or other debts whatsoever . . .

Had the Revolution not occurred, Britain might have reached a solution
of colonial monetary problems. As early as 1754, Richard Jackson and
Franklin exchanged plans to form one or more land banks based on
capital loaned from the Bank of England or subscribed by private
investors. It was expected that land bank notes would provide a circulating medium for the continent. Later, when the Stamp Act was under
discussion, Franklin and Thomas Pownall broached a similar scheme, as
an alternative way of gaining a revenue from the colonies. They envisaged
a continental land bank with a branch office in each province, centrally
managed in Britain. The bank was to issue legal tender notes on loan at 5
per cent interest, the principal to be repaid over a period of ten years. The
notes would circulate as currency throughout the American colonies.
Franklin and Pownall pressed this scheme for three or four years.[83]

By 1767, it appears that the Secretary of Trade concurred in the idea
that the restraining act of 1764 should be modified to permit the colonies
to establish loan offices which would emit legal tender notes valid for all
transactions except payment of sterling debts. A bill for this purpose was
being prepared and the ground laid for its introduction into the House of
Commons, when the colonial agents learned that the Commons would
probably seize the opportunity to declare the income arising from the loan
offices subject to the appropriation of the crown. As the colonial agents
could not risk this outcome, they gave up the project. Saying he had
hoped to make better use of his plan for a continental land bank, Pownall
published the details of it in the 1768 edition of his *Administration of the
Colonies.*[84]

Any solution of the money problem under British auspices was fore-
stalled by the Revolution. When it was too late, the British government
instructed its peace commissioners of 1778 in a number of schemes which
might have borne fruit if attempted earlier.[85]

A view of the evidence suggests that generations of historical scholarship have fostered a mistaken impression of the monetary practices of the

[83] Van Doren, *Letters of Franklin and Jackson,* 41–54; Carey, *Franklin's Economic
Views,* 19–20; Verner Crane, "Benjamin Franklin and the Stamp Act," Colonial Society
of Massachusetts, *Transactions,* XXXII, 58–59; Pownall, *Administration of the Colonies,* 186–187, 230–253. See [John Dickinson], *Political Writings of John Dickinson,*
I, 58.

[84] See preceding citation, also Franklin to Joseph Galloway, June 13, 1767, Smythe,
Works of Franklin, V, 25–28; Osgood Hanbury and Capel Hanbury to Charles Hammond, George Steuart, and John Brice, May 6 and May 21, 1767, Black Books, V, 19,
20, Maryland Hall of Records.

[85] Samuel E. Morison, ed., *Sources and Documents Illustrating the American Revolution, 1764–1788,* 2nd ed. (Oxford, 1929), 195–197, contains the instructions.

colonies. The efforts of the American provinces to create a medium of
exchange, erect a system of agricultural credit, and equip their governments with the means of incurring and discharging responsibilities, hardly
constitute a "dark and disgraceful" picture; nor, on the whole, is the
record one of failure. Most of the colonies handled their currency with
discretion and were successful in realizing the purposes associated with its
use. Except for New England, where depreciation had given it a bad
name, paper money was the "ancient system," which had long served well
the needs of trade and the ordinary processes of government. Although
mindful of its dangers, men of property accepted it as useful and
necessary. In time of war, all the colonies but one were fully prepared to
adopt the methods of currency finance as the only way of meeting an
emergency. Emissions might then be over-large, as the Revolution was to
prove, but the common need precluded any nice regard for the effect on
contracts.

The Economic Advantages of Empire

7. British Mercantilism and the Economic Development of the Thirteen Colonies

Curtis P. Nettels

Mercantilism is defined for this discussion as a policy of government
that expressed in the economic sphere the spirit of nationalism that
animated the growth of the national state in early modern times. The
policy aimed to gain for the nation a high degree of security or self-
sufficiency, especially as regards food supply, raw materials needed for
essential industries, and the sinews of war. This end was to be achieved in
large measure by means of an effective control over the external activities
and resources upon which the nation was dependent. In turn, that urge
impelled the mercantilists to prefer colonial dependencies to independent
foreign countries in seeking sources of supply. If the state could not free

   "British Mercantilism and the Economic Development of the Thirteen Colonies,"
by Curtis P. Nettels, is reprinted by permission from Journal of Economic History,
XII (Spring, 1952), 105–114.

itself completely from trade with foreign nations, it sought to control that trade in its own interest as much as possible. To realize such objectives, mercantilism embraced three subordinate and related policies. The Corn Laws fostered the nation's agriculture and aimed to realize the ideal of self-sufficiency as regards food supply. State aids to manufacturing industries, such as the protective tariff, sought to provide essential finished goods, including the sinews of war. The Navigation Acts were intended to assure that foreign trade would be carried on in such a way as to yield the maximum advantage to the state concerned.

Since the mercantilist states of Europe lacked the resources for complete self-sufficiency, they could not free themselves from dependence on foreign supplies. Economic growth therefore increased the importance of external trade, and the preference for colonies over foreign countries intensified the struggle for dependent possessions. The importance in mercantilism of a favorable balance of trade and of a large supply of the precious metals is a familiar theme. We need only to remind ourselves that the mercantilists considered it the duty of government to obtain and to retain for the nation both a favorable trade balance and an adequate stock of gold and silver. To this end the state should help to build up a national merchant marine and should foster domestic manufacturing industries. The chief means of procuring raw materials, a favorable trade balance, and an ample supply of the precious metals was that of exporting high-priced manufactured goods and shipping services.

Despite its emphasis on government action, mercantilism was not socialism. In England, the system invoked the initiative and enterprise of private citizens. It encouraged the merchants, shippers, and manufacturers by conferring benefits upon them and by identifying their private interests with the highest needs of the state. So close was this identification that one may properly regard the theory of mercantilism as a rationalization of the special interests of dominant groups of the time. The mercantilist policy was an expression of an accord between landowners and merchant-capitalists in alliance with the Crown.

Is it possible to measure the influence of government on the economic development of an area? Whether such influence be large or small, it must necessarily be only one factor at work in the process of economic change. The range of influence of even the most powerful government is limited, whereas economic activity is world-wide in its scope and ramifications. Thus far no scheme of statecraft has succeeded in bending all the members of the perverse human family to its designs. To many students of economic affairs it may seem futile to attempt to isolate and to measure the effect of only one factor in the immensely intricate, varied, and shifting activities that are involved in the development of a large area, such as the thirteen colonies. But perhaps such an effort may serve a purpose. It at least stimulates thought, which is essential to intellectual growth, and growth—not final answers or ultimate solutions—is all that one can expect to attain in this world of perpetual change.

To begin with, we note that the thirteen colonies experienced a phenomenal development during the 150 years in which they were subject to the regulating policies of English mercantilism. Adam Smith said in 1776:

> A nation may import to a greater value than it exports for half a century, perhaps, together; the gold and silver which comes into it during all this time may be all immediately sent out of it; its circulating coin may gradually decay, different sorts of paper money being substituted in its place, and even the debts, too, which it contracts with the principal nations with whom it deals, may be gradually increasing; and yet its real wealth, the exchangeable value of the annual produce of its lands and labor, may, during the same period, have been increasing in much greater proportion. The state of our North American colonies, and of the trade which they carried on with Great Britain, before the commencement of the present disturbances, may serve as a proof that this is by no means an impossible supposition.

To what extent did English mercantilism contribute to this "real wealth"—this "exchangeable value of the annual produce of . . . lands and labor?" Lands and labor. Two of the most fundamental factors in the growth of the thirteen colonies were the character of the people and the nature of the land and resources to which they applied their labor. The connecting link between the two that gave the thirteen colonies their unique character was the system of small individual holdings that came into being, usually at the start of settlement. It provided a strong incentive to labor and was therefore a major factor in their development. Crèvecoeur spoke of "that restless industry which is the principal characteristic of these colonies," and observed: "Here the rewards of . . . [the farmer's] industry follow with equal steps the progress of his labor; his labor is founded on the basis of nature, self-interest, can it want a stronger allurement . . . ? As farmers they will be careful and anxious to get as much as they can, because what they get is their own."

Although the land system of the thirteen colonies has not usually been considered an element of mercantilism, yet it was not divorced from it. Why did the English Government grant to its colonies a benefit that was not commonly bestowed on settlers by the other colonizing powers? Small holdings inspired the colonists to work; their labor expanded production; and increased production enlarged English commerce. The resulting trade was more susceptible to control by the state than a comparable trade with foreign countries would have been. For this reason, the colonial land system may be regarded as an expression of mercantilist policy. Viewed in this light, mercantilism contributed directly to the growth of the settlements.

Such also was the effect of the policy of England with reference to the peopling of its part of America. The government opened the doors to immigrants of many nationalities and creeds. Its liberality in this respect was unique. It harmonized with the mercantilist doctrine. The Crown admitted dissenters and foreigners in order to expand colonial production and trade. Such immigrants were, to a large extent, industrious, progressive, and energetic. Their productivity was stimulated by the climate of freedom in which they lived—a climate that was made possible in good measure by the indulgence of the government. The resulting growth of English trade served the needs of the state as they were viewed by the mercantilists.

We shall next consider the effects of specific mercantilist laws and government actions on the economic development of the thirteen colonies. It appears at once that such laws and actions did not create or sustain any important industry or trade in Colonial America. The major economic pursuits of the colonies grew out of, and were shaped by, the nature of the resources of the land, the needs of the settlers, and the general state of world trade in the seventeenth century. No important colonial activity owed its birth or existence to English law. The statutes and policies of mercantilism, with an exception or two, sought to control, to regulate, to restrain, to stimulate, or to protect. In the great majority of instances it was not the role of the government to initiate, to originate, to create. All the important mercantilist laws were adopted in response to a development that had occurred. They undertook to encourage, or to regulate, or to suppress some industry, practice, or trade that had been initiated by private citizens and which they had proved to be profitable. When the origins of enterprise in America are considered, it appears that every important industry got its start by reason of the natural resources of an area, by virtue of the demand for a product, or because of such factors of trade as transportation or location. Ordinarily, the government did not subject a colonial activity to regulation by law until it had proved itself to be profitable. In Virginia, for instance, the government did not initiate the tobacco industry or attempt to stimulate its early development. Rather, the Crown sought to discourage it. After it had taken root under the influence of general economic conditions, the government stepped in to regulate it. The major Navigation Act was passed in response to the success of the Dutch in world commerce. The English Government did not legislate against certain industries in the colonies until they had grown of their own accord to the extent that they menaced their English counterparts. The currency policy which England applied to its colonies was worked out not in a vacuum but in answer to practices in which the colonists were engaging.

The effects of mercantilist laws naturally depended upon their enforcement. Since they almost invariably sought to prevent something that the colonists had found to be profitable, the task of enforcement was difficult. It required the exercise of force and vigilance.

In a general way, the government attained a reasonable success in its efforts to enforce the policies that bore directly on the southern mainland colonies, whereas the principal acts which were designed for the Middle Colonies and New England could not be made effective.

The program for the plantation area embraced several policies. The Navigation Act of 1661 excluded from its trade all foreign merchants and foreign vessels. By the terms of the Staple Act of 1663 the planters must buy most of their manufactured goods from England. Slaves must be bought from English slave traders. The area must depend upon English sources for capital and credit, and the planters could not avail themselves of legal devices in order to ease their burdens of debt.

The government made a strenuous effort to enforce these policies. The decisive action centered in the three Dutch wars between 1652 and 1675. The defeat of the Dutch drove them from the southern trade and enabled the English merchants to hold it as in a vise. After 1665 the development of the plantation colonies proceeded in conformity with the tenets of mercantilism. The effect was to retard that development, since the planters were subjected to a virtual English monopoly and were denied the benefits of competitive bidding for their crops and the privilege of buying foreign goods and shipping services in the cheapest market.

Certain conditions of the period 1675 to 1775 favored the English mercantilists in their efforts to enforce the southern policy. The geography of the Chesapeake country made it easy to exclude foreign vessels, since the English navy had to control only the narrow entrance to the bay in order to keep foreign vessels from reaching the plantations. That the tobacco ships had to move slowly along the rivers made concealment impossible for interlopers. Secondly, there was the factor of debt. Once a planter had become indebted to an English merchant, he was obliged to market his crops through his creditor in order to obtain new supplies. Hence he lost the advantage of competitive bidding for his export produce. And finally, the four wars with France, 1689–1763, served to rivet the plantation area to Britain, as mercantilism intended. The British navy provided convoys for the tobacco ships, and the expenditures of the Crown in America for military purposes provided the planters with additional buying power for English goods, thereby increasing their dependence on British merchants, vessels, and supplies.

By reason of the acts of government, the economic development of the southern colonies exhibited after 1665 about as clear an example of effective political control of economic activity as one can find. The trade of the southern colonies was centered in Britain. They were obliged to employ British shipping, to depend on British merchants, and to look only to British sources for capital and credit. They were not permitted to interfere with the British slave trade. British investments enjoyed a sheltered market in that the Crown excluded the foreign investor from the area and prohibited the colonists from taking any legal steps that would impair the claims of British creditors. The resulting dependence of the plantation country gave it a strongly British character, retarded its development, fostered discontent, and goaded the planters to resistance and revolt.

The initial enforcement of the Navigation Acts in the 1660's reduced the profits of the tobacco planters and forced them to cut the costs of production. Slavery was the answer. Appropriately at this time the English Government undertook to furnish its colonies with an ample supply of slaves. The planters were obliged to buy them on credit—a main factor in reducing them to a state of commercial bondage. The English Government forbade the planters to curtail the nefarious traffic. American slavery was thus one of the outstanding legacies of English mercantilism. That resolute foe of English mercantilist policy, George Washington, subscribed to the following resolve in 1774: "We take this opportunity of declaring our most earnest wishes to see an entire stop forever put to such a wicked, cruel, and unnatural trade."

In another sense the Navigation Act of 1661 had a discernible effect on American development. It stimulated the shipbuilding and shipping industries in New England and the Middle Colonies. It did not, however, create those industries. But the English Government drove the Dutch from the trade of English America before English shipping could meet the full needs of the colonies. The Navigation Act gave to English colonial shipbuilders and shipowners the same privileges that were given to English shipbuilders and shipowners. Undoubtedly this favored treatment spurred on the shipping industries of New England. Shipbuilding flourished there, since the colonial builders were permitted to sell their product to English merchants, and New England shipowners could employ their American-built vessels in the trade of the whole empire. New England benefited directly from the expulsion of the Dutch from the trade of English America. After New England's shipbuilding industry had become fully established (and had proved itself more efficient than its English rival) the British Government refused to heed the pleas of British shipowners who wished to subject it to crippling restraints.

English policy for the plantation area was essentially negative. It did not originate enterprises. With one exception it did not attempt to direct economic development into new channels. The exception appears in the bounty granted for indigo—a form of aid that made the production of that commodity profitable and sustained it in the lower South until the time of the Revolution, when the industry expired with the cessation of the bounty.

The policies that affected the Middle Colonies and New England differed materially in character and effect from the policies that were applied to the South. The northern area received the privilege of exporting its chief surplus products—fish, meats, cereals, livestock, lumber—directly to foreign markets. As already noted, the northern maritime industries flourished under the benefits conferred upon them by the Navigation Acts. Freedom to export the staples of the area in company with vigorous shipbuilding and shipping industries induced the northerners to engage in a varied foreign trade. This outcome, however, was in part a result of certain restrictive measures of the English Government. It prohibited the importation into England of American meats and cereals, thereby forcing the colonists to seek foreign markets for their surplus.

The resulting trade of the northern area—with southern Europe, the Wine Islands, Africa, and the foreign West Indies—did not prove satisfactory to the English mercantilists. It built up in the colonies a mercantile interest that threatened to compete successfully with English traders and shipowners. It carried with it the danger that the northerners might nullify those features of the Navigation Acts which aimed to center most of the trade of English America in England. Nor did their reliance on foreign trade prove to be entirely satisfactory to the colonists. In time of war, their vessels were exposed to the depredations of the French. The English navy could not protect the diverse northern trades with convoys, as it protected the simpler, more concentrated commerce of the plantation area. The wartime disruption of the northern trade deprived the area of the foreign money and products that in peacetime its merchants carried to England for the purpose of buying English goods for the colonial market. The resulting decline of the exportation of English merchandise was then deplored by the English mercantilists. Unable to procure finished goods in England, the northerners were driven to manufacture for themselves. Thence arose what the mercantilists regarded as a fatal danger—the prospect that the colonies would manufacture for themselves, decrease their purchases in England, and produce a surplus of finished goods that would compete with English wares in the markets of the world.

To avoid this danger, the English mercantilists devised their major experiment in state planning of the early eighteenth century. They undertook to foster the production of naval stores in the Middle Colonies and New England. Such products would be sent directly to England as a means of paying for English goods. They would divert the colonists from domestic manufacturing and free them from their dependence on diverse foreign trades. They would transform the commerce of the northern area in such a way that it would resemble that of the plantation area—a simple, direct exchange of American raw products for English finished goods.

The naval-stores program was constructive in intent. The government sought to shape the development of the northern area, thereby solving a serious problem. But the policy failed. It did not stimulate the production of naval stores in the northern area sufficiently to provide it with adequate payments for English goods, or to divert the northerners from their foreign trades, or to halt the trend toward home manufacturing.

This failure led the mercantilists to embrace a purely negative policy. As the trade of the northern area with the foreign West Indies increased, the English Government undertook to stop it altogether. Such was its intent in imposing upon the colonies the Molasses Act of 1733. But that effort did not succeed. Again, a mercantilist policy failed to bear its expected fruit.

The early policies of mercantilism had a marked effect on the growth of the northern area. But the result turned out to be unpleasing to the English authorities. Their endeavors to give a new direction to the development of the area failed completely after 1700. A problem had arisen for which English mercantilism never found a solution.

The main element in this problem was the trend in the northern area toward domestic manufacturing. Since that trend menaced all the essentials of mercantilism, the English Government did its best to thwart it. Thus there was no more important ingredient in English policy than the determined effort to retard or prevent the growth in America of industries that would produce the sort of goods that England could export at the greatest profit. Such, chiefly, were cloth, ironware, hats, and leather goods. The effectiveness of the laws and orders against colonial manufacturing is a subject of dispute. It is difficult to prove why something did not happen. If the colonies were slow in developing manufacturing industries, was it the result of English policy or of other factors? The writer believes that English policies had a strong retarding influence. The barriers erected were extensive and formidable. British statutes restrained the American woolen, iron, and hat industries. The colonies could not impose protective tariffs on imports from England. They could not operate mints, create manufacturing corporations, or establish commercial banks—institutions that are essential to the progress of manufacturing.

It was easier to enforce a policy against American fabricating industries than a policy that aimed to regulate maritime trade. A vessel could slip in and out of the northern ports. A manufacturing plant and its operations could not be concealed, unless, as in later times, it was engaged in mountain moonshining. The exposure of factories to the gaze of officials undoubtedly deterred investors from building them in defiance of the law.

New industries in an economically backward country commonly needed the positive encouragement and protection of government. It was the rule of mercantilism that handicaps to home manufacturing should be overcome by tariffs, bounties, and other forms of state aid. Such stimuli were denied to the colonies while they were subject to English mercantilism. Not only was the imperial government hostile; equally important, the colonial governments were not allowed to extend assistance to American promoters who wished to establish industries on the basis of efficient, large-scale operations.

An important aspect of the influence of state policy is its effect on the attitude of the people who are subjected to its benefits and restraints. The colonists as a whole were not seriously antagonized by the British imperium prior to 1763. Its most detrimental policy—that of the Molasses Act—was not enforced. In time of war (which meant thirty-five years of the period from 1689 to 1763) the military expenditures of the Crown in America helped to solve the most crucial problem of the colonies by supplying them with funds with which they could pay their debts and buy needed supplies in England. The shipbuilders and shipowners of the northern area shared in the national monopoly of imperial trade. Underlying all policy and legislation was the extremely liberal action of the English Government in making land available to settlers on easy terms and of admitting into the colonies immigrants of diverse nationalities and varied religious faiths.

After 1763 the story is different. The colonies no longer received the sort of easy money that they had obtained from military expenditures during the wars. Instead, they were called upon to support through British taxes the defense establishment that was to be maintained in America after the war. Britain now abandoned its old liberal practice regarding land and immigration and replaced it with restrictive measures suggestive of the colonial policies of France and Spain. The Crown proceeded to enforce with vigor all the restraints it had previously imposed on colonial enterprise. Most of the features of the imperial rule that had placated the colonists were to be done away with. Not only were the old restraints to be more strictly enforced, they were to be accompained by a host of new ones. The policies of Britain after 1763 merely intensified the central difficulty of the trade of the colonies. How might they find the means of paying for the manufactured goods that they must buy from England? If they could not get adequate returns, they would have to manufacture for themselves.

In its total effect, British policy as it affected the colonies after 1763 was restrictive, injurious, negative. It offered no solutions of problems. In the meantime, the colonists, having lived so long under the rule of mercantilism, had become imbued with mercantilist ideas. If the British imperium would not allow them to grow and expand, if it would not provide a solution of the central problem of the American economy, the colonists would have to take to themselves the right and the power to guide their economic development. They would find it necessary to create a new authority that would foster American shipping and commerce, make possible the continued growth of settlement, and above all stimulate the growth of domestic manufacturing industries. Thus another result of English mercantilism was the American Revolution and the creation thereafter of a new mercantilist state on this side of the Atlantic.

Effects of the Revolution

8. The American Revolution Considered as an Economic Movement

Clarence L. Ver Steeg

Historians for a generation or more have been so sensitive to economic influences during the Revolutionary period that a modern scholar places his reputation in jeopardy if he fails to take account of such forces, regardless of what phase of political, social, or cultural life he is investigating. Although this sensitivity did not have its birth with the notable works of Charles A. Beard, they assuredly stand as an unmistakable landmark. The results, in the main, have been good. Our perspective of the Revolutionary generation has broadened, our understanding deepened; and the main stream of events has often been magnificently illuminated.

In contrast, historians have tended to neglect the other side of the coin, giving relatively little, if any, attention to the influences that political, social, and cultural forces might have had upon economic development. Even studies embracing what are normally considered "economic" subjects—such as the role of merchants, the course of trade, the change in the land systems—have almost invariably been oriented toward a distinct vantage point: What effect did a change in land policy have upon social structure? How did the course of trade affect diplomatic policy? How significant was the position of the merchant in the formulation of political decisions? As illuminating as such studies have been, the results have given us only a partial view, for we have yet to answer the questions which arise when economic developments are approached from the reverse, and what many economists would call the proper perspective. Did the modification of political institutions affect the economy? Did political action influence economic change? Were social theories produced that modified the actions of merchant and planter capitalists? Did American society by its very structure circumscribe or direct the course of economic change? How significant was the American Revolution generally upon the rise of capitalism in America? If historians are to assess the impact of the American Revolution upon the whole of American life, these questions and others of equal importance need more precise answers than we now possess.

"The American Revolution Considered as an Economic Movement," by Clarence L. Ver Steeg, is reprinted by permission from *Huntington Library Quarterly*, XX (August, 1957), 361–372.

To illustrate the lack of balance in current historical writing, one need only compare the emphasis given by scholars to the social rather than the economic consequences of the Revolution. Numerous monographic and more general works covering the period could be cited to support this point, but textbooks in United States history give as reliable a testimony as one would wish. Whereas none would be considered complete without its section neatly entitled "Social Impact of the Revolution," or something similar, followed by appropriate paragraphs of description and analysis, no textbook examined by the writer has a similar section devoted to the economic impact. Indeed, it is rare when the possibility of economic results is so much as mentioned. The textbooks in American economic history offer little more. A chapter on the Revolution is seldom included. When it is, too often its focus is "economic causation"; in fact, most economic histories are organized in such a way that one would scarcely realize that a Revolution had taken place. Let it be quickly said that this comparison casts no reflection whatsoever on the textbook writers; the texts, quite properly, merely show the trend of scholarship. Although individual scholars, treating isolated subjects, have sometimes attempted to evaluate the economic effect of the Revolution, no major attempt has been made to bring together the existing material, much less to strike out into unexplored areas where fresh insights and new material would provide the ingredients for a solid synthesis. The only possible exception in the literature of the Revolution is Evarts B. Greene's helpful chapter on "The War's Economic Effects" in his *The Revolutionary Generation, 1763–1790* (New York, 1943). Greene gives a useful summary of some of the scholarship, but his approach is rather limited. Furthermore, Greene's chapter has never caught the attention of scholars; it has not been a departure point for new investigation.[1]

What becomes increasingly obvious, therefore, is that this significant theme, the impact of the Revolution upon the course of economic development, rates a thorough book-length study. This article can be little more than an introduction to an exciting historical problem. Its primary purpose is to focus attention upon the importance of the theme in terms of an area for research and in terms of a more complete understanding of the Revolutionary epoch. It will also attempt to indicate possible approaches to the problem, to make a preliminary assessment of some of the existing material, and, on occasion, to suggest additional theses that might help to define the problem. Part of the following discussion, therefore, will view

[1] It will be interesting to see whether or not the volume in Rinehart's series on the *Economic History of the United States*, covering the period 1776–1815, will grapple with this problem or whether it will be a straight narrative. There are three places where a summary of the general economic development for these years can be found: Edward Channing, *History of the United States* (New York, 1912), III, ch. iii; Clarence L. Ver Steeg, *Robert Morris, Revolutionary Financier* (Philadelphia, 1954), ch. iii, stressing the period up to 1781; and Merrill Jensen, *The New Nation* (New York, 1950), pp. 179–244, stressing the Confederation period.

familiar material from a somewhat different perspective, while other parts will suggest areas that seem to deserve more elaborate consideration if historians are eventually to make a realistic evaluation, and to see the Revolution in its fullest context.[2]

One of the most obvious, but largely overlooked, changes brought by the Revolution, carrying with it the broadest economic implications, was the new relationship between the rights of private property and mineral rights or, to use a broader term, natural resources. A careful study of this transition has never been made, but it is clear that whereas mineral rights in colonial times resided with the sovereign, to be granted or reserved as circumstances dictated, the Revolution saw such rights brought eventually within the purview of private property. The control of natural resources, therefore, was secured more firmly by private enterprisers.

It will be recalled that the charters of most colonies, though granting the rights to minerals and mines, contained a clause reserving the fifth part for the crown. This figure was more than a token; it represented an acknowledgment that the crown, when it disposed of land, possessed the power to grant or retain natural resources under the soil. That such grants were made at all merely indicates that the crown did not believe such resources existed in quantity and, in consequence, it could be generous with an added "inducement" to colonization. As a result, there was some mining activity in the majority of colonies before the Revolution. It is interesting, however, to speculate how magnanimous the crown would have been in granting any mineral rights if precious metals, the priority minerals of the seventeenth and eighteenth centuries, had suddenly been discovered in the colonies; given the basic mercantile position of the mother country it is safe to say that its terms would have been somewhat less liberal.

From the point of view of this article, it is significant that the sovereign right of the central government over mineral resources, though retained as a matter of form, apparently was not preserved in substance. So far as my investigation goes, there seems to be no discussion of this point in the exhaustive debates that took place on the land question during the Revolution. The Land Ordinance of 1785, it is true, reserved "one-third part of all gold, silver, lead, and copper mines" for the national government, but if a scholar relies on the standard monographs on the national land system, nothing seems to have come of it. Although the problem requires more exhaustive study, it would seem that one of the legacies of the Revolution, established almost by default, made an incalculable impact on American society where the command of critical natural resources—coal, iron ore, oil and gas, precious metals, and many others—has been a key factor.

---

[2] Because of the exploratory nature of this article, only a few citations have been made.

Two of the basic elements in eighteenth-century economic life, farming and land policy, were also greatly influenced by the Revolution. Quite naturally, the celebrated Land Ordinance of 1785 comes immediately to mind, for it was largely responsible for "institutionalizing" the basic productive unit in Midwestern agriculture, the family farm. What this meant for the course of economic development is significant; interestingly enough, arguments are still raging as to the merits of the established family farm as compared with a much larger unit, seemingly more suitable to the complex economy of modern times. The Land Ordinance is only the most obvious of more subtle changes from the land practices of the colonial period, some of them procedural and others substantive, depending upon the region studied. Moreover, the stimulus given to land speculation by some of the interstate and international business groups—an area in which additional research would clarify many issues—is of great importance in itself.[3]

Farming, at least in two regions, the South and New England, underwent a profound change. That historian of agriculture, Lewis C. Gray, whose discriminating analysis and careful judgment commands respect if not always agreement, goes so far as to assert: "For the South it [the American Revolution] was also a great economic Revolution."[4] He particularly emphasizes that general farming, as distinguished from the production of staples in certain areas, was stimulated; and he stresses the importance of the new internal lines of communication and trade. Gray has received additional ammunition from Professor Lawrence Harper who has traced the relative production of specific staples. Indigo, for example, ceased to be produced soon after the Revolution, not so much because indigo failed to enjoy the British subsidy of colonial times, but rather because the British subsidy after the Revolution, applying as it did only to producers within the empire, resulted in a price advantage that the South could not meet.[5] It is also well to remember that the damage caused by the fighting—the crops and livestock destroyed, and the wasted fields—meant that the South needed time to rebuild its plantation economy, especially in South Carolina and Georgia. Indeed, the desperate search for new staples to replace the loss of indigo, together with the limited geographical area where rice could be produced, helps to explain

---

[3] Payson J. Treat's standard monograph, *The National Land System, 1785–1820* (New York, 1910), ch. ii, makes some comparison between colonial land systems and that evolved after the Revolution. It is entirely possible, however, that the "New England influence" on the national land system has been overstated. It was a thesis that was given wide currency before new research revised some previously accepted assumptions on eighteenth-century New England land policy.

[4] Lewis C. Gray, *History of Agriculture in the Southern United States to 1860* (New York, 1941), II, 613.

[5] Lawrence A. Harper, "The Effect of the Navigation Acts on the Thirteen Colonies," in *The Era of the American Revolution*, ed. R. B. Morris (New York, 1939), pp. 24–25, and n. 61.

the renewed interest in cotton, which had been experimented with for a century previous to independence but never produced in quantity.

Although the New England farmer generally was not asked to face the ravages caused by military engagements, the Revolution had a profound effect upon New England agriculture. The decisive change that occurred when its customary marketing outlets were eliminated, especially those to the West Indies, was not immediately apparent, for until 1780 war-born markets took up the slack. With the sharp cutback in wartime markets starting late in 1781, and with no comparable peacetime markets to replace them, the New England farmer suffered a blow from which he never fully recovered. It is highly probable that the despair and discontent of agrarian New England in the 1780's is largely explicable in terms of the economic consequences of the Revolution.[6]

Trade, as well as agriculture and land policy, was never the same as a result of the Revolution. In some areas it was greatly broadened; in others it was sharply restricted. Furthermore the lines of trade were modified and mercantile connections were altered to meet the new circumstances. Although this effect of the Revolution has received some attention, more exacting studies are needed before it can be adequately measured.

The opening of the China trade, for example, was a direct consequence of the Revolution. In colonial times, the British imperial system made any notion of such a trade an unattainable dream. With the elimination of the British restrictions, this new vista was opened; and the business enterprisers of the new republic, anticipating its promise of rich rewards, rushed to exploit it. It matters not that their hopes were, in part, built upon illusions, for these illusions were quickly dispelled. What is significant is that the Asiatic trade introduced new products, created new demands, and, in some respects, educated this country's merchants in new trading techniques. William B. Weeden's apt statement deserves to be quoted; he asserts that the Revolution marked a break where one passes "from the Peter Faneuils, the negro and rum dealers of the middle century, to the Derbys, Perkinses, Thorndikes. . . . These men brought the far Eastern world home to its new counterpart in the West."[7] The influence of this trade, of course, was not confined to New England. It was a Pennsylvanian, Robert Morris, who was mainly responsible for outfitting the first American ship to Asiatic waters, and it was a New Yorker, John Jacob Astor, whose career was built upon the rewards of this trade.

[6] There is some difference of opinion among scholars who have recently surveyed this problem. Oscar and Mary Handlin's *Commonwealth: A Study of the Role of Government in the American Economy: Massachusetts, 1774–1861* (New York and London, 1947), pp. 1–52, is a good evaluation for the whole New England economy. Percy Bidwell and John Falconer's *History of Agriculture in the Northern United States to 1860* (Washington, 1925), is of no help.

[7] William B. Weeden, *Economic and Social History of New England, 1620–1789* (Boston and New York, 1890), II, 821–822.

Whereas the Pacific trade was opened, the Caribbean trade was sharply reduced. Many factors were responsible, not the least of course being the British and French imperial systems, which automatically established a barrier against commodities from the new nation. Where the West Indies had served as an important market for fisheries, livestock, lumber, rum, and other goods during the colonial period and had acted as the crucial entrepôt during the War of Independence itself, it was suddenly closed to American products. How significant this result was for the economy of the new country has often been suggested, but it is a theme that still requires more elaborate and precise investigation.[8]

When trade is basically modified, it is axiomatic that mercantile connections are modified as well. As the most casual reading of the recently published volumes on eighteenth-century merchants will testify, the impact of the Revolution was profound. Some trading connections were completely changed; in others the nature of the trade itself was altered; in still other cases, a particular merchant or merchant group either won or lost its relative position in the trading community. The Pepperrells of Piscataqua, remaining loyal to Britain, abandoned American shores; the Browns of Providence, though they maintained their important position in the trading community, modified their business connections and adjusted their manufacturing interest to suit the new era; in New York City, James Beekman, whose business was seriously crippled during the Revolution when he was forced to flee from New York City to escape the British, found after the war that the pattern of trade relationships he used with success before 1776 was no longer applicable; Robert Morris, whose relative position within the mercantile community had improved so significantly that he could properly be called the Prince of Merchants, found it not only necessary after 1783 to establish a new network of business partnerships to adjust to the times, but also advantageous to expand his business operations and diversify his investments.[9]

General business organization, as well as the careers of individual merchants, was influenced by the Revolution. Robert East's indispensable book has demonstrated the intricate connections between business groups during the Revolution; but he was primarily interested in their political and to some extent social impact.[10] Using some of the identical material, it is possible to reverse the coin and see the results upon economic life: the rise of multiple partnerships and the beginnings of the corporate struc-

[8] Merrill Jensen believes that there was less disruption to the West India trade than most scholars have asserted (op. cit., pp. 198–199).

[9] Byron Fairchild, Messrs. William Pepperrell: Merchants at Piscataqua (Ithaca, N. Y., 1954). James B. Hedges, The Browns of Providence Plantations: Colonial Years (Cambridge, Mass., 1952), pp. 285–286, p. 306. Philip L. White, The Beekmans of New York (New York, 1956), pp. 441–530; Clarence L. Ver Steeg, Robert Morris, Revolutionary Financier (Philadelphia, 1954), ch. x.

[10] Business Enterprise in the American Revolutionary Era (New York, 1938), passim.

ture; the expansion of business groups to include every major marketing center; and the modification of these connections to meet new trade and business opportunities. When the Revolution so profoundly affected so many of its most representative mercantile leaders and the structure of business generally, how can it ever be said that it had little impact upon the economic development of the United States or the rise of commercial capitalism in the young republic!

A discussion of trade during the Revolution inevitably leads to the subject of interstate commerce, especially of course to the fact that its control was placed within the framework of the national government. This subject has become so commonplace that there is a tendency to dismiss it without relating its significance to the rise of commercial capitalism. During the first six decades of the eighteenth century one of the key signs of economic maturation and of developing commercial capitalism was the increased specialization that occurred within the colonies. Each region—New England, the Middle Colonies, and the South—was producing commodities for market that were best suited to its resources. This specialization, among other things, stimulated intercolonial trade. When the Revolution placed its blessing upon this development by giving control of interstate commerce to the national government (the Articles of Confederation in allocating this power to the individual states were actually running counter to the colonial experience and, it should be added, to reality) the consequences were so significant as to be almost incalculable. An unlimited, unfettered, internal market not only stimulated the fruition of commercial captialism, but also laid down the basic pattern that was to provide an expanding market for the industrial America that would eventually emerge.

The problem of money and money supply and its relation to economic development is a theme that runs through American history, but we still need an evaluation of the effect of the financial experience and policies of the Revolution upon the economic development of the nation. For a nation based upon a money economy, the mere act of transfer, shifting the financial problems from Britain to the United States, is obviously important for the direction of economic development, but scholars have yet to study the finances in this context.

There are, however, other promising approaches, one of which could focus around the concept of an expanding economy. It is possible, for example, that the extensive use of paper money—far outreaching any colonial experience—stimulated general economic activity, although this thesis requires a more precise examination before it can be accepted. Moreover, a number of alert minds during these formative years explored the relationship between national credit and an expanded national economy—Peletiah Webster, Robert Morris, Gouverneur Morris, and Alexander Hamilton, to cite the most obvious. Still another part of the story is the creation of commercial banks, made possible only by the act of Independence. Although the Bank of North America, chartered in 1781, was first, it was quickly imitated by banks in Massachusetts and New York and plans were laid to create others. The critical role played by these institutions is a matter of record, particularly in their credit experience and their role in the expansion of the economy. Without question, such ideas, practices, policies, and institutions in financial affairs—the result of the Revolution—played a significant role in the economic development of the period; indeed, it is possible that careful study and analysis will find that not nearly enough stress has been placed on their far reaching effects.

Another area requiring further research is manufactures.[11] At first glance this plea may appear unnecessary, for numerous historians assert that manufacturing was greatly extended, often supporting such claims with some specific illustrations. What is overlooked, however, is how often historians are merely quoting each other. The few basic economic studies that have included a section on manufacturing—so far as the writer knows, no single monograph on manufacturing in the Revolution exists—are sadly in need of revision. In addition, scholars have failed to distinguish between an increase in production and an increase in total "plant" capacity, a crucial feature of the industrial expansion in the First and Second World Wars. It is logical to assume that the demand for guns, wagons, tents, clothing, and other articles brought an expansion in total productive capacity, but the evidence is not conclusive; nor is there so much as a well-informed estimate as to the degree of expansion.

Another factor that remains virtually unnoticed is the expansion of foreign investments in the United States during and after the Revolution. Before independence, quite naturally, neither French nor Dutch capital was invested in American enterprise; almost immediately upon the outbreak of war, however, key figures in both countries appeared to exploit the opportunities opening up in the new nation. In France such great names as that of Chaumont were prominent; in Holland, the Willinks and the Van Stapenhorsts. Some of the investment was purely speculative— the "investments" in currency, for example. In other cases, it was geared to more lasting enterprises, such as the French financial backing given to several new commercial houses. It can also be assumed that foreign investment in American securities must have played some part in capital formation during this period, but there has not been so much as a

---

[11] It is of interest to note that J. Franklin Jameson, *The American Revolution Considered as a Social Movement* (Princeton, 1926), spends an entire chapter on "Industry and Commerce," although it is difficult to see how he relates it directly to social change, except to state that the "Revolution brought ultimate benefit to the agriculture, the manufactures, and the commerce of the United States of America" (p. 114). The focus of this article, in contrast, is upon those areas where the Revolution may have altered the direction or emphasis of economic development.

scholarly guess as to how significant a part. More important, the question of British investment has been neglected. Leland Jenks's fine study of the migration of British capital to the United States begins too late to throw much light on the Revolutionary epoch, with the result that our information is less than sketchy for the prewar as well as the immediate postwar period. Although historians have not given the entire subject of foreign investment its due, and in consequence we cannot speak of the results with confidence, it most certainly is an area of almost limitless possibilities.

Another promising approach, but one that has attracted little attention, is to use material normally discussed in terms of social history. The abolition of primogeniture and entail is a case in point. In most discussions the social consequences of these acts are emphasized: making the stratification produced by a set land system more flexible and thereby encouraging democratization. Seldom, if ever, is the abolition of primogeniture and entail considered in terms of its economic impact, a perspective of equal, if not greater, importance. To encourage a flexible land system where more efficient producers using up-to-date techniques can thrive, in contrast to a static system that settles for the status quo, is surely a matter of some importance. Indeed, it is instructive that historians have recently discovered that the abolition of primogeniture and entail in Virginia had minor social significance and that support for this act was more universal than had been assumed.[12] It might well be another way of saying that these acts were more important for economic than for social results. More study is needed before a final conclusion can be drawn, but it is evident that a number of topics customarily considered in a social context will be rewarding avenues of exploration for the historian evaluating the economic consequences of the Revolution.

In fact, the number of essential questions requiring answers that only a thorough investigation can provide is a bit overwhelming. Historians have acknowledged that recent depressions, that of the 1930's in particular, have brought about some profound changes, but they have yet to appraise the lasting effect of the immediate postwar depression upon the course of economic development. Historians have written about the rise of the port of Baltimore, when the British blockade of Philadelphia brought new opportunities to its Maryland neighbor, but they have yet to assess the total effect of the Revolution upon the marketing centers of the new nation, including New York City. Historians have noted the decline of fisheries in New England, the change that took place in whaling, and the move from the outports of Massachusetts to Boston, yet they have been slow to determine whether or not the economy of one region of the nation

---

[12] A choice example is to trace the increasing firmness with which this new thesis is accepted in the works of Irving Brant, Dumas Malone, and Nathan Schachner on Madison and Jefferson respectively.

received a more durable impress from the Revolution than did the others. Historians talk about American society with confidence, but they have never asked whether it contained within itself certain special characteristics that would decisively determine the course of economic life in the New Nation.

These considerations re-emphasize not only the importance of the theme but also the vast number of questions that will need to be asked—and, if possible, answered—if we are to assess the full impact of the Revolution. Although this article is merely an introduction rather than a *summa* and any conclusions are, at best, tentative, the evidence concerning the economic consequences of the Revolution is impressive. It is entirely possible that when scholars have completed their investigations, they will conclude that the American Revolution is of greater importance for its economic consequences, where the surface has scarcely been scratched, than for its social consequences, where the research in the Revolution has been concentrated in recent decades. To use the celebrated phrase of that pioneer in the field, J. Franklin Jameson, as a model, a phrase that has made scholars acutely conscious of the social aspects of the Revolution—the time seems overdue for historians to recognize and develop the idea of "The American Revolution Considered as an Economic Movement."

Foundation of Industrialization: The Leading Urban Families

9.   The Entrepreneur and the Community [*]

Robert K. Lamb

III

In Providence, the leading family on the eve of the Revolution was that of the Browns, whose ancestors had been among its first settlers. By the

[*] By permission of its editors, I have used here in considerably altered form certain material published under the title "Entrepreneurship in the Community," appearing in *Explorations in Entrepreneurial History,* vol. II, No. 3, pp. 114–127, a publication of the Research Center in Entrepreneurial History, Harvard University, Cambridge,

1760's four Brown brothers, Nicholas, Joseph, John, and Moses, were trading in rum, slaves, and other West India goods through the firm their father James Brown and his brother Obadiah had formed thirty years earlier.[2] By 1763 the four brothers were at the center of a "trust," the Spermaceti Candle Manufacturers, operating in Providence, Newport, Boston, and Philadelphia. Moses' three brothers became active Patriots, and his brother John was widely believed to have been the ringleader in the *Gaspee* affair. But in 1773, after his wife (Obadiah's daughter) died, Moses Brown withdrew from the family firm and turned Quaker, objecting to slave trading and war profiteering.

When war broke out, and the Secret Committee of the Continental Congress gave out Rhode Island war contracts through his brother Nicholas, Moses did not share in them. Instead he turned his attention to manufacturing experiments. The Browns were ready, when the federated American states achieved a national union, to make Providence a center for commercial activity at home and abroad comparable to its rival Newport before the Revolution. Among the four Brown brothers, Moses was prepared to go even further, and to lay foundations for Providence as a manufacturing center.

The Lowells of Boston [3] show a family system like that of the Browns in Providence, their founding entrepreneur being John Lowell, son of the Reverend John Lowell of Newburyport. After graduating from Harvard in 1760, and studying law in Boston, young John Lowell returned to Newburyport to practice and quickly became attorney for the town's leading merchants, Patrick Tracy and Tristram Dalton. In January 1767, he married Sarah Higginson, daughter of Stephen Higginson and Elizabeth Cabot of Salem. Sarah Higginson Lowell died in 1772, and John Lowell married her cousin Susan Cabot. In 1775, John and Susan had a son, Francis Cabot Lowell, whose mother died within two years; in 1778 John Lowell took Mrs. Rebecca Russell Tyng, a widow, as his third wife.

By his father's three marriages to a Higginson, a Cabot, and a Russell, Francis Cabot Lowell grew up in an extended-kinship group second to none in Boston and its satellite towns on the North Shore, a family connection based upon several generations of merchant-shipowning. The

---

Massachusetts. See also my essay on "Entrepreneurship and Community Development," in *Explorations in Economics* (Notes and Essays Contributed in Honor of F. W. Taussig, New York: McGraw-Hill, 1936); and my unpublished doctoral dissertation at Harvard's Widener Library on "The Development of Entrepreneurship in Fall River, Massachusetts: 1813–1859," submitted to Harvard University in 1935.

[2] On the Browns of Providence, I am indebted to the work of Professor James B. Hedges of Brown University; and on the relations of Moses Brown and Samuel Slater, I have referred to G. S. White, *Memoir of Samuel Slater* (Philadelphia, 1836).

[3] On the Lowells of Boston, I rely especially on Ferris Greenslet, *The Lowells and their Seven Worlds* (Boston: Houghton, Mifflin, 1946).

marriages of Francis and the other sons and daughters of the Judge were to enlarge that family circle. Families like the Higginsons of Salem, the Cabots of Beverly, the Russells of Charlestown, were active in the same trade on which the Browns of Providence founded their fortunes. They were not all among the earliest to defy the Crown, but were handsomely rewarded for their American patriotism through war contracts and privateering.

During the war Judge Lowell served as attorney for various Loyalist estates, including that of former Governor Hutchinson—chief target of the rebels Sam Adams and James Otis. Lowell also found time to act as counsel for his privateering relatives by marriage, the Higginsons, Cabots, and Russells, and personally filed seven hundred of the eleven hundred libels against prize vessels in the Boston court, being concerned as assistant counsel in nearly half the rest. We can understand why he was one of the first to move up from the North Shore to Boston when the Tories sailed away to Halifax; they left opportunities in the legal and mercantile life of Boston for able men with financial backing.

Lowell served in the Continental Congress in 1782, where he became familiar with John Brown of Providence, Alexander Hamilton and other New Yorkers, and the Philadelphia group around Robert Morris and his partner Thomas Willing, who a year earlier founded the Bank of North America hoping to make it a national central bank patterned after the Bank of England. Late in 1782 Lowell was given a congressional appointment as judge of appeals in admiralty cases; on returning to Boston he joined with his family connection in organizing the Massachusetts Bank, the first bank in Boston. It was opened in 1784. His cousin, also named John Lowell, was made its teller, and the "judge" served for a while as cashier.

Judge Lowell, according to his son and partner John Lowell, accumulated during the war upwards of $200,000, but held much of it in continental paper money. He and his relatives by marriage became, after peace was signed, leaders of the group seeking a constitutional convention and a new national union to replace the Confederation. His relatives, and especially his brother-in-law George Cabot, were spokesmen for the Essex Junto which elected James Bowdoin as the first Federalist Governor of Massachusetts in 1785, and went on to put down Shays's rebellion the next year.

The Judge died on May 6, 1802. Four years earlier his son Francis had married Hannah Jackson, daughter of the Judge's old friend and neighbor Jonathan Jackson, and granddaughter of Lowell's wealthy client, Patrick Tracy. Francis had already assumed responsibility for investing the Judge's fortune, chiefly in "Adventures at Sea," and was established as a Boston merchant-shipowner operating eight vessels; his brother-in-law Patrick Tracy Jackson was his partner.[4]

[4] As a boy Francis Cabot Lowell visited his uncle George Cabot's horse-driven

Beginning with the first Continental Congress in 1774, a national economy was formed by the efforts of provincial leaders like the Browns in Providence and John Lowell and his family connection in Boston. After these local entrepreneurs became active in the national war effort, by a series of gradual changes they created a new economy to fill the vacuum left by separation of the American colonies from London's metropolitan economy. During the war this new economy enabled Americans to trade with France and other continental nations, and their island possessions; once war ended, the problem became: how to compete in trade abroad in the face of the growing industrial revolution in Great Britain, and how to restore the disrupted peacetime economies of the individual American states.

By 1789, when President Washington was inaugurated, the aristocratic family groups consolidated by the American Revolution had tacitly agreed on one chief economic spokesman: young Alexander Hamilton who in 1780 had married General Philip Schuyler's daughter Betsey. From 1772, when Hamilton arrived in New Jersey as a boy, he was the protégé of the Livingston-Schuyler-Van Rensselaer connection, chief manorial families of New York and New Jersey. During the war he served as Washington's military secretary, forming a more extensive acquaintance among leading Americans than did any other young man of his generation.

Building on these connections, Hamilton became at a remarkably early age one of the three or four chief exponents of a constitutional convention, and one of its youngest delegates. He had been proposed for the Superintendency of Finance in 1781, at the age of twenty-four, when Robert Morris was chosen. Once the new nation was formed, Hamilton was a logical candidate for the Secretaryship of the Treasury in the first Washington Administration, as head of an alliance between the leading mercantile and landed families of New York and Pennsylvania. Included in this alliance were mercantile families in other cities; for example, the Browns of Providence and the Lowell family connection in Boston.

Hamilton was now in a position to become the great entrepreneur of the new American national economy. With the aid of William Duer (the first Assistant Secretary of the Treasury), Tench Coxe (Duer's successor, a protégé of Morris, Willing, and Benjamin Franklin), and other representatives of his alliance, Hamilton established the original financial patterns for the new nation, and in a series of famous reports laid down its original economic programs and principles. Working together they

---

cotton factory at Beverly, and may have gained there his continuing interest in the possibilities of American manufacture of cotton textiles. That Beverly mill was in operation a year before Moses Brown hired Samuel Slater to work with Ozias Wilkinson at Pawtucket, and Brown knew about the Beverly experiment. George Cabot was one of the three appraisers of John Lowell's estate (the old Judge, drawer of wills, died intestate).

defined the structure and function of the Federal Treasury, the first Bank of the United States, the New York and Philadelphia money markets, a national currency, and the outlines for a protective tariff. Within this national structure, the regional groups centered in the chief towns could organize their own new patterns of entrepreneurial activity. We exaggerate if we argue that this was a singlehanded performance of one financial genius. What Hamilton and his friends were able to do was to complete by their initiative the work of a generation.

IV

One of the chief problems of the group around Hamilton was how to restore economic connections with London, without sacrificing political independence. The struggle between the Federalist party led by Hamilton and the Democratic-Republican party led by Jefferson revolved around the terms on which the United States would come back into the orbit of the London economy. As author of the *Report on Manufactures*, Hamilton was a strong advocate of the need for tariff protection for "infant industries," like the textile industry of which his Society for Useful Manufactures at Paterson, New Jersey, and his New York Manufacturing Society were early (but financially unsuccessful) promoters. Hamilton's efforts to restore good trade relations between the United States and Britain were hampered by Britain's practice of forbidding her mechanics to emigrate, and by her prevention of the export of textile machines, models, or blueprints.

It was paradoxical, but true, that Hamilton, Tench Coxe, and others who worked successfully within the Federal government and the New York and Philadelphia money markets to create a new national economy failed to launch a manufacturing industry. Nevertheless, they provided the national setting wherein Moses Brown of Providence, by employing Samuel Slater, became the first great entrepreneur of the American cotton textile industry.

Alexander Hamilton was appointed Secretary of the Treasury on September 11, 1789. Two days later a young Englishman, Samuel Slater, boarded a vessel bound for America, where he was first employed by the New York Manufacturing Society. Quickly disappointed by its incompetent management, Slater wrote in the first week of December to Moses Brown in Providence, Rhode Island (a state not yet admitted to the federal union), saying:

A few days ago I was informed that you wanted a manager of *cotton spinning*, etc., in which business I flatter myself that I can give the greatest satisfaction, in making machinery, making good yarn, either for *stockings* or *twist*, as any that is made in England; as I have had opportunity, and an oversight, of Sir Richard Arkwright's works, and in Mr. Strutt's mill upwards of eight years. If you are not provided for, should be glad to serve you. . . .

Brown and Slater with the aid of the Wilkinsons, a Pawtucket family of ingenious mechanics, were able within a year to start 72 spindles on a water-frame, driven by an old fulling-mill wheel. This success depended on the knowledge Slater had smuggled out of England in his head, defying the British regulation against emigration of skilled mechanics. He had first been drawn to emigrate by an English reprint from a Philadelphia paper saying that a society there was aiding the growth of cotton textile manufacturing in the United States by offering bounties to native and foreign mechanics trained in the methods of that industry. This was probably the Pennsylvania Society for the Encouragement of Manufactures and Useful Arts, which had been founded in Philadelphia in 1787 while the Constitutional Convention was sitting there and which had the blessing of Benjamin Franklin and the support of Tench Coxe, later Hamilton's Assistant Secretary of the Treasury. Coxe used the Slater mill as one of his chief examples in drafting Hamilton's Report on Manufactures.

By 1793 the firm of Almy, Brown and Slater had built a small factory of their own in Pawtucket (and Slater had become a son-in-law of Ozias Wilkinson). Their operations were pitifully small compared to those Slater had left behind in England, where Arkwright throughout a generation had operated a dozen or more mills, some of them with 600 workmen. Nevertheless, thanks to Slater, America was launched on the cotton textile industry as a young rival of the British. The infant industry flourished in the small-scale operations of the Blackstone Valley where it could rely on skillful mechanics, small water powers, and a close identity between capital and management. The United States was not ready for large-scale corporate manufacturing experiments, such as those of Hamilton and his friends.

The other Browns were more immediately influenced by Hamilton's national experiments than by those of Slater and their brother Moses in Pawtucket. In 1791 the Browns helped found the Providence Bank (modeled on those in Philadelphia, New York, and Boston); in 1794 they built the *John Jay*, and launched her in the trade to India. It was not until 1804 that Nicholas Brown, Jr. considered his uncle's manufacturing venture sufficiently successful to justify the firm of Brown and Ives in buying its first water rights on the Blackstone River, above Providence.

v

This Blackstone Manufacturing Company quickened the interest of small merchants and mechanics as far away as Fall River, Massachusetts, on the Rhode Island border. By the time of Jefferson's embargo, the mills built at Pawtucket and elsewhere by Almy, Brown and Slater had become "schools" for machinists from the region twenty or thirty miles around Providence. The men they trained harnessed small streams to turn mill wheels and drive cotton-spinning water-frames; small textile villages grew up about these mills.

In 1808 a twenty-two-year-old named David Anthony, who hailed from near Fall River, went to work for Slater and the Wilkinsons. In 1813 Anthony and his cousin Dexter Wheeler, the mechanic, started the Fall River Manufactory, first cotton mill on the Quequechan River in the village of Fall River, on land belonging to Thomas Borden—later to be Anthony's father-in-law. That same year the blacksmith Nathaniel Wheeler, Dexter's brother, helped organize the Troy Cotton and Woollen Manufactory at the head of the stream, on land owned by the family of Simeon Borden.

The chief family structure in the village of Fall River at this time was an extended-kinship group centering around a series of intermarriages over several generations between members of the Borden and Durfee family connection whose ancestors were among the original settlers of Freetown after the Freeman's Purchase in 1658. By 1803, when the township of Fall River was carved out of adjoining Freetown and Tiverton by the legislature, there were eighteen dwelling-houses near the sites of the first two mills on the stream, and nine of the family heads had the name of Borden, while one was a Durfee.

The two Fall River mills founded in 1813, and a neighboring mill set up in 1811 in Tiverton, were all organized by members of this family connection. They had operated grist and sawmills on the Quequechan for generations, and traded with the Browns and other Providence merchants by sloop; through Anthony and others they established close relations with the Pawtucket experiment; and in the years to come maintained them. Thus the Fall River mills and families grew from the seed-bed of the American textile industry, and through Slater and the Providence-Pawtucket system derived their skills directly from the original British cotton textile industry founded by Arkwright and the Strutts.

Studies of entrepreneurship which place heavy emphasis upon the "creative personality" of the *individual* entrepreneur are apt to underestimate the importance of the *group* from which these entrepreneurs derive so much of their strength. The key group in the establishment and development of Fall River was the already described extended-kinship family system joining together its early entrepreneurs. For fifty years after the founding of the first mills, or until the panic of 1873 struck the city, this family structure founded in the seventeenth and eighteenth centuries was still close-knit. Its individual members usually exerted personal control over the major institutions formed there during that half century. The bad times in the 1870's forced a period we may call "trusteeship" when a few local members of the family modernized the institutional structure by which they held control. Then the group directing the family's affairs accepted the leadership of an outstanding member of their oncoming generation who had earlier been sent to represent them in New York, and he thereafter dominated the life of the town until the outbreak of the First World War, exercising final control from New York through his family connections in Fall River.

This process of growth goes through a number of stages, marked by an increasing impersonalization and institutionalization of the family as a social control group. The Fall River Iron Works was the chief local institution through which this control was exercised until after the Civil War. This company founded by the Borden-Durfee group in 1825 included, until the economic crisis of 1829, two of the Wilkinson brothers from Pawtucket: Abraham and Isaac. They brought to the company their knowledge of textile machine manufacture (notably that of the Scotch loom, long produced by their brother David), their skill in iron-making, and especially their father's nail-making machine.

The year of the formation of the Iron Works marked also a period of transition when the family generation of the founders, who had grown up in the shadow of Samuel Slater, Ozias Wilkinson, and Moses Brown, began to move into strategic positions in the newly formed local bank and savings bank founded by the family, or to concentrate on side lines like the running of a steamboat line to Providence (and later to New York). Thus the family was extending its influence within and outside the local community.

Prior to 1825 it would be difficult to point to any single member of the family group as the leader in local developments. Thereafter, right down to 1914, there was usually one member of the family whom we can designate as the prime mover in community affairs; frequently this was by no means the eldest member of the active group, but usually that one whose capacities and working experience best fitted him to give the kind of leadership needed at a given stage of community growth. This pattern of family control, rooted in the customary ways of the group on the land or in shipping ventures, was reinforced by their use of the joint-stock, limited liability corporation.

When the founding generation of entrepreneurs turned over control of manufacturing after formation of the Iron Works in 1825, a new generation of the family led by Holder Borden took charge. He had two claims to a central role in the family: first, though he was a bachelor, his three sisters had married Durfee cousins, while his mother's second husband was Major Bradford Durfee, another cousin; second, he was in 1825, at the age of 26, a success in the eyes of the Borden-Durfee family connection because of his responsible position in Providence with Brown and Ives. He continued this connection for over a decade, while dominating the Fall River scene. He made his major contribution to the growth of the community by extending the family interest to textile printing.

Known in Fall River and Providence as a great "driver" he appears to have hastened his death from consumption by "commuting" behind a fast horse, changed halfway between the two cities (it is said he chain-smoked cigars). Holder left his estate (apparently in equal shares; there is no will) to his three Durfee brothers-in-law and his Durfee stepfather, no doubt because of the restrictions on married women as estate-holders. By these legacies he helped to concentrate control of the family enterprises in the Borden-Durfee connection. This was compounded by his great-uncle William Valentine, a few years later, who left his estate including his Iron Works shares in trust, and made Jefferson Borden (Holder's uncle) his principal trustee.

Bradford Durfee followed Holder in the family leadership and provided a new impetus towards practical engineering; he made his chief contribution on the mechanical side of the cotton industry, by importing and helping perfect the English "mule" for the fine-spinning of cotton thread. By the time he died in 1845 after overexertion at a major fire in Fall River, he had begun the connection of the town with the Old Colony Railroad. Leadership of the Iron Works group passed with his death to his brothers-in-law, Richard and Jefferson Borden. Richard was the dominant one, but they worked out a division of labor, with Jefferson specializing in the "finishing" end of the cotton industry (he founded the bleachery and ran the American Print Works), and expanding the family's banking role.

By the 1850's, most of the nephews and nieces of Richard and Jefferson Borden had married cousins, keeping their Iron Works shares within the family connection of the Bordens and Durfees. There were in 1856 only 32 Iron Works shares outstanding, with a book value of $960,000 as against the original investment of $24,000; each *share* now had an individual value of $30,000. Nephews and nieces who held fractions of a share (e.g., $\frac{3}{4}$ of $\frac{1}{32}$) wanted to use these as security for bank loans; they also wanted to be represented at the Iron Works when decisions were made about their shares. The family created a board of directors, and arranged a stock split-up, issuing 300 shares of a par value of $100 each in exchange for every one of the 32 shares outstanding, or 9600 shares in all. These changes shifted the company from close-knit family control to a more impersonal basis of financing and control, more subject to outside pressure from banks, and other creditors. The full effect of this was not felt until after the panic of 1873.

During the thirty-year regime of Richard and Jefferson Borden, the Borden-Durfee connection maintained its leadership in Fall River, in spite of the financial crash in 1857, and the textile boom of the Civil War with its mushroom growth of rival mills. Richard's death in 1874 and that of his younger brother Jefferson in 1879 revealed, however, the failure of the family to provide adequate local successors to their leadership. The crash also disclosed the financial weakness and overextension of some of the lesser members of the family group, especially the incompetent business operations of their nephew, Dr. Nathan Durfee, founder of the first steam-driven cotton mill in the city. He and his sons-in-law proved to have used the family connection as a basis for speculative financial dealings which nearly brought down the whole structure of family investments during the panic's aftermath. Only the creation of a family "trusteeship" enabled the Iron Works group to survive the financial storm.

After 1845 a generation of Yankees from rocky farms surrounding Fall River founded their own commercial banks and savings banks and during and after the Civil War built new textile mills. Until the war, more than two-thirds of the local mill operatives and their families were Yankee, largely drawn from these neighboring farm areas. The managerial group in mills, banks, and stores was also composed overwhelmingly of Yankees, tied by blood or marriage to the first or second generation of bank clerks, store owners, mechanics, and superintendents who ran local enterprises for the Borden-Durfee family connection. Their sons became the backbone of the new group of entrepreneurs of the Civil War generation, rapidly enlarged Fall River's mill-working population, and changed the sources from which the town drew its workers. The manufacturers continued to rely on rural family groups, but began sending agents to Canada and overseas. In less than twenty years the town grew from 15,000 to 45,000 residents, largely drawn from French Canada and the British Isles but increasingly from the European continent.

After the crisis of the 1870's struck, Fall River's recovery was slow; it waited for the appearance of a new entrepreneur, who could provide a wider horizon for its textile industry. The driving force to set the town back on its rapid upward expansion of mill-building was supplied by Matthew Chaloner Durfee Borden, who represented the Borden-Durfee family interests in New York. He realigned the family businesses in Fall River so as to make that city an industrial satellite of New York. Through association with Low, Harriman and Company, the large New York firm merchandizing cotton goods, he had a thorough knowledge of the marketing system growing up in that metropolis. Through his wider outlook the Bordens, rather than the newer men, held top leadership in Fall River.

M. C. D. Borden's allies back home included the Brayton brothers, whose sister Mary had been the second wife of Bradford Durfee. The Braytons' nephew, Bradford Matthew Chaloner Durfee, was due to come of age in 1864; in 1863 his Brayton uncles, as trustees for his estate (based on Iron Works shares), founded the B. M. C. Durfee Trust Company; they used its financial backing to build the Durfee mill, first of a series of their family holdings. M. C. D. Borden made the B. M. C. Durfee Trust Company his chief financial agency in Fall River, and relied heavily on the advice of the Braytons in his local operations. He converted the Fall River Iron Works, no longer able to compete in iron manufacture, into a cotton manufactory, and built the largest textile corporation in the United States, operating before the First World War about a million spindles.

We can conclude our Fall River example with a few statistics showing the extraordinary growth fostered by the Borden-Durfee connection. A community of less than 100 in 1815 became a city of over 100,000 by 1915, primarily devoted to the manufacture of cotton-textiles. When the textile depression set in after 1923, the town went through the financial wringer. Such cotton textile manufacturing as survived did so in plants tied to large nation-wide companies operating chains of mills, North and South; their product was marketed through close connections with the head offices of wholesalers and department-store chains in New York City.

VI

We turn from the Fall River example of the growth of a textile community out of the extended-kinship system of the surrounding countryside to that of Boston as a different type of community growth, one based directly on the family system operating in shipping and overseas trade. Comparison of Fall River with Boston shows a fundamental difference in the structure and function of these communities, and a comparable difference between the contributions made by their entrepreneurs to the growth of the American textile industry. Fall River's first mills were founded while Francis Cabot Lowell of Boston and Paul Moody were experimenting with their power loom in Waltham. Chronologically, the two experiments started together; their patterns of development, however, were decades apart.

The Bordens' influence on the growth of the textile industry was confined to Fall River until after 1880; the Lowells, operating from their Boston base, had a regional influence from the start. If we contrast the Boston region after 1814 with Boston and Providence after 1789 we shall see the stimulus to American manufactures of Jefferson's embargo and of the Louisiana Purchase. The treaty with Britain after the War of 1812, by reducing economic dependence of the United States upon London and removing restraints on westward expansion, changed the pace of American economic development and expanded national markets for cotton textiles. This was the period when the Fall River and Waltham mills got their start. In these years, also, after the Hartford Convention (chaired by Lowell's uncle George Cabot) the New England Federalists abandoned their close alliance with the British economy, and many Federalist families shifted into manufacturing, under Lowell's leadership.

The Fall River process of converting the extended-kinship family rooted in the soil into an economic institution dominating a whole community had certain inherent limitations not present when a family of merchant-shipowners undertook to give comparable leadership. Francis Cabot Lowell in 1814 started shifting the whole direction of Boston's entrepreneurial activities from overseas trade to manufacturing, and channeled them into a series of ventures modeled on his "Waltham plan."

Abroad in 1811, with some such plan in mind, he studied intensively the operations of the British textile industry, especially the new power looms then just in the final stages of experiment. His mathematical skill and remarkable memory enabled him to imitate Slater by evading British restrictions on export of machinery or models and, after his return to Boston, to invent a loom of his own. He set it going in an old paper mill in Waltham with the aid of Paul Moody's mechanical abilities. Lowell enlisted his brother-in-law Patrick Tracy Jackson, and secured some financial support from Nathan Appleton, a Boston merchant with whom he had discussed his plans while both were abroad.

When Lowell's power loom enabled his Boston associates to organize the production of cotton cloth at Waltham within one factory (instead of putting out the yarn to weavers, or letting yarn-buyers weave their own cloth), Jackson, Appleton, and Lowell were already experienced in the merchandising of cotton cloth, British and Indian. Available Boston capital derived from overseas commerce started the Boston Manufacturing Company with a capitalization larger than that of Brown and Ivcs' venture in 1804, and far larger than that in Fall River. By 1816 the Waltham experiment was acknowledged by members of the Lowell family connection to have succeeded. That year Francis Lowell lobbied the tariff on cotton cloth through Congress, a few months before his death at forty-two.

With his death, Lowell's associates Patrick Jackson [5] and Nathan Appleton faced new problems in carrying the experiment forward. By 1821 Paul Moody, under their direction, had harnessed all the available falls at Waltham, and they sought a new water-power site. Capital for the expansion was not a major consideration: by 1822 the Boston Manufacturing Company had paid dividends of 102.5 per cent on the original investment of $400,000. This large initial capital was in itself a demonstration of the difference between the new textile industry projected from Boston and that growing up simultaneously in Fall River. The Borden-Durfee group was forced to accumulate most of its capital locally, and to use members of its extended-kinship group as workers in its cotton mills.

Appleton, Jackson, and Moody found the new water power at Chelmsford, where a thirty-foot fall was owned by "The Proprietors of the Locks and Canals on Merrimack River." When on February 27, 1822, the first meeting of stockholders of the Merrimack Manufacturing Company [6]

[5] On the career of Patrick Tracy Jackson, cf. K. W. Porter, *The Jacksons and the Lees*, vols. I and II (Cambridge: Harvard University Press, 1937), *passim*.
[6] Of the stock of the new Merrimack Company, 25 per cent was subscribed by the Boston Manufacturing Company, and in later years Francis' nephew John Amory

elected a board of directors, the Lowell connection was well represented: it included Francis Lowell's brothers-in-law Patrick Tracy Jackson, Benjamin Gorham, and Warren Dutton, who was named president.

In memory of Francis Cabot Lowell the company town, incorporated by the legislature in 1826, was named Lowell. It established a new pattern of industrial community life in the United States. Around Providence and Pawtucket had grown up a regional congeries of mill villages, each dependent on a small water power, and each drawing its workers from the near-by farm families. These villages were in no sense "plantations," but stemmed directly out of the existing rural structure. At Lowell, the Boston proprietors built dormitories for workers, and recruited their "help" from rural areas as far away as New Hampshire. They preferred young farm girls who wanted to supplement the family income. A much more rootless community was thus created, controlled by the superintendents of the companies' mills.

The foundation of Lowell in 1822 marked a turning point for Boston: a general movement began, spreading the manufacturing interests of Boston to the large water powers of New England. Later in 1822 some of the stockholders of the Merrimack Company started a similar development at Chicopee, with some capitalists from the Connecticut River Valley. Both at Lowell and at Chicopee new mills rose in rapid succession, as the Boston associates saw markets expand in pace with their output. Within the next fifteen years the Boston group developed other water powers at Taunton, Massachusetts; Manchester and Somersworth, New Hampshire; Saco and Biddeford, Maine; and elsewhere. As steamboating on the Mississippi, grain traffic on the Great Lakes, and the building of the Erie Canal boomed western lands, the population of the country grew rapidly and the textile industry boomed also. This boom collapsed in 1837, but was soon revived by the railway expansion of the two decades before the Civil War.

The group of entrepreneurs who create a new community provide the most spectacular example of the role of the entrepreneur in relation to the community. Once the site was chosen and the town launched, these entrepreneurs among the Boston associates carried through their age-old entrepreneurial functions of organizing new institutions such as local banks, savings banks, real estate companies, manufacturing corporations, branch railroads, and the like. Meanwhile, these economic and social institutions within the local communities were being duplicated in Boston

---

Lowell and Francis' sons John, "Junior" and Francis, Jr. were to become large stockholders; John Amory Lowell served from 1827 to 1844 as its Treasurer and thereafter until 1877 as its President. Patrick Tracy Jackson felt he could not leave the Waltham mill, and recommended instead Kirk Boott, who was made treasurer and clerk, and engaged to lay out the new manufacturing community. The Boott family, English merchants in Boston, had given John Amory Lowell his first job.

to tie the new industrial towns to their regional metropolitan capital. The growth of the region, stimulated by the "plantation" of these new towns, was accelerated after the development of the railroad and the importation of new working populations from abroad. New England differed from areas further west, however, by reason of the close-knit relationships between these long-established mercantile families and the newcomers whom they associated with their group. Town building assumed one pattern in the more settled regions of the east and another along the lines of railway expansion in the west; the resulting communities show to this day important differences in their patterns of entrepreneurship.

Years before the expansionist effects of the coming railway age could be felt in New England, the Boston associates turned to the federal government for tariff protection following the panic of 1829. In the Providence-Pawtucket center of the industry, the panic bankrupted Abraham and Isaac Wilkinson (and forced them to sell to Bordens and Durfees their shares in the Fall River Iron Works); Samuel Slater and many others were threatened. Fears of similar troubles undoubtedly strengthened the protectionist forces in Boston and elsewhere. The national political significance of the pattern of absentee ownership and the founding of company towns by the Boston associates was demonstrated to the people of Massachusetts in 1830. In that election the free traders supported Henry Lee for election to Congress from the Boston seat against Nathan Appleton, candidate of the protectionists. This campaign shook the old-family structure of Boston to its foundations: Henry Lee, for example, was the brother-in-law of Appleton's associate Patrick Tracy Jackson; Appleton's victory marked the permanent ascendancy of the protectionist interest in the city.

To consolidate the position of the Lowell associates as leaders of the textile industry, and the position of Boston as the metropolis of the growing region, many new entrepreneurial advances had to be made. New banking methods were needed, so Nathan Appleton, John Amory Lowell, and their friends originated the Suffolk Banking System to stabilize banknote currency throughout New England. Appleton had a long career as exponent of "sound money."[7] He was an original subscriber to the Suffolk Bank, along with his brother William; the list included John W. Boott, Patrick Tracy Jackson, and Amos and Abbott Lawrence.

Abbott Lawrence and Nathan Appleton, self-made men, were interlopers on the Boston scene by comparison with the Lowell family connec-

---

[7] Appleton had been chiefly responsible in 1808 for bringing down the financial house-of-cards created by Andrew Dexter among country banks through the Boston Exchange Office, which manipulated their notes circulating in Boston. During similar crises in 1814 and 1819 Appleton, as a director of the Boston Bank, held his fellow bankers to the payment of specie, and in 1819 when suspension was general he wrote a number of newspaper articles, contrasting the sound banks of Boston with the unreliable banks farther south.

tion. Their personal histories show many parallels with those of the Bordens and Durfees in Fall River, but within the Boston setting they entered the charmed economic circle of the merchant-shipowner group by their careers as overseas merchants. They were accepted as social near-equals of the ruling group, however, by reason of the marriages of their children.[8] By their manufacturing careers, Appleton and Lawrence gave a driving force to the expansion of Boston's entrepreneurial role which would probably otherwise have been lacking to the operations of the Lowell family group after the death of Francis Cabot Lowell.

Nathan Appleton and Abbott Lawrence showed many parallels in their careers, but Lawrence started his in Boston fourteen years after Appleton arrived in 1794. Like Appleton, Lawrence as a boy entered his older brother's Boston commercial house, bringing a bundle of clothes under his arm and a fortune of three dollars in his pocket.[9] The children of two rural deacons became the founders of the two greatest textile centers spawned by Boston; unlike Fall River, however, the cities created by Appleton and Lawrence were company towns, controlled by the methods of absentee ownership fostered by the Lowell family connection at Waltham. Neither Appleton nor Lawrence used his ancestral acres, as did the Bordens, to raise up a community with which they mingled the lives of their family connection, except remotely as mill treasurers and corporate directors.

After the panic of 1829, Nathan Appleton felt that the time had come to enlist the support of new capital and persuaded Abbott Lawrence and his brothers, who had acted as merchandizers of textiles for the mills of Lowell, to join "The Proprietors of the Locks and Canals on Merrimack River," and build their own mills to take advantage of the remaining water power. From this moment Lawrence moved up to take his place beside Appleton and John Amory Lowell as a leading cotton manufacturer. Fifteen years passed, however, before the Lawrences were ready to found a textile city bearing their name.

[8] When Appleton's daughter married Professor Henry Wadsworth Longfellow of Harvard, her fortune assisted him in buying Craigie House, where he settled down to the writing of poetry; Lawrence's daughter Katherine married Augustus Lowell, promising son of John Amory Lowell, who fulfilled his promise during the panic of '57 and succeeded his father in his many directorships and trusteeships after the panic of '73. The greatest contributions of Augustus and Katherine Lawrence Lowell to the Lowell family were their famous children: Percival, the astronomer; Amy, the poet; and Abbott Lawrence Lowell, President of Harvard.

[9] Nathan and Abbott each attended the private academy in his town, each missed out on more advanced education; both were to become benefactors of Harvard; their monuments were Appleton Chapel and the Lawrence Scientific School. The first Appleton and the first Lawrence, both Puritans, came from the county of Suffolk, England in 1635. Deacon Appleton had twelve children who grew up in New Ipswich, New Hampshire; Deacon Lawrence had nine who farmed his acres in Groton, Massachusetts. The families of the Appletons and Lawrences were joined on March 31, 1842, by the marriage of Abbott's nephew, Amos Adams Lawrence, son of his brother Amos, to Nathan's niece, Sarah Elizabeth, daughter of William Appleton.

On March 20, 1845, fourteen leading Bostonians,[10] including Nathan Appleton, Patrick Jackson, and Abbott Lawrence, set out on an "excursion" by rail to inspect a new power site on the Merrimack River, some distance short of the city of Lowell. The new industrial city of Lawrence was built at a time when the characteristics of the mill workers of Massachusetts were changing, and Lawrence became at the start a more heterogeneous community than Lowell. Mill girls, a majority of the workers at Lowell in the 1830's, were drawn chiefly from the farms of New England; they worked to supplement the declining income of their farm families, and to save money for their own dowries. By the 1840's their places were being taken by English and Irish immigrants whose families joined them as mill workers. With the decline of working and living conditions after the panic of 1837, strikes commenced to plague the proprietors.

That there were other troubles we can see from a letter written in July 1842 by Henry Lee, Sr. (whom Nathan Appleton had defeated for Congress in 1830) to his son Henry Lee, Jr., then in Paris. The senior Henry Lee had begun in 1841 converting a fortune made in commerce into active investments in manufacturing and railroad stocks, continuing for at least the next ten years. He writes:

> A *reforming party* has been at work with Wm. Appleton—at its head & sustained by Geo. Lyman, Col. Perkins, the Brooks, E. Francis, H. Cabot, Geo. How(e)—and nearly all the independent men who don't get salaries & are not influenced by those who do—They have been resisted by the combined power of Lawrence, N. Appleton, the Lowells & the Jacksons & their allies—but it was *inffectual*. Salaries are reduced (operatives were 6 mo ago) more work done at the factories.[11]

This letter shows how the insiders who dominated the operations of the Boston associates in Lowell, Lawrence, Chicopee, and elsewhere struggled against the outsiders drawn from the ranks of the overseas merchants, who like Lee had become investors in mill stocks. On the wave of recovery after the panic of 1837, new stockholders like Henry Lee helped found the city of Lawrence in 1845. Thereafter until the Civil War the growth of industry in New England continued within the pattern laid down by the Boston associates.

After the start of the railway age, the Boston associates linked their

[10] In the party of fourteen there were, besides Jackson and Appleton, three Lawrences—Abbott, William, and Samuel—two Lowells—John Amory and his cousin Francis Cabot Lowell, Jr.—and Charles Storer Storrow, a civil engineer trained at the Ecole des Ponts et Chaussees in Paris, who was to build their new industrial city. Storrow's qualifications as an engineer entitled him to an appointment as builder of Lawrence, but his wife was Lydia Cabot Jackson, granddaughter of Jonathan Jackson, and daughter of Dr. James Jackson and Elizabeth Cabot; hence she was the niece of Patrick Tracy Jackson.

[11] K. W. Porter, *The Jacksons and the Lees*, I, 125.

metropolitan center to its regional hinterland; they planted textile cities at available water powers and tied them together by a railroad network. The proprietors of Lowell led this movement in 1830 by projecting the Boston and Lowell road, and Patrick Tracy Jackson climbed back into harness to direct its construction. With the completion of its links to its neighboring cities, and especially its span across the Berkshires to the Hudson River, Boston had laid the foundations for its position as "The Hub" city.[12]

Thomas Handasyd Perkins, who deserves much of the credit for joining Boston and Albany by rail, kept himself in the background of most of the ventures in which he was interested.[13] He was outstanding among the merchant-shipowners who became investors in textile manufacturing on the second wave (he was probably the "Col. Perkins" of Henry Lee's letter). A leading Boston merchant, long prominent in the China trade, he appears in 1828 as an incorporator of the new mills of the Lowell and Appleton companies in the town of Lowell.

The most important result of Perkins' interest in railways was its effect on his nephew John Murray Forbes, who while a boy had followed his uncle as a China merchant, returning by the age of twenty-four with a comfortable fortune. Through Forbes the entrepreneurs of Boston leapt over the Hudson with their railway investments, before they spanned it by a railway bridge. The career of John Forbes, promoter of the Michigan Central, and the Chicago, Burlington and Quincy Railroads, directed the attention of Bostonians to the expanding West at a time when they would probably otherwise have devoted their major energies to further industrializing of New England. The result was to launch Boston as a national source of investment funds, although the city did not mature in that role until after the Civil War, when several old-family firms (among whom Lee, Higginson was foremost) became active traders in the securities of Western railroads, mines, real estate, and lumber companies outside of New England.

By the end of the Civil War the original "Boston associates" who established their city as textile capital of the United States were dead: Patrick Tracy Jackson died in 1847, followed in 1855 by Abbott Lawrence.

[12] The year 1835 saw the formal celebration of the completion of three railroads, the Boston & Province on June 11, the Boston & Lowell on June 27, and the Boston & Worcester on July 4. It also marked the opening of a drive to connect Boston, through Worcester, with Albany and the Hudson River over a line to be called the Western Railroad. At a mass meeting held in Faneuil Hall on October 7, 1835, Abbott Lawrence presided, and Nathan Appleton offered a report and resolutions, starting the new campaign for subscriptions. The road was completed in 1841.

[13] Perkins was first interested in a railway to the Hudson in 1825, during the effort to complete the Bunker Hill Monument, when he helped underwrite the tramway for hauling granite from Quincy, and became convinced that a railway would be more feasible than the canal then being projected to join Boston and Albany. In 1826 he petitioned the Legislature to make a survey for what later became the Western Railroad; he succeeded during the next few years in blocking a parallel movement for a canal—the fever of the Erie Canal was in Boston's blood.

In July 1861, three months after the firing on Fort Sumter, the Boston Merchants' Exchange held a memorial meeting for Nathan Appleton, dead at eighty-one. John Amory Lowell, presiding, said:

> [The name of Nathan Appleton] is too intimately connected with finance, with commerce, with all the great industrial pursuits of New England, to need eulogium from any one; but it is a privilege which we, his fellow citizens, could not willingly forego, to bear our ready testimony to those qualities which have done more than those of perhaps any other one man to enhance the estimation and promote the prosperity, not of this city only, not of this State, nor of New England, but of the whole of our common country, North, East, West, ay, and South.

John Amory Lowell had already assumed the responsibilities previously carried by Nathan Appleton and Abbott Lawrence for directing the widespread concerns of the Boston associates of the Lowell family connection. Enterprises he directed included the whole gamut of operations from manufacturing textile machinery and steam engines in the Lowell Machine Shops, distributing water power through the Locks and Canals, railroading on the Boston and Lowell Railroad, cotton manufacturing in the Boott, Massachusetts, and other mills, banking in the Suffolk Bank, insurance in the Massachusetts Mutual, and the Massachusetts Hospital Life Insurance Companies, to cotton goods merchandizing through J. K. Mills and Company and other firms. Meanwhile he found time to oversee the affairs of the Boston associates through his son, Augustus, his cousins and other members of the Lowell family group. He remained active as the acknowledged head of the family throughout the Civil War and the panic of 1873, retiring in 1877 in favor of his son Augustus, then forty-seven.[14]

Boston, the political and economic capital city for much of colonial America, was stimulated by post-Revolutionary trade to the Far East and by the expanding textile industries. It ranked in the first four cities of our country right down to the Civil War but, after 1845 and the growth of western railroads, steadily lost headway to its more westerly rivals. It retained, and retains, its character as the metropolitan capital of a regional economy. While Fall River has continued throughout its career to be a satellite, first to Providence, and then to New York, Boston maintained a large measure of economic independence until quite recently. Much of the credit for this must go to the close-knit system of old-family leadership established before the Civil War.

[14] The late seventies saw recovery and new expansion in the multifarious enterprises and social and charitable institutions over which John Amory Lowell had so long presided, including Harvard College, then headed by Charles William Eliot. By 1877 Lowell had served on the Harvard Corporation for 40 years, with six different Presidents of the College; the year of his retirement from the Harvard Corporation he saw his grandson, Abbott Lawrence Lowell, graduate 32 years before that grandson succeeded Eliot as President of the University.

Prior to the Civil War, in Boston as in Fall River, a new generation of self-made men founded banks and business corporations, and spread their influence throughout the region centered upon Boston, enlarging its structure and functions. It was not, however, until after the Civil War that this group began effectively to challenge the group we have called the Boston associates.[15] The Lowell family connection met this challenge and, while its absolute importance declined, successfully maintained a central position in Boston through collateral branches such as those of the Lees, Higginsons, Cabots, Jacksons, and Storrows.

VII

After this examination of the development of the pre-Civil War generations of entrepreneurs who created the American textile industry, and our glimpse at some of the communities they helped expand, we are ready to return to the questions we asked at the start of this essay: How was the organizing of the structures and functions of our national economic system related to the development of the textile industry? How did certain communities, mercantile centers before the Revolution, become regional textile-industry capitals after the ratification of the Constitution? What entrepreneurs were responsible for these developments, and how much did they depend on other groups in their local or regional communities, or in the national community?

The development of the American textile industry between 1789 and 1815 was directly related to the formation of the national economic system. Providence began its shift from mercantile to manufacturing activity as a regional capital for the textile industry because of the entrepreneurial skills of Moses Brown; however, Brown needed not only the genius of Samuel Slater and the Wilkinsons but also the commercial capital and experience accumulated by the Brown family, and their connections with the new national economy. Fall River was only the most outstanding of a number of textile communities which grew from the Providence-Pawtucket experiment, but its entrepreneurs were rooted in a rural extended-kinship system which channeled the growth of a whole community. Boston's history, like that of Providence, depended upon the regional development of a mercantile capital city but especially upon the leadership provided by one group of merchant-shipowners who combined

[15] This phrase, "the Boston associates," is used on p. 54 and thereafter in Vera Shlakman, *Economic History of a Factory Town: A Study of Chicopee, Massachusetts*, Smith College Studies in History (Northampton, Mass., 1936). This excellent study goes far beyond the story of Chicopee in its description of the pre-Civil War generation of Bostonians who founded its regional textile industry. Our essay cannot hope to describe the leaders of the post-Civil War generations in Boston. We can note only that many of the most important of their members were drawn from the families with whom John Lowell formed his connections by marriage in the years before and during the Revolution.

the extended-kinship system with the wider horizon of a family group engaged in overseas trade. The success of the Lowells as entrepreneurs of the textile industry began twenty-five years after the Browns, because it depended upon the arrival of a new stage in manufacturing: the operation of an integrated factory and the plantation of company towns. It depended also on the reorganization of the national economy which followed the War of 1812 (a reorganization marked by the tariff of 1816 and the formation of the Second Bank of the United States).

The Business Ethic Triumphant

10.   The Basic Democrat: A Version of Tocqueville

Marvin Meyers

Alexis de Tocqueville's commentary on democracy has become a political classic consulted by American historians for every purpose but the simplest: as a key to the immediate subject of the work, Jacksonian America. In the view of sober history Tocqueville exists as a philosopher, as a (fallible) prophet, as a personage, and as a source of brilliant phrases. Evidently, the advantage would be great if one could restore to him the office of observer, interpreting the scene he visited between the spring of 1831 and the late winter of 1832. The return in data would be negligible; Tocqueville has wrung his text almost dry of discrete particulars. What might be found is just the resource most needed by the student of Jacksonian times: an integrative view of society and character, grounded in experience.[1]

The general neglect of Tocqueville for this limited historical use is not mysterious; indeed the author invited it in his introductory confession that "in America I saw more than America; I sought there the image of democracy itself, with its inclinations, its character, its prejudices, and its

---

[1] *Democracy in America*, edited by Phillips Bradley, 2 vols. (New York, 1948). All references in this article, unless otherwise indicated, are to the Bradley edition. The *Democracy* consists primarily of judgments formed "upon the mass of evidence," as the Introduction states, and rarely preserves particulars in the text, I, 16.

"The Basic Democrat: A Version of Tocqueville," by Marvin Meyers, is reprinted by permission from *Political Science Quarterly*, LXXII (March, 1957), 50–70.

passions, in order to learn what we have to fear or to hope from its progress."[2] The approach is alternately hortatory, speculative, analytic, descriptive; the contents present a seeming chaos of latent and manifest, essential and accidental traits, of French and American experiences, of glacial movements of democracy over seven centuries and the events of a decade. Yet the difficulties in handling the *Democracy* as a historical source, real enough, are not so overwhelming as the common avoidance of the task would suggest. One deals here with a clear mind and a lucid style.

Without attempting an elaborate defense of Tocqueville as historical guide, I shall briefly indicate the leading general objections and estimate their force. Tocqueville's interest in "more than America," in "the image of democracy itself," has encouraged a too simple assessment of the work as abstract, deductive, only incidentally related to the scene of his travels. In terms of the author's manifest intention, this is a one-sided interpretation: he maintains in the opening sentences of the Introduction that "the study of American society" shaped his conception of the great democratic revolution,[3] and repeatedly he specifies the link between America and democracy not as something casual but exactly as the relationship between the case and the class. America could reveal "the image of democracy" because there the social revolution "seems to have nearly reached its natural limits," and this "without having had the revolution itself."[4] "I have selected the nation . . . in which its development has been the most peaceful and the most complete, in order to discern its natural consequences. . . ."[5] Tocqueville's modest apology is entirely consistent, at least in principle, with the design of his work: "I do not know whether I have succeeded in making known what I saw in America, but I am certain that such has been my sincere desire, and that I have never, knowingly, moulded facts to ideas, instead of ideas to facts."[6]

At a more complex level, the objection—from the viewpoint of historical usefulness—to Tocqueville's generality and abstractness does raise serious problems of method. He is by no means an empirical reporter of the American scene; a scheme of democracy informs every part of his work. Indeed, Tocqueville accuses himself of attempting, on rhetorical considerations, "to carry all his ideas to their utmost theoretical conclusions, and often to the verge of what is false or impracticable"[7]—a comment on political reasoning which has some bearing on the method of social inquiry. This is not, however, to be taken as a crude confusion of

[2] I, 14.
[3] I, 3.
[4] I, 13.
[5] I, 14.
[6] I, 15.
[7] I, 16; also II, v–vi, where Tocqueville concedes more than is necessary to critics of his monistic thesis.

logic and experience. The large conception of democracy is drawn from historical evidence, given theoretical elaboration and tried out upon the materials of observation. The question, in short, is not one of "abstraction" versus "reality" but of the value of Tocqueville's thesis in organizing and explaining American phenomena. Seldom is the careful reader left in doubt as to when the text is developing the logic of the type, when characterizing the American (or French) situation, when bringing the two things into single focus.

Tocqueville's conception of the "fatal circle" of human possibilities in democratic times—that is, his idea of democracy as a type of social system with necessary tendencies and limits—does not exclude the significance of accident and art in the determination of actual consequences. On the contrary, he insists upon the "wide verge" of the circle, within which history, place and rational invention exercise decisive influence. Thus with reference to the discussion of America, the basic democratic situation is the constant point of departure for an analysis always open to the play of contingent circumstance and reasoned choice.[8] Indeed, one may propose a novel criticism of the *Democracy:* that, beginning with a general conception of democracy, and then allowing for the unique varieties of American experience, it does not attempt a second integration of both elements. At most one finds a series of American themes, variously juxtaposed according to the subject of observation, all rather loosely related to a common point of departure in the framework theory.

Other familiar criticisms of Tocqueville as a guide to Jacksonian society are, I think, less serious. His manifest concern with French prospects in the midst of American life tends to sharpen, not confuse, the discussion, for he is led to distinguish American, French and universal-democratic elements in order to discover a prudent policy for France.[9] The further question of aristocratic bias has generally—and rightly—been resolved in Tocqueville's favor: beyond a rare capacity to enter sympathetically into another realm of values, he had the art of using deliberately the contrast between object and observer to reveal essential and determinative traits.[10] Finally, the rebuke to Tocqueville's gullibility—that he was taken in by tendentious conservative informants—has some truth and little consequence. The catologue of Tocqueville's "errors"—some of which are far from obviously wrong—refers primarily to chapters in the first volume constituting a kind of manual of American government for foreigners; refers, that is, to sections of the work which now hold least interest and value for the historian. The discussion of the "customs of the people"—"a central point in the range of observation, and the common termination of all by inquiries"—has errors and omissions, of course; but no critic, to my

[8] II, 334; see also I, 319–322. A fuller discussion will be found *infra,* pp. 56–59.
[9] See, e.g., I, 323–330.
[10] See, e.g., his candid airing of the problem, I, 252–253; II, 331–334.

knowledge, has traced these to a systematic American Whig bias.[11] It would be marvelous indeed to find Tocqueville's views flowing from informants who had given no sign of understanding them in the same way.

These preliminary remarks are not intended to absolve the *Democracy* of all faults, but simply to clear a way through certain general objections, toward a critical employment of an immensely valuable historical source. My object here shall be to take from Tocqueville a portrait of the democrat as American, beginning with a brief account of the basic democratic situation; then searching for the American-democratic synthesis as expressed in social character. I have called all of this a version of Tocqueville to emphasize the obvious fact that I have selected and re-ordered the contents of the *Democracy* to satisfy my own purpose.

THE DEMOCRATIC SITUATION

America is an illuminating case and not a realized blueprint of democratic development: a case uniquely valuable as the fully recorded experience of a nation born equal, tranquilly unfolding its original endowment, and now arrived at a measure of equality unknown to history. The great democratic revolution in the Western world, extending over seven centuries, has thrown America into its advance guard to explore, within a special history and place, varieties upon a providential theme: equality. Tocqueville's general analysis of democracy represents an effort to define the common social situation created by equality, through which accident and choice must operate.

Every page of Tocqueville, beginning with the first sentence of the Introduction, is an argument that equality of condition "is the fundamental fact from which all others seem to be derived"—at once the principle and the substance of the great seven-century social revolution.[12] Condition is, in this usage, the total social situation:

> Gradually the distinctions of rank are done away with; the barriers that once severed mankind are falling; property is divided, power is shared by many, the light of intelligence spreads, and the capacities of all classes tend towards equality. Society becomes democratic, and the empire of democracy is slowly and peaceably introduced into institutions and customs.[13]

The primary theoretical task for Tocqueville is to discover how equality, the primal active element, can constitute a social system, democracy.

---

[11] I, 322. Tocqueville defines "customs" to include "habits, opinions, usages, and beliefs," *ibid.* Or in a still broader formulation: "The moral and intellectual characteristics of men in society." I, 319 fn.

[12] I, 3.

[13] I, 9.

In searching out the social design of democracy, Tocqueville confronts the possibility that equality does not create a community at all, but the negation of community. Radical equality is a solvent of bonds: of tradition, hierarchy, authority, and every joint articulating contemporaries and generations. Viewed strictly, from the elevation of an ideal aristocracy, democracy would seem a state of bedlam, a vast aberration, with system only in the mode of its departure from the norms of human association. Approaching democracy from above and behind, Tocqueville in America, one feels, could never quite put down a sense of shock at what he saw: not a black void but a viable human condition with remarkable powers of expansion and persistence. It is as if a man removed the main supports of a massive structure and felt its terrible weight in his own hands: then withdrew and saw it still standing. Here I think Tocqueville's aristocratic values served him wonderfully, at first to find the essential contrast of the old and new condition; and then to force him to construct in theory a coherent order out of chaos.

In a dazzling passage Tocqueville sketches the primary response to leveled condition:

> Among democratic nations new families are constantly springing up, others are constantly falling away, and all that remain change their condition; the woof of time is every instant broken and the track of generations effaced. Those who went before are soon forgotten; of those who will come after, no one has any idea: the interest of man is confined to those in close propinquity to himself. As each class gradually approaches others and mingles with them, its members become undifferentiated and lose their class identity for each other. Aristocracy had made a chain of all the members of the community, from the peasant to the king; democracy breaks that chain and severs every link of it. . . .
>
> Thus not only does democracy make every man forget his ancestors, but it hides his descendants and separates his contemporaries from him; it throws him back forever upon himself alone and threatens in the end to confine him entirely within the solitude of his own heart.[14]

This is the original democratic chaos—"individualism"—from which Tocqueville derives the essential pattern of the new order. Men set apart upon a social plain confront their strength and then their weakness. To think and act alone breeds boundless independence. To doubt or fail in independence out of common human insufficiency compels submission to the only eminence equality permits, the equal brotherhood. The masterless of democratic times invent the only authority tolerable, even conceivable, in their condition: themselves *en masse*.[15] In the absence of counter-

[14] II, 99.
[15] I, 254–270; II, 8–12, 258–263, 316–321.

vailing influence extrinsic to the social structure, Tocqueville expects always to find democracy somewhere in the passage from an insupportable liberty-in-isolation toward an abject dependence on the majority. This logic of development cannot be reversed; at most its consequences can be modified, and then only by understanding the process, accepting its limits, and employing the peculiar means which it presents.[16] Thus the urgent call: "A new science of politics is needed for a new world." [17]

I do not wish to impose more rigor and completeness upon Tocqueville's ideal conception of the democratic situation than the author himself intended. The *Democracy* never pulls together a formal structure with all elements nicely integrated and all tendencies precisely specified. Perhaps it is misleading to apply the term "ideal type" to a broad characterization of a historical trend, used as a kind of wire master-key to understanding strange new things. At any rate my purpose here has been not to systematize Tocqueville's system—a major theoretical task in its own right—but to locate its central theme as an aid to recognition of the democrat as American.

American Departures

The *Democracy* is so full of paradox that the casual reader is moved to suspect the author either of a muddled head or of a willful eccentricity. Man in his pride, portrayed in burning primaries, gives way to man reduced to a gray mass; then reappears; then disappears again. There is no simple formula in Tocqueville for composing the antagonistic figures in a single frame; yet there are guides which bring the difference within the range of comprehension. The fundamental source of paradox lies in the double potentiality of the democratic situation: toward radical independence; toward submergence in the brotherhood. The most powerful and enduring tendency in "pure" democracy is the passage from the former toward the latter: toward a soft totalitarianism peopled by shapeless hollow men. If all the counterforces of accident and statecraft should converge, there could not be a second coming of the aristocratic virtues. Uniformity, conformity, mediocrity, and the rule of the felicific calculus are fixed returns of equalitarian society.[18]

And yet, within the democratic range, variety remains significant: the independence unloosed by killing off the gods of traditional society persists in varying degrees, in different spheres of social action, according to the reinforcements brought by history, place and the creative use of political means available to democratic leaders. Thus the American of the

---

[16] I, 418; II, 287–296, 316–321.
[17] I, 7.
[18] I, 252–253; II, 332–334.

Democracy is the compound product of the universal democratic situation and a unique national experience. If the fundamental fact of American history has been the quiet unfolding of an equalitarian society [19]—the basic democratic situation—there are lesser facts which, in aggregate, weigh heavily upon the outcome. A historical beginning in the modern era, under conditions of substantial equality and middle-class homogeneity, has meant in Tocqueville's view not only the quick and thorough elaboration of a democratic society, but a unique deliverance from social revolution and its special consequences—notably, class hatred and a strengthened state. The English-Puritan heritage transplanted to America carried the most advanced democratic elements of the old world, to shape the new exclusively along democratic lines; but, further, the heritage brought special gifts which altered importantly the course of democratic development: especially, the values of individual liberty, local freedom, and morality grounded in religious belief.[20] It is to me amazing that critics should suggest that Tocqueville neglected the English influence upon American life: "I think I see the destiny of America embodied in the first Puritan who landed on those shores. . . ."[21]

Historical influences count in giving American democracy a distinctive turn only as they are grounded in customs and institutions. Tocqueville credits America with several political inventions of critical importance for preserving its historical gifts: the most brilliant innovation, perhaps, the design of the dual federal system, with a wide distribution of administrative functions. The constitutional separation of church and state, the guarantee of private rights, and the assignment of important functions to the judiciary are further instances of a prudent statecraft, effecting the translation from historical possibility, through legal and institutional forms, into "habits of the heart" and mind which alter the consequences of the basic democratic situation.[22] And yet the greatest achievement of the American democracy in recasting its fate Tocqueville sees as an unintended process, a fortunate result of choices made with other ends in view. Returning to the fundamental analysis of the leveled society, contrasted with a model aristocracy, Tocqueville recalls the essential feature of nonarticulation, of shapelessness—"individualism" when expressed in terms of members' responses. Through local freedom, the broad extension of political rights, and a bold commitment to almost unlimited civil liberty, the Americans have fallen upon the chief expedient in democratic times for avoiding the new despotism: voluntary association. Ironically, the leading virtue of political democracy in America turns out to be the capacity to penetrate the citizen's isolation, join his self-interest to a wider

[19] I, 46–54.
[20] I, 26–29, 30–35, 43–44, 62–67, 290–291; II, 6–7, 101, 243–244, 256, 247–299.
[21] Bradley Introduction, p. xciv; I, 290.
[22] I, 244–247, 271–272, 280, 299, 300–314, 324–325.

group, and educate him in the decisive skills of organization; thus to fill the void between the weak individual and the overbearing mass with a buzzing congeries of private ("civil") associations.[23]

So history and art intervene to give variety to providence, and the look of paradox to Tocqueville's pages. The accidents of geography have less autonomous influence: Tocqueville anticipates the recent critics of Turner by asking why comparable conditions in South America, Canada and the United States have yielded such different national careers; and finds the answers in decisive differences of law and above all custom, introduced by variant historical beginnings.[24] The gift of space, rich resources and unmenaced borders has meant a free field for the fulfillment of the democratic revolution: specifically, a full provision for material equality; a wide margin for error; and elbow room for liberty.[25] In Tocqueville's phrase: "Nature herself favors the cause of the people." [26] The sheer abundance of the natural endowment—"a field for human effort far more extensive than any sum of labor that can be applied to work it" [27]—preserves the recessive tendency in democracy, toward independence. In a sense, the American environment perpetuates the democratic state of nature—the world of liberated equal isolates—by promising fabulous rewards to brave spirits: Brave *economic* spirits, one should add, excited by the material rewards which loom so large in the city of equality—not independent minds and characters.

Venturous Conservative

American departures work selectively upon the basic democratic situation to give a mixed, even a paradoxical, aspect to American society in Tocqueville's wide perspective. Here one could close the analysis with the judgment that the double potentiality in democracy—toward independence, toward dependence—made possible a certain interesting and in some respects hopeful variety in American life, which Tocqueville rendered in alternating images of equalitarian freedom and servitude. To use this handy exit would, I think, cost us some of the most powerful historical insights in the *Democracy*. Primarily, it would miss Tocqueville's most ambitious and—I think—most fruitful effort toward a concrete synthesis of American character; that is, his recurrent attempt to identify a patterned response to the American situation, in both its typical democratic and its unique American features. The phrase, "venturous conservative," is mine, and the assembled argument for using it as a central expression

[23] I, 191–198, 241–244, 248–252; II, 102–120.
[24] I, 319–323; see also pp. 316–317.
[25] I, 288–298.
[26] I, 291.
[27] I, 297.

for the antithetic elements in American character is mine again, derived from scattered interpretations in the text suggestive of a common theme.

"They love change," Tocqueville's provocative formula for the American democrat goes, "but they dread revolutions."[28] Thus:

> Two things are surprising in the United States: the mutability of the greater part of human actions, and the singular stability of certain principles. Men are in constant motion; the mind of man appears almost unmoved. . . . In the United States general principles in religion, philosophy, morality, and even politics do not vary, or at least are only modified by a hidden and often an imperceptible process; even the grossest prejudices are obliterated with incredible slowness amid the continual friction of men and things.[29]

In elucidating the distinction between change and revolution, in exploring the interplay of mutable actions and frozen principles, Tocqueville provides a brilliant lead for the understanding of Jacksonian Americans.

Speaking from his full elevation—the French aristocrat looking down upon a provincial soap opera—Tocqueville sometimes—rarely—dismisses his own problem with a noble yawn. What does all the shuffling of possessions, laws and notions amount to in the scale of dramatic high policy, philosophic heresy, great revolution?

> It is true that they [democracies] are subject to great and frequent vicissitudes, but as the same events of good or adverse fortune are continually recurring, only the name of the actors is changed, the piece is always the same. The aspect of American society is animated because men and things are always changing, but it is monotonous because all these changes are alike.[30]

But sympathy and curiosity force Tocqueville beyond pained boredom: the soap opera is man's fate, all of reality which can reasonably be expected to appear, and therefore a thing to be understood internally. Indeed, I would argue—and this is controversial—that Tocqueville often, in unguarded moments, forgot that he was conceding the world reluctantly to the providential dictum: the lesser good for the greatest number; and that he gaped and marveled at the American miracle—the continuous social explosion which contained itself, and prospered mightily.

The ultimate sources of American character are found in that radical equality of condition which makes men masterless and separate. Everything seems possible, nothing certain, and life short: the American "clutches everything, he holds nothing fast, but soon loosens his grasp to pursue fresh gratifications."[31] As traders the Americans overwhelm their

[28] II, 255.
[29] II, 257.
[30] II, 228–229.
[31] II, 136.

rivals with the audacity of French Revolutionary generals;[32] as workers they are never "more attached to one line of operation than to another" and have "no rooted habits."[33] Commercial business is "like a vast lottery."[34] Turner's famous sketches of a Westering people are almost watery beside the restless image in the *Democracy*, of a "continuous removal of the human race" without parallel since "those irruptions which caused the fall of the Roman Empire."[35] Thus:

> It would be difficult to describe the avidity with which the American rushes forward to secure this immense booty that fortune offers. . . . Before him lies a boundless continent, and he urges onward as if time pressed and he was afraid of finding no room for his exertions. . . . They early broke the ties that bound them to their natal earth, and they have contracted no fresh ones on their way. Emigration was at first necessary to them; and it soon becomes a sort of game of chance, which they pursue for the emotions it excites as much as for the gain it procures.[36]

All this rootless, anxious, driving quality Tocqueville invests in a panoramic view of American careers:

> In the United States a man builds a house in which to spend his old age, and he sells it before the roof is on; he plants a garden and lets it just as the trees are coming into bearing; he brings a field into tillage and leaves other men to gather the crops; he embraces a profession and gives it up; he settles in a place, which he soon afterwards leaves to carry his changeable longings elsewhere. If his private affairs leave him any leisure, he instantly plunges into the vortex of politics; and if at the end of a year of unremitting labor he finds he has a few days' vacation, his eager curiosity whirls him over the vast extent of the United States, and he will travel fifteen hundred miles in a few days to shake off his happiness. Death at length overtakes him, but it is before he is weary of his bootless chase of that complete felicity which forever escapes him.[37]

So far the social basis of American character, equality of condition, has been treated in a generalized way, as the unstructured social environment playing into a rich and spacious physical environment, giving to American life the qualities of "a game of chance, a revolutionary crisis, or a battle," and shaping the American as "a man of singular warmth in his desires, enterprising, fond of adventure and, above all, of novelty."[38] It is equally clear that restlessness, anxiety, insatiability are permanently embedded in

[32] I, 422–425.
[33] I, 425.
[34] II, 236.
[35] I, 293.
[36] I, 294–295.
[37] II, 136–137.
[38] I, 426.

an enterprising nature: Tocqueville's venturous American is no more the heroic Renaissance individual than he is a flexible Poor Richard, deriving his actions from his balance sheet. A grinding tension is inherent in that bold pursuit of a success which

> perpetually retires from before them, yet without hiding itself from their sight, and in retiring draws them on. At every moment they think they are about to grasp it; it escapes at every moment from their hold. They are near enough to see its charms, but too far off to enjoy them; and before they have fully tasted its delights, they die. . . .
>
> In democratic times enjoyments are more intense than in the ages of aristocracy, and the number of those who partake in them is vastly larger; but, on the other hand, it must be admitted that man's hopes and desires are oftener blasted, the soul is more stricken and perturbed, and care itself more keen.[39]

In America Tocqueville saw "the freest and most enlightened men placed in the happiest circumstances that the world affords; it seemed to me as if a cloud habitually hung upon their brow, and I thought them serious and almost sad, even in their pleasures."[40] Indeed, so central was this worried quality in American experience that Tocqueville suspected life "would have no relish for them if they were delivered from the anxieties which harass them."[41]

Perhaps it is already evident how Tocqueville will discover tameness in the marrow of the tiger. But the case will be clearer if first we trace the argument from condition to character along a more concrete line. All the previous references involve—what I have not stopped to specify—the pursuit of material success, the handling of material things. This is not, of course, accidental to Tocqueville's thesis. Most democratic energies, heightened by the extraordinary flux and freedom of American life, are channeled into one outlet: the direct pursuit of rank, privilege, honor, power, intellectual distinction has an aristocratic taint; money and goods alone are legitimate counters for the social competition of dissociated equals. The existence of competition is a given democratic fact: human energies must go somewhere in a society which does not prescribe fixed places and goals, which makes everything possible. But its intensity and direction are best understood from the conception of a social order in which men see first themselves and then a mass of almost-equals.[42]

In Tocqueville's penetrating analysis:

> Whatever efforts a people may make, they will never succeed in reducing all the conditions of society to a perfect level. . . . However democratic, then, the social state and the political constitution

[39] II, 138–139.
[40] II, 136.
[41] II, 222.
[42] II, 128–130, 136–139, 154–157, 228–229, 244–247.

of a people may be, it is certain that every member of the community will always find out several points about him which overlook his own position; and we may foresee that his looks will be doggedly fixed in that direction. When inequality of conditions is the common law of society, the most marked inequalities do not strike the eye; when everything is nearly on the same level, the slightest are marked enough to hurt it. Hence the desire of equality always becomes more insatiable in proportion as equality is more complete.[43]

Thus the intensity of democratic-American striving. The direction, already partially explained, can now be given fuller definition. A major component of social equality in America is the narrowed spread of property differences, with a heavy concentration in the middle range: the typical figures are "eager and apprehensive men of small property." "As they are still almost within the reach of poverty, they see its privations near at hand and dread them; between poverty and themselves there is nothing but a scanty fortune, upon which they immediately fix their apprehensions and their hopes." [44] The case is very similar for the democratic rich and poor: "When . . . the distinctions of ranks are obliterated and privileges are destroyed, when hereditary property is subdivided and education and freedom are widely diffused, the desire of acquiring the comforts of the world haunts the imagination of the poor, and the dread of losing them that of the rich." [45] In total effect, "The love of well-being has now become the predominant taste of the nation; the great current of human passions runs in that channel and sweeps everything along in its course." [46]

With the urgent, worried striving for indefinite material success Tocqueville finds a marked propensity toward industrial and commercial callings; that is, toward the most flexible pursuits which afford the quickest openings to large returns.[47] The seeming contradiction, in the heavy predominance of agricultural employment among Americans, Tocqueville resolves first by pointing to the rapid rate of growth in nonagricultural lines and, more effectively, by attaching a special meaning to American farming.

> Almost all the farmers of the United States combine some trade with agriculture; most of them make agriculture itself a trade. It seldom happens that an American farmer settles for good upon the land which he occupies; especially in the districts of the Far [i.e., Middle] West, he brings land into tillage in order to sell it again, and not to farm it: he builds a farmhouse on the speculation that, as the state of the country will soon be changed by the increase of population, a

[43] II, 138.
[44] II, 253.
[45] II, 129.
[46] II, 130.
[47] II, 154–157.

good price may be obtained for it. . . . Thus the Americans carry their businesslike qualities into agriculture, and their trading passions are displayed in that as in their other pursuits.[48]

Tocqueville does not hesitate to accept one of the sweeping consequences of his argument: that America is essentially a one-dimensional society, with a single basic life-style, a single character-type. Equality of condition, American-style, defines a common social situation and enforces a common pattern of response (along the lines sketched above). Examining the possibility of sectional variation, Tocqueville concludes that the American South alone has preserved a unique social universe, founded upon the glaring anomaly (within a democratic order) of Negro slavery —and even this difference must collapse eventually. The West is partially distinct in nature and effects, yet basically within the unitary pattern.[49] In a fascinating set of wilderness notes [50] (which some future editor of the *Democracy* ought to append to the text), Tocqueville wrote that he had indeed expected geography to count for more in America, and abandoned this among other "traveller's illusions" only in the face of strong evidence.

> In America, even more than in Europe, there is only one society. It may be either rich or poor, humble or brilliant, trading or agricultural; but it is composed everywhere of the same elements. The plane of a uniform civilization has passed over it. The man you left in New York you find again in almost impenetrable solitudes: same clothes, same attitude, same language, same habits, same pleasures. Nothing rustic, nothing naive, nothing which smells of the wilderness, nothing even resembling our [French] villages. . . . Those who inhabit these isolated places have arrived there since yesterday; they have come with the customs, the ideas, the needs of civilization. They only yield to savagery that which the imperious necessity of things exacts from them. . . .[51]

The most remarkable quality of the West, in short, is not its somewhat looser, rougher ways, but its capacity to reproduce almost from the moment of settlement the typical society and character of American democracy.[52]

At the center of this spinning turbulence Tocqueville exposes—what he scarcely expected his French readers to credit—the soul of an archconservative: the steady citizen, the meek thinker, the pillar of property and propriety. To deal convincingly with such a strange compound he calls upon all his explanatory resources in history, politics, sociology and psychology. His point is, not to distinguish differences and place them

[48] II, 157.
[49] I, 356–381, 392–395, 405.
[50] Quoted in George Pierson, *Tocqueville and Beaumont in America* (New York, 1938), pp. 231–284.
[51] *Ibid.*, pp. 236–237.
[52] I, 290–292, 297, 316–317.

separately upon plausible grounds, but to reconstruct a dynamic whole, a venturous conservative.

The men of the middle, preponderant in democratic times and uniquely so in America, are unquiet souls, whipped into motion by acquisitive hunger and then arrested by possessive fears.[53] When Tocqueville portrays such as the "natural enemies of violent commotions," [54] he has in mind no inert lump of a dozing bourgeois but a nervous striver whose apprehensions mount with his success. The democratic competitor, shifting his efforts fluidly toward the quick opening to relative economic success (as the key to all felicity), finds himself in the midst of a universal competition of equals. With all the parts of his universe (himself included) in erratic motion, with no fixed terminus and no secure resting place, the democrat develops an acute awareness of loss and failure. He is never the contented success; rarely the jealous miser; and typically the unrelenting acquisitor, casting a nervous backward glance at what he has already gained.[55] The economic radical—in terms of work-style—becomes in this sense the property-conservative: "between poverty and themselves there is nothing but a scanty fortune, upon which they immediately fix their apprehensions and their hopes." [56]

In the basic democratic situation, the strenuous pursuit of private welfare means the draining of vital concern from alternative engagements, notably with ideas and politics. There is simply a low minimum of attention available to revolutionary agitation.[57] This analysis has only a limited application to America, however, where free, democratic political institutions infuse the habits of freedom into almost the entire population: [58] "but if an American were condemned to confine his activity to his own affairs, he would be robbed of one half of his existence; he would feel an immense void in the life which he is accustomed to lead, and his wretchedness would be unbearable." [59] It is not, then, political apathy which tames the American; instead he shapes the quality of his political participation to correspond to and conserve his private-welfare interests.

An American attends to his private concerns as if he were alone in the world, and the next minute he gives himself up to the common welfare as if he had forgotten them. At one time he seems animated

[53] II, 252–253, 128–130.
[54] II, 252.
[55] II, 154–157, 244–248, 228–229, 136–139.
[56] II, 253. Even failure is not a clean-cut, ultimate catastrophe leading to emotional rejection of the economic system. The bankrupt has fallen in an equal competition, has a standing offer of new chances in new places, and so responds normally by renewing the struggle, abnormally by escape into insanity, almost never by overt rebelliousness. II, 139, 236.
[57] II, 253–255, 260.
[58] I, 249–252.
[59] I, 250.

by the most selfish cupidity; at another, by the most lively patriotism. The human heart cannot be thus divided. The inhabitants of the United States alternately display so strong and so similar a passion for their own welfare and for their freedom that it may be supposed that these passions are united and mingled in some part of their character. And indeed the Americans believe their freedom to be the best instrument and surest safeguard of their welfare; they are attached to the one by the other. They by no means think that they are not called upon to take a part in public affairs; they believe, on the contrary, that their chief business is to secure for themselves a government which will allow them to acquire the things they covet and which will not debar them from the peaceful enjoyment of those possessions which they have already acquired.[60]

With such passionate devotion to the gains he has and seeks, the venturous American creates within himself a counterforce to his furious energies: "They love change but they dread revolutions."[61] Under a régime of almost unlimited political and civil liberty, the American democrat is perhaps the safest citizen in the world. Yet this is not the full measure of American conservatism: "amid the continual friction of men and things," Tocqueville observes, "the mind of man appears almost unmoved."[62] Here his classic analysis of equalitarian conformity, scarcely modified by anything unique to the American situation, records the suicide of individuality unbounded.[63] If elsewhere Tocqueville emphasizes the "wide verge" of the "fatal circle" defined by a democratic social condition, it now becomes clear that accident and choice are critically significant only in one direction: the avoidance of political despotism (the total domination of "an immense and tutelary power"), mainly by releasing and focusing vast stores of private energy for the nonpolitical accomplishment of social tasks. Against the natural tendency of democracy to press minds into a dead uniformity Tocqueville's "new science of politics" uncovers no deep-rooted, viable restraints.[64]

The leveling of society, especially when accomplished through a violent revolutionary episode, initially unhinges all authority-relations. But the shock of leveled liberty puts an insupportable strain upon the democrat:[65] "A principle of authority must then always occur, under all circumstances, in some part or other of the moral and intellectual world."[66] The location is determined by the basic democratic situation:

[60] II, 142.
[61] II, 255.
[62] II, 257.
[63] See *supra*, pp. 55–56.
[64] II, 318, 332–333.
[65] II, 3–12.
[66] II, 9.

When the inhabitant of a democratic country compares himself individually with all those about him, he feels with pride that he is the equal of any one of them; but when he comes to survey the totality of his fellows and to place himself in contrast with so huge a body, he is instantly overwhelmed by the sense of his own insignificance and weakness. The same equality that renders him independent of each of his fellow citizens, taken severally, exposes him alone and unprotected to the influence of the greater number. The public, therefore, among a democratic people, has a singular power, which aristocratic nations cannot conceive; for it does not persuade others to its beliefs, but it imposes them and makes them permeate the thinking of everyone by a sort of enormous pressure of the mind of all upon the individual intelligence.[67]

Thus democrats—and Americans—turn toward public opinion as their source of moral and intellectual authority.[68] That a pervasive public opinion should exist in democratic society, to assume the functions of authority, is understood by Tocqueville as a simple consequence of equality:

Men who are equal in rights, in education, in fortune, or, to comprise all in one word, in their social condition, have necessarily wants, habits, and tastes that are hardly dissimilar. As they look at objects under the same aspect, their minds naturally tend to similar conclusions; and though each of them may deviate from his contemporaries and form opinions of his own, they will involuntarily and unconsciously concur in a certain number of received opinions. . . . The leading opinions of men become similar in proportion as their conditions assimilate: such appears to me to be the general and permanent law; the rest is casual and transient.[69]

The democratic heretic who seeks a public hearing must speak at once to all: he has a legal permit, but no special platform—no claim to the attention of a busily preoccupied crowd, no initial concession of confidence in private intellectual authority to build upon.[70] "He strains himself to rouse the indifferent and distracted multitude and finds at last that he is reduced to impotence, not because he is conquered, but because he is alone."[71]

[67] II, 10.
[68] I, 263–265.
[69] II, 258. See I, 303–307, II, 6, 10–11, 26–28, on the conservative reinforcement provided by religion, adapted to democratic circumstance and accepted "as a commonly received opinion."
[70] II, 258–263.
[71] II, 255.

In Summary [72]

The image of the democrat as American which I have assembled from Tocqueville's pages represents a most ambitious attempt to derive from the basic social situation of democracy (with local variations) a characteristic pattern of psychological response manifested broadly in the laws, customs, opinions, manners and life-style of Jacksonian Americans. Certainly the boldest, possibly the most revealing, feature of the portrait is the joining in dynamic tension of two major tendencies—toward independence, toward dependence. Tocqueville discovers the antithetic trends in the basic democratic situation, finds them in varying relations through every aspect of American life, and sees them exposed again in that duality of character which I have summed up in the phrase, "venturous conservative." Condensing drastically, I would suggest that Tocqueville sees the process shaping the venturous conservative in two related ways. A comprehensive social equality is the common point of departure. Along one line: a world of almost-equals, creates an anxious, urgent, flexible seeker of the next, most precious, most elusive increment of wealth and status; a seeker who, out of fear for his possessions and hope for his opportunities, becomes a firm property-conservative; and one who, from the depth of his material engagements, has little concern for radical revaluations of his moral universe. Along a second line: the masterless man, free to invent a fresh world, finds all the important value-answers—and many petty ones—given in familiar, comfortable form by his own self-image, magnified to authoritative dimensions—by the majority. In this direction little adventure survives; only a sort of surface confusion disguising a frozen mass of values.

Tocqueville's venturous conservative is a historical type, perceived in wide focus. The portrait is built out of Jacksonian materials, but composed primarily to elucidate the enduring family traits of the democrat, with special reference to the American branch. It would be foolish to expect from the *Democracy* a direct solution for detailed problems of Jacksonian history. As Tocqueville abstracted the democratic type from his Jacksonian observations, so I think one can profitably reverse the process, reviewing Jacksonian times in the light of Tocqueville's synthesis. One need not seek—what history so rarely yields—the neat confirmation of a rigorous hypothesis. It would be enough to gain some clues to the meaning of certain central actions and reactions.

Tocqueville does not himself make the connection between social situation, typical response, and the specific content of the Jacksonian political

---

[72] For an interpretation of Jacksonian Democracy, developing the theme suggested below, see Marvin Meyers, "The Jacksonian Persuasion," *American Quarterly*, V (Spring 1953), 3–15.

appeal. Yet it seems to me a highly plausible association. The American who was involved in the continuous re-creation of his social world, the continuous re-location of his place within it, became the anxious witness of his own audacity. The consequence, Tocqueville suggests, was the renewal of frenetic activity and, at the same time, a passionate attachment to property. A further response is evidenced, I would propose, by the effectiveness of the Jacksonian political appeal: to hard money, personal enterprise and credit, rural simplicity, and—broadly—to the pristine values of the Old Republic.

PART TWO

A National Economy Takes Shape

As THE change in ethical attitudes toward business—described in *Part One*—accelerated during the early national period, a commercial society gradually took form in America. This "commercial revolution" met less resistance and occurred at a faster pace here than in western Europe. By the time of President Andrew Jackson, the commercial tone of American society was well defined. A vital, even aggressive, economic individualism held sway almost everywhere, reflected not only in everyday business but also in the prevailing morality, law, and institutions of society.

In interpreting the dynamics of this period,[1] economic historians until recently have assumed that the role of government was secondary, passive, or permissive in character. Federal land and tariff policies and the failure in this period to establish permanent national control over banking have been characterized in this way. Relatively little attention has been given to state and local governments, whose economic policy was assumed to have had the same general character as national policy.[2] By the 1830's, however, almost all

[1] A very helpful bibliographical discussion of the recent writings on this period is contained in Carter Goodrich, "Recent Contributions to Economic History: The United States, 1789–1860," *Journal of Economic History*, XIX (March, 1959), 25–43. The same issue contains useful bibliographical essays on contributions to other periods of American economic history written since 1945.

[2] An article written as early as 1902 indicated very clearly that state government had played a major role in early American economic development. Guy S. Callender, "The Early Transportation and Banking Enterprises of States in Relation to the Growth of Corporations," *Quarterly Journal of Economics*, XVII (November, 1902), 111–162. However, Callender's promising interpretation was neglected for

171

adult (white) males could vote and hold office, and this political democracy became an important factor in speeding economic development. As the selections in this section illustrate, Americans insisted upon (in Tocqueville's words) "a government which will allow them to acquire the things they covet." Enormous popular pressure was exerted on politicians and government officials at all levels to survey and open new lands and to promote transportation facilities, so that individuals could acquire wealth. Such government actions lowered the cost of getting goods to market and raised land values, preventing the areas concerned from being left behind in the quest for profits.

Robert A. Lively, in *Selection Eleven*, presents a comprehensive analysis of the role played by government in American economic development prior to the Civil War. Although he raises interesting questions of historiography and needed research, he concludes from the research already completed that government at every level, federal, state, and local, actively promoted business enterprise and economic growth during this period. This research deals mainly with the developmental activities of state and local government, especially in the field of internal improvements but also in banking and the regulation of corporations. Many governmental units dug canals, built railroads, operated banks, and engaged in extensive regulatory and public-service activities. They often invested in "mixed enterprises" and subsidized private transportation projects. These governmental activities were designed to aid business enterprise and were welcomed without any agitation about *laissez-faire* principles. Lively states that "government everywhere undertook the role put on it by the people, that of planner, promoter, investor, and regulator." Furthermore, he suggests that this early "public support of business development" may be part of a grand continuity running from Alexander Hamilton's plans to the mixed economy of today.

One of the major contributors whose work is reviewed by Lively is Carter Goodrich, who devoted his presidential address to the Economic History Association in 1956 (*Selection Twelve*) to "American development policy" in the field of internal improve-

---

half a century. The great interest in research on this subject since the 1940's has undoubtedly been generated in good part by concern about the expanding role of government and the problems of economic development here and in other countries.

ments. Goodrich asserts that in this field "the aim was directly and unmistakably developmental and the amount and variety of governmental activity quite extraordinary." He assesses the uneven fulfillment of this developmental aim in public construction, financing, and other assistance of transportation projects throughout the nineteenth century. He suggests that "Government activity in internal improvements was in large measure a frontier phenomenon, a great instance of frontier collectivism." Furthermore, local rivalries, civic pride, and "boosterism" have always influenced government developmental activities. The resulting American experience is thus unique as regards the extensive reliance on local government and the voluntary efforts of civic groups. There is seeming paradox in Goodrich's conclusion that government promotion of internal improvements was strongly influenced by "the American traditions of individualism, of localism, and of the habit of voluntary association." [3]

However, state and local government had no monopoly on public aid to economic development during the early national period. Indeed, Forest G. Hill (*Selection Thirteen*) shows how the federal government in many varied ways actively promoted the growth of science, technology, and enterprise. National defense as well as economic development stood to benefit from a more rapid advance and diffusion of technical knowledge; and several federal agencies, both military and civil, were extensively drawn into these endeavors. [4] Among the agencies which played such a role were the Patent Office, the Coast Survey, the Smithsonian Institution, the Lighthouse Board, and the technical branches of the War and Navy Departments. Agency personnel were often engaged in the exploration of the West, surveys and engineering aid for transportation projects, the charting of bays and oceans, the acquiring of European technological knowledge, and the collection of information about the country's natural resources and weather. Hill concludes that "When these many activities bearing on the promotion and applica-

---

[3] See also Carter Goodrich, *Government Promotion of American Canals and Railroads, 1800–1890* (New York: Columbia University Press, 1960) as well as his numerous articles.

[4] Concerning early federal support of science, see A. Hunter Dupree, *Science in the Federal Government* (Cambridge, Mass.: The Belknap Press of Harvard University Press, 1957).

tion of science are put in perspective, it becomes clear that the government's early scientific endeavors were extremely important for territorial and industrial expansion." He also suggests that this early period provides "instructive parallels to the present day's close relationships of government and defense to science and private enterprise."

The "bank war," or destruction of the second Bank of the United States in the 1830's, generated great political controversy at the time and also much controversy of historical interpretation later. The first Bank of the United States had been chartered by Congress in 1791 for twenty years upon Hamilton's recommendation. It drew frequent charges of unconstitutionality, favoritism, and "money monopoly" and was not rechartered. The War of 1812 again demonstrated the need for such an institution, and in 1816 the second Bank was given a twenty-year charter. During the administration of Andrew Jackson, it became a highly controversial issue, attracting the same charges as its predecessor. Under the direction of Nicholas Biddle this "public bank" operated essentially as a central bank and also served as a depository for federal funds, issued bank notes, and carried on a large private banking business through its many branches. Arthur M. Schlesinger, Jr. asserts that the second Bank was far too powerful, that Jackson was right in opposing it, that Jackson and his political lieutenants opposed it because of their hard-money views, and that Jackson's victory in the "bank war" was due mainly to the support of eastern workingmen and intellectuals. Bray Hammond questions Schlesinger's interpretation.[5] In *Selection Fourteen* Hammond argues that the second Bank, under Biddle, performed well as a central bank, avoiding inflation by regulating the note issue and lending of other banks. Hammond says, "It was notorious that large and influential numbers of the private banks and official state banks resented this regulation of their lending power." In his view, these bankers seized upon the Jackson-Biddle fight to eliminate the Bank of the United States as both their regulator and their competitor in the expanding field of private

---

[5] Arthur M. Schlesinger, Jr., *The Age of Jackson* (Boston: Little, Brown and Co., 1945). For Hammond's very critical review article on this book, see Bray Hammond, "Public Policy and National Banks," *Journal of Economic History*, VI (May, 1946), 79–84.

banking. Although Jackson's "hard-money agrarians" delighted in the defeat of the Bank, in reality "they helped an acquisitive democracy take over the conservative system of bank credit introduced by Hamilton and by the merchants of New York and Philadelphia and limber it up to suit the popular wish to get rich quick." Whatever Jackson intended in crushing the second Bank, the result was a triumph for *laissez faire* and rugged individualism, plus many years of monetary troubles.

Although Hammond believes that Jackson's monetary actions and the bank war triggered "the Jacksonian inflation," the resulting panic of 1837, and the ensuing monetary troubles, other writers trace these financial difficulties to more basic economic forces. Jeffrey G. Williamson and George Macesich (*Selections Fifteen and Sixteen*) assign scant causal significance to the demise of the second Bank in their opposing analyses of monetary disturbances during the 1830's and 1840's. Instead, they emphasize—despite the differences in their analytical frameworks—changing levels of production, foreign trade, capital inflow, bank credit, and prices. The debate between Williamson and Macesich raises important methodological and analytical questions which economic historians often must face. On substantive grounds their interpretations differ greatly. Macesich attributes causal priority to external influences in the world capital market which controlled the flow of capital into the United States; then he focuses attention on the resulting internal adaptations in monetary conditions, price levels, and foreign trade balances. Williamson, in contrast, assigns a central causal role to changing rates of growth in domestic production in response to changes in foreign markets for American products. He believes that the rise and fall in the price and export earnings of cotton during the 1830's stimulated and then retarded the inflow of foreign capital for investment in transportation facilities and cotton production. These developments, in turn, caused major shifts in domestic levels of production, prices, incomes, and imports. In this manner alternating cotton booms produced "long swings" of economic growth prior to the Civil War.

Williamson draws extensively on the work of Douglass C. North.[6]

[6] See Douglass C. North, *The Economic Growth of the United States, 1790–1860* (Englewood Cliffs, N. J.: Prentice-Hall, Inc., 1961).

These authors emphasize that throughout the nineteenth century there was a fundamental interdependence among agricultural production for the market, transportation improvements, and urban-commercial development. This close interdependence necessarily limited as well as stimulated economic growth; whenever domestic production increased at a faster pace than foreign markets, especially British, the penalty was a reduced rate of domestic growth. In *Selection Seventeen* North explains how agricultural expansion along regional lines stimulated economic development. The South and the West had the natural endowment to produce export staples which were in demand outside the region, especially abroad. As a result, the output of cotton in the South and wheat and other foodstuffs in the West expanded rapidly, thereby encouraging many activities such as transportation improvements, trading and service enterprises, and the import of needed equipment. In his analysis, North emphasizes the differential responses of regions to these market stimuli. The West's agricultural growth prompted extensive diversification of production, growth of cities, and rise of new industries. However, the plantation system, specialization in one export staple, and unequal incomes prevented the South from benefiting extensively from its huge cotton trade.

Eugene D. Genovese (*Selection Eighteen*) stresses certain retardative effects of slavery on the South's economic development.[7] He asks, ". . . who could deny that slavery gave rise to a distinct politics, ideology, and pattern of social behavior and that these had immense economic consequences?" Yet his investigation is much more limited than this query would imply. Among the many influences of plantation slavery on economic growth, he selects one specific factor "which in itself provides an adequate explanation of the slave South's inability to industrialize: the retardation of the home market for both industrial and agricultural commodities." The South lacked a large urban market, and its rural population had low purchasing power. Regardless of its other problems, what industry the South had could not expand in the face of a thinly scattered demand; this condition alone discouraged urbanization and industrialization.

---

[7] For a different approach to this question, see Alfred H. Conrad and John R. Meyer, "The Economic Effects of Slavery in the Ante Bellum South," *Journal of Political Economy*, LXVI (April, 1958), 95–122.

Furthermore, Genovese notes, "An agrarianism uncompromisingly hostile to industry and urbanization—to what was called 'manufacturing as a system'—existed only in the South and can not be separated from the ideological leadership of the slaveholding planters."

John E. Sawyer (*Selection Nineteen*) finds that there was no such pervasive ideological barrier to industrialization in the Northeast. Instead, he concludes from his researches that many social and cultural conditions actively fostered the development of what soon came to be known as the "American system of manufacturing." Among these conditions were attitudes favorable to efficiency, specialization, ingenuity, mobility, entrepreneurship, and economic success. Sawyer finds that European observers in America were reporting in 1850 as well as in 1950 that "the new horizons and ways of working, organizing, and consuming were facilitated by the prevailing social framework"; these visitors of more than a hundred years ago "show no equivocation in assigning a very central place to the goals and values and structural characteristics of the American social order in explaining the distinctive manufacturing developments under review."

Several of the authors in this section compare or contrast the determinants and problems of economic growth in our early national period with those prevailing today in this country or in the developing nations. We were then beginning to industrialize, incurring rapid economic growth, struggling with problems of transportation and banking and capital shortage, and adapting our social values and institutions to the needs of economic development. In critical areas the role of government was often important, while market forces were at work in a powerful way. But government and market functioned in an environment of changing values and institutions in which *laissez faire* and individual initiative became increasingly dominant. The economic historian seeking determinants of economic development can find in American experience of the early nineteenth century very challenging materials for reinterpretation.

The Role of Government

11. The American System: A Review Article

Robert A. Lively

The role of government in the ante-bellum American economy has been boldly redefined in a score of books and articles published during the past decade.[1] Close analysis of state and local sponsorship of enterprise, initi-

[1] The following list of books and articles reviewed is arranged to serve as an index to specific data employed in the text. Review-style citation is utilized, where reference is to material in the subject literature. The several contributions of a single author are numbered to simplify identification of the work cited. E. C. Kirkland's study of New England railroads, G. R. Taylor's general history of the ante-bellum period, and G. S. Callender's seminal article are grouped with the works below so that they can be cited conveniently, but no effort is made to summarize their generally known contributions.

Earl S. Beard, "Local Aid to Railroads in Iowa," *Iowa Journal of History*, L (1952), 1–34.

John W. Cadman, Jr., *The Corporation in New Jersey. Business and Politics 1791–1875* (Cambridge, 1949).

Guy S. Callender, "The Early Transportation and Banking Enterprises of the States in Relation to the Growth of Corporations," *Quarterly Journal of Economics*, XVII (1902–1903), 111–62.

Carter Goodrich
1. "Public Spirit and American Improvements," *Proceedings of the American Philosophical Society*, XCII (1948), 305–9.
2. "National Planning of Internal Improvements," *Political Science Quarterly*, LXIII (1948), 16–44.
3. "The Virginia System of Mixed Enterprise. A Study of State Planning of Internal Improvements," *Political Science Quarterly*, LXIV (1949), 355–87.
4. "Local Planning of Internal Improvements," *Political Science Quarterly*, LXVI (1951), 411–45.
5. With Harvey H. Segal, "Baltimore's Aid to Railroads. A Study in the Municipal Planning of Internal Improvements," *Journal of Economic History*, XIII (1953), 2–35.
6. "The Revulsion Against Internal Improvements," *Journal of Economic History*, X (1950), 145–69.

Bray Hammond
1. "Banking in the Early West: Monopoly, Prohibition and Laissez Faire," *Journal of Economic History*, VIII (1948), 1–25.
2. "Jackson, Biddle, and the Bank of the United States," *Journal of Economic History*, VII (1947), 1–23.
3. "Free Banks and Corporations: The New York Free Banking Act of 1838," *Journal of Political Economy*, XLIV (1936), 184–209.

Oscar Handlin
1. "Laissez-Faire Thought in Massachusetts, 1790–1880," *Journal of Economic History*, III, *Supplement* (1943), 55–65.
2. With Mary Flug Handlin, "Origins of the American Business Corporation," *Journal of Economic History*, V (1945), 1–23.

"The American System: A Review Article," by Robert A. Lively, is reprinted by permission from *The Business History Review*, XXIX (March, 1955), 81–96. Copyright, 1955.

ated and supported by the Committee on Research in Economic History,[2] has suggested a thesis that appears to invite a new view of American capitalism in its formative years. Taken together, the works here reviewed form a consistent report of economic endeavor in an almost unfamiliar land. There, the elected public official replaced the individual enterpriser as the key figure in the release of capitalist energy; the public treasury, rather than private saving, became the major source of venture capital; and community purpose outweighed personal ambition in the selection of large goals for local economies. "Mixed" enterprise was the customary organization for important innovations, and government everywhere undertook the role put on it by the people, that of planner, promoter, investor, and regulator.

No scholar has yet attempted a general description of an America so dependent on its public authorities. The several authors who have conducted the recent surveys of little known state and local functions have carefully qualified their findings, and each has confined himself to a specific area or a selected problem in his restatement of the relation of government to enterprise. The most ambitious and inclusive accounts of positive state endeavors may be found in the articles and monographs of Louis Hartz, and Oscar and Mary Handlin. Concerned primarily with what the people wanted from their governments, rather than with what

---

3. With Mary Flug Handlin, *Commonwealth: A Study of the Role of Government in the American Economy, Massachusetts, 1774–1861* (New York, 1947).
Louis Hartz
    1. "Laissez Faire Thought in Pennsylvania, 1776–1860," *Journal of Economic History*, III, Supplement (1943), 66–77.
    2. *Economic Policy and Democratic Thought: Pennsylvania, 1776–1860* (Cambridge, 1948).
Milton S. Heath
    1. "Public Railroad Construction and the Development of Private Enterprise in the South before 1861," *Journal of Economic History*, X, Supplement (1950), 40–53.
    2. "Public Co-operation in Railroad Construction in the Southern United States to 1861" (unpublished Ph.D. dissertation, Harvard University, 1937).
    3. Laissez Faire in Georgia, 1732–1860," *Journal of Economic History*, III, Supplement (1943), 78–100.
Frederick K. Henrich, "The Development of American Laissez Faire. A General View of the Age of Washington," *Journal of Economic History*, III, Supplement (1943), 51–54.
Edward Chase Kirkland, *Men, Cities, and Transportation. A Study in New England History 1820–1900* (Cambridge, 1948).
Harry H. Pierce, *Railroads of New York. A Study of Government Aid, 1826–1875* (Cambridge, 1953).
James Neal Primm, *Economic Policy in the Development of a Western State. Missouri, 1820–1860* (Cambridge, 1954).
George Rogers Taylor, *The Transportation Revolution 1815–1860*, Vol. 4, *The Economic History of the United States* (New York, 1951).
  [2] Arthur H. Cole, "Committee on Research in Economic History. A Description of Its Purposes, Activities, and Organization," *Journal of Economic History*, XIII (1953), 79–87.

they got, Hartz and the Handlins were free to let their speculations carry them to extreme views. More limited but more impelling conclusions are presented in the works of Carter Goodrich and Milton Heath: their restraint lends force to their views of the carefully defined issues they analyze. Harry Pierce, John Cadman, James Neal Primm, Earl Beard, and others avoid bold generalizations, but add essential detail to the Goodrich-Heath story. These authors are united in their belief that the activities of state and local governments were of crucial importance in the stimulation of enterprise in the United States. Their variations on this theme are so numerous that the principal concern to which all return is surprisingly familiar. Their common specific task is the rescue of the internal improvements movement from the political historian, and the inflation of this issue as primary evidence for their new view of America's economic organization. In their report of the struggle of communities and states for control of inland produce or for access to markets, they document the emergence of a sturdy tradition of public responsibility for economic growth. The tradition as they describe it, persistent to the very end of the nineteenth century, was so extensively employed that it seems expanded in no theoretical respect by its modern uses in the Tennessee Valley or in the exploitation of atomic energy.

*   *   *

Recent notice of the age and respectability of this tradition began with attack on what Louis Hartz called the " 'laissez faire' cliche" that "has done much to distort the traditional analysis of our early democratic thought" (Hartz, 2, xi). Historians, according to Hartz and others, have compounded this distortion by concentration on national issues, and by excessive concern with limitations put by the Constitution or by jealous sections on the Federal government. The story obscured, meanwhile, has been that of the broad uses to which the ante-bellum states put the powers reserved to them in a Federal system. In three papers read to the 1943 meeting of the Economic History Association, Oscar Handlin, Hartz, and Milton Heath reported that the states of Massachusetts, Pennsylvania, and Georgia were in no way inhibited by laissez-faire notions. "In the realm of the practical," observed Handlin, "there never was a period in Massachusetts history when this conception was of the slightest consequence. From the very first organization of the Commonwealth in 1780, the state actively and vigorously engaged in all the economic affairs of the area, sometimes as participant, sometimes as regulator" (Handlin, 1, 55). Of Pennsylvania, Hartz later said that, "Far from being limited, the objectives of the state in the economic field were usually so broad that they were beyond its administrative power to achieve" (Hartz, 2, 292). Milton Heath concurred, though with variations, when he concluded that of Georgia "it may be said that during the early decades there developed no definite philosophies defending the exclusive validity of either individual or public action" (Heath, 3, 100).

King Laissez Faire, then, was according to these reports not only dead; the hallowed report of his reign had all been a mistake. The error was one of monumental proportions, a mixture of overlooked data, interested distortion, and persistent preconception. Scholars who tried to set the story right, moreover, found the void before them yawning constantly wider. Authors of the first major books addressed to the issue met with boldness and imagination the problem of guiding readers through a land from which theoretical signposts had been removed. Oscar and Mary Handlin, and Louis Hartz, who published their full-length studies of Massachusetts and Pennsylvania in 1947 and 1948, were engaged by hypotheses that outreached their evidence, but the shock effect of their works was a useful stimulant to fresh and original thought about the role of government in early state history. It now seems evident that the Handlins and Hartz, in their enthusiasm for the demolition of laissez-faire mythology, substituted new theories almost as unsatisfactory as the ones they so adequately undermined. They were victims, in a way, of the assumptions they discovered to be false when employed in description of the ante-bellum period. Instead of eliminating the laissez-faire theme from analysis of public policy, they merely changed its chronology. Each assumed general adherence to the philosophy *after* the mid-century point at which their studies ended; and with this presupposition they gave to their account of earlier alternative policies a tone more appropriate for description of antique curiosities than for revelation of continuing themes in American economic history. They wrote as though state sponsorship of economic development had been an all or nothing proposition, a point of view that obligated them to demonstrate the total collapse and failure of the schemes and visions they had discovered.

In this respect the Handlins' work was the more portentous: they were quick to admit that the "commonwealth" policies (their name for persisting elements of mercantilist theory and practice in Massachusetts) were doomed from the start. According to their theory Massachusetts emerged from the Revolution composed of many diverse interests, but polity in the state was dominated by the "fact that transcending the interests of all its constituents was the interest of society . . ." (Handlin, 3, 30). This "unity behind diversity" was to be expressed by a "government prominent in the direction and management of productive enterprise" (Handlin, 3, 261). Ambition for bold public endeavors, however, was cramped by a narrow public purse and popular fear of debt. The state therefore operated through the grant of privilege or the gift of incorporation to private groups. Rapid extension of these grants weakened the concept of common interest, and led inevitably to the growth of a body of private rights with which the government could not interfere. The state matched its original broad purpose with growing policy in only one area, that of humanitarian reform—or, as the Handlins would have it, in "police state" functions. Otherwise their analysis of policies from the Revolution to the Civil War reveals a story of shrinking public ambitions, of "transition from the Commonwealth to the police state, from mercantilism to liberalism . . ." (Handlin, 3, 262).

The Hartz analysis revealed that in Pennsylvania there was equally persistent faith in mercantilist theory; there, as in Massachusetts, the Revolution simply meant belief in the "need for utilizing that principle exclusively for colonial ends" (Hartz, 2, 6). Pennsylvania, however, implemented faith with a remarkable array of plans, controls, investments, and public works. Policies of the state affected "virtually every phase of business activity, were the constant preoccupation of politicians and entrepreneurs, and they evoked interest struggles of the first magnitude. Government assumed the job of shaping decisively the contours of economic life" (Hartz, 2, 289). Through its chartering policy it registered influential opinions on the character and shape of banking and transport enterprises, and then on an increasing variety of industrial developments. As investing partner of enterprisers, it placed public directors on the boards of over 150 "mixed" corporations by 1844. Further, by the sale of public lands, and by the investment of more than $100 million in the public works system, the state, in its "entrepreneurial function . . . assumed major proportions" (Hartz, 2, 290). Humane regulatory policy was equally extensive, from the abolition of slavery in 1785 to the limiting of child labor in the 1850's. The state, in fact, acquired such extensive responsibilities that its bureaucratic machinery broke down; a "stable and expert administrative system . . . did not develop" (Hartz, 2, 293). Administrative failure was compounded by sectional jealousies within the state; the public credit was critically threatened by the hard times of the late thirties and early forties; and in the end the theorists of public enterprise were driven from the field by their erstwhile partners, the private directors of mixed corporations. Confident, mature, and no longer dependent on the public treasury for their existence, the now "private" corporations clothed themselves in individualist theory, and launched with "messianic vigor" a successful assault on the whole theory of state participation in enterprise.

Unhappily for a critic in search of a documented hypothesis, the image of the positive state thus revealed in the Hartz and Handlin monographs is limited by the authors' intentions to the status of an engaging speculation rather than a demonstrated reality. The authors set out to describe what the people of Massachusetts and Pennsylvania conceived to be the role of their governments, rather than to outline government activity; and with this definition of their work as exercises in intellectual history, they very often relegated principal economic themes to the position of supporting detail. For the Handlins this approach permitted convenient and specific disavowal of any effort to "assess the effects of government action upon economic trends" (Handlin, 3, xii). Selection of the "commonwealth" theme permitted adequate proof for their belief that the state government was for many years expected to show formal interest in every public and private endeavor of material consequence—but from the evidence they present this concern was displayed without cash content or interested administration. Bemused with the curiosity about the Commonwealth pattern, they avoided analysis of substantial public aid to the emerging corporations whose legal form and rights they understand so well. Louis Hartz, on the other hand, was very much concerned with positive state policies, but only insofar as these policies would illustrate the half-century of debate that led on the eve of the Civil War to the emergence of a full-blown laissez-faire philosophy. Along the way he documented Pennsylvania's extraordinary excursions into state-sponsored transportation development, but the heart of his study lies not in what the state did, but in the story of how individual enterprisers and public planners alike lost control of both their theories and good works to the private corporations that supplanted them.

The Hartz-Handlin interpretation of the rise and decline of state ambition has not been adopted by students investigating related material. Scholars at work on similar themes have found that a smaller canvas and more thorough development of relevant detail brings them to conclusions quite different from those of the works just summarized. An effort to demonstrate the practice as well as the theory of state enterprise has required them to rely on more conclusive evidence than a summary of popular hopes and complaints; and they have found that achievements, as distinct from vague desires, were the products of somewhat more orthodox capitalist purpose.

The data repeatedly employed in analysis of state endeavors has been sought in study of public aids to railroads. No other public undertakings excited such extensive argument, nor attracted, in the end, so great a share of the public's capital. Careful review of causes and effects in the story of railroad aid became for Milton Heath and Carter Goodrich a means to general analysis of the role of government in ante-bellum economic development. Heath described in his 1937 Ph.D. dissertation the railroad building efforts of communities and states throughout the South. Goodrich, in six recently published articles, surveyed the hopes, methods, and achievements of officials directing government assistance at every level of public administration. Both men, writing as economists and students of planning, sought a contemporary relevance in the familiar story of "internal improvements." In the nineteenth-century American experience they hoped to find lessons that might prove useful to modern underdeveloped countries that are also faced with problems too great for the skill and capital of their private organizations. In applying the word "planning" to ante-bellum practices, they quite consciously gave the word its modern meaning—that is, the adoption by communities of "deliberate and concerted policies . . . designed to promote economic expansion or prosperity and in which positive action to provide favorable condtions for economic activity is emphasized more strongly than negative regulation or the correction of abuses" (Goodrich, 2, 16; Heath, 2, 1).

The end to which the planners aspired was neither the achievement of an all-embracing "commonwealth," after the Handlin definition, nor yet the creation of a permanent public stake in enterprise, according to the Hartz pattern. Rather, "public railroad promotion took on the character of positive planning for a freer private enterprise" (Heath, 1, 46; Goodrich, 3, 355). In the America they described there was no particular disposition to question the propriety of public enterprise, where private efforts proved inadequate to meet public needs. There was little positive preference, on the other hand, for public works as something inherently superior to private endeavors. States or localities undertook roles for which no other agency was fitted, and then waited for the time when the public might "conveniently exchange its position as proprietor for that of regulator" (Heath, 2, 43). Milton Heath's observations on the normal cycle of municipal investment revealed a chronology and a purpose that were repeated at each level of government operation:

> . . . the public function was viewed as an initial, developmental one. After enterprises became established on a profitable basis, city governments tended to transfer their investments to new projects, and so, normally, a transition from public or quasi-public to private ownership and operation took place (Heath, 1, 49).

Local and state governments assumed the "role of the primary entrepreneurs" as part of their normal functions (Heath, 1, 51). When public-spirited citizens met to discuss the need for projects of public utility, they turned naturally toward some variety of the public corporation as the agency best fitted for large efforts (Goodrich, 1, 307). The need for capital was the factor that most frequently determined government entry into the field of enterprise; only public authorities could command sufficient credit at a reasonable interest rate for works of the size demanded. Subordinate considerations were usually present, of course: glib promoters reached eagerly for public funds; hopeful administrators sought state investments so profitable that taxes could be reduced; and in a day when works of public utility were by definition regarded as monopolistic, a people suspicious of power generally were sure to insist that their governments guide these developments with a firm regulatory hand. But underlying every justification for state endeavor was the hope that by public effort businessmen of a locality would prosper, that land values would rise, and that the competitive position of the area would be improved. The whole business community was dependent on state execution of the general investment functions necessary to economic growth; it was by state endeavor that "idle resources could be brought into employment and the social income maximized" (Heath, 1, 47–48).

Discharge of these practical functions required state governments more active, if anything, than those that might have undertaken the theoretical responsibilities discussed by Hartz and the Handlins. The Goodrich and Heath hypothesis, moreover, enjoys the advantage of superior documentation by measurable facts—and contains, at the same time, a plausible explanation for most of the impulses described by the earlier reporters. Above all, the Goodrich-Heath theme is consistent with subsequent developments in the nation's economic history. After the states handed over their projects to private direction, the Federal government emerged as the chief sponsor of transcontinental enterprise, and local governments pledged their credit to the completion of the interlacing railroad net. The terms for these later grants of aid were substantially altered by the maturity and strength of the post-Civil War private corporation, but the established role of government was if anything enlarged.

✿   ✿   ✿

However varied the explanations for public sponsorship of enterprise, the facts supporting these stories can be summarized in one generalization: the movement was virtually unlimited both as to time and place. From Missouri to Maine, from the beginning to the end of the nineteenth century, governments were deeply involved in lending, borrowing, building, and regulating. Beyond this observation summary is difficult. Accurate measure of the public's stake in enterprise, for instance, cannot be taken from the evidence here reviewed. The statistics employed by the several authors are of an illustrative rather than a conclusive sort. Diligent in their analysis of the total figures involved in public investment, they have not undertaken similar analysis of the private contribution to mixed corporations. They show a tendency to rely on reported book values in their estimates of total construction costs, and they thus ignore both the enormous discounts involved in marketing stock to private groups, and the extensive practice by which "investors" offered overvalued construction services rather than cash for their share of developments.

Milton Heath's estimate of the cost of the Southern railroad net represents an unusual effort to take these latter factors into account. According to the Census of 1860, the cost of the South's 9,211-mile system had been $245,212,229. Of this approximate cost, the public had supplied 55 per cent through its official agencies. Further refinement of this estimate, however, suggests that private investment was so often in labor and kind that public authorities actually supplied about three-fourths of the cash

required (Heath, 2, 253). In contrast, Harry Pierce emphasizes the importance of state and local investment of $47,150,035.46 in New York's
railroads, but he sets total construction costs at $400,000,000, a figure left
uncriticized either as to type or time of investment (Pierce, 25, 5).

The bulk of references to the extent of public endeavors, however, are
presented without the foregoing bases of comparison. A review of the
statistics of state and local investment suggests how generally the movement was shared, and how great a burden governments undertook, but it
affords no decisive measure of the government role in contrast to that of
private investors. Even with their use thus qualified, the figures are
impressive. Pennsylvania was probably the most active, not so much for
her investment of $6,171,416 in 150-odd mixed corporations, but for her
expenditure of $101,611,234 on the construction and operation of the
Main Line canal and railroad system. New Jersey, on the other hand, was
one of the few states that stayed almost completely out of the movement
(Goodrich, 3, 357; Cadman, passim.). In New England, Massachusetts,
the only notable state investor, put $8,200,000 in eight railroads by 1860;
and she had just begun the celebrated Hoosac Tunnel Project, in which
she was to invest $28,856,396 by the turn of the century (Kirkland, I, 324,
432). To the West, Missouri had pledged $23,101,000 to improvements by
1860, a sum estimated by James Neal Primm at 25 times the state's
average annual income (Primm, 105). These undertakings of the late
forties and the fifties have hitherto been obscured by the familiar story of
panic and retrenchment in states throughout the Union after 1837–1839.

The most impressive revelation in the detailed analysis of the improvement program is the degree to which local governments maintained and
extended the responsibilities relinquished by many states on the eve of
the Civil War. The local aid movement, authorized by 2,200 laws in 36
states, appears to have dwarfed better-known state endeavors (Goodrich,
4, 412–23). The bulk of local aid, further, was given after the Civil War;
enterprise demanded and received vital support from public treasuries so
long as there was a mile of American railroad track to be laid. In Maine,
for instance, the legislative delegation of Aroostook County was electing
public members of the Bangor and Aroostook's Board of Directors in the
1890's, and thus defending the County's new $728,000 stake in the road's
future (Kirkland, I, 491).

Harry H. Pierce, in his outstanding study of the railroads of New York,
1826–1875, has taken the only satisfactory measure of the local aid movement. In an account drawn from scattered town records, railroad books
and correspondence, legislative records, and court reports, Pierce found
that 315 of New York's municipalities pledged $36,841,390.69 toward the
construction of the state's roads. The conclusions he drew from study of
hundreds of specific projects are arresting:

. . . the importance of these subsidies lies not in their amount but in their timeliness. In practically every instance the aid was proffered at a critical moment in the company's history. It is significant that, with the exception of the city of Albany, neither the state nor any municipality ever assisted a railroad that was already in operation. Public money in New York always pioneered the way. It took the initial risk. . . . Government aid to railroads not only facilitated the raising of money, but also greatly reduced the cost of financing them. In many cases, particularly in the building of marginal lines, public subsidies made possible the construction of roads that would not otherwise have been built. In an even greater number of instances, it permitted the completion of projects at a much earlier date than would have been possible with private capital alone (Pierce, 25).

Other students agree that local aids were very considerable, but some assert that they were given when public subsidies were of diminishing importance (Goodrich, 4, 435). E. C. Kirkland, for instance, reveals in a few pages the mixed views with which the postwar grants have been described. He concludes that New England communities were "so extravagant and so generous that the pre-war years in comparison were but a diminutive forerunner." By reference to the total capitalization of the roads, however, he minimizes the effect of the new public investments. Although Connecticut towns subscribed 60 per cent of the new railroad securities issued in the state between 1868 and 1877, the town percentage of total capitalization in 1877 "was only nine." In his general summary of New England efforts, on the other hand, he appears to credit the aids with more decisive effect; no other policy, he reports, "public or private, produced so many useless railroads" (Kirkland, II, 309–16).

Local efforts were extensive throughout the Union. Louis Hartz concluded that in Pennsylvania, state investment was at its height "of minor significance compared with investments by cities and counties" (Hartz, 2, 86). Ante-bellum southern cities and counties contributed $45,625,512.05 out of total southern aids of $144,148,684.92 (Heath, 1, 41). James Neal Primm concluded that most of the stock "sold" in the 1850's by the state-aided railroads of Missouri was sold to the municipalities and counties through which the roads would pass (Primm, 106). The major undertakings of Baltimore are well-known; the city invested about $20 million in railroad development between 1827 and 1886 (Goodrich & Segal, 5, 2). The indications are that cities and counties to the west were increasingly lavish in their grants as the years passed. Cincinnati exceeded Baltimore in expenditures on her municipally owned road; the city of Milwaukee, with a population of 45,246 in 1860, lent $1,614,000 in 1858. Earl Beard's recent analysis of local aid in Iowa reports as an "educated guess" a total of $50 million spent there by the 1890's (Beard, 32). More than adequate figures are at hand, it seems, to support the recent conclusion by Carter Goodrich that the generally employed estimates on the extent of public aid published in 1938 by the Federal Coordinator of Transportation are far too low[3] (Goodrich, 4, 430).

*   *   *

Detailed analysis of railroad development has not been duplicated in studies of state promotion in other fields. In the four states for which general policy has been described—Massachusetts, Pennsylvania, Georgia, and Missouri—the passage rather than the administration of promotional laws has been offered as evidence of state achievement. Grant of the privilege of incorporation, with attendant alienation of certain public powers, is perhaps the only other major concern subjected to careful definition. There were laws on every conceivable subject, but without an account of enforcement machinery there is no means by which their effect can be judged.

Massachusetts, for instance, used licensing laws to grant monopoly privileges to selected entrepreneurs; the pioneer glass manufacturers of the state were promised years of freedom from competition (Handlin, 3, 81–82). Bounties were given quite freely by several states, particularly to agriculture. Maine paid out $150,000 in the year 1839 alone to wheat and corn producers; nine states subsidized silk culture (Taylor, 380); and Massachusetts aided fisheries and naval stores production (Handlin, 3, 83–84). Tax exemptions and relief of workers from poll taxes or from militia and jury duty were other means by which industries in certain states were encouraged. Pennsylvania was active for a number of years after the Revolution in fixing prices for certain goods and services (Hartz, 2, 206). Many states encouraged quality production by inspection laws, affecting in particular goods consigned to interstate commerce. Georgia maintained 30 public warehouses for the grading and marketing of tobacco by 1800 (Heath, 3, 85); and Missouri inspected virtually all tobacco exported after she constructed a $25,000 tobacco warehouse at St. Louis in 1843 (Primm, 118). Stay laws, relief laws, and public loan offices were familiar phenomena after the Panic of 1819.

The authors cited have skirted warily around one type of major undertaking comparable in scope to the internal improvements effort. Enterprise throughout the union depended heavily on the credit provided by the investment of state capital in banking operations. Recent reappraisals of the operations of the Second Bank of the United States, however, have not been followed by more than casual summaries of the way in which states put their resources behind public or mixed banking systems. A series of articles by Bray Hammond has swept away some of the my-

[3] Federal Coordinator of Transportation, *Public Aids to Transportation*, I (Washington, 1938), 18–19.

thology surrounding these state adventures, but effort to give the movement a proper place in the general story of state enterprise has been
limited (Hammond, 1, 2, 3). No one, for instance, has developed the
challenging conclusion offered by Guy S. Callender more than 50 years
ago, to the effect that the southwestern states, in their large-scale grants of
credit to commercial agriculture, maintained responsibilities comparable
to the canal and railroad building efforts of the middle states (Callender,
161–62). The amount of money invested has usually been estimated, and
banking as a political issue described, but the day-to-day operations and
achievements of partially or wholly owned state systems remain a field for
research demanding all the support now promised by the Committee on
Research in Economic History.

   Opinions expressed casually about forces apart from central themes
developed in the subject literature seem in some cases more important
than specific illustrations of state enterprise. The role of private capital,
suggested in scarcely more than parenthetical references, is quite anoma-
lous. The authors take repeated note of the "unwillingness of private
investors to risk their money in railroad securities . . ." (Pierce, 4).
Initiative in new adventures was left to the state, partly because of the
general inadequacy of private investment funds (Heath, 1, 47–48), but
just as often because individuals seeking profit are pictured as cautious to
the point of timidity. Even where such a financial community as New
York made available more than adequate liquid capital, the spirit of
caution prevailed. William H. Aspinwall, John V. L. Pruyn, Edwin D.
Morgan, Cornelius Vanderbilt, and Russell Sage moved in to form the
New York Central after communities had taken the initial risks, and not
before (Pierce, 10). Further, the movement of the substantial private
capital that was invested before 1860 is ascribed to community spirit
rather than to the hope of gain (Heath, 1, 44–46). Merchants of Baltimore, Charleston, or Savannah sponsored connections with the interior as
a program of "metropolitan mercantilism" that would benefit them in a
general rather than a particular way. Similarly, the farmers of Wisconsin
had not turned speculators when, between 1850 and 1857, they gave
nearly $5,000,000 in mortgage notes to railroad builders; they were invest-
ing in regional prosperity (Taylor, 98).

   These opinions are disquieting in view of the current interest in "entrepreneurial" history. The reviewer is certain that the right hand of the
Committee on Research in Economic History knows what its left hand is
doing, but there is little evidence to prove it. For instance, in the most
important recent contribution from the entrepreneurial school, Thomas C.
Cochran's *Railroad Leaders, 1845–1890*, the author takes only incidental
and inconclusive notice of public aids other than land grants.[4] This iso-

---

[4] Thomas C. Cochran, *Railroad Leaders 1845–1890. The Business Mind in Action*
(Cambridge, 1953), pp. 17–18, 96–98, 184, 189–94, 200–1.

lation of individual endeavours from public efforts seems all the more curious in view of the fact that the Goodrich-Health hypothesis describes an American System in which state and private initiative are fully compatible. Continued separation of the themes prevents desirable refinement of both. Greater offenders in this regard are the authors reviewed here whose exclusive concern with public aspects of the mixed corporation permits them to avoid analysis of its private parts. The corporate agency for community action was so mixed an instrument that neither description from the point of view of the state nor analysis from the position of the entrepreneur can alone give a proper view of its growth. Public efforts to employ corporations for social ends deserve their overdue notice, but private contributions remain matters of consequence.

As an early American institution, to be sure, the corporation was a public school for enterprise. Its graduates were never very loyal, but they were no less obligated to it for their experience with major engineering projects, their knowledge of managerial problems, and their skill at gathering and handling large capital. Its modern "private" form was a very late achievement:

> The attributes of peculiar economic efficiency, of limited liability, and of perpetual freedom from state interference were . . . not present at the birth of the American business corporation. Divested of these characteristics, the form assumes a new significance. At its origin in Massachusetts the corporation was conceived as an agency of the government, endowed with public attributes, exclusive privileges, and political power, and designed to serve a social function for the State. Turnpikes, not trade, banks, not land speculation, were its province because the community, not the enterprising capitalists, marked out its sphere of activity (Handlin, 2, 22).

In Pennsylvania, of 2,333 business corporations chartered by special act, 1790–1860, 64.17 per cent were in the field of transport, 7.2 per cent in banking, 11.14 per cent in insurance, 7.72 per cent for manufacturing, 2.79 per cent for water, 3.21 per cent for gas, and 3.77 per cent in miscellaneous categories—the form, in other words, was predominantly employed for works of public utility (Hartz, 2, 38). Society, in creating agents to perform social services, attempted through the several states to keep a firm hand both on the evolving corporate agents, and on the quality of the services the agents rendered. At the very least cities and states attempted to protect their investments in transportation companies, and at most they attempted to harness and direct growing corporate power. Both the minimum and maximum attempts were on the whole failures. In the end, society sought the measure of its achievement in the intangibles of community growth and prosperity; there were no other measures, for communities lost their money and they lost control of their corporations.

The state struggle to maintain controls, however, left the issue in doubt for a very long time. In the first place the chartering power was maintained until after the Civil War as a means of potential corporate regulation. The Dartmouth College Doctrine did not break legislative power over the state's creations; it only invited more careful charter limitations (Cadman, 426, 429; Hartz, 2, 236–52; Primm, 35–52). Corporate charters included detailed specifications on the size and power of directorates, the liability of stockholders and officers, the nature of capital structures, and on the details of the operations the organizations might attempt. Regulation of corporate services was generally undertaken. Banks were restricted to collection of interest rates specified in charters, and were often required to reserve a certain part of their loans for named classes. Dividends were controlled by law, especially when specie payments had been suspended (Hartz, 2, 258; Primm, 26–28). Public utilities were subjected to rate regulation, to requirements that certain customers get preferential treatment, and to the maintenance of minimum service schedules (Hartz, 2, 258–60). Illustration of the extent of detailed control might be expanded indefinitely for there were almost as many specific regulations as there were charters.

Effective administration of these laws proved possible only when the regulating authority worked toward reasonably defined and sensibly limited ends. Pennsylvania, equipped with the most ambitious regulatory program, failed in almost all her objectives. The reporting system by which the state's auditor-general kept in touch with state investments broke down completely; state officials responsible for public shares in mixed corporations were assigned more duties than they could identify, much less discharge; and legislative investigating committees proved to be clumsy and inadequate instruments of control (Hartz, 2, 96–103, 262–67). In Virginia, on the other hand, an excellent reporting system was maintained. The Virginia Board of Public Works avoided detailed problems in the administration of mixed corporations, and concentrated on the protection of the state's financial interests, and on the provision of expert engineering services to enterprise. Even when the board controlled a majority interest in a project, it left to private hands the detailed responsibilities of management (Goodrich, 3, 378–83). In Maryland, where the state and the City of Baltimore selected a majority of the B & O directors until 1867, a similarly effective review of financial and engineering detail was maintained. Baltimore treated the road as a public institution as long as the city had a stake in it; the City Council was seeking wage raises for B & O employees as late as 1880 (Goodrich & Segal, 5, 27).

The nature of the alliance between politics and trade cannot be revealed by facts drawn only from the records of public authorities. For one thing, public directors in mixed corporations were often private stockholders in their own right: the Virginia Board, in fact, required such a display of "interest" by its agents after 1847 (Goodrich, 3, 378–9). The distinction between politician and entrepreneur was consistently vague; three mayors of Baltimore, for instance, served as presidents of railroads aided by the city. John W. Barrett, president of the B & O from 1858 to 1884, was not master of his railroad until he was master of the state of Maryland. He continued then to welcome public subscriptions to the road's development, but he preferred control to remain in private hands (Goodrich & Segal, 5, 19–20, 28–32). Harry Pierce's analysis of the battle between capitalists of Albany and Troy, New York, for control of the western trade, reveals the difficulty of judging such public endeavors as Troy's municipally owned road in the narrow context of either "public" or "private" enterprise (Pierce, 60–81).

Analysis of the intimate association of public and private officials has for the most part been avoided by the authors considered; they have tended to concentrate instead on themes demonstrating a sharp division between public and private interests. In particular they have emphasized the persistent anticorporate spirit evident throughout the nation until deep into the nineteenth century. Abundant evidence has been resurrected to demonstrate popular expression of traditional hostility to concentrated power, to the grant of privilege and monopoly, and to the mysterious or dishonest manipulations by which irresponsible corporate managers maintained themselves. Small businessmen and conservative investors feared corporations, and the public often felt misused by them. These sentiments, however, appear not to have controlled state policies; chartering programs were constantly expanded, and the form was made available to every type of business. The most distinct policy change related to the anticorporate spirit was the frequent adoption of general incorporation laws. Studies of the general incorporation movement in Massachusetts, New Jersey, Pennsylvania, and Missouri, however, reveal it to be something other than a Jacksonian extension of privilege to all comers. For enterprisers, general laws in these states were rigid and unwelcome rules written by men who wanted to restrict corporate power and growth. They were not employed by businessmen, who continued to seek and get the special charters given freely until after the Civil War. Even the Democrats, who tended to be authors of the laws, seemed to be satisfying emotional needs rather than executing serious policy; they passed general laws, and then continued in the same sessions to grant special privileges on request (Handlin, 3, 233–5; Cadman, 431–8; Hartz, 2, 38–42; Primm, 54–62).

While communities indulged their anticorporate emotions, they continued to charter, regulate, and subsidize in their search for necessary social services. The retreat from public investment came only after the railroads had been built, and usually under the pressure of major economic crises. Increasingly, though, the regulatory effort was designed for the protection of public funds, rather than for the direction of corporate behavior. Massachusetts, in fact, demonstrated no other purpose from the start (Kirkland, I, 325). State activity declined sharply in the early 1840's, and then revived for a briefer season in the 1850's. The local aid movement reached its climax after the Civil War, before the substantial reaction of the 1870's (Goodrich, 6, 145–52). The retreat from aid by the cities was accompanied by widespread effort to dishonor municipal bonds; communities were without scruple in their efforts to repudiate debts blamed on dishonest promoters, incapable builders, and venal public officials (Pierce, 84–86; Goodrich, 6, 152–5; Beard, 16).

The retreat was not universal, and the sense of having been cheated was not generally shared. Bangor and Baltimore continued to subsidize, and in the southern states the Civil War only delayed for a season the Reconstruction climax of state aid. The financial record of the southern states had been good, the roads well built, and the hope of public profit reasonable (Health, 2, 250–2). Communities, moreover, had never staked their hopes on business balance sheets. Only one city in 25 made a profit from railroad investments in New York, but 85 per cent of the cities subsidizing got the improved transport for which they had worked. Public losses were probably no greater than those of early private investors, and the communities had more to show for their effort (Pierce, 127). Massachusetts suffered a $9,500,000 loss on her $28,856,396 Hoosac Tunnel expenditures; profits went to the "tunnel ring" in the northwestern part of the state. But early in the twentieth century 60 per cent of Boston's exports flowed east through the "great bore" of Massachusetts politics, and all New England depended heavily on this gateway to the West (Kirkland, I, 430–2). In Virginia a committee of the Senate, balancing profit and loss on the ante-bellum effort, concluded in 1876 that state investments had been justified by the increased wealth of the whole area served (Goodrich, 3, 387). The state-owned and operated Western and Atlantic Railroad of Georgia was not only the first railroad to penetrate the Appalachian Chain; the road won for the state control of western imports into the eastern cotton belt. Georgia, whose public planners share with the builders of the Erie Canal the greatest reputations in the improvements field, has long been recognized as the executor of a "master-stroke in railway policy." [5]

＊   ＊   ＊

Conclusions invited by summary of the 25 books and articles digested in the preceding pages tend to take the form of questions rather than assertions. The significance of the literature reviewed cannot be established until the themes suggested are tested in a more general synthesis than has been attempted by any of the authors referred to here. At present

[5] Ulrich Bonnell Phillips, *A History of Transportation in the East Cotton Belt to 1860* (New York, 1913), p. 334.

the works present an extended and more exact analysis of the spirit, policies, and achievements of the internal improvements era. This much is clear gain. The considerable influence of the newly reported theory and detail is measured by the prominence accorded government as sponsor of enterprise by George Rogers Taylor in the most recent volume of the Rinehart *Economic History of the United States.* But the most basic reappraisal of the internal improvements movement can scarcely be regarded as "new" in any bold sense; the subject is too much a staple of American economic history, and has for too long been a principal retreat for Ph.D. students seeking thesis topics. Also, more than 50 years have passed since Guy S. Callender contributed a brilliant explanation for state accumulation of $200,000,000 in capital for investment in ante-bellum industrial development, and if two more generations pass before the current version of the Callender thesis is further refined, then the recent burst of scholarly energy may not seem very significant.

One can hope for alternative developments. Taken together, the works reviewed now end on a tentative note, and leave unresolved some of the more fundamental questions they raise. Studies of the theory and practice of local aid, for instance, reveal no changes in the public mind that justify continued use of the Civil War as a convenient point to close off the story of government activity. The absence of the Federal government from the new literature is inexplicable, particularly during the 1860's and 1870's, when Washington assumed for the states so many of their services to enterprise. A fresh approach to Federal sponsorship of economic growth, undertaken in knowledge of the traditions that descended to national officers from the era of state aid, might give a new look to Radical Republican policy. The decade of monetary reform, tariff revolution, and resource alienation has been so rudely handled in the liberal historical tradition that the postwar era is remembered for corrupt deviations, rather than as a time for logical extension of established public procedures. Yet the story of public risk-taking and private profit-making does not appear to have been altered very much by transfer of the issues to the Federal sphere. The Goodrich-Heath explanations and chronology for government intervention and withdrawal might add as much meaning to Federal policy as they did to the lesser efforts by states and cities. A further test of the thesis certainly seems merited; controversies on the role of government seem almost interchangeable as the decades pass. The same angry words echo out of debates in widely separated eras, whether the subject is the delivery of monopoly powers to the Camden and Amboy, the sale of the Main Line System to the Pennsylvania Railroad, the alienation of the trans-Mississippi West, or, for that matter, the negotiation of the Dixon-Yates Contract. Perhaps historians, in their dismay at certain memories they report, have too long delayed resignation before a persistent theme in the nation's economic development—the incorrigible willingness of American public officials to seek the public good through private negotiations.

The detail of these negotiations should be pursued with infinite care. No one has undertaken extended or precise description of the way public and private obligations were combined by officers and public guardians of ante-bellum mixed corporations. Their compromise of sometimes contradictory duties, nonetheless, established ruling conventions for postwar economic organization. The mixed railroad corporation was not only parent to "big" business in the United States; its leaders also defined the character of business-government relationships, the duties of corporation to public, and the responsibility of manager to investor. Customary procedures and standards of behavior for managers of the modern corporation were thus conceived in ideological twilight, and had become habitual before the individual entrepreneur achieved a firm grip on the corporate form. Perhaps from the divided loyalties of the public-spirited men who planned so boldly for early community growth there emerged the ethical confusion characteristic of subsequent corporate behavior. Speculation on this point needs support from more abundant and specific fact than is yet available from the era of the mixed corporation.

To studies of the continuing association of government and enterprise should be added the equally unbroken theme of state regulatory efforts. The hiatus between stories of state control policies before and after the war becomes increasingly hard to justify, particularly after recent indictment of the view that "Granger" laws were the product of agrarian discontent.[6] Just as individual enterprisers of the forties and fifties had joined in unsuccessful efforts to reduce corporate power, so, in the sixties and seventies, merchants and shippers maintained and strengthened control mechanisms. The considerable complexity of the postwar laws may possibly reflect long years of uninterrupted experience and concern with protection of the public interest. The only major break in regulatory policy appears to lie in the uneven assumption by the Federal government of earlier state responsibilities. Even at Washington, state patterns were repeated; controls, whatever the level of government, tended to lag about a generation behind aids.

The substantial energies of government, though, were employed more often for help than for hindrance to enterprise. The broad and well-documented theme reviewed here is that of public support for business development. Official vision and public resources have been associated so regularly with private skill and individual desire that the combination may be said to constitute a principal determinant of American economic growth. Internal improvements dominated the association in ante-bellum years, but opportunities for broader use of the alliance multiplied as

[6] George H. Miller, "Origins of the Iowa Granger Law," *Mississippi Valley Historical Review*, XL (1954), 657–80.

controls over the economy became more centralized. Resolute Federal decision was in time revealed to be a key to remarkable productive achievement, most notably during the wars of the twentieth century. States and cities meanwhile transformed their record of debt from millions to billions as they constructed the nation's highways and public buildings, and extended their public services; B. U. Ratchford's analysis of American state debts might serve as an outline for a score of theses on the influence of Keynesian experiments, before Keynes. Rising constantly from the impulse to public-spirited undertakings, moreover, was the neomercantilism of regions and provinces of the American economy which came to replace the earlier and simpler competition of cities and states. Commercial clubs in the cities, industrial commissions in the states, and governors' conferences in the regions all joined in sponsorship of industrial expansion.[7] The story sprawls out to ungovernable proportions, to tax exemptions, police-guaranteed labor discipline, municipal power-plant construction, and on to RFC, TVA, and AEC. Even communities in Mississippi, the very oldest and deepest of the southern states, have in the past 14 years spent $29,206,000 in the construction of free factories for 92 enterprises who have agreed to locate there. From the grass roots putting up shoots before Chamber of Commerce buildings to the Office of the President's Council of Economic Advisors there can be documented the unceasing pressure for public sponsorship of economic growth.

Milton Heath, in the earliest contribution to the literature here considered, described the public aid movement of ante-bellum years as possibly the "last great associative effort on American soil" (Heath, 2, 60). In this judgment he was probably as wrong as other authors who have analyzed the internal improvements effort as something unique in the American experience. The distant historical phenomenon they report proves very close at hand. Instead of the last great associative effort, they have revealed theory and practice for the first of continuing efforts to associate the massive powers of government with the skill of enterprise. Historians have been unaccountably slow in seeking the general themes of this story; they catalogue the plans of a Hamilton, a Gallatin, or a Clay, but they have ignored the rapid translation of these schemes into essential elements of a lasting American System. The notable accomplishment of the authors reviewed lies in the bold step they have taken down the road that leads from Hamiltonian dreams toward the mixed economy of contemporary America. This road is not yet fully marked, but its general direction is now clear. Further studies of government's partnership with enterprise may reveal it to be one of the major routes connecting early American hopes with recent material achievements.

[7] Robert A. Lively, "The South and Freight Rates: Political Settlement of an Economic Argument," *Journal of Southern History*, XIV (1948), 357–84.

Government and Transportation

12. American Development Policy: The Case of Internal Improvements *

Carter Goodrich

The subject I should like to discuss grows directly out of the theme of the meetings as a whole. They have been concerned with the American West as an Underdeveloped Region, and the title was intended to suggest the analogy between the United States of an earlier period and the so-called underdeveloped nations of the present day. To many it would suggest a contrast in policy. These other nations are now in many cases striving to achieve economic development by national planning and deliberate measures of governmental policy. On the other hand the United States achieved its massive economic development without over-all economic planning, without five-year plans or explicit national targets of input and output, and—it is sometimes believed—without the adoption of policies deliberately intended to promote development.

Yet the contrast is not as complete as this statement would suggest. It is not quite true that the United States just "growed" like Topsy or that the American empire of the West was settled and developed in a fit of absence of mind. Throughout our history statesmen have been concerned with devising measures to promote economic growth, and individuals and corporations have often come to governmental agencies with demands for encouragement and assistance. Many of the great debates on political issues have turned on what would today be described as development policy. Hamilton's *Report on Manufactures* is an obvious case in point. Its well-remembered argument for protection and its almost-forgotten plea

* The author's study has been carried on under the auspices of the Council for Research in the Social Sciences of Columbia University. The paper draws on the materials of articles previously published: in *Journal of Economic History*, "The Revulsion Against Internal Improvements," X (November, 1950), 145–169; (with Harvey H. Segal) "Baltimore's Aid to Railroads: A Study in the Municipal Planning of Internal Improvements," XII (Winter, 1953), 2–35; in the *Political Science Quarterly*, "National Planning of Internal Improvements," XLIII (March, 1948), 15–44; "The Virginia System of Mixed Enterprise: A Study of State Planning of Internal Improvements," XLIV (September, 1949), 355–387; "Local Government Planning of Internal Improvements," XLVI (September, 1951), 411–445; "Public Aid to Railroads in the Reconstruction South," LI (September, 1956), 407–442; in the *Proceedings of the American Philosophical Society*, XCII (October 25, 1948), 305–309.

"American Development Policy: The Case of Internal Improvements," by Carter Goodrich, is reprinted by permission from *Journal of Economic History*, XVI (December, 1956), 449–460. Presidential address, Economic History Association, September 8, 1956.

for encouraging the importation of technical improvements from abroad are both commonly duplicated in the underdeveloped nations of today. Hamilton's plea for the Funding System, that it would in effect provide a favorable climate for foreign investment, reminds us of what is so commonly urged on capital-hungry nations today. It is perhaps more difficult to disentangle explicit developmental considerations in the bitter nineteenth-century debates over monetary and banking issues. In national policy there was nothing to suggest comparison with the Development Banks, *Corporaciones de Fomento,* and National Investment Funds that play so large a role in the current plans of the less developed countries, though on the state level Milton Heath's reappraisal of the Central Bank of Georgia and Carter Golembe's study of early Middle-Western banking may suggest that we have underestimated the influence of conscious development policy.[1] With respect to land, the great decisions down through the nineteenth century were concerned with the conditions under which the national domain was to be turned over to individuals and corporations. This was the main issue of land policy, not land use, not conservation, not "land reform" in the explosive twentieth-century sense—unless you choose to regard the emancipation of the slaves as the most completely unplanned land reform in history! Yet the public domain was itself so magnificent that the manner of its disposition could not fail to be a major factor in influencing development, and explicit considerations of the rapidity and the desirable type of settlement dominated the debates from the Ordinance of 1787 to the Homestead Act, including expressions of deliberate preference for a particular type of social structure, that represented by the independent small farmer.

In an examination of American development policy, I believe that particular interest attaches to the case of internal improvements. Here the aim was directly and unmistakably developmental and the amount and variety of governmental activity quite extraordinary. Recent studies have increased our knowledge of the number of cases, and they have shown that the volume of government investment was greater than had been believed, both in absolute figures and in relation to total canal and railroad investment, to total national investment, and to the total budgets of governmental authorities.[2] Yet, half a century ago, the first modern

[1] Milton S. Heath, *Constructive Liberalism: The Role of the State in Economic Development in Georgia to 1860* (Cambridge: Harvard University Press, 1954), ch. 9. Carter H. Golembe, "State Banks and the Economic Development of the West, 1830–1844," unpublished dissertation, Columbia University, 1952.

[2] Professor Lively is right in pointing out that too little has been done with the comparison with private investment. Robert A. Lively, "The American System: A Review Article," *Business History Review,* XXIX (March 1955), 81–96. He cites Heath's figures on the ante-bellum South as a notable exception. See Milton S. Heath, "Public Railroad Construction and the Development of Private Enterprise in the South before 1861," *Journal of Economic History,* X (Supplement, 1950), 40–53.

An approach to the comparison with total national investment has been made in Harvey H. Segal, "Canal Cycles, 1834–1861: Public Construction Experience in New York, Pennsylvania and Ohio" (unpublished dissertation, Columbia University, 1956),

student of the subject, Guy Stevens Callender, was able to point out that our supposedly individualistic America had had in the early and middle nineteenth century a certain world prominence as an example of the extension of the activity of the state into industry. He asked what conditions had given "rise to this remarkable movement towards State enterprise here in America, where of all places in the world"—he said—"we should least expect to find it." [3]

This movement, however, appears less paradoxical if it is examined in the light of the economics of development. The conspicuous contrast was with England. English canals and railways were built entirely by private enterprise. American canals and railways were for the most part products of governmental or mixed enterprise or the recipients of government aid. But consider the difference in economic circumstance. A railway between London and Liverpool ran through settled country and connected established centers of trade. It could expect substantial traffic as soon as completed. On the other hand, a route across the Appalachians to the largely unsettled West or a railroad running from Chicago west across almost empty plains could hardly be profitable until settlement took place along its route and at its terminus. Jerome Cranmer uses the words "exploitative" and "developmental" for these two types of enterprise.[4] Exploitative canals or railroads were built to take advantage of an existing opportunity. With them early returns could be expected and private enterprise could operate without subsidy. On the other hand the developmental undertaking depended for most of its traffic on the settlement that its own construction was to bring about. But such development could not in the nature of the case be immediate, and substantial early returns on the investment were hardly possible. The ultimate benefits might be very large but they were certain to be deferred and likely to be widely diffused. Such undertakings, therefore, could hardly be carried to success by unaided private means. They required either government enterprise, subsidy to private enterprise, or else extraordinary illusions on the part of the original investors.[5]

A survey of the history of railroad building around the world illustrates this distinction and tends to confirm these observations. Few countries

which relates the canal expenditures to several estimates of capital formation and construction.

Heath, *Constructive Liberalism*, ch. 15, relates improvement expenditures to the state budget of Georgia; and Goodrich and Segal, "Baltimore's Aid to Railroads," relate them to the city budget.

[3] Guy Stevens Callender, "The Early Transportation and Banking Enterprises of the States in Relation to the Growth of Corporations," *Quarterly Journal of Economics,* XVII (November, 1902), 111–162. Reprinted in Joseph T. Lambie and Richard V. Clemence (eds.), *Economic Change in America* (Harrisburg: The Stackpole Co., 1954), 552–559. The quotation is from p. 554.

[4] H. Jerome Cranmer, "The New Jersey Canals: A Study of the Role of Government in Economic Development," unpublished dissertation, Columbia University, 1955.

[5] This last alternative is noted in Frank W. Fetter, "History of Public Debt in Latin America," *American Economic Review,* XXXVII (May, 1947), 147–148.

copied the British example. Certainly it was seldom followed where the problem was one of opening up unsettled areas or of achieving economic development in a preindustrial region. The railroads of Australia and New Zealand are state enterprises. Throughout most of the rest of the world the greater part of the railroad network has been built either on government account or with different forms of government aid or subsidy. One variant of the latter, government guarantee of return on the private investment, which Daniel Thorner has described as "Private Enterprise at Public Risk," was employed in India and Brazil as well as in France.[6] The purely private enterprises have been typically those that exploited obvious economic opportunities—to carry the produce of the pampas to Buenos Aires, or sugar from Cuban fields to the ports, or coffee to Santos. In Bolivia, for example, the pattern is precisely illustrated. The two railroads that take the tin from the great mines to the coast were built and are still owned and operated by private British interests, while the others are entirely governmental.

Nineteenth-century America displayed a similar pattern. There were certain railroad companies, particularly on the Atlantic seaboard, exploiting the opportunities of trade between established centers, which were profitable from the beginning and neither asked nor needed government aid. For New England, Kirkland described these as "dowager railroads" and cited the Boston and Lowell as one of the examples.[7] The Camden and Amboy was a similar case, and its partner the Delaware and Hudson might be described as a dowager canal—both exploiting the trade between New York and Philadelphia. But these were exceptions. Most of the canals and early railroads depended for their traffic on the growth of the areas into which they were extended. They were developmental in character and, like developmental undertakings almost everywhere, they were in considerable part built with government funds and credit.

The same distinction supplies one important clue to the understanding of the complex and apparently irregular timing of internal improvements activity. In this there were, to be sure, many cross currents. Reversals of state policy sometimes resulted, though less often than is sometimes believed, when power shifted from Whigs to Democrats, or vice versa, or when "Redemption" ended Reconstruction regimes in the South. More often improvements policy varied with the phase of the business cycle. Ambitious programs were abandoned in depression years, and failures were followed by "revulsion" and constitutional prohibitions. The collapse of the Illinois railroad program gave a lesson of caution to neighboring Iowa. On the other hand, New York's success with the Erie Canal had

---

[6] Daniel Thorner, *Investment in Empire: British Railway and Steam Shipping Enterprise in India, 1825–1940* (Philadelphia: University of Pennsylvania Press, 1950), ch. 7. Julian Smith Duncan, *Public and Private Operation of Railways in Brazil* (New York: Columbia University Press, 1932).

[7] Edward C. Kirkland, *Men, Cities and Transportation: A Study in New England History, 1820–1900* (Cambridge: Harvard University Press, 1948).

earlier inspired imitation up and down the entire Atlantic seaboard. Aid was given by local authorities, in varying amounts, in every state that formed part of the Union before 1890;[8] and in some fourteen states it continued to be given after the abandonment of state programs.[9] It may be said that governmental participation at one level or another persisted in most sections of the country as long as "developmental" conditions continued to exist, and perhaps in some cases beyond that point.

In general the relationship between developmental conditions and the various waves of government activity can be readily traced. For the Federal Government the building of the National Road and the formulation of the comprehensive internal improvement plans of Gallatin and Calhoun took place when the geographical obstacle to development was the Appalachian Mountains; and the major extension of actual aid to the transcontinental railroads took place when the obstacle was that of the Rocky Mountains and the Great Plains. Government activity in internal improvements was in large measure a frontier phenomenon, a great instance of frontier collectivism. In any given area it tended to diminish and die out as settlement and traffic became more dense and also as the business corporations themselves grew in strength and in the ability to raise large sums of money and commit them for long periods. As early as the 1850's, the *American Railroad Journal* was emphasizing this distinction. "In the infancy of our railroads," it said, "it was frequently necessary for the community to aid them in its collective capacity." Such a need continued in the South and in the West, declared the *Journal,* but in the North and East there was "abundant capital . . . for all legitimate enterprise," and public aid was no longer required.[10] To this doctrine it was not a real exception that Maine should vie with Oregon in furnishing some of the very latest cases of local government aid, since eastern Maine remained no less of a frontier than the Far West. Somewhat more surprising were the large amounts of money that Massachusetts poured out after the Civil War for the construction of the Hoosac Tunnel route and the extraordinary outpouring of municipal bonds for the building of the New York Midland. Yet in each case this represented an improvement for the less developed part of a highly developed state; and it may be added that in the case of the latter a new bankruptcy and the failure of plans for reorganization, occurring since the publication of Harry Pierce's book, tend to confirm his account of the selection of the route![11]

[8] In Colorado only during the territorial period.

[9] States of which this was substantially true include Georgia, Illinois, Indiana, Maryland, Michigan, Minnesota, Mississippi, Missouri, Nebraska, New York, North Carolina, South Carolina, Tennessee, and Virginia. Local aid was also given in states that had not had state programs. On the other hand, Alabama, Arkansas, Colorado, Ohio, and Pennsylvania adopted constitutional prohibitions against local aid at the same time as against state aid.

[10] *American Railroad Journal,* XXVII (1854), 449; XXVIII (1855), 281.

[11] Harry H. Pierce, *Railroads of New York: A Study of Government Aid, 1826–1875* (Cambridge: Harvard University Press, 1953).

If, then, we think of nineteenth-century America as a country in process of development, the experience of other countries in a similar situation suggests that extensive government investment in the means of transportation was not paradoxical but something entirely to be expected. What would really have been surprising would have been the spectacle of communities eager for rapid development but waiting patiently for their canals and railroads until the way was clear for prudent private investment to go forward without assistance. Yet neither an analysis of the economics of development nor analogy from foreign experience would account for all the peculiar forms and shapes taken by the American movement for internal improvements. Among its characteristics were three general shortcomings that would at once be obvious to anyone attempting to advise the underdeveloped countries of today on the organization of their programs of public improvement.

The first of these deficiencies was the failure to develop a workable economic criterion for the selection of projects for government support. Perhaps the sheer abundance of developmental opportunities made the question seem less crucial than it is for countries with more limited resources. There was, to be sure, no lack of statements of the reasons why short-run return on the investment itself was not a sufficient test. In addition to arguments based on the political advantages of closer connection between sections, which would strike a familiar note in many underdeveloped countries, expenditure on developmental transportation was defended on economic grounds. These statements called attention, often in thoroughly sophisticated terms, to its various benefits, not all of which could be appropriated by the collection of tolls or fares and freight charges. These included gains to the government itself in the enlargement of its tax base and the enhanced value of its lands, the diffused gains to the population at large in opportunities for income and employment, and in general the external economies provided to business as a whole by the provision of adequate transportation. But how should these broader and vaguer benefits be balanced against the expected costs? How were expenditures on unnecessary projects to be prevented? If prospective profit was not to be the conclusive test, how much immediate loss—and under what conditions—should the public authorities be prepared to incur in order to obtain these general advantages? On these questions I have so far found no serious contemporary statement.

A second shortcoming was the failure to develop and apply criteria for the assignment of projects to the different levels of government authority—federal, state, and local. Gallatin's admirable attempt to define a national project had little or no practical effect, and his program of federal action foundered largely on unresolved conflicts of state and regional interests. Within the several states, the problem of competing local interests was hardly less acute. Virginia attempted to operate on the theory of state support on equal terms to all local projects meeting certain specified conditions. In Pennsylvania and elsewhere there were bitter conflicts between proponents of a main or trunk line development and the advocates of aid to miscellaneous minor projects. Ante-bellum Georgia offered the unique example of confining its contribution almost entirely to a single strategically located state railroad, leaving connecting lines to local aid and private enterprise.[12] The extensive resort to the agencies of local government, the several thousand cases of railroad subscriptions and subsidies on the part of cities, counties, towns, and villages, can hardly be explained as the result of the application of any reasoned criteria as to which authorities were best fitted to make the necessary decisions. Aside from the early projects of the ambitious eastern seaports, each eager to carve out its part of the western empire, the recourse to local aid was in most cases a final expedient adopted after state aid had been prohibited, but when public demand for improvements, skillfully abetted by the companies themselves, still remained irrepressible. The extreme example of this type of causation is that of the citizenry of Cincinnati who, discovering that prohibition against *aiding* a railroad did not prevent them from *building* one, proceeded to construct the Cincinnati Southern as a successful municipal enterprise.

The third shortcoming lay in the nature of the government agencies themselves. They were sometimes subject to corruption, the danger of which increased as the railroad corporations graduated from the stage of infant enterprises. Moreover, they were in most cases poorly equipped to discharge the responsibilities of planning programs of internal improvement and of operating the undertakings effectively or of protecting the public interest in those that received public support. There were, to be sure, a considerable number of notable exceptions. The Gallatin Plan, prepared by the Secretary of the Treasury and a few clerks, would stand comparison with any twentieth-century plan for the development of a nation's communications. The present location of the trunk line railroads is eloquent testimony to its geographic foresight. New York's state enterprise, the Erie Canal, was both a financial and a technological success. The engineers who learned the job on the Erie carried their technique to other undertakings. The United States Army Engineers gave technical assistance to a large number of railroads; [13] and, in its early days, the Virginia Board of Public Works furnished engineering services to local enterprises. Georgia's state railroad, the Western and Atlantic, not only earned a good return on its investment but also provided for the other railroads of the state their indispensable connection with the West. Baltimore's City Council made serious and persistent efforts to guard its

[12] Heath, *Constructive Liberalism*, ch. 11.
[13] Forest G. Hill, "Government Engineering Aid to Railroads before the Civil War," *Journal of Economic History*, XI (Summer, 1951), 235–246.

railroad investments. Cincinnati's success has already been cited. Other examples could of course be named. Yet it can hardly be denied that in general the governments of the time, with small budgets and small staffs with little expert personnel and without civil service traditions, lacked what would now be regarded as the essential means for the effective supervision of improvement programs. The deficiency became more glaring as public aid came more and more to rest on the decisions of local authorities. Little planning could be expected of village or township boards deciding whether to recommend "whacking up" the contribution demanded by the railroad agent, or to risk letting the road go through the neighboring crossroads instead. Their chance to protect the public interest consisted mainly in making sure that the company really ran cars through their village in exchange for the contribution.

To contemporaries the lightness or feebleness of the supervisory hand of government did not always appear a disadvantage. Shortly after the Federal Government had begun the practice of making land grants to railroads, a British official, reporting enthusiastically to the Privy Council's Committee for Trade and Foreign Plantations, suggested its adoption in the British colonies precisely on the ground that it gave needed assistance without imposing the penalty of interference with management. The *American Railroad Journal* often advocated public aid but consistently argued that governments should not take a direct part in improvement enterprises. As president of the Baltimore and Ohio Railroad, John W. Garrett protested indignantly against what he regarded as interference by the public directors at a time when a substantial majority of the company's stock belonged to the State of Maryland and the City of Baltimore. If these attitudes are to be discounted as *ex parte*, there is evidence that legislators often shared these views and argued for them on grounds of public interest.

Virginia's system of mixed enterprise was explicitly based on the principle that the purpose of the state subscription was to draw out individual wealth for purposes of public improvement, and that the Commonwealth's control over the enterprises should extend no further than the correction of obvious abuses. With this in view, the state's participation in stock and voting rights was first limited to two fifths of the whole. When it appeared necessary to raise the state contribution to three fifths, the voting power of the state proxy in the stockholders' meeting was deliberately limited to two fifths, in accordance with the philosophy of the original law. A similar attitude was illustrated in the local aid statutes of a number of states that provided that the shares of stock subscribed to by the local governments should be distributed pro rata to the individual taxpayers. It was believed inexpedient to leave the administration of this stock in the hands of the local authorities, and that its distribution to private individuals would stimulate them to a vigilant supervision of the conduct of the work.[14]

As long as the common purpose was that of getting the much-desired improvement made, those who took part in the movement were not very much concerned if in many cases the method employed came close to being public enterprise under private management. To the Missourians on whom James N. Primm reports, as to many other Americans of the period, "The details of ownership and control were secondary . . . to the principal objective, the establishment of a comprehensive system of public improvement in the interests of the general welfare." [15]

Popular interest in this objective was very widely diffused. This was conspicuous in the support given to the many state programs and perhaps even more clearly in the willingness of the citizens to vote to assume local taxes in so many local elections. In these campaigns the appeals were typically couched in terms of public spirit and local patriotism. "Call meetings," urged a Mississippi paper. "Vote county, city, corporation and individual aid in bonds, money and land." A newspaper from a neighboring state added its plea: "Let the Mississippians come up strong to the work" on election day.[16] Projects were planned and campaigns organized in state or regional railroad conventions and in innumerable local railroad meetings. Boards of trade and chambers of commerce took leading parts in the movement. In a number of cases, after local government aid had been made illegal, unofficial bodies like these raised subscriptions in the same spirit and by appeal to the same arguments. It was they who took over the function of negotiating with the railroads over the location of their lines, shops, or roundhouses.

Throughout the developmental period individual citizens donated land for railroad rights of way, permitted the use of stone and timber from their lands, and supplied the labor of their slaves or their teams—occasionally even their own labor—to what was considered the common cause. Often, though not always, these services were paid for in shares of the stock of the enterprise. Appeals for cash subscriptions to canal or railroad stock were frequently based on grounds of civic duty as well as on prospects of financial return. Citizens were urged to bear an honorable part in what was often described as a great state or national work. In 1857 the president of a North Carolina railroad reproved his private stockholders for clamoring for dividends as if they had invested as capitalists rather than as citizens eager to promote the development of their state. As late as

[14] An alternative explanation, that of evading a constitutional prohibition against government stock ownership, has been suggested for the Iowa statute. See Earl S. Beard, "Local Aid to Railroads in Iowa," *Iowa Journal of History*, L (1952), 1–34.

[15] James Neal Primm, *Economic Policy in the Development of a Western State: Missouri, 1820–1860* (Cambridge: Harvard University Press, 1954), p. 113.

[16] Jackson *Mississippi Daily Pilot*, May 15, 1871. Mobile *Register*, October 24, 1871.

1870, the editor of a Nashville paper declared that "no individual in this country outside of the Lunatic Asylum ever subscribed to the capital stock of a railroad expecting to receive a profit on the investment in the way of dividends." This is of course not to be taken as literal truth. By the time the editor wrote, many investors had received good returns on railroad stock, and no doubt others were bitterly disappointed that they had not done so. But it remains true that for many private subscribers, as well as for those who urged government action, "the object," as he said, or at least one great object, "was to develop the country, enhance the value of their lands, and create cheap transporation of their produce."[17]

I am sure that no one would urge the underdeveloped countries of today to pattern their programs of transporation development upon the very disorderly history of American action in the field. One may hope that they will succeed in avoiding the three shortcomings I have noted, though they will not find it easy to do so. Most students believe that they will need to use the powers and the borrowing power of government even more than in the American case. But they would be fortunate indeed if they found their citizens as ready to support the undertakings with their own savings and the forced savings of taxation and if they could enlist as widespread an interest and participation in transportation development as was taken by the people of the United States. In this the local governments, for all their mistakes and inadequacies, and also the voluntary associations, played a considerable part. The building of the American network of transportation gained support from the local patriotism and the booster spirit of the city, town, and small community. It may be pointed out that the Communist practice of carrying regimentation and the party apparatus down into the smallest units, and the very different methods of "community development" of India and other countries, represent deliberate efforts to obtain popular participation at the local level in the processes of economic development. In the United States, vigorous local participation took instead the spontaneous forms that have been described.

On this occasion it is customary to consider The Tasks of Economic History. May I suggest that one such task is the examination of the economic effects of this American "boosterism," of this local civic pride, and to ask how much of its rather noisy activity canceled out in cross purposes and duplication of effort,[18] and to what extent its energy made a positive contribution to economic development. Since a large part of this

[17] Nashville *Union and American,* February 11, 1870.

[18] The effect of local rivalries in impeding the formation of a fully connected national railroad system, by perpetuating differences in gauge and delaying physical connections between lines, is discussed in George Rogers Taylor and Irene D. Neu, *The American Railway Network, 1861–1890* (Cambridge: Harvard University Press, 1956). The text refers to the "long continued parochialism of the cities" (p. 51) and quotes a comment on "village peevishness" (p. 53).

activity has been carried on by voluntary and unofficial organizations, the subject has rather fallen between the stools of the historians of politics and the historians of business. The records of these bodies are less accessible than those of governments, and their accomplishments are less measurable than those of business firms. Yet exploration of the subject, whatever the difficulties, seems to me essential for the understanding of a unique characteristic of American life.

My discussion of internal improvements began by citing the comment that the amount of government activity and expenditure in this field appeared astonishing in so individualistic a country. It ends on a quite different note, by suggesting that the nature and manner of this extensive government activity have been in close conformity with certain special characteristics of American development. Our record demonstrates a preference, though by no means universal or doctrinaire, for government partnership or subsidy rather than for purely public enterprise, and for leaving management largely in the hands of individuals and corporations. In this, American experience differs from that of many foreign countries but not of all. Our record also shows that a large amount of this government action was taken by local governments, often of small communities. In this, American experience is unique. In our case, moreover, governmental effort has been accompanied and abetted by the voluntary activity of a host of unofficial civic organizations, for which I am sure no parallel can be found in the history of other developing countries. Our policy with respect to internal improvements has thus been profoundly affected—for better or worse—by the traditional American characteristics of individualism, of localism, and of the habit of voluntary association.

Government and Science

13.   Formative Relations of American Enterprise, Government and Science

Forest G. Hill

How large a part did the federal government play in the early advancement of science, and thereby of private enterprise as well? This question bears on the larger perspective now needed to understand the greatly expanded federal promotion of science and technology, especially in the field of scientific research and development. Recent historical work has shown that the government at all levels, federal, state and local, actively promoted business and economic development in the period before the Civil War.[1] Such public action for the benefit of transportation, industry and agriculture, as well as national defense, was often closely related to the growth of science in this country. Since progress in these areas of federal support both required and stimulated scientific advances, the government was forced to take heed of the nation's needs as well as its potential for developing and diffusing scientific knowledge. This support of science became a major avenue for the encouragement of private enterprise.

A great deal more needs to be known, however, about government promotion of scientific development and the resulting stimulus to enterprise. How early did the government take a hand in fostering scientific advance? Why did it assume this rôle? What methods did it use to aid the growth of science? How great was the stimulus to industrial development? This survey can only suggest the general scope and character of this early promotion of science, thereby indicating how much remains to be done to secure an adequate understanding of the close relation between government and science and enterprise which prevailed before the Civil War.[2]

[1] Of great value here are recent studies by Carter Goodrich, Oscar Handlin, Louis Hartz, and Milton S. Heath.

[2] The most comprehensive study of government and science is A. Hunter Dupree, *Science in the Federal Government* (Cambridge, 1957). For the early period see Brooke Hindle, *The Pursuit of Science in Revolutionary America* (Chapel Hill, 1956). Two other useful works of recent date are Whitfield J. Bell, Jr., *Early American Science: Needs and Opportunities for Study* (Williamsburg, 1955), and Don K. Price, *Government and Science: Their Dynamic Relation in American Democracy* (New York, 1954).

"Formative Relations of American Enterprise, Government and Science," by Forest G. Hill, is reprinted by permission from *Political Science Quarterly*, LXXV (September, 1960), 400–419.

Early Interest in Public Support of Science

Even before the American Revolution a considerable interest in science prevailed in the American Colonies. The varied work of Benjamin Franklin, particularly his research in electricity, is quite significant in this regard. Several colonial members of the Royal Society of London, including Franklin, carried on active correspondence with members in England. George Washington and Thomas Jefferson were typical of a group of Americans with strong interests in exploration, surveying, and the application of science to agriculture.

The American Revolution, somewhat like the French Revolution later, produced an acute concern for the prestige and the needs of science in a country fighting for its independence and asserting its cultural nationalism. The Continental Army required men of science for several of its major activities. Military engineers were desperately needed, and this country had to look mainly to Europe for its trained engineers, France being the chief supplier of this talent. Military surveying was required, and geographers and surveyors of roads had to be secured. Artillerists and armorers were likewise in great demand. David Rittenhouse, early physicist and astronomer, rendered valuable ordnance service during the war by supervising the casting of cannon and the manufacture of gunpowder.[3] Among those who showed a great interest in the support of science at this time were Franklin, Washington, Jefferson, Alexander Hamilton and Benjamin Rush.

President Washington and his successors down to John Quincy Adams strongly urged the establishment of a national university which would be well grounded in the sciences.[4] They also advocated military schools designed to promote military science and engineering. Jefferson was instrumental in founding the Military Academy at West Point, to which James Madison and James Monroe in turn gave firm support. Particularly under Monroe, West Point assumed importance as a school of engineering. John C. Calhoun, Monroe's Secretary of War, actively fostered its improvement and favored the creation of military schools of practice. With the backing of Jefferson and Albert Gallatin, Ferdinand Rudolph Hassler, the Swiss mathematician, was selected to organize the Coast Survey. He planned its work before the War of 1812 and initiated actual operations following the war. Jefferson selected Jared Mansfield, noted

[3] I. Bernard Cohen, "American Physicists at War: From the Revolution to the World Wars," *American Journal of Physics*, XIII (1945), 224–235. Earlier Rittenhouse had made a number of colonial boundary surveys. Hindle, *op. cit.*, pp. 134, 174–175, 229–230.

[4] See Edgar B. Wesley, *Proposed: The University of the United States* (Minneapolis, 1936), pp. 3–10; Dupree, *op. cit.*, pp. 14–15, 33, 40–42.

mathematician and scientist, to be a professor at West Point and then Surveyor-General of the United States. Mansfield subsequently made the astronomical observations required to place federal land surveying on an accurate basis. For many years John Quincy Adams insistently sought the establishment of a national observatory.

The early Federalists or Hamiltonians were notable for their strong concern about science and its promotion by government. Although the Jeffersonians were perhaps less militant in this regard, Jefferson's own fond interest in science and its support by government was quite outstanding. Madison and Monroe took much the same official position, especially the latter after the War of 1812. This official concern with the progress of science seems to have waned considerably in the age of Jackson. The Jeffersonians consequently resembled the Federalists more than they did the Jacksonians in this sympathy for public sponsorship of science.[5] The idea of a national university became less popular after the 1820's and was finally dropped, at least in the formal utterances of presidents and other leading officials. The Military Academy, however, was rapidly developed after 1815 into a systematic school of military science, including engineering and its application to internal improvements. The view may be taken that, at least in the field of science, West Point was allowed to serve in lieu of a national university.

GOVERNMENT EFFORTS TO ADVANCE SCIENCE

The American Revolution clearly demonstrated the urgency of science in a new country which had to protect itself and improve its means of communication. This war particularly revealed the need for military engineers, geographers, and experts in the manufacture and use of artillery. To meet this lack of engineers, foreigners had to be employed during the Revolution, and to some extent for four or five decades thereafter. Their chief postwar services were in the construction of coastal defenses and the teaching of military science and engineering at West Point.[6] The public domain had to be surveyed and boundaries determined, which were major functions of government carried on primarily by native Americans. Under the Articles of Confederation, problems of coinage and weights and measures also led to complications.

The Constitution gave explicit recognition to a number of these pressing scientific matters. It made provisions for determining standards of weights and measures, developing a system of coinage, issuing patents

[5] Cf. Bell, op. cit., pp. 33–36; Price, op. cit., pp. 4–9.
[6] William E. Birkhimer, Historical Sketch of the Organization, Administration, Matériel and Tactics of the Artillery, United States Army (Washington, 1884), pp. 1–33, 108–115, 166–167, 183–185, 191–192; Hindle, op. cit., pp. 240–243.

and copyrights, and taking a census of the population. Soon after the Constitution was adopted, attention had to be given to several pressing technical problems, including land surveying, coastal fortifications, the survey of the coast, the development of military schools, and the creation of national armories and arsenals. In addition, the Cumberland Road was commenced as a federal project, and there was widespread advocacy of a national university.

Continued demands for a military school led in 1802 to the creation by law of the United States Military Academy, which was to devote itself primarily to the training of engineers and artillerists, the most technical or scientific branches of the military establishment. As early as 1794 a Corps of Artillerists and Engineers had been created to promote technical instruction in these services and to build harbor defenses. The act of 1802 creating the Military Academy separated the Corps of Engineers from the Artillery, and an Ordnance Department was later instituted. National armories were established at Springfield, Massachusetts, and Harpers Ferry, Virginia; and a program for procuring small arms on long-term contract was designed for the express purpose of creating a domestic small-arms industry. The national armories were operated in such a way as to foster this private industry; they coöperated closely in technical matters to aid the private armorers of New England and the Pennsylvania–Harpers Ferry area.[7]

STIMULUS OF THE WAR OF 1812

The War of 1812 acutely impressed upon government leaders the urgency of a number of major technical problems. Among the outstanding needs it demonstrated were those for improved inland transportation, seacoast fortifications, domestic manufacture of armaments, and skilled artillerists and engineers. Greatly increased attention was given to the development of industry, and in 1816 a protective tariff was enacted to stimulate the growth of American manufacturing. At this time the government took vigorous steps to develop West Point as a leading school of science and engineering. Concerted action was taken to secure an elaborate scheme of coastal defenses and to fortify strategic points along the Mississippi and the Great Lakes. The government acted on a wide front to improve transportation to the interior. It started using troops to build roads to the frontier military posts, and it commenced extending the Cumberland or National Road toward the Mississippi. It also gave finan-

[7] Felicia Johnson Deyrup, *Arms Makers of the Connecticut Valley* (Northampton, 1948), pp. 5, 37–38, 41–50, 66–67; Constance McLaughlin Green, *Eli Whitney and the Birth of American Technology* (Boston, 1956), pp. 101–109, 123–130, 143–156, 167–175.

cial assistance to a few canal companies, and in 1824 it assigned numerous Army engineers to the work of improving rivers and harbors and surveying routes for roads and canals to be built by state or private enterprise. These transportation improvements followed the plan laid down by Secretary of War Calhoun in his report of 1819 on roads and canals, which in turn incorporated the essentials of Secretary of the Treasury Gallatin's 1808 report on internal improvements.[8]

Government officials and military leaders worked out what was, in effect, a general plan of national defense following the War of 1812. This plan embodied coastal fortifications, interior defenses, the regular Army, the militia, the Navy, and transportation improvements, as well as the promotion of science and domestic industry. Much of this planning was centered in the Board of Engineers for Fortifications, which was created in 1816. The year before, two distinguished Army engineers, Colonel William McRee and Major Sylvanus Thayer, were sent to Europe to procure knowledge and treatises on military science and engineering. After meeting two of Napoleon's outstanding engineers, Simon Bernard and Claudius Crozet, they joined with Gallatin and Lafayette in recommending that the government employ these two French engineers to help in developing a strong system of national defense.[9]

General Bernard was brought to this country in 1816 as Assistant Engineer in the same rank as General Joseph G. Swift, the Chief Engineer. The Board of Engineers for Fortifications was formed around General Bernard as its chief member, along with Colonels McRee and Joseph G. Totten. This board carefully examined the needs for coastal and interior fortifications and then formulated plans for a general system of coastal defenses and the project plans for individual works. They used several brigades of Army engineers to make topographical and hydrographic surveys, upon which their detailed plans were based. This planning of seaboard defenses was coördinated with Hassler's survey of the coast, upon which still other topographical engineers were employed. The General Survey Act was passed in 1824 to provide surveying for roads and canals of military and commercial importance. Bernard became the leading member of the Board of Engineers for Internal Improvements, created that year to direct these new surveying and planning activities. He served on these two interrelated boards with distinction and made many important surveys and tours of inspection throughout the country prior to his return to France in 1831.[10]

[8] See Carter Goodrich, "National Planning of Internal Improvements," *Political Science Quarterly*, LXIII (1948), pp. 16–44.
[9] R. Ernest Dupuy, *The West Point Tradition in American Life* (New York, 1940), pp. 81, 92–100.
[10] William H. Carter, "Bernard," *Journal of the Military Service Institution of the United States*, LI (1912), pp. 147–155; J. G. Barnard, "Eulogy of the Late Joseph G. Totten . . . ," Smithsonian Institution, *Annual Report . . . 1865* (Washington, 1872), pp. 137–172.

Crozet also came with Bernard to the United States in 1816 and became professor of engineering at West Point. Not long after Major Thayer returned from Europe, President Monroe installed Thayer as Superintendent of the Military Academy. With the firm support of Secretary of War Calhoun, West Point was rapidly built into an effective school of engineering through the efforts of Thayer, Crozet, Jared Mansfield, and the enlarged academic staff. Crozet introduced descriptive geometry and materials on military and civil engineering which he had acquired at France's famed Polytechnic School in Paris. In 1823 he left West Point to commence a long career as state engineer of Virginia. He was the leading founder of the Virginia Military Institute, which was developed as a military and engineering school upon the model of West Point and the Polytechnic School.[11]

The War of 1812, which stimulated this acute interest in national defense and economic development, actually initiated a systematic transfer of military science from Europe to the United States. Other Frenchmen in addition to Crozet taught at West Point in the next decade or two. French textbooks on engineering and mathematics were used at West Point, sometimes first in the original French and then in English translations. During the 1820's and in each later decade prior to the Civil War, American military men, particularly engineer and ordnance officers, followed McRee and Thayer to Europe to examine military schools and other military and technical institutions. In this way the country gained a great deal of technical knowledge about European scientific schools, fortifications, ordnance systems, industrial plants, and civil works, including canals, railways, harbors, and river improvements.[12]

Rôle of the Military in Promoting Science

The War Department, as is now evident, was responsible for several major functions which were obviously quite technical in character. Among these were the construction of fortifications, exploration of the West, development of artillery and ordnance equipment, operation of West Point as an engineering and scientific school, and the execution of various civil-works programs. Of particular importance were the Engineer Department, including the Military Academy and Topographical Bureau, the Artillery, the Ordnance Department, and the national armories. The work of these military agencies encompassed the transfer of technical knowledge from Europe, specialized training of Army officers for techni-

[11] Crozet's career is treated by William Couper in *Claudius Crozet: Scholar-Soldier-Educator-Engineer* (Charlottesville, 1936), and *One Hundred Years at V.M.I.* (Richmond, 1939–1940).

[12] Dupuy, *op. cit.*, pp. 137–138, 161, 191–201; Dirk J. Struik, *Yankee Science in the Making* (Boston, 1948), pp. 244–245.

cal duties, military medicine, aid to the Coast Survey, and a wide range of activities in exploring, surveying, and constructing public works. These agencies were reasonably well protected from political pressures, had the aura of military justification, were often beneficial to industrial or business interests, and received considerable support from the Executive and Congress.[13]

The exploration carried on by Army officers was most varied and far-flung. It was designed to gain knowledge along many lines—geographical, topographical, hydrographical, geological, mineralogical, botanical, zoological and meteorological, also ethnological. The early expedition by Captains Lewis and Clark, planned by President Jefferson to explore the Louisiana Purchase, had scientific as well as geographical and political objectives. Among several other western explorations before the War of 1812 were those by Lieutenant Zebulon M. Pike. These expeditions in the West increased rapidly in number following the War of 1812, involving such Army explorers as Stephen H. Long, Bonneville and Fremont.[14]

The Army sponsored explorations by Schoolcraft, Edwin James, Nicollet, Featherstonhaugh, and others which produced considerable knowledge about the geology and mineral resources of the western country. Through the Treasury Department, ordnance officers, and Army engineers, the government after 1820 gave much attention to the lead mine regions of the Mississippi Valley. The lead lands of Illinois, Iowa and Missouri were explored, surveyed and frequently inspected as part of a program for leasing them to private miners for rapid exploitation. Soon after gold was discovered in California in 1848, mineralogical surveys were made there by government officials and Army officers. In these and other ways, the government had a significant part in advancing mineralogical knowledge and science, thereby aiding the mining industry for more than half a century before the United States Geological Survey was established in 1879.[15]

The knowledge contributed by these military explorations in the West went far beyond geography and natural resources. Materials were accumulated, for instance, concerning the Indian tribes, weather, botany and zoology of the regions explored. The western agents of the General Land Office also added to this knowledge. The Indian Office, which was part of the War Department until the Interior Department was created in 1849, amassed many ethnological and mineralogical data. The most sys-

[13] Price, op. cit., pp. 21–26.

[14] The work of Army explorers is evaluated in Edmund W. Gilbert, The Exploration of Western America, 1800–1850: An Historical Geography (Cambridge, England, 1933).

[15] Institute for Government Research, The U. S. Geological Survey (New York, 1918), pp. 1–9; George Otis Smith, "A Century of Government Geological Surveys," A Century of Science in America (New Haven, 1918), pp. 193–216.

tematic and highly organized exploration undertaken in this period consisted of the Pacific railroad surveys, commenced by the War Department in 1853. Several surveying parties were busy almost to the Civil War examining alternative routes for a railroad from the Mississippi to the Pacific. These railroad explorers collected detailed knowledge of the minerals, climate, agricultural resources, and plant and animal life along the several routes surveyed. Geologists, natural scientists, and other experts accompanied these surveying parties, as they had often done on earlier western expeditions.

The War Department also executed a wide variety of civil works in the period before 1860. The General Survey Act of 1824 involved the Army engineers in two decades of active surveying for major transportation projects, at the height of the nation-wide movement for internal improvements. Government engineers made surveys for innumerable roads and canals, even though built mainly by state or private enterprise. They also surveyed at government expense the routes for some forty or fifty railroads between 1827 and 1840 and were sometimes furloughed to locate and construct private or state-owned railroad and canal lines.[16]

The Engineer and Quartermaster Departments carried on extensive road building in the West, often with the labor of troops. They constructed military and territorial roads in the Mississippi Valley and Great Lakes regions, connecting the Army posts on the Indian frontier with the settled areas. For two decades the Engineer Department supervised the extension of the National Road westward to the Mississippi. The War and Interior Departments continued to build territorial roads in the Far West until well after the Civil War.[17] In this road work and the surveying for canals and railroads, the Army engineers made effective use of their engineering training and experience. In fact, their talents were in great demand by states, territories and transportation companies. Since trained civil engineers were then very scarce, the work of these military engineers was extremely significant in advancing the nation's transportation system.

The Army engineers found another major outlet for their engineering skills in river and harbor improvements. Starting in 1824, they greatly improved steamboat navigation on the Ohio, Mississippi, Missouri and Red Rivers and completed numerous harbor and breakwater projects along the Atlantic Coast and the Great Lakes.[18] These works gave employment and training to many civilian engineers, while the Army engineers

[16] Forest G. Hill, "Government Engineering Aid to Railroads Before the Civil War," *Journal of Economic History*, XI (1951), pp. 235–246.

[17] *Cf.* W. Turrentine Jackson, *Wagon Roads West: A Study of Federal Road Survey and Construction in the Trans-Mississippi West, 1846–1869* (Berkeley and Los Angeles, 1952).

[18] See W. Stull Holt, *The Office of the Chief of Engineers* (Baltimore, 1923), and Louis C. Hunter, *Steamboats on the Western Rivers* (Cambridge, 1949).

developed many methods, such as snag removal, dredging, and use of cement and other building materials, which aided the advance of construction techniques and civil engineering generally. They served as the chief construction agency for several government departments, particularly the Treasury. They supervised the erection of lighthouses along the Atlantic and the Great Lakes, thereby assuming a major rôle in the lighthouse program.[19] They likewise built custom houses, marine hospitals and post offices; and in Washington they supervised the construction of the Capitol and other public buildings, as well as the Washington Aqueduct.[20]

Army officers trained in military and civil engineering often resigned at an early age to enter private employment. West Point graduates became leading civil engineers and occupied influential positions in transportation, industry and scientific schools. War Department officials continually praised the work they did, not only in the scientific, technical and civil-works programs of the government, but also in their private careers. The government visualized that it was providing the skilled technicians required to promote the nation's industry, transportation and scientific education. It felt that through both their public service and civil careers, West Pointers were helping to disseminate science and accelerate economic development.[21] This favorable attitude toward the rôle of the military in disseminating science was prominently expressed in the messages of the Presidents and the annual reports of the Secretaries of War, Engineer Department, and Boards of Visitors to the Military Academy.

Why did the military establishment assume this major rôle in promoting and disseminating science? From the beginning the Army had to fulfill technical functions which required a good deal of scientific knowledge. Military men had the education, experience and discipline to carry on technical or scientific work required for both military and economic purposes.[22] Their work aided the westward movement, strengthened the militia, and facilitated industrial and educational progress. Furthermore, there was widespread popular approval of the military for assuming this highly beneficial rôle. There had always been great public hostility toward a large standing army, which would place a heavy economic burden on the country and might endanger individual freedoms. These objections, however, were happily offset by letting military personnel usefully promote the nation's science and industrial wealth.

[19] Arnold B. Johnson, *The Modern Light-House Service* (Washington, 1889), pp. 15–27; George Weiss, *The Lighthouse Service* (Baltimore, 1926), pp. 1–15.

[20] The varied civil activities of the topographical engineers are summarized in Henry P. Beers, "A History of the U. S. Topographical Engineers, 1813–1863," *Military Engineer*, XXXIV (1942), pp. 287–291, 348–352.

[21] Dupuy, *op. cit.*, pp. 368–369, 378–379, 382–384. The technical work of the Army engineers prior to the Civil War is discussed in Forest G. Hill, *Roads, Rails and Waterways: The Army Engineers and Early Transportation* (Norman, 1957).

[22] See Price, *op. cit.*, pp. 20–23, 123.

Like the War Department, the Navy came to have major technical or scientific functions and interests. Although the Navy was commenced in the 1790's and achieved separate departmental status by 1798, it remained quite small until the War of 1812. While the widespread fear of a regular army hardly applied to the Navy, the compelling urge for governmental economy affected it adversely. Furthermore, the Navy was not immediately beneficial to westward expansion or domestic transportation and industry. Officers of the Navy envied the predominance of the War Department, particularly its highly organized and influential bureaus and Military Academy. After many years of insistent pleas by naval officers, the bureau system for separate functions was instituted in 1842, and the Naval Academy was finally created in 1845. Like West Point, it developed a scientific curriculum designed to provide the technical skills needed in the naval service, especially in navigation, marine architecture and mechanical engineering.[23]

The Navy took a strong interest in the survey and charting of coastal waters. It was active in securing breakwaters, harbors of refuge, dry docks and navy yards along the coasts. Naval officers worked closely with military engineers on various boards to select sites and design plans for these coastal installations, as well as lighthouses and harbor defenses. Navy yards were established at Portsmouth, Boston, New York, Philadelphia, Washington, Norfolk and Charleston on the Atlantic Coast and at Pensacola on the Gulf, while in the early 1850's the Mare Island Navy Yard was opened on the Pacific near San Francisco. These yards not only built and repaired vessels, but also worked on problems of naval artillery and ordnance. Before the Civil War the Washington Navy Yard made considerable progress in ordnance work, one of its major achievements being the rifled naval gun. The Navy's Bureau of Ordnance, created in 1842, actively experimented with improvements in its field. Naval experts also devoted some attention to protective armor and problems of steam power and iron vessels before the Civil War.

The Navy Department by the 1830's started gathering a large volume of nautical information, securing data from both merchant and naval vessels. The Depot of Charts and Instruments was created in 1830 to collect, test, correct and issue charts, instruments and nautical books. Out of this Depot developed the Hydrographic Office and the Naval Observatory. It made hydrographic surveys in various parts of the world and prepared and distributed its own ocean charts. The Depot was headed in turn by Lieutenants L. M. Goldsborough, Charles Wilkes, James M. Gilliss and Matthew Fontaine Maury. Under their direction it made great strides in collecting and supplying hydrographic and navigational data for the Navy and the merchant marine. It also made systematic observations in astronomy, magnetism and meteorology. Maury became distinguished as

[23] The evolution of the Naval Academy is discussed in John Crane and James F. Kieley, *United States Naval Academy: The First Hundred Years* (New York, 1945).

a hydrographer and meteorologist; his Wind and Current Charts and his Sailing Directions were of great value to the nation's ocean shipping interests as well as the Navy.

Although John Quincy Adams could never persuade Congress to authorize a national observatory, the Navy Department finally succeeded in this endeavor. The Depot of Charts and Instruments started making astronomical observations in the 1830's; and by 1844 it secured the permanent Naval Observatory in Washington, built under the supervision of Gilliss. In planning for the Observatory, he went abroad and consulted noted European astronomers. From 1845 onward the Observatory did systematic astronomical work, gaining international recognition by the 1850's. This work permitted the preparation of a nautical almanac and the publication of other astronomical data, valuable alike to the merchant marine, other scientists, and the Navy itself. In the years 1849–1852 Gilliss made an astronomical expedition to Chile, which yielded much scientific information about that country.

The first scientific expedition and large-scale hydrographic surveying made by the United States Navy was the Wilkes Exploring Expedition to the Pacific Ocean and South Seas in the years 1838–1842. Wilkes took along a scientific staff and made detailed hydrographic, meteorological and magnetic observations. His work included the location of islands, reefs, whaling grounds and sailing routes; and the scientific results of the expedition were published in a series of detailed reports. Commodore Matthew C. Perry made an expedition to Japan in 1852–1854, which had scientific as well as diplomatic objectives. Extensive nautical and scientific surveys and observations were made around Japan. The North Pacific Exploring Expedition, 1853–1859, was directed in turn by Commodore Cadwalader Ringgold and Commander John Rodgers. This expedition carried on comprehensive surveying, charting and scientific work around Japan, the Bering Sea and the Arctic Ocean. After a late start, the Navy rapidly contributed its share to charting the oceans and enlarging the knowledge of meteorology, astronomy and terrestrial magnetism.[24] Its work was very beneficial to, and greatly favored by, the nation's commercial and shipping interests as American trade spread around the globe.

Other Government Scientific Activities

The early scientific work of the War and Navy Departments is less difficult to comprehend than that scattered through a number of civilian departments and agencies. However diffused and piecemeal these other

[24] The early scientific work of the Navy is described by Gustavus A. Weber in *The Hydrographic Office* and *The Naval Observatory* (both published at Baltimore, 1926).

scientific activities may have been, they were nevetheless quite important. They need to be outlined here in their variety and major concentrations, in order to have a more balanced picture of early government promotion of science and enterprise.

The Treasury Department came to have a number of scientific functions. These included coinage and the mints, the Coast Survey, standards of weights and measures, lighthouse construction, leasing of the lead mines in the Mississippi Valley, and construction and operation of marine hospitals. In many of these activities, including the construction of public works, the Treasury used the services of Army engineers. Hassler was teaching at West Point when he was selected by President Jefferson and Secretary of the Treasury Gallatin to institute the survey of the coast. In 1843 he was succeeded by Alexander Dallas Bache, noted scientist and educator who was a West Pointer and briefly an Army engineer. Hassler and Bache employed Army engineers and naval officers in their triangulation and hydrographic surveys along the coasts. Especially under Bache, the Coast Survey carried on a wide range of scientific investigations and gained great prestige. These two men in turn headed the Office of Weights and Measures, the forerunner of the National Bureau of Standards. They did extensive work in determining, standardizing and publicizing accurate weights and measures. In connection with the Coast Survey, the Treasury possessed the instruments and trained personnel for this work in the science of measurement, which was a practical necessity in the operation of the custom houses and the conduct of foreign trade.[25]

The State Department played a significant rôle in the transfer of scientific knowledge from Europe to America. As Secretaries of State, Jefferson and John Quincy Adams made elaborate reports on weights and measures in 1790 and 1821, respectively. The Secretaries of State made other scientific reports, secured technical information and agricultural plants and seeds through American ministers in Europe, and arranged for Army and Navy officers to make scientific investigations there. The State Department was instrumental in acquiring technical treatises, models of weights and measures, and scientific instruments abroad for government use. Its various boundary commissions employed topographical engineers and astronomers who gained valuable training and geographical knowledge. The Secretaries of State also directed the early censuses and accumulated data about the Indian tribes and organized territories of the West through handling treaty relations with the Indians and official relations with territorial governments.

[25] See Benjamin A. Gould, "Address in Commemoration of Alexander Dallas Bache," American Association for the Advancement of Science, *Proceedings*, XVII (1868), pp. 1–56; Gustavus A. Weber's two monographs on *The Bureau of Standards* and *The Coast and Geodetic Survey* (Baltimore, 1925 and 1923, respectively); Dupree, *op. cit.*, pp. 29–33, 51–56, 100–105.

There was inevitably a strong scientific aspect to the work of the General Land Office, which yielded further knowledge about the West. It surveyed the public domain on a systematic basis, classified lands, and supervised their sale or disposition. Notably in the special-purpose survey and control of mineral and timber lands, the Land Office produced extensive information on the country's natural resources. It supervised the reservation of certain forest lands for naval purposes, the genesis of the government's work in forestry. Land agents also contributed geological data and reported weather observations from an early period. The Land Office thus aided the early growth of meteorology, alongside the Army engineers, post surgeons, Navy Hydrographic Office, Patent Office and Smithsonian Institution.[26]

The Smithsonian looms quite large in the history of government efforts to promote science. It was founded in 1846 to use the bequest left by the Englishman James Smithson for advancing and disseminating science in this country. Government scientists such as Bache and Totten were among its founders; and Joseph Henry, foremost physicist of the day, became its director in the capacity of secretary. Congressional sentiments of the Jacksonian era prevented use of this bequest to found a national university or observatory. Instead, the Smithsonian promoted research in several scientific fields, notably geology, mineralogy, ethnology and meteorology. Before the Civil War it commenced preparing weather maps and forecasts based on telegraphic reports from various points.[27] The Smithsonian worked in close liaison with the Coast Survey, Engineer Department, Lighthouse Board, and other scientific agencies; and it maintained contact with such private scientific groups as the American Association for the Advancement of Science, the American Philosophical Society, and the Franklin Institute. The Smithsonian thus rendered valuable service by associating together the scientific men in public and private life.[28]

This communication and exchange between government and private scientists bore fruit during the Civil War in the coordination of scientific research and advice for war purposes. President Lincoln actively supported the Smithsonian Institution, Coast Survey, Army and Navy Ordnance Bureaus, and other technical agencies in their research and experimentation on military equipment and techniques.[29] Coördination of this work became the task of a special commission, headed by Henry of the Smithsonian, Bache of the Coast Survey, and Admiral Charles Henry Davis, formerly Bache's assistant on the Coast Survey and the first editor

[26] Cf. Gustavus A. Weber, The Weather Bureau (New York, 1922), pp. 1–3; Dupree, op. cit., pp. 109–114.

[27] Weber, The Weather Bureau, pp. 1–3.

[28] Cohen, op. cit., pp. 227–229; Price, op. cit., pp. 16–18; Dupree, op. cit., pp. 66–90.

[29] Robert V. Bruce, Lincoln and the Tools of War (Indianapolis and New York, 1956).

of the Navy's *American Ephemeris and Nautical Almanac.* In 1863 these men were instrumental in chartering the National Academy of Sciences, founded largely as an agency to assist and advise the government on scientific problems. The function of the National Academy of Sciences as scientific adviser to the government was continued on a diminished scale in peacetime. A notable instance of this was its detailed study and plan of 1878 to consolidate within two agencies, the Coast and Geodetic Survey and the Geological Survey, the government's proliferated surveying activities. Its recommendations led to the creation of the latter in 1879.[30]

The Steamboat Inspection Service represents the development of a government technical function of a regulatory character. Frequent boiler explosions on river and lake steamers prompted demands for the government to correct this hazard to navigation. To assure the safety of passengers on steam vessels, legislation as early as 1838 required the inspection of hulls, boilers, safety equipment and competency of crews. This work was the subject of frequent laws and, like similar technical functions, was made the responsibility of the Treasury Department. A "Steamboat Act" of 1852 set up a system of nine supervising inspectors who met annually as a board and employed numerous local inspectors in their respective districts.[31] The government showed a strong interest in the improvement not only of steamboats, but also of the telegraph, railroads, agricultural science, and other technological advances of similar economic significance.

The work of the Patent Office clearly revealed this concern of government for the progress of invention and science. The first patent law of 1790 placed the issuance of patents under the charge of the Secretary of State, and Jefferson took a keen interest in the work. Patent law was basically improved in 1836, when the Patent Office became a separate bureau in the State Department, until its transfer to the new Department of Interior in 1849. After 1836 the Patent Office developed technical competence, a scientific library, a collection of models, and a regular staff of examiners. It coöperated with the Smithsonian Institution in collecting and publishing meteorological data from many voluntary observers in the United States and neighboring countries. The Patent Office as early as 1836 secured plants and seeds abroad for distribution to farmers, often through individual Congressmen. After 1841 its Agricultural Division developed a research program in agricultural chemistry—soils, fertilizers, plant nutrition, animal feeding, the analysis of cereals, the culture of cotton, sugar cane and tobacco, and related subjects. The agricultural section of the Patent Office's annual reports carried the results of these

---

[30] Cohen, *op. cit.,* pp. 223, 229–232; Dupree, *op. cit.,* pp. 132–148; Price, *op. cit.,* pp. 18–20.

[31] Lloyd M. Short, *Steamboat-Inspection Service* (New York, 1922), pp. 1–16; Price, *op. cit.,* pp. 10–11.

scientific investigations, along with agricultural and meteorological statistics. It thus developed the scientific and informational aids to agriculture which became the work of the Department of Agriculture in 1862.[32]

Government activity was by no means lacking in the social sciences prior to the Civil War. Perhaps the most notable work was the decennial censuses, directed by the State Department until the Interior Department was established. Although the Census Office initially dealt in crude fashion with population alone, it gradually expanded the demographic detail on a more comprehensive basis. At the same time, it introduced broader inquiries on manufacturing, agriculture, commerce, mining, fisheries and education. By the Civil War the census was thus yielding an enlarged range of useful demographic, social and economic statistics.[33]

Valuable economic data resulted from the operation of still other government agencies. The Treasury Department amassed materials relating to foreign and domestic commerce, shipping, internal revenues, mining, and related subjects. Its collection of import duties, excise taxes and local tonnage duties enabled it to compile related data on a systematic and useful basis; and Congress often called upon it for special reports on the merchant marine, imports, exports and domestic manufacturing. The Army engineers collected data on inland transportation and trade, especially on the western rivers and the Great Lakes. The Interior Department, including the General Land Office, increased the knowledge of natural resources as to their location, extent and exploitation. The Indian Office was quite interested in the Indian trade and made contributions in the field of ethnology. Annual and special reports of government agencies promoted the gradual accumulation and use of economic and social knowledge. The enormous collection of congressional documents indicates how varied and extensive this government work became. These documents are of immense value for study of the country's economic and social development, including the growth of science and its dissemination in the interest of industry and trade.[34]

SIGNIFICANCE OF GOVERNMENT PROMOTION OF SCIENCE

When these many activities bearing on the promotion and application of science are put in perspective, it becomes clear that the government's early scientific endeavors were extremely important for territorial and

[32] Dupree, *op. cit.*, pp. 47, 109–114; Price, *op. cit.*, pp. 13–14; Gustavus A. Weber, *The Bureau of Chemistry and Soils*, pp. 1–13, and *The Patent Office* (Baltimore, 1928 and 1924, respectively), pp. 1–15.

[33] W. Stull Holt, *The Bureau of the Census* (Washington, 1929), pp. 1–18.

[34] The technical work of various government agencies is treated in the series of Service Monographs of the United States Government, prepared by the Institute for Government Research; several of these are cited above. See also Dupree, *op. cit.*

industrial expansion. Federal officials often took a highly purposeful attitude toward the development and dissemination of scientific knowledge and skills. Various agencies, particularly the technical bureaus of the War and Navy Departments, played a large part in this work. They actively borrowed technical knowledge from Europe, developed education and training functions, and carried on extensive investigation and research activities. Elsewhere in the government, the most significant scientific work was found in the Coast Survey, Smithsonian Institution, and Patent Office. Other agencies deserving notice for their scientific interests were the Lighthouse Board and the Land, Indian, and Census Offices.

In this broad concern of government with the advancement of science, the United States resembled and was influenced by France even more than Great Britain. The industrial revolution in Britain produced many self-taught craftsmen and engineers who filled the technical needs of private industry in manufacturing and public services such as transportation and communication. In France, however, the government assumed major responsibility for training technical experts and employing them in military institutions and public utilities, as well as in many industrial activities.[35] American officials often took these French technical schools and public services as models as well as sources of technical knowledge and even of trained experts.

The Civil War roughly marks a major transition in American science and industry. The modern factory system was rapidly emerging by this time, and the experimental or laboratory sciences quickly came to the forefront of scientific and technological advance. Because of their close relation to manufacturing, the crucial fields of scientific endeavor were physics and chemistry. Even during the Civil War most governmental calls for scientific help from the Smithsonian and the National Academy of Sciences fell within these two fields.[36] By and large, the government's earlier scientific work had been adapted chiefly to the practical needs of a preindustrial era. Although its activities in civil engineering, geology, mineralogy, astronomy, meteorology and agronomy continued to increase after 1865, they had to adapt to the experimental methods of pure science and the pace-setting advances in chemistry, physics and industrial technology. Meanwhile private scientists, industrial laboratories, and the new or reinvigorated universities and technological schools took the decisive lead in these latter fields and made great inroads into those in which the federal government had done much of the earlier pioneering. In this new, peaceful industrial era the scientific activities of government for several decades became considerably less crucial for the continued growth of

[35] See Arthur L. Dunham, *The Industrial Revolution in France, 1815–1848* (New York, 1955), pp. 13–15, 60, 66, 89, 399–407.
[36] Cohen, *op. cit.*, pp. 223, 229–232.

industry than had been the case before the Civil War.[37] As a consequence, the era of 140 or 160 years ago exceeds that of 70 or 80 years ago in providing instructive parallels to the present day's close relationships of government and defense to science and private enterprise.

[37] As Dupree (*op. cit.*, p. 2) observes, "Indeed, before the rise of the universities, private foundations, and industrial laboratories, the fate of science rested more exclusively with the government than it did later."

Government and Banking

14.   Jackson, Biddle, and the Bank of the United States

Bray Hammond

More than forty years have passed since Catterall's monograph on the second Bank of the United States was published, and, though that account has never been superseded, it antedates all recent literature on central banking and therefore presents inadequately the public purposes of the bank. Furthermore, it includes nothing about the bank's Pennsylvania successor, which failed, and thus omits the denouement of Biddle's conflict with Jackson. The inevitable effect of the failure, in the rough justice of history, was to make Jackson seem right and Biddle wrong; and this impression, especially in the absence of attention to the purpose and functions of the bank, seems in recent years to have been strengthened. I think it needs correction.

I

The Bank of the United States—the B.U.S. as Biddle and others often called it—was a national institution of complex beginnings, for its establishment in 1816 derived from the extreme fiscal needs of the federal government, the disorder of an unregulated currency, and the promotional ambitions of businessmen.[1] The bank had an immense amount of

[1] On the organization of the bank, besides R. C. H. Catterall, *Second Bank of the U. S.* (Chicago: The University of Chicago Press, 1903), see Raymond Walters, Jr., "Origin of the Second Bank of the U. S.," *The Journal of Political Economy*, LIII (1945), 115.

"Jackson, Biddle, and the Bank of the United States," by Bray Hammond, is reprinted by permission from *Journal of Economic History*, VII (May, 1947), 1–23.

private business—as all central banks then had and as many still have—yet it was even more definitely a government bank than was the Bank of England, the Bank of France, or any other similar institution at the time. The federal government owned one fifth of its capital and was its largest single stockholder, whereas the capital of other central banks was wholly private. Government ownership of central-bank stock has become common only in very recent years.[2] Five of the bank's twenty-five directors, under the terms of its charter, were appointed by the President of the United States, and no one of these five might be a director of any other bank. Two of its three successive presidents—William Jones and Nicholas Biddle—were chosen from among these government directors. The charter made the bank depository of the government and accountable to Congress and the Secretary of the Treasury.

On this depository relation hinged control over the extension of credit by banks in general, which is the essential function of a central bank. The government's receipts arose principally from taxes paid by importers to customs collectors;[3] these tax payments were in bank notes, the use of checks not then being the rule; the bank notes were mostly those of private banks, which were numerous and provided the bulk of the money in circulation; the B.U.S. received these notes on deposit from the customs collectors and, becoming thereby creditor of the private banks that issued them, presented them to the latter for payment. Banks that extended credit properly and maintained adequate gold and silver reserves were able to pay their obligations promptly on demand. Those that overextended themselves were not. The pressure of the central bank upon the private banks was constant, and its effect was to restrict their lending and their issue of notes. In this fashion, it curbed the tendency of the banks to lend too much and so depreciate their circulation.[4] Its regulatory powers were dependent on the private banks' falling currently into debt to it. The regulatory powers now in effect under the Federal Reserve Act depend upon the opposite relation—that is, upon the private banks' maintaining balances with the Federal Reserve Banks. The private banks were then debtors to the central bank; they are now creditors. The regulatory

[2] The Bank of England and the Bank of France came under government ownership in 1945. The modern term "central bank" was not used till nearly a century after Biddle's death. Hamilton used the term "public bank," and the nineteenth-century equivalent was "bank of issue."

[3] E. R. Taus, *Central Banking Functions of the U. S. Treasury, 1789–1941* (New York: Columbia University Press, 1943), Appendix III and IV; Davis R. Dewey, *Financial History of the U. S.* (New York: Longmans, Green and Company, 1931), p. 168; John Spencer Bassett, *The Life of Andrew Jackson* (New York: The Macmillan Company, 1931), p. 586.

[4] I use the term "private banks" in preference to the common term "state banks" because it brings out the essential differences between the central bank and the units of the banking system regulated by it. I therefore include as private those "state banks" proper owned in whole or part by state governments; for functionally these "state banks" proper differed little if any from the private banks.

powers of the United States Bank were simpler, more direct, and perhaps more effective than those of the Federal Reserve Banks, though they would not be so under present-day conditions.

It was notorious that large and influential numbers of the private banks and official state banks resented this regulation of their lending power. All but the more conservative found it intolerable to be let and hindered by the dunning of the B.U.S. and forced to reduce their debts instead of enlarging their loans. Many of them had the effrontery to insist as a matter of right that they be allowed to pay the central bank if and when they pleased.[5] The effort of various states, especially Maryland and Ohio, to levy prohibitory taxes on the United States Bank's branches reflects this desire of the private banks to escape regulation quite as much as it reflects the states' jealousy of their "invaded" sovereignty; the efforts were economic as well as political.[6]

In 1831, Gallatin commended the bank for its conduct during the twenties; it had "effectually checked excessive issues" by the state banks; "that very purpose" for which it had been established had been fulfilled. On the regulatory operation of the bank, "which requires particular attention and vigilance and must be carried on with great firmness and due forbearance, depends almost exclusively the stability of the currency. . . ." The country's "reliance for a sound currency and, therefore, for a just performance of contracts rests on that institution."[7] In 1833 he wrote to Horsley Palmer, of the Bank of England, that "the Bank of the United States must not be considered as affording a complete remedy," for the ills of overexpansion, "but as the best and most practicable which can be applied"; and its action "had been irreproachable" in maintaining a proper reserve position "as late as November 1830."[8] Though Gallatin did not say so, this was in effect praise of Nicholas Biddle's administration of the bank.

The powerful expansion of the economy in the nineteenth century made it necessary for the regulatory action of the bank to be mostly one of restraint, but there was occasion also for it to afford ease as holder of the ultimate reserves and lender of last resort. One of the first things it did was to end the general suspension that the country had been enduring for more than two years; and a crucial factor in the willingness and ability of the private banks to resume payment of their obligations was the pledge of the United States Bank that it would support them.[9] This, Vera Smith

---

[5] R. C. H. Catterall, *Second Bank*, p. 85.

[6] *McCulloch* v. *Maryland* (1819), 4 Wheaton, p. 315; *Osborn* v. *Bank of the United States* (1824), 9 Wheaton, p. 737. The arguments in these cases were constitutional, not economic.

[7] Albert Gallatin, *Writings*, ed. Henry Adams (Philadelphia: J. B. Lippincott and Company, 1879), III, 304, 336, 390; II, 426.

[8] *Ibid.*, II, 461. See also *Niles' Weekly Register*, XXXV (1828–29), 37.

[9] R. C. H. Catterall, *Second Bank*, pp. 24–26; American State Papers, *Finance* (Washington: Gales and Seaton, 1858), IV, 768–69.

writes, was "a very early declaration of the view that it is the duty of the central bank to act as lender of last resort."[10]

The regulatory functions of the bank were not always well performed. Its first president, William Jones, was a politician who extended credit recklessly, rendered the bank impotent to keep the private banks in line, and nearly bankrupted it—all in a matter of three years. Langdon Cheves put the bank back in a sound condition by stern procedures that were unavoidably unpopular. When Nicholas Biddle succeeded Cheves in 1823, the bank was strong in every respect but good will. Biddle repressed the desires of the stockholders for larger dividends, keeping the rate down and accumulating reserves. The art of central banking was not so clearly recognized then as it has since become, but Biddle advanced it, and with better luck he might well be memorable for having developed means of mitigating the tendency to disastrous, periodic crises characteristic of the nineteenth century in the United States.[11]

But Biddle, with all his superior talents, was not very discreet. He had an airy way of speaking that shocked his more credulous enemies and did him irreparable harm; and, when he described the functions of the bank, he contrived to give a livelier impression of its power than of its usefulness. Once when asked by a Senate committee if the B.U.S. ever oppressed the state banks, he said, "never": although nearly all of them might have been destroyed, many had been saved and still more had been relieved. This was ineffable in a man of Biddle's exceptional abilities. It put a normal situation in a sinister and uncouth light. A wanton abuse of regulatory powers is always possible, and abstention from it is not to be boasted of—any more than a decent man would boast of not choosing to be a burglar. By talking so, Biddle made his opponents feel sure he had let the cat out of the bag. For Thomas Hart Benton he had proved entirely too much—that he had a dangerous power "over the business and fortunes of nearly all the people."[12] Jackson referred in his veto to Biddle's remark, and Roger Taney was still shuddering at the disclosure many years later. He believed then and he believed still, he wrote, that there was a scheme to close every state bank in the Union. He believed "that the matter had been thought of, and that the manner in which it could be done was well understood."[13] That people believed such things, Biddle had his own jauntiness, naïveté, and political ineptitude to thank.

[10] Vera C. Smith, *Rationale of Central Banking* (London: P. S. King and Son, 1936), p. 40.

[11] Statements on Biddle's central-bank policy will be found in Reginald C. McGrane, *Correspondence of Nicholas Biddle* (Boston: Houghton Mifflin Company, 1919), pp. 34–36, 51, 56–58. Catterall discusses the subject admirably in his chapter v, with the limitation that central banking was no better understood in his day than in Biddle's—if as well. See also J. S. Bassett, *Andrew Jackson*, pp. 585–86.

[12] T. H. Benton, *Thirty Years' View* (New York: D. Appleton and Company, 1897), I, 159.

[13] C. B. Swisher, *Life of Taney* (New York: The Macmillan Company, 1935), pp. 166–69.

II

When Jackson became president in 1829, the B.U.S. had survived what then seemed its most crucial difficulties. The Supreme Court had affirmed and reaffirmed its constitutionality and ended the attempts of unfriendly states to interfere with it. The Treasury had long recognized its efficient services as official depository. The currency was in excellent condition. Yet in his first annual message, Jackson told Congress that "both the constitutionality and the expediency of the law creating the bank were well questioned by a large portion of our fellow-citizens, and it must be admitted by all that it has failed in the great end of establishing a uniform and sound currency."

There is nothing remarkable about Jackson's doubts of the bank's constitutionality, for he did not defer his own judgment to John Marshall's nor, in general, had the Supreme Court's opinions attained their later prestige.[14] His statement that the bank had failed in establishing a good currency is more difficult to understand, for it was plainly untrue in the usual sense of the words. But he was evidently using the words in the special sense of locofoco hard-money doctrine, according to which the only good money was gold and silver; the Constitution authorized Congress to coin it and regulate its value; the states were forbidden to issue paper and the federal government was not empowered to do so. Jackson, wrote C. J. Ingersoll, "considers all the state banks unconstitutional and impolitic and thinks that there should be no currency but coin. . . ."[15] There were practical considerations no less important than the legal. It was evident to the antibank people that banking was a means by which a relatively small number of persons enjoyed the privilege of creating money to be lent, for the money obtained by borrowers at banks was in the form of the banks' own notes. The fruits of the abuse were obvious: notes were overissued, their redemption was evaded, they lost their value, and the innocent husbandman and mechanic who were paid in them were cheated and pauperized. "It is absurd," wrote Taney, "to talk about a sound and stable paper currency."[16] There was no such thing. So, in Jackson's opinion, if the United States Bank was not establishing a metallic currency, it was not establishing a constitutional or sound and uniform one. His words might seem wild to the contaminated, like Gallatin and

[14] Even Gallatin in 1831 took pains to defend the bank's constitutionality without a reference to the court's decisions, of which he remarked in a footnote he had not known. Gallatin, *Writings*, III, 327. He was in Europe when *McCulloch* v. *Maryland* was decided, but not *Osborn* v. *Bank of the United States*. It is notable that he would discuss constitutionality without learning till he was through that the Supreme Court had said something on the subject.

[15] R. C. McGrane, *Correspondence of Biddle*, 172. For Benton's ideas, see his *Thirty Years' View*, I, 436.

[16] J. S. Bassett, *Correspondence of Andrew Jackson* (Washington, D. C.: Carnegie Institution, 1931), V, 491; Benton, *Thirty Years' View*, I, 436.

Biddle, but they were plain gospel truth to his sturdy antibank, hard-money agrarians.[17]

Hard money was a cardinal tenet of the left wing of the Democratic party. It belonged with an idealism in which America was still a land of refuge and freedom rather than a place to make money. Its aim was to clip the wings of commerce and finance by restricting the credit that paper money enabled them to obtain. There would then be no vast debt, no inflation, no demoralizing price changes; there would be no fluctuant or disappearing values, no swollen fortunes, and no grinding poverty. The precious metals would impose an automatic and uncompromising limit on the volatile tendencies of trade. "When there was a gold and silver circulation," said an agrarian in the Iowa constitutional convention of 1844, "there were no fluctuations; everything moved on smoothly and harmoniously." [18] The Jacksonians were even more devoted to the discipline of gold than the monetary conservatives of the present century.

There was also a pro-bank, "paper-money wing," which harbored the Democratic party's less spiritual virtues.[19] Its strength lay with free enterprise, that is, with the new generation of businessmen, promoters, and speculators, who found the old Hamiltonian order of the Federalists too stodgy and confining. These were 'Democrats by trade," as distinguished from "Democrats in principle"; one of the latter wrote sarcastically in the *Democratic Review* in 1838, "Being a good Democrat, that is to say, a Democrat *by trade* (Heaven forefend that any son of mine should be a Democrat *in principle*)—being a good Democrat by trade, he got a snug slice of the public deposites." [20] Fifty years before, business had fostered the erection of a strong federal government and inclined toward monopoly; in the early nineteenth century it began to appreciate the advantages offered by laissez faire and to feel that it had more to gain and less to fear from the states than from the federal government. This led it to take on the coloration and vocabulary of Jacksonian democracy and to exalt the rugged individualism of the entrepreneur and speculator along with that of the pioneer.

The private banks and their friends had helped to kill the first Bank of the United States twenty years before, but the strength they could muster

[17] The principal argument against the bank's constitutionality was not this, of course, but that Congress had no power to charter a bank outside the District of Columbia.

[18] Benjamin F. Shambaugh, *Fragments of the Debates of the Iowa Constitutional Conventions of 1844 and 1846* (Iowa City: State Historical Society of Iowa, 1900), pp. 69, 70, 71.

[19] Col. Benton on Banks and Currency, *Hunt's Merchants' Magazine*, XXXVIII (January 1858), 560–61.

[20] *The United States Magazine and Democratic Review* (Washington: Langtree and O'Sullivan, December 1838), III, 368. Alexander Hamilton's son, James A. Hamilton, a friend of Jackson and a speculator in New York real estate, seems to have been a Democrat by trade.

against the second was much greater. Herein lies the principal difference between the situation of the old bank when Jefferson became president in 1801 and the situation of the second when Jackson became president in 1829. Both men disapproved of the national bank and yet were inhibited by its being accepted in their own party and performing well its evidently important functions. There were also the differences that Jefferson was more amendable to reason than Jackson, that he had in Gallatin a better adviser than any Jackson had, and that the bank was under a more passive management in his day than in Jackson's. But of most importance was the greater pressure the private banks were able to exert in Jackson's time than in Jefferson's. Between 1801 and 1829 their number had greatly increased, as had the volume of their business and the demand for credit. The records indicate that in 1801 there were 31 banks, in 1829 there were 329, and in 1837 there were 788—an increase of 140 per cent during Jackson's administration alone.[21] These banks were associated to a marked extent with the Democratic party, especially in New York. Their opposition to federal regulation was therefore far greater in 1829 than in 1801, and it did more for Jackson's victory over the national bank than did the zeal of his hard-money locofocos. De Tocqueville wrote that "the slightest observation" enabled one to see the advantages of the B.U.S to the country and mentioned as most striking the uniform value of the currency it furnished. But the private banks, he said, submitted with impatience to "this salutary control" exercised by the B.U.S. They bought over newspapers. "They roused the local passions and the blind democratic instinct of the country to aid their cause. . . ." [22] Without them, it is doubtful if the Jacksonians could have destroyed the B.U.S.

The Jacksonian effort to realize the hard-money ideals was admirable, viewed as Quixotism. For however much good one may find in these ideals, nothing could have been more unsuited than they were to the American setting. In an austere land or among a contemplative and self-denying people they might have survived but not in one so amply endowed as the United States and so much dominated by an energetic and acquisitive European stock. Nowhere on earth was the spirit of enterprise to be more fierce, the urge for exploitation more restless, or the demand for credit more importunate. The rise of these reprobated forces spurred the agrarians, and as business itself grew they came to seek nothing less than complete prohibition of banking.[23] Yet they chose to destroy first the institution which was curbing the ills they disapproved,

---

[21] United States Comptroller of the Currency, *Annual Report*, 1916, pp. 913–14.
[22] Alexis de Tocqueville, *Democracy in America*, ed. Phillips Bradley (New York: Albert A. Knopf and Company, 1945), I, 409.
[23] In a number of western states and territories they achieved prohibition: in Arkansas, Illinois, Iowa, Wisconsin, California, and Oregon—though in the last two the impetus was more than agrarian.

and to that end they leagued with the perpetrators of those ills.[24] Jackson made himself, as de Tocqueville observed, the instrument of the private banks.[25] He took the government's funds out of the central bank, where they were less liable to speculative use and put them in the private banks, where they were fuel to the fire.[26] He pressed the retirement of the public debt, and he acquiesced in distribution of the federal surplus.[27] These things fomented the very evils he deplored and made the Jacksonian inflation one of the worst in American history. They quite outweighed the Maysville veto, which checked federal expenditures on internal improvements, and the specie circular, which crudely and belatedly paralyzed bank credit.

As a result, Jackson's presidency escaped by only two months from ending like Hoover's in 1933. Far from reaching the happy point where the private banks could be extirpated and the hands of the exploiters and speculators could be tied, Jackson succeeded only in leaving the house swept and garnished for them; and the last state of the economy was worse than the first. He professed to be the deliverer of his people from the oppressions of the mammoth—but instead he delivered the private banks from federal control and his people to speculation. No more striking example could be found of a leader fostering the very evil he was angrily wishing out of the way.[28]

But this was the inevitable result of the agrarian effort to ride two horses bound in opposite directions: one being monetary policy and the other states' rights. Monetary policy must be national, as the Constitution doubly provides. The agrarians wanted the policy to be national, but they eschewed the practicable way of making it that, and, instead of strengthening the national authority over the monetary system, they destroyed it. Where they were unencumbered by this fatal aversion to centralized

[24] T. H. Benton, *Thirty Years' View*, I, 158.

[25] Alexis de Tocqueville, *Democracy in America*, I, 409.

[26] Taney made himself ridiculous: he told the pet banks the government funds would enable them to lend more, he gave them checks on the B.U.S. to protect them from the monster, and then he helplessly asked them not to use the checks.—R. C. H. Catterall, *Second Bank*, pp. 302–5. United States Secretary of the Treasury, *Annual Reports* (1833), III, 369; 23d Congress, 1st Session, *Senate Document No. 16*, 321 ff.

[27] Retirement of the public debt was inflationary in that it spread a feeling of elate satisfaction and closed a field for conservative investment. Gallatin had thought the retirement would be a good thing but later found to his dismay that it was "a signal for an astonishing increase in the indebtedness of the community at large."—Henry Adams, *Life of Albert Gallatin* (Philadelphia: J. B. Lippincott and Company, 1879), p. 656.

[28] See a contemporary English observer, "Causes and Consequences of the Crisis in the American Trade," *Edinburgh Review*, LXV (July 1837), 227–28. The impetus given new banks by the prospect of closing the B.U.S. was observed everywhere. Benton exclaimed that he had not joined in putting it down in order "to put up a wilderness of local banks."—24th Congress, 2d Session, January 1837, *Register of Debates*, p. 610. See also Jabez Hammond, *History of Political Parties in New York* (Cooperstown: H. and E. Phinney, 1846), II, 434, 489.

power, they accomplished considerable. In Indiana they set up an official State Bank, with branches, which from 1834 to 1853 was the only source of bank credit permitted and yet was ample for all but the most aggressive money-makers, who finally ended its monopoly. In Missouri, they established the Bank of Missouri, with branches, a state monopoly which lasted from 1837 to 1857, when it too succumbed to free enterprise. And in Iowa, another monopoly, the Bank of Iowa, with branches, was in operation from 1858 till 1865, when free banking penetrated the state under authority of the National Bank Act. These instances indicate that if the hard-money agrarians had had a conception of national government less incompatible with their social purposes, they might have tempered rather than worsened the rampant excesses of nineteenth-century expansion that so offended them.[29]

But as it was, they helped an acquisitive democracy take over the conservative system of bank credit introduced by Hamilton and by the merchants of Philadelphia and New York and limber it up to suit the popular wish to get rich quick. Wringing their hands, they let bank credit become the convenient key to wealth—the means of making capital accessible in abundance to millions of go-getting Americans who otherwise could not have exploited their natural resources with such whirlwind energy. The excesses of that energy have forced the Jacksonian hard-money heroics to be slowly undone: the federal government's authority over money, the Treasury's close operating contact with the banking system, and the central-bank controls over credit have been haltingly restored. Credit itself, in the surviving American tradition, is not the virus the agrarians held it to be but the lifeblood of business and agriculture, and the Jacksonian hard-money philosophy has been completely forgotten, especially by Jackson's own political posterity.

III

Jackson had not committed himself against the bank during the early part of his first term but worried both those who wanted him to support recharter and those who wanted him to prevent it. In November 1829 he was friendly to Biddle and assured him that he had no more against the B.U.S. than against "all banks." The next month he slurred the bank in his message to Congress. In 1831 when the cabinet was changed, two important portfolios went to friends of Biddle: Livingston became Secretary of State and McLane Secretary of the Treasury. Both wanted the bank continued and hoped to influence Jackson. Biddle deferred to their hopes, but the tension was evidently too severe for him. The bank's enemies were

[29] See Hugh McCulloch, *Men and Measures of Half a Century* (New York: Charles Scribner's Sons, 1889); John Ray Cable, *The Bank of the State of Missouri* (New York: Columbia University Press, 1923); Howard H. Preston, *History of Banking in Iowa* (Iowa City: State Historical Society of Iowa, 1922).

growing more provocative, and in the summer of 1831 his brother, a director of the bank's St. Louis branch, was killed in a duel, more than usually shocking, which arose from the controversy over recharter.[30] Whatever the reasons, he let impatience get the upper hand and decided that the bank, without further temporizing, should ask Congress that the charter be renewed.[31]

Jackson was offended by this direct action, and notwithstanding improvements in the new charter and concessions to his views, he vetoed the bill of renewal. The economic reasoning of the veto message was, in Catterall's language, "beneath contempt," and the most appealing allegations in it were "demonstrably and grossly false." [32] Biddle was deluded enough to have 30,000 copies printed and distributed in the bank's own interest. One may regard this as evidence of contempt for Jackson or of a faith in the democracy as sincere as Jackson's own; but it is also evidence of the limitations on Biddle's political sense. In the election that fall the bank was the leading issue, and hopes for recharter went to nothing with Jackson's overwhelming majority. Jackson's purpose now was to stop using the bank as government depository. How firmly accepted it was in Washington as the peculiar agency of the government is indicated by the resistance he encountered. He had to get rid of two Treasury heads successively before he found a third who would execute his wishes, the law giving only the Secretary of the Treasury the power to remove the government's deposits from the bank; and he had also to disregard a House resolution declaring that the government deposits were safe as they were.

With loss of the deposits, the bank lost the means of regulating the private banks' extension of credit. Biddle had made enough mistakes already, but he now made the fatal one of failing to resign and let the bank be liquidated; there is a limit beyond which the head of a central bank cannot decently go against the head of the government, even when he is right and the head of the government is wrong. Moreover, although a central bank is a very useful institution, it never possesses the kind of virtues that count in conflict against an intensely popular leader. By resigning, Biddle would have stultified Jackson and justified himself, as it turned out; for when the panic came in 1837, Jackson would have got the blame, with considerable justice. Furthermore, Biddle would have spared himself a tragic end. The bank was in a better condition than it came to be later, and conditions were much more favorable for liquidation, in spite of the recession of 1833–1834. Incidentally, this recession was produced, it

[30] *St. Louis Beacon,* September 1, 1831, September 22, 1831; *Niles' Weekly Register,* September 17, 1831, p. 37. The duel was fought with pistols at five feet, Major Biddle being nearsighted, and each man killed the other.

[31] R. C. H. Catterall, *Second Bank,* pp. 214 ff.

[32] *Ibid.,* p. 239.

was averred, by a vindictive curtailment of the bank's loans. There certainly was resentment mixed into the bank's policy, but on the other hand, the bank could not go out of existence, as its enemies desired, without curtailing its credit, and curtailment is always unpopular, scarcely less in a period of general expansion than in one of depression.

Instead of going out of existence the bank became a private corporation under Pennsylvania charter in February 1836, a fortnight before its federal charter expired.[33] A little more than a year later the panic of 1837 broke. It began May 10 and involved all the banks in the country, about 800 in number, with an aggregate circulation of $150,000,000 and deposits of $125,000,000. It precipitated three distinct monetary programs—one of hard money by the anti-bank administration in Washington, one of easy money by Biddle in Philadelphia, and one of convertibility by the banks of Wall Street under the sage but incongruous leadership of the venerable Jeffersonian, Albert Gallatin.

The administration, with Van Buren now president, took the opportunity to urge an independent Treasury system, with complete "divorce of bank and state." Its course was that urged by Jackson, who wrote, July 9, 1837:

> Now is the time to separate the Government from all banks, receive and disburse the revenue in nothing but gold and silver coin, and the circulation of our coin through all public disbursements will regulate the currency forever hereafter. Keep the Government free from all embarrassments, whilst it leaves the commercial community to trade upon its own capital, and the banks to accommodate it with such exchange and credit as best suits their own interests—both being money making concerns, devoid of patriotism, looking alone to their own interests—regardless of all others. It has been, and ever will be a curse to the Government to have any entanglement or interest with either, more than a general superintending care of all.[34]

Wall Street paid little attention to this program but set about preparations to resume specie payments as soon as possible, getting its own house in order and urging the banks elsewhere to send delegates to a convention "for the purpose," in Gallatin's words, "of agreeing on a uniform course of measures and on the time when the resumption should take place."[35]

Nicholas Biddle took a course opposed to that of both Wall Street and

[33] The authorized capital of the bank under Pennsylvania charter was $35,000,000, as it had been under national charter. It appears, however, that the shares ($7,000,000 par) held by the government under the national charter were not reissued to new owners and that the actual paid-in capital of the Pennsylvania corporation was only $28,000,000.—John J. Knox, *History of Banking* (New York: Bradford, Rhodes, and Company, 1903), pp. 78–79.

[34] J. S. Bassett, *Correspondence of Jackson*, V, 495, 498, 500, 504 ff.; Condy Raguet, *Financial Register*, II (Philadelphia: Adam Waldie, 1838), 58.

[35] Albert Gallatin, *Writings*, III, 398.

the administration. He demanded that the Treasury scheme be abandoned and the specie circular repealed. He contended that Jackson's policies were responsible for the financial distress and that the basic condition of recovery was their repudiation by Congress. Till these things were done, the banks should not resume redemption of their notes. Wall Street's program he denounced as premature and sacrificial. He advocated instead an active and flexible policy that should be remedial for the prostrate economy—that should check the credit contraction and the fall of prices. His own objects during the past eighteen months, he wrote James Gordon Bennett, October 1838, had been "to sustain the national character abroad by paying our debts and at the same time to protect the securities and the staples of the country from the ruinous depreciation to which they were inevitably sinking." [36] It was evident to him, he wrote John Quincy Adams in December, "that if resort was had to rigid curtailments, the ability to pay would be proportionally diminished; . . . . the only true system was to keep the country as much at ease as consisted with its safety, so as to enable the debtors to collect their resources for the discharge of their debts." [37] Lenity for the banks would mean lenity for their debtors, foreclosures and bankruptcies would be avoided, and values protected from collapse. Suspension, he had already said, was "wholly conventional between the banks and the community" and arose from "their mutual conviction that it is for their mutual benefit." [38]

The situation was one in which the more conservative settled back to let deflation, as it came to be called a century later, run its bitter course; and the hard-money agrarians sardonically joined them in hoping for the worst. But both the agrarians and Wall Street testified to the popularity of Biddle's ideas. Governor Ford of Illinois observed, with the sarcasm of a hard-money Democrat, that although the banks owed more than they could pay and although the people owed each other and the banks more than they could pay, "yet if the whole people could be persuaded to believe the incredible falsehood that all were able to pay, this was 'confidence.'" [39] In Wall Street it was said that suspension made lawbreakers of every one. "Instead of the permanent and uniform standard of value provided by the Constitution, and by which all contracts were intended to be regulated, we have at once fifty different and fluctuating standards, agreeing only in one respect, that of impairing the sanctity of contracts." [40] The believers in Biddle were themselves eloquent in the new faith. Following the later debacle of the B.U.S., the Philadelphia *Gazette*

[36] Presidents' Letter Book, No. I, 542, Biddle MSS, Library of Congress.
[37] 29th Congress, 1st Session, *House Document No. 226*, p. 405
[38] Condy Raguet, *Financial Register*, I, 342–46.
[39] Thomas Ford, *History of Illinois* (Chicago: S. C. Griggs and Company; New York: Ivison and Phinney, 1854), p. 227.
[40] Report of delegates to the Bank Convention, New York, November 1837; Condy Raguet, *Financial Register*, I, 229.

said: "The immediate effect of the suspension will be an ease in the money market, a cessation of those cares and disquietudes with which the business men of our community have been annoyed. . . . . The great error . . . . to which all subsequent errors are in a measure to be traced was in the premature resumption in August 1838. . . . . The banks are just as good, and better and more solid, under a season of suspension as under its opposite." [41]

Meanwhile, the New York banks had succeeded in resuming payment of their obligations, May 10, 1838, the anniversary of the suspension. This was a real hard-money achievement, due largely to Gallatin and the Bank of England, in which the professedly hard-money administration had little if any part. Instead it had to violate with its eyes open the professions that Jackson had violated without knowing what he was doing. While still trying to distribute a federal "surplus" which had turned into a deficit, it had to resort to issues of Treasury notes, which its hard-money zealots believed unconstitutional. It had to go still further and tolerate what Biddle had demanded: the specie circular was repealed in May 1838, the subtreasury bill was defeated in June, and in July the Treasury had to accept—to its substantial relief—a credit of four to five million dollars on the books of the Bank of the United States in anticipated payment of amounts due the government in liquidation of its shares.[42] This last transaction made the bank a depository of the government some five years after Jackson had ordered that its predecessor, a better institution, cease to be used as depository.

By the fall of 1838, banks everywhere were back on a specie basis, and, although this was mainly due to the efforts of Wall Street and Albert Gallatin, it was Biddle who had the prestige. He was riding on the crest. "All that it was designed to do has been done," he wrote John Quincy Adams in December 1838; and he was about to retire.[43] Two months later, February 1839, he was Van Buren's guest of honor at the White House. "This dinner went off very well," according to James A. Hamilton, "Biddle evidently feeling as the conqueror. He was facetious and in intimate converse with the President." [44] A month later Biddle retired from the

[41] *Philadelphia Gazette,* October 10, 1839.

[42] These represented payment of $7,900,000 to the government for its stock in the bank. This sum included a premium of about $1,000,000, besides which the government had received dividends of over $7,000,000 during the twenty years of the bank's existence. The net gain to the government from its original investment of $7,000,000, which it paid for in bonds, is estimated by Knox at $6,000,000 and by Catterall at $8,000,000.—John J. Knox, *History of Banking,* p. 79; R. C. H. Catterall, *Second Bank,* p. 474. In the settlement for the government stock, agreed upon in 1837 (Catterall, *Second Bank,* pp. 373–75), the administration had held out for a premium in a way which indicated it had no doubt of the bank's solvency.

[43] 29th Congress, 1st Session, *House Document No. 226,* p. 408

[44] R. C. McGrane, *Correspondence of Biddle,* p. 337; *Reminiscenses of James A. Hamilton* (New York: Charles Scribner's Sons, 1869), p. 312.

bank, its affairs being, he said, in a state of great prosperity and in able hands.[45] The same day the directors were unanimous in describing him as one who had "performed so much and so faithfully" and was leaving the bank "prosperous in all its relations . . . . and secure in the respect and esteem of all who are connected with it in foreign or domestic inter-course." [46]

Six months later, in the fall of 1839, the bank suspended payment of its obligations. It resumed and then suspended again. In 1841, after two years of dismayed inquiry and recrimination, it was assigned to trustees for liquidation.

The stockholders were stunned, and then they turned on Biddle. In the summer of 1840 he was told that he owed the bank an "over-advance" of about $320,000 on an old account. This he denied. Nevertheless, "though he did not recognize the claim" and although "neither law or equity made it necessary to pay," he did so—mostly in Texas bonds which were accepted at more than market value. The stockholders next turned to litigation and thereafter seem to have kept Biddle continuously in the courts. In January 1842, he and former associates in the bank were arrested on charges of criminal conspiracy and put on $10,000 bail each. The charge was that they had conspired "to cheat and defraud the bank by obtaining therefrom large advances upon shipments of cotton to Europe," and "by the unlawful receipt and expenditure of large sums of money, the application of which is not specified upon the books." [47] The court of General Sessions was occupied two weeks with habeas corpus hearings, twenty witnesses being examined and "all the books and papers of the bank brought into court, where they underwent a most searching investigation." Biddle's attorneys let his case stand on the evidence of the prosecutors. "As soon as the testimony for the prosecution was finished, the counsel for Mr. Biddle offered to leave the matter to the court without argument." [48] The court found evidence lacking that the acts charged involved fraud; for they were known to the directors and approved by them. Of any fraudulent coalition it found nothing to justify even a reasonable suspicion.[49] Two judges concurred in this decision; one dissented.

A few weeks later another suit was instituted. The stockholders filed a bill of equity in which they asked that Biddle and one of his former associates be required to account for $400,000 of the bank's funds. The bill

[45] *Niles' Weekly Register,* LVI (April 6, 1839), p. 84.
[46] 29th Congress, 1st Session, *House Document No. 226,* p. 486.
[47] 29th Congress, 1st Session, *House Document No. 226,* 419 ff., 475 ff.; also opinion of Judge Barton, *Philadelphia Inquirer,* May 10, 1842.
[48] *Philadelphia Public Ledger,* April 11, 1842.
[49] *Philadelphia Public Ledger,* April 30, 1842. The court had much to say of "the singularly loose method" by which the directors had conducted the business of the corporation.

was dismissed December 1844, the court holding that information which might incriminate the defendants could not be required of them.[50] But Biddle was no longer living. He had died ten months before, February 27, 1844, aged fifty-eight.

IV

The failure of the B.U.S. leaves two questions one would like to have answered: What was the actual condition of the bank? How responsible was Biddle for it? The Jacksonians had easy answers, of course, and jeered triumphantly; matters had proved to be even worse than they had said, Biddle had known the bank was rotten, and having enriched himself he had striven to leap clear in time but had been caught. The Democratic press was hot with invective and ribald ridicule of the great Regulator, the old Nick, the prestidigitatorial wizard who had crowned a career of astounding performances by consummately destroying everything he had done, and himself with it.[51]

To say with Biddle's political enemies that the bank was "rotten" is putting it both vigorously and vaguely. No one can be precise in such a matter, for in a long and complicated liquidation involving suits and technical decisions respecting the admissibility of claims, the completeness of the settlement must be subject to interpretation. But, according to a trustee quoted by Knox, the creditors were paid in full, principal and interest, though the bank's capital was entirely absorbed, and the stockholders got nothing.[52] This would mean a shrinkage of about one fourth of the value of the bank's assets, roughly speaking. The 7,000 bank failures in the United States in the ten years, 1921–1930, entailed estimated losses of about one third of the total deposit liabilities.[53] The comparison is crude, but I think it warrants the opinion that the condition of the B.U.S. was rotten only in a hyperbolical sense. Moreover, it is to be borne in mind that values usually diminish in liquidation, that the portfolio to be liquidated was the country's largest, and that the process, which ran to 1856, had to be undertaken in a period when buyers were not eager nor prices buoyant. The stockholders in 1841 insisted to the legislature that the bank could pay all its creditors and requested lenity so that losses might be minimized.[54] These things make me think that the bank in 1839 may have been in a situation little if any worse than that which Jones had got its predecessor into twenty years before and from which Cheves rescued it.

[50] Bank of the United States v. Biddle, Parsons' Select Cases in Equity (Philadelphia, 1888), II, 33 ff.

[51] Democratic Review, II (December 1838), 372–73.

[52] John J. Knox, History of Banking, p. 79.

[53] Federal Deposit Insurance Corporation, Annual Report (Washington, 1940), p. 66.

[54] 29th Congress, 1st Session, House Document No. 226, p. 533.

As for the second question—Biddle's responsibility—it seems to me clear that policies put into effect by him led to the bank's failure but that he had no realization or suspicion of what was developing. The policies included prodigal loans on stocks, especially to officers and directors of the bank, heavy investments in corporate stocks and speculative bonds, and purchases of cotton and other agricultural commodities for export. The cotton transactions were undertaken in the emergency of 1837 as a means of sustaining domestic commodity prices and providing European exchange. They succeeded initially, but once begun they were hard to stop, and they produced loss, litigation, and recrimination that was probably more damaging to Biddle himself than to the bank. The loan and investment policy was begun as early as 1835 when it looked as if the bank would have to liquidate: the active assets were converted into loans on stocks in preparation for a long period of liquidation. But when the Pennsylvania charter was obtained, the policy was not abandoned. Instead it was adapted to the vaster prospects of manifest destiny and empire building. Loans were made with a lax grandiosity. "It seems to have been sufficient," according to a stockholders' committee report later, "to obtain money on loan, to pledge the stock of 'an incorporated company', however remote its operations or uncertain its prospects." Partly from choice and partly from the extortionate requirements of its charter —which Biddle should never have accepted—the bank also became the owner of such stocks outright; in 1840 it had shares in more than twenty other banks, some of which it wholly controlled, and great holdings in railways, toll bridges, turnpikes, and canals, besides speculative bonds issued to finance "public improvements." [55] These investments immobilized the bank's funds so that it was without active means to repay the government for its stock, to honor its $20,000,000 of circulating notes, which soon began to be rapidly presented for redemption, and to meet its charter obligations, which in five years made it divert more than a third of its capital "to purposes of the state." To meet these requirements, the bank was driven into the market as borrower, both at home and abroad. These borrowings were begun by Biddle, and his successors turned to them more and more. Hence the bank came to be progressively incurring new obligations harder to meet than the old. The pressure mounted swiftly, so that a situation of apparent comfort in the spring of 1839 had passed into

[55] Laws of Pennsylvania 1835–36, p. 43; 29th Congress, 1st Session, *House Document No. 226*, p. 532. See report of the stockholders' committee, April 3, 1841, 29th Congress, 1st Session, *House Document No. 226*, esp. pp. 414–16, 425 ff. This report confirms, it seems to me, the opinion of Judge Barton a year later. I do not go into the cotton transactions, which Judge Barton discusses at length, because to discuss them adequately takes too much space. They show Biddle's audacity, ingenuity, and casuistry, but it is not clear that they cost the bank much, except indirectly by deterioration of management. The loan policy, though less irregular, did the bank more direct damage.

one of agony in the fall. These were the six months between Biddle's retirement and the bank's suspension. The bank had for years been growing more and more illiquid, but the condition had remained concealed by confidence. Once the illiquidity was suspected, however, the bank's creditors woke up with a start, and its obligations became instantly menacing. The suddenness of the change depended not on existence of the condition but on recognition of it.

According to one view, Biddle cannot be blamed for the bank's failure —it happened six months after he had retired. Well, granted that Biddle was gone, the bank was in the hands of successors who besides being heirs to his policies had been trained in his school. And this school, according to the evidence of stockholders' reports and court records, was one of extreme administrative inefficiency. The directors, dazzled by Biddle, knew nothing and approved everything. There were special procedures for special transactions, items being carried in the teller's drawer till it was expedient to post them. Accounts of the old bank were continued on the books of the new as if the corporate continuity was unbroken; and the notes of the old were kept in circulation by the new—a practice which particularly outraged Gallatin. It was in this atmosphere that Biddle's successors learned to manage the bank, and if they came to grief it cannot be said that it was merely because they had not his ability. He would have come to grief himself.[56]

That Biddle must bear responsibility for the bank's condition is one thing; but that he had a guilty consciousness of its condition is quite another. Although the tradition of his dishonesty is held both by the Jacksonian partisans and by some scholars, I think it rests on a trite and stiffly moralistic view of the facts. If he realized how seriously wrong things were, it was an instance of objective analysis and cold self-appraisal unique in his career. I cannot believe him capable of it. He was eminently of a sanguine disposition, as is emphasized in the characterization of him by Catterall, who has given him more attention than any other historian. Caution and modesty were probably never among his more conspicuous virtues, and Jackson's attack did not enhance them. In the years 1836 to 1839, when he was laying down a new course for the bank, he was at the height of his career, it then seemed, and flushed with victory. He had blundered when he forced the issue of recharter in 1832, and Jackson had whipped him in the elections that year, in the veto, and in the removal of the deposits in 1833. But by 1838 he seemed to have retrieved his blunder and defeat. He had found sanctuary for the bank in the Pennsylvania jurisdiction, where Jackson could only gnash his teeth at it. He could point scornfully at the situation compounded of the panic of

[56] For some account of the bank's methods, see Sister M. Grace Madeleine, *Monetary and Banking Theories of Jacksonian Democracy* (Philadelphia: The Dolphin Press, 1943), chaps. iv and v. The author seems to believe Biddle morally culpable.

1837, the specie circular, and distribution of the federal surplus. By 1839 he was the honored guest of Van Buren in the White House, and he could boast that the bank was again a government depository, that the independent Treasury scheme was rejected, and that the specie circular was repealed. He had triumphed over the Jacksonians on the points he cared most about. He even claimed credit for resumption, patronized Wall Street, and acted as the impresario of national monetary policy. It was in the fatuous mood of wishful thinking and expansive imagination stimulated by these illusive developments that he administered the bank after the failure of Jackson's attempt to annihilate him. If Biddle, at the height of his success in the winter of 1838–1839, examined his achievements objectively and concluded that all he had done mounted up to either a colossal fraud or a colossal mistake, he must have been a very remarkable character indeed. Yet that is what the tradition of his moral guilt requires one to believe. I find more credible the less dramatic possibility that, being a man of very sanguine susceptibilities, he was simply carried away by success and self-confidence, by the grand scale of his activities, and by the daily exercise of more power, as he put it, than the President of the United States possessed. I believe he had lost the faculty of recognizing his own mistakes. The series of letters he wrote in 1841—prolix, specious, declamatory compositions in which he unconvincingly insisted that the bank had been in sound condition when he left it—seem to me the pathetic efforts of a man confounded by other things than guilt: by surprise, incredulousness, grief, anxiety, and shock.[57] His friends were at no less a loss; the most they could say in his favor was to protest at those who had been his sycophants while hoping to prosper but who turned against him with a "malicious prosecution" when their common fortunes collapsed.[58]

The hostility of Jackson to the Bank of the United States was in the first instance a matter of principle, the bank belonging to a monetary system and to a theory of federal powers which he disapproved; but later he and his followers could allege also that the bank was rotten and Biddle dishonest. That allegation was, in fact, emphasized more than the original principle. But if the bank was not rotten and Biddle was not dishonest, then what may be called the moral grounds for Jackson's action disappear leaving no defense except in charity to his good intentions. All he did was destroy a wisely developed monetary system. The administration of that system by the B.U.S. was admirable but might have been strengthened and improved had not Jackson's views been so radical and his temper so intransigent. In particular, had his demoralizing attack never been made Biddle would not have been stimulated to undertake his later grandiose and tragic course. But the blame must be shared by Biddle. The fury and

[57] 29th Congress, 1st Session, *House Document No. 226*, pp. 475–516.
[58] *Philadelphia Public Ledger*, April 1, 1842.

the folly of these two ruined an excellent monetary system—as good as any the country has ever possessed—and left a reckless, booming anarchy.

When the career of Nicholas Biddle is given the study its importance deserves, it may appear that the earlier part of it, when he was a central banker, was something less than brilliant and that the later part, when he was an empire builder, was something worse than overweening. But, as it is, the evidence indicates an inventive, facile, dynamic person—vain and not too painfully honest under pressure—who encountered a bigoted interference with his extremely able management of an institution purposing to restrain the inflationary abuse of bank credit; who naïvely trusted the rightness of his position, contemned his adversary, defied him, and, after a smart defeat which he refused to acknowledge, achieved an illusory victory; who then, with overblown confidence in his own judgment, in the economic future of the country, and in the alchemic powers of bank credit, committed himself to empire building; who did things the ingenious if not the right way; and who reckoned on a faster and less fluctuant growth than the country actually had. In all this he went with the times. When an opposition that was locofoco on one side and laissez faire on the other overcame him, he joined the latter and likelier of the two. Having been stripped of the Hamiltonian garments of central control, he gladly put on the gayer ones of free enterprise. Yet Biddle was attracted more by the statesmanship of enterprise than by enterprise itself. As a central banker, his policy had been governed properly by public interest rather than profit.[59] As empire builder also, he led the bank into affairs of national scope and purpose.[60] He upheld the nation's foreign financial obligations. He intervened with both parties on behalf of Texas, whose government he had financed.[61] He resisted Jackson's monetary measures with a determination more patriotic than discreet. His retirement from the bank at the age of fifty-three must have been greatly influenced, and very reasonably, by political ambitions. Only a few weeks before announcing that he would retire, he had been advised by Thomas Cooper that his candidacy for president of the United States was not immediately practicable because of the "prevailing ignorance and prejudice about banks"—the general suspension being still a recent matter—and that "some years hence" prospects might be better.[62] The bank's difficulties from 1839 on blanked out these prospects wholly. They did

---

[59] See his criticism of "mere men of business" as administrators of the B.U.S.—R. C. McGrane, *Correspondence of Biddle*, p. 27.

[60] It will be recalled that, in his earlier literary days, he prepared a popular edition of the Lewis and Clark journals.

[61] R. C. McGrane, *Correspondence of Biddle*, pp. 325, 333, 335; C. H. Van Tyne, *Letters of Daniel Webster* (New York: McClure, Phillips and Company, 1902), p. 213.

[62] R. C. McGrane, *Correspondence of Biddle*, p. 333. See also earlier correspondence with Thomas Cooper regarding the presidency, pp. 272, 277–282, 293, 296, 323.

more. Biddle had rebounded from the earlier frustration that ended his career as central banker; from the disaster to his later career he had no power to turn. John Quincy Adams had dinner with him *en famille,* November 22, 1840, and talked long with him. "Biddle," he wrote, "broods with smiling face and stifled groans over the wreck of splendid blasted expectations and ruined hopes. A fair mind, a brilliant genius, a generous temper, an honest heart, waylaid and led astray by prosperity, suffering the penalty of scarcely voluntary error—'tis piteous to behold." [63] He died a little more than three years later, in reduced circumstances if not insolvent.

Besides the Jacksonian view of Biddle and the view that I have opposed to it, there is another I have already mentioned. Its distinction is its calm silence about the unhappy events, whether discreditable or tragic, of Biddle's last years. In R. C. McGrane's *The Panic of 1837,* the bank's failure is alluded to, and Biddle's connection with it is dismissed in a footnote: "It should be noted that Biddle was now out of office, and can not be held responsible for what the bank did at this period." In the published correspondence of Nicholas Biddle, edited by Mr. McGrane, there is nothing that deals with the things that made Biddle's last years so miserably unlike those of his prime—the bank's failure, the loss of money and esteem, the prosecution of suits against him. And similarly in the article on Biddle in the *Dictionary of American Biography,* no mention is made of his last years' being clouded by any trouble whatsoever. Such reticence and piety contrast genteelly with the bitterness he actually suffered and with the judgment that he belonged in jail.[64]

Two things combined to give Biddle's fall a supererogatory blackness. One was the sheer drama of the event. The largest corporation in the country—one of the largest in the world—had fallen suddenly from its splendid success into sprawling collapse at the very feet of the genius who had only recently with grand gestures relinquished its management. It was a denouement that stimulated the imagination to make worse what was already bad enough. The other aggravation of the story came from political motives. Biddle and the bank had never been warmed to by the Whigs, and Biddle's own ties were less with them than with the Democrats, but the latter naturally sought to make the bank seem Whig.[65] They

[63] John Quincy Adams, *Memoirs,* ed. C. F. Adams (Philadelphia: J. B. Lippincott and Company, 1876), X, 361.

[64] Reginald C. McGrane, *The Panic of 1837; Some Financial Problems of the Jacksonian Era* (Chicago: The University of Chicago Press, 1924), p. 205; R. C. McGrane, *Correspondence of Biddle.* The Jacksonian opinion of Biddle is reflected in Arthur M. Schlesinger, Jr.'s, *Age of Jackson* (Boston: Little, Brown and Company, 1945), which I have not referred to in this essay because I reviewed it in the May 1946 issue of this JOURNAL.

[65] It is not clear which party Biddle supposed might make him president. The second Bank of the United States was both nurtured and destroyed within the Democratic party. Its creators and friends included Madison, Monroe, Gallatin, and Crawford;

had great success; the debacle helped to distintegrate the Whigs and strengthened the Jacksonians immeasurably. As a result, partisan views have dominated subsequent judgments and given Biddle the incidental and thankless role of darkened background to the glories of Andrew Jackson; and his achievements in credit policy, especially in the earlier and more admirable phase when he was a pioneer central banker, have been forgotten. Nowhere has he been studied adequately in his own right as a man of significant accomplishments, shortcomings, and misfortunes. Yet, in intellectual capacity, force of character, public spirit, and lasting influence, he was comparable with any of the contemporaries of his prime.

The withering that overtook Biddle's fame did not extend to his philosophy and example, which turned out to be triumphant, though with no acknowledgment to him. The monetary views of Gallatin and of Jackson are both obsolete, but Biddle's have a sort of pragmatic orthodoxy. He sought to make monetary policy flexible and compensatory rather than rigid. His easy-money doctrine had its source in a vision of national development to which abundant credit was essential. The majority of his countrymen have agreed with him. They have dismissed the man, but they have followed his ideas, especially his worse ones. They have shared his bullishness and his energy. They have not liked Jackson's primitive ideals of a simple, agrarian society, except in their nostalgic moods. They have not understood Gallatin's noble aversion for the fierce spirit of enterprise. They have exploited the country's resources with abandon, they have plunged into all the debt they could, they have realized a fantastic growth, and they have slighted its cost. Gallatin personified the country's intelligence and Jackson its folklore, but Biddle personified its behavior. They closed their careers in high honor—he closed his in opprobrium and bewilderment.

---

its three presidents, Jones, Cheves, and Biddle, were party members. Its greatest enemies were likewise pillars of the party—Jackson himself, Benton, and Taney. Jackson's cabinet was divided. The Whigs championed the bank less for its own sake than because Jackson's course left them no choice, and they abandoned it with relief as soon as they could. They were not interested in having bank credit restricted.

Foreign Markets and Economic Growth

15. International Trade and United States Economic Development: 1827–1843 *

Jeffrey G. Williamson

The decades of the 1820's, 1830's and early 1840's form a fascinating period in the process of American nineteenth-century development. In many ways that era represents a classic case of interdependence between developed and underdeveloped economies through the movements of factors, goods and specie. During these formative years in American development, the United States was predominantly a single primary product exporter, her rate of economic expansion very much a function of the state of the external market for cotton. The flow of capital moves in the classic fashion, from capital-rich Great Britain to capital-scarce America, but varying with relative degrees of expected returns; that is, varying with the relative rate of development between the two countries. But the period from the 1820's to 1840's exhibits another interesting aspect as well: it reveals the first substantial evidence of a long swing in the rate of American economic development.[1]

In a recent issue of this *Journal*, George Macesich presented a somewhat unusual argument concerning external influences on domestic monetary fluctuations over the period 1834–1845, appealing to a highly simplified gold standard model.[2] Macesich begins his analysis with the evidence of large capital inflows in the period 1834–1838 and the subsequent outflow in the 1840's. From this evidence Macesich feels there is sufficient proof to support the hypothesis that the monetary difficulties of the 1830's and 1840's are not primarily attributable to the struggle between Jackson's "hard currency" and Nicholas Biddle's "Second Bank" supporters. Rather, he argues, the monetary variations in the 1830's and 1840's reflect mainly the operation of the Hume specie-price mechanism in

* I wish to thank Moses Abramovitz and Edward S. Shaw, who have offered wise advice, both of whom, of course, should not share my responsibility for statements made here.

[1] I do not wish to imply that the American long swing mechanism began during this period, but only that the evidence of such a mechanism prior to the mid-1820's is much more difficult to find.

[2] George Macesich, "Sources of Monetary Disturbances in the United States, 1834–1845," *The Journal of Economic History*, XX, No. 3 (Sept. 1960), 407–34.

"International Trade and United States Economic Development: 1827–1843," by Jeffrey G. Williamson, is reprinted by permission from *Journal of Economic History*, XXI (September, 1961), 372–383.

affecting the real transfer concomitant with the (unexplained) fluctuation in the inflow of British capital.

The purpose of this article is twofold. I would like to take issue with Mr. Macesich on a number of points, but especially with some important, but what I feel are erroneous, inferences which he derives from his research. Then I will attempt to present an alternative explanatory model, more complex than Macesich's but providing, I hope, a more realistic explanation of the observed interactions between external and internal conditions during the 1830's and 1840's. I must admit that in doing so I have the advantage of using aggregate net capital import estimates recently published by Douglass C. North.[3]

I am most disturbed by Macesich's seemingly complete disregard for income movements and possible alternations in the pace of United States development. Indeed, the only reference to an income effect upon the flow of goods and the trade balance (*as well as* the flow of American securities abroad) is in a footnote recognizing the possibility that the inflow of foreign funds "causes money income and expenditure to rise in the United States and, as income rises, imports rise still further and exports fall."[4] In the spirit of his argument and in explicit statement, Macesich seems to feel that from 1834–1845 secular income movements are only results, caused by capital flows, that facilitate the real transfer: and only a minor explanation of trade balance movements at that.

Macesich's position seems best stated by his own words:

> One would expect on theoretical grounds that the United States balance of trade position would become unfavorable (or less favorable) as a result of continuous and heavy inflows; and conversely, one would expect on theoretical grounds that the balance of trade would become ultimately favorable (or less unfavorable) as a result of capital outflows. When capital is imported steadily over a long period, a new trade equilibrium must be reached by the movement of goods. In the long run commodity imports and exports are the flexible items in the balance of payments . . . when capital inflows ceased the balance of trade became for the most part active. In general, the balance of trade seems to conform to the expectation of theory.[5]

And again his view is clearly expressed earlier in his article:

> Given the specie standard, we should expect that an inflow of capital and the corresponding increased supply of foreign exchange would drive the exchange rate in the United States to the specie-import point; the inflow of specie would cause the money supply in the United States to rise, and consequent price changes would cause im-

[3] Douglass C. North, "The United States Balance of Payments, 1790–1860," *Trends in the American Economy in the Nineteenth Century.* Vol. 24, *Studies in Income and Wealth,* National Bureau of Economic Research (Princeton: Princeton University Press, 1960), pp. 573–627.

[4] Macesich, p. 419, note 29.

[5] *Ibid.,* p. 420.

ports to rise and exports to fall. In this way the trade balance would be turned against the United States thus enabling the real transfer of capital . . . to occur.[6]

It is my contention that one can hardly ignore domestic income movements over the decade 1834–1845 and particularly over a longer period of more relevance, the 1820's to the 1840's. This twenty-year period is not the place for verification of an essentially *static* experiment in economic theory. Those capital flows did not occur autonomously and in a vacuum.[7] Nor did the trade balance react passively to net capital movements. It seems more correct to consider balance-of-payments movements during this period in the context of real growth. Could it not be that *both* trade balance and capital movements were functions of a third variable, the rate of real development and income-output movements? Would it not still be consistent with the revealed positive correlation between gold flows and capital imports (and income), to assume a general equilibrium model which includes in it a money (gold) demand function? Macesich, it seems to me, has applied a short-run disequilibrium model to a long-run growth problem.

To begin with then, I would have stated the problem somewhat differently. Almost a decade prior to the first year of Macesich's examination, 1834, there is evidence of a quickening in the pace of American development. From the mid-1820's until the late 1830's there is ample evidence of acceleration and subsequent gradual retardation in the rate of growth of the American economy, terminating in the 1840's with a disastrous and prolonged secular depression. Nor does the description of this period seem to occupy a unique position in the process of nineteenth-century United States development. Kuznets, Abramovitz, Lewis, Thomas, Burns, North and Berry, among others, all have indicated evidence of a long swing in the process of American development averaging about fifteen-twenty years in duration: the apparent long swing beginning in the mid-1820's and terminating with the early 1840's is only the first (for which adequate data are avaliable) in a series of five long waves in the pace of this country's development from 1820 to 1915.[8]

[6] *Ibid.*, p. 413.

[7] Incidentally, when Macesich does suggest an explanation for those variations in capital flows, at only one point in his paper, he appeals to supply conditions in Great Britain. Prior to the Civil War, however, there is little correlation between British capital exports and American capital imports over long periods of twenty years, suggesting that it is demand conditions in the American states which are the important causative variable. *Ibid.*, p. 414.

[8] Moses Abramovitz, "Resources and Output Trends in the United States Since 1870," *Am. Ec. Rev.*, XLVI, No. 2, *Papers and Proceedings* (May 1956), 5–23; "The Nature and Significance of Kuznets Cycles," *Economic Development and Cultural Change*, IX, No. 3 (April 1961), 225–49; and "Long Swings in United States Growth," *38th Annual Report* of the National Bureau of Economic Research (New York: National Bureau of Economic Research, 1958), pp. 47–56. Simon Kuznets, *Secular Movements in Production Prices* (New York: Houghton-Mifflin, 1930). W. A. Lewis and P. J. O'Leary, "Secular Swings in Production and Trade, 1870–1913," *The*

The long swing of the 1830's and 1840's is perhaps most striking in the balance of payments; there is no other time after 1830–1840 when international trade plays a greater role in the American economy.[9] Furthermore, long swings [10] in the flow of goods and capital over United States borders are very closely correlated with those in domestic activity such as the small sample in Table 1 which includes incorporations, public land sales, immigration, building and transportation. Table 2 shows imports moving positively with general income movements, rising from low levels in the 1820's to a secular peak in the late 1830's before falling to low levels in the early 1840's, for a duration of twenty-two years. This same secular pattern is also reflected in net capital imports, and, perhaps surprisingly, in export movements. The long swing in exports, incidentally, is not found in the post-Civil War era. The trade balance is dominated by import movements, since first differences in imports are greater than exports, and the trade balance exhibits a long swing with a peak deficit in the late 1830's. Given a domestic long swing, which evidence does suggest, the balance of payments moves precisely as we might have predicted, except for the unusual fluctuation in exports.

TABLE 1[a]

	Incorporations	Building	Public Land Sales	Immigration	Transport
Trough	1820–22	....	1823	1823	1825
Peak	1837	1836	1836	1834	1832
Trough	1842	1843	1842	1838	1843
Peak	1852–54	1853	1854	1854	1856

[a] Taken from North, "The United States Balance of Payments, 1790–1860," Table 4, p. 587.

Manchester School of Economic and Social Studies, XIII (May 1955), 113–52. Brinley Thomas, Migration and Economic Growth (Cambridge: Cambridge University Press, 1954). Arthur F. Burns, Production Trends in the United States Since 1870 (New York: National Bureau of Economic Research, 1934).

Pertaining to this period in particular (1830's and 1840's): Douglass C. North, "International Capital Flows and the Development of the American West," The Journal of Economic History, XVI, No. 4 (December 1956), 493–505; more recently, see his The Economic Growth of the United States, 1790–1860 (Englewood Cliffs, N. J.: Prentice-Hall, Inc., 1961). T. S. Berry, Western Prices Before 1861: A Study of the Cincinnati Market (Cambridge: Harvard University Press, 1943).

[9] K. W. Deutsch and A. Eckstein estimate that American external trade, exports and imports of goods, was 15–20 per cent of national income from 1819 to 1839. "National Industrialization and the Declining Share of the International Economic Sector, 1890–1959," World Politics, XIII (January 1961), 267–99.

[10] Although I argue throughout this note that the period from the 1820's to the 1840's was only part of a recurring long swing mechanism which pervades all of American nineteenth-century development, it is not indispensable to the general criticism of Macesich's article. The prejudiced reader may consider it an episodic variation in growth rates.

TABLE 2ª

(millions $)	Exports (current value)	Imports (current value)	Trade Balance	Net Capital Imports (+)
1821	54.6	54.5	.5	−5.0
1822	61.4	79.9	−18.2	8.3
1823	68.3	72.5	−3.7	−2.0
1824	69.0	72.2	−2.6	−1.0
1825	90.7	90.2	1.0	−6.8
1826	72.9	78.1	−4.5	2.6
1827	74.3	71.3	4.0	−10.0
1828	64.0	81.1	−16.4	11.4
1829	67.4	67.1	.5	−1.5
1830	71.7	62.7	9.5	−7.9
1831	72.3	95.9	−23.1	14.1
1832	81.5	97.0	−15.2	6.8
1833	87.5	103.1	−15.5	13.5
1834	102.3	110.8	−8.3	18.8
1835	115.2	139.5	−23.9	30.0
1836	124.3	180.1	−55.3	62.2
1837	111.4	133.1	−21.2	22.6
1838	105.0	97.9	7.4	4.2
1839	112.3	159.6	−47.0	49.1
1840	123.7	100.2	24.2	−30.8
1841	111.8	125.4	−13.0	−4.4
1842	99.9	98.0	2.3	−18.2
1843	82.8	43.3	39.9	−22.2
1844	105.7	104.7	1.4	−4.7
1845	106.0	115.4	−9.0	−3.8
1846	109.6	122.6	−12.5	−.8
1847	156.7	127.3	30.3	−18.6
1848	138.2	154.6	−15.8	2.3
1849	140.4	146.9	−5.9	−2.8
1850	144.4	180.5	−35.4	28.9
1851	188.9	219.2	−29.5	7.5

ª Taken from North, "The United States Balance of Payments, 1790–1860," Table 3, p. 581.

This positive correlation between the rate of domestic expansion and balance-of-payments fluctuations persists throughout the nineteenth century, and, incidentally, is not isolated to United States experience. With Imlah's estimates of British balance of payments, there is a strong suggestion of an inverse correlation between British and American domestic growth and their balance of payments.[11]

[11] Albert H. Imlah, "British Balance of Payments and Exports of Capital, 1816–1913," *Ec. Hist. Rev.*, Series 2, V (1952–1953), 204–39, and more recently, *Economic Elements in the Pax Britannica* (Cambridge: Harvard University Press, 1958). Perhaps the best-known investigations of the interaction of the Atlantic economy are in Brinley Thomas' *Migration and Economic Growth*, and in A. K. Cairncross' *Home and Foreign Investment, 1870–1913* (Cambridge: Cambridge University Press, 1953).

One of the arguments presented in this note is that movements in the merchandise trade balance are hardly primarily explained by the specie-price mechanism. Rather I would argue that it is mainly a long swing in the pace of real domestic development which is the major cause for (and effect of!) *both* capital flows and fluctuations in the trade balance. Not only is it likely that general price level movements play only a secondary role, but it is not clearly evident that the flow of specie is consistently an important determinant of long-term price fluctuations concomitant with the long swing in real variables. It is not my main purpose, however, to press the point that the correlation between specie flow and the money supply is poor (1834–1845)—Macesich admits this—but to suggest to Macesich an alternative explanation for those specie flows.

In the place of a static model which suggests that the trade balance passively responds to autonomous net capital flows, which cause variations in the money supply via "residual" specie flows, consider a general equilibrium model constructed on the presumption of variations in real growth however explained. With rapid real growth, the 1820's to 1830's, an excess supply of securities is generated along with an excess demand for goods, reflected respectively with an increasing inflow of capital and a worsening in the trade balance. But concomitant with real growth, there is a tendency to generate excess demands for real money balances, reflected, under a gold-standard system, by an increasing inflow of gold. The solution is a general equilibrium one: the flow of gold does not necessarily reflect a potential movement back to equilibrium in the balance of payments, but a movement to equilibrium which removes excess demands and supplies in the domestic economy without excessive price variation. In fact, it seems that the flow of gold *may* have oversatisfied excess demands in the money market generated by real income growth, since the upswing to the 1830's is accompanied by price inflation. Given alternations in the growth of real income over a period of twenty years, why treat gold flows as fortuitous and as "residuals"? In the long run all elements in the balance of payments are flexible, and demands for money (gold), goods and securities must be solved simultaneously in a general equilibrium context.[12] It remains then to briefly describe the nature of the long swing in real growth from the 1820's to the 1840's.

The long swing in net capital imports, or Kuznets cycle as Arthur Lewis prefers to call it, rises very sharply in the quinquennially averaged data from a trough in 1825 to a peak in 1837 and falls to a trough in 1842 for a duration of seventeen years. Like other long waves in international factor movements over the nineteenth century, this long swing in capital imports has an extreme amplitude in both the annual and smoothed data. In 1825 there is a relatively insignificant outflow of capital of about $6.8 million, in 1837 it attains a peak inflow of $62.2 million, and finally reaches a

---

[12] In the long-run context of growth, it is not true that "commodity imports and exports are the flexible items in the balance of payments." Macesich, p. 420.

maximum outflow in the trough of the 1840's amounting to $30.8 million.

Although the time shape of capital inflow in the 1830's and 1840's was not unique, since alternations in the import of factors are closely related to the domestic long swing throughout the nineteenth century, this period reflects the first large sustained net import. Indeed, so large was the inflow of foreign funds in the decade 1830–1839 that North terms it "relative to the size of the economy it was probably the most significant inflow of capital during the nineteenth century." [13]

A major argument pursued in this paper has been that the movements in the balance of payments were interrelated with the long swing in domestic development, 1820–1845. But not only does the external balance *reflect* the domestic long swing, primarily in net capital and commodity import movements, but it is also a major *source* of the long swing. The export market, primarily cotton, was intimately related with American demands for foreign capital. Indeed, the major explanation for these domestic swings can be found in the varying profitability of primary producing lands. "It was the expected return upon cotton in the Southwest and upon wheat, corn, and hogs (and the manufacture thereof) in the Northeast," which in turn was dependent upon foodstuff demands in the South, "that was the most fundamental factor" effecting the pace of American development.[14]

What kinds of foreign investments were being made? There can be little doubt that over the nineteenth century as a whole foreign investment was primarily interested in, and facilitated the development of, our transportation network. But after the Civil War and even in the 1850's, foreign funds went directly into the securities issued by the rails. Prior to the 1850's, the story is a little different; the majority of foreign funds was funneled into the purchase of state and local bond issues. A large portion of these security issues was used to finance an expanding transportation network, and for many reasons too extensive to cover here the state and local governments acted as both financial intermediaries and entrepreneurs. This type of bond was attractive to foreigners in part due to its *apparent* low risk (with government backing and guarantee) and in part due to British familiarity with the profitability of transportation development derived from their own internal experience.

Even as late as 1853, when estimates first become available, as much as 68 per cent of foreign long-term holdings was in the form of state and local bonds.[15]

The Erie Canal was the first major state enterprise financed by foreign

[13] "The United States Balance of Payments, 1790–1860," p. 585.

[14] North, "International Capital Flows and the Development of the American West," p. 498.

[15] Cleona Lewis, *America's Stake in International Investment* (Washington: The Brookings Institution, 1938), pp. 521–22.

funds. From 1817–1825, seven million dollars worth of New York bonds issued to finance this spectacular state-owned and constructed venture passed into English hands. It is historically evident that New York benefited from the ensuing trade with the western states. But perhaps more important, the lucrative example of this enterprise set a precedent for future state issues. Philadelphia and Baltimore were clamoring for state enterprise and foreign capital to construct canals to the interior, with Washington and Richmond quickly recognizing this competition. Maryland gave bonds and guarantees to private companies for both the Chesapeake and Ohio Canal and the Baltimore and Ohio Railroad.[16] In the Middle West, state canal systems were planned on a comprehensive scale, supported by Federal land grants, in Ohio, Indiana, Illinois, Michigan and Kentucky.[17]

> Only the Pennsylvania coal routes, the Schuykill Coal and Navigation Company, the Philadelphia and Reading Railroad, with some short railroads in New England and central New York, ventured to proceed with neither guarantee nor bonds from a paternal legislature. Before 1836 over 90 million dollars had been invested in canals and railways in the North, of which more than half was a charge upon public credit. The bulk of this capital had been procured from England.[18]

In the South, the forces of expansion were different but the states still acted as financial intermediaries—just as they did in the North. Capital was desired mainly for cotton expansion. By 1824 Louisiana initiated the idea of the state land bank, the prominent recipient of foreign investment in the South throughout the 1830's and 1840's, which issued bonds in the East and in London to secure working capital. All the southern states became deeply concerned in the land banks and most of the loans for these undertakings directly or indirectly were sought in London.[19]

But if the outstanding portion of foreign investment in the American states from 1830 to 1839 was in the form of state and local bonds, it is also evident that the types of state-owned and state-sponsored enterprises financed by external funds were regionally quite different. Whereas the investment in the Northeast and Northwest was mainly for social enterprise and expansion of the existing transportation-communication network (to facilitate trade with the South for the West's foodstuffs as well as a future market for the West's products across the Atlantic and in the East), the investment of foreign funds in the South was mainly of a more short-term sort. Either these funds were used to facilitate the immediate

---

[16] *Ibid.*, p. 17.
[17] Leland H. Jenks, *The Migration of British Capital to 1875* (New York: A. A. Knopf, 1927), p. 74.
[18] *Ibid.*, p. 75.
[19] *Ibid.*, pp. 75–76.

production of the South's cotton for European consumption through state land banks, or they were even shorter-term loans financing the marketing period between production and sale.

The private southern economy even in the boom years of the mid 1830's did not have access to long-term capital. Almost all of its foreign sources were to support the state banks. The South's chief sources of loanable funds, then, "were the commercial banks and mercantile houses that were limited by the character of their business to short-time advances." [20] Even the Bank of the United States, which was later to attempt to encourage the flow of short-term capital from Europe after the 1837 panic, and which was an important source of funds for the South, did not supply anything other than more liquid loans.[21]

This apparent difference between the final expenditure out of state and local debts financed by foreign capital should not imply independent economic development between the two regions. The South opened up an extremely lucrative field for the employment of labor and capital in that section. Its effect upon the northern states, and especially the Northwest, was nevertheless important. It was the initial expansion of the South which gave the Northeast and Northwest their first important market and supplied a requisite for their economic development.[22] I suspect Matthews would stress the interdependence between North and South, and the dominance of the latter, even more strongly.

> The central position occupied by cotton in the boom of the mid-1830's in the South was inevitable in view of its dominance in the Southern agricultural economy. Should we go further and say that cotton was the progenitor of the entire boom throughout the country or even its mainstay during the whole of its course? [23]

Since the net capital imports were a function of the expansion of cotton production directly, with foreign investment in the southern land banks, or indirectly, with investment in the North to facilitate the supply of food-stuffs to the South, it should occasion no surprise to find net capital movements extremely sensitive to the state of the cotton market. In early 1837 the fall in cotton prices (25 per cent in February and March of 1837) finally exceeded the rise in bales produced and export revenues began to fall. Now whether an earlier bad turn in cotton prices (late 1835) caused a downward readjustment of foreign investors' expectations or whether the fall in export revenue directly interfered with the interest payments,

[20] Milton S. Heath, "Public Railroad Construction and the Development of Private Enterprise in the South Before 1861," *The Journal of Economic History*, Supplement IX (1949), 48.

[21] Berry, pp. 410–11.

[22] G. S. Callender, "The Early Transportation and Banking Enterprises of the States in Relation to the Growth of Corporations," *Q.J.E.*, XVII (1903), 125.

[23] R. C. O. Matthews, *A Study in Trade Cycle History: 1833–1842* (Cambridge: Cambridge University Press, 1954), p. 51.

European purchases of American securities came to a pause. Lewis believes, as I do, that it was the latter. British houses specializing in American securities were badly hit since a large share of American payments on commercial debts and for interest and dividends payable abroad was provided by the export revenue from cotton.[24] It therefore seems likely that foreign investors, especially British, were less impressed by the movements in cotton prices than by the lagging fall in cotton export revenues. American cotton prices begin to fall late in 1835 and the English in 1836, but net capital imports rise to a peak in 1836 which is double its 1835 level. At any rate, for reasons stressed here and earlier, it does not seem likely that supply conditions abroad played a crucial role in the dictating of the flow of capital.

If the rate of capital imports was dependent upon the state of the export or cotton market both directly, via the southern land banks, and indirectly, via northern investment in transportation improvement which in turn was mainly a function of southern demands for foodstuffs, what mechanism could there possibly be in the cotton industry which could make it the primary cause for the long swing in American development from the 1820's to the 1840's? The position assumed by the present author is similar to that taken by North,

> . . . that surges in westward development were initiated by long-run favorable movements of the prices of key staple commodities [cotton, 1820–1845]. However, an increased supply of these staples could only be obtained by heavy capital expenditure in internal improvements and plantation development. Long-term foreign capital played an important role in meeting this need by directing real resources into the needed social overhead investment and making possible an import surplus of consumer and capital goods during these expansive periods.[25]

The answer to the question lies in America's monopolistic position in cotton and supply response to price.

The most recent description of the importance of cotton in early American growth, and the self-generating long swing mechanism contained in cotton expansion, can be found in a new publication by North.[26] Only a brief description of the interaction is attempted here. There seems to be a clear relationship between cotton supply and prices; over-expansion and long periods of lagging readjustment cause long swings in prices interacting with long swings in the rate of growth of quantum production with consistent lags. Quantum cotton produced and exported grows at increasingly rapid rates from 1829–1835, and export values with

[24] Lewis, p. 25.
[25] North, "International Capital Flows and the Development of the American West," p. 494.
[26] North, The Economic Growth of the United States, 1790–1860.

them. After that point, an overexpansion is generated and cotton prices begin to fall in 1835 and continue to do so until 1843. It is not until the latter part of the 1830's that the rate of supply expansion begins to adjust to price movements: from 1843–1850, production and export of cotton bales remains at low (almost zero) growth rates. Export values begin falling in 1837, when the fall in prices exceeds quantum expansion, and continue falling until 1843. After that point, prices recover, causing exports in current prices to improve as well but supply expansion does not respond until 1850. And thus the lagged cycle prevails over the period 1820–1860.

This brings us back to our initial criticism of Macesich's argument. He should recognize, it seems to me, that the flow of capital and trade balance movements from the 1820's to the 1840's must be considered in a context of growth. Indeed, it is precisely that growth pattern of real income alternating rapid to the late 1830's and slow in the 1840's, which primarily dictates the flow of capital. The trade balance also seems to be a function of real income growth and cannot be simply responding passively to net capital flows via the Hume specie-flow mechanism. But although the external balance adjusts to long swings in the pace of American development in a way consistent with later years, the movements in exports are quite unusual compared to post-Civil War evidence. Whereas in the long swings after the 1860's, movements in the balance of payments only reflect variations in domestic growth, prior to the Civil War and especially over this first long swing not only do net capital and merchandise imports *respond* to domestic growth patterns, but it seems that exports play an important role in dictating the pace of real growth.

Furthermore, it does not seem reasonable to treat gold flows over long periods simply as residuals which balance heavy capital movements. Secularly, no element in the balance of payments is an arithmetic residual: all elements in the external balance are flexible in the long run. Rapid growth has a tendency to generate excess demands for money (gold) and goods (trade balance deficit), as well as excess supplies of securities (net capital inflow). No one of these elements should be treated with more importance than another, and the equilibrium solution must be general. Gold inflows do not necessarily reflect disequilibrium in the balance of payments, but may simply reflect a tendency towards excess demands for money in a rapidly growing economy.

As far as Macesich's argument concerning the importance of specie flows in determining the money supply goes, there is little room here for an extensive discussion. I would, however, like to make two comments. First, in the period of the 1850's, another long swing in American development, there is also a tremendous inflow of foreign capital. But why is it that during this later period there are increasing outflows of specie? Although the answer is obvious, it is not explained by Macesich's simple

Hume specie-price mechanism. In a general equilibrium context, there are excess *supplies* of real money balances concomitant with the gold discoveries in the West; thus an outflow of gold. Second, Macesich suggests a reasonable hypothesis for the poor correlation between specie flow and additions to the money stock by appealing to the possible movements of short-term holdings (a gold reserve substitute). But in the period 1879–1904, gold flows and changes in the money supply have almost a perfect correlation. Can the difference between these two periods be easily explained by the immaturity of the American money market?

Foreign Capital and Economic Growth

16.   International Trade and United States Economic Development Revisited*

George Macesich

Mr. Williamson's comments on my article leave the issue between us ambiguous.[1] I welcome this opportunity further to develop my own views regarding the turbulent period of the 1830's and early 1840's.

First of all, I believe that Williamson has overstated his case in attributing to me disregard of the importance of internal events in the United States. I advanced the hypothesis that the primary disturbing factor in the period 1834–1845 was an increase, and then a decrease, in the flow of funds into the United States, and the problem I wished to examine was the response in the American economy to this initial disturbance. As indicated in my article, the emphasis placed on external factors does not mean that internal events in the United States were negligible.[2]

* I am indebted to Marshall R. Colberg for useful comments and suggestions.

[1] George Macesich, "Sources of Monetary Disturbances in the United States, 1834–1845," *The Journal of Economic History*, XX, No. 3 (Sept. 1960), 407–34.

[2] Indeed they suggest that on occasion changes in the supply of money, for example, can be brought about by internal events that can hardly be attributed to contemporary changes in income, for example, the alteration in the American monetary system in 1834. For a discussion of this episode, see W. B. Smith and A. H. Cole, *Fluctuations in American Business, 1790–1860* (Cambridge: Harvard University Press, 1935), p. 78, and especially J. L. Laughlin, *History of Bimetallism in the United States* (Chicago: University of Chicago Press, 1901).

"International Trade and United States Economic Development Revisited," by George Macesich, is reprinted by permission from *Journal of Economic History*, XXI (September, 1961), 384–385.

If I understand Williamson correctly, he considers it more plausible to argue that the rapid expansion of the American economy during the period attracted an inflow of funds. Now it should be obvious that if the foreign funds had not been forthcoming the American boom in the 1830's would have been halted, as it indeed was halted after 1839 when the inflow of foreign funds was drastically reduced. These two forces are inextricably linked together over the whole period. Mr. Williamson's comments have not settled the issue of priority, much less the issue of causality. Indeed such information as we do have suggests that the initial speedup in the flow of funds into the United States was apparently occasioned by unfortunate events elsewhere in the world.

Following 1815, London became the leading source of long-term capital.[3] Listings on the London exchange indicate trends in overseas investment. Immediately after the Napoleonic War, British foreign investments were made in European issues. In the 1820's bond issues of the newly created South American states were popular. When these went into default, London turned toward the United States. From 1815 to 1830, the only American issues traded extensively in London were three issues of the United States Government, stock of the Second Bank of the United States, bond issues of four states, and bond issues of two municipalities. In 1840, however, the London exchange listed forty-six bond issues of sixteen states and the stocks or bonds of twenty-five canals, railroads, and banks.

In the second place, my purpose in the article was not to "prove" the price-specie mechanism of international trade theory. Inadequacies of available data do not permit rigorous tests to be applied. The data, as far as they go, are at least consistent with a number of hypotheses derived from international trade theory, and this is the principal message contained in the article. It has been recognized for some time now that the income effect modifies but does not necessarily alter conclusions derived from classical trade theory except under some rather weird assumptions.[4] The incorporation of the income effect helps to explain the speed of adjustment and so the smaller specie flows required to accomplish the real transfer of capital.

The point that Williamson believes he has discovered is one stated some time ago by J. C. Ingram.[5] Essentially, Ingram's point is that the classical and modern parts of the theory of adjustment yield a prediction that exports will decline as a result of capital transfer. In the United States

---

[3] The material in the following two paragraphs is from Leland H. Jenks, *The Migration of British Capital to 1875* (New York: A. A. Knopf, 1927), Chs. II–IV.

[4] See, for example, L. A. Metzler, "The Theory of International Trade," in H. S. Ellis (ed.), *Survey of Contemporary Economics* (Philadelphia: The Blakiston Company, 1948), I, 211–22.

[5] James C. Ingram, "Capital Imports and the Balance of Payments," *Southern Economic Journal*, XXII (April 1956), 411–25, and "Growth in Capacity and Canada's Balance of Payments," *Am. Ec. Rev.*, XLVII, No. 2 (March 1957), 93–104.

exports increased in the period 1834–1837; they moved up and down until 1843 and increased in the remaining years under review.[6] The rise in imports, however, exceeded the rise in exports and thus enabled the real transfer of capital to occur. In this respect the years 1834–1837, when the largest capital inflow occurred, are particularly conspicuous. A slight modification along lines set out by Ingram is required to enable the theory to account for this behavior of exports.

Modifying the theory of transfers is necessary because both the price-specie flow analysis and income analysis do not explicity take into account changes in the receiving country's productive capacity. In short-run adjustments, these changes can perhaps be ignored, but not over "long swings." I would argue that such waves, if they did exist in the rhythms of the nineteenth century, may have been produced by shifts in the direction of foreign investment and propagated through monetary mechanisms.

[6] Douglass C. North, "The United States Balance of Payments, 1790–1860," *Trends in the American Economy in the Nineteenth Century*. Vol. 24, *Studies in Income and Wealth*, National Bureau of Economic Research (Princeton: Princeton University Press, 1960), Table 3, p. 581; cited by J. G. Williamson, "International Trade and United States Economic Development: 1827–1843," *The Journal of Economic History*, XXI, No. 2 (Sept. 1961), Table 2.

Agricultural Markets and Economic Growth

17.   Agriculture in Regional Economic Growth

Douglass C. North

I

Despite the existence of a few dissenters there seems to be agreement amongst many economists that agriculture contributes little to economic growth. The argument has developed along two lines: The first equates economic growth with an industrial revolution and argues that a "take off" into industrialization "fails to occur mainly because the comparative advantage of exploiting productive land and other natural resources delays the time when self-reinforcing industrial growth can profitably get

"Agriculture in Regional Economic Growth," by Douglass C. North, is reprinted by permission from *Journal of Farm Economics*, XLI (December, 1959), 943–958.

under way."[1] The argument stems from the classic view of diminishing returns in agriculture, the greater productivity of manufacturing and the difficulties associated with the shift of resources into secondary activities when diminishing returns obtain.[2]

The second argument is quite different and indeed stems from different theoretical underpinnings.[3] It has been most cogently stated by Professor Theodore Schultz as the following hypothesis: "(1) Economic development occurs in a specific locational matrix; there may be one or more such matrices in a particular economy. This means that the process of economic growth does not necessarily occur in the same way, at the same time, or at the same rate in different locations. (2) These locational matrices are primarily industrial-urban in composition; as centers in which economic development occurs, they are not mainly out in rural or farming areas although some farming areas are situated more favorably than are others in relation to such centers. (3) The existing economic organization works best at or near the center of a particular matrix of economic development and it also works best in those parts of agriculture which are situated favorably in relation to such a center; and it works less satisfactorily in those parts of agriculture which are situated at the periphery of such a matrix."[4] This hypothesis in effect states that it is industrial development which is the prime mover in economic growth and that agriculture is a dependent variable in the overall pattern of industrial urban growth.

I find parts of both hypotheses attractive and indeed there is abundant evidence to support particular illustrations that add weight to them.[5] Yet neither will stand generalization either in historical application or as policy guides in contemporary problems of economic growth. In this paper I shall argue that the successful production of agricultural (or indeed most extractive) commodities for sale without the region can be and under certain conditions has been the prime influence inducing economic growth, the development of external economies, urbanization, and eventually industrial development.

[1] W. W. Rostow, "The Takeoff into Self-sustained Economic Growth," *The Economic Journal*, Vol. LXVI, March, 1956, p. 28.

[2] The whole stage sequence of regional growth implicitly accepts this argument. See E. M. Hoover and J. Fisher, "Research in Regional Economic Growth" in *Problems in the Study of Economic Growth* (New York: National Bureau of Economic Research, 1949).

[3] The notion of diminishing returns is conspicuously absent. It is imperfections in the factor market rather than a relatively fixed factor supply which is strategic to the argument.

[4] Theodore Schultz, *The Economic Organization of Agriculture* (New York: McGraw-Hill, 1953), p. 147.

[5] See Rostow, *op. cit.*, for supporting evidence. In connection with the United States, however, see my critical note, "A Note on Professor Rostow's 'Take-off' into Self-sustained Economic Growth." *The Manchester School*, January, 1958. In connection with Schultz's thesis see Anthony Tang, *Economic Development in the Southern Piedmont 1860–1950* (Chapel Hill: University of North Carolina Press, 1958).

The argument baldly stated is as follows: (1) Specialization and division of labor have been the most important factor in the initial expansion of regions. (2) Production of goods for sale without the region has induced this specialization and (3) involvement in the developing international economy (or national in the case of some regions in the United States) of the past two centuries has been the way by which regions and nations have accomplished economic development. The argument is of course the classic one of Adam Smith as succinctly restated recently in the title of an article by George Stigler, "The Division of Labor is Limited by the Extent of the Market." [6] While I have no quarrel with Schultz that manufactured goods (and particularly fabricated as contrasted with processed goods) have enjoyed the most rapid expansion in demand in recent U.S. economic history, in contrast to the income inelasticity in demand for farm goods, the expanding demand for agricultural goods in the 19th century and the prospects for many primary commodities in world agriculture in the present century makes the case of the United States (and some other industrial nations) in recent years atypical. Whether we look at Denmark between 1865–1900,[7] the Pacific Northwest between 1880–1920,[8] the Canadian economy between 1900–1913 [9] or indeed any of a myriad of other possible illustrations, it has been the expansion from one or more agricultural commodities which has been the prime mover in initiating expansion. Since I have discussed the role of export industries in promoting regional economic growth in an earlier article in the *Journal of Political Economy,* an extended discussion here is unnecessary.[10] However, my original argument was incomplete. While the expansion of an export industry is a necessary condition for regional growth it is not a sufficient one. I should like to take this opportunity to elaborate the argument before returning to a specific rebuttal of the two hypotheses outlined above.

II

The first step in the analysis of regional economic growth consists of an exploration of the determinants of the export sector of the region. However, a necessary additional step is to examine the disposition of the income received from without the region. Certainly one of the perplexing

[6] *Journal of Political Economy,* Vol. LIX, June, 1951, pp. 185–193.
[7] A. J. Youngson, *The Possibilities of Economic Progress* (Cambridge, The University Press, 1959), pp. 191–230.
[8] See the brief description in my article "Location Theory and Regional Economic Growth," *Journal of Political Economy,* Vol. LXIII, June, 1955.
[9] G. M. Meier, "Economic Development and the Transfer Mechanism," *Canadian Journal of Economics and Political Science,* XIX, Feb., 1953.
[10] In addition to the original article, "Location Theory and Regional Economic Growth," *loc. cit.,* see the discussion with Charles Tiebout in the same *Journal,* Vol. LXIV, No. 2, April, 1955, pp. 160–69.

problems in the study of economic growth has been the differential progress as amongst different regions resulting from an increment to income from the export sector. Why does one area remain tied to a single export staple while another diversifies its production and becomes an urbanized, industrialized region? Regions that remained tied to a single export commodity almost inevitably do not achieve sustained expansion. Not only will there be a slowing down in the rate of growth in the industry which will adversely affect the region, but the very fact that it remains tied to a single export industry will mean that specialization and division of labor are limited outside that industry. Historically it has meant that a larger share of the populace has remained outside the market economy. The answer lies (a) in the natural endowments of the region (at any given level of technology), (b) in the character of the export industry, and (c) in changes in technology and transfer costs. It is worthwhile to examine each of these in turn.

The natural endowments of the region dictate the initial export commodities of the area. If these endowments are such as to result in a tremendous comparative advantage in one commodity over any other, then the immediate consequence will be for resources to concentrate upon its production. If, on the other hand, the region has broad production possibilities such that the rate of return upon the production of a number of goods and services is not too much less than upon the initial export commodity, then with the growth of the region and accompanying change in factor proportions the production of other goods and services is likely to be a simple process.

The character of the export commodity in influencing regional growth is more complicated since there are several facets to it. A number of important consequences stem from the technological nature of the production function. If the export commodity is a "plantation" type commodity which is relatively labor intensive and in which there are significant increasing returns to scale, then the development will be in marked contrast to one in which the export commodity may be produced most efficiently on a family-size farm with relatively less absolute amounts of labor required.[11] In the first case there will tend to result an extremely unequal distribution of income with the bulk of the population devoting most of their income to foodstuff and simple necessities (much of which may be self-sufficient production). At the other end of the income scale, the plantation owners will tend to spend most of their income upon luxury consumption goods which will be imported. In short, there will be little encouragement of residentiary types of economic activity. With the more equitable distribution of incomes, there is a demand for a broad range of

[11] This argument has been explored by R. E. Baldwin in some detail. See "Patterns of Development in Newly Settled Regions," *The Manchester School of Economic and Social Studies*, Vol. XXIV, No. 2, May, 1956, pp. 161–79.

goods and services, part of which will be residentiary, thus inducing investment in other types of economic activities. There will tend to develop trading centers to provide a wide variety of such goods and services, in contrast to the plantation economy which will merely develop a few urban areas devoted to the export of the staple commodity and the distribution of imports.

A natural consequence of the divergent patterns described in the previous paragraph will be the attitude towards investment in knowledge.[12] Under the plantation type with very unequal income distribution, the planter will be extremely reluctant to devote his tax monies to expenditures for education or research other than that related to the staple commodity. As a consequence skills and knowledge not directly related to the export commodity will be at a low level. In contrast, the region with more equitable income distribution will be well aware of the stake in improving its comparative position through education and research and will accordingly be willing to devote public expenditures in these directions. The result will be to relatively improve its comparative position in a variety of types of economic activity and therefore broaden the resultant economic base.

Equally important is the investment induced by the export commodity or service. If the export is such as to require substantial investment in transport, warehousing, port facilities and other types of social overhead investment, then the external economies are created which facilitate the development of other exports. Furthermore, if the export industry induces growth of subsidiary industries and if technology, transport costs and resource endowments permit these to be locally produced rather than imported, then this will induce further development. Both in the case of social overhead investment and investment in subsidiary industry the consequence is to promote urbanization and increased specialization and development of additional residentiary activity geared to the increasing local demand for consumption goods and services. At the other extreme is the export industry which requires only the immediate development of a few centers for the collection and export of the commodity and entails the development of little subsidiary industry or perhaps entails the development of such subsidiary industry and marketing facilities, but they are of a nature to be most efficiently imported.[13]

Changes in technology and transport may completely alter the region's comparative advantage either favorably or unfavorably.[14] Technological change may increase the potential rate of return in the production of other

---

[12] I am in Professor Schultz's debt for focusing my attention on this problem in the course of a series of very stimulating discussions this past Spring.

[13] In part at least, therefore, the development of subsidiary industry depends upon the first point discussed above, the natural endowments of the region.

[14] A further discussion of this point is to be found in my article, "Location Theory and Regional Economic Growth," *loc. cit.*, pp. 254–56.

goods and services and lead to the exploitation of new resources and a shift of resources away from the old export industry. The initial development of transportation facilities to implement the export industry tends to reinforce dependence upon it and inhibit more diversified economic activity in several ways. The early development of transport typically (under competitive conditions) leads to a rapid fall in the transport rate and therefore increases the comparative advantage of the export commodity.[15] Moreover, with newly settled regions the transportation is typically one way. The outward shipment of a bulky product having no counterpart in the inward shipment which must be made mostly empty or in ballast. In consequence, inward freights are very low and compete with locally produced goods. As a result a good deal of local industry which had been protected by high transport costs or might develop if high transport costs continued, faces effective competition from imports.[16] In summary the disposition of income earned from export industry plays a decisive role in the growth of the region. Related to this argument is the region's propensity to import. To the extent that a region's income directly flows out in the purchase of goods and services rather than having a regional multiplier-accelerator effect,[17] then it is inducing growth elsewhere, but reaping few of the benefits of increased income from the export sector itself.

Let me briefly illustrate the argument of the preceding pages by contrasting the economic structure of the South and the West in the years prior to the Civil War.[18]

Both regions enjoyed a thriving export trade in the years between the end of the second war with England and the Civil War. The cotton trade of the South accounted for more than half of total U. S. exports during the period, with rice, sugar and tobacco as subsidiary commodity exports. The value of cotton exports alone increased from $17.5 million in 1815 to $191.8 million in 1860. The West enjoyed an expanding trade in wheat and corn and derivatives thereof (pork, bacon, lard, flour, whisky) first with the South and then increasingly after the mid 1840's with the Northeast and Europe. However, at this point their similarity ends. Let me point up the contrasts.

1. The South was characterized by its concentrated production for the

[15] See my article "Ocean Freight Rates and Economic Development 1750–1913," *The Journal of Economic History,* December, 1958, for a discussion on this point.

[16] The early sanguine hopes of Gallatin and Tench Coxe which rested upon the burgeoning development of manufacturing during the Embargo as reported in the 1810 census was in good part for the local market and completely unable to compete with imports following the end of the 2nd War with England.

[17] See J. S. Duesenberry, "Some Aspects of the Theory of Economic Development," *Explorations in Entrepreneurial History,* Vol. III, No. 2, December, 1950.

[18] This very brief account is a summary from two chapters of a study I am completing on U. S. economic growth from 1790–1860. Of necessity the supporting statistical and qualitative evidence cannot be presented in this short paper.

market of a single export staple with a comparative advantage so great that even in periods of low cotton prices, resources could not receive an equal return from alternative types of economic activity. The West had no overwhelming comparative advantage in a single commodity but rather branched out into mining (lead in Missouri, copper in Michigan and iron at Pittsburgh) and various kinds of processing.

2. Large scale organization typified the southern plantation and a resultant extremely unequal pattern of income distribution reinforced, of course, by the institution of slavery. Wheat and corn in the West could be produced most efficiently on the "family size farm" given early 19th century technology. In consequence the pattern of consumer demand was markedly different. The South was almost totally lacking in urban development during the period (with the exception of New Orleans which served as an entrepôt for western foodstuff for the southern planter and as a port for cotton exports), and its states were conspicuously at the bottom of the list of retail stores per thousand population in the 1840 census. A large percentage of the South's population remained outside the market economy. In contrast small community centers dotted the West to serve the local populace and served as nuclei for residentiary industry and trade and services. While these early developed to serve local consumer needs, with the gradual expansion of the market and the development of external economies many came to serve an increasingly large area and become export industries. With each surge of expansion in the West (1816–18, 1832–39, 1849–57), an increasing percentage of western farmers shifted out of self-sufficiency and became a part of the market economy.

A further consequence of these contrasting structures was the differential investment in education. The South had the highest illiteracy rate (as a percentage of the white population), the lowest ratio of pupils to (white) population, and the smallest number of libraries. Even western states that were just emerging from the pioneer stage were conspicuously higher than the South in educational investment.[19]

3. Little additional investment was necessary for the efficient export of southern cotton. Neither transportation development nor extensive subsidiary industry were required. The Factor with his ties with northern credit and shipping served as both the exporter of the planter's cotton, and importer of his foodstuff (from the West) and manufactures (from the Northeast and Europe). Large scale investment in the South was devoted solely to the opening up of new cotton lands and the acquisition of slaves. Extensive investment in transportation (as well as other facilities to implement the export of goods) was essential to opening up the West. Moreover, there were important locational advantages to processing wheat and corn products into flour, corn meal, ham, bacon, salt pork, lard,

[19] For interesting figures on investment in knowledge see H. R. Helper *The Impending Crisis of the South* (New York: A. P. Burdick, 1860), pp. 144, 288–89.

and whisky within the region rather than without. In consequence a variety of such manufacturing grew up and promoted urban development in the West.

4. The unique characteristics of the ocean freight trade which resulted in one-way cargoes from the cotton ports resulted in back hauls of manufactured goods being imported into the cotton region at very low rates. As a result there was no protection for local consumer oriented industries from the cheap imports of the Northeast and Europe. In contrast manufactures had to come to the West either over land or via the long route back up the Mississippi, and the protection thereby assisted the early development of consumer oriented industries in the West.

Is this purely historical argument with little relevance for the contemporary scene? I think not. The special institution of slavery like the special characteristics of land tenure systems is capable of being examined in terms of economic analysis and we only beg analytical answers by retreating to the institution per se as an explanation.[20] The characteristics described above go far to explain the differential success of regional economies in the contemporary world. A positive restatement of the thesis elaborated above is that the development of a successful agricultural export industry will result in an increase in income to the region, and under the favorable conditions outlined above will lead to:

(1) Specialization and division of labor with a widening of the regional market;

(2) The growth of facilities and subsidiary industry to efficiently produce and market the export commodity;

(3) The development of residentiary industry to serve local consumers, some of which may, in consequence of expanding markets and external economies developed in association with the export industry, lead to a broadening in the export base;

(4) As a natural consequence of the above conditions, the growth of urban areas and facilities;

(5) An expanded investment in education and research to broaden the region's potential.

Under these circumstances, a good deal of industrial development will occur naturally as a consequence of the conditions described above. Indeed as the regional market increases in size, more and more manufacturing firms will find it feasible to establish branch plants there.

Where the unfavorable conditions outlined above obtain, then there is room for effective governmental policy to modify them. The alteration of land tenure systems (which should not be done at the expense of productivity, however) and the redirection of public expenditure into

[20] See A. H. Conrad and J. A. Meyer, "The Economics of Slavery in the Ante-Bellum South," *The Journal of Political Economy*, Vol. LXVI, No. 2, April, 1958.

research, technology, and education promise to yield very handsome returns.[21]

III

Let me point up the differences between the argument advanced in this paper and the two hypotheses of Professors Rostow and Schultz. My argument with Rostow is, I think, the more fundamental. Rostow's thesis is, in effect, the same as one presented at the annual meetings of this Association in 1951 by Professor J. K. Galbraith in a paper entitled "Conditions for Economic Change in Underdeveloped Countries." [22] Growth is associated with industrialization and stagnation with agriculture. It is my contention that this misses the whole problem of economic change and reflects a basic misreading of the economic history of the past two centuries.[23] Involvement in the larger market economies, despite the evident hazards entailed, has been the classic way by which regional economies have expanded. It has resulted in specialization, external economies, the development of residentiary industry, and the growth of vertical "dis-integration" as a result of the widening of the market to which Professor Stigler rightly attributes a good deal of the increase of manufacturing productivity.[24] I have made clear in the previous section the factors that can prevent successful regional expansion, but it should also be clear that these are not synonymous with agriculture per se.

My quarrel with Professor Schultz is not over the application of his "retardation hypothesis" to the contemporary American scene, but rather with his contention that economic history strongly supports his argument that economic development has taken place in primarily industrial-urban matrices.[25] I don't think that the 19th century economic history of the Midwest from 1815–1860, the Pacific Northwest from 1880–1920, or even California from 1848–1900 (where it was first the impetus of mining and then agriculture) support his argument. There is certainly not the space in this paper to explore the relative shifts in demand and supply, and the income elasticities, which make for the difference of opinion, and indeed it is not necessary at this point since the facts of the matter are that these (and other U.S.) regions grew up, developed urban centers, external economies, and manufacturing in consequence of a successful agricultural export trade. I have no quarrel with Professor Schultz's argument with respect to imperfections in the factor market and the importance of

[21] See Arnold C. Harberger, "Using the Resources at Hand More Effectively," *Proceedings of the American Economic Association*, May, 1959, pp. 134–46.

[22] This *Journal, Proceedings*, Nov., 1951, pp. 689–96.

[23] See A. J. Youngson, *Possibilities of Economic Progress* (Cambridge: The University Press, 1959), for evidence from the economic history of four regions to support this argument.

[24] Stigler, *op. cit.*, p. 190.

[25] Schultz, *op. cit.*, p. 147.

investment in human capital, and indeed I believe that they fit in very well with the argument I made in the previous section of this paper. I would simply argue that a successful agricultural export trade can and has induced urbanization, improvements in the factor markets, and a more effective allocation of investment funds.

In conclusion I should like to restate the positive position that the relevant problems of regional economic development revolve around the issues raised in the main body of this paper. They are not issues of agriculture versus industrialization but rather revolve around a region's ability to become integrated into the larger markets of the world through exports, and of the resultant structure of the regional economy which will influence its ability to achieve sustained growth and a diversified pattern of economic activity.

Slavery and Economic Growth

18. The Significance of the Slave Plantation for Southern Economic Development

Eugene D. Genovese

Historians are no longer sure that plantation slavery was responsible for the economic woes of the Old South. The revisionist doubts rest on two propositions of dubious relevance. The first is that slave labor could have been applied successfully to pursuits other than the raising of plantation staples; the second is that slave agriculture was possibly as profitable as were alternative industries and can not be held responsible for the unwillingness of Southerners to use their profits more wisely.[1] The first confuses slave labor and its direct effects with the slave system and its total effects; it is the latter that is at issue, and the versatility of slave labor

[1] See, for example, the well known writings of R. R. Russel, including his "The General Effects of Slavery upon Southern Economic Progress," *Journal of Southern History*, IV (February 1938), 34–54, or the more recent statement of Alfred H. Conrad and John R. Meyer, "The Economics of Slavery in the Ante-Bellum South," *Journal of Political Economy*, LXVI (April 1958), 95–130.

"The Significance of the Slave Plantation for Southern Economic Development," by Eugene D. Genovese, is reprinted by permission from *Journal of Southern History*, XXVIII (November, 1962), 422–437.

is a secondary consideration. The second rests on the assumption that the master-slave relationship was purely economic and not essentially different from an employer-worker relationship. Yet, when confronted with the issue direct, who could deny that slavery gave rise to a distinct politics, ideology, and pattern of social behavior and that these had immense economic consequences?

We need not examine at the moment the precise relationship between slavery and the plantation. Certainly, plantation economies presuppose considerable complusion, if only of the *de facto* type now prevalent in Latin America. The historical fact of an ante bellum plantation-based slave economy is our immediate concern, although, undoubtedly, post bellum developments preserved some of the retardative effects of ante bellum slavery.

Those retardative effects were too many even to be summarized here. A low level of capital accumulation, the planters' high propensity to consume luxuries, the shortage of liquid capital aggravated by the steady drain of funds out of the region, the low productivity of slave labor, the need to concentrate on a few staples, the anti-industrial, antiurban ideology of the dominant planters, the reduction of Southern banking, industry, and commerce to the position of auxiliaries of the planatation economy—all these are familiar and yet need restudy in the light of the important work being done on the economics of underdeveloped countries. For the present let us focus on another factor, which in itself provides an adequate explanation of the slave South's inability to industrialize: the retardation of the home market for both industrial and agricultural commodities.

Thirty years ago Elizabeth W. Gilboy complained that economic historians studying the process of industrialization were too much concerned with supply and insufficiently concerned with demand.[2] Her complaint was justified despite brilliant work on the problem of markets by a few outstanding men from Karl Marx to R. H. Tawney and Paul Mantoux. Since then, demand has received much more attention, although possibly not so much as it deserves. Important essays by Maurice Dobb, Simon Kuznets, H. J. Habakkuk, and Gunnar Myrdal, among others, have helped to correct the imbalance,[3] as has new research on European industrialization and the economics of underdeveloped countries. If there

[2] Elizabeth W. Gilboy, "Demand As a Factor in the Industrial Revolution" in *Facts and Factors in Economic History; Articles by the Former Students of Edwin F. Gay* (Cambridge, Mass., 1932), 620–39.

[3] Maurice Dobb, *Studies in the Development of Capitalism* (New York, 1947), 6 ff, 87 ff, 98 ff, 290–96; Simon Kuznets, "Toward a Theory of Economic Growth" in Robert Lekachman (ed.), *National Policy for Economic Welfare at Home and Abroad* (New York, 1955), 12–77; H. J. Habakkuk, "The Historical Experience on the Basic Conditions of Economic Progress" in L. H. Dupriez (ed.), *Economic Progress* (Louvain, Belgium, 1955), 149–69; Gunnar Myrdal, *Rich Lands and Poor* (New York, 1957), *passim*, 23–38 especially.

is one lesson to be learned from the experience of both developed and underdeveloped countries it is that industrialization is unthinkable without an agrarian revolution which shatters the old regime of the countryside. While the peasantry is tied to the land, burdened with debt, and limited to minimal purchasing power, the labor recruitment and market pre-conditions for extensive manufacturing are missing. "Land reform"— *i.e.* an agrarian revolution—is the essential first step in the creation of an urban working class, the reorganization of agriculture to feed growing cities, and the development of a home market.

There are several ways in which agricultural reorganization can provide markets for manufactures; for our immediate purposes we may consider two. First, when the laborers are separated from the land, as they were during the English enclosures, they necessarily increase the demand for clothing and other essentials formerly produced at home. Paradoxically, this expansion of the market is compatible with a marked reduction in the laborers' standard of living. Second, the farmers left on the countryside to produce for growing urban markets provide an increased demand for textiles, agricultural equipment, and so forth.

The rapid extension of the rural market was the way of the North, but the slave plantations dominated the South until such time as reorganization was imposed from without by a predatory foe interested primarily in a new system of rural exploitation. An adequate home market could not arise in the ante bellum South and has only evolved slowly and painfully during the last century.

In 1860 about seventy-five per cent of the Southern cotton crop was exported; during no ante bellum year did the grain exports of the United States exceed five per cent of the grain crop. No doubt, cotton profits were an important element in the financing of America's economic growth. The question is, were the profits siphoned off to build up the Northern economy? We know that the credit mechanisms alone, to a considerable extent, did just that. The South's dependence on the export trade, in contradistinction to the North's primary reliance on its home market, indicates not merely a social division of labor but the economic exploitation of the exporting South.

Robert G. Albion, in his excellent examination of the colonial bondage of the South to the North, concludes that the South's lack of direct trade with Europe constituted an irrational arrangement secured by the impudence of New York's aggressive entrepreneurs. We can agree that, had the South imported from abroad as much as the North and West, there could have been no sensible reason to route through New York either the South's cotton or its share of European goods; but Albion's assumption of a rough equality of imports, an assumption shared by contemporaries like George McDuffie and T. P. Kettell, can not be substantiated. The slave South's total market for manufactured goods was small relative to that of the free states; and even though the South depended upon Europe as well as the North for manufactured goods, its imports from Europe were smaller in value than imports into the North and West and smaller in bulk than the staples it exported. If the ships carrying cotton had sailed from Southern ports direct to Europe and back, they would have had to return in ballast.[4] New York's domination of the South's export trade was, therefore, not accidental. Furthermore, if the South's share in American imports had been as Albion suggests, and if the coastal trade had been as large as he implies, the greater part of the goods sent from New Orleans to the plantation areas would have originated in Europe and been reshipped through New York rather than being—as is known—of Western origin.[5]

Albion's acceptance of the assumption of nearly equal imports is the more surprising in view of the evidence of restricted Southern demand. The Southern cotton, iron, paper, wool, and railroad industries—to mention a few—struggled with indifferent results against a low level of Southern patronage. Antislavery leaders like Henry Ruffner and Cassius M. Clay made slavery's effects on the home market a cardinal point in their indictment. Thoughtful proslavery Southerners also commented frequently on the market problem. The opinion of the editor of the *Southern Agriculturalist* in 1828 that the South lacked sufficient customers to sustain a high level of manufacturing was echoed throughout the ante bellum period. The speech of Col. Andrew P. Calhoun to the Pendleton, South Carolina, Farmers' Society in 1855, for example, was strikingly similar in tone and content. On the other side, someone like Beverley Tucker would occasionally argue that Northerners would never risk a war

[4] See Robert Greenhalgh Albion, *The Rise of New York Port, 1815–1860* (New York, 1939) and Albion, *Square-Riggers on Schedule; the New York Sailing Packets to England, France, and the Cotton Ports* (Princeton, 1938). For similar arguments presented by contemporaries, see James E. B. De Bow (ed.), *The Industrial Resources, etc., of the Southern and Western States . . .* (3 vols., New Orleans, 1852–1853), 125, 365; and *De Bow's Review*, IV (1847), 208–25, 339, 351. For a perceptive Northern reply, see the anonymous pamphlet, *The Effects of Secession upon the Commercial Relations Between the North and South and upon Each Section* (New York, 1861), 15. For the weakness of the Southern import trade, see George Rogers Taylor, *The Transportation Revolution, 1815–1860* (New York, 1951), 198; Philip S. Foner, *Business & Slavery; the New York Merchants & the Irrepressible Conflict* (Chapel Hill, 1941), 6–7; and Samuel Eliot Morison, *The Maritime History of Massachusetts, 1783–1860* (Boston, 1921), 298–99. Many of the lines carrying cotton from Northern ports were deeply involved in bringing immigrants to the United States, which was one of the reasons why their ships did not have to return from Europe in ballast. John G. B. Hutchins, *The American Maritime Industries and Public Policy, 1789–1914; an Economic History* (Cambridge, Mass., 1941), 262–63.

[5] Emory R. Johnson and others, *History of the Domestic and Foreign Commerce of the United States* (2 vols., Washington, 1915), I, 242; R. B. Way, "The Commerce of the Lower Mississippi in the Period 1830–1860," *Mississippi Valley Historical Association, Proceedings*, X (1918–1919), 62; Louis Bernard Schmidt, "The Internal Grain Trade of the United States, 1850–1860," *Iowa Journal of History and Politics*, XVIII (January 1920), 110–11.

"which, while it lasted, would shut them out from the best market in the world."[6] It is difficult to imagine that many, even those who adopted such arguments for political purposes, took seriously a proposition so palpably false.

Alfred Glaze Smith, Jr., and Douglass C. North have traced the low level of Southern demand, in part, to plantation self-sufficiency. This view is not borne out by the data in the manuscript census returns from the cotton belt, which reveal only trivial amounts of home manufactures on even the largest plantations and which bear out the judgments of Rolla M. Tryon and Mary Elizabeth Massey on the weakness of Southern house-hold industry.[7] In De Soto and Marshall counties, Mississippi, the big planters (those with thirty-one or more slaves) averaged only seventy-six dollars worth of home manufactures in 1860, and farmers and small planters averaged much less. In Dougherty and Thomas counties, Georgia, the small planters (those with from twenty-one to thirty slaves) led other groups of slaveholders with one hundred and twenty-seven dollars, and the big planters produced only about half as much. Most of the planters in both clusters of counties recorded no home manufactures at all.[8] Sample studies from Virginia's tobacco area, wheat area, and tide-

[6] *Southern Agriculturalist* (Charleston), I (September 1828), 404; *Farmer and Planter*, VI (December 1855), 270–71; *Southern Quarterly Review*, XVIII (September 1850), 218.

[7] Alfred G. Smith, *Economic Readjustment of an Old Cotton State: South Carolina, 1820–1860* (Columbia, S. C., 1958), 134; Douglass C. North, *The Economic Growth of the United States, 1790–1860* (Englewood Cliffs, N. J., 1961), 132–33; Rolla M. Tryon, *Household Manufacturers in the United States, 1640–1860; a Study in Industrial History* (Chicago, 1917); Mary Elizabeth Massey, *Ersatz in the Confederacy* (Columbia, 1952), 80, 98.

[8] From the five Mississippi and the five Georgia cotton belt counties regarded as typical by Lewis C. Gray in his *History of Agriculture in the Southern United States to 1860* (2 vols., Washington, 1933), I, 334–35, II, 918–21, I have analyzed for each state the two that come closest to the mode in the only variable for which there is clear evidence, the size of slaveholdings. A review of the economic and natural conditions of the South reveals nothing to suggest that the four counties so chosen are not roughly typical of the cotton belt. I have used the four counties primarily for an investigation of purchasing power—to gain clues to the general structure of the market—and the insignificant expenditures recorded indicate that even with due allowance for the possibility of a wide, say 50%, deviation in other counties and for incorrect reporting in the census returns, the results could not conceivably be substantially different.

As a random sample, I selected the first ten names on each page of U. S. Census, 1860, Georgia, Schedule 4, Productions of Agriculture, Dougherty and Thomas counties (Library, Duke University, Durham, North Carolina) and U. S. Census, 1860, Mississippi, Schedule 4, De Soto and Marshall counties (Mississippi State Archives, Jackson). From the U. S. Census, 1860, Georgia, Schedule 2, Slave Inhabitants, Dougherty and Thomas counties, and U. S. Census, 1860, Mississippi, Schedule 2, De Soto and Marshall counties (National Archives, Washington), I determined the number of slaves held by each agriculturist in my sample. Where Schedule 4 gave the amount of produce but not its monetary value, I used a specially prepared price schedule in order to translate the amounts into dollar values. See Eugene D. Genovese, The Limits of Agrarian Reform in the Slave South (unpublished Ph.D. thesis, Columbia University, 1959), appendixes.

water reveal the same situation. Plantation manuscripts show surprisingly frequent, and often quite large, expenditures for artisans' services and suggest that plantations were much less self-sufficient and exhibited much less division of labor than is generally appreciated.[9] The root of the insufficient demand must be sought in the poverty of the rural majority composed of slaves, subsistence farmers, and poor whites.

In nineteenth-century America as a whole both capital and labor were in short supply. Industrial development was spurred by farmers who provided a large market for goods and tools, and manufacturing arose on the foundation of this immense rural demand. Eastern manufacturers gradually awoke to their dependence on this rural market and by 1854 were supporting homestead legislation not only to gain support for higher tariffs and for purposes of speculation but to expand the market for their goods. Farmers in New England saw their futures linked with industrial development, and their hostility toward commercial middlemen was not usually transferred to the manufacturers.[10] The same was true in the West. As the shrewd Achille Murat noted in the 1830's, the manufacturing interest of the West "is not constituted by the manufactories which exist, but those which they look forward to in prospective."[11] An agrarianism uncompromisingly hostile to industry and urbanization—to what was called "manufacturing as a system"—existed only in the South and can not be separated from the ideological leadership of the slaveholding planters. Even there, those seriously interested in economic progress saw the link between agricultural reform and industrialization and tried to work out proposals for increased manufactures that would be palatable to their fellow slaveholders.[12]

[9] These expenditures were for blacksmiths' services, road building, cabin building, and even for such trivial tasks as the erection of door frames. The accounts often run into hundreds of dollars. See, for example, Moses St. John R. Liddell and Family Papers (Library, Louisiana State University, Baton Rouge), Haller Nutt Papers (Library, Duke University, Durham, N. C.), Everard Green Baker Papers (Southern Historical Collection, University of North Carolina, Chapel Hill), I, 139; Killona Plantation Journals (Mississippi State Department of Archives and History, Jackson), I, 60 ff.

[10] Roy M. Robbins, *Our Landed Heritage; the Public Domain, 1776–1936* (New York, 1950), 177; Joseph Brennan, *Social Conditions in Industrial Rhode Island, 1820–1860* (Washington, 1940), 18; Samuel Reznck, "The Rise and Early Development of Industrial Consciousness in the United States, 1760–1830," *Journal of Economic and Business History*, IV (1932), 784–811; Isaac Lippincott, *A History of Manufactures in the Ohio Valley to the Year 1860* . . . (New York, 1914), 63–65; Grace Pierpont Fuller, *An Introduction to the History of Connecticut As a Manufacturing State* (Northampton, Mass., 1915), 45; James Neal Primm, *Economic Policy in a Development of a Western State, Missouri* (Cambridge, Mass., 1954), 56–59; Frank W. Taussig, *The Tariff History of the United States* (7th ed., New York, 1923), 68–108; and Bray Hammond, *Banks and Politics in America, from the Revolution to the Civil War* (Princeton, 1957).

[11] Achille Murat, *America and the Americans* (New York, 1849), 19.

[12] For examples, see the remarks of M. W. Philips and John J. Williams, *Mississippi Planter and Mechanic*, II (May 1858), 157–58; of Thomas J. Lemay, *Arator*, I (November, 1855), 237; and of Andrew Johnson, *Congressional Globe*, XXIII, 312.

The West was able to import capital because Eastern manufacturers and European creditors were confident of her growth and prosperity. Outside credits at that time had to be accumulated by the importation of commodities and the maintenance of an unfavorable trade balance. The immense internal market guaranteed the West an import surplus until 1850. Its insatiable demand for manufactured articles contributed to the unfavorable trade balance of the United States, but on the whole this was not a serious problem for the country because American importers were strong enough to obtain long-term credits on relatively easy terms; and, during the 1850's, profits from shipping and other invisible gains largely restored the balance.[13] Thus, on the one hand, the national economy was sufficiently strong to overcome the worst effects of a trade deficit, and, on the other hand, the agrarian West was able to obtain the credits required for industrial development. The South did not benefit from this arrangement. It provided an exportable surplus, which, although of great help to the national economy in offsetting the large quantity of imports, was exploited by Northern capital. The invisible gains that were so important to national growth were made partly at the expense of the South.

The population statistics for 1860 offer a clue to the structure of the market. If we exclude Maryland, in which slavery was declining, and Delaware, which was a slave state in name only, the median population per square mile in the slave states was 18, and Kentucky was high with 31. In comparison, Massachusetts had a population of 158 per square mile; Rhode Island, 138; Connecticut, 98; New York, 84; New Jersey, 81; and so forth. In the West, Ohio had 59; Indiana, 40; and Illinois, 31.

These figures do not tell the important part of the story. A country that is sparsely settled, in absolute terms, may have a high population density, in economic terms, if its system of transportation and commodity production are well developed and integrated. For example, the Northern states in 1860 had a much higher population density—from an economic point of view—than the thickly populated countries of Asia. When we consider the superiority of Northern transportation and economic integration, relative to those of the South, we must conclude that the difference in the magnitude of the market greatly exceeded that suggested by the population figures.

Historians have long appreciated—at least since the pioneer researches of U. B. Phillips—that the Southern transportation system tied the staple-producing areas to the ports and that this was the best possible arrangement for the planters. The planters controlled the state legislatures in an era in which state participation was decisive in railroad construction and generally refused to assume the tax burden necessary to open the back country and thereby encourage and strengthen politically suspect farmers.

---

[13] See Simon S. Kuznets, *Economic Change; Selected Essays in Business Cycles, National Income, and Economic Growth* (New York, 1953), 307 ff; and Charles F. Dunbar, *Economic Essays* (New York, 1904), 268.

Without a fully developed railroad network tying the South into an economic unit, the absorption of nonstaple producers into the market economy, except in a peripheral way, was impossible. Poor transportation was, for example, one important factor in the retardation of the Southern cotton textile industry.[14]

With good reason alert Southerners spoke of the connection among railroads, markets, diversified agriculture, and manufacturing. James Robb pointedly described improved transportation and greater industry as necessary ingredients in the process of unifying the South. Oscar M. Lieber noted that without an adequate transportation system South Carolina farmers were prevented from entering the market as corn producers. John Bell warmly supported federal land grants to railroads to strengthen the bonds of commodity production.[15] Within the South these men could, at best, expect to be received with an impatient silence. Where their message was sometimes listened to attentively was in the upper South, as for example in what came to be West Virginia; the subsequent construction of road and railroad links to existing markets generally bound parts of the upper South to the free states and helped remove them from the slaveholders' domain.

In the slave South the home market consisted primarily of the plantations, which bought foodstuffs from the West and manufactured goods from the East. The planters needed increased Southern manufacturing but only for certain purposes. They needed cheap slave clothing, cotton gins and a few crude agricultural implements, rope for cotton bagging, and so forth. This narrow market could not compare with the tremendous Western demand for industrial commodities of all kinds, especially for agricultural implements and machinery on the more capital-intensive Western farms. The Northeast had the capital and skilled labor for fairly large-scale production and had established its control over existing markets in the North and West. Southern manufacturers could not hope to compete with Northern outside the South, and the same conditions that brought about Northern control of the Northern market made possible Northern penetration of the Southern market despite the costs of transportation.

The South was caught in a contradiction similar to that facing many underdeveloped countries today. On the one hand, it provided a market for outside industry. On the other hand, that very market was too small to

[14] See Milton S. Heath, *Constructive Liberalism; the Role of the State in Economic Development in Georgia to 1860* (Cambridge, Mass., 1954), 290–91, and Seth Hammond, "Location Theory and the Cotton Industry," *Journal of Economic History,* II (1942), Supp., 101–17. The opposition of entrenched landowning classes to the extension of transportation has been general in colonial, underdeveloped countries. See George Wythe, *Industry in Latin America* (New York, 1945), 4.

[15] De Bow (ed.), *Industrial Resources,* II, 154; Oscar M. Lieber, *Report on the Survey of South Carolina . . . 1857* (Columbia, 1858), 106; *Congressional Globe,* XXI, pt. 1, 867–68.

sustain industry on a scale large enough to compete with outsiders who could draw upon wider markets. Only one fifth of the manufacturing establishments of the United States were in the South, and their average capitalization was well below that of the manufacturing establishments of the free states. Consider the situation in two industries of special importance to the South—cotton textiles and agricultural implements. New England had almost three times as many cotton factories as the entire South in 1860, and yet the average capitalization was almost twice as great. The concentration in this industry had proceeded so far by 1850 that of the more than 1,000 cotton factories in the United States only forty-one had one half the total capital investment. As for the agricultural implement and machinery industry, New York, Pennsylvania, Ohio, and Illinois each had a greater total capital investment than did the entire South, and in three of these the average capitalization was between two and two and a half times as great as the average in the South.[16] This Northern advantage led Edmund Ruffin and T. L. Clingman, among others, to look forward to a Southern confederacy protected by high tariffs against Northern goods.[17]

In view of the nature of the plantation market it is not surprising that data on the cotton textile industry almost invariably reveal that Southern producers concentrated upon the production of the cheapest and coarsest kind of cloth to be used in the making of slave clothing.[18] Even so, local industrialists had to compete for this market with Northerners who sometimes shipped direct and sometimes established Southern branches and who had facilities for the collection and processing of second-hand clothing.[19] Just as New England supplied much of the South's "Negro cloth," so it supplied much of the boots and shoes. Firms like Batchellor

[16] U. S. Census Office, *Manufactures of the United States in 1860 . . .* (Washington, 1865), xxi, ccxvii, lxxiii, 729–30; Evelyn H. Knowlton, *Pepperell's Progress; History of a Cotton Textile Company, 1844–1945* (Cambridge, Mass., 1948), 32. The average capitalization of manufacturing establishments was in 1850 more than 25% higher in the free states and territories than in the slave states, and the gap widened in the 1850's when the increase in average capital investment was 68% in the free states and territories and only 51% in the slave states. The lower South (North Carolina, South Carolina, Georgia, Florida, Alabama, Mississippi, Louisiana, and Texas) fell even further behind. The average capitalization here, 38% less than in the free states in 1850, was 47% less by 1860. Furthermore, the rate of increase in the number of establishments during this decade was appreciably greater in the North than in the South.

[17] Edmund Ruffin, Incidents of My Life, 19–20, in Edmund Ruffin Papers (Southern Historical Collection, University of North Carolina); T. L. Clingman's speech to the House of Representatives, January 22, 1850, in *Selections from the Speeches and Writings of Hon. Thomas L. Clingman of North Carolina . . .* (Raleigh, N. C., 1877), 233–54, especially 250.

[18] See Patent Office, *Annual Report, 1857, Agriculture*, Senate Exec. Docs., 35 Cong., 1 Sess., No. 30, pt. 4 (Serial 928), 308–309, 318; and Richard H. Shryock, "The Early Industrial Revolution in the Empire State," *Georgia Historical Quarterly*, XI (June 1927), 128.

[19] Jesse Eliphalet Pope, *The Clothing Industry in New York* (Columbia, Mo., 1905), 6–7.

Brothers of Brookfield produced cheap shoes especially for the Southern market and as early as 1837 opened a branch at Mobile to consolidate its Southern market.[20]

Producers of better cotton goods had little hope of making a living in the South. Occasionally, a William Gregg could penetrate Northern markets successfully, but Southern demand for such goods was too small to have much effect on the industry generally. Northern firms like the Pepperell Manufacturing Company or A. A. Lawrence Company did little business in the South. On the other hand a rising demand for textiles in the agrarian West had greatly influenced the New England cotton industry since 1814.[21]

The Southern iron industry, hampered as it was by the restricted railroad development in the slave states, also had a poor time of it. American iron producers generally were handicapped because much of the country's railroad iron was being imported. The small scale of operations and resultant cost schedule, which hurt the industry nationally, hit the Southern manufacturers especially hard. Dependent upon a weak local market, Southern iron manufacturers had great difficulty holding their own even during the prosperous 1850's.

No wonder the Augusta, Georgia, Commercial Convention added to its demand that Southerners buy Southern goods the qualification, unless you can get Northern cheaper. And no wonder the proposal was ridiculed as amounting to "Never kiss the maid if you can kiss the mistress, unless you like the maid better." [22]

We can not measure precisely the extent of the Southern market nor even make a reliable, general, quantitative comparison between the Southern and Western rural markets, but we can glean from various sources some notion of the immense difference. For example, Phelps, Dodge & Co., a prominent cotton shipping firm that also distributed metals, tools, machinery, clothing, and an assortment of other items, reported at the beginning of the Civil War that only five per cent of its sales were to the South and that those were primarily to the noncotton states. We do not know the extent of the firm's participation in the cotton export trade, but it was considerable. Phelps, Dodge & Co. was in an excellent position to exchange industrial goods for cotton, but the Southern demand for imported goods could not compare in bulk or value with the supply of cotton. In the West, on the other hand, farmers and

---

[20] Blanche Evans Hazard, *The Organization of the Boot and Shoe Industry in Massachusetts Before 1875* (Cambridge, Mass., 1921), 57–58.

[21] Knowlton, *Pepperell's Progress*, 83–84; Caroline F. Ware, *The Early New England Cotton Manufacture; a Study in Industrial Beginnings* (Boston, 1931), 48, 55.

[22] Herbert Wender, *Southern Commercial Conventions, 1837–1859* (Baltimore, 1930), 25.

townsmen provided a growing and lucrative market, and the firm had more customers in Ohio than in any state except New York.[23]

An examination of the 1860 manuscript census returns and other primary sources pertaining to two representative cotton counties in Mississippi and to two in Georgia permits us to judge roughly the extent of the market in the cotton belt by estimating the expenditures made by planters and farmers in these counties. (See above, note 8.) The estimates are the most generous possible and exaggerate the extent of the Southern rural market in relation to the Western in two ways: There were far more rural poor with little or no purchasing power in the cotton belt than in the West, and the concentration of landholdings in the South resulted in fewer landowners than could be found in a Western area of comparable size. Thus, even if the estimate of the expenditures made by these Southern planters and farmers had been larger than the expenditures of a similar group of individual proprietors in the West—which was by no means true—the total purchased in each county would still have been far less than in a comparable Western area. Furthermore, as food was a major item in the expenditures of the Southerners, the market for industrial commodities was much smaller than might appear.

The concentration of landholding and slaveholding in the Mississippi counties meant that six per cent of the landowners commanded one third of the gross income and probably a much higher percentage of the net. That is, the majority of landowners were faced with a disproportionately small portion of the total income accruing to the cotton economy as a whole.

Only the largest planters—ten per cent of the landowners—spent more than $1,000 a year for food and supplies, and they rarely spent more. These expenditures include the total purchases for the slaves. The slaveholding farms and plantations in Mississippi annually spent about thirty or thirty-five dollars per person for food and supplies; nonslaveholders spent about twenty-five dollars per person. In Georgia slaveholding farms and plantations spent about twenty-five dollars per person, and nonslaveholders were just about self sufficient.[24] In contrast, Philip Foner reports that contemporary newspapers and other sources indicate that the small farmers who made up the great majority of the rural population of the West accumulated store bills of from one hundred to six hundred dollars.[25] Even if we allow for considerable exaggeration and assume that the accounts were generally closer to the lower estimate, these figures, which are exclusive of cash purchases, mail orders, payments to drum-

---

[23] Richard Lowitt, *A Merchant Prince of the Nineteenth Century, William E. Dodge* (New York, 1954), 31 ff, 37.

[24] In Mississippi a sample of 584 units with 7,289 slaves and an estimated 2,480 whites spent about $316,500; in Georgia a sample of 100 units with 2,354 slaves and an estimated 710 whites spent about $73,300.

[25] Foner, *Business & Slavery*, 143.

mers, and so forth, are at least a clue to the impressive purchasing power of the Western countryside.

However imprecise the estimates for the South may be, they indicate the lack of purchasing power among the rural population of the cotton belt and demonstrate how greatly the situation there differed from that in the West. With such a home market the slave economy could not sustain more than the lowest level of commodity production apart from that of a few staples. The success of William Gregg as a textile manufacturer in South Carolina and the data produced by Professor John Hebron Moore showing that a cotton textile industry could and did exist in ante bellum Mississippi would seem to contradict this conclusion; but Gregg, who was aware of the modest proportions of the home market, warned Southerners against trying to produce for local needs and suggested that they focus on the wholesale market. His own company at Graniteville, South Carolina, produced fine cotton goods that sold much better in New York than in the South. Gregg's success in the Northern market could not easily be duplicated by others, and when he discussed the Southern market, he felt compelled, as did Benjamin L. C. Wailes and other astute observers, to advocate production of cheap cotton goods for the plantations.[26] Moore's conclusion that his data prove the adaptability of manufacturing to the lower South requires for substantiation more than evidence of particular successes, no matter how impressive;[27] it requires evidence that Southern producers were strong enough to drive out Northern competition and, more important, that the market was large enough to sustain more than a few firms.

The plantation system did have its small compensations for industry. The planters' taste for luxuries, for example, proved a boon to the Petersburg iron industry, which supplied plantations with cast-iron fences, lawn ornaments, balconies, fancy gates, and other decorative articles.[28] A silk industry emerged briefly but was destroyed by climatic conditions as well as by a shortage of capital.[29] The hemp industry, which sup-

[26] William Gregg, *Essays on Domestic Industry; or An Inquiry into the Expediency of Establishing Cotton Manufactures in South-Carolina* (Graniteville, S. C., 1841), 4; Benjamin L. C. Wailes, *Address Delivered in the College Chapel Before the Agricultural, Horticultural and Botanical Society, of Jefferson College* (Natchez, Miss., 1841), 22–23; *De Bow's Review*, XXIX (October 1860), 496–97; Broadus Mitchell, *William Gregg, Factory Master of the Old South* (Chapel Hill, N. C., 1928), 106.

[27] John Hebron Moore, "Mississippi's Ante-Bellum Textile Industry," *Journal of Mississippi History*, XVI (April 1954), 81.

[28] Edward A. Wyatt, IV, "Rise of Industry in Ante-Bellum Petersburg," *William and Mary College Quarterly*, third series, XVII (January 1937), 32.

[29] Southerners were very much interested in silk cultivation and manufacture and saw fine market possibilities. See Charles G. Parsons, *Inside View of Slavery; or a Tour Among the Planters* (Boston, 1855), 71 ff; C. O. Cathey, "Sidney Weller: Ante-Bellum Promoter of Agricultural Reform," *North Carolina Historical Review*, XXI (January 1954), 6; Spaulding Trafton, "Silk Culture in Henderson County, Kentucky," *Filson Club History Quarterly*, IV (October 1930), 184–89.

plied rope for cotton baling, depended heavily on the plantation market.

Some Southern industrialists, especially those in the border states, did good business in the North. Louisville tobacco and hemp manufacturers sold much of their output in Ohio. Botts and Burfoot of Richmond, Virginia, reported the sale of $1,000-worth of straw cutters in the North during a six-month period. The more successful Southern iron producers were those of the upper South, who were able to sell outside the slave states. Smith and Perkins of Alexandria, Virginia, began production of locomotives and railroad cars in the 1850's and obtained a good many orders from the North; but the company failed because shipping costs made consolidation of its Northern market difficult and because only a few orders were forthcoming from the South. Similarly, the paper industry in South Carolina did well until the 1850's, when Northern orders dropped and no Southern orders appeared.[30] The political dangers of these links with the free states were widely appreciated. The Virginia Commercial Convention, for example, reported that West Virginia was being cut off from the South in this way.[31] During the Civil War, William Henry Holcombe, a thoughtful doctor from Natchez, listed in his diary various reasons for the adherence of the border states to the Union and placed close commercial ties high on the list.[32] One suspects that there was more than hindsight here, for politically sophisticated Southerners were alert to the danger well before 1861. But what could they have done about it?

The inability of the slave South to generate an adequate rural market inhibited industrialization and urbanization, which in turn limited the market for agricultural produce and undermined attempts at diversification. With the exception of New Orleans and Baltimore, the slave states had no large cities, and few reached the size of 15,000. The urban population of the South could not compare with that of the Northeast, as is generally appreciated; but, more to the point, it could not compare with that of the agrarian West either. The urban population of the lower South in 1860 was only seven per cent of the total population, and in the western part of the lower South, embracing most of the cotton belt, there was a relative decline during the preceding twenty years. In New England, the percentage was thirty-seven; in the Middle Atlantic states, including

[30] Lippincott, *Manufactures in the Ohio Valley*, 64; *Southern Planter*, III (April 1843), advertisement on back cover; Lester J. Cappon, "Trend of the Southern Iron Industry Under the Plantation System," *Journal of Economic and Business History*, II (February 1930), 361, 371, 376; Carrol H. Quenzel, "The Manufacture of Locomotives and Cars in Alexandria in the 1850's," *Virginia Magazine of History and Biography*, LXII (April 1954), 182 ff; Ernest M. Lander, Jr., "Paper Manufacturing in South Carolina Before the Civil War," *North Carolina Historical Review*, XXIX (April 1952), 225 ff.

[31] De Bow (ed.), *Industrial Resources*, III, 465.

[32] William Henry Holcombe Diary (Southern Manuscript Collection, University of North Carolina), entry for September 6, 1855, but obviously written in 1861.

Ohio, thirty-five; and perhaps most significantly, in Indiana, Illinois, Michigan, and Wisconsin, fourteen.[33]

The urban market in the South was even less developed than these figures suggest. If we except New Orleans, which was a special case, three cities of the lower South had a population of 15,000 or more: Mobile, Charleston, and Savannah, with a combined population of 92,000. Of this number, thirty-seven per cent were slaves and free Negroes, who may be assumed to have represented only minimal purchasing power. In the 1850's American families certainly did not spend less than forty per cent of their incomes on food, and the importance of a large urban market for foodstuffs may be judged accordingly.[34]

Eugene W. Hilgard, state geologist of Mississippi, explained his state's failure to develop a cattle industry largely by the absence of a local market. Similarly, Oscar M. Lieber, state geologist of South Carolina, warned farmers in a state that was never comfortably self-sufficient in corn not to produce more corn than they could consume, for there was no place to market the surplus. Charles Yancey of Buckingham County, Virginia, wrote that planters and farmers would not grow oats because the only possibility of disposing of them lay in person to person barter.[35]

The weakness of the market for agricultural produce had many detrimental consequences for the South, of which we may mention only two. First, those sections of the border states which found markets in the Northern cities were increasingly drawn into the political-economic orbit of the free states at the very moment when the slave states required maximum solidarity to preserve their system. Second, the weakness of the market doomed the hopes of agricultural reformers and transformed their cry for diversification into a cry for a backward step toward natural economy.

When that great antislavery Kentuckian, Cassius M. Clay, finally receives from historians the honor and attention that he deserves, he will surely be recognized as one of the most penetrating commentators on the economics of slavery. Consider his remarks on the problem of markets, with which we are presently concerned:

Lawyers, merchants, mechanics, laborers, who are your consumers; Robert Wickliffe's two hundred slaves? How many clients do you

[33] Urban area defined as incorporated places of 2,500 or more. See U. S. Bureau of the Census, *Urban Population in the U. S. from the First Census* (1790) *to the Fifteenth Census* (1930) . . . (Washington, 1939).
[34] This estimate is from Edgar W. Martin, *The Standard of Living in 1860* (Chicago, 1942), 11–12, and may greatly underestimate the situation in urban households. According to Richard O. Cummings, laborers in Massachusetts probably spent about three fourths of their weekly wages on food in 1860. R. O. Cummings, *The American and His Food; a History of Food Habits in the United States* (Chicago, 1941), 266.
[35] Eugene W. Hilgard, *Report on the Geology and Agriculture of the State of Mississippi* (Jackson, 1860), 250–51; Lieber, *Report,* 106. See also Patent Office, *Annual Report, 1849, Agriculture,* Senate Exec. Docs., 31 Cong., 1 Sess., No. 15, pt. 2 (Serial 556), 137.

find, how many goods do you sell, how many hats, coats, saddles, and trunks do you make for these two hundred slaves? Does Mr. Wickliffe lay out as much for himself and his two hundred slaves as two hundred freemen do? . . . All our towns dwindle, and our farmers lose, in consequence, all home markets. Every farmer bought out by the slave system send off the consumers of the manufacturers of the town: when the consumers are gone, the mechanic must go also. . . . . A home market cannot exist in a slave state.[36]

Plantation slavery, then, so limited the purchasing power of the South that it could not sustain much industry. That industry which could be raised usually lacked a home market of sufficient scope to permit large-scale operation; the resultant cost of production was often too high for success in competition with Northern firms drawing on much wider markets. Without sufficient industry to support urbanization, a general and extensive diversification of agriculture was unthinkable. Whatever other factors need to be considered in a complete analysis, the low level of demand in this plantation-based slave society was sufficient to retard the economic development of the South.

[36] Horace Greeley (ed.), *The Writings of Cassius Marcellus Clay* . . . (New York, 1848), 179, 227. For a recent biography, see David L. Smiley, *Lion of White Hall: The Life of Cassius M. Clay* (Madison, Wis., 1962).

Social Values and Economic Growth

19. The Social Basis of the American System of Manufacturing[*]

John E. Sawyer

I

Of the many tasks confronting economic history, none are more shrouded in uncertainty than those encompassed in the theme "Institutional and Cultural Factors in Economic History." We have in general

[*] I should like to express my appreciation to the many individuals who offered helpful comments following the oral presentation of my briefer paper; to Carl Sapers, Ann Satterthwaite, and Emily McWhinney for helpful assistance at various points; and to the Carnegie Corporation for a grant that enabled me to embark on this project.

"The Social Basis of the American System of Manufacturing," by John E. Sawyer, is reprinted by permission from *Journal of Economic History*, XIV (December, 1954), 361–379.

treated these factors respectfully, but as a profession we have preferred to work in areas more clearly defined and with tools more fully developed. As a result few areas have received less sustained attention than the zones where we must seek the interplay of economic, social, and cultural forces.

My general question is whether for analyzing problems of differential economic growth—and particularly cases of sustained indigenous development that is neither imposed from without nor centrally controlled or financed from within—we may not have to give greater attention to areas lying beyond traditional economic categories and familiar quantities, to probe further into the ways in which social and cultural factors bear upon economic processes, stimulating or retarding the beginnings of growth, and acting to sustain or dampen out phases of growth once under way.

There are good reasons behind caution in the past, and for caution in the future, in venturing beyond the side of the street better lit to date by both theory and statistics, and expectations of what is likely to be promptly or firmly proved had best be modest. But the darker areas on the other side of the street, which the newer psychological and social sciences have been exploring, seem too important to economic history to be left either to the poets and novelists of successive generations, or solely to bold spirits, like Weber or Schumpeter, who have at intervals swept across our horizon.

II

The particular case to which I would like to turn the discussion is one close to home—a case centering on the American system of manufacturing and the possible part that social and cultural factors may have played in its origins or in its persisting features. My concern at this point is not with final evaluations—the subject is too big and complex and still needs too much examination for that—but rather with developing the question as it has presented itself in two substantial sets of evidence more than a century apart, one from our own day and one from the period of its beginnings.

Perhaps the most pointed and most considerable body of recent evidence on this problem is that which emerged from the experience with the American foreign aid programs in the years since the Second World War (under the E.C.A.—the Marshall Plan—and its successor agencies, M.S.A. and F.O.A.).[1] This experience may be roughly divided into two parts, that of Americans abroad and that of Europeans here.

The relevant parts of the record of American operations overseas have

---

[1] A gradually changing range of functions has been successively handled by the European Cooperation Administration, the Mutual Security Administration, and, since August 1953, by the Foreign Operations Administration. In another connection I have had occasion to review certain aspects of this experience, and I should like to indicate my debt to the officials here and abroad who discussed these problems with me.

now become sufficiently familiar to need no extensive review. Aid programs which got under way under assumptions that the task was largely one of dollars and tools, and that a given input of these would yield given results, again and again were confronted by evidence of unexpected sharpness on the extent to which these, while essential, were not enough. A given allocation of funds or equipment or technical assistance simply did not produce anticipated results. In some instances even virtually identical plants that had been set up abroad by American firms had shown conspicuously lower output records than their counterparts at home. Gradually, in case after case and country after country, those closest to the task found themselves struggling with the more intangible aspects of productivity. They found their attention directed not just to the formal framework of credit, market, and business organization but beyond that to a full range of considerations that we would place under the headings of social and cultural factors: the ways in which prevailing value systems, family patterns, social stratification, and a network of social relationships extending far beyond the place of work affected not only the character of the firm and of the market but the behavior and aspirations of various participants in the economic process—entrepreneurs, investors, technicians, workers, jobbers, retailers, and, not least, consumers.

Out of this disparate but very practical experience emerged a new light on the American scene, a reverse light pointing to the economic significance of attitudes and social arrangements at home that had received only perfunctory attention.

More significant for our special example is the supporting evidence from the other side of the coin, the second major part of the record, the positive observations of the now hundreds of European "productivity teams" who have come to the United States since 1949 to look into the highways and byways of American economic life. Of their findings and conclusions we are fortunate in having an extensive published record, now totaling several hundreds of reports and many thousands of pages.[2] This mass of reports, particularly some of the major series like the British and the French, when taken together with the American reports from abroad, constitute an unusually extensive and detailed body of observations on *comparative* industrial practices. Although these reports need a great deal of sifting and correction for obvious limitations inherent in such visits and reports, for uneven depth and quality, and for certain predispositions or private interests, they are in the main the serious work

[2] These missions, varying in size and composition and in the length of their visit from a few weeks to more than a year, have generally published their reports through their respective national productivity agency or under the auspices of the O.E.E.C. They include both "industry" reports and reports of "specialists" on particular functions (like training, accounting, packaging, materials handling, and so forth). Since 1953 the F.O.A. has broadened the program to include a growing number of non-European missions.

of responsible economic agents thoroughly familiar with their home industries—executives, engineers, foremen, and others—who quite generally came here with real and practical problems in mind, to find out all they could about the nature of and reasons for whatever superiority the United States might have in their several lines of activity.

I have not surveyed the whole of this literature. I can, however, report from a significant sample of the major series that their reports present social and cultural factors in at least as strong an image as did those on European countries. The importance assigned to social and cultural conditions and pressures, in trying to explain differences in productivity, is both persistent and considerable. A British writer, reviewing the entire series published in England by the Anglo-American Council on Productivity, concludes:

> When the sixty-six A.A.C.P. Teams between 1949 and 1952 made comprehensive inquiries in so many American industries (most of which they already knew by their own technical experience) not one could report that the U. S. prodigies of production were achieved by methods unknown, or technically impossible, in Britain.[3]

Though technical materials were typically the initial focus of investigation, and the lengthy explanations they require occupy a large part of the space, few reports, no matter how technical their starting points, fail to turn to social and cultural themes.

III

A careful examination of twenty-five reports selected from this British series as being relevant to our problem shows sociocultural categories of explanation given major place in roughly two thirds, and what appears to be a still more crucial role in about half of these.[4] An example of this over-all emphasis may be chosen from the report on an industry that has not always fared so well at home, the building industry, where the findings were summarized as follows:

> . . . in this Report we have examined the main psychological, organizational and technical differences between the British and American building industries with the object of isolating the factors which

[3] Graham Hutton, *We Too Can Prosper: The Promise of Productivity* (London: Allen and Unwin, 1953), p. 18. L. Rostas in his earlier and more formal study is primarily concerned with problems of method and measurement of physical and technical factors, and only briefly refers to the dimensions we are pursuing.—*Comparative Productivity in British and American Industry*, National Institute of Economic and Social Research, Occasional Papers, XIII (Cambridge: The University Press, 1948), pp. 66–67.

[4] Though not a complete selection, see such diverse reports from this series as those on *The Brassfoundry, Building, The British Cotton Industry, Machine Tools, Retailing, Trade Unions*, or the *Training of Supervisors;* or any of the additional titles cited below.

make for high productivity in the United States. In our opinion, the most important, but not the only, factors are (i) . . . pre-planning . . . (ii) . . . coordination . . . (iii) the adequacy of supplies . . . (iv) . . . mechanical aids (v) . . . continuous research . . . and (vi) the nation-wide stimulus of the American industrial climate. . . .

This last reason . . . is perhaps the most important of all. Acceptance of the need for high productivity as an essential factor in industrial life is universal in America, and it permeates the will and action of the operatives as well as of the employer groups.[5]

Statements in like vein can be duplicated in the British or other reports. Any one report, however, is subject to many possible distortions. It therefore appears more useful to try to illustrate a range of particular themes that recur again and again in a wide variety of reports; and, without attempting any full tally, to do this in sufficient fullness both to make clear some of the kinds of things that struck foreign observers as important today and to indicate themes that an earlier run of evidence suggests have been of persisting significance.

Thus on the general outlook of Americans toward economic life: [6]

[Productivity] is part of the American way of life, an article of faith as much as a matter of economics. . . . Americans believe that it is their mission to lead the world in production efficiency. Every small town has its own newspaper and radio station, and the performance of local industries is daily news. Individuals, trade unions and management are equally convinced that their different ends will be served only by high productivity. . . . (*Coal*, p. 4.)

There, the feeling that "the sky is the limit" still prevails and Americans generally seem to believe not only in the possibility of self-advancement by individual effort but also in the desirability of making that effort. (*Freight Handling*, p. 50.)

In an average American factory there seems to be . . . a sense of urgency and aliveness. . . . It is characteristic of Americans that they seldom hesitate to make changes. . . . The executive is keenly aware that better methods are always possible, and labour believes that the more there is produced the more there is to divide. (*Furniture*, p. 70.)

. . . there seems to be no feeling in America, as there so often is here, that a sojourn at a university has unfitted the graduate for the rigours of a business life . . . . there is a lack of snobbishness among educational bodies and the American people in general about success in business, which is as highly regarded as professional success. (*Retailing*, p. 72.)

[5] *Building*, p. 63. See also the Introduction and pp. 55–56. This Report can at once illustrate the emphasis in question and some of the cautions in order in using this material.

[6] All references in this section are to the Reports indicated in the British (A.A.C.P.) series. What cannot be reproduced here is the weight of emphasis arising from repeated attention to these themes.

On entrepreneurs and the executive role:

> Amongst the top executives we met, we encountered a freshness and breadth of outlook . . . a readiness to encourage and pass on knowledge to juniors. It is accepted that industry offers an excellent career for people possessing brains, character, and ability. (*Hosiery and Knitwear*, p. 8.)
>
> "Cost-consciousness". . . does not simply mean cutting costs. . . . It also means not missing opportunities. He will just as readily embark on large-scale and ambitious expenditure if the rewards . . . appear sufficient. (*Management Accounting*, p. 37.)
>
> American managements look continually towards the future. They base their decisions on an intelligent anticipation of trends rather than wait until the pressure of current events forces them to make decisons. (*Production Control*, pp. 7, 17.)
>
> We found that the principal would unhesitatingly change his specialist supplier, even if the association had been lengthy, whenever a similar product at lower cost or of superior quality was available from another quarter. (*Simplification in Industry*, p. 9.)
>
> American managers have such a different conception of their job. . . . [He] conceives it to be his duty above all else to increase his sales. . . . This concentration on turnover leads naturally to a conception of retailing as an aggressive process; something the retailer does to his customers rather than something they do to him. (*Retailing*, p. 46.)
>
> The U. S. has outpaced the U. K. in the matter of increasing national productivity because U.S. management has, overall, shown much more foresight, courage and vigour in taking and applying the various decisions to make progress round the spiral. (*Machine Tools*, p. 44.)

On staff and the lower levels of management:

> The managerial candidate tends to receive education of a more general character to a later age than is customary in Britain, and to acquire his technical knowledge by actual service. . . . He is thus led by training and circumstance to seek the widest personal exchange of knowledge and views on technical and administrative practices . . . and this habit, early acquired, appears to continue. . . . (*Hosiery and Knitwear*, pp. 6–7.)
>
> . . . we are convinced that the American foreman as defined is better informed about company policy and tends to have wider responsibility. . . . It is both the policy and practice of American management to bring a well-informed responsible member of management into closer day to day contact with the operative than is possible in most British factories. (*Training of Supervisors*, p. 7; also p. 10.)

On labor and the attitudes of workers and toward workers:

> . . . in not a single case did we find serious opposition to the introduction of new methods of materials handling or mechanical aids.

Trade union officials generally expressed the view that such changes were inevitable and that progress could not be impeded. (*Materials Handling in Industry,* p. 39.)

We found a very positive attitude to work, with tea breaks uncommon and lunch breaks of only half-an-hour. Moreover, we found that the American worker appears to have no objection to overtime, nor to shift work: a great number of firms were working two or three shifts. (*Packet Foods,* p. 64.)

An American feels that he can, if he chooses, move from one industry to another. . . . In Britain the "tradesman" values the position he has gained by his years of apprenticeship and training; in America the workman equally values his position of independence in industry. (*Furniture,* p. 5.)

American unions' attitude to company profits is typical of their acceptance of a capitalist economy. . . . Usually, high profits are considered a sign of efficiency . . . and the main concern of unions is to obtain a fair share of them. (*Trade Unions and Productivity,* p. 52.)

The American workman is not a mere workman; he is an American and he aims to live as well as, and, to use his own expression, to "have fun" to the same extent as any other American. There is not that social distinction between management and worker which is found in Britain. (*The Brassfoundry,* p. 6.)

On consumption patterns and pressures:

The American's social status is measured in terms of ownership, not so much of money as of material goods . . . [and] is most important to Americans, especially to women. They are fond of their homes, fond of good clothes, fond of going one better than the family next door. In this respect there is far greater competition than is found in Britain, and it is the womenfolk who promote this competition and urge their men to make it possible. (*The Brassfoundry,* p. 6.)

. . . the American housewife is less conservative and more adventurous, and seems always willing to buy something new or different. (*Retailing,* p. 7.)

In the lively American economy, the market continuously exercises great pressure on the producer for new textile products, with novelty, with eye-appeal, and/or of low price. From this pressure results a receptivity to new ideas, methods, devices and equipment on the part of both management and workers, which we found most refreshing. (*Hosiery and Knitwear,* p. 7.)

On certain characteristics of the American system of manufacturing:

. . . one common characteristic which seems to emerge: . . . a conscious effort by the manufacturer to achieve greater productivity by studied methods and not by ad hoc improvements. (*Packet Foods,* p. 62.)

As low cost is the main object of American industry no premium is placed on craftsmanship for its own sake. Only so much accuracy and refinement of finish are put into the article as are necessary if it is to meet the standard of the quality range for which it was originally designed. (*Management Accounting,* p. 7.)

We attempted to find the key to this unexpected alliance of variety and standardisation . . . standardisation and simplification, as we saw them operated in the United States, are nothing more than means towards mechanisation. (*Packaging,* p. 25.)

The marked machine consciousness in America. . . . Whilst the cost of the equipment is naturally taken into account, the returns on it are calculated not merely in the narrow sense of money but in the wider sense of adding to the firm's general resources and improving the working conditions of the staff. (*Freight Handling,* pp. 49, 50.)

The principles and methods which American management applies are well known in this country but are practiced much more universally and vigorously in America. (*Management Accounting,* p. 14.)

The list could be multiplied, or similar citations presented from other series. A sampling of the comparable French materials, for example (some of them of book length), strongly confirms themes emphasized above in the British reports, though reflecting problems of French society in their special attention to the worker and the ways in which the American social order favorably affects his status, attitudes, and integration in the industrial effort.[7] When all the proper discounts have been made, an impressive number of interested and qualified European observers from all levels, who often came here with other explanations in mind, went away giving high place in their list to the surrounding social framework; or, as French reports have phrased it, to the impress of the culture on the human factor.

IV

This review may have already sufficiently indicated a problem of the first order for economic history—or rather the importance of the host of problems involved in trying to break into, analyze, and assess the part played by varying social or cultural influences in particular patterns of economic activity.

We have thus far, however, been dealing with a highly contemporary world and with evidence subject to special cautions. I am therefore concerned about the skeptic who might argue that, lacking dimension in time, simplifying Americans abroad and impressionable Europeans here have misjudged the signs and read effects as causes, mistaking the social consequences of different economic growth as significant causes contributing thereto. We would, of course, readily agree with the important measure of truth behind this. Both cause and effect are obviously present

[7] See, for example, *Aspects de l'entreprise américaine* or *L'Industrie de la Machine-Outil* in the French series, published by La Société Auxiliaire pour la Diffusion des Editions de Productivité (S.A.D.E.P.) in Paris.

in these cases and materials. The extent to which the social character of modern America has been shaped and sustained by abundant resources and extraordinary rates of economic growth needs no laboring here. But I should not want to see our problem slither away under a screen of sound insistence on historical interaction into the underbrush where inquiry halts before the truism that everything influences everything else, nor see it reduced to a problem of concern only to those whose interest is in the results of economic growth rather than its causes.

In the balance of this paper I would therefore like to move backwards in time to see if we cannot find there a second bearing on our question, a parallel run of evidence, that will help "fix" this problem as of central causal significance for economic history.

The prodigious and distinctive growth of American industries in the decades since 1870 might be a good case to examine. Here again the accounts of travelers and foreign industrial missions give heavy emphasis to social and cultural conditions among the determinants. Both the prevailing creed and the open structure of American society were surely mightily at work in the developments of this era, in the release and channeling of men's energies. It is, however, a most difficult period in which to assign these factors a proper place. For this is also the period in which the standard "big" explanations of American growth become so clearly operative and tend to occupy the scene—the period when the thunder of the railroads at first tends to drown out all else, when vast continental resources come into play, when population growth and rising incomes make a bigger internal market than European countries had known, and heavy industry grows apace. These latter developments loom so large and loud, and explanations tied to scale, size, and rates of growth so fill the stage, that to insist on giving sociocultural factors their due, however appropriate, presents many of the difficulties of listening for the strings in a Wagnerian crescendo.

It therefore seems more fruitful to turn further back to earlier and quieter decades, before these explanations geared to bigness in effect "take over" American economic history, and to seek the point at which a distinctive pattern of American manufacturing first appears and the reasons advanced in contemporary accounts for its appearance.

v

We find that during the first half of the nineteenth century there emerged patterns of producing (and marketing) manufactured goods that by the 1850's had become widely known abroad as the "American system of manufacturing." Centering in southern New England and in the light metalworking industries, notably in firearms, clocks, watches, locks, and tools of various kinds, and then spreading into neighboring states and a broadening range of industries, there came into being the basic elements and patterns of modern mass manufacturing; that is, the principles and practice of quantity manufacture of standardized products characterized by interchangeable parts and the use of a growing array of machine tools and specialized jigs and fixtures, along with power, to substitute simplified and, as far as possible, mechanized operations for the craftsman's arts. Hand in hand with the technical advances [8] went parallel developments in the organization of productive effort and in the new methods necessary to market standardized quantity products.[9]

While we do not have answers to many questions that interest us, the substantial material set forth in the literature thus far [10] seems to provide a sufficient basis for the following general propositions: (1) that a distinctive pattern of manufacturing had come into being in the United States in the period *before* the Civil War, having many of the characteristics, technical, economic, and social, that the world today associates with contemporary American manufacturing; (2) that while there were both anticipations and parallel developments abroad, and the debt to Europe remained heavy and continuous, the new society made important *independent* contributions to the development of this system throughout the early decades of the nineteenth century, in tools, techniques, and above all in ways of approaching and organizing both production and distribution; (3) that these early American innovators often seem to have more clearly seen the general principles and potentialities of their departures from traditional ways than their contemporaries elsewhere; [11] (4) that

[8] Primarily worked out, according to Joseph W. Roe, in England and New England in the decades between 1800 and 1850.—*English and American Tool Builders* (New Haven: Yale University Press, 1916), pp. 4–5 and ff. In these early decades, of course, "tolerances" in no way approached those associated with precision manufacturing today.

[9] On the latter phase the early history of the Connecticut clock industry offiers an interesting example of the cases in which a market had to be created in order that the economies of quantity manufacture might be realized.

[10] Most notably in the writings and researches of Joseph W. Roe, Charles H. Fitch, D. L. Burn, A. P. Usher, V. S. Clark, A. H. Cole, Felicia Deyrup, and others conveniently cited and briefly summarized in the Bibliography of the very useful recent book by George R. Taylor, *The Transportation Revolution, 1815–1860* (New York: Rinehart and Co., 1951), pp. 220 ff. and 418–24. To titles there listed may be added two additional books of a somewhat different nature, Siegfried Giedion, *Mechanization Takes Command* (New York: Oxford University Press, 1948), and Jeannette Mirsky and Allan Nevins, *The World of Eli Whitney* (New York: The Macmillan Co., 1952).

[11] Eli Whitney, for example, thus wrote in 1812 (somewhat naïvely and boastfully) in seeking a new government contract for 15,000 muskets:

The subscriber begs leave further to remark that he has for the last 12 years been engaged in manufacturing muskets; that he now has the most respectable private establishment in the United States for carrying on this important branch of business. That this establishment was commenced and has been carried on upon a plan which is unknown in Europe, and the great leading object of which is to substitute correct and effective operations of machinery for that skill of the artist which is acquired only by long practice and experience; a species of skill which is not possessed in this country to any considerable extent.—

Roe, *English and American Tool Builders*, pp. 132–33. Such contracts and financing played a critical part in Whitney's remarkable early development of quantity manufacturing on the principle of interchangeable parts.

these new patterns and the extensive social transformation that they involved met with far less resistance here than abroad; on the contrary, that the new horizons and ways of working, organizing, and consuming were facilitated by the prevailing social framework and accepted and encouraged as the natural way of doing things, with an ease and generality that was unique.

The basic features of all this were in being by the mid-century and successfully applied to a broadening range of industries among the Northern states. A rising "industrial consciousness" that gave early support to practical education and a technical literature hastened their spread.[12] The Crystal Palace Exhibition of 1851 served as a kind of milestone where the world began to discover and to record its reactions to what "the colonists" had done.[13] Examination of its records and those of the industrial exhibitions held by Western nations in the years between 1851 and 1867 shows more than twenty industries in which an "American system of manufacturing" was recognized. Agricultural machinery, firearms, sewing machines, rubber goods, and woodworking and other machine and hand tools were most prominent, but the list ranged ever wider from certain textile machinery through cutlery and precision instruments to carriages, pianos, and paper bags. European comment often gave much attention to the crudity, the lack of finish, the use of wood in place of metal, or the light construction of various articles; but admiration for their simplicity, originality, effectiveness, and above all their economy and volume of production led not only to recognition at the world fairs but to the increasing entrance of American products and methods into European markets as imports, or through licensing or notably less formal practices. American manufacturers also began to establish plants abroad in this era, and the factory that Colt set up in England in 1851 quite literally astounded professional opinion.[14] Finally, as early as 1853 European industrial commissions began arriving in the United States to report on the American system of manufacturing, and the British Ordnance Committee of 1854 initiated a widening stream of European commissions that came not only to observe but to buy tools and equipment and borrow personnel and methods as well.[15]

[12] For an interesting discussion of the early phases of this, which already had considerable momentum by 1830, see Samuel Rezneck, "The Rise of Industrial Consciousness in the United States, 1760–1830," *Journal of Economic and Business History*, IV, No. 4 (August 1932), 784–811.

[13] Merle Curti, "America at the World Fairs, 1851–1893," *American Historical Review*, LV, No. 4 (July 1950), 833–56, provides an instructive overview of the longer period and many leads into the literature. The American showing in 1851 was both late and very incomplete. The comments below draw on the official and unofficial materials arising from the five exhibitions held between 1851 and 1867.

[14] See the remarks of James Nasmyth quoted below, pp. 296–97.

[15] Charles H. Fitch, "Report on the Manufactures of Interchangeable Mechanism," *Tenth Census of the United States [1880]: Manufactures* II, 619–20.

The kind of things that caught the attention of expert European machine makers and manufacturers is clearly and briefly illuminated in the reports of the British commissions that came here in 1853 and 1854. These reports have the special value of bringing to bear on American developments the perspectives of highly qualified judgment from the acknowledged leading industrial nation of the time. The single "Report of the Committee on the Machinery of the United States of America" (1854) will here serve our purpose.[16]

Arising from the concern of the Ordnance Department with the inefficiency of small-arms production in Britain, this committee, with John Anderson, Inspector of Machinery, as its central figure, conducted an extensive survey of standardized manufacturing in the Northeastern states in the spring and summer of 1854. While their assignment led to a special focus on the manufacture of firearms in both private plants and national armories—and calls attention to the role of large government contracts, funds, and facilities in the early development of this particular field—their observations fortunately ranged far beyond. Even in covering their formal mission, they did not stop with the examination and purchase of machine tools employed but went on to study the systematic organization of the flow of work and the more general features of the system— from its bookkeeping to the speed of production and the facility with which interchangeable parts were finally "assembled." To this end, their Report notes many details:

> Besides the machinery and tools which have been enumerated, there are hundreds of valuable instruments and gauges. . . .
> The Committee also observed that everything that could be done to reduce labour in the movement of materials from one point to another was adopted. This includes mechanical arrangements for lifting material, &c., from one floor to another, carriages for conveying material on the same floor, and such like.
> Many of the parts . . . are polished on buffs, in the same manner as practised in England; but on the whole less attention is bestowed on . . . high finish given to the parts, only to please the eye.[17]

[16] Parliamentary Papers, House of Commons, Accounts and Papers (21), 1854–1855, L. For convenience, page references follow those of the Report itself. D. L. Burn summarized many of the essentials of both this Report and those of the British Commissioners to the New York Industrial Exhibition of 1853 in an interesting article nearly twenty-five years ago, "The Genesis of American Engineering Competition, 1850–1870," *Economic History*, II (January 1931), 292–311. For our purposes they deserve attention in their entirety.

[17] *Committee on Machinery*, pp. 38 and 42. (The verb "assemble" is regularly put in quotes.) They were particularly impressed by an ingenious sequence of sixteen machines for producing gunstocks, "devised and set to work with its present degree of perfection." In the course of their trip they placed orders for approximately $100,000 worth of tools and equipment (1854 dollars).

But apart from praise for the best machinery seen in the small-arms industry, the Report is studded with references on *other* fronts to new tools or new ways of adapting and using machinery, which "struck the Committee as useful or new" as it moved about. Thus, in the first few pages they specifically enumerate for later discussion:

A peculiar shaped screw augur. . . . Extensive rope spinning machinery. . . . An apparatus for cleaning metal. . . . A new sort of trip hammer. . . . A new sort of steam tilt hammer. . . . Machine for polishing lasts. . . . A vertical saw, for cutting irregular forms. . . . An apparatus for testing the quantity of power required to work a machine. . . . A machine for sifting sand. . . . Patent magnetic sewing machine. . . . Yankee chaff cutter. . . . Tourbine waterwheel. . . . Machine for cutting files. . . . Cask making machinery. . . . Packing up machinery.[18]

Of greatest significance is the diversity of industries in which they found the "thorough application" of the manufacturing principles we are discussing. Thus for New Haven, in addition to Whitney's armory, their Report reads:

Jerome's Clock Manufactory. In this establishment clocks are made in immense quantities for home use and exportation; 600 per diem being the yield, with 250 men employed.
Machinery is most extensively used in all parts of the manufacture, and the clocks produced at a very low price, the movements of some costing only $1.
Messrs. Davenport and Mallory's Works. This [is] a manufactory of padlocks and locks; and the same system of special machinery is applied to every particular part; and all . . . can be interchanged.
The work is turned out at very low cost, some padlocks being made for 5 cents (2½ d), and 2000 produced daily.
Messrs. Candie [sic] and Company's Factory. This is a manufactory of india-rubber shoes, in which machinery is applied as far as practicable, and with 175 hands 2000 pair are daily produced.[19]

As the committee went its round, on to New York, Philadelphia, Pittsburgh, Buffalo, Utica, and back to New England, the list grows impressively. It includes a stone works where "machinery has been extensively applied"; a chandelier and lamp factory with "all the work carried on on a manufacturing principle"; an accoutrements works similar to those in England "except [for] the extent of the premises and work-rooms, and the wholesale way in which the work was conducted"; "a large manufactory of leather in which machinery was extensively applied"; biscuits "made in larger quantities, and machinery used in almost all the processes"; and so

[18] *Ibid.*, pp. 8–12.
[19] *Ibid.*, pp. 11–12. A later passage duly explains that the *keys* were not identical.

on for spades and shovels; wagon building; nails made by a boy at 200 per minute; railway spikes, whips, and melodions, all made on the factory principle; pails and tubs where "machinery is used most extensively, by means of which 1000 buckets are produced daily at a very cheap rate, and exceedingly well made"; railway cars, doors and sash, wooden pegs, screws "made by self-acting machinery which is particularly good . . . Nettlefold's is perhaps the best Screw Manufactory in England, but very inferior to Mr. Grigg's"; and so on to furniture, bedsteads produced at 15,000 yearly, boot trees, boat oars, carriages and other items, all found in production on similar lines.[20]

The committee also recorded its disappointments with certain fields (like sewing machines for their purposes, for example), and at many points noted that equipment was rough or quality poor. More significant, however, are the repeated recommendations that particular American methods and standards should be adopted in England. Perhaps the most concise over-all assessment offered is the following:

> As regards the class of machinery usually employed by engineers and machine makers, they [the Americans] are upon the whole behind those of England, but in the adaptation of special apparatus to a single operation in almost all branches of industry, the Americans display an amount of ingenuity, combined with undaunted energy, which as a nation we would do well to imitate, if we mean to hold our present position in the great market of the world.[21]

The Report as a whole reaches far beyond machinery in its emphasis on speed and efficiency, on ingenuity, simplicity, and specialization, perhaps above all, on "the admirable system everywhere adopted, even in those branches of trade which are not usually considered of much importance." [22]

VI

All this, it will be remembered, had emerged in the period *before* the "big" explanations became operative and at a time when principles of comparative advantage might have argued for other lines of growth—before the transcontinentals and the open hearths; before the ores of the Mesabi or the opening up of oil; before the great capital accumulations associated with later decades; and, most important, *before* that always-cited bigger American market had come into existence. Until after the mid-century the total internal American market was smaller than that of leading European countries and markedly reduced as an effective market

---

[20] *Ibid.*, pp. 13–20. Also see Chapter iv for fuller discussion of the manufacturing of many of these items. Particularly interesting for our purposes are those on pails, nails, spikes, screws, or, for the break with craft traditions, melodions.

[21] *Ibid.*, p. 32.

[22] *Ibid.*, p. 84.

by geographical spread.[23] In fact the germ of the pattern, the basic principles and features of the whole, and their successful application, took shape before 1850 in small industries in sparse New England towns, which often had to sell their products in thin and scattered markets.

Yet it was in this place and time that the "underdeveloped" country— the country for whose manufacturing future Lord Sheffield and others had not long before recorded such dismal views—overleaped the more mature economies of the leading countries of Europe in certain distinctive patterns of manufacturing and marketing. While output in these lines was of small import in the *volume* of the world's trade in 1850, they represented a growing front of high importance for the future of manufacturing. We have here a massive fact requiring explanation.

Major parts of such an answer, of course, lie within traditional economic spheres—the high cost of labor and shortage of traditional skills, the rapidly expanding market for cheap manufactures, improving transportation, the new technological possibilities, and the range of factors associated with differential rates and timing of growth. But I do not think these considerations, nor the favorable formal political and legal framework of the young Republic, will begin to carry us far enough in trying to understand why the United States jumped so rapidly from home and handicraft and imported manufactures into such patterns as we have seen; why it did not longer follow its predicted history; or why these developments in manufacturing came as they did, where they did, and when they did.

VII

Directions which we must press further seem once again to be most clearly suggested in the contemporary accounts of European observers who over the first half of the nineteenth century, as today, have left a massive record of their findings and of their views on the reasons why. While again requiring caution and correction, what they saw and thought deserves our serious attention.

Here I have turned to three main bodies of evidence from the early or middle decades of the nineteenth century, each carrying within it the comparative perspectives of the Old World on the New: the great and varied literature of the general travelers who came and passed judgment upon us and upon our economic life in profusion; the official reports and unofficial commentaries arising from the international exhibitions; and the

---

[23] Though understating the case in omitting the factor of established overseas markets, population figures by "countries" crudely reflect the relatively smaller market of American producers through the first half of the century as compared to those in leading European countries. Thus for 1850 population for the United States is given 23.2 millions, 27.5 for the United Kingdom, and 35.8 for France.—W. S. and E. S. Woytinsky, *World Population and Production* (New York: Twentieth Century Fund, 1953), p. 44.

various specialized reports of industrial commissions that came to examine our methods of manufacture, such as that reviewed above. While I am still mid-stream in these materials and thus shall defer any full appraisal, I can report from an extensive screening to date: first, the overriding weight of testimony supporting the basic social and cultural themes familiar from the classical accounts of Crèvecoeur, Tocqueville, and others; and, second, the cross-consistency among these three bodies of contemporaneous material. This extends, thus far, both to the general emphasis on a distinctive social order in explaining distinctive economic patterns and results and to particular characteristics of the new society that are felt to have pressed on these results.

Experts commenting on our machinery or industrial commissions studying our techniques of standardized manufacturing sustain the prevailing themes of the general traveler. In much the same vein and many of the same words, their reports turn to differences in the nature and diffusion of education in America; the absence of rigidities and restraints of class and craft; the freedom from hereditary definitions of the tasks or hardened ways of going about them; the high focus on personal advancement and drives to higher material welfare; and the mobility, flexibility, adaptability of Americans and their boundless belief in progress. These and closely related patterns are linked directly to economic behavior and economic results—to initiative, originality, systematic effort, and boldness; the "eager resort to machinery" and productive use of small capital, at a time when small capital was decisive; the ceaseless search and ready adoption of the new and more efficient; the intense responsiveness to shifting opportunities and expanding horizons; the "go-aheadism" that visitors from all categories so often placed at the root of the "immense drive" of American manufacturing.[24]

Not all comment was laudatory by any means, in tone or intent. Large numbers of observers freely expressed their displeasure or even disgust with American institutions and American ways. But whether they talked of "a noble desire to elevate one's station" or "vulgar dollar chasing," and whether they liked or denounced a society in which business rode high and a wide open social structure fostered mobility, rootlessness, restlessness, and the like, and gave enhanced significance to the visible results of economic success, they were pointing to social values and a social order uniquely favorable to the particular patterns of manufacturing that we have been discussing.

Some of Europe's best-qualified observers made the connections most sharply of all. Thus James Nasmyth, one of England's outstanding ma-

---

[24] These observations are based on each and all of the three bodies of evidence mentioned at the beginning of the preceding paragraph.

chine makers, told a Parliamentary Committee that he had been humbled by the experience of going through the factory Colt established in England in 1851.

> The acquaintance with correct principles has been carried out in a fearless and masterly manner, and they have been pushed to their full extent; and the result is the attainment of perfection and economy such as I have never seen before. [Many English mechanics knew the correct principles] but there is a certain degree of timidity resulting from traditional notions, and attachment to old systems, even among the most talented persons, that they keep considerably behind. . . . In many cases young men mind four machines. One had been a butcher, another a tailor, another a gentleman's servant. . . . You do not depend on dexterity—all you want is intellect.[25]

Or to return to the findings of John Anderson and those associated in the British Ordnance Committee on the Machinery of the United States of 1854:

> . . . indeed every workman seems to be continually devising some new thing to assist him in his work, and there being a strong desire, both with masters and workman all through the New England States, to be "posted up" in every new improvement, they seem to be much better acquainted with each other all through the trade than is the case in England.[26]

Again in their conclusions they give special attention to

> . . . the dissatisfaction frequently expressed in America with regard to present attainment in the manufacture and application of labour-saving machinery, and the avidity with which any new idea is laid hold of, and improved upon, a spirit occasionally carried to excess, but on the whole productive of more good than evil.

And to working conditions and results, noting, for example:

> The care universally bestowed on the comfort of the workpeople, particularly attracted the notice of the Committee; clean places for washing . . . , presses to contain their change of clothes, and an abundant supply of good drinking water, in many cases cooled with ice.
> The regular attendance and cleanliness of the workmen, and the rigid exactness with which the work is continued up to the last minute of the working hours.[27]

---

[25] Before a Parliamentary *Select Committee on Small Arms,* 1854, XVIII, Q. 1367, as quoted in D. L. Burn, "The Genesis of American Engineering Competition," 296–97.
[26] *Loc. cit.,* p. 38.
[27] *Ibid.,* p. 85. At another point, however, higher absenteeism is mentioned.

While we cannot begin now to exploit additional sources, a single passage from the British Commissioners' reports on the New York Exhibition of 1853 may offer an appropriate place at which to stop:

> As there is no apprenticeship system, properly so called, the more useful the youth engaged in any industrial pursuit becomes to his employer, the more profitable it is for himself. Bringing a mind prepared by thorough school discipline, and educated up to a far higher standard than those of a much superior social grade in society in the Old World, the American working boy develops rapidly into the skilled artizan, and having once mastered one part of his business, he is never content until he has mastered all. . . . The restless activity of mind and body—the anxiety to improve his own department of industry—the facts constantly before him of ingenious men who have solved economic and mechanical problems to their own profit and elevation, are all stimulative and encouraging; and it may be said that there is not a working boy of average ability in the New England States, at least, who has not an idea of some mechanical invention or improvement in manufactures, by which, in good time, he hopes to better his position, or rise to fortune and social distinction.
> On this intelligent understanding of the true position of things, and the requirements of the social system around him, the skilled workman rests his position.[28]

Though these and like observers give appropriate emphasis to other causes as well—notably the shortage of skilled labor—they show no equivocation in assigning a very central place to the goals and values and structural characteristics of the American social order in explaining the distinctive manufacturing developments under review.

VIII

More significant still for our larger question are the similarities that appear between these earlier accounts relating to the nineteenth-century beginnings of the "American system of manufacturing" and the comparable accounts of European observers of recent years with which we began this discussion. New notes have, of course, appeared. Much more striking to me, however, is the stability, the parallelism in what European observers have emphasized about the American scene in 1850 and 1950. This stands out—as perhaps the quotations have suggested—for both the characteristics of American manufacturers and the system that produced them. It stands out also for particular social and cultural characteristics that are felt to have fostered these results.

[28] *New York Industrial Exhibition: Special Report of Mr. George Wallis*, Parliamentary Papers, House of Commons, Command Paper, 1854, XXXVI, p. 3 (of Mr. Wallis' Report). The balance of his introduction or the "Conclusion" of the corresponding Report by Joseph Whitworth offers impressive testimony in this vein.

There is no need to strain the case, I believe. Giving allowance to the influence of stereotypes, and noting changes that also are visible, the extraordinary similarities in gross emphasis and in detail in these bodies of observations more than a century apart suggest that we have here no fleeting phenomena, no marginal factors in economic history. They suggest that we are dealing here, in Professor Kuznets' words, with both *antecedent* and *sustaining* conditions of economic growth. And in so doing, they point to a task for economic history stretching far ahead.

PART THREE

The Struggle Toward
Economic Maturity

THE American economy was already in the process of industrialization before the Civil War.[1] The war itself in some ways impeded, but perhaps ultimately stimulated, this industrialization. The same forces which had encouraged prewar industrial growth— improved transportation, agricultural expansion, available markets, and a favorable climate of social values and government policies —were all the more encouraging after the war. Although the environment was favorable to rapid growth, there was also great tension and imbalance as various industries and groups struggled for power and profit.[2]

The traditional view among historians has held that northeastern businessmen during the period of Radical Reconstruction kept southern representatives out of Congress while they shaped national policy to their liking in such crucial fields as tariffs, currency, and access to southern resources. In *Selection Twenty* Stanley Cohen subjects this view to critical examination. He finds that north-

[1] See Douglass C. North, *The Economic Growth of the United States, 1790–1860* (Englewood Cliffs, N. J.: Prentice-Hall, Inc., 1961) and W. W. Rostow, *The Stages of Economic Growth* (Cambridge: Cambridge University Press, 1960).

[2] For bibliographical aid, see Thomas LeDuc, "Recent Contributions to Economic History: The United States, 1861–1900" and Thomas C. Cochran, "Recent Contributions to Economic History: The United States, The Twentieth Century," *Journal of Economic History*, XIX (March, 1959), 44–63 and 64–75.

301

eastern business groups and Radical legislators were far too divided among themselves on major policy issues to agree on a unified program. Far from desiring to exploit the fallen South, the most
influential northern capitalists wanted an end to the Radical experiment; meanwhile they found far more interesting areas for investment in the rapidly-developing, politically stable North and West.
Coben therefore concludes that "the reconstruction program of the
Radicals cannot be explained as an organized attempt by the business interests of the Northeast either to preserve and promote their
own economic advantages or to obtain protection for economic exploitation of the South." However, these business interests were
acutely concerned over the impact of national economic legislation,
as evidenced, for example, by their involvement in the struggles
over tariff rates and currency. As Coben's analysis demonstrates,
business groups which had little interest in the continuation of Reconstruction exercised enormous political influence in attempting
to align other national policies with their diverse special interests.

By the time the South had rehabilitated its agriculture after the
Civil War, the nation's agriculture was facing severe difficulties.[3]
In bold strokes Theodore Saloutos (*Selection Twenty-One*) sets
forth the major forces responsible for the agricultural maladjustments which emerged after the Civil War. Among the factors he
stresses are a "faulty land policy," the "rank individualism" of
farmers, the high tariff policy, and, ultimately, the decline of agricultural exports. He states, "If we had anything that came close to
resembling a policy, it was that of throwing open vast quantities of
public and private lands to cultivation which resulted in maladjustments that made it difficult, if not impossible, for farmers to
adjust themselves to capitalistic methods of production and distribution." As individualistic farmers eagerly grabbed up land, the results were overexpanded production, falling prices, marketing difficulties, credit problems, farm foreclosures, and tenancy. Even
though this rapid agricultural expansion had promoted industrial
growth, our high tariff policy and rapid industrialization jointly

[3] For a good survey of this subject, see Fred A. Shannon, *The Farmer's Last Frontier* (New York: Farrar and Rinehart, 1945).

contributed to "the drastic decline in farm exports" which commenced around 1900.

These agricultural changes gave rise to another serious problem, a growing number of transient seasonal farm workers. In 1914 the Industrial Workers of the World decided to try to organize the thousands of migratory workers in the western wheat belt. Philip Taft (*Selection Twenty-Two*) describes this unusual organizing drive which extended from Oklahoma and Kansas to the Dakotas between 1915 and 1917 and which was finally curtailed by the wartime suppression of the I.W.W. Taft says that I.W.W. secretary-treasurer "Big Bill" Haywood "regarded the migratory worker in the harvest belt as making up the elite which would regenerate the labor movement and as fitted to carry out the more difficult tasks of organization." The I.W.W. also wanted to organize such groups as lumber workers, metal miners, maritime workers, and oil-field roustabouts, many of whom worked seasonally in the grain harvest. Since these migratory workers moved from job to job on freight trains, I.W.W. organizers were stationed at western railroad centers and even on moving freights where they demanded that migratories have I.W.W. membership cards. But for the wartime suppression, Taft speculates, the I.W.W. "might have been able to carve out a place for itself in the industrial sectors which had, up to the thirties, been unattractive to the old line labor organizations." In that case it "would have been transformed into an economic organization of predominantly unskilled and semi-skilled workers."

The orthodox philosophy of the American labor movement, to which the radical I.W.W. was so foreign, is sympathetically expounded by Selig Perlman in *Selection Twenty-Three*. This is essentially the philosophy of Samuel Gompers, founder of the American Federation of Labor.[4] It upholds capitalism, rejects political activism or a labor party, and embraces "job consciousness" or control over job opportunities as the basis for winning economic gains for union members through collective bargaining. As the AFL's early

---

[4] Perlman makes this philosophy the touchstone of the "Wisconsin School" of labor economics, founded by John R. Commons.

development shows, adequate job control and organizational strength first became possible in the crafts or skilled trades. Perlman is convinced that American labor history has proved the viability and virtues of conservative, job-conscious unions despite the New Deal Revolution and labor's unfortunate civil war when the Congress of Industrial Organizations emerged in the 1930's. According to Perlman, the AFL had learned since the 1880's what the CIO soon began to learn: the labor movement, in order to survive and be relatively effective in the American environment, had to remain independent of management, of government, and of party politics, relying primarily on job-conscious unionism for its success.

Although trade unionism, as Perlman emphasizes, had great difficulty gaining and then maintaining a foothold during the latter part of the nineteenth century, big business was in the ascendancy and had great economic power as well as political influence. However, many economic historians, including Edward C. Kirkland (*Selection Twenty-Four*), have become very critical of the "muckraker" or "robber-baron" interpretation of the early triumphs by big business. Kirkland feels that this era has been grossly distorted, that revision is sorely needed, and that ample materials exist for this reinterpretation. He warns against any "a priori wish to condone or condemn" or reliance on "some variant of economic determinism." Since "the attack upon big business was a politically motivated attack" and since businessmen held strong although divergent views about government policy toward business (see *Selections Twenty and Twenty-Eight*), Kirkland suggests that the analysis should run largely in political terms: ". . . revisionism will be most fruitful if it enters the period by the gate of politics."

Gabriel Kolko (*Selection Twenty-Five*), however, severely criticizes the "Business Revisionists" of the past two or three decades for their use, often implicitly, of value judgments which serve to justify the development and present character of big business. To say the least, he poses serious questions of methodology for the economic historian and especially for the entrepreneurial school of business history. He insists that business revisionists actually rationalize the status quo, including "monopolization and aggressive capital accumulation," and give moral absolution to business leaders, including the "robber barons," by employing notions of economic necessity or inevitability and of "realistic morality" or practical business ethics. Indeed, he asserts that in these respects the business revisionists' approach closely parallels the economic determinism of the Marxists.[5] Kolko states, for instance, that "the very concept of the validity, progressiveness, and inevitability of the process of capital accumulation . . . which relates the values of the Business Revisionist viewpoint to Marxism, is utilized to neutralize all attacks on the capitalist system itself."

In *Selection Twenty-Six* Alfred D. Chandler, Jr. analyzes the development of big business into the early twentieth century in terms of the dynamic forces promoting big business and the resulting innovations in function and organization. In the late nineteenth century the fundamental dynamic factors promoting large-scale business were the westward expansion of population, the completion of a national railroad network, and the consequent development of a national and primarily urban market. Early in the twentieth century the key forces were the application of electricity and the internal combustion engine and the coming of organized research and development activities. The resulting innovations produced the giant industrial corporation. Expanding urban markets prompted extensive merging or horizontal combination of firms and the development of nationwide marketing organizations. Large-scale vertical integration was instituted to assure raw materials and to coordinate production processes. Managerial centralization and departmentalization of functions along highly bureaucratic lines ensued. The result was that "Major industries were dominated by a few firms that had become great, vertically integrated, centralized enterprises."[6]

John P. Roche (*Selection Twenty-Seven*) asserts that leading businessmen of the period 1880–1910 were not doctrinaire, ruggedly individualistic supporters of *laissez faire*. "On the contrary, this elite lived at the public trough, was nourished by state protection, and devoted most of its time and energies to evading Adam Smith's individualistic injunctions." This group was "totally opportunistic: It

---

[5] Kolko adds that this same historicism permeates the work on the conservative Social Darwinians as well as the "Wisconsin school" of labor economists as exemplified by Selig Perlman (see *Selection Twenty-Three*).

[6] See also Alfred D. Chandler, Jr., *Strategy and Structure: Chapters in the History of the Industrial Enterprise* (Cambridge, Mass.: Massachusetts Institute of Technology Press, 1962).

demanded and applauded vigorous state action in behalf of its key values, and denounced state intervention in behalf of its enemies." It obtained court injunctions against strikes and court protection against union organizing, public utility regulation, and social legislation. "Entrepreneurial liberty" was written into the Constitution when the courts defined the right of contract as property in terms of the due process clause. The courts, for instance, initially ruled that wages and hours laws infringed the freedom of contract of firms and employees. Companies had their workers sign "yellow dog" contracts agreeing not to join a union; then the courts issued injunctions prohibiting unions from urging any breach of contract. As Roche says, "The Constitution was not, in short, adapted to the needs of laissez-faire 'conservatism' . . . but to the exigent needs of the great private governments."

Businessmen held conflicting views on public policy issues during the Progressive era before World War I, according to Robert H. Wiebe (*Selection Twenty-Eight*), just as they had done during the Reconstruction era (see *Selection Twenty*). Business did not stand united against government regulation, as might be inferred from Roche (*Selection Twenty-Seven*). Internal conflicts within the business community developed, as Wiebe shows, concerning reform proposals for reorganizing the banking system, regulating railroads, and controlling the trusts. Conflicts over these reforms "illustrate how the business community split into hostile factions over problems which threatened a redistribution of power among its members." The conflicts ran not only in terms of the participants' specific economic interests but also along broader urban-rural and regional lines and by size and industrial or functional character of business firms. Wiebe, thus, generalizes that "an examination of businessmen's reactions to the Progressive movement indicates that far from forming a cohesive group they differed widely over the proper solution to America's problems and expended a large portion of their energies in internal conflicts."

The forward thrust of the maturing industrial economy between the Civil War and World War I brought uneven fortunes to the various groups struggling for position or profit. The conflicts were political and ideological as well as economic or market-centered. Rival groups sought government favor for themselves and regulation of opposing interests, while trying to avoid regulation themselves. The business community was immersed in political and governmental affairs, often to its advantage although it was never unified or consistent in its efforts. The individualistic farmers expanded acreage and output, only to encounter price and market dislocations; and some of them sank into tenancy. Agricultural laborers, blocked off from farm ownership, became increasingly numerous and demoralized. Urban workers in the skilled crafts fared reasonably well with the success of job-conscious unionism, but most unskilled and semiskilled workers remained unorganized. The greatest triumphs were achieved by the manufacturers, who developed large-scale producing and marketing organizations characterized by horizontal combination, vertical integration, and centralized management. The new industrial era was dominated by big business: bureaucratic, efficient, profitable, oligopolistic, usually disliked and misunderstood, and sometimes threatened by increased government regulation.

Government and Business: Reconstruction Era

20.   Northeastern Business and Radical Reconstruction: A Re-examination

Stanley Coben

Historians generally have accepted the view that Radical Reconstruction "was a successful attempt by northeastern business, acting through the Republican party, to control the national government for its own economic ends: notably, the protective tariff, the national banks, [and] a 'sound' currency." [1] The Radical program is also said to have been "the method by which the 'Masters of Capital'. . . expected to exploit the resources of the southern states" behind federal protection. [2] Western hostility to these eastern business designs was avoided by large appropriations for rivers, harbors, railroads, free land, and pensions, and by use of the ever-potent "bloody shirt." Thus is supposed to have been prevented a union of western and southern agrarian opposition to the industrial and financial masters of the East. [3]

This thesis has met with little serious challenge and has been subjected to only occasional qualification. It continues to influence studies of the political and economic history of the post-Civil War era. [4] Yet a closer

[1] This is the conclusion of the most recent survey of historians' attitudes toward Radical Reconstruction. T. Harry Williams, "An Analysis of Some Reconstruction Attitudes," *Journal of Southern History* (Baton Rouge), XII (November, 1946), 470. Williams calls this the "Beale thesis," because it has been most completely developed by Howard K. Beale in his *The Critical Year: A Study of Andrew Johnson and Reconstruction* (New York, 1930), and his "On Rewriting Reconstruction History," *American Historical Review* (New York), XLV (July, 1940), 807–27.

[2] William B. Hesseltine, "Economic Factors in the Abandonment of Reconstruction," *Mississippi Valley Historical Review* (Cedar Rapids), XXII (September, 1935), 191.

[3] Helen J. and T. Harry Williams, "Wisconsin Republicans and Reconstruction, 1865–1870," *Wisconsin Magazine of History* (Madison), XXIII (September, 1939), 17–39.

[4] For recent expressions of the "Beale thesis," see C. Vann Woodward, *Origins of the New South, 1877–1913* (Baton Rouge, 1951), 23–24; George R. Bentley, *A History of the Feedmen's Bureau* (Philadelphia, 1955), 34–36; William B. Hesseltine, *Confederate Leaders in the New South* (Baton Rouge, 1950), 136; Arthur S. Link, *American Epoch: A History of the United States since the 1890's* (New York, 1955), 4–5; George R. Woolfolk, *The Cotton Regency: The Northern Merchants and Reconstruction, 1865–1880* (New York, 1958).

Earlier statements of the thesis may be found in Charles A. and Mary R. Beard, *The Rise of American Civilization* (2 vols., New York, 1927), II, Chap. XX; Louis M.

"Northeastern Business and Radical Reconstruction: A Re-examination," by Stanley Coben, is reprinted by permission from *Mississippi Valley Historical Review*, XLVI (June, 1959), 67–90.

examination of the important economic legislation and congressional battles of the period, and of the attitudes of businessmen and influential business groups, reveals serious divisions on economic issues among Radical legislators and northeastern businessmen alike. Certainly neither business leaders nor Radicals were united in support of any specific set of economic aims. Considerable evidence also suggests that the divisions among businessmen often cut across sectional as well as industrial lines. Furthermore, evidence indicates that few northeastern business groups were interested in southern investments in the early postwar years, and that these few were hostile to Radical Reconstruction.

The evident need for new interpretations of the motivation of northern Radicals and of the economic history of the entire period is demonstrated by a re-examination of the most important of the "economic ends" usually agreed upon as motives for Radical Reconstruction: the tariff and the currency issues, and the charge that northern business interests sought federal protection for the exploitation of the South.

The tariff split northeastern businessmen more than any other issue.[5] So fierce was business competition in this era, and so eager were the antagonists to use every possible means of winning an advantage, that almost all important tariff schedules became battlegrounds between industries, as well as between firms within the same industry. The copper, iron, linseed, and woolen textile industries, for example, were bitterly divided on crucial tariff schedules. The most significant split, however, was between certain highly protectionist Pennsylvania interests on one side and influential low-tariff groups in New England and New York on the other. Pennsylvania coal mine operators feared the competition of rich Nova Scotia deposits, mined by low-wage labor, close to major American markets. Iron and steel manufacturers, the largest highly protected interest, were faced with the competition of long-established, technologically advanced English producers, whose wage scale was only a fraction of that of the Americans. Pennsylvania carpet, glass, and wool industries demanded protection for similar reasons. The Keystone State was the largest extractor of iron ore and coal, the largest manufacturer of every form of iron and steel, of carpets, glass, and chemicals. On the other hand, powerful opposition to the tariff objectives of the Pennsylvanians came from the cotton and many of the woolen textile manufacturers of New England, and from the intertwined importing, financial, and railroad interests of New York.

Hacker, *The Triumph of American Capitalism* (New York, 1940), Chap. 25; Richard N. Current, *Old Thad Stevens: A Story of Ambition* (Madison, 1942), Introduction, Chap. IV, and pp. 226, 249, 260; Mathew Josephson, *The Politicos, 1865–1896* (New York, 1938), Chap. I. James S. Allen, *Reconstruction: The Battle for Democracy, 1865–1867* (New York, 1937), is a Marxist version of the thesis.

[5] For a very different point of view, see Howard K. Beale, "The Tariff and Reconstruction," *American Historical Review*, XXXV (January, 1930), 276–94.

New Englanders had become strong advocates of lower tariffs in the 1850's. The sharp tariff reductions of 1857 were accomplished chiefly by southern and New England votes.[6] New England manufacturers, especially textile producers, desired cheap imported raw materials in order to lower the price of their finished goods on the international market. Furthermore, they agreed to reduced rates on manufactured goods to discourage the growth of domestic competition.[7] Among American manufacturers, New England producers as a group were farthest from domestic sources of raw materials, closest to sources of cheap foreign commodities. Cheap supplies of coal, lumber, flaxseed, building stone, fine wool, and other commodities were available in nearby Canada and Nova Scotia. Scottish and British iron, Indian linseed, and Russian and Philippine hemp were imported into Boston in large quantities for the benefit of manufacturers.[8] Hardly any wool for the finer grades of cloth was produced in America, either before or after the war; nor were the rough, lowest grades, used in carpets and blankets, available at home.[9] By the end of the war, northeastern cotton manufacturers were importing the cheap Indian Surat cotton already widely used in England.[10]

English textile manufacturers, rivals of the New Englanders both in world markets and in America, obtained their raw materials free of duty.[11] There were good reasons for northeastern producers to believe that only the American system of imposts kept them from equaling the British in world trade. By the 1850's, many American mills had been in operation for three generations. They had experienced managers and weavers, cheap and abundant credit, modern machinery and production methods. In

[6] Davis R. Dewey, *Financial History of the United States* (New York, 1903), 263. Dewey calculated the House vote for the 1857 tariff by section: New England 18 to 9 in favor, South 60 to 2 in favor, West 14 to 33 opposed, Middle States 24 to 28 opposed. There was no roll call on the final vote in the Senate, but see speeches by Senator Henry Wilson of Massachusetts, *Cong. Globe*, 34 Cong., 3 Sess., Appendix, 333–34 (February 26, 1857), and Senator Daniel Clark of New Hampshire, *ibid.*, 36 Cong., 2 Sess., 1023 (February 19, 1861). See also Richard Hofstadter, "The Tariff Issue on the Eve of the Civil War," *American Historical Review*, XLIV (October, 1938), 50–55.

[7] George W. Bond and George Livermore, *Report of the Boston Board of Trade on Wool for 1859* (Boston, 1860), 2; Frank W. Taussig, *The Tariff History of the United States* (8th ed., New York, 1931), 142; Melvin T. Copeland, *The Cotton Manufacturing Industry of the United States* (Cambridge, 1912), 14.

[8] See, for example, "Review of the Boston Market for the Year 1865," *Twelfth Annual Report of the Boston Board of Trade* (Boston, 1866), 72–95.

[9] Arthur H. Cole, *The American Wool Manufacture* (2 vols., Cambridge, 1926), II, 310, 319, 330; John L. Hayes, *Statement of Fact Relative to Canada Wools and the Manufacture of Worsted* (Boston, 1866), 10, 19.

[10] "It may soon become imperatively necessary to us to be able to obtain foreign cotton on even terms with English manufacturers if we expect to compete with them in other markets." *Boston Board of Trade: Report of a Committee upon the Cotton Tax* (Boston, 1867); *Ninth Annual Report of the Boston Board of Trade* (Boston, 1863), Appendix, 99.

[11] Shepard B. Clough and Charles W. Cole, *Economic History of Europe* (3rd ed., Boston, 1952), 472–76, 605–607.

cotton cloth manufacturing, for which machinery could be used most extensively, New England labor was the most productive in the world. By 1860, the average number of looms per weaver was four in America, two in Great Britain. French and German manufacturers lagged even farther behind in methods and machinery.[12]

In addition to high productivity which made their goods competitive in the world markets, and the need to import cheap raw materials, many New England manufacturers preferred low tariffs from a fear that high textile duties would foster the growth of new competitors at home. New producers might bring cutthroat competition and periodic chaos to the industry by their poor judgment of market conditions. A special committee of the Boston Board of Trade acknowledged in 1858 that New England textile manufacturers had potentially dangerous rivals, especially in Pennsylvania; but the committee concluded that the tariff reduction of 1857 removed any immediate threat. "Under the impulse of a high protective tariff they accomplished so little, that now, under a change of policy, there seems no present cause of alarm." [13] When the higher Morrill duties came before the House in 1860, Representative Alexander H. Rice of Massachusetts, speaking for the manufacturers of his state, declared that "excessive protection" would stimulate "ruinous and irresponsible competition at home." In the Senate, textile manufacturer Henry Wilson proclaimed: "A high protective policy . . . is calculated to raise up rivals at home, and is more injurious to us than foreign competition." [14]

After the war, fear of the growth of protected competition continued to influence New England tariff sentiment. Edward Atkinson, president of the Cotton Spinners of New England, and a director of the Boston Board of Trade, wrote to Henry Wilson in 1866: "The strongest men in the trade are more afraid of the unskillful competition built up at home by high duties than they are of foreign competition." [15] Enoch R. Mudge, one of the most influential New England textile men, told the organizing meeting of the National Association of Cotton Manufacturers and Planters in 1868: "When we speak of protection, I think it should be given only at the point where the cotton manufacturer requires it." [16] For well-established,

[12] Copeland, *Cotton Manufacturing Industry*, 10. "What this country wants," Massachusetts cotton manufacturer Edward Atkinsion wrote Senator Henry Wilson in 1866, "is cheap iron. Our cotton mills now cost to build $30 per spindle complete with looms, etc., etc., against $10 to $12 in England." Atkinson to Wilson, July 7, 1866, Harold F. Williamson, *Edward Atkinson: The Biography of an American Liberal* (Boston, 1934), 67.

[13] *Fifth Annual Report of the Boston Board of Trade* (Boston, 1859), 96–97.

[14] *Cong. Globe*, 36 Cong., 1 Sess., 1867 (April 26, 1860); *ibid.*, 36 Cong., 2 Sess., 1026 (February 19, 1861). Rice later became president of the Boston Board of Trade, then governor of Massachusetts.

[15] Atkinson to Wilson, July 7, 1866, Williamson, *Atkinson*, 67–68.

[16] *Proceedings of a Convention for the Purpose of Organizing the National Association of Cotton Manufacturers and Planters* (Boston, 1868), 13.

efficient New England producers, of course, there were comparatively few points at which protection was necessary. They had seen evidence of the success of their low tariff theories in the few years the 1857 schedules were in force. "The operation of the tariff of 1857 has contributed largely to the prosperity of our woolen manufactures," one of Boston's largest wool dealers reported in 1859.[17] Exports of cotton cloth had risen steadily, from an average of $7,000,000 in the years 1851 through 1856, to almost $11,000,000 in 1860.[18]

The government's need for revenue allowed protectionists an almost unchallenged ascendancy during the Civil War,[19] but the battle between northeastern business groups over tariff schedules was resumed after Appomattox. For example, when a resolution for lower tariffs was placed before the National Board of Trade Convention in 1869, delegates from the Boston Board of Trade and Boston Corn Exchange voted 6 to 1 for the resolution; Philadelphia delegates voted 7 to 0 against it.[20] The Boston Board of Trade also worked unsuccessfully to prevent abrogation of the reciprocity treaty with Canada; Philadelphia's Board joined western agricultural interests in demanding an end to reciprocity.[21]

These divisions within the business community were likewise reflected in the congressional debates and voting on important tariff schedules. Cotton manufacturers resumed their prewar demands for lower schedules, even for cotton textiles. Senator William Sprague, whose sprawling Rhode Island mills were relatively inefficient, protested against the 25 per cent cut in cotton textile duties proposed in 1867. He was answered by Senator William P. Fessenden of Maine, sponsor of the measure: "I am informed by the commissioner [Revenue Commissioner David A. Wells] that these duties were fixed at a rate perfectly satisfactory to those engaged in the manufacture of cottons, who appeared before him. . . . The cotton interest of this country has got so that it can stand of itself pretty much." [22]

Schedules on coal similarly came under attack. As power looms replaced hand looms, and steam power replaced water power, New England manufacturers became increasingly interested in lower coal duties.[23]

[17] Bond and Livermore, Report on Wool, 2.

[18] Copeland, Cotton Manufacturing Industry, 14; Taussig, Tariff History, 142.

[19] Dewey, Financial History, 265–67, 272, 301–304; Taussig, Tariff History, 150, 159–62; Edward Stanwood, American Tariff Controversies in the Nineteenth Century (2 vols., Boston, 1903), II, 130.

[20] Proceedings of the Second Annual Meeting of the National Board of Trade (Boston, 1870), 321.

[21] Eleventh Annual Report of the Boston Board of Trade (Boston, 1865), 42; Thirteenth Annual Report of the Boston Board of Trade (Boston, 1867), 2–3; Thirty-first Annual Report of the Philadelphia Board of Trade (Philadelphia, 1864), 17.

[22] Cong. Globe, 39 Cong. 2 Sess., 709, 744 (January 24, 25, 1867).

[23] Copeland, Cotton Manufacturing Industry, 29; J. Herbert Burgy, The New England Cotton Textile Industry: A Study in Industrial Geography (Baltimore, 1932), 24, 30, 34, 100.

Under reciprocity and the low tariff of 1857, imports of coal into Boston rose steadily from 88,531 tons in 1858, to 209,225 tons in 1865, most of this being cheap Nova Scotia fuel.[24] Representative George S. Boutwell and Senator Charles Sumner of Massachusetts tried in vain to prevent higher coal schedules from being placed in the proposed tariffs of 1866 and 1867. Sumner acknowledged that there was a lot of coal in Pennsylvania, West Virginia, and the West. "But why," he asked, "should New England, which has a natural resource comparatively near at home, be compelled at a great sacrifice to drag her coal from these distant supplies?" Sumner's amendment was defeated 11 to 25, with eight New Englanders, both New Yorkers, and one senator from Oregon comprising those favoring lower duties on coal.[25]

Many other schedules in the proposed bills of 1866 and 1867 were fought out by competing or conflicting business interests. Manufacturers, especially New Englanders, dependent upon cheap imported raw materials, were continually in opposition to the combined efforts of raw material producers and competing manufacturers closer to these native sources of supply. When Senator Benjamin F. Wade of Ohio moved to raise the duty on linseed, largely grown in the West, Fessenden of Maine accused him of asking the higher rate "for this simple, selfish reason: that the trade of crushing seed and manufacturing oil on the sea-coast may be utterly destroyed for the benefit of crushers of seed and the manufacturers of oil in the West." [26]

Rolling mills, chiefly eastern, which controlled the American Iron and Steel Association,[27] almost forced through an extremely low duty on scrap iron. Such a duty would allow the mills to import huge quantities of cheap European used rails, and to re-roll them in lieu of using domestic pig iron for new rails. Senator Zachariah Chandler, from the iron producing state of Michigan, demanded that the proposed duty on wrought scrap iron be quadrupled, and the duty on cast scrap be almost tripled. Lower schedules, he declared, would close the iron mines, put out every blast furnace, and mean "total ruin to the iron interests of the United States. . . . It is a bill gotten up to suit the railroad rolling-mills, and to sacrifice every other iron interest in the United States." The rolling mills won one Senate vote, but Chandler forced another, which was won by those sympathetic with

[24] *Twelfth Annual Report of the Boston Board of Trade* (Boston, 1866), 75.

[25] *Cong. Globe*, 39 Cong., 1 Sess., 3569 (July 3, 1866); 39 Cong., 2 Sess., 830, 857 (January 29, 30, 1867).

[26] *Ibid.*, 39 Cong., 2 Sess., 705 (January 24, 1867). Linseed oil was important in the manufacture of paints, dyes, and varnishes.

[27] Pig iron producers, still the dominant segment of the iron and steel industry in the early 1870's, withdrew from the American Iron and Steel Association in 1871 and formed their own association, which by 1873 numbered two hundred firms. For the sharp division which this Association saw between itself and the American Iron and Steel Association, see *The American Pig Iron Manufacturing Association, Meeting Held in New York City, February 19, 1873* (Philadelphia, 1873), 32, 64.

the mine operators and pig iron producers. Almost all the western senators and both Pennsylvanians voted for higher duties on scrap metal. All but one senator from New England and New York voted for the low schedule.[28]

The only tariff adjustment besides the wool and woolens bill to become law in the early postwar years was a measure passed in 1869, greatly increasing the duties on copper. Eastern smelters, who used a combination of eastern and cheap South American ores, were forced out of business by this bill, passed for the benefit of Lake Superior mine operators, whose domestic ores did not require smelting. The Lake Superior mine owners, some of whom were eastern financiers, were thus given a monopoly of the American market. They were thereby enabled to charge much higher than world prices at home and to dump their surplus abroad at much lower prices.[29] Similar conflicts among business interests developed on tariff schedules for salt (used for scouring wool), zinc, lead, nickel, and building stones.[30]

The wool and woolens bill of 1867, which considerably raised most schedules, has been cited as a prime example of the co-operation of business interests, because it was devised in a conference between a committee of wool growers and representatives of the National Association of Wool Manufacturers. What has generally been overlooked is the fact that the manufacturers' association, like the American Iron and Steel Association, was dominated by a well-organized segment of the industry, in this case by worsted and carpet manufacturers, whose interests conflicted with those of other important groups within the woolen industry.

Most influential of the men who negotiated the agreement for the manufacturers were Erastus B. Bigelow, president and founder of the Association, and America's leading carpet manufacturer; John L. Hayes, permanent secretary of the Association; and J. Wiley Edmonds, treasurer of the giant Pacific Mills, a leading worsted producer. Hayes reported to the membership that "for six months Mr. Bigelow gave himself unremittingly to the great work . . . [and to him they] must attribute the happy results of the conference." Before this "happy" conclusion, Hayes conceded, most woolen manufacturers "were becoming more and more disposed to look abroad for the chief supply of raw material . . . and were inclined to advocate the British policy of free trade in raw materials, in-

---

[28] *Cong. Globe*, 39 Cong., 2 Sess., 799–801 (January 28, 1867), 860–62 (January 30, 1867).

[29] Taussig, *Tariff History*, 219–21; *Letter of Henry Martin, Esq., President of the Baltimore Copper Company to the Senate of the United States in Opposition to the Bill Increasing the Duty on Imported Copper Ores* (Baltimore, 1869); Bliss Perry, *Life and Letters of Henry Lee Higginson* (Boston, 1921), 263–64; William B. Gates, *Michigan Copper and Boston Dollars* (Cambridge, 1951), 33–35, 45–47.

[30] *Cong. Globe*, 39 Cong., 2 Sess., 680, 765, 793, 798, 821 (January 23, 26, 28, 29, 1867).

cluding wool." [31] Certainly the results of the conference were not so happy for manufacturers of woolen cloth, the largest item of domestic woolen output. These producers would be forced to pay much higher rates for imported raw wool than the worsted manufacturers with whom they competed. Carpet and blanket manufacturers would pay by far the lowest rates.[32]

The largest manufacturer of wool cloth taking part in the negotiations with the growers was Edward Harris of the Harris Manufacturing Company, Woonsocket, Rhode Island. Harris later declared that he had no part in deciding the schedules, and that his name had been appended to the agreement without his knowledge or consent.[33] Senator Henry Wilson of Massachusetts, a manufacturer of fine woolen cloth, told the Senate Finance Committee if the new schedules were put into effect, he would have to close his factory. He subsequently declared in the Senate: "Some of the very ablest men in Massachusetts and in England earnestly believe that this bill, so far as it concerns two thirds of the woolen manufacturers of the country, is not so good as the present tariff. [Only] the carpet manufacturers are abundantly satisfied." Wilson's statement was reinforced by other New England senators. William Sprague of Rhode Island, William P. Fessenden of Maine, and Lot M. Morrill of Maine reported similar opinions of the wool and woolens bill among the cloth manufacturers in their constituencies.[34] Nevertheless, there was no organized opposition in Washington to the energetic Hayes or to the large number of western congressmen who were anxious to honor an agreement which gave protection to wool growers. The wool and woolens bill passed easily despite adverse votes from men like Wilson, Sumner, and Sprague who had close associations with the New England woolen industry.[35]

Northeastern opposition to the cloth schedules continued after the

[31] *Transactions of the National Association of Wool Manufacturers, Second Annual Report* (Boston, 1866), 12, 20. For interesting evidence of Edmonds' part in this agreement, see speech by Senator Jonathan P. Dolliver, *Cong. Record*, 61 Cong., 1 Sess., 1717 (May 4, 1909). For the protectionist ideas of Bigelow and Hayes, see Erastus B. Bigelow, *Objects and Plan of the National Association of Wool Manufacturers* (Boston, 1865), 3–4; John L. Hayes, *The Fleece and the Loom: An Address before the National Association of Wool Manufacturers at the First Annual Meeting in Philadelphia, September 6, 1865* (Boston, 1866), 60.

[32] For more detailed discussion of the schedules, see Chester W. Wright, *Wool Growing and the Tariff* (Cambridge, 1910), 213–15; Haldor R. Mohat, *The Tariff on Wool* (Madison, 1935), 23–25; Taussig, *Tariff History*, 195–218.

[33] Edward Harris, *Memorial of Manufacturers of Woolen Goods to the Committee on Ways and Means* (Washington, 1872), 22.

[34] *Cong. Globe*, 39 Cong., 2 Sess., 909–11 (January 31, 1867).

[35] *Ibid.*, 1958 (March 2, 1867). A relatively small but well-informed and organized group within the woolen industry was able to write schedules to suit itself because they had to be phrased in complicated, technical language. See Senator Dolliver's comments on this subject, *Cong. Record*, 61 Cong., 1 Sess., 1715 (May 4, 1909). The major reason for passage, however, was the fact that the schedules pleased leading wool growers.

passage of the bill, and the winter of 1869–1870, Edward Harris and forty-three other New England woolen manufacturers petitioned Congress to reduce the duties on wool for cloth as low as carpet wool duties, which were one-fifth as high. On reaching Washington with this petition, Harris was informed that the wool growers and John Hayes, who said he represented three hundred companies and individuals associated with the woolen industry, had first claim on congressmen's votes.[36] In 1889, the woolen cloth manufacturers obtained 530 signatures from wool manufacturers and dealers asking for lower duties—and again failed. Finally, in 1909, the cloth manufacturers formed a separate organization to do permanent battle in Washington with the worsted and carpet interests.[37]

For somewhat different reasons a low-tariff sentiment similar to that in New England was also strong in New York City, by far the largest importing and financial center in the country. New York merchants, shippers, and those who financed their activities opposed tariffs which might restrict imports, while the railroad financiers protested that under the proposed tariff of 1866 the Erie and the New York Central systems alone would have to pay out annually "about two million dollars by way of protection." [38] The New York Chamber of Commerce had opposed the Morrill bill of 1861 as "a radical change in the tariff policy of the country," but had patriotically refrained from strenuous protests as tariff rates steadily rose during the war.[39] In listing the organization's postwar objectives, however, Secretary John Austin Stevens declared: "The principles of free, unshackled trade, which it has ever upheld, must be reaffirrmed." [40] A few months after the war's end, the *Commercial and Financial Chronicle* observed: "Signs are not wanting that the subject of Free Trade will be made the text of the next political agitation in this country." The *Journal of Commerce* also began agitating for lower tariffs soon after the war; and the introduction of the first postwar tariff bill, providing for generally increased rates, naturally brought a strong protest from the New York Chamber of Commerce.[41]

[36] Edward Harris, *The Tariff and How It Effects the Woolen Cloth Manufacture and Wool Growers* (Woonsocket, 1871), 14–15; *Carded Wool Bulletin* (Boston), I (May, 1910), 6; Edward Atkinson, *Reply to the Argument by Mr. John L. Hayes* (Woonsocket, 1872).

[37] Mohat, *Tariff on Wool*, 19; Taussig, *Tariff History*, 316–17.

[38] Statement of Representative Henry J. Raymond of New York, *Cong. Globe*, 39 Cong., 1 Sess., 3516 (June 30, 1866).

[39] *Fourth Annual Report of the Chamber of Commerce of the State of New York* (New York, 1862), 2–3; *Fifth Annual Report of the Chamber of Commerce of the State of New York* (New York, 1863), 4–5. Senator Edwin D. Morgan, a member of the Chamber, voted for tariff increases during the war, then reverted to fighting high schedules in 1866. James A. Rawley, *Edwin D. Morgan, 1811–1883: Merchant in Politics* (New York, 1955), 207–209.

[40] *Centennial Celebration of the Chamber of Commerce of the State of New York . . . : Report of Proceedings* (New York, 1868), 21; also, *Ninth Annual Report of the Chamber of Commerce of the State of New York* (New York, 1867), Part I, p. 5.

[41] *Commercial and Financial Chronicle* (New York), I (July 8, 1865), 38; New York *Journal of Commerce*, May 23, 1865; *Ninth Annual Report of the Chamber of*

Clearly, then, New England cotton manufacturers and many wool and other manufacturers preferred and worked for lower tariff schedules—as did most of New York's financial and mercantile community. This fact was obvious to contemporary protectionists, especially the fervent Pennsylvanians. They recognized the role New Yorkers and New Englanders played in reducing many schedules, and in defeating, by obstructionist tactics, bills of which they disapproved. A delegate from Philadelphia's Board of Trade complained to the National Board of Trade in 1869 that New England's industries had been built up behind tariff walls. "Now they are marked disciples of free trade. . . . They overlook the interests yet in their infancy. . . . Is this right? Is this just?" [42] Henry C. Carey, leading spokesman for Pennsylvania iron, coal, and other protected interests, charged in 1867 that for twenty years, on tariff questions, "It has pleased the representatives of Massachusetts to array themselves on the side of cotton planters, slave owners, railroad monopolists." [43]

Northeastern businessmen were thus far from united in support of high tariffs after the Civil War. Leading business interests of New England and New York believed that they lost more than they gained from high postwar tariffs. Had reconstruction politics allowed them a choice, it seems likely that these important groups would have preferred a return to the coalition which had produced the low tariff of 1857—a coalition which included the South. Certainly they would not have opposed the return of southern representatives in order to retain high imposts.

The business interests of the Northeast were divided into fiercely competing groups not only by the tariff issue, but by currency questions as well. These conflicts were brought into the open shortly after the Civil War by attempts to contract the swollen wartime currency. Secretary of the Treasury Hugh McCulloch's proposals for contraction, designed for quick resumption of specie payments, won a cordial response from many importers and financiers, who would gain materially from the elimination

---

Commerce of the State of New York, Part I, pp. 29, 30, 60, 61. The Chamber's protest could not be ignored. The organizations membership included many of the largest campaign contributors to both parties, including, in 1866, such merchants and importers as Moses Grinnell, Alexander T. Stewart, William E. Dodge, Horace Claflin, and Senator Edwin D. Morgan; and such financiers as Henry Clews, Levi P. Morton, John Austin Stevens, Moses Taylor, John J. Cisco, and J. Pierpont Morgan.

[42] *Proceedings of the Second Annual Meeting of the National Board of Trade* (Boston, 1870), 312. For a justification of their low tariff policies, see the comments by New England textile men in *First Annual Meeting of the National Board of Trade* (Boston, 1869), 127–34.

[43] Henry C. Carey, *Reconstruction: Industrial, Financial and Political, Letters to the Hon. Henry Wilson, Senator from Massachusetts* (Philadelphia, 1867), 34. As Carey observed, votes on the complex tariff bills of 1866 and 1867 were not an accurate indication of tariff sentiment. Some additional insight into these bills is provided by Herbert R. Ferleger, *David A. Wells and the American Revenue System, 1865–1870* (New York, 1942), 22–168; Williamson, *Atkinson*, 64–71; Taussig, *Tariff History*, 175–77. Carey was especially hurt by what he considered the apostasy of his friend, Revenue Commissioner Wells, who went over to the camp of the low-tariff New Englanders in 1866–1867.

of the premium on gold and a consequent rise in the market value of government bonds.[44] Many businessmen longed for the currency stability they believed resumption would bring. But McCulloch met with warnings and protests from other important northeastern business groups. The Philadelphia Board of Trade immediately warned against hasty action, "lest by injudicious measures and rapid contraction," the people's interests should be sacrificed. A few weeks later, the *Commercial and Financial Chronicle*, a firm advocate of hard money, was forced to admit: "There is little doubt that the depression in public confidence, of which a proof will be found in our account of the week's fluctuation in the Stock Market, is closely connected with the anticipated effects of the contraction movement of the Secretary of the Treasury." [45]

Although only a moderate amount of currency was taken out of circulation, businessmen continued to fear that goods bought at high prices with inflated greenbacks might have to be sold at much lower prices if McCulloch were allowed to proceed with contraction. Wholesale prices fell sharply after January, 1866, confirming their fears.[46] As general price depreciation continued through 1866 and 1867, businessmen's objections to contraction became increasingly loud and widespread. The Commercial Exchange of Philadelphia adopted a resolution in January, 1867, "That premature resumption will prove a curse and not a blessing." A vice-president of the New York Chamber of Commerce, who approved contraction, recalled "living in the midst of the clamor against that process, where almost every man I met was denouncing the Secretary and predicting ruin upon all the interests of the country unless the policy was discontinued." [47]

Opposition to McCulloch's policy spread to Congress, where Representative William D. Kelley of Pennsylvania called it the "road to bankruptcy." [48] Finally, in January, 1868, Senator John Sherman of Ohio

[44] It should be noted that while immediate resumption would have raised the market value of federal bonds, it would also have reduced the value of interest payments, which were made in gold. Important dealers in government bonds, like Henry Clews and Jay Cooke, opposed contraction. Cooke wrote his brother in 1867, "As to getting back to specie payments, the least said about that the better, as it is the premium on gold that enables us to sell the 5-20's." Jay Cooke to Henry D. Cooke, September 20, 1867, Henrietta M. Larson, *Jay Cooke: Private Banker* (Cambridge, 1936), 204, 209-10.

[45] *Thirty-third Annual Report of the Philadelphia Board of Trade* (Philadelphia, 1866), 1. *Commercial and Financial Chronicle*, II (January 13, 1866), 31; *Iron Age* (New York), V (November 7, 1867), 2, 4.

[46] Wesley C. Mitchell, *Gold, Prices, and Wages under the Greenback Standard* (Berkeley, 1909), 26; "Review of the Boston Market for the Year 1866," *Thirteenth Annual Report of the Boston Board of Trade* (Boston, 1867), 43. Wholesale prices fell fastest, affecting manufacturers and the larger merchants and importers more than retailers. Both wholesale and retail prices fell faster than wages and farm prices.

[47] *Proceedings of the First Annual Meeting of the National Board of Trade* (Boston, 1869), 114, 173.

[48] "Contraction, the Road to Bankruptcy," reprinted in William D. Kelley, *Speeches, Addresses, and Letters on Industrial and Financial Questions* (Philadelphia, 1872), 210.

introduced legislation to end contraction. "We hear the complaint from all parts of the country," he said, "from all branches of industry . . . that industry for some reason is paralyzed and that trade and enterprise are not so well rewarded as they were. Many, perhaps erroneously, attribute all this to the contraction of the currency." [49]

Passage of Sherman's measure, however, did not end the conflict among northeastern businessmen over currency. Most seem to have favored a stable money supply, and to have opposed currency expansion and quick resumption alike. Many of the more conservative bankers, importers, and merchants, however, continued to support an early return to specie payments. There was also an influential and vocal group of businessmen which persistently called for currency inflation. This last group found adherents among those manufacturers and merchants who sought to take advantage of great postwar demand for their products, but who had difficulty obtaining capital for plant and inventory expansion, even at extremely high interest rates. Many of those who borrowed large sums for investments in factories, mines, and railroads, were apt to favor currency expansion, which they believed would lower interest rates, raise prices, and make debts easier to pay. Radical Senator Sprague, for example, in control of a Rhode Island empire of factories, real estate, utilities, and banks, complained to the Senate that "The interest paid by the borrower today is just double what it was at the close of the War." He placed the blame on "the power centralized in New York." [50]

It is significant that Jay Cooke, once an ardent hard money man, became something of an inflationist after he borrowed millions to build the Northern Pacific, and saw his corporation become a huge land speculator through government grants. In a letter to his brother and partner, written in 1868, Cooke called for moderate currency expansion which would keep pace "with the new habits and enlarged area of Country." "Why," he asked, "should this grand and Glorious Country be stunted and dwarfed—its activities chilled and its very life blood curdled by these miserable 'hard coin' theories—the musty theories of a by gone age?" [51]

Pennsylvania iron and steel men, through their representatives and periodicals, led eastern demands for an increased supply of currency. Their industry was expanding rapidly behind high tariff walls, stimulated by the postwar spurt in railroad building. Iron manufacturer Thaddeus Stevens was a leader in congressional schemes to inflate the currency. Both Stevens and Kelley of Pennsylvania supported textile manufacturer Benjamin F. Butler's resolution to pay the wartime bonds in paper rather than gold. [52] Representative Daniel J. Morrell, a bank president as well as

[49] *Cong. Globe*, 40 Cong., 2 Sess., 407, 537, 674 (January 9, 15, 22, 1868).

[50] *Ibid.*, 40 Cong., 1 Sess., 65, 361 (March 15, 30, 1867). Sprague's overextended empire went into bankruptcy in 1873 when his loans were called in. Zechariah Chafee, Jr., "Weathering the Panic of '73," *Dorr Pamphlets* (Providence), No. 4 (1942).

[51] Jay Cooke to Henry D. Cooke, November 23, 1869, Larson, *Jay Cooke*, 205.

[52] *Cong. Globe*, 40 Cong., 2 Sess., 212–13 (December 16, 1867).

former general manager of the giant Cambria Iron Works in Pennsylvania, called for more circulation, and contended that under a program of inflation "Capital would be less valuable, and a larger share of the increase in wealth would go to the enterprise and labor which created it." [53] Pennsylvania iron and steel periodicals took up the fight against the bankers. "In the seaboard cities," said *Iron Age* in 1867, "the money power seeks to attain a position of irresistible control, and to subdue and subordinate to itself all the interests of industry." [54] The lines of battle were perhaps drawn most succinctly and cogently in a speech by Representative Kelley in January, 1867. "The contest," he said, "is between the creditor and the debtor class—the men of investments and the men of enterprise." [55]

The issue, however, was not as simple as Kelley put it. Most foreign goods were paid for with gold, not greenbacks. Customs duties were also payable in gold. As long as specie payments could be postponed, the premium on gold would remain. In the early postwar years, the premium fluctuated between 30 and 40 per cent. The effect was to raise the cost of foreign goods about one-third above what their cost would be if specie resumption should occur.[56] Monetary inflation would tend to raise the premium and consequently the price of imports even higher. This fact was not lost on the Pennsylvanians. As early as 1863, the Philadelphia Board of Trade noted that the "premium on foreign exchange adds greatly to tariff and transportation costs." [57] In 1864, Samuel J. Reeves, iron manufacturer and chairman of the executive committee of the American Iron and Steel Association, wrote the Commissioner of Internal Revenue: "The constant advance in the price of gold has acted as so much protection to the home manufacturer above the duty. . . . The iron manufacture now finds its safety only in the high cost of gold; what is to become of it when there will be no premium on gold?" [58] The answer, so far as many iron manufacturers were concerned, was to retain the premium on gold.

The significance of the Pennsylvanians' currency policies was obvious to importers, financiers, and many manufacturers in New York and New England. Most of these favored hard money and low tariffs. The Boston

[53] *Ibid.*, 41 Cong., 2 Sess., Appendix, 142 (March 10, 1870).
[54] *Iron Age*, V (October 24, 1867), 4; *ibid.* (November 7, 1867), 4; *Industrial Bulletin* (Philadelphia), VIII (November, 1871), 4.
[55] Kelley, *Speeches, Addresses, and Letters*, 226.
[56] See statement of costs of English rails in *Bulletin of the American Iron and Steel Association* (Philadelphia), No. 2 Supplement (February 6, 1867), 186. The Association's figures show the premium to have been a greater share of total cost than was the tariff duty.
[57] *Thirtieth Annual Report of the Philadelphia Board of Trade* (Philadelphia, 1863), 40.
[58] "Extracts from a letter to the Hon. Joseph J. Lewis . . . from Samuel J. Reeves," *Thirty-second Annual Report of the Philadelphia Board of Trade* (Philadelphia, 1865), 76.

Board of Trade's "Wool Report" for 1863 noted the effect of the gold premium on the price of wool.[59] New York merchants protested that the high price of gold seriously discouraged imports, and the city's Chamber of Commerce adopted a resolution charging that "Powerful interests are striving to perpetuate the existing depreciation of the currency." [60]

When contraction was abruptly ended and tariff reform failed, in 1867–1868, some businessmen in New York and New England felt that the government's policies were falling under the control of high tariff and paper money men. On the other hand, Henry C. Carey, spokesman for Pennsylvania protectionists, charged that New England, aided by New Yorkers, was attempting to create a monopoly in money and manufacturing. One instrument of the monopolists, said Carey, was a low tariff, which New England manufacturers could afford because of their low interest charges and modern machinery, and which they used to ruin domestic competition and to obtain cheap foreign raw materials to aid New England producers. A second instrument, he continued, was the banking system—"a great money monopoly for the especial benefit of the Trading States." Even with this monopoly, Carey complained, the traders wished to contract the currency, further reducing the pittance allowed Pennsylvania and further raising interest charges manufacturers would have to pay. Either the New Englanders would change their ways, he warned, or they would be compelled to do so by a combination of southern, western, and middle states, in which Pennsylvania would take the lead.[61] In reply, cotton manufacturer Edward Atkinson "rejoiced" at this analysis of New England's advantage, and assured Carey that henceforth the New England representatives would support the low tariff and hard money policies even more strongly. Instead of fearing the threatened combination of sections under Pennsylvania's leadership against those policies, he prophesied that New England would join with the South and the West in promoting them.[62]

Both Carey and Atkinson overstated the unity of New England manufacturers, oversimplified the varied and conflicting interests in the West,

[59] Bond and Livermore, Report on Wool, 3.

[60] Eighth Annual Report of the Chamber of Commerce of the State of New York (New York, 1866), Part II, p. 90; Memorial to the Honorable the Senate and House of Representatives (New York, 1869), signed by A. A. Low and Samuel Babcock for the New York City Chamber of Commerce; remarks by A. A. Low in Eight Annual Report of the New York Chamber of Commerce (New York, 1866), Part I, p. 28; and Ninth Annual Report of the New York Chamber of Commerce (New York, 1867), Part I, pp. 74, 76.

[61] Carey, Reconstruction, 4, 8, 21, 24–26, 50, 53–58, 67–68.

[62] Atkinson to Carey, November 11, 1867, Williamson, Atkinson, 79–80. For further details of this controversy see Henry Wilson to Carey, September 21, 1867; Carey to Wilson, September 25, 1867; George L. Ward to Carey, October 16, 1867; Carey to Ward, October 18, 1867; David A. Wells to Carey, November 1, 6, 1867; Carey to Atkinson, November 18, 1867, Henry C. Carey Papers, Edward Carey Gardiner Collection (Historical Society of Pennsylvania, Philadelphia).

and conjectured about the probable political and economic alignments of the postwar South. Nevertheless, both were more realistic than historians who have explained northeastern leadership of Radical Reconstruction in terms of a unified northeastern business interest anxious to keep the South out of the Union in order to protect high tariffs and hard money.

Nor can the direction and support which northeastern representatives gave to Radical Reconstruction be accurately explained as an attempt to "make easy the road for northern economic penetration and exploitation of the South." [63] Few important northeastern capitalists had any desire to place their money in a war-torn, unsettled region. Eventually, northerners invested huge sums in southern factories, mines, railroads, and real estate; but it is significant that only a small number did so as long as Radicals controlled southern state legislatures.

Many southern leaders and periodicals recognized the need for northern capital after the Civil War, and numerous cordial invitations were extended.[64] That such invitations were futile was obvious to businessmen, North and South. "We want capital attracted to the South," said the *Commercial and Financial Chronicle* of New York City, "and this cannot be, so long as the States are under semi-military rule." And from the South *De Bow's Review* echoed, "It is idle to ask capital to venture until order is restored." South Carolina exempted manufacturers from all state and local taxation, but failed to attract northern capital partly because of the uncertainties of Reconstruction.[65] Thomas W. Conway, a former Freedmen's Bureau official, who toured the North in 1866 trying to induce businessmen to make southern investments, reported to the New York Chamber of Commerce, which had encouraged his mission: "The substantial men met by me in all parts of the country are sick of the delay in regard to the settlement of our national political difficulties." Until such settlement occurred, he predicted, there would be continued uncertainty and violence in the South, and poor prospects for northern investment.[66]

Even Pennsylvania's Representative William D. Kelley, who was both a Radical leader and an enthusiastic advocate of northern investments in the postwar South, soon found that Radical Reconstruction interfered with southern industrial growth. In March, 1868, Kelley demanded immediate readmission of Alabama—a potential economic paradise, he said,

[63] Hesseltine, *Confederate Leaders in the New South*, 136.
[64] For example, see Petersburg (Va.) *News*, quoted in New York *Journal of Commerce*, May 20, 1865. A number of similar appeals for northern capital are cited in John F. Stover, *The Railroads of the South, 1865–1900: A Study in Finance and Control* (Chapel Hill, 1955), 54–55. See also Broadus Mitchell, *The Rise of Cotton Mills in the South* (Baltimore, 1921), 237.
[65] *Commercial and Financial Chronicle*, II (February 17, 1866), 198; *De Bow's Review* (Nashville), After the War Series, Vol. IV (November, 1867), 451; Francis B. Simkins and Robert H. Woody, *South Carolina during Reconstruction* (Chapel Hill, 1932), 290–91.
[66] Thomas W. Conway, "Introduction of Capital and Men into the Southern States of the Union," *Ninth Annual Report of the Chamber of Commerce of the State of New York* (New York, 1867), Part II, pp. 8–13.

whose wealth was "paralyzed" while Reconstruction ran its violent course. Thaddeus Stevens, less interested in southern industrial development than was Kelley, fought against his colleague's haste, insisting that Alabama must first guarantee the suffrage rights of Negroes.[67]

New England cotton manufacturers, dealers, and shippers feared that northerners' refusal to send their capital south would result in an insufficient cotton crop. Edward S. Tobey, Boston cotton merchant and manufacturer, recommended that the Freedmen's Bureau be authorized to take over the role of private capital in organizing Negro labor for cotton cultivation. The South's deficiency of capital, Tobey told the Boston Board of Trade in a famous speech in November, 1865, was proved by "frequent applications from Southern men to Northern capitalists to invest in cotton lands at low prices." It would be ideal if private investors could supply this want; but capital, Tobey observed, "is seldom placed by its possessors where society is disorganized and life and property comparatively unprotected by a stable and efficient government." The Board approved Tobey's suggestion.[68]

A few months after Tobey's speech, however, the New Englanders' plans were changed by a sudden shift in the cotton market. The southern cotton crop was larger than expected. Furthermore, the English, with new machinery and methods for manufacturing with cheap Indian Surat cotton, had become increasingly less dependent upon American producers. New England manufacturers and dealers were caught with large supplies of cotton as the price dropped almost 40 per cent in the first four months of 1866.[69] The momentary interest New England businessmen had shown in reconstruction legislation dropped with the price of cotton. The Boston Board of Trade's "Review of the Boston Market for the Year 1867," declared: "Business men, generally, are loud in their complaints against the course of legislation for two years past. Important interests have been neglected by Congress, and too much time has been wasted on questions which only led to discord and bad feeling in the different branches of the Government." [70]

Most large northern investors, instead of being concerned over the difficulties of investing in the South, turned their attention to the many lucrative opportunities elsewhere—in Minnesota timberlands, Michigan iron and copper mines, Pennsylvania coal and oil, and railroads in almost

[67] Cong. Globe, 40 Cong., 2 Sess., 2139–41 (March 26, 1868). For another significant conflict between Kelley and Stevens see ibid., 39 Cong., 1 Sess., 3687–88 (July 9, 1866).

[68] Edward S. Tobey, The Industry of the South . . . : A Speech Delivered before the Boston Board of Trade, November 27, 1865 (Boston, 1878). See also Twelfth Annual Report of the Boston Board of Trade (Boston, 1866), 57.

[69] Thirteenth Annual Report of the Boston Board of Trade (Boston, 1867), 47.

[70] Fourteenth Annual Report of the Boston Board of Trade (Boston, 1868), 122. For further evidence of the New Englander's rapid change of heart, see Williamson, Atkinson, 59–61, and Boston Board of Trade, Report of a Committee upon the Cotton Tax (Boston, 1867).

every state. Significantly, the Pennsylvania Railroad, with abundant capital and great influence in Congress, did not attempt to create its "Southern empire" until Radical Reconstruction was nearing its conclusion. Until 1871, the Pennsylvania preferred to take advantage of investment opportunities in the Northwest. When Thomas A. Scott, who guided the railroad's expansion, decided to move south, he dealt with Conservative governors and legislators in the South as successfully as he had with Democrats and Republicans in the North and West.[71]

Only one important northeastern business group was strongly attracted by investment opportunities in the South immediately after the war: New York financiers, the true "masters of capital," who had long-standing commercial ties with the South, and had sufficient funds to risk large amounts in a turbulent area. New York merchants, shippers, and financiers were as interested as Bostonians in large postwar cotton crops, but they emphatically disagreed with the Boston proposal to use the Freedmen's Bureau to grow cotton. When Tobey's plan was put before the executive committee of the New York Chamber of Commerce, the committee reported: "Our best reliance for attaining the desired end is to present the capitalists this most inviting field." [72]

In so far as northern capital was invested in southern railroads, both before and immediately after the war, most of it was provided by New Yorkers. A recent study shows, for example, that of some 280 directors of twenty-five major southern lines in 1867–1868 only eleven were northerners, and ten of these were from New York.[73] Two important New York investors in southern railroads were elected to Congress and were thus in a position to speak publicly about reconstruction legislation. One of the two was William E. Dodge, metal importer, iron manufacturer, land speculator, railroad investor, and president of the New York Chamber of Commerce; the other was William W. Phelps, director of four large banks and eight railroads.[74] The evidence suggests that the opinions these men

[71] Stover, *Railroads of the South*, 99–121. According to Stover, "While many southerners in the postwar years had eagerly sought northern capital for their stricken railways, their entreaties up to 1870 had rarely resulted in more than visits of railroad carpetbaggers." John F. Stover, "The Pennsylvania Railroad's Southern Rail Empire," *Pennsylvania Magazine of History and Biography* (Philadelphia), LXXXI (January, 1957), 28.

[72] *Eighth Annual Report of the Chamber of Commerce of the State of New York* (New York, 1866), Part I, p. 70. One of the few influential New Englanders interested in "exploiting" the South was former abolitionist, Governor John A. Andrew of Massachusetts. His small American Land Company and Agency was forced out of business in 1866. Andrew was not sympathetic to the Radicals' program, and favored turning southern state governments over to the old leaders of southern society—businessmen, politicians, former Confederate officers. Henry G. Pearson, *The Life of John A. Andrew* (2 vols., Boston, 1904), II, 267, 270, 273.

[73] Stover, *Railroads of the South*, 38.

[74] For one example of southern railroad investments by Dodge and Phelps see Hugh M. Herrick (comp.), *William Walter Phelps: His Life and Public Service* (New York, 1904), 31–32. The other two men who took part in this investment were Moses Taylor, president of the National City Bank, and John J. Cisco, investment banker

expressed of Radical Reconstruction were typical of those held by New York's financial leaders.

When Thaddeus Stevens' bill for dividing the South into military districts reached the floor of the House in January, 1867, Dodge voted against it; and in explaining his vote he told his Republican colleagues: "I claim to be as loyal as any other man . . . [but] if these southern states are still to be kept year after year in this state of disquietude we at the North, sympathizing with them in our social and business relations, must to a certain extent suffer with them." Furthermore, said Dodge, business-men believed that this bill would result in continued high taxation to support an army of occupation in ten states.[75] And in the debate on Butler's civil rights bill in 1875, Phelps—one of three Republicans to vote against it in the House—expressed sentiments long held in the New York financial community. "You are trying to do," he said, "what it seems to me this House everlastingly tries in one form or another to do—to legislate against human nature. You are trying to legislate against human preju-dice, and you cannot do it. . . . Let us end this cruel policy." [76]

Many New York financiers made public their support of President Andrew Johnson in his battle against the Radicals. When Johnson vetoed the bill for the continuation of the Freedmen's Bureau, in February, 1866, a mass meeting to celebrate the veto was arranged by the city's business leaders, and a committee was sent to Washington to offer the President New York's aid. Among those on the committee were Moses Taylor, dean of New York bankers, and William B. Astor, known as the "landlord of New York." [77] Six months later, when Johnson visited New York as part of his "swing around the circle," a grand dinner was given for him at Delmonico's. Chairman of arrangements was Alexander T. Stewart, the "dry goods king"; treasurer for the dinner was Henry Clews, probably second only to Jay Cooke as a dealer in government bonds, and second to none as a dealer in southern railroad securities. A large number of New York's leading businessmen attended the dinner.[78] This was followed on September 17, 1866, by a giant National Union celebration to demonstrate the city's support of the President at the height of his crucial campaign

and treasurer of Credit Mobilier. Both Taylor and Cisco also opposed Radical Recon-struction.

[75] *Cong. Globe*, 39 Cong., 2 Sess., 627–29 (January 21, 1867).

[76] *Ibid.*, 43 Cong., 2 Sess., 1002 (February 4, 1875). For similar earlier statements see *Commercial and Financial Chronicle*, I (August 26, 1865), 260; New York *Journal of Commerce*, May 25, 1865.

[77] New York *Morning Herald*, February 23, 1866. Among the organizers of the meeting were Dodge; banker and brokerage house president George Opdyke; Dodge's predecessor as Chamber of Commerce president, A. A. Low; and financier mer-chant Moses Grinnell. See also George Fort Milton, *The Age of Hate: Andrew Johnson and the Radicals* (New York, 1930), 289–96.

[78] *Dinner to the President of the United States in Honor of His Visit to the City of New York, August 29, 1866*, printed program in Samuel J. Tilden Papers (New York Public Library); also Henry Clews to Samuel J. Tilden, September 6, 1866, Tilden Papers. In Philadelphia, banker Anthony J. Drexel met with other leading business-

against the Radicals. The reception committee for this impressive meeting included Stewart, Taylor, Clews, Edwards Pierrepont, and August Belmont. Among those who gave public notice of their approval of Johnson's policies by allowing their names to be listed as vice-presidents of the meeting were such well-known financiers as William H. Aspinwall, Cornelius Vanderbilt, John J. Cisco, and Henry Grinnell, as well as numerous important merchants and manufacturers.[79]

Similar indications of support or approval of the presidential reconstruction program rather than that of Congress also came from the New York Chamber of Commerce and from the financial press. In 1866 the Chamber of Commerce adopted a resolution, introduced by the banker brother of Radical leader Roscoe Conkling, which expressed the hope that Reconstruction "may be everywhere signalized by magnanimity and clemency and that it may nowhere be stained by a single act which will be condemned as needlessly harsh or revengeful." A copy of this resolution was sent to Washington as encouragement to the President.[80] As early as July, 1865, *Hunt's Merchants Magazine* and the *Commercial and Financial Chronicle*—two of the leading business journals of the period—had applauded Johnson's program for the speedy restoration of the seceded states. As the Radicals gathered their forces in the fall of 1865, the *American Railroad Journal* announced that Reconstruction "is going on as well as could be hoped. The President . . . sets the example of kindness and benignity and a large majority of both parties . . . are evidently disposed to support his policy." And in January, 1866, the *Journal of Commerce* proclaimed its support of Johnson.[81]

---

men in the Merchant's Exchange and planned Johnson's welcome to the city. Philadelphia *Age*, August 28, 1866. For evidence of Jay Cooke's disgust with Radical Reconstruction, see Ellis P. Oberholtzer, *Jay Cooke: Financier of the Civil War* (2 vols., Philadelphia, 1907), II, 22.

[79] *National Union Celebration at Union Square, September 17, 1866* (New York, 1866). After the 1866 election, when it was apparent that Johnson could not be re-elected in 1868, these men began to switch their support to Grant, who was known to be safe and sound on the currency, and who seemed most likely to bring peace to the South. Many northern businessmen were antagonized by Johnson's undignified campaign. New York *Tribune*, December 5, 1867.

[80] *Eight Annual Report of the Chamber of Commerce of the State of New York* (New York, 1866), Part I, p. 4.

[81] *Hunt's Merchants Magazine and Commercial Review* (New York), LIII (July, 1865), 28–30, 43; *Commercial and Financial Chronicle*, I (July 1, 1865), 3, 5; (July 29, 1865), 133; *American Railroad Journal* (New York), XXXIII (October 7, 1865), 949; New York *Journal of Commerce*, January 9, 1866.

Although lack of space necessitated the omission from this article of discussions of government bonds and national banks, the antagonism to Radical Reconstruction of the great financiers, their organizations and periodicals, is perhaps the best evidence of the remote relationship between these financial issues and congressional reconstruction policies. For the negative attitude of the New York bankers toward the national banking system, both during and after the Civil War, see Fritz Redlich, *The Molding of American Banking: Men and Ideas* (2 vols., New York, 1951), II, 105, 106, 108, 121, 140–46; Larson, *Jay Cooke*, 140–42.

From evidence such as this, the reconstruction program of the Radicals cannot be explained as an organized attempt by the business interests of the Northeast either to preserve and promote their own economic advantages or to obtain protection for economic exploitation of the South. Actually, northeastern businessmen had no unified economic program to promote. Important business groups within the region opposed each other on almost every significant economic question, and this lack of a common interest was likewise reflected in the economic views of Radical congressmen. Thaddeus Stevens, for example, dominant Radical leader in the House, was a fervent protectionist and a proponent of paper money inflation; Charles Sumner, Senate Radical leader, spoke and voted for lower tariff schedules and for resumption of specie payments. With both the businessmen and the legislators thus divided on economic issues, and with the New York merchants and financiers—who were in a position to gain most from economic exploitation of the South—definitely critical of the Radicals' program, it seems clear that factors other than the economic interests of the Northeast must be used to explain the motivation and aims of Radical Reconstruction.

Agricultural Maladjustments

21. Land Policy and Its Relation to Agricultural Production and Distribution, 1862 to 1933

Theodore Saloutos

If by land policy we mean a comprehensive, well-thought-out plan that made for an efficient long-range use of our agricultural resources, we are reasonably safe in saying we had none.[1] If we had anything that came close to resembling a policy, it was that of throwing open vast quantities of public and private lands to cultivation which resulted in maladjustments that made it difficult, if not impossible, for many farmers to adjust themselves to capitalistic methods of production and distribution. The

[1] L. C. Gray, "The Causes: Traditional Attitudes and Institutions," *Soil and Men. Yearbook of Agriculture, 1938* (Washington: Govt. Printing Office, 1938), p. 111.

"Land Policy and Its Relation to Agricultural Production and Distribution, 1862 to 1933," by Theodore Saloutos, is reprinted by permission from *Journal of Economic History*, XXII (December, 1962), 445–460.

extent of these maladjustments may be gauged in part by observing the status of agriculture on the eve of the New Deal. Shrinking foreign markets, world-wide competition, rising tariff walls, poor farm management practices, and excessive production and distribution costs were accompanied by sharp increases in indebtedness, farm foreclosures, and tenancy. Agriculture was receiving a dwindling share of the national income, capital formation was being discouraged, and farming had been relegated to a subordinate position within the economy.

From the outset it should be made plain that our land laws were hardly as liberal to the farmers as once had been imagined. And even if these laws had been more liberally administered to satisfy their immediate and long-range needs, it is doubtful whether they would have been spared from many of the vicissitudes of commercial farming. More than cheap land was needed to acquire full ownership and to retain it. A far-sighted policy that would have made for a seasoned settlement of the areas thrown open to cultivation and taken legitimate credit needs into account conceivably might have mitigated, but not necessarily eliminated, the difficulties of the settlers. Too many other elements were involved.

As suggested, the phrase land policy suggests something definite, well planned, unified, and long-range in character. But the most cursory investigation bears out that insofar as the Federal Government was concerned this hardly was the case. Policies were, and still are, formulated by Congress, the President of the United States, and directly or indirectly influenced by the decisions of the courts. As a rule, Federal legislation has been the result of compromise between conflicting factions and the President rather than an expression of "a uniform philosophy" and "coherent and consistent aims." Bureaucratic agencies likewise had a hand in elaborating upon the details of a general policy. Several departments were responsible for the administration of programs or the development of research aimed at influencing the course of agricultural land policy. And these departments were not necessarily agreed in their objectives or distinguished for their consistency.[2]

In theory we were committed to the philosophy that every man had the right to the unrestricted ownership of a piece of land, and that our democratic institutions should be rooted in a nation comprised of small family-sized farms. We believed it wise to turn over all lands, agricultural and nonagricultural, to private hands on the theory that in this manner they would be used to greatest advantage. We gave little, if any, consideration to controlling the settlement of these lands in a manner that would have prevented an overexpansion of agriculture, or guiding would-be farmers into areas most suited to agriculture. We believed that private

---

[2] L. C. Gray, "Objectives in the Land Use Planning Programs of the United States Government," *Proceedings* of the Western Farm Economics Association, Seventh Annual Meeting (Berkeley, 1934), p. 1.

ownership would make for an effective utilization of the land, a maximum of wealth and a satisfactory distribution of it, and a wholesome community life. We were so overpowered by our strongly individualistic way of life that it was difficult for us to heed to the warnings of a John Wesley Powell. The seemingly inexhaustible supply of our land resources did not inspire thoughts of conservation. In an age when labor was scarce and land plentiful, it was believed economical to avoid the immediate consequences of waste and destruction by moving on to fresh soil.[3]

The weaknesses of our land laws have been spelled out in considerable detail by historians, land economists, and others; there is little point in belaboring the obvious. Hindsight and years of suffering have made obvious what foresight could not make obvious to policymakers at an earlier date. Authorities are generally agreed that the application of the homestead policy to the Great Plains was a serious mistake. The 160-acre units that were suited to farming conditions in the humid Mississippi valley proved highly unsuited to the arid conditions of the West.[4]

Apart from the Federal land laws numerous other pressures of a private or quasi-private nature were at work. These included the activities of the railroads, the state and territorial immigration commissions, the real estate agents, the "go West young man" tradition, technological improvements, the growing export market—at least down to the end of the nineteenth century—the progress in converting hard spring wheat into flour of superior quality, the influence of the agricultural colleges, experiment stations, and private agencies, and the exhortations of the poets and politicians.

The arguments employed in attracting settlers were persuasive, to say the least. No efforts were spared and no class of people overlooked; the hale and the hearty, the frail and the frustrated were appealed to. Sufferers from "pulmonary, bronchial and malarial diseases," "dyspeptic, hollow-chested" young Easterners, and neurotic young ladies who wanted to restore their health and in the process acquire a husband with a slice of government land were urged to come. The ubiquitous real estate agent was prepared with his pencil and paper to explain the advantages of farm over city life. The farmer enjoyed lower living costs; his farm was his home as well as his place of business, and this entailed little additional expense; his livelihood came mostly from the land, and he needed less cash; food from the farm was fresher and the atmosphere healthier.

Illusions of quick riches also were encouraged by bonanza farms sponsored or worked in co-operation with the railroads; they were backed by adequate capital, and operated by skilled managers using the most mod-

[3] Paul Gates, "Recent Land Policies of the Federal Government," *National Resources Board, Land Planning Committee,* Part VII (Washington: Govt. Printing Office, 1935), p. 60.

[4] Gray, "Objectives in the Land Use Planning Programs," p. 4.

ern methods and implements, and farming the most fertile lands. Appealing likewise was the argument that wheat raising provided the farmers with ample leisure; seeding, harvesting, and threshing were the busy periods, and the rest of the time was their own. In 1895 the Northwest was advertised as being capable of supporting a hundred times its population. "Come to the Great Bread Basket of the World. Come ye, and eat!" was the admonition.[5]

Many, if not most, of the settlers hardly were of a select variety capable of applying managerial skills in farming lands that taxed the resources of even the most efficient producers; many had their difficulties in the older communities, and now they exposed themselves to farming in the sub-humid areas with which they were unfamiliar. Land was sold to anyone capable of meeting the minimum financial requirements. The purchasers were not required to demonstrate any proficiency as managers.

The effects of this nonselective process were graphically demonstrated during the First World War, when abnormally high prices accelerated the movement of "nonfarmers" and "misfits" onto marginal and submarginal lands. Investigators discovered that in one of the areas of greatest failure sixty-three occupations other than farming were represented, and that 51 per cent of those who took up land were without capital. Among the nonfarmers were "two circus musicians, a paper hanger, sailor, sea-going engineer, two wrestlers, two barbers, a cigar-maker, a race horse man, a bricklayer, an undertaker, a deep-sea diver, six 'old maids,' a milliner, and a professional gambler." Such an onrush onto the land made it impossible to foster a seasoned economic development which was based on careful planning and consideration to costs, prices, and returns to labor and investments.[6]

Between 1850 and 1930, as a result of the activities of private groups, and Federal and state legislation, the area of all land in farms had more than tripled, and the area of improved land in farms almost quintupled. When this eighty-year period is broken down into smaller time spans, we find that the area opened up to cultivation reached its greatest dimensions during the 1880's and 1890's. Between 1870 and 1900, the total area of all farm lands increased from 408 to 823 million acres, the improved lands from 189 to 414 million acres, and the improved lands per capita from 4.9 to 5.5 acres.[7]

After 1900 the pace of expansion slackened considerably. Only forty-four million acres were added during the first decade of the twentieth century, and another seventy-seven million acres during the second decade. The Federal reclamation program launched in 1902 was a means of

[5] Theodore Saloutos, "The Spring Wheat Farmer in a Maturing Economy, 1870–1920," *The Journal of Economic History*, VI, No. 2 (Nov. 1946), 173–75.

[6] *Ibid.*, pp. 176–77.

[7] Richard T. Ely and George S. Wehrwein, *Land Economics* (New York: Macmillan Co., 1940), pp. 172–73.

extending homesteading opportunities to lands too arid for cultivation; and this perhaps was influenced by the neo-Malthusian belief that the population of the nation would continue to increase indefinitely. In due time this reclamation program was extended to apply to land in private as well as public ownership; and under the spell of speculators, chambers of commerce, and railroads, it became more local in scope. Frequently the program operated more to the benefit of the land speculator and private interest groups than the farmers. It was responsible, among other things, for the creation of a number of communities that probably would have never come into existence, and for saddling many of them with impossible debt burdens and fantastic capital structures.[8]

During the 1920's and the first half of the 1930's the actual area added to farms increased more than the improved lands, while the per capita acreage of improved lands per capita declined. In 1920 the acreage of all land in farms was 956 million, in 1930—987 million, and in 1935—1,055 million; the improved lands in farms during these years were 503 million, 522 million, and 514 million acres, respectively. Meanwhile, the improved land in farms per capita had dropped from 4.8 acres in 1920 to 4.3 acres in 1930, and 4.0 acres in 1935.[9]

According to Tostlebe's study for the National Bureau of Economic Research, the physical capital in agriculture, consisting chiefly of land and measured in terms of 1910–1914 prices, grew steadily from 1870 to 1910. Although this growth varied from section to section and decade to decade, the rate of growth diminished steadily from 41 per cent during the 1870's to about 10 per cent during the 1910's. Then there followed two decades of no increase or slight decrease.

In the post-Civil War decades, much barren land was brought into productive use through public expense and the efforts of farmers who plowed their time, money, and energies into fertilizing and draining wet land, irrigating dry land, clearing away brush, stumps, and stones, or bringing their land closer to markets by building roads, railroads, and other means of transportation. The extent of this gain can be found in the productivity of the land under cultivation, the increase in the improved land, and the rising land values.

Fluctuating prices seem to have had little influence on the growth of farm capital during these earlier expansive years of agriculture. Capital formation, according to Tostlebe, proceeded at a faster pace during these earlier years than in any subsequent period, despite the fact that the prices the farmers received were declining a good deal of the time. The obvious reason for this is that the Federal and state governments, the railroads and timber companies, made land available to farmers at relatively minimum costs.

The availability of good cheap land persuaded many to establish farms,

[8] Gray, "Objectives in Land Use Planning Programs," p. 4.
[9] Ely and Wehrwein, Land Economics, pp. 172–73.

despite the scarcity and costliness of capital. The prospects of high income and capital gain once the farm was placed in operation, appealed to the older farmers and their children who were ready to start out on their own. This was equally true of men in other occupations and other countries who had the necessary capital and credit to make a start. The incentive to establish an independent farm was strong in bad times and good, for the urge to establish an independent livelihood on cheap land always had wide appeal.[10]

Veblen pointed out that it was common practice for the farmer to take up more land than he could cultivate. This increased his need for equipment to cultivate the land and for credit to meet expenses incident to holding idle and semi-idle land. "All this," wrote Veblen,

> . . . has had the effect of raising the cost of production of farm products; partly by making the individual farm that much more unwieldy as an instrument of production, partly by further enforcing the insufficiency and the make-shift character for which American farm equipment is justly famed, and partly also by increasing the distances over which the farm supplies and the farm products have had to be moved.[11]

The passing of the so-called era of cheap lands was felt by the farmers. Well before the twentieth century, it became progressively difficult for one to establish a farm with a small capital outlay. By 1920, it was almost impossible to obtain good land cheaply or improve it with one's own labor. During the 1920's and 1930's it was rare for one to turn to farming as a means of obtaining land cheaply, or for farmers from the older regions to make a fresh start in newer areas. After the First World War capital formation occurred, as a rule, either on well-established farms which more or less were improved, stocked, and equipped; or else it gave way to the more immediate needs of the farmer and family.[12]

Meanwhile, shifts occurred in the geographical areas of production and in the intensive utilization of resources that altered the proportion in which land, machinery, livestock, and stored crops were used; and they had an effect on the basic composition of agricultural credit. Farm real estate comprised between 78 and 82 per cent of the total physical assets from 1870 to 1935. Then, financing farm real estate was more important than financing capital items, such as machinery and power, that came into greater prominence after 1935.

The farmers, to a very appreciable extent, financed the increases in farm capital with their own savings and incomes. Beginning in 1900, but

---

[10] Alvin S. Tostlebe, *Capital in Agriculture: Its Formation and Financing Since 1870* (Princeton: Princeton Univ. Press, 1957), pp. 4–5, 11–14.

[11] Thorstein Veblen, *Absentee Ownership* (New York: B. W. Huebsch, 1923), p. 136.

[12] Tostlebe, *Capital in Agriculture*, pp. 11–14.

omitting the years 1910 to 1919, this new capital came from the gross income of the farmers, and to a lesser extent from loans and book credit. The volume of new farm capital financed with credit was always important, but it was relatively small when compared with the self-financing efforts of the farmers.

After the First World War a noticeable change occurred in the sources of outside credit. This was especially true after 1920 when Federal and federally-sponsored agencies made available large sums of money to the farmers, and the reliance on local banks, individuals, and mortgage companies diminished. This trend was accelerated during the 1930's and on down to the end of the Second World War.[13]

Also bearing upon the productivity of the soil, and reflecting upon the wisdom of our land policy, was the size of the farm labor force. In 1870 some 6,800,000 persons, comprising 53 per cent of the total labor force of the nation, worked on farms as operators, hired hands, or unpaid family laborers. Their numbers increased steadily until they reached an all-time high of 11,592,000 in 1910. Meanwhile, the number of those engaged in nonagricultural pursuits increased at a much faster rate, so that those engaged in agriculture comprised about 31 per cent of the total labor force. By 1930, the number actually engaged in agricultural pursuits had declined to 10,472,000 or 21 per cent of the persons engaged in all occupations.[14]

The output of agricultural products continued to rise after 1920, when a period of capital stagnation set in about as rapidly as when the farm labor force and capital formation were expanding. This continued rise in productivity, despite the decline in the traditional factors of production, that is, land, labor, and capital, merely emphasizes the impact that technology was having on agriculture.

The increase in the farm output after 1920 is attributable not to an increase in the land area, as was the case during the earlier expansive years, but to the assumption by the nonfarming sectors of the economy of some of the functions formerly performed by the farmers themselves. A conspicuous illustration of this is the supplanting of animal power with tractors, motor vehicles, and fuel provided by industry. Also important were the changes in methods, equipment, livestock, and crops that conserved both capital and labor while they increased the farm output.[15]

Especially noteworthy is that the rate of output was accelerated after 1920, despite the shrinkage in the size of the labor force, chiefly as a result of the rise in capital per farm worker. The national average of capital per person engaged in farming rose from $2,900 in 1870 to $4,400 in 1920.[16]

[13] *Ibid.*, pp. 19–20.
[14] *Ibid.*, pp. 46–47.
[15] *Ibid.*, pp. 20–21.
[16] This is expressed in terms of 1910–1914 prices.

The rate of increase was about 10 per cent per decade, and this was maintained despite the 68 per cent increase in the number of persons in farming. This upward trend in capital per worker continued after 1920, when capital formation was checked or actually declined, owing to the dwindling size of the labor force. This continued until the 1940's when farm capital began forming at a very vigorous rate.[17]

As indicated, land policy or the lack of it, in itself, cannot be blamed for everything that ailed agriculture. More than land entered into the raising and marketing the products of the farm and in influencing the over-all effects. The highly individualistic nature of agriculture, the world-wide character of the competition, the weather and the climate, the peculiar production and distribution problems of the farmers, the policies of foreign governments, the difficulties involved in attempting to adjust production to demand, as well as an over-extended land area all had a hand. It is difficult to state precisely to what degree a faulty land policy, as against the aforementioned influences, contributed to the maladjustment between production and distribution. Suffice it to say that it was a significant contributing force.

One of the obvious consequences of our uninhibited expansion was the spread of commercial agriculture and the growing dependence of the producer on the market. Once the farmer left his subsistence basis and risked all on staples such as wheat, he assumed the characteristics of an ordinary businessman with all his risks and anxieties. As a commercial producer, he found himself handicapped in his dealings with men and markets. In the self-sufficing state his daily tasks revolved around his family, which he dominated in theory if not always in fact; in the commercial stage, he was confronted with the problem already alluded to and a host of other interrelated matters to which he once believed himself immune. His subsistence psychology carried over into an industry that was hazardous, unstable, and highly competitive.[18]

The farmer was one of the most individualistic, independent, and "unbunched person" in the world. Contact with the world had given him stiffness in the backbone which, on occasions, made him assertive; but generally speaking he stood, thought, planned, and struggled as an individual, ignorant of the deep economic currents at work, unable to communicate with other farmers, and found himself at the mercy of organized groups that were prepared to exploit him.[19]

The divergent interests within agriculture aggravated matters, and made it literally impossible to weld the farmers into a cohesive, well-integrated group. Their orientation was comparable to that of the trade unionist; it was narrow, limited, circumscribed, and selfish; they thought

[17] Tostlebe, *Capital in Agriculture*, pp. 22–23.
[18] Ralph E. Flanders, *Platform for America* (New York: Whittlesey House, 1936), pp. 8–10.
[19] Gove Hambidge, "The Meat in the Agricultural Stew," *Harper's*, CLXXI (July 1935), 245.

and behaved primarily as corn-hog producers, wheat growers, cotton planters, and dairy farmers. Narrow commodity interests such as these found the producers of certain crops working at cross-purposes with the producers of other crops.[20]

There was little hope of the farmers benefiting from the advantages of mass production and distribution. Agriculture gave slight indication of being able to concentrate itself, at this particular time, into massive productive and distributive units comparable to those of General Motors, United States Steel, and Standard Oil. At the peak of the Great Depression, more than 6,000,000 un-co-ordinated farm units were engaged in a mad scramble for markets.

As for organizing them, the farmers were far more difficult to bring together than the laborers, and even more difficult to keep organized. The distances between farms, the rank individualism of the farmers, past failures in organization, recurrent depressions, and a consequent unwillingness to pay dues, and prohibitive organization expenses, were insurmountable barriers. There never was "any glue strong enough to keep the elements in most farm groups stuck together." [21]

American scholars have been less appreciative of the drastic decline in farm exports that set in about the turn of the twentieth century and the possible relationship of the passing of the era of cheap lands. Perhaps this oversight has been due to the fact that the total decline in exports was less pronounced than the decline of specific commodities such as cereals and meats.

These changes in exports partially reflected the unavailability of desirable lands that could be farmed at costs which would enable American farmers to compete with foreign producers, and also in part the effects of a high tariff policy. The diminished importance of American grains and livestock in foreign markets is proof that our framers were encountering stiff competition in these commodities. The occupation of our most productive lands and the consequent rise in the costs of production enabled newer nations such as Argentina, Australia, and Canada to step in and provide the additional food and raw material needs of the Europeans at less cost, since they had a greater reserve of unused fertile lands. On the other hand, the increase in cotton and tobacco exports emphasized the dependence of the Europeans on the South for goods their own farmers were unable to produce.[22]

Our rapid industrialization, which was accelerated in part by our

[20] Harry Schwartz, "On the Wage Structure of Agriculture," *Political Science Quarterly*, LVII, No. 3 (Sept. 1942), 413; see also, Eric Englund, "The Dilemma of the Corn Belt," *World's Work*, LIII (Nov. 1926), 46–47.

[21] Theodore Saloutos, "The American Farm Bureau Federation and Farm Policy: 1933–1945," *Southwestern Social Science Quarterly*, XXVIII, No. 4 (March 1948), 316; Hambidge, "The Meat in the Agricultural Stew," p. 245.

[22] "Agricultural Exports in Relation to Land Policy," *Supplementary Report of the Land Planning Committee to the National Resources Board*, Part II (Washington: Govt. Printing Office, 1935), p. 6.

expanding land area, had an adverse effect on the demand for American farm products abroad. This is a phase in our economic history that needs great emphasis. Up to 1898 our cereals, livestock products, cotton and tobacco found an insatiable European market because American obligations were repaid to a very considerable extent with the products of the farm. We were providing the greatest bargain-basement counter in the history of American agriculture, and our English and continental creditors were taking advantage of it. These goods went to Europe without the United States receiving an equivalent in kind.[23]

By the opening of the twentieth century this one-way traffic began tapering off. As our dependence on English and European manufactures declined and American tariff walls rose, the Europeans struck back by curtailing their imports of American farm products.

The agrarian policies of the major European nations likewise accounted in part for the decline in the foreign market. France's geographic position and fear of a blockade in the event of a war drove her toward self-sufficiency. Germany, which occupied a geographic position less favorable than France, was inspired by similar motives and likewise committed herself to a policy of self-sufficiency. Tariffs, bounties, and special transportation rates were framed to enable German farmers to face foreign competition.

The reasons a farm crisis did not develop, while the foreign market in wheat and meat was contracting, are to be found in our population increases, the growing demands of an industrial society for food, and the belief that our food supplies were barely keeping pace with our population increases. Our rapid industrialization, for the time being, seems to have whittled down the excessive supply of farm products. Furthermore, the exchange ratio of farm products for those of industry was steadily rising, to the advantage of the farmers, who were receiving a good return on their investment.[24]

By 1933, there was no notable increase in the total consumption of farm products per capita since the opening of the twentieth century, and no sizeable net increase in the crop or pasture area, despite a population increase of 22,000,000 since 1917. The growing use of the automobile and tractor, and the substitution of gasoline for horse feed, released some 30,000,000 acres of crop land for meat and milk animals. Improvements in animal husbandry brought about a greater production of meat and milk

[23] *Farmers in a Changing World, Yearbook of American Agriculture* (Washington: Govt. Printing Office, 1940), p. 571.

[24] J. L. Coulter, "Agricultural Development in the United States, 1900–1910," in T. N. Carver, ed., *Readings in Rural Economics* (Boston: Ginn & Co., 1916), p. 322; Edwin G. Nourse, "Agriculture," in *Recent Economic Changes in the United States,* II (New York: National Bureau of Economic Research, 1929), 553; Nourse, *American Agriculture and the European Market* (New York: McGraw-Hill Book Co., 1924), p. 42.

that resulted in an economy of approximately 25,000,000 acres of crop land. Other contributing causes were the shifts from the less productive to the more productive crops, that is, from corn to cotton in the South, from wheat to corn in the western corn belt, and from beef cattle and sheep to dairy cattle and swine. Farm exports that had been shrinking to new low levels required less than 10 per cent of the farm land for their production. It appeared at the time that the population of the nation, and not foreign demand, would remain the dominant factor influencing the use of land for crops and pasture.[25]

Meanwhile, the progress that farmers had made in the distribution of their farm products was essentially this. Considerable progress had been made in the co-operative marketing of livestock, wheat, dairy products, and fruits, under the influence of general farmer organizations, independent co-operative associations, the agricultural colleges, and the Federal Government. Enabling legislation was enacted by many, if not the majority of the states, to encourage the more efficient marketing of crops; the Capper-Volstead Act proved a great help in interstate commerce; and the Agricultural Marketing Act, under President Hoover, provided a revolving fund of half a billion dollars to encourage large-scale marketing, and engage in price-stabilization operations. But the co-operatives, useful as they were from a long-range point of view in bringing to the farmers a larger share of the consumer's dollar, really were not the answer to the maladjustments in production and demand that had been brought about in part by an overexpansion of the land area.[26]

It is hardly surprising that agriculture became less important as a source of national income. In 1909, income from agriculture constituted almost 19 per cent of the total from all sources, but during the agricultural boom of the war and postwar period, 1918–1919, it rose to 20.5 per cent. However, with the drastic decline in farm prices beginning late in 1920, the percentage of national income derived from farms fell to 12.6 per cent in 1921. By 1929 it dropped as low as 10.4 per cent, and continued its downward course after that.[27]

The average prices the farmers received from 1869 to 1929 were influenced primarily by the general financial and business conditions of the times, and only partially by changes in the aggregate volume of agricultural production. In the cases of some individual commodities, the variations in production assumed greater importance as price factors. Average farm prices were affected by the downward course of farm production in general. During the late 1870's, the late 1880's, and the late 1890's, when

[25] O. E. Baker, "Land Utilization," *Encyclopaedia of the Social Sciences*, IX (New York: Macmillan Co., 1937), 132–33.

[26] Theodore Saloutos and John D. Hicks, *Agricultural Discontent in the Middle West, 1900–1939* (Madison: Univ. of Wisconsin Press, 1951), pp. 128–30, 554–56.

[27] Maurice Leven, Harold G. Moulton, and Clark Warburton, *America's Capacity to Consume* (Washington: The Brookings Institution, 1934), pp. 19–21.

production exceeded the long-time trend, prices took a dip. During the late 1870's and 1890's, the large volume of production intensified the decline in farm prices that was due to other causes. During the late 1880's, on the other hand, the large volume of production prevented farm prices from fully responding to the prosperity conditions in the domestic market.

The rise in farm prices from 1890 to 1914 was somewhat more regular than the decline in the years after the Civil War. But here, too, the effect on prices of volume in excess of normal was apparent, especially from 1904 to 1906.

From 1914 to 1932, three distinct periods in price levels stand out: the inflation and deflation associated with the First World War, the relatively stable price situation of the 1920's, and the second major price collapse between 1929 and 1932.

The entire period after the First World War was one in which farm prices and income followed a downward course as they did after the Civil War, with two periods of price and income markedly below the general downward trend, those of 1921 and 1932, and one period, that of 1925–1929, when prices and income were above the course of the downward trend.[28]

A comparison between the composition of the total gross income for the calendar years 1869 and 1929 indicates the changes in the relative importance of the various groups of commodities. For 1869 the estimated gross income of the commodities studied was about $2,350,000,000; and for 1929 it was more than $10,700,000,000, or an increase of 350 per cent. The income from textile raw materials rose by about the same percentage, and the income from staple food products and slaughtered livestock by slightly more than 200 per cent; while the income from dairy and poultry products and fruits increased more than 800 and 1,000 per cent respectively.[29]

Prior to 1933, the most outstanding modifications in Federal land policy applied chiefly to nonagricultural lands. The setting aside of millions of acres of public lands in the West of scenic, scientific or historical interest was recognition that individual ownership and utilization of land was not always consistent with the general welfare. Little by little, this principle of public ownership and administration of land was extended to justify acquisition by the Federal Government of lands in private ownership. But generally speaking, little if any progress was made in formulating a policy with respect to agricultural lands.[30]

A study of the protests of farmer organizations indicates that relatively

[28] Frederick Strauss and Louis H. Bean, *Gross Farm Income and Indices of Farm Production and Prices in the United States, 1869–1937*, U. S. Agriculture Dept., Technical Bulletin No. 703 (1940), p. 6.

[29] *Ibid.*

[30] Gray, "Objectives in the Land Use Planning Programs," p. 4.

few attributed the problems of overproduction and poor distribution to an overexpanded land area. The organized farmers, through their leaders, emphasized the growth of trusts and combinations, the inability of farmers to fix prices, the army of middlemen that preyed on the producers, the lack of credit, the tariff and related topics. Scholars tended to emphasize farm management practices, scientific agriculture, a cleaner rural life, the finding of new markets, home demonstration work, and the like. While the farmers, through their general organizations, were quicker to emphasize the distribution aspects of agriculture, the scholars, the agricultural press, the better educated farmers, and the agricultural colleges tended to stress the need for bigger and better production. About the only concern expressed over the land was in keeping it out of the hand of monopolists, corporations, speculators, and foreigners. An examination of farmer-organization and farmer-politician demands during the 1920's shows a heavy emphasis on topics such as tariff equality, a fair-exchange ratio for the products of the farm, large-scale co-operative marketing, and liberalized credit facilities. There were, to be sure, demands such as retiring acres from cultivation, but these were the demands of a vocal but ineffective minority.[31]

Even though the interest in land utilization increased throughout the 1920's, and the wisdom of John Wesley Powell's recommendations was belatedly recognized, the entire subject was in its formative stages as late as 1933. This made it difficult to determine what elements were to enter into a land policy that was reflective of the changed demographic, social, and economic conditions of the nation. The general assumption was that if economic conditions warranted, progress in the techniques of production would continue at an accelerated pace. In view of this, the former Federal and state policies of land utilization were obsolete, if not injurious. Among the extreme recommendations to emerge from the conference on land utilization in 1931 was one asking for the licensing and regulating of all land development and settlement enterprises.

By 1933, several dominant thoughts occupied the minds of the policy-makers in the matter of land needs. The foreign market for farm products had dropped to a minimum, and it then appeared unlikely that any portion of it would be recovered in the immediate future; our population was growing at a relatively slow rate and the human needs for food were limited; techniques of agricultural production had been greatly improved; and our capabilities of producing had greatly outstripped our capacities to absorb these products at a profit to the producers. The belief was growing that the adjustment of production to demand could be achieved through acreage retirement, help undo some of the effects of

[31] Saloutos and Hicks, *Agricultural Discontent in the Middle West,* pp. 128–30, 554–56; John D. Hicks, *The Populist Revolt* (Minneapolis: Univ. of Minnesota Press, 1931), pp. 427–44.

faulty land policies and thus partially compensate for the errors of the past.[32]

In summary, our agricultural land policies had a distinct bearing on production and distribution, but it is difficult if not impossible to segregate faulty land policy from other contributing factors, and fairly assess upon each the degree to which it was responsible for the maladjustments in production and distribution. The significance of land policy cannot be underestimated, but it would be misleading to make it the doormat for everything that ailed agriculture.

Our agricultural land policies had failed to bring about as wide a diffusion of land ownership among farm families as once had been thought desirable. The advocates of the homestead policy hoped that once a settler acquired ownership of the land he would see to it that it remained in the family for years to come. Some settlers succeeded in doing this, others failed, and still others did not even try. Mounting capital requirements, inflexible credit terms, the need for drastic adjustments in farm sizes, changing farming methods, machinery and technology, and the laws of inheritance made it difficult for the owner-operator to function within the original limits of the homestead act, and to retain the farm. Changes in the size and ownership of the farm became necessary. Many settlers had to sell or go into debt to purchase additional land at terms that were ill-adapted to their needs. Farm tenancy and farm foreclosures became common.

Tenancy increased in two regions in which homesteads were created: in the North Central states, where the proportion of farms operated by tenants rose from 20 per cent in 1880 to 40 per cent in 1930, and in the West South Central states, where tenancy increased from 35 to 62 per cent over the same period. We cannot blame this solely on the Federal homestead policy, for large areas had been granted to railroads, the states, and other agencies, which in turn sold land to investors, speculators, or settlers. Perhaps these nonhomesteaded areas contributed more than their proportionate share to the growth of tenancy. In the South, factors unrelated to the homestead policy contributed to the rise of tenancy after the Civil War. Many wondered whether this trend, if permitted to continue, would undermine the position of the family farm.

B. H. Hibbard wrote in rather strident tone about the over-all effects of our homestead policy. "All in all, the homestead acts served to spread population too rapidly over a wide stretch of territory. Social relationships suffered, education lagged and, most basically, the prices of farm products collapsed. Land was being used too soon and in too great quantities in relation to other occupations and developments. The economic machine was thrown out of balance." Of course, this same argument can be

---

[32] Baker, "Land Utilization," *Encyclopaedia of the Social Sciences*, IX, 136. See also Edward A. Duddy, *Conference on Economic Policy for American Agriculture* (Chicago: Univ. of Chicago Press, 1932).

levelled at the land-sales policies of the railroads, private land companies, and various other agencies that were instrumental in peopling the new farm areas.

Might-have-beens do not fall within the province of the historian, but one cannot help but ask whether the restless political climate of the time would have tolerated the slow, deliberate, and seasoned program of settlement that scholarly hindsight bears out as being the more desirable. It appears unlikely. It is not a question of which was the more desirable policy, but what policy was acceptable in the light of existing conditions.[33]

At the same time, it would be unfair to ignore some of the contributions that were rendered by what many of us consider to have been a short-sighted land policy. The rapid settlement of the land contributed to the relative abundance of cheap food, which in turn hastened the economic growth of the nation. Much of our national progress during the latter part of the nineteenth century may be attributed, at least in part, to the expansion of the agricultural areas of the nation. The agricultural base on which so much of the industrial expansion of the nation has been built has been too often overlooked by the historian.

In the final analysis, it appears that it was not simply a faulty land policy that was to blame, as much as it was a growing inability on the part of a large number of small farmers to adapt themselves to capitalistic methods of production and distribution.

[33] Rainer Schickele, *Agricultural Policy* (New York: McGraw-Hill Book Co., 1954), pp. 364–67.

Migratory Labor

22. The I.W.W. in the Grain Belt

Philip Taft

The withdrawal of the Western Federation of Miners in 1907 marked a turning point in the history of the Industrial Workers of the World. After the Federation's departure, the I.W.W. developed into an organization whose energies were largely devoted to agitation. Members of the I.W.W. played a prominent role in taking over the leadership of spontaneous

"The I.W.W. in the Grain Belt," by Philip Taft, is reprinted by permission from *Labor History*, I (Winter, 1960), 53–67.

strikes of unorganized workers who left their jobs in protest against conditions they could no longer bear. McKees Rock, Lawrence, Paterson, Little Falls and Akron are inextricably linked with this phase of I.W.W. activity. The free speech fight was another type of agitation prominently carried on in the period between 1909 and 1915. Attempts by local authorities to restrict or suppress street corner meetings led to passive resistance, which usually flared into free speech fights. Hundreds of footloose free speech fighters would flock to the scene of the disorder, mount soap boxes, and court arrest. Local communities found it expensive to fill the jails and sometimes, as in San Diego, California, reacted with brutal violence. Spokane, Fresno, and Sioux City were the scenes of other spectacular free speech demonstrations.

The free speech fights attracted widespread attention and even aroused sympathy among many who were otherwise hostile to the doctrine and activities of the I.W.W., but they did not have any significant organizational results. Except for a few former members of the Western Federation of Miners and a scattering of others like William E. Troutmann, a former leader of the Brewery Workers, who left the I.W.W. after the Lawrence strike, soapboxers dominated the organization during this period. Their conception of the function of the I.W.W. is reflected in the comment of James P. Thompson, for a time general organizer, on the Lawrence textile strike. An extremely effective street orator, Thompson was called in to help run the strike. For him, the strike was "one big propaganda meeting. Every hour that the strike lasted the One Big Union idea was spreading like wildfire. The strikers of Lawrence were actually teaching the country how to fight."[1]

Propaganda had become the main function of the I.W.W., which had virtually developed into a propaganda league. Some of its leading members felt that it should abandon any pretense of being an economic organization and devote its energies exclusively to agitation and, wherever possible, to boring-from-within the conservative unions of the American Federation of Labor.

Curiously, while at this time the I.W.W. was ineffective as an economic labor organization, on a minuscule scale it showed some of the symptoms usually associated with business unionism. In 1912 complaints were heard that "several of the Locals have suffered in the past year from defaulting secretaries."[2] The Lawrence textile strike, which began in January 1912, was not unattended by scandal. Over $68,000 was expended on the relief of strikers and their families, but some of the funds collected for these purposes were misused.

In 1914, the I.W.W. seemed completely spent. True, this was only a year after the spectacular Paterson silk strike, a struggle which aroused

[1] *Solidarity*, October 19, 1912.
[2] *Industrial Worker*, October 24, 1912.

national attention. But neither this nor the previous dramatic strikes had led to the creation or establishment of permanent unions in the industries involved. A notable exception occurred in Philadelphia, where a group of dock workers, the majority Negroes, had applied for a charter, and struck for recognition on May 13, 1913. After a strike of two weeks, the dock workers won recognition of their union and the right to bargain collectively. The I.W.W. was opposed to signing agreements, but the Philadelphia longshoremen were able to agree to contract terms, and they carried out their agreement faithfully.

From the start the Philadelphia dock workers encountered a number of difficult problems because of their affiliation with the I.W.W. These eventually led to a severance of their affiliation. The I.W.W. required that its constituent units accept the card of a member of another branch without additional charges for initiation. This free transfer system meant that a member could shift from one division to any other, as long as he had or sought employment in an area in which an I.W.W. unit operated. The desire of many footloose members to transfer at different times to the Philadelphia longshoremen's local inevitably created a problem. When the I.W.W. insisted the local reduce the initiation fee, which had been raised to $25.00 to limit new entrants, it withdrew.

The Philadelphia longshoremen's branch and a local of Italian bakery workers in New York were the only stable unions the I.W.W. was able to establish prior to 1916. The low state of I.W.W. fortunes in 1914 may be inferred from the fact that less than 1,700 votes were cast in the election for secretary-treasurer, the highest office in the organization.[3] (Publicly the I.W.W. claimed 25,000 or more members.) Vincent St. John, who had been the previous secretary-treasurer, refused to be a candidate for re-election. Since he was a veteran unionist, his refusal was perhaps an expression of disillusionment with the possibilities of building an economic organization independent of the traditional unions. In any event, the record of the I.W.W. made it abundantly clear that it could not build viable "on the job" organizations. It was much better adapted to engaging in colorful battles with police and local authorities than to recruiting and organizing stable and steady workers.

It was during this ebb in its fortunes that there occurred a development which, were it not for the intervention of World War I, might have transformed the I.W.W. into a powerful economic organization of unskilled and semi-skilled workers. During the convention of 1914, Frank Little, a member of the General Executive Board suggested that "some means should be taken for concerted and efficient action in the harvest fields next year. It was proposed that a conference be held composed of members from different locals bordering the harvest district, and that this

[3] *Solidarity,* March 10, 1914.

conference [devise] ways and means for harmonious grouping of hitherto spasmodic efforts of harvest organizations." [4]

At harvest time, farmers in the Middle Western grain belt found it necessary to hire considerable additional labor. Not all of this labor could be provided by the cities and towns in the area; hence the farmers depended upon thousands of workers who migrated from cities such as Kansas City, Omaha, etc., although some workers came from even more distant points. The harvesting of winter wheat would begin in Southern Oklahoma in late May or early June, depending upon the season; and gradually expand into Eastern, Central, and Western Kansas and into the grain-growing areas of Nebraska. A minority of harvest hands would remain for the threshing, but the larger group would move in a series of northward jumps so as to be on hand for employment in the spring wheat areas of Minnesota, the Dakotas, and Eastern Montana; some would move as far north as Saskatchewan and Alberta. Not all harvest hands started in the fields of Oklahoma or Kansas; there were those who worked only in one or in several adjacent states.

Farmers with one hundred acres in grain might require five to seven extra men for harvesting. On the average, a harvest hand might be able to get from seven to fourteen days work from a single job. As the grain ripened simultaneously in the same area, most harvesters would be compelled to move North and West once they finished a job in a given section of a state. The fortunate ones might finish the season as members of a threshing crew with twenty-five to sixty days of steady work. Threshing was carried on by crews from fourteen to twenty-two men, some of them usually from the surrounding farms or the immediate area. Some workers were hired by the farmer and the rest of the crew by the contractor.[5]

After finishing the grain harvest, some men usually moved into Iowa and Nebraska for corn husking. Others would try their luck at potato picking in Western and Central Minnesota, and still others would seek employment in the sugar beet factories of Western Nebraska. The oil field worker went back to Kansas and Oklahoma, Texas or Louisiana, and the lumberjack normally found his way back to the woods in the Middle Western lumbering areas or to the short logs in Montana and Idaho. Many harvesters sought only a "stake" large enough to enable them to move into a housekeeping room in one of the cities adjacent to the grain belt. By frugal management, they hoped to go through the winter with a minimum of work. Such hopes were often not realized; inadequate earnings, as well as danger and temptation, were the frequent lot of the harvest hand.

The harvest fields were a magnet for thousands of workers. Some came from places hundreds and even thousands of miles distant. Men who

[4] Ibid., October 10, 1914.
[5] Don D. Lescohier, "Conditions Affecting the Demand for Labor in the Grain Belt," United States Department of Agriculture Bulletin 1230, April 1924, pp. 6–13.

worked at strawberry picking in Arkansas might come into Southern Oklahoma to replenish their income. There were also those who "made" the harvest annually: the oil field pipe liner or roustabout, the lumber worker, the mule skinner without a road job, and the migrant who moved from place to place picking up an occasional job. The ranks of the perennials would be swelled by a scattering of college students in search of tuition and adventure and, in times of more than normal unemployment, by more venturesome factory workers. The large mass of strangers who invaded the grain areas inevitably attracted a number of undesirables. These included the tinhorn gambler, the highjack (the term came from the orders of the stickup man, who addressing his victim as "Jack," told him to raise his hands "high"), and in dry areas, the bootlegger. Railroad brakemen were also a problem. The men who came to the harvest would usually steal rides on top of freight trains, and the brakeman might ask: "What are you riding on?" The question was, in effect, a request for a dollar, although some brakemen would recognize a union card in lieu of payment.

Until they got work, most harvest hands arriving in the grain area would be forced to sleep in box cars and eat in "jungles," areas adjacent to the local stockyards or beside a brook or a spring. Through use of tin cans and makeshift frying pans, it would be possible to prepare an inexpensive cooperative meal which might be shared with those without money. Upon completion of a job, the men would return to the jungles to "boil up," that is wash and mend their clothes, before moving to the next point. The bootlegger and cardsharp infested the jungles hoping, and often succeeding, to separate the harvester from his hard-earned wages. Highjacks rode the trains, relieving the hapless victims of their monies and sometimes seriously injuring those whom they compelled to leave the train while it was moving rapidly through the countryside. The communities in which the harvest hands congregated were not always overjoyed at the presence of their out-of-town guests. Of course, the welfare of the town might depend upon the availability of harvest labor, for otherwise it might not be possible to bring in the crops. But many of the workers created police and sanitary problems, and the best the harvest hands would normally receive was a grudging welcome from the townspeople.

Distribution of harvest labor was imperfect. A short crop or a large supply of hands meant a surplus of labor, and forced many to remain in town without employment or funds to support themselves. Begging or stealing inevitably aroused the local populace which might order the unwelcome strangers out of town. On the other hand, a sudden ripening of grain over a wide area might deplete the available labor supply and lead to a serious shortage of help.

The I.W.W. at the time consisted mainly of independent local industrial unions and recruiting unions. The latter were analogous to the federal labor unions of the A.F.L. in that workers of every type and grade joined one unit. The difference was that the A.F.L. regarded these units as temporary organizational devices whose members would eventually be distributed among various affiliates. The local industrial unions and re-cruiting unions of the I.W.W. contained relatively few members and were of no significance as unions. There were also a few national industrial unions in the I.W.W., largely paper organizations of no importance.

The locals in such places as Kansas City and St. Joseph, Missouri; Omaha, Nebraska; and Minneapolis, Minnesota, which bordered on the Middle Western grain belt, usually sent their delegates into the harvest fields in a competitive endeavor to recruit members among the thousands of migratory workers who annually flocked to these areas in search of employment. The proposal of Frank Little to the 1914 convention was thus designed to establish cooperation among the different locals on a common organizational program in the grain fields.

Soon after the adjournment of the 1914 convention, William D. ("Big Bill") Haywood, the new secretary-treasurer, announced the I.W.W. would establish a Bureau of Migratory Workers. He declared that "an organized effort will be made to circumvent the schemes of the labor bureaus and employment sharks." He attacked the existing exploitation of the migrant worker and described the procedures followed by I.W.W. members in the harvest belt during the crop season. "The I.W.W.," Haywood said, "form in groups and establish what may be called com-munity life in the jungles. When a crowd of members of this organization leave a train near the station, they go to the outskirts of the town or the bank of a stream if convenient. There a meeting is called, a Camp Committee is elected, the formation of which is to see the camp is kept clean and sanitary. A job committee is selected to rustle the town for work. . . . Every man is expected to do some work around camp, though there are some of parasitic nature who accept service without giving service; these are called 'Jungle Buzzards.' But they are not tolerated for long by the I.W.W. Gamblers and 'Stick-ups' infest all harvest gangs, but in the I.W.W. camps the rule, No Gambling, is strictly observed." [6]

As directed by the convention, Secretary-Treasurer Haywood convened a conference in Kansas City of locals adjacent to the grain belt. The conference took place on April 21, 1915. Its purpose was to work out a unified organization program for the harvest fields. Earlier Haywood had suggested that the conference might establish a central office separate from the locals, and that a general organizer should be appointed to direct the organizing campaign. He also recommended the application of uni-form dues and initiation schedules throughout the entire Middle Western

[6] William D. Haywood, "To Migratory Workers," *Solidarity*, November 28, 1914.

grain belt. The individual locals would be prohibited from following their own inclinations in these matters.

Nine locals were represented at the conference, and the delegates established the Agricultural Workers Organization 400. Haywood later declared that the number "400" had been suggested by him because he regarded the migratory worker in the harvest belt as making up the elite which would regenerate the labor movement and as fitted to carry out the more difficult tasks of organization. A secretary and an agitation committee, later to become the organization committee, were chosen. The conference voted, "if there is any surplus of finances at the end of the season in the treasury of the Agricultural Workers Organization, that it be used for organizing work among the migratory workers." [7] The conference formulated the following demands: A minimum wage of $3.00 a day; 50 cents overtime for every hour worked above ten in one day; adequate board and good places to sleep; and no discrimination against members of the I.W.W.

The first organizing campaign got under way in June in Oklahoma and Kansas.[8] A statement issued by the agitation committee, "Harvesting the Harvesters," declared that "Kansas is full of tin-horn gamblers and crooks of all kinds. These human vultures follow up the harvest in order to harvest the harvesters. They go ahead with their business unmolested. . . . Gambling and holdups are in full swing. It seems as if the authorities are encouraging it, as there is nothing done in the way of stopping it. . . . The I.W.W. organization is referred to as 'I won't work' and the members are charged with that they never work. But gamblers don't work and they are OK. . . . And the only reason the employers are against the I.W.W.'s is that they Do Work." [9] The agitation committee asked all I.W.W. members to transfer to the Agricultural Workers' Organization 400.

The tactics pursued by A.W.O. 400 were highly successful. From July 1, 1915 to December 31, 1915, the A.W.O. initiated 2,208 members and accumulated $14,113.06 in its treasury.[10] Such prosperity had seldom been enjoyed by any unit of the I.W.W. since the departure of the Western Federation of Miners. And this comparison is somewhat misleading, since the Western Federation of Miners was a going concern long before the I.W.W. had been established. The initiation of more than two thousand workers in a period of several months—most of the newly organized were recruited between June and October—may not appear to be a striking feat, but by the usual organizing standards of the I.W.W., it was of great

[7] *Solidarity*, April 24, 1915.
[8] *Ibid.*, June 26, 1915.
[9] *Ibid.*, July 10, 1915.
[10] *Ibid.*, March 18, 1916.

significance. Few units of the I.W.W. had up to that time been able to do as well organizationally and financially, although relief and defense expenditures in several of the strikes were considerably greater.[11]

The success of the drive in the harvest fields had repercussions in other parts of the organization. The *Monthly Bulletin* issued by the General Office "suggested that in view of the successful work of the A.W.O., similar methods should be adopted for the lumber, mining and other migratory workers' industries." [12]

In the summer of 1916 the A.W.O. organizing campaign in the harvest fields went in to high gear. Under the slogan "Come on 400," the A.W.O. began the forced initiation of thousands of harvest workers. Organizers and their aids, some armed with clubs, pickhandles and guns, virtually took over the freight trains entering the harvest fields. No one was allowed to ride unless he could show a card issued by the A.W.O. 400 or another I.W.W. unit. In many instances, men who refused to join were unloaded, forced to get off the trains, or denied use of the jungles.

The campaign was directed by the A.W.O. Organization Committee whose members were each given a territory to supervise. Stationary delegates were located at the principal points in the grain belt during the harvest season; among others, Enid, Oklahoma; Wichita and Ellis, Kansas; Fargo and Minot, North Dakota; Aberdeen, South Dakota. The actual organizing work was carried on by delegates or volunteers who were given credentials by the stationary delegates or by members of the organization committee. Groups of these delegates and their supporters combed the freight trains in search for non-members, who were requested or forced to join. Since commissions were paid for new members, an incentive beyond mere loyalty to the I.W.W. prompted the use of force.

These organizational methods led to a sharp increase in income and membership, and the monies were used to expand organization work in industries utilizing migratory labor. Nevertheless, not all members were happy with the new approach. Forrest Edwards, who was elected secretary of the A.W.O. in 1916, obliquely defended it. "Objections are frequently made to the methods of the '400.' Some say the methods are too severe. In fact, this seems to be the general opinion of oldtime I.W.W. men. This new blood is putting over stuff and getting away with it so that the old wobbly seem amazed at it." The organizers of the A.W.O. established what they called an 800-mile picket line "that reached from Kansas to Aberdeen, South Dakota. The longest picket line . . . simply represented an effort to keep non-union men off the job." [13] Nevertheless the strong arm tactics created serious dangers for the organization. The older

---

[11] *Ibid.*, January 8, 1916.
[12] *Ibid.*, August 28, 1915.
[13] Forrest Edwards, "The Class War in Harvest Country," *Solidarity*, August 19, 1916.

members recognized forceful recruiting techniques were not effective ways of promoting loyalty and stability. Joining, they felt, should be a voluntary act based upon sympathy for, and understanding of, the principles of the I.W.W. Yet the large increase in revenue and members obscured for many the dangers which the ruthless shock tactics held. The undesirables, who were a menace to the safety of the honest harvest hand, frequently took out a card for the protection which membership gave them. In a letter to *Solidarity*, a correspondent described the shooting and robbing of a member of the A.W.O. by a bandit who had "joined the organization merely as a shield and with the view of using the Union as a means of self-protection. Whatever good such characters have ever done for the Union has been upset by later actions." [14] Nor was this an isolated incident, for as the writer indicates, many tinhorns, highjacks and other undesirables joined the I.W.W. as a cover for their criminal activities. The "working stiffs" were bitterly opposed to the influx of this alien element. Bitter debates on the attitude to be taken towards these men took place, but the issue was never resolved.

These "holdup" tactics, which could hardly be morally justified, had nevertheless a stimulating effect upon the general organization. Even more important was the comparatively large increase in monies flowing into the treasury of the A.W.O. The new resources enabled the I.W.W., aided by the Agricultural Workers Organization, to undertake campaigns in the lumber industry and in others as well.

At a mass conference, held by the A.W.O. in October 1916, it was reported that 18,000 members had been initiated since April 1915. The meeting decided to establish an industrial union, and elected an organization [executive] committee. [15] Elsewhere the effect of the campaign in the harvest fields was noted from increases in income received at the general headquarters of the I.W.W. For the year ending August 31, 1915, the income of the I.W.W. was $8,934.47; for the next fiscal year it reached $49,114.84. [16] The additional revenue enabled the I.W.W. to multiply its activity severalfold. During the fiscal year, largely in 1916, it issued 116 charters, the largest number ever issued within a comparable period. [17]

An examination of the journals and the literature of the I.W.W. during this time shows a clear shift in the orientation of the organization. The shift was noted by the editor of *Solidarity* who remarked that the "10th Convention [1916] is remarkable as denoting the decline of the 'soap boxer' as a dominant element." [18]

The 1916 convention of the I.W.W. was largely controlled by the

[14] *Ibid.*, December 22, 1916.
[15] *Ibid.*, November 18, 1916.
[16] *Proceedings of the Tenth Convention of the Industrial Workers of the World, November 10, 1916 to December 1, 1916* (Chicago, 1917), p. 32.
[17] *Ibid.*, p. 36.
[18] *Solidarity*, December 2, 1916.

Agricultural Workers Organization whose 7 delegates held 252 of the 335 votes. The treasury had a cash surplus of $18,000. As a result, for the first time in years the convention witnessed a debate on the size of the salary to be paid the organization's top official.

Inspired by the success of the drives in the harvest fields, the convention voted to reorganize its structure. Under the revised constitution, the I.W.W. was to be made up of industrial departments, industrial unions and their branches, and recruiting unions. The latter were to be composed of wage workers in whose respective industries no industrial union existed. Despite the influence of the A.W.O., Secretary-Treasurer Haywood expressed some misgivings over its widespread activity, which he claimed was more like that of a mass organization than an industrial union. He suggested that the A.W.O. abstain from organizing non-agricultural workers.[19]

In the meantime, the A.W.O. was achieving some success in other industries. In February 1916, Lumber Workers Local No. 315 became part of the A.W.O., and as a consequence the A.W.O. supported financially and organizationally a campaign in the lumber industry. A number of new locals were established. In March 1917, 13 delegates representing A.W.O. branches in Eastern Washington, Idaho, and Western Montana; the Middle Western lumber states of Michigan, Minnesota and Wisconsin, as well as the lumber areas around Seattle and Tacoma, established Lumber Workers Industrial Union No. 500. The initial finances and manpower for this venture were provided by the Agricultural Workers' Organization.[20]

Now for the first time in its history the I.W.W. was functioning regularly as a labor organization. It was using its finances and many new recruits to organize slowly and systematically some of the industrial areas it had staked out for itself. I.W.W. publications of the time reflect this change. Instead of emphasizing free speech fights, they now urged members "to get on the job." They stressed the virtues of employment, of improving conditions on the job, and of organizing new members.

The organizing work of the A.W.O. aroused considerable opposition in the grain belt. About 100 members were arrested in Kansas and in Oklahoma in 1915, most of whom were released after a day or two in jail. Some towns took steps to counteract the demands for a given wage, and recalcitrants might be asked to leave the community. In 1916, several grain belt communities took more vigorous action. But the Non-Partisan League, a farmer's political group functioning at the time mainly in North Dakota, suggested in the spring of 1917 that committees from the League and the I.W.W. meet and work out a schedule of wages, hours of work,

[19] Ibid., p. 4. Preamble and Constitution of the Industrial Workers of the World, 1908, p. 5; 1916, pp. 4–5.
[20] James Rowan, The I.W.W. in the Lumber Industry (no place or date or publisher), p. 25.

and other conditions. A preliminary meeting was actually held. At the same time, the I.W.W.[21] chartered the Metal Mine Workers Industrial Union No. 490 which was to embark upon its stormy career in Montana and Arizona.

Despite opposition from employers, the I.W.W. made its greatest organizational progress in 1916 and early 1917. Its shift away from the resultless, even though dramatic, free speech fights, and its concentration upon organization of the unorganized seemed to hold promise that it would be able to sink roots in some of the industries employing a large complement of unskilled labor. The harvest hands themselves did not always help in promoting organization, even though for several years they provided substantial funds. They were always a serious problem to those who were permanently attached to an industry and hoped to improve conditions through "organizing on the job." The "400 cats," as they were called, were seldom interested in steady employment; they were footloose, undisciplined, had few ties and fewer responsibilities. They were both envious and contemptuous of the steady-working "home guard," and his wife and brood. It was not unusual for the members of 400 "to blow up" a job, that is stage a spontaneous and purposeless "walkoff" or mass resignation. Such action usually came when a number were beginning to tire of the work after several weeks of employment; the "walkoffs" were unaccompanied by demands for improvement.

But the I.W.W. was reaching out for the lumber worker, the road construction hand, the metal miner and both the shoreside and sea-going maritime worker. These workers had considerable attachment to their industry, and normally thought in terms of job improvement as a means of permanent self-improvement. The same was true of the pipe liner and roustabout in the oil fields, largely semi-skilled and unskilled workers permanently attached to an industry, although they were likely to be more mobile than the average industrial employee.

Of course, the industries the I.W.W. sought to win were very difficult to penetrate. Except for the metal mines there was not much of a tradition of labor unionism in most of them. Employees in these industries had, moreover, fewer resources than the average industrial worker, and very likely a lower propensity for remaining organized. Yet it might have been possible to establish some foothold in at least parts of these industrial divisions had not World War I intervened. World War I came when the I.W.W. had partially completed the first extensive organization campaign in the lumber industry, and had established several units in the metal mining camps of the North and Southwest. The lumber and metalliferous strikes, in which it would have been difficult to gain victory under the most favorable circumstances, came in the summer of 1917 at a time when the country was in the first throes of war fever, whipped up by the burgeoning advertising arts. The I.W.W. espousal of direct action and

[21] *Solidarity,* June 9, 1917.

sabotage was interpreted as a violation of the criminal syndicalist laws, which the legislatures of the Northwestern states began to enact in 1917. In addition, the federal government indicted in June 1917 the entire top leadership of the I.W.W., and the secondary leaders who replaced the first group were often subjected to prosecution and harassment largely by the federal authorities during World War I and under state criminal syndicalist statutes throughout the 1920s.

During World War I, I.W.W. publications were suppressed and many of the halls forcibly closed. The hostility against radicalism, expressed by the Palmer Raids in the period after World War I (they were directed by United States Attorney General A. Mitchell Palmer), fell heavily upon the I.W.W. Yet the organization was able to survive and actually staged a minor comeback after World War I.[22] But the postwar suppression through the criminal syndicalist laws continued to rob the I.W.W. of its potential leaders. Organizing became increasingly difficult and the organization slowly withered away, after an enervating controversy over whether the federal prisoners should accept conditional pardons.

The Communists had little effect upon the I.W.W. The average wobbly was not temperamentally good material for Communist discipline. Most members of the I.W.W., especially the non-foreigners who comprised the largest part of the organization, were extreme individualists who would not subject themselves voluntarily to the orders of their organizational superiors upon which Communist discipline is based. With the exception of Haywood and several of the editors of foreign language papers who fled to the Soviet Union after their conviction under the espionage law, few leaders of the I.W.W. went over to the Communist Party. Among the more than 150 who were convicted of violating the espionage law during World War I, only Harrison George and George Hardy became permanently active in the Communist movement. George became an active Communist journalist, and Hardy, a Comintern agent. Charles Ashleigh, who had returned to England after his release from federal prison, was for a time active in the British Communist movement. While serving as a correspondent in Moscow, he was asked to leave the Soviet Union for non-political reasons. The I.W.W. delegate to the founding convention of the Red Labor Union International, George Williams, bitterly assailed the "delegate packing" he had witnessed in Moscow, as well as the arrogance and officiousness of the promoters of the Red Trade Union International.[23] Williams declared that the Congress had been filled with delegates from non-existing organizations, and that the Red Labor Union International would inevitably be dominated by the Communist Party. On December

---

[22] The General Defense Committee estimated that at the beginning of 1920 more than 2,000 members of the I.W.W. were in jail on charges of vagrancy, criminal syndicalism and sedition. *New Solidarity*, January 17, 1920.

[23] *The First Congress of the Red Trade Union International: A Report of the Proceedings by George Williams, Delegate from the Industrial Workers of the World* (Chicago, Illinois: Industrial Workers of the World, no date).

10, 1921, the General Executive Board recommended that "this organization do not affiliate in any manner with the Red Trade Union International." [24] The view was reiterated in the following year, when the Board
again rejected affiliation.[25] There is thus no evidence that the Communists
had much influence on members of the I.W.W.

It is, therefore, possible to assume that if events had not overwhelmed
the I.W.W., it might have been able to carve out a place for itself in the
industrial sectors which had, up to the thirties, been unattractive to the
old line labor organizations. Indeed it is possible that were it not for the
effects of World War I, the I.W.W. would have been transformed into an
economic organization of predominantly unskilled and semi-skilled workers. It is unlikely that the I.W.W. would have ever presented a serious
challenge to the hegemony of the A.F.L. But were it not for wartime
persecution, it might have achieved the status of the Swedish syndicalist
organization, the Central Organization of Labor. It is also likely that with
the winning of job control, the free transfer of members between unions,
which was bound to arouse opposition from those in control of a labor
market, might have been repealed. Even the signing of contracts might
have been accepted as an evil necessary for the exercise of job control. But
events foreclosed these possibilities.

[24] Williams, op. cit., p. 55.
[25] The I.W.W. Reply to the Red Trade Union International (Moscow) by the
General Executive Board (Chicago, Illinois: Industrial Workers of the World, 1922).

Trade Unionism: Gaining a Foothold

23.   The Basic Philosophy of the American Labor Movement

Selig Perlman

THE SCHOOLS

For better or for worse, attempting to formulate anew the philosophy of
labor means taking a position on at least a few of the schools of thought
which have arisen. The Wisconsin School, founded by John R. Commons,
is somewhere in the center of their array from left to right. So, Marxism-

"The Basic Philosophy of the American Labor Movement," by Selig Perlman, is
reprinted by permission from *The Annals of the American Academy of Political and
Social Science*, Vol. 274 (March, 1951), 57–63.

Leninism and Fabianism are to its left, Hobsonism-Keynesianism a somewhat close neighbor, and Elton Mayoism and the school of neoclassical economic theory to its right.

Neoclassical Economic Theory

Let us start with a much-discussed recent version of the last-named school. The Wisconsin School feels dubious about Professor Lindblom's [1] thesis that American trade unionism, in continually pressing for improved conditions of employment, is bound to raise costs above the productivity point and, either through mass unemployment or else through inflation, ultimately cause a collapse of the private enterprise system. This prophecy of doom assumes that management is completely devoid of the power to hold back the pressure by the unions and that it lacks the wits to get in exchange for the "packages" granted to the unions the freedom to introduce cost-reducing changes in production methods, and further, that unions have inexhaustible strike funds and will be so purblind as to persist in digging their own, as well as their industry's, grave.

True, the political wage is not unknown in America, as shown by the several rounds after 1945. But it has had at least two playmates, one of which is already quite ripe in years: the political prices of farm commodities in vogue since 1933, and the political manufacturing profits traceable as far back as the time Daniel Webster changed his stand on the tariff. Consequently, there is more than one potential culprit in the death of capitalism, should it actually come to pass, and among these, labor is the one which, in the nature of the situation, would be obliged to commit its fatal transgressions more publicly and more dramatically than the others.[2]

The Wisconsin School admires the research methods of the industrial sociologists aiming to reach the individual worker's tensions and motives, and it endorses their objective of a higher productivity through industrial harmony. Yet, the Wisconsin School wonders why so many of this truly pathbreaking school have failed to find a place for historical unionism, not only in their schemes for the future, but even in their very awareness.

Fabianism

The Wisconsin School is grateful for detailed and well-arranged personal data [3] about the leaders of labor, especially the younger generation

[1] Charles E. Lindblom, *Unions and Capitalism*, New Haven: Yale University Press, 1949.

[2] Walter A. Morton, "Trade Unionism, Full Employment, and Inflation," in *American Economic Review*, March 1950, pp. 13–39.

[3] C. Wright Mills, *The New Men of Power—America's Labor Leaders* (New York: Harcourt, Brace & Co., 1948).

among them. Yet Mills's designation "The New Men of Power" seems greatly overdrawn. It is not clear whether the book of this title is a tocsin call to a Trotskyite "Permament Revolution" or to a labor party activism. If the former, it would be an incitement to suicide. But, even if it were only the latter, it would still be unrealistic, since it would overlook the strong overrepresentation of the rural and small-town populations in the state and national legislative chambers and their latent, when not actual, fear of an expanding labor movement. A typical example of the incompatibility of farmers and labor, closely observed by this writer, occurred some twenty years ago in the lower house in the Wisconsin legislature— then dominated by farmer "progressives"—when an eight-hour-day bill, introduced by a Milwaukee member, was done to death amid joyous mockery by attaching to it several dozen amendments.

It is true that the leaders of the newer unions, in response to altered conditions (this is treated at length below), to their own outlook, and to the noncraftsman nature of most of their membership, eagerly turn to political action and thus could be optimistically groomed for the "New Men of Power." But, as there is as yet no sign of the removal of the old roadblocks to labor on the political highway—antiurbanism and the adverse feeling of the middle classes as a whole—frustration rather than success will be the likely end result. It is only when these so-called "New Men of Power" join forces with a realistic and fair-dealing political leader of an old political party, especially one with the power of the nation's executive at his command, that they can make an impress on the public process at all! And such a political leader could not even grasp the hankering of some of these new leaders of labor for the intellectually all-inclusive objective instilled in their thinking by an earlier socialistic training. Nor should one underrate the political conservatism within labor itself, even among seasoned unionists. So much for American Fabianism and near-Fabianism.

Modern Marxism

Contiguous to Fabianism is Laski's "Marxism." Laski has never espoused Lenin's methods of recruiting the faithful nor of dictatorship by a revolutionary elite, but his intellectual position is, avowedly, a Marxian one. In his *The American Democracy*,[4] he asks whether America, as she is now, could be trusted with the defense of democracy, and replies that so long as America is business dominated, her custodianship of democracy is, to put it mildly, most uncertain, and that once her capitalists feel endangered, she might even become the breeder of another world war. In his own words "The free enterprise system, the American businessman's

[4] Harold J. Laski, *The American Democracy* (New York: Viking Press, 1948), pp. 200–264.

euphemism for capitalism from which most of the world is seeking to free itself, leads by inexorable stages through crisis to war." [5] Only on condition that American labor take over the reins of power from the business class would America cease to be a menace to democracy and to peace. Now, Laski could not really have been so naïve as to suppose that the America which we now have could be laborized in time to stave off the disaster which he was foretelling as a high possibility, if not a probability. Hence, his stipulation amounted, in effect, to urging upon all genuine democrats a policy of neutrality in the current struggle between the USSR and the USA.

THE MATERIAL UNDERLYING THE WISCONSIN THEORY

The Wisconsin School is a history-conscious school. The individual workman leaves no historical records, but the labor movement does. That is the closest one can get to the experimental method in dealing with social movements. The labor leaders who make policy decisions are virtually experimenters, although obliged to operate without controls. They experiment with the public, which can put them in the doghouse; with the employers, who may decide either to crush them or to deal with them; with the politicians, who may further their cause, act neutral, or worse; and above all, with the loyalty of their membership, who may show battle fatigue sooner or later. The laboratory notes, often discontinuous and scattered, bring out the tensions engendered by the changed conditions, especially those of an economic nature resulting in the rise of bargaining classes. In his Shoemaker article,[6] Professor Commons has reconstructed, after the manner of the paleontologist, the sequence of industrial stages. But the material is wider than the mere economic data; it is, in fact, the whole stream of American history, notably the ideological factors.

The problem of organizing and of staying organized has continued the paramount problem of the American labor movement. In America, we lacked the rigid class divisions to assist capitalism in producing a made-to-order revolutionary working class or even a labor cohesiveness for mere meliorative purposes. The life of the American labor movement was strictly in its own hands, and the American society, with its horizontal and vertical mobility, was indeed a most difficult environment. The leader was, therefore, forever making decisions upon which the very survival of his organization depended. Should Gompers have heeded the call to mobilize the American Federation of Labor to aid the American Railway

---

[5] *Ibid.*, p. 546.
[6] John R. Commons, *Labor and Administration* (New York: The Macmillan Company, 1913), Chapter XIV.

Union in the deadly grip of the Railway Managers' Association and of Attorney-General Richard Olney? Should he have permitted DeLeon to walk off with the AFL? Should he have treated the injunction as merely another one of the devices capitalism will employ to stifle labor, with relief coming when a labor political victory wipes out all oppression, or should he have invoked the traditional American hatred for government by usurpation and have concentrated upon its immediate abolition with the aid of a Bryan or a Woodrow Wilson? Or what position should the AFL have assumed towards the war with Germany in 1917?

These were the questions which life threw at Samuel Gompers, under whose guiding hand American labor has first emerged stable in purpose, if not in size. He called his philosophy "voluntarism" and "trade unionism, pure and simple." This the Wisconsin School has renamed "job consciousness," but with an undiminished admiration for the author.

Dynamic Job Consciousness

The assailants of America's job conscious unionism, from Daniel DeLeon's day to our own, have consistently viewed it as a phenomenon in labor movement pathology. To this writer, job consciousness is primarily an emphasis on what is nuclear, what is the central core of labor's interest, which under the spur of changing conditions is likely to compel a widening of the area of labor interest. At the same time, American labor history teaches us that the job interest must remain the nuclear one if the movement is not to weaken or disintegrate.

The art of building fortifications and their defense offers a good analogy of how change in basic circumstances compels change in strategy, even if the objective remains unaltered. Prior to the airplane, it was enough to fortify a limited area, to garrison it adequately, and to await confidently the assault. Today, to be impregnable, a fortress must control an area with a radius of many hundreds of miles, even aside from the consideration of the wider strategy of protecting the whole country. The mere "nuclear" interest, the holding of the fortress, has thus compelled the erection of outlying strong points to keep away enemy bombers.

Economic and Political Influences

The Gompersian job consciousness had been the product of more than half a century's effort by the American labor movement to attain stability and a real foothold, from the organization of the first workingmen's parties in the 1820's to the triumph of the AFL over the Knights of Labor in the 1880's. The struggling unions had to learn to cut the cord that tied them to the farmer and to other middle-class anti-monopoly movements, with which they had shared an overweening passion for self-employment and a burning faith in salvation through political parties thrust up by the "producing classes," a most unstable conglomerate when tested in action. Labor had to learn to avoid such enthusiasms and "sure" paths to victory and to concentrate on the job interest as the only hard reality in the wage earner's life. Labor's historical experimenting also extended to the American community as a whole—the public—to the employers, and to the government.

Labor learned that an attack, or even what might be misconstrued as an intended attack, on private property and enterprise as institutions would only be a free gift to its enemies; that employers, if the gods were willing, could be coerced or sometimes cajoled into a joint job administration under a trade agreement; that the structure of political action in the United States doomed a labor party set up in competition with the "old" parties but opened a possibility for carrying collective bargaining into politics and even for infiltrating the old parties; and finally, that the American government with its states' rights, judicial review, and general checks and balances was a very limited instrument for labor's good and often a menace to be warded off (for example, the Sherman Anti-Trust Act). But if the government of the land was to be handled with caution and fear, labor could still go ahead building up two kinds of unofficial "governments," each around the job interest.

One was a government for the labor movement itself, erected on the principle of exclusive union jurisdiction, setting up the labor movement as a job empire with affiliated job kingdoms, duchies, and baronies, and held together through the absolute and pitiless suppression of dual or illegitimate unions. The other kind of government, dealing as it did with the conditions of employment, had to reckon with the employers, but under it the unions sought, wherever possible, full possession of the job territory through the closed or union shop.

Such was American unionism when the sovereignty of American government was confronted with the apparently stronger sovereignty of American business; when labor believed that the economic system including job opportunities was being kept up and expanded by private enterprise alone. Under those circumstances, labor saw its task clearly as building its union fortifications over the several job territories, mostly craft, a few covering an industry. Unionism of that period saw little lying outside the immediate economic area that could either improve the conditions of the job or multiply job opportunities.

Yet, as early as 1906, Gompers saw himself compelled to mix his economism with forays into politics in order to attempt to influence Congress to curtail the court injunction so restrictive of the unions' economism. That government would ever be eager to lend its strength to unionism and virtually force union recognition upon the biggest employers of the land, as happened in the 1930's, could not then be dreamed even by the most uncontrolled dreamers in the labor movement, and Gompers would have certainly looked such a gift horse in the mouth.

Through Civil War in the Labor Ranks

The New Deal has literally opened to unionism the doors to the heretofore barred mass production industries. Unfortunately for the labor movement, the leaders of the AFL have managed to couple this windfall with the curse of a civil war in the labor ranks. Under Gompers, the AFL had faced the demand of the socialist industrialists for a complete recasting of the structure of the movement, a demand which, if granted, would have undone the internal order obtained with great effort. By contrast the "industrialists" of 1935 were organization-wise and there was no reason whatsoever why a constitutional crisis in the labor movement should have arisen, at this time. At bottom, that crisis was the joint fault of the self-appointed "constitutional lawyers" and pseudo historians within the high official leadership, and of the leaders of lesser rank, eager for dues and power.

As regards the labor program as such, however, no startling change has emerged. The Congress of Industrial Organizations unions, mass production and others, while utterly contemptuous of the crafts' phantom partitions, have largely reproduced the old procedures of job administration, including seniority, job sharing, and so forth. Even Harry Bridges' Longshoremen's and Warehousemen's Union, of leftist renown, has failed to proclaim the jobs in that occupation free to all comers. The culmination of this sameness with the AFL came within the past two years when the CIO abandoned its initial effort to provide a home for all unions regardless of ideology and turned to expelling communist-controlled unions en bloc.

The same community of pattern is found in conjunction with union-management co-operation, the reward for the farsightedness of both management and union leadership: the Baltimore and Ohio—shopcraft's prototype of the 1920's—rules the CIO versions. On the all-important issue of management prerogatives again both labor movements have taken a common position. While neither AFL nor CIO is willing to surrender the right of scrutiny of any managerial area, since it might possibly affect the job control and, therefore, warrant the demand for right of codetermination, neither even questions the necessity for derivation of the basic management mandate independent of government or labor.

It is this which marks off the American labor movement from most other national movements; it is a labor movement upholding capitalism, not only in practice, but in principle as well.

While labor's views on the social order have thus remained unaltered, the earlier pure and simple pattern has shown a definite adaptation to the Roosevelt "revolution" in government yet not at all in the direction of independent political action through a third or labor party.

The New Deal has effected a veritable revolution in American government, comparable to the Jeffersonian and Jacksonian revolutions. Roosevelt's attack on the United States Supreme Court, followed as it was by a counter-reformation in the Court's decisions in 1937, has brought together the *disjecta membra* of American government and fashioned them into a powerful instrument. Congress could now abolish regional differentials at the lowest wage level, as well as bestow other boons on the weaker groups.

In a New Political Climate

For the bulk of the labor movement this spelled a new political climate, which even raised in some optimistic minds the hope that at long last American labor was coming round to conform to the West-European model, with its political class organization. Such glowing expectations might have been checked by a knowledge of American labor history. For decades before the New Deal, railway and other conservative unions, under conditions where government was a decisive factor in their job control activities, have without fear of departure from safe labor orthodoxy resorted to political pressures, most frequently to arrest adverse interference. Living under one government instead of under forty-nine, and thus finding favorable legislation more attainable, they had in essence become politicized even before World War I—not because of their defection from job consciousness, but because of their very fealty to it. This went hand in hand with the conviction that the indirect method of collective bargaining with a major party was the road to follow—not the direct method of setting up a political shop in competition with the old parties. The support of the independent candidacy of La Follette in 1924—indeed, not alone by the railway unions but also by the AFL under Gompers' pressure—was a move of despair and not labor's first choice.

With Americans' ingrained aversion to "class" parties and with the labor pattern of action still alien to the majority, especially the overrepresented nonmetropolitan groups, America can have a government actively favorable to the labor movement only under an exceptionally able leadership. That leadership must itself be free of any "class" label, above all of the "labor" label; it must know how to convince the underprivileged of its deep concern over their woes; and it must be skillful enough, on the one hand to resolve the mutual antagonisms, material and sentimental, among labor and the middle classes, and on the other hand to influence its own party managers to permit the nomination of trust-inspiring candidates—perhaps the most difficult assignment of all. And any boastful claims by labor leaders about their importance in the counsels of the party or in the administration are almost certain to jeopardize their political partner's success.

On the still more cheerless side for labor is the fact that what political action has given to labor under a government free since 1937 of its former constitutional limitations, political action has already begun to take back from labor. It is, therefore, not improbable that after the latest (1950) frustrating experience with lobbying and election campaigns, some, if not a majority, of the labor leaders, now that the gates of big industry have been opened to them, may come to hanker for the simpler days of "economism." Yet the very new powers vested in government render it unlikely that the indicator should ever again be permitted to rest on neutral. Opponents of the Fair Deal may find these powers just as useful as did their recently defeated foes and thus compel labor to stay on for a political defensive.

The Outlook

Broadly speaking, the American labor movement has so far shown little indication of breaking away from the Compersian moorings, if these are considered in the sense of the basic social order it favors and of the method it employs in its political action. Yet Gompers has been the *bête noire,* not only of intellectuals, but of practical experimenters of his own type such as Sidney Hillman. With the pride of a member of a more recently arrived ethnic group than the "older" Americans on the AFL's Executive Council, upon whom Gompers' mantle had fallen, Hillman forever delighted in displaying his superior mastery in shaping new American institutions. Hillman was the anti-Gompers par excellence in his own mind and in the eyes of the public, notably in his molding of his own union as a union with a wider awareness than the regular AFL unions, an industry consciousness—in effect, forcing the employers towards a superior managerialism under the union's gracious patronage. As labor's pioneers, however, Gompers and Hillman really did not stand far apart: both excelled in grasping the minds of labor and management and the social topography of America as well. Today, many believe that Walter P. Reuther, of the United Automobile Workers, is in that illustrious line of American labor's great experimenters. He has been identified with a new broadening out of labor's horizon to include the consumer interest and has expressly spelled this out during the long General Motors strike. For those who have had an upbringing like his own that strike must have held a muted socialist appeal, while seeming to those not of the "faith" perhaps to be mere keen "public relations." For the present, the role of experimenter in that great industry seems to have fallen less to Reuther than to the General Motors management, bent on bringing back the Welfare Capitalism [7] of the 1920's, with the sophisticated substitution of a national union for a company union. In the meantime, something suspiciously akin to the old-fashioned job consciousness has revealed itself in the hot protest of the UAW against the Federal Reserve Board's move to combat inflation by tightening the credit terms in the sales of automobiles.[8]

In the grasp of the Wisconsin School, the American labor program, indicative of its basic philosophy, has shown remarkable steadfastness through times of rapid external change. The objective, as said above, has been unaltered since Gompers' day; the methods, even outside the immediate vicinity of the job interest, show no more change than can be accounted for by the changing environment. This steadiness of labor's self-integration into the evolving American society is of significance, not only to the labor movement itself and to its theorists, but even more importantly, for its defense of democracy against totalitarianism. As labor in this country utterly rejects any idea of "class hegemony," it is thus a bulwark of the principle of "unity in diversity," upon which Western civilization rests.

[7] S. Perlman, *A Theory of the Labor Movement* (New York: The Macmillan Company, 1928, 1949), pp. 207–209.
[8] *The New York Times,* Oct. 22, 1950.

The Case for Business Revisionism

24.   The Robber Barons Revisited

Edward C. Kirkland

There are many reasons for revising an estimate or an impression of a period. An a priori wish to condone or condemn it hardly seems a legitimate one, though the partisan purpose may be masked for the occasion in the erudition of a frame-of-reference theory or the assertion that every generation must write its own history. More commendable as a reason for revision is the discovery or availability of new sources and other material. Such availability has been of peculiar importance in the case of business or company history and of biographies of business

"The Robber Barons Revisited," by Edward C. Kirkland, is reprinted by permission from *The American Historical Review,* LXVI (October, 1960), 68–73.

leaders. For the business titans in the robber baron generation there have thus resulted two successive two-volume studies of John D. Rockefeller by Allan Nevins.[1] The occasion for the second of these books thirteen years after the first was "the fortunate discovery of an immense additional body of correspondence, long thought lost." At the same time Ralph and Muriel Hidy, under the sponsorship of the Business History Foundation, were chosen to write, from the corporate records, the history of the Standard Oil Company of New Jersey and affiliated or related corporations.[2] They elected to regard their narrative as a series "of decisions made in response to a succession of prods and pressures" and they abjured any "systematic effort to correct specific errors and misconceptions about Standard Oil and its leaders" on the ground that "to have done so would have required a second volume as large as this one, a prospect as appalling to the authors as to potential readers." Though the introduction of decisions, sometimes characterized by others as "entrepreneurial decisions," introduces a variable into the history of this era as hard to nail down as that puzzling newcomer "the Protestant ethic" is in all periods of American history, the facts here set forth speak for themselves. A third study of comparable significance is that of the philosophy and, to a lesser extent, the practice of railroad leaders by Thomas C. Cochran.[3] Though the author insists that he could not have written the book without relying upon the concept of role playing, I think the volume valuable for its levies upon the corporate records and official correspondence of sixty-one railroad executives and the arrangement of the resulting treasure of new material in categories that would have occurred to any investigator of common sense.

Granted that the works hitherto cited throw light from a different angle upon the age of the robber barons, it does not follow that the availability of new material automatically involves any extensive revisionism. Julius Grodinsky in his study of Jay Gould [4] utilized masses of new material and made clear how the business decisions and methods of this particular business leader worked. But as a personality and businessman of his times, Gould remains a financial scamp or a compulsive acquisitor with a pathetic sense of loneliness—depending upon the point of view.

Nor is all new material in business archives and correspondence. The refulgence of square-deal muckraking, coupled with the myopia of our

[1] Allan Nevins, *John D. Rockefeller: The Heroic Age of American Enterprise* (2 vols., New York, 1940) and *Study in Power: John D. Rockefeller, Industrialist and Philanthropist* (2 vols., New York, 1953).

[2] Ralph W. and Muriel E. Hidy, *Pioneering in Big Business, 1882–1911: History of Standard Oil Company (New Jersey)* (New York, 1955).

[3] Thomas C. Cochran, *Railroad Leaders, 1845–1890: The Business Mind in Action* (Cambridge, Mass., 1953).

[4] Julius Grodinsky, *Jay Gould: His Business Career, 1867–1892* (Philadelphia, 1957).

historians of literature, has left the impression that the periodicals of the late nineteenth century were compendia of genteel pieces. Actually periodicals like the *Forum, North American Review, Atlantic,* and *Popular Science Monthly* were crowded with articles on religion, education, technology, housing, the division of wealth, the nature of the ideal society, and political and economic issues. Though partisan participants often wrote these articles, they were generally as discerning and more responsible than articles by Ida M. Tarbell and Lincoln Steffens. Reliance upon periodical material is one of the outstanding characteristics of Sidney Fine's highly useful volume.[5] While the book is neither revisionist in premises or tone, it introduces one innovation: a considerable statement of the "laissez-faire" or business point of view. Using the editorials and obituaries of a wide sample of newspapers, Sigmund Diamond[6] has demonstrated among other things that on death three robber barons were less censured than two business leaders from the previous generation of capitalists.

The cause of revisionism must be more broadly based than upon the mere tumbling of new material into the scholarly market place. Some inherent paradox of inconsistency in the period itself must nag the observer into efforts to discover a clue that will reconcile the contradictions. In this period, according to the old consensus, business was greedy and without social purpose, businessmen were at best selfish and at worst dishonest, management exploited labor, the rich grew richer while the poor grew poorer, and "things are in the saddle and ride mankind." At least this would seem to be the upshot of the interpretations of Charles and Mary Beard and Vernon Parrington.[7] Both of these works were of the late twenties or soon thereafter. It is unnecessary to cite the numerous and popular textbooks derived from these two pacemakers. Wherever stated, it is hard to reconcile these general assertions with the fact that nationally the Republican party, the party of big business, enjoyed almost uninterrupted political success and was as strong under McKinley at the end of the period as it was under Grant at the beginning. The Cleveland interim was no ideological exception to this generalization. One by one the bridges of explanation that were thrown across this gap—"waving the bloody shirt," buying the election in a whole state, for example, Indiana, or the widespread intimidation of voters as in 1896—did not reach the other side or exhibited other imperfections. Perhaps it is simpler to

---

[5] Sidney Fine, *Laissez Faire and the General-Welfare State: A Study of Conflict in American Thought, 1865–1901* (Ann Arbor, Mich., 1956).

[6] Sigmund Diamond, *The Reputation of the Businessman* (Cambridge, Mass., 1955).

[7] Charles A. and Mary R. Beard, *The Rise of American Civilization* (2 vols., New York, 1927); Vernon L. Parrington, *Main Currents in American Thought* (3 vols., New York, 1927–30), III. *The Beginning of Critical Realism in America, 1860–1920.*

believe that the performance of the economy during this era was not as bad as pictured and in general won popular endorsement.

  It is doubtful if a revision of the robber baron period will be initiated by a single volume. For the pre-Civil War era a work like Charles A. Beard's *An Economic Interpretation of the Constitution* is so much a foundation stone that its refutation would shake the treatment of the Federalists and the Jacksonians. And certainly if the cases of Robert E. Brown and Forrest McDonald [8] can be made to stick, extensive changes in the interpretation of later history are in order. For the post-Civil War era there is no comparable key volume. Nevins and the Hidys may well correct the narrative and reverse the judgments of Ida M. Tarbell,[9] and a careful reading, coupled with an analysis of his rhetorical devices, discredit Henry Demarest Lloyd.[10] Such procedures will only shake down a little plaster. It is no use undermining the big over-all works of this period by Rhodes and Oberholtzer, for both were comparatively unconcerned with economic changes. For example, the former was once chided, somewhat unjustly, for devoting more space to an operation on Cleveland's jaw than to the history of the AF of L. Matthew Josephson's two volumes are in a somewhat different category.[11] They have not enjoyed much repute among historians for some reason. Perhaps they are too gay and flippant about serious matters; perhaps they handled rumor and gossip as evidence; perhaps they reveal traces of the doctrinaire; perhaps they are too interestingly written. But it is the fashion to dismiss them as "journalistic" —an adjective reserved for books not written by professional historians.

  A few years ago the hope for a new synthesis of the history of this period would have been said to lie in breaking down the barriers between disciplines and in raiding sociology, economics, anthropology, and psychology for their insights, methodology, and less frequently their rhetoric. There are signs the vogue for this prescription is waning. One of the statesmen of our profession, Merle Curti, has discovered in his study of Trempealeau County, Wisconsin,[12] that quantitative and qualitative methods—to wit, diaries, newspapers—yield much the same conclusions or at least the methods confirm each other; and a sociologist, C. Wright Mills, though he has some doubts about the historical specificity of American history, is exhorting sociologists to write like historians.[13]

  Perhaps the barriers best burned away are those between specialities

  [8] Robert E. Brown, *Charles Beard and the Constitution: A Critical Analysis of "An Economic Interpretation of the Constitution"* (Princeton, N. J., 1956); Forrest McDonald, *We the People: The Economic Origins of the Constitution* (Chicago, 1958).
  [9] Ida M. Tarbell, *The History of the Standard Oil Company* (New York, 1904).
  [10] Henry D. Lloyd, *Wealth against Commonwealth* (New York, 1894).
  [11] Matthew Josephson, *The Politicos, 1865–1896* (New York, 1938), and *The Robber Barons: The Great American Capitalists, 1861–1901* (New York, 1934).
  [12] Merle Curti, *The Making of an American Community: A Case Study of Democracy in a Frontier County* (Stanford, Calif., 1959).
  [13] C. Wright Mills, *The Sociological Imagination* (New York, 1959).

within the field of history. We are getting too partitioned off even within our own single discipline. Instances of the advantages of combining historical specialties are demonstrated in Samuel P. Hays, *Response to Industrialism*,[14] which though fragmentary in its revisionism remains the most perceptive account of the robber baron period; in Henry F. May, *Protestant Churches and Industrial America*,[15] which, like most books on this theme, hurries too rapidly over other attitudes in order to reach the social gospelers, a minority group; and in Willard Hurst's highly original volume,[16] which dissipates the stock conventionalities,[17] repeated time out of mind, about the relations of the law and courts to business enterprise. How advantageous it would be if someone not an educationalist would integrate our educational advance, the public schools, and practical education in this era with the demands and needs of the business community and an industrial order. For higher education Walter Metzger has demonstrated that "business control" was neither as sinister nor mischievous as readers of Upton Sinclair's *Goose Step* would have anticipated.[18] Still to cover the whole field, a history of higher education and business should include technical and practical education, changes in the liberal arts institutions, and the growth of collegiate athletics and other so-called "activities."

But there will always remain a human tendency to select one note as dominant for the period of the robber barons. Since economic events were then so dramatic and overpowering and there seems to be an inborn inclination to explain things in terms of economic life, historians have tended to put at the forefront in interpreting this period some variant of economic determinism. Indeed one gifted supervisor of undergraduates at Cambridge University left his students with the impression that if they knew the history of business and industry after the Civil War they knew all. In view of the overemphasis on politics in American history instruction in Great Britain, this alleged dictum was startling and commendable. Nevertheless revisionism will be most fruitful if it enters the period by the gate of politics. I do not mean by this a mere analysis of political structure and performance—though these have a place—but an emphasis upon what Edward Atkinson, one of the most thoughtful businessmen in this period, once called "our whole democratic organization." It was this as ideal and practice that enabled the labor union movement to appeal to

[14] Samuel P. Hays, *The Response to Industrialism, 1885–1914* (Chicago, 1957).

[15] Henry F. May, *Protestant Churches and Industrial America* (New York, 1949).

[16] J. Willard Hurst, *Law and the Conditions of Freedom in the Nineteenth-Century United States* (Madison, Wis., 1956).

[17] For example, the essay on Stephen J. Field in Robert McCloskey, *American Conservatism in the Age of Enterprise: A Study of William Graham Sumner, Stephen J. Field, and Andrew Carnegie* (Cambridge, Mass., 1951).

[18] Richard Hofstadter and Walter P. Metzger, *The Development of Academic Freedom in the United States* (New York, 1955).

fellow laborers and to middle-class sympathizers as successfully as it did. The enlarging participation of the government in scientific activities reflected, among other pressures, the democratic spirit; findings accumulated and publicized by government belonged to everybody, not to private individuals. Hunter Dupree [19] has incidentally illuminated this facet of the period. Since the economy was, on the whole, functioning to the satisfaction of the majority by making more goods at cheaper prices, the attack upon big business was a politically motivated attack. It was feared that the innumerable business relationships with government would spoil our whole democratic organization. The Sherman Anti-Trust Act was as much a political and social measure as an economic one.[20] Conversely the very strong undercurrent against democracy flowing through these years opposed government intervention in business not because it was intervention by government but because it was intervention by democracy. At least this would seem to be the upshot of the argument by Charles Francis Adams, Jr. If our government had been a different sort, intervention might have been feasible and palatable.

Not the least advantage of a political approach is that it reveals so much about business. Specifically it shows the folly of writing as an entity about a "business program" or "what businessmen wanted." Thus Lee Benson's volume [21] shows not only that eastern farmers felt differently than western farmers about railroad practices or abuses, but unveils as well the highly ludicrous spectacle of railroad leaders condemning the proposals of merchants and others as "communistic." Stanley Coben in his article in the *Mississippi Valley Historical Review* [22] reveals other cracks in the business monolith on the subject of sound money and the tariff. Of all the themes that need to be rescued from the assumptions of nineteenth-century liberalism and from the overemphasis of antibusiness critics, the tariff is the most important.

How far should revisionism go? When will the task of revisionism be done? The frame-of-reference boys will logically reply "Never!" Since history depends upon the context of the writer, the present pitch to revisionism will prove but a passing phase. Averting his gaze from this picture of eternal restlessness and flux, the revisionist can hardly expect historical writing to paint Jim Fisk as a capitalist with a sense of social responsibility; he is entitled to hope Fisk will not be christened "emblem-

[19] A. Hunter Dupree, *Science in the Federal Government: A History of Policies and Activities to 1940* (Cambridge, Mass., 1957).

[20] Hans B. Thorelli, *The Federal Antitrust Policy: Organization of an American Tradition* (Baltimore, Md., 1955). See also my forthcoming *The Coming of the Industrial Age: Business, Labor, and Public Policy, 1860–1897*, in the Rinehart Economic History Series.

[21] Lee Benson, *Merchants, Farmers, and Railroads: Railroad Regulation and New York Politics, 1850–1887* (Cambridge, Mass., 1955).

[22] Stanley Coben, "Northeastern Business and Radical Reconstruction: A Re-examination," *Mississippi Valley Historical Review*, XLVI (June 1959), 67–90.

atic" of his business generation.[23] I have a different litmus paper to test the acidity of historical judgment of the robber barons. In 1902 George F. ("Divine-Right") Baer wrote: "The rights and interests of the laboring man will be protected and cared for—not by labor agitators but by the Christian men to whom God in His infinite wisdom has given the control of the property interests of the country." When textbooks writers stop quoting Mr. Dooley on this inept statement and recognize that instead of being entirely presumptuous, it is based upon the pious premise that the economic arrangements of this earth flowed from natural law which was of divine ordination and that the beneficiaries of natural law had an obligation for Christian stewardship, I will know that revisionism has made its dent.

[23] As in W. A. Swanberg, *Jim Fisk: The Career of an Improbable Rascal* (New York, 1959).

The Case against Business Revisionism

25.   The Premises of Business Revisionism

Gabriel Kolko

If there is one issue upon which the opposing sides in the debate over relativism agree, it is that all historians have values and that the denial of their influence in written history serves no useful purpose. Disagreements would immediately arise, of course, whether the validity of a statement or a history is lessened because of the value biases of the historian, but for the purposes of this article the reasons for unanimity are the more significant.[1] The primary reason for theoretical agreement, as distinguished

[1] There have been innumerable participants in the battle, but some representative discussions can be found in Morris R. Cohen, *The Meaning of Human History* (La Salle, Ill., 1947), p. 80 ff.; Ernest Nagel, "The Logic of Historical Analysis," in *Readings in the Philosophy of Science,* Herbert Feigl, ed. (New York, 1953); Bert James Loewenberg, "Some Problems Raised by Historical Relativism," *The Journal of Modern History* (March, 1949); Gunnar Myrdal, "The Relation Between Social Theory and Social Policy," *The British Journal of Sociology* (Sept., 1953), pp. 238–242 ff.; Charles A. Beard, "A Memorandum on Social Philosophy," *Journal of Social Philosophy* (Oct., 1939); Committee on Historiography, *Theory and Practice in Historical Study* (New York, 1946), pp. 117, 125–127.

"The Premises of Business Revisionism," by Gabriel Kolko, is reprinted by permission from *Business History Review*, XXXIII (Autumn, 1959), 330–344. Copyright 1959.

from practical application, is the belief that unspecified values allowed to pass as the objective findings of the historian create the real danger of written history becoming a mere reflection of an individual's idiosyncrasies or ideology. Even though the historian may deny that his researches have any contemporary implications or function, and in innumerable fields he may be correct, the historian of recent times has no defense on this count, for every causal statement, every sequence, and every use of the word "because" amounts, implicitly or explicitly, to an evaluation of the nature and direction of history. Whether that evaluation is right or wrong is irrelevant, for the fact remains it is made.

Although the debate over methodology among historians has subsided in the past decade, the need to understand the constant importance of value premises in historical writing is still indispensable for those desiring to sift the grain from the chaff in historical research. The focus of this article is on the value premises of the historians of American corporations and business leadership who have broken with the critical view of American economic development which dominated historical writing up to about the Second World War. For convenience I shall label this tendency as Business Revisionism. It is my thesis that this school, though generally unorganized, reflects a rather detailed set of unacknowledged value assumptions and, despite their general claim to objectivity, these premises have far-reaching implications to functional social theory and are, in effect, conservative. To help illustrate the nature of their values I shall make comparisons between some of the major assumptions and analyses of Business Revisionism and aspects of Marxism, and attempt to show how conclusions and generalizations not sustained by the analyses upon which they purport to be based are often finally dependent on implicit value judgments. It is not my aim, needless to say, to show that in all particulars Business Revisionism parallels Marxism in all its ideas or methodological principles. Yet strongly identical elements enter into both analyses, and for the sake of examining the basic premises of the Business Revisionists it is the similarities rather than the substantial disagreements which will be stressed.

*　　*　　*

One of the legacies of the tradition of Progress which Marx accepted was the notion that an inevitable chain of interdependent changes in the social structure, whether caused by technology, ideas, or both, would result in a final social order in which the dynamics of change would end and, in Marxism's case, the socialist society would be realized. Although he enmeshed it with Hegelian dialectics and gave each phase a vastly more concrete and detailed economic and sociological consideration, thereby taking, as Marx believed, dialectics off its head and standing it upright, Dialectical Materialism is still very much in the millennial tradition of Condorcet's ten epochs of human development or Comte's three stages of human knowledge.

Since the economic factor is dominant "in the last analysis," as Engels phrased it, human actions, protests, and ideas cannot change the basic course of economic and historical development. As part of an interdependent process, the present stage of economic development, and human suffering, was inexorably determined by its precedent. "Men are not free to choose their productive forces; for every productive force is an acquired force, the product of former activity." [2] This conception of man's invariable role in an inevitable historical and economic development moves history into, as Karl Popper has suggested, "The Kingdom of Necessity." The person who dissents, who asserts that man can make history as well, is, as the orthodox Marxist would have it, an idealist.

This necessity was so fixed in the course of history that any attempt to circumvent the workings of the process of capital accumulation, to end the basic cause of human suffering before monopolization had taken place, would be premature and destructive. As J. Martov, Lenin's leading adversary within the Russian Marxist movement correctly interpreted Marx, ". . . the proletariat can score a victory over the bourgeoisie—and not for the bourgeoisie—only when 'the march of history will have elaborated the material factors that create the *necessity* . . . of putting an end to the bourgeois methods of production.'" [3]

If history moves inevitably and irresistibly toward the final synthesis—a most desirable end—what happens today cannot *really* be wrong or evil, however cruel it may seem in and of itself and however much it grates our sensibilities. For implicit in Marx is a rationalization of the present for the future. Virtually built into the concept of Historical Materialism is the assumption that the end of history is known and every economic change today, even if it involves human suffering, brings us closer to a desirable tomorrow, and is in this sense progressive. Although the capitalist is not necessarily absolved morally—Marx does not say this explicitly—he nevertheless is absolved functionally by virtue of the basic role he *must* play in the necessary and desirable process of capital accumulation. After all, the task of the exploiter is to exploit, and a man moved by the laws of history (which move him, and not vice versa) is no more the fit subject of moral condemnation than the psychotic who steals or murders.

Marx' writings are therefore understandably saturated with oblique admiration for the capitalist and his material achievements. "The bourgeoisie, historically, has played a most revolutionary part." [4] Capping this compliment Marx adds: "It has been the first to show what man's activity

---

[2] Karl Marx, quoted in V. Gordon Childe, *What is History?* (New York, 1953), p. 78.

[3] J. Martov, *The State and the Socialist Revolution* (New York, 1938), p. 59. (Italics in original.)

[4] From "The Communist Manifesto" reprinted in Karl Marx, *Capital, The Communist Manifesto and Other Writings*, Max Eastman, ed. (New York, 1932), p. 323.

can bring about. It has accomplished wonders far surpassing Egyptian pyramids, Roman aqueducts, and Gothic cathedrals. . . ." [5] "The bourgeoisie, during its rule of scarce one hundred years, has created more massive and more colossal productive forces than have all preceding generations together." [6] The logical outcome of this reasoning was a doctrine which made industrialization a fetishistic means to a utopian end which has yet to be realized in practice.

❉   ❉   ❉

In terms of an attitude toward capital accumulation, the outspoken admiration of the process and belief in its inevitability which characterizes Marxism, and which is so much a part of its theory of historical dynamics, finds striking parallels in a "secularized" version among some American historians today. As the most prominent and active revisionist of American business history, Allan Nevins states it: [7]

> It will yet be realized that the industrial revolution in the United States came none too soon, and none too fast; and that the ensuing mass production revolution as yet so little understood by Americans, was not born a day too soon. . . . We shall also come to realize that the turmoil and human suffering which *inescapably* accompanied the industrial revolution were not after all a tremendous price to pay for the benefits. Great business aggregations are not built without frustrating, crushing, or absoring multitudinous small enterprises. To many caught in the midst of the transformation, its destructive and exploitive aspects seem paramount. The leaders of the process appeared as "robber barons" and the process itself the "great barbecue." This is one facet of the truth, but there are others. The constructive aspects of the transformation were in the long run more important than the destructive; the development of new wealth far outweighed the wastes of existing wealth.

The beginning of a major reinterpretation of the value of the American business leader and capital accumulation was perhaps anticipated by Ida Tarbell in 1936, when she wrote "Still clearer was it that the leadership of strong men was the price the country was paying for its rapid development as well as for more abundant comforts and cheaper luxuries." [8] A

[5] *Ibid.*, p. 324.
[6] *Ibid.*, p. 326.
[7] Allan Nevins, "New Lamps For Old in History," *The American Archivist* (Jan., 1954), p. 12. Allan Nevins, *Study in Power: John D. Rockefeller, Industrialist and Philanthropist* (New York, 1953), Vol. I, p. viii. [Italics: G. Kolko.] "In the field of business history moral strictures, however enticing, cannot be substituted for a scientific study of *rigid economic causes and compulsions*. Lloyd, failing to understand that the movement for industrial concentration was primarily a reaction against deep-seated evils and a response to *irresistible economic forces* . . . fails to do any justice to its beneficial side." Allan Nevins, letter in *The American Historical Review* (April, 1945), p. 688. [Italics: G. Kolko.]
[8] Ida Tarbell, *The Nationalizing of Business: 1878–1898* (New York, 1936), p. 268.

few years later Louis Hacker, upon leaving the editorship of *The Marxist Quarterly*, wrote an intellectually ambivalent history of American economic growth which perhaps best captures the parallel logic of the Marxists and the Business Revisionists. Using such descriptive terms as "unearned increment," "hard bitten and dangerous antagonists," "corrupting government officials," etc., Hacker concluded that "The capitalism I have described gave us the physical means of achieving abundance. . . ." [9] Allan Nevins, in his two-volume history of John D. Rockefeller and Standard Oil, in 1940 saw in Rockefeller's ability to rationalize the oil industry a value in itself—"Quite apart from this issue of ethics, the time was to come when the Standard would be praised for its pioneering qualities and for its demonstration of the useful possibilities of large scale organization." [10] And, all valuations apart, ". . . from the vantage point of a later day we can see that many crusaders were blind to the larger tendencies of the time. They did not realize that industrial concentration was now a world-wide movement. . . ." [11]

Marxism is monolithic in its theory of economic causation—monopolization and large-scale capital accumulation is the necessary outcome of definable historical law. Despite the absence in their philosophy of anything quite as sophisticated and mechanistic as Historical Materialism, most Business Revisionists nevertheless accept monopolization and aggressive capital accumulation as inevitable, and thereby preserve the content of Marxism even though it loses much of its form. Concomitant to this is the mutual admiration of capitalists, and not merely capitalism, as organizationally and technologically progressive, which was also a characteristic of Marx. Frederick Lewis Allen, in his discussion of Pierpont Morgan, reflected this view when he wrote: [12]

> . . . he was constantly intervening in business to reform and strengthen [it] in his own way. . . . In a real sense it was he and the other fabricators of giant industries, and the lawyers and legislative draftsmen [*sic!*] inventing new corporate devices, who were the radicals of the day, changing the face of America; it was those objected to the results who were conservatives seeking to preserve the individual opportunities and the folkways of an earlier time.

✿   ✿   ✿

Marxism does not suffer from ambivalence as to the problem of justifying, in terms of humanist and liberal values, the role of capitalists as

[9] Louis M. Hacker, *The Triumph of American Capitalism* (New York, 1940), p. 434.

[10] Allan Nevins, *John D. Rockefeller: The Heroic Age of American Enterprise* (New York, 1940), Vol. I, p. 683.

[11] *Ibid.*, Vol. II, p. 127. See Tarbell, *Nationalizing*, p. 270, for the same theme.

[12] Fredcrick Lewis Allen, *The Great Pierpont Morgan* (New York, 1949), p. 77. See Nevins, *Study in Power*, Vol. II, pp. 36, 436, and Edwatd C. Kirkland, *Dream and Thought in the Business Community, 1860–1900* (Ithaca, N. Y., 1956), p. 167, for the same theme.

individuals and capitalism as a system. Although it is politically necessary to do so, orthodox Marxists in certain respects should have little to criticize in the over-all trends within capitalism. As for the individual entrepreneur, "My stand-point, from which the evolution of the economic formation of society is viewed as a process of natural history, can less than any other make the individual responsible for relations whose creature he socially remains, however much he may subjectively raise himself above them." [13] And with the larger historical developments being part of a necessary and progressive process which society ". . . can neither clear by bold leaps, nor remove by legal enactments . . . ," condemnation is pointless.[14] Indeed, as I will indicate later, the implications of this necessitarianism virtually destroys the need and efficacy of individual and group social action, save under very limited conditions.

Although done very unsystematically, the Business Revisionists manage to achieve the same moral absolution for the business leaders as do the Marxists. The first aspect of this line of thought is to assert the historical relativity of business ethics in each epoch, and our consequent inability to project our own values in judging past events. It has been further stimulated by the application of structural-functionalist theory to historical inquiry under the guidance of interdisciplinary "entrepreneurial historians." On the assumption of structural-functionalism that society is fairly stable, equipped with behavioral norms which exert effective social control and place limitations on accepted individual behavior, the entrepreneurial historians assume "The individual entrepreneur, like all other social actors, is oriented to this total social situation. The range of decisions he normally considers, and his evaluation of the alternatives thus defined are functions of it." [15] The businessman, in short, merely reflects the values of his age.

To condemn the businessman, therefore, is to demand unreasonable,

---

[13] Karl Marx, *Capital* (Chicago, 1906), Vol. I, p. 15.

[14] *Ibid.*, p. 14. This historicism is not restricted to Marxists or Business Revisionists, but has also been explicitly formulated both by conservative Social Darwinians and the dominant "Wisconsin school" of labor theorists under John R. Commons and Selig Perlman, the latter as an alleged alternative to Marxism. For a detailed analysis, see Gabriel Kolko, "Unionism Reconsidered: A Critical Appraisal of Its Philosophy," *Institute of Social Studies Bulletin,* Vol. II (Winter, 1954), Vol. III (Spring, 1955).

[15] John E. Sawyer, "The Entrepreneur and the Social Order," in *Men in Business,* William Miller, ed. (Cambridge, Mass., 1952), p. 9. This is a systematic statement of the formal assumptions of the entrepreneurial historians. See Wayne Hield, "The Study of Change in Social Science," *The British Journal of Sociology* (March, 1954). Hield's criticism of structural-functionalism as being concerned with presumably static social structures, and being essentially conservative in its beliefs in doctrinal and institutional continuity, is just as true of the enterepreneurial historians as Talcott Parsons. Robert Merton, in his discussion of deviance in "Social Structure and Anomie," *Social Theory and Social Structure* (Glencoe, Ill., 1949), attempts to introduce a concept of dynamics and change into functionalism, and elsewhere he asserts that the theory is neither conservative or radical, but a neutral technique. He admits, however, that most advocates of structural-functionalism (in Merton's term, "Functional analysis") have been interested in stability and are, implicitly, conservative.

nonconformist behavior on his part. "The interest in discussing them [robber barons]," writes Thomas Cochran, "is to illustrate business malpractices, and presumably to convey moralistic warnings against such activities, rather than to understand the business process in society."[16] In this context, to explain, if indeed that is what is done, is to justify. For the unversally accepted social norms dictate business behavior under all circumstances, and structural-functionalists tend to deny the existence of alternate norms or inherent conflicts or opposition within a social structure which might radically change the character of that structure's basic institutions or social sanctions; ". . . those who denied the value of these major themes, seem during these years to have been a relatively small, or at least uninfluential, portion of the population."[17] With Max Weber, who was one with Marx in viewing the rationalization of the industrial and business structure as inevitable, the entrepreneurial historians see an inexorable process in which actions directed toward business consolidation appear to be normal. Further influenced by George Herbert Mead and recent studies of role determination of individual behavior, they tend to take the businessman's statements and conceptions of his "self" and social role as the reflection of socially accepted norms. Disparities between beliefs and actions, and the consequent disturbing implications for a static concept of the social structure, are minimized. The businessman's analysis of himself, in a sort of historical opinion poll which disregards the truth or falsity of such self-analysis in relation to an independent historical study, is taken as the basis of evaluation of his actual social role.[18]

[16] Thomas C. Cochran, "The Legend of the Robber Barons," *Explorations in Entrepreneurial History* (May, 1949), p. 2.

[17] *Ibid.* Ironically, Cochran's own historical studies are the best refutation of entrepreneurial, and his own, theory. The assumption that social and business norms of behavior are not specifically class phenomena, and have wider acceptance throughout the social structure, is effectively refuted by Cochran: "In examining the prescribing group for our nineteenth-century railroad executives we found it composed of other top officers plus the members of the board of directors. And among the latter the opinions of the general entrepreneurs with wealth and power were the most important in defining the executive role. . . . And among these men [operating managers] themselves the opinions of their fellows, their daily acquaintances of Wall and State Streets, counted for more than those of anyone else." *Railroad Leaders, 1845–1890* (Cambridge, Mass., 1953), pp. 13–14. ". . . those who denied the value of these major themes . . ." may have been "uninfluential," but this was undoubtedly due to the fact, as Cochran so ably shows (pp. 185–189, 193–197), the railroads purchased editors and maintained "lobbies" whenever public opposition to their goals warranted it. As for the purported unity and implicitly classless social sanctions upon which business action is rationalized: "By 1870, as many writers have shown, the public was becoming highly critical of railroad management. The long depression of the seventies heightened this feeling. . . . While the hostility to railroads waned somewhat in the prosperity of the eighties, it remained a force to be reckoned with by managers in every section. Added to the popular distrust of railroad entrepreneurs was a suspicion of corporations in general and monopolistic corporations in particular." *Ibid.,* p. 184.

[18] Cochran's *Railroad Leaders* is one form of this. Kirkland's *Dream and Thought,* p. viii ff. displays the same tendency. The most systematic discussion of the idea can

The less methodologically inclined historians advance a concept of "realistic morality" which declares that to succeed a businessman must do so on terms of the prevailing economic ethos, ethos he cannot personally assume responsibility for. ". . . in sometimes employing ruthless methods," writes Nevins, "they to a great extent acted according to the economic ethics of the time; if they had not used these weapons, still more ruthless men would have used them against the Standard organizers." [19] And, finally, the very concept of the validity, progressiveness, and inevitability of the process of capital accumulation mentioned earlier, and which relates the values of the Business Revisionist viewpoint to Marxism, is utilized to neutralize all attacks on the capitalist system itself. Skeptics and critics must not fail, says Edward Saveth, ". . . to recognize that abuses in business practices were byproducts of the tremendous efforts of men who, with limited capital in a relatively poor and vast country, performed miracles of material accomplishment. . . ." [20]

❊   ❊   ❊

The ideological analysis of knowledge is an aspect of intellectual craftsmanship peculiar to the twentieth century.[21] Although Marxists often discussed ideas, especially in aesthetics, as reflections of class needs or dilemmas, or as having some ominous ulterior political purpose, it was not until the impact of Beard's economic interpretations of the Constitution and Jeffersonian democracy that the technique was systematically discussed and comprehended as a distinct intellectual tool among American historians. The pointing out of economic and political interest as the basis

be found in Leland Jenks, "Role Structure of Entrepreneurial Personality," Harvard University Research Center in Entrepreneurial History, *Change and the Entrepreneur: Postulates and Patterns in Entrepreneurial History* (Cambridge, 1949).

For an analysis of related problems in Weber, see Gabriel Kolko, "A Critique of Max Weber's Philosophy of History," *Ethics* (October, 1959). For the disparity between business statements and behavior in a specific instance and its relevance to the validity of entrepreneurial theory, see his "American Business and Germany, 1930–1941," *Western Political Quarterly* (December, 1962).

[19] Nevins, *Rockefeller*, Vol. I, pp. 266–267. Also see *ibid.*, Vol. II, p. 710.

[20] Edward Saveth, "What Historians Teach About Business," *Fortune* (April, 1952), p. 165.

[21] In this sense, "ideology" is equivalent to Karl Mannheim's "sociology of knowledge"—". . . the question when and where social structures come to express themselves in the structure of assertions, and in what sense the former concretely determine the latter." *Ideology and Utopia* (London, 1936), p. 239. In addition to "social structures," I think it correct to add "political parties, status and economic interest groups." "Ideological analysis" is to be understood as the evaluation of the function ideas play in expressing the needs, sentiments, or aspirations of these groups. Calculations as to the invidious role of ideas consciously manipulated may also come under this heading, although Mannheim declared his sociology was little concerned with criticizing this thought "on the level of the assertions themselves." "Ideology" is sometimes used as an equivalent for "ideas" without regard to their function, and sometimes freely used in both senses by the same person. See, for example, Adolf Grunbaum, "Science and Ideology," *The Scientific Monthly* (July, 1954).

of actions and ideas was, as Beard suggested, at least as old as Harrington and Madison, but not until the twentieth century was its use formalized among historians. The impact of Freudianism on intellectuals only strengthened the interest in the ulterior in historical analysis, and broadened its dimensions to include psychological as well as class needs as causes of historically significant actions.

The ideological analysis, needless to say, does not and should not obviate the need to examine events and especially ideas beyond their relational context in the hope of discovering the validity of their claims and significance, irrespective of their class or psychological function. The theory of relativity, for example, cannot be explained away, or proved, by a class or psychoanalytical study of Einstein. But in practice the ideological analysis has been utilized both as a tool of understanding and, at the best, criticism from the vantage of the critic's value preferences. One has only to recall the furious attacks in the form of class analyses by Marx, who has done as much as anyone to formulate the technique, on Bakunin and Lasalle to understand the dual possibilities of this potentially useful tool. In more recent times, Karl Mannheim's *Ideology and Utopia,* which is not only a discussion of the sociology of knowledge but a critique of conservatism and liberalism, has shown the confusion of those interested in promoting the use of a value-free ideological analysis. And, unfortunately, all too often the assertion of an ulterior, albeit unconscious, function of an idea or action tends to raise conspiratorial and sinister associations in the minds of many.

In America the ideological analysis of historical writing has in recent years been utilized by the school of historians under consideration. Unfortunately, the fact this technique is being used, and the role of their values, is little recognized by its adherents. As a result, few of the advantageous possibilities of an ideological analysis are exploited. In consequence of this fact, it is the negative aspect of the tradition which emerges, and far more heat than light is generated.

The task of reinterpreting the nature of American business history and capital accumulation has included not merely the work of writing history anew, or reinterpreting it, but a criticism of those historians who have been most active in shaping the critical view of America's industrialization and the role of business leadership in it. Allan Nevins has expressed perhaps the mildest judgment on the topic when he wrote: "To assail Rockefeller was to some extent a mere habit in which millions unthinkingly joined. In part it rose from a justifiable antagonism to monopoly and Standard's methods. But in part the ceaseless hue and cry was deliberately maintained by journalists who had learned that it boosted circulation and politicians who knew there were votes in it." [22] Louis Hacker, in

[22] Nevins, *Rockefeller,* Vol. II, p. 515.

discussing the "Anticapitalist Bias of American Historians," has presented an even stronger ideological analysis when he writes of Charles Beard, the *bete noir* of the Business Revisionists: "Beard, in effect, took over the agrarian prejudices of his own Indiana boyhood to the capitalist processes. . . . No effort is made to analyze or comprehend the contributions of capitalism to America's extraordinary growth." [23] In the case of historians who were friendly or even neutral in their writings in Populism, we have ". . . an anticapitalist bias not for economic reasons but for political and moral ones." [24]

The most systematic exploitation of the ideological analysis has been made by Edward N. Saveth, who has explained the reasons for the anticapitalist bias of historians from Parkman on. His analysis is an economic interpretation and ideological attack as rigid as any used by a Marxist.[25]

> As long ago as the first quarter of the nineteenth century, historians were finding business and businessmen rather distasteful. At that time the commercial and agrarian basis of New England's economy was beginning to shift to a dominant manufacturing pattern. Eventually the industrialists were to get the upper hand, economically and socially. Unfortunately for their reputations, however, it was the descendants of the merchant princes they displaced in power who took to writing history. Francis Parkman, William Hickling Prescott, and John Lothrop Motley were all born in Massachusetts, around the beginning of the nineteenth century, and were descendant of families whose wealth derived from trade.

Stating that the public image of the businessman was created by the Muckrakers, an assertion whose validity it is not in place to consider here, Saveth deems it relevant to the validity of their history to explore the motives of the Muckrakers and their publishers. Thus McClure encouraged sensationalism because he profited from it. "Thomas Lawson, author of *Frenzied Finance* . . . was a publicity-mad millionaire who, at the same time, turned against the system that had enriched him. . . . Ida Tarbell's father had been an independent oilman who had come out second best after a tussle with Standard." [26] The total impression given is that the persons allegedly most responsible for the critical portrayal of capitalism were primarily opportunists, sour apples or, what is worse, occasionally fellow-travelers.

The revisionist trend in American business history is not an isolated

[23] L. M. Hacker in *Capitalism and the Historians*, F. A. Hayek, ed. (Chicago, 1954), pp. 80–81.

[24] *Ibid.*, p. 89.

[25] See the remarkably similar discussion of the same group of historians in Herbert Aptheker, *Laureates of Imperialism* (New York, 1954), pp. 16–17; Saveth, *Fortune*, p. 118.

[26] *Ibid.*, p. 119.

phenomenon, and can best be understood as a part of a change in the intellectual scene over the past several decades. In sociology, for example, many of the most influential writers now tell us the United States is a classless and very prosperous society existing within a socially responsible big business economy. The writings of A. A. Berle, John K. Galbraith, and David Lilienthal have accepted the large corporation as an integral part of the American scene, which it most certainly is, and asserted its alleged virtues. The trend in all of the social sciences has been towards a narrowing focus, a specialized microcosmic view of problems, and this in turn has restricted the possibility of theory and generalization which might criticize accepted institutions and beliefs. One must remember that it is only in the past decade and a half that the large corporation has received any significant acceptance in the academy, and this is especially true of historians who, whether conservative or liberal, generally had been critical of the manners or the function of big business in a democracy.

In part the sympathy for the large corporation is a result of a growing conviction among historians, and social scientists in general, that despite the problem of democratic control and the danger of economic concentration which was central in the minds of Populists and Progressives, the advantages of massive productive power in an age of totalitarianism, war, and hunger make the seemingly efficient large-scale economic unit take on virtues never fully appreciated in the past. The Business Revisionist school is not the product of consciously conservative historians, although in the hands of Saveth and Hacker it has become a branch of the amorphous New Conservatism as well, but often the response of liberals to some of these larger problems. But I do think that a hesitant judgment which started out as an either-or choice between lesser evils has, in a good number of instances, turned into a militant assertion of positive good.

Ultimately, I believe, the major impetus behind the reconsideration of the nature of American business and the role of the businessman is the belief on the part of many, especially the liberal historians, that the status quo achieved those economic and social goals which they once thought might be better reached by more radical means. A decade of seeming prosperity has resulted in a social order which, it is widely believed, eliminated poverty and serious economic instability and created a society in which abundance has replaced scarcity and insecurity. The productive machine which achieved this end was a positive good and a means of progress. Frederick Lewis Allen's *The Big Change* (1952) is nothing short of a eulogy of this entire phenomenon. As Allan Nevins put it in discussing Ford, ". . . they had done more than all other manufacturers combined to make the automobile a democratic possession; they had been the first to bring mass production, the reshaper of modern life, to birth. . . ."[27] To Edward Saveth, it appeared that, ". . . the national resources of a great

[27] Allan Nevins, *Ford: The Times, the Man, the Company* (New York, 1954), p. 587.

land were harnessed; consumers' goods were turned out in variety, quantity, and at a low price; real wages increased. . . ."[28] Capitalism, wrote Louis Hacker, is ". . . a system and a set of attitudes which have made possible material progress and the alleviation of human suffering."[29]

These are, however, assertions of the alleged success of the present economy, and they can be proved or disproved only in economic terms. They do not, I believe, justify a qualitative reinterpretation of essentially the same storehouse of historical facts only remotely related to judgments on the distributive or productive efficiency of the present American economy. Similarly, I do not believe that the assertions on the recent economic situation have any relevance to the nature and relationship of the occurrences of the 1870's. At least they should not. Nor is the application of sociological analyses which are fairly consistently conservative in their results either a relevant reinterpretation of our existing store of information or an especially valid basis for approaching new information.

❋   ❋   ❋

One of the dilemmas which some Marxists realized was inherent in Historical Materialism, its certitude and absolute predictability, was its anesthetizing consequences to individual and social action. Both Marx and Martov, as I suggested earlier, minimized the efficacy of premature human intervention in the social structure. The result was a sort of absolution of injustice and cruelty, at least insofar as the mechanics of Dialectics were concerned. As Bertrand Russell has correctly pointed out: "He might have said that he did not advocate Socialism, but only prophesied it. . . . He undoubtedly believed every dialectical movement to be, in some impersonal sense, a progress, and he certainly held that Socialism, once established, would minister to human happiness more than either feudalism or capitalism have done. These . . . beliefs remained largely in the background so far as his writings are concerned."[30]

The average Marxist has not been attracted or repelled by these academic conflicts, since of all the political liabilities of socialism, doctrinal inconsistencies have perhaps been the least important. Not until 1898 did

[28] Saveth, *Fortune*, p. 165.

[29] Hacker, *Capitalism and the Historians*, p. 75. Also see Kirkland, *Dream and Thought*, p. 167 and Thomas C. Cochran, *The American Business System: A Historical Perspective, 1900–1950* (Cambridge, Mass., 1957), pp. 110, 156–157, 186–187. "In a number of ways the problem of business consolidation now presents itself, even to liberals and reformers, in different forms from those in which it appeared to the men of the Progressive generation. . . . Product competition has in some respects replaced the old price competition. The great distributive agencies, themselves giant concerns, have given consumers some protection from the exactions of monopoly. Big business has shown itself to be what the Progressives of the Brandeis School resolutely denied it would be—technologically more progressive than the smaller units it has replaced. The political power of capital has been more satisfactorily matched by an enormous growth in labor organization." Richard Hofstadter, *The Age of Reform* (New York, 1955), pp. 252–253.

[30] Bertrand Russell, *History of Western Philosophy* (London, 1946), p. 816.

George Plekhanov, a Russian orthodox Marxist, attempt to prove that the
". . . materialist conception of the human will is quite compatible with
the most vigorous practical activity." [31] In an important tract which, save
for Dialectics replacing God, in form and substance imitated Jonathan
Edwards' attack on the Arminian heresy 150 years earlier, Plekhanov
asserted that,[32]

> . . . in my mind, necessity becomes identified with freedom and
> freedom with necessity; and then, I am unfree only in the sense that
> I cannot disturb this identity between freedom and necessity. I can-
> not oppose one to the other, I cannot feel the restraint of necessity.
> But such a lack of freedom is at the same time its fullest manifesta-
> tion.

Thus Plekhanov seemingly saved Marxism from one of its inherent political liabilities without appearing, at least in his own mind, excessively
monolithic about it. In a brilliant application of Hegel's unity of opposites
man was declared to be free, but not free, at the same time.

Although it would be absurd to expect to find a parallel discussion of
free will in any of the writings of the Business Revisionists, I do believe
strong similarities in procedure and logic appear even here. For despite
the political necessity to condemn the capitalist in moral terms, without
the capitalist the Marxist would not have Marxism. Regardless of the
knowledge of the direction of societal development purported to be
known by Historical Materialists, each historic and economic period has
its own function to play in the total complex, and each period has its own
economic morality involved in fulfilling that function. Without having
similar cosmic predictions as to the fate of our economy, the concept of
"realistic morality," which is simply a variant of the same cultural relativism of Marxism, is utilized by the Business Revisionists to rationalize the
status quo.

But the real question here is: Was there, so to speak, an "economic free
will" which might have allowed American industrial development to take
a different course had its leaders so desired? Or was the economic development necessitated by inflexible laws and conditions which determined
the actions of men, rather than vice versa? If the answer is negative, then
we face the classic dilemma involving moral judgment which Jonathan
Edwards and all those denying the existence of freedom faced two
centuries ago. If there is no freedom of action, then criticism or moral
condemnation is irrelevant, for the institution or person condemned is not
responsible for the consequences of their acts. The response of the Marx-

---

[31] George Plekhanov, *The Role of the Individual in History* (New York, 1940),
p. 11.
[32] *Ibid.*, p. 10. Plekhanov was familiar with the debate on free will in Christian
theology. Plekhanov, obviously, wanted to have his cake (of freedom to inspire
political action and condemn the capitalist) and eat it too (by being certain of the
outcome of "history").

ists is clear. And as I have attempted to show in my discussion of the Business Revisionists' belief in the inevitability of abuse in capital accumulation, in its ultimately progressive function, and in "realistic morality" or structural-functionalism, the Business Revisionists would agree with them. Indeed, given the economic hedonism which is the basic psychological determinant of individual behavior in classical, Keynesian, and Marxian economic theory, the agreement on this question as well should not surprise one.

If there was no "economic free will," the present economy, with all its concomitants, was at worst inevitable, at best desirable and inevitable. In Marxism this inevitability is a part of the Dialectic, and grudgingly good insofar as it heralds even better things in the Future. In Business Revisionism the status quo is asserted as a positive good, and insofar as there is a Revisionist dialectic or concept of economic evolution, our present society is about as close to economic utopia as reasonable men can hope to come. The basis of their assertion is not founded on any philosophical exegesis such as the Marxist might perform, but on a causal explanation and value bias which offers moral absolution on the assumption we know too much to condemn. But whether the Business Revisionists realize it or not, their viewpoint has both method and formal preconceptions in many respects similar to Marxism in form and consequence.

Business Combination: Causes and Consequences

26.   The Beginnings of "Big Business" in American Industry *

Alfred D. Chandler, Jr.

CRITERIA FOR SELECTION AND ANALYSIS

The historian, by the very nature of his task, must be concerned with change. What made for change? Why did it come when it did, and in the way it did? These are characteristically historians' questions. For the

* This study was supported by the Sloan Research Fund of The School of Industrial Management and the Center for International Studies, Massachusetts Institute of Technology.

student of American business history, these basic questions can be put a little more precisely. What in the American past has given businessmen the opportunity or created the need for them to change what they were doing or the way they were doing it? In other words, what stimulated them to develop new products, new markets, new sources of raw materials, new ways of procuring, processing, or marketing the goods they handled? What encouraged them to find new methods of financing, new ways of managing or organizing their businesses? What turned them to altering their relations with their working force, their customers and competitors, and with the larger American public?

The question of what constitutes the dynamic factors in American business history, dynamic in the sense of stimulating change and innovation, can be more clearly defined if the country's land, natural resources, and cultural patterns are taken as given. Land and resources were the raw materials with which the businessmen had to work, and the cultural attitudes and values helped set the legal and ethical rules of the game they had to play. Within this cultural and geographic environment a number of historical developments appear to have stimulated change. These provide a framework around which historical data can be compiled and analyzed.

The following major dynamic forces are visible in the American business economy since 1815: the western expansion of population; the construction and initial operation of the national railroad network; the development of a national and increasingly urban market; the application of two new sources of power: the internal combustion engine and electricity, to industry and transportation; and the systematic application of the natural and physical sciences, particularly chemistry and physics, to industry through the institutionalizing of research and development activities.

The first, the westward expansion, appears to have provided the primary impetus, except possibly in New England, to business innovation in the years from 1815 to about 1850; the building of the railroads appears to have been the major factor from the 1850's to the late 1870's; the growth of the national and urban market from the 1880's until a little after 1900; the coming of electricity and the internal combustion engine from the early 1900's to the 1920's; and, finally, the growth of systematic and institutionalized research and development since the 1920's.

These five factors are essentially aspects of fundamental population changes and technological advances. There were, of course, other factors that encouraged business innovation and change. The coming of the new machines and mechanical devices may have been a more important stimulant to innovation in New England than the growth of her markets and sources of supply in the expanding South and West. Wars usually precipitated change. The business cycle, flow of capital, government policy and legislation all played a significant part in business innovation. But such political and financial developments appear to have intensified or delayed the more basic changes encouraged initially by fundamental population shifts and technological achievements.

The purpose of making such a list is, however, not to argue that one development was more dynamic than the other. Nor are these five factors to be considered as "causes" for change; nor are they "theses" to be argued as representing reality, nor "theories" to provide an over-all explanation of change or possibly of predicting change. They are, rather, a framework on which historical information can be tied and inter-related. They provide a consistent basis upon which meaningful questions can be asked of the data.

This framework and these questions are, it should be emphasized, concerned only with fundamental changes and innovation in the business economy. They do not deal with the day-to-day activities to which businessmen must devote nearly all of their time. They are not concerned with the continuous adaptation to the constant variations of the market, sources of supply, availability of capital, and technological developments. Nor do they consider why some businesses and businessmen responded quickly and creatively to the basic population and technological changes and others did not. But an understanding of the continuous response and adjustment would seem to require first an awareness of the meaning of the more fundamental or "discontinuous" changes.

Since historical compilation and analysis must be selective, it is impossible to undertake any historical study without some criteria either implicit or explicit for selection. Further study and analysis, by indicating the defects of this approach and framework, will suggest more satisfactory ones. In the process, an analysis and interpretation of change in the American business past should come a little nearer to reality.

The purpose of this article then is, by using the framework of basic, dynamic forces, to look a little more closely at the years that witnessed the beginnings of big business in American industry. What types of changes came during these years in the ways of marketing, purchasing, processing, and in the forms of business organization? Why did these changes come when they did in the way they did? Was the growth of the national market a major prerequisite for such innovation and change? If not, what then was? How did these innovations relate to the growth of the railroad network or the coming of electricity and the internal combustion engine?

In addition to secondary works on this period, the data used in seeking answers to these questions have been annual and other corporation reports, government documents, articles in periodicals, histories, and biographies concerning the 50 largest industrial companies in the country in 1909. Nearly all these companies, listed in Table I, had their beginnings in the last years of the nineteenth century.

Major Changes in American Industry at the End of the Nineteenth Century

Between the depression of the 1870's and the beginning of the twentieth century, American industry underwent a significant transformation. In the 1870's, the major industries serviced an agrarian economy. Except for a few companies equipping the rapidly expanding railroad network, the leading industrial firms processed agricultural products and provided farmers with food and clothing. These firms tended to be small, and bought their raw materials and sold their finished goods locally. Where they manufactured for a market more than a few miles away from the factory, they bought and sold through commissioned agents who handled the business of several other similar firms.

By the beginning of the twentieth century, many more companies were making producers' goods, to be used in industry rather than on the farm or by the ultimate consumer. Most of the major industries had become dominated by a few large enterprises. These great industrial corporations no longer purchased and sold through agents, but had their own nationwide buying and marketing organizations. Many, primarily those in the extractive industries, had come to control their own raw materials. In other words, the business economy had become industrial. Major industries were dominated by a few firms that had become great, vertically integrated, centralized enterprises.

In the terms of the economist and sociologist a significant sector of American industry had become bureaucratic, in the sense that business decisions were made within large hierarchical structures. Externally, oligopoly was prevalent, the decision-makers being as much concerned with the actions of the few other large firms in the industry as with over-all changes in markets, sources of supplies, and technological improvements.

These basic changes came only after the railroads had created a national market. The railroad network, in turn, had grown swiftly primarily because of the near desperate requirements for efficient transportation created by the movement of population westward after 1815.[1] Except for the Atlantic seaboard between Boston and Washington, the construction of the American railroads was stimulated almost wholly by the demand for better transportation to move crops, to bring farmers supplies, and to open up new territories to commercial agriculture.

By greatly expanding the scope of the agrarian economy, the railroads

[1] The factors stimulating the growth of the American railroad network and the impact of the earlier construction and operation of this network on the American business economy and business institutions is suggested in Chandler, *Henry Varnum Poor—Business Editor, Analyst, and Reformer* (Cambridge, 1956), especially chaps. 4, 6–9.

quickened the growth of the older commercial centers, such as New York, Philadelphia, Cincinnati, Cleveland, and St. Louis, and helped create new cities like Chicago, Indianapolis, Atlanta, Kansas City, Dallas, and the Twin Cities. This rapid urban expansion intensified the demand for the products of the older consumer goods industries—particularly those which processed the crops of the farmer and planter into food, stimulants, and clothing.

At the same time, railroad construction developed the first large market in this country for producers' goods. Except for the making of relatively few textile machines, steamboat engines, and ordnance, the iron and nonferrous manufacturers had before 1850 concentrated on providing metals and simple tools for merchants and farmers. Even textile machinery was usually made by the cloth manufacturers themselves. However, by 1860, only a decade after beginning America's first major railroad construction boom, railroad companies had already replaced the blacksmiths as the primary market for iron products, and had become far and away the most important market for the heavy engineering industries. By then, too, the locomotive was competing with the Connecticut brass industry as a major consumer of copper. More than this, the railroads, with their huge capital outlay, their fixed operating costs, the large size of their labor and management force, and the technical complexity of their operations, pioneered in the new ways of oligopolistic competition and large-scale, professionalized, bureaucratized management.

The new nation-wide market created by the construction of the railroad network became an increasingly urban one. From 1850 on, if not before, urban areas were growing more rapidly than rural ones. In the four decades from 1840 to 1880 the proportion of urban population rose from 11 per cent to 28 per cent of the total population, or about 4 per cent a decade. In the two decades from 1880 to 1900 it grew from 28 per cent to 40 per cent or an increase of 6 per cent a decade. Was this new urban and national market, then, the primary stimulant for business innovation and change, and for the coming of big business to American industry?

Changes in the Consumers' Goods Industries

The industries first to become dominated by great business enterprises were those making consumer goods, the majority of which were processed from products grown on the farm and sold in the urban markets. Consolidation and centralization in the consumers' goods industries were well under way by 1893. The unit that appeared was one which integrated within a single business organization the major economic processes: production or purchasing of raw materials, manufacturing, distribution, and finance.

Such vertically integrated organizations came in two quite different ways. Where the product tended to be somewhat new in kind and especially fitted for the urban market, its makers created their businesses by first building large marketing and then purchasing organizations. This technique appears to have been true of the manufacturers or distributors of fresh meat, cigarettes, high-grade flour, bananas, harvesters, sewing machines, and typewriters. Where the products were established staple items, horizontal combination tended to precede vertical integration. In the sugar, salt, leather, whiskey, glucose, starch, biscuit, kerosene, fertilizer, and rubber industries a large number of small manufacturers first combined into large business units and then created their marketing and buying organizations. For a number of reasons the makers of the newer types of products found the older outlets less satisfactory and felt more of a need for direct marketing than did the manufacturers of the long-established goods.

Integration via the Creation of Marketing Organization

The story of the changes and the possible reasons behind them can be more clearly understood by examining briefly the experience of a few innovating firms. First, consider the experience of companies that grew large through the creation of a nation-wide marketing and distributing organization. Here the story of Gustavus F. Swift and his brother Edwin is a significant one. Gustavus F. Swift, an Easterner, came relatively late to the Chicago meat-packing business. Possibly because he was from Massachusetts, he appreciated the potential market for fresh western meat in the eastern cities.[2] For after the Civil War, Boston, New York, Philadelphia, and other cities were rapidly outrunning their local meat supply. At the same time, great herds of cattle were gathering on the western plains. Swift saw the possibilities of connecting the new market with the new source of supply by the use of the refrigerated railroad car. In 1878, shortly after his first experimental shipment of refrigerated meat, he formed a partnership with his younger brother, Edwin, to market fresh western meat in the eastern cities.

For the next decade, Swift struggled hard to carry out his plans, the essence of which was the creation, during the 1880's, of the nation-wide distributing and marketing organization built around a network of branch

[2] Swift's story as outlined in Louis F. Swift in collaboration with Arthur Van Vlissingen, *The Yankee of the Yards—the Biography of Gustavus Franklin Swift* (New York, 1928). The United States Bureau of Corporations, *Report of the Commissioner of Corporations on the Beef Industry, March 3, 1905* (Washington, 1905), is excellent on the internal operations and external activities of the large meat-packing firms. There is additional information in the later three-volume *Report of the Federal Trade Commission on the Meat Packing Industry* (Washington, 1918–1919). R. A. Clemen, *The American Livestock and Meat Industry* (New York, 1923) has some useful background data.

houses. Each "house" had its storage plant and its own marketing organization. The latter included outlets in major towns and cities, often managed by Swift's own salaried representatives. In marketing the product, Swift had to break down, through advertising and other means, the prejudices against eating meat killed more than a thousand miles away and many weeks earlier. At the same time he had to combat boycotts of local butchers and the concerted efforts of the National Butchers' Protective Association to prevent the sale of his meat in the urban markets.

To make effective use of the branch house network, the company soon began to market products other than beef. The "full line" soon came to include lamb, mutton, pork, and, some time later, poultry, eggs, and dairy products. The growing distributing organization soon demanded an increase in supply. So between 1888 and 1892, the Swifts set up meat-packing establishments in Kansas City, Omaha, and St. Louis, and, after the depression of the 1890's, three more in St. Joseph, St. Paul, and Ft. Worth. At the same time, the company systematized the buying of its cattle and other products at the stockyards. In the 1890's, too, Swift began a concerted effort to make more profitable use of by-products.

Before the end of the 1890's, then, Swift had effectively fashioned a great, vertically integrated organization. The major departments—marketing, processing, purchasing, and accounting—were all tightly controlled from the central office in Chicago. A report of the Commissioner of Corporations published in 1905 makes clear the reason for such control: [3]

> Differences in quality of animals and of their products are so great that the closest supervision of the Central Office is necessary to enforce the exercise of skill and sound judgement on the part of the agents who buy the stock, and the agents who sell the meat. With this object, the branches of the Selling and Accounting Department of those packing companies which have charge of the purchasing, killing, and dressing and selling of fresh meat, are organized in the most extensive and thorough manner. The Central Office is in constant telegraphic correspondence with the distributing houses, with a view to adjusting the supply of meat and the price as nearly as possible to the demand.

As this statement suggests, the other meat packers followed Swift's example. To compete effectively, Armour, Morris, Cudahy, and Schwarzschild & Sulzberger had to build up similar integrated organizations. Those that did not follow the Swift model were destined to remain small local companies. Thus by the middle of the 1890's, the meat-packing industry, with the rapid growth of these great vertically integrated firms had become oligopolistic (the "Big Five" had the major share of the market) and bureaucratic; each of the five had its many departments and several levels of management.

[3] *Report of Commissioner of Corporations on the Beef Industry*, p. 21.

This story has parallels in other industries processing agricultural products. In tobacco, James B. Duke was the first to appreciate the growing market for the cigarette, a new product which was sold almost wholly in the cities.[4] However, after he had applied machinery to the manufacture of cigarettes, production soon outran supply. Duke then concentrated on expanding the market through extensive advertising and the creation of a national and world-wide selling organization. In 1884, he left Durham, North Carolina, for New York City, where he set up factories, sales, and administrative offices. New York was closer to his major urban markets, and was the more logical place to manage an international advertising campaign than Durham. While he was building his marketing department, Duke was also creating the network of warehouses and buyers in the tobacco-growing areas of the country.

In 1890, he merged his company with five smaller competitors in the cigarette business to form the American Tobacco Company. By 1895 the activities of these firms had been consolidated into the manufacturing, marketing, purchasing, and finance departments of the single operating structure Duke had earlier fashioned. Duke next undertook development of a full line by handling all types of smoking and chewing tobacco. By the end of the century, his company completely dominated the tobacco business. Only two other firms, R. J. Reynolds & Company and P. Lorillard & Company had been able to build up comparable vertically integrated organizations. When they merged with American Tobacco they continued to retain the separate operating organizations. When the 1911 antitrust decree split these and other units off from the American company, the tobacco industry had become, like the meat-packing business, oligopolistic, and its dominant firms bureaucratic.

What Duke and Swift did for their industries, James S. Bell of the Washburn-Crosby Company did during these same years in the making and selling of high-grade flour to the urban bakeries and housewives, and Andrew J. Preston achieved in growing, transporting, and selling another new product for the urban market, the banana.[5] Like Swift and Duke, both these men made their major innovations in marketing, and then went on to create large-scale, departmentalized, vertically integrated structures.

The innovators in new consumer durables followed much the same pattern. Both Cyrus McCormick, pioneer harvester manufacturer, and William Clark, the business brains of Singer Sewing Machine Company,

---

[4] Some information on James B. Duke and the American Tobacco Company can be found in John W. Jenkins, *James B. Duke, Master Builder* (New York, 1927), chaps. 5–7, 10. More useful was the United States Bureau of Corporations, *Report of the Commissioner of Corporations on the Tobacco Industry* (Washington, 1909).

[5] The story of Bell is outlined in James Gray, *Business Without Boundary, the Story of General Mills* (Minneapolis, 1954), and of Preston in Charles M. Wilson, *Empire in Green and Gold* (New York, 1947).

first sold through commissioned agents. Clark soon discovered that salaried men, working out of branch offices, could more effectively and at less cost display, demonstrate, and service sewing machines than could the agents.[6] Just as important, the branch offices were able to provide the customer with essential credit. McCormick, while retaining the dealer to handle the final sales, came to appreciate the need for a strong selling and distributing organization, with warehouses, servicing facilities, and a large salaried force, to stand behind the dealer.[7] So in the years following the Civil War, both McCormick and Singer Sewing Machine Company concentrated on building up national and then world-wide marketing departments. As they purchased their raw materials from a few industrial companies rather than from a mass of farmers, their purchasing departments were smaller, and required less attention than those in the firms processing farmers' products. But the net result was the creation of a very similar type of organization.

Integration via Horizontal Combination

In those industries making more standard goods, the creation of marketing organizations usually followed large-scale combinations of a number of small manufacturing firms. For these small firms, the coming of the railroad had in many cases enlarged their markets but simultaneously brought them for the first time into competition with many other companies. Most of these firms appear to have expanded production in order to take advantage of the new markets. As a result, the industries became plagued with overproduction and excess capacity; that is, continued production at full capacity threatened to drop prices below the cost of production. So in the 1880's and early 1890's, many small manufacturers in the leather, sugar, salt, distilling and other corn products, linseed and cotton oil, biscuit, petroleum, fertilizer and rubber boot and glove industries, joined in large horizontal combinations.

In most of these industries, combination was followed by consolidation and vertical integration, and the pattern was comparatively consistent. First, the new combinations concentrated their manufacturing activities in locations more advantageously situated to meet the new growing urban demands. Next they systematized and standardized their manufacturing processes. Then, except in the case of sugar and corn products (glucose and starch), the combinations began to build large distributing and smaller purchasing departments. In so doing, many dropped their initial

[6] The early Singer Sewing Machine experience is well analyzed in Andrew B. Jack, "The Channels of Distribution for an Innovation: the Sewing Machine Industry in America, 1860–1865," *Explorations in Entrepreneurial History,* Vol. IX (Feb., 1957), pp. 113–141.
[7] William T. Hutchinson, *Cyrus Hall McCormick* (New York, 1935), Vol. II, pp. 704–712.

efforts to buy out competitors or to drive them out of business by price-cutting. Instead they concentrated on the creation of a more efficient flow from the producers of their raw materials to the ultimate consumer, and of the development and maintenance of markets through brand names and advertising. Since the large majority of these combinations began as regional groupings, most industries came to have more than one great firm. Only oil, sugar, and corn products remained long dominated by a single company. By World War I, partly because of the dissolutions under the Sherman Act, these industries had also become oligopolistic, and their leading firms vertically integrated.

Specific illustrations help to make these generalizations more precise. The best-known is the story of the oil industry, but equally illustrative is the experience of the leading distilling, baking, and rubber companies.

The first permanent combination in the whiskey industry came in 1887 when a large number of Midwestern distillers, operating more than 80 small plants, formed the Distillers' and Cattle Feeders' Trust.[8] Like other trusts, it adopted the more staisfactory legal form of a holding company shortly after New Jersey in 1889 passed the general incorporation law for holding companies. The major efforts of the Distillers Company were, first, to concentrate production in a relatively few plants. By 1895 only 21 were operating. The managers maintained that the large volume per plant permitted by such concentration would mean lower costs, and also that the location of few plants more advantageously in relation to supply and marketing would still reduce expenses further. However, the company kept the price of whiskey up, and since the cost of setting up a distillery was small, it soon had competition from small local plants. The company's answer was to purchase the new competitors and to cut prices. This strategy proved so expensive that the enterprise was unable to survive the depression of the 1890's.

Shortly before going into receivership in 1896, the Distillers Company had begun to think more about marketing. In 1895, it had planned to spend a million dollars to build up a distributing and selling organization in the urban East—the company's largest market. In 1898, through the purchase of the Standard Distilling & Distributing Company and the Spirits Distributing Company, it did acquire a marketing organization based in New York City. In 1903, the marketing and manufacturing units

[8] The major sources of information on combination and consolidation in the distilling industry are Jeremiah W. Jenks, "The Development of the Whiskey Trust," *Political Science Quarterly,* Vol. IV (June, 1889), pp. 296–319; J. W. Jenks and W. E. Clark, *The Trust Problem* (rev. ed.; New York, 1917), pp. 141–149. The annual reports of the Distilling and Cattle Feeding Company and its various successors provide some useful additional data, as does the Industrial Commission, *Preliminary Report on Trusts and Industrial Combinations* (Washington, 1900), Vol. I, pp. 74–89, 167–259, 813–848, and Victor S. Clark, *History of Manufactures in the United States* (New York, 1929), Vol. II, pp. 505–506. Changes in taxes on liquors also affected the company's policies in the early 1890's.

were combined into a single operating organization under the direction of the Distillers Securities Company. At the same time, the company's president announced plans to concentrate on the development of brand names and specialties, particularly through advertising and packaging.[9] By the early years of the twentieth centruy, then, the Distillers Company had become a vertically integrated, departmentalized, centralized operating organization, competing in the modern manner, more through advertising and product differentiation than price.

The experience of the biscuit industry is even more explicit. The National Biscuit Company came into being in 1898 as a merger of three regional combinations: the New York Biscuit Company formed in 1890, the American Biscuit and Manufacturing Company, and the United States Biscuit Company founded a little later.[10] Its initial objective was to control price and production, but as in the case of the Distillers Company, this strategy proved too expensive. The Annual Report for 1901 suggests why National Biscuit shifted its basic policies: [11]

> This Company is four years old and it may be of interest to shortly review its history. . . . When the Company started, it was an aggregation of plants. It is now an organized business. When we look back over the four years, we find that a radical change has been wrought in our methods of business. In the past, the managers of large merchandising corporations have found it necessary, for success, to control or limit competition. So when this company started, it was thought that we must control competition, and that to do this we must either fight competition or buy it. The first meant a ruinous war of prices, and a great loss of profit; the second, a constantly increasing capitalization. Experience soon proved to us that, instead of bringing success, either of those courses, if persevered in, must bring disaster. This led us to reflect whether it was necessary to control competition. . . . we soon satisfied ourselves that within the Company itself we must look for success.
>
> We turned our attention and bent our energies to improving the internal management of our business, to getting full benefit from purchasing our raw materials in large quantities, to economizing the expenses of manufacture, to systematizing and rendering more effective our selling department; and above all things and before all

[9] *Annual Report of the President of the Distillers Securities Company* for 1903.
[10] The information on National Biscuit comes largely from its annual reports.
[11] *Annual Report of the National Biscuit Company for the Year Ending December, 1901*, January 3, 1902. References to centralizing of manufacturing facilities appear in several early annual reports. As this was written before Theodore Roosevelt had started to make the Sherman Act an effective antitrust instrument and Ida Tarbell and other journalists had begun to make "muck raking" of big business popular and profitable, the Biscuit Company's shift in policy could hardly have been the result of the pressure of public opinion or the threat of government action.

things to improve the quality of our goods and the condition in which they should reach the customer.

It became the settled policy of this Company to buy out no competition. . . .

In concentrating on distribution, the company first changed its policy from selling in bulk to wholesalers to marketing small packages to retailers. It developed the various "Uneeda Biscuit" brands, which immediately became popular. "The next point," the same Annual Report continued, "was to reach the customer. Thinking we had something that the customer wanted, we had to advise the customer of its existence. We did this by extensive advertising." This new packaging and advertising not only quickly created a profitable business, but also required the building of a sizable marketing organization. Since flour could be quickly and easily purchased in quantity from large milling firms, the purchasing requirements were less complex, and so the company needed a smaller purchasing organization. On the other hand, it spent much energy after 1901 in improving plant layout and manufacturing processes in order to cut production costs and to improve and standardize quality. Throughout the first decade of its history, National Biscuit continued the policy of "centralizing" manufacturing operations, particularly in its great New York and Chicago plants.

In the rubber boot, shoe, and glove industries, the story is much the same. Expansion of manufacturing facilities and increasing competition as early as 1874, led to the formation, by several leading firms, of the Associated Rubber Shoe Companies—an organization for setting price and production schedules through its board of directors.[12] This company continued until 1886. Its successor, the Rubber Boot and Shoe Company, which lasted only a year, attempted, besides controlling prices and production, to handle marketing, which had always been done by commissioned agents. After five years of uncontrolled competition, four of the five firms that had organized the selling company again combined, this time with the assistance of a large rubber importer, Charles A. Flint. The resulting United States Rubber Company came, by 1898, to control 75 per cent of the nation's rubber boot, shoe, and glove output.

At first the new company remained a decentralized holding company. Each constituent company retained its corporate identity with much freedom of action, including the purchasing of raw materials and the

[12] The background for the creation of the United States Rubber Company can be found in Nancy P. Norton, "Industrial Pioneer: The Goodyear Metallic Rubber Shoe Company" (Ph.D. thesis, Radcliffe College, 1950), Constance McL. Green, *History of Naugatuck, Connecticut* (New Haven, 1948), pp. 126–131, 193–194, and Clark, *History of Manufactures,* Vol. II, pp. 479–481, Vol. III, pp. 235–237. The company's annual reports provide most of the information on its activities.

selling of finished products, which was done, as before, through jobbers. The central office's concern was primarily with controlling price and production schedules. Very soon, however, the company began, in the words of the 1896 Annual Report, a policy of "perfecting consolidation of purchasing, selling, and manufacturing." [13] This was to be accomplished in four ways. First, as the 1895 Annual Report had pointed out, the managers agreed "so far as practicable, to consolidate the purchasing of all supplies of raw materials for the various manufacturies into one single buying agency, believing that the purchase of large quantities of goods can be made at more advantageous figures than the buying of small isolated lots." [14] The second new "general policy" was "to undertake to reduce the number of brands of goods manufactured, and to consolidate the manufacturing of the remaining brands in those factories which have demonstrated superior facilities for production or advantageous labor conditions. This course was for the purpose of utilizing the most efficient instruments of production and closing those that were inefficient and unprofitable." The third policy was to consolidate sales through the formation of a "Selling Department," which was to handle all goods made by the constituent companies in order to achieve "economy in the distribution expense." Selling was now to be handled by a central office in the New York City headquarters, with branch offices throughout the United States and Europe. Of the three great new departments, actually manufacturing was the slowest to be fully consolidated and centralized. Finally, the treasurer's office at headquarters began to obtain accurate data on profit and loss through the institution of uniform, centralized cost accounting.

Thus United States Rubber, National Biscuit, and the Distillers Securities Company soon came to have organizational structures paralleling those of Swift and American Tobacco. By the first decade of the twentieth century, the leading firms in many consumers' goods industries had become departmentalized and centralized. This was the organizational concomitant to vertical integration. Each major function, manufacturing, sales, purchasing, and finance, became managed by a single and separate department head, usually a vice president, who, assisted by a director or a manager, had full authority and responsibility for the activities of his unit. These departmental chiefs, with the president, coordinated and evaluated the work of the different functional units, and made policy for the company as a whole. In coordinating, appraising, and policy-making, the president and the vice presidents in charge of departments came to rely

[13] *The Fifth Annual Report of the United States Rubber Company, March 31, 1897,* pp. 6–7.

[14] This and the following quotations are from the *Fourth Annual Report of the United States Rubber Company, May 25, 1896,* pp. 4–5, 7–8.

more and more on the accounting and statistical information, usually provided by the finance department, on costs, output, purchases, and sales.

CHANGES IN THE PRODUCERS' GOODS INDUSTRIES

Bureaucracy and oligopoly came to the producers' goods industries somewhat later than to those making products for the mass market. Until the depression of the 1890's, most of the combinations and consolidations had been in the consumers' goods industries. After that, the major changes came in those industries selling to other businesses and industrialists. The reason for the time difference seems to be that the city took a little longer to become a major market for producers' goods. Throughout the 1880's, railroad construction and operation continued to take the larger share of the output of steel, copper, power machinery, explosives, and other heavy industries. Then in the 1890's, as railroad construction declined the rapidly growing American cities became the primary market. The insatiable demand for urban lighting, communication, heat, power, transportation, water, sewerage, and other services directly and indirectly took ever growing quantities of electric lighting apparatus, telephones, copper wire, newsprint, streetcars, coal, and iron, steel, copper, and lead piping, structures and fixtures; while the constantly expanding urban construction created new calls on the power machinery and explosives as well as the metals industries. Carnegie's decision in 1887 to shift the Homestead Works, the nation's largest and most modern steel plant, from rails to structures, symbolized the coming change in the market.[15]

Also the new combinations and consolidations in the consumers' goods industries increased the demand for producers' products in the urban areas. Standard Oil, American Tobacco, Swift and other meat packers, McCormick's Harvesting Machinery and other farm implement firms, American Sugar, Singer Sewing Machine, and many other great consumer goods companies concentrated their production in or near major cities, particularly New York and Chicago.

The changes after 1897 differed from the earlier ones not only in types of industries in which they occurred but also in the way they were promoted and financed. Combinations and vertical integration in the consumer goods industries before 1897 had been almost all engineered and financed by the manufacturers themselves, so the stock control remained in the hands of the industrialists. After 1897, however, outside funds and often outside promoters, who were usually Wall Street financiers, played an increasingly significant role in industrial combination and consolidation. The change reflected a new attitude of investor and finan-

15 Clark, *History of Manufactures,* Vol. II, chap. 19.

cier who controlled capital toward the value of industrial securities.[16] Before the depression of the 1890's investment and speculation had been overwhelmingly in railroad stocks and bonds. The institutionalizing of the American security market in Wall Street had come, in fact, as a response to the needs for financing the first great railroad boom in the 1850's.

The railroads, however, had made a poor showing financially in the middle years of the 1890's when one-third of the nation's trackage went through receivership and financial reorganization. The dividend records of some of the new large industrial corporations, on the other hand, proved unexpectedly satisfactory. Moreover, railroad construction was slowing, and the major financial and administrative reorganizations of the 1890's had pretty well stabilized the industry. So there was less demand for investment bankers and brokers to market new issues of railroad securities.

Industrials were obviously the coming field, and by 1898 there was a rush in Wall Street to get in on this new business. The sudden availability of funds stimulated, and undoubtedly overstimulated, industrial combination. Many of the mergers in the years after 1897 came more from the desire of financiers for promotional profits, and because combination had become the thing to do, and less from the special needs and opportunities in the several industries. Moreover, as the financiers and promoters began to provide funds for mergers and expansion, they began to acquire, for the first time, the same type of control over industrial corporations that they had enjoyed in railroads since the 1850's.

The changes in the producers' goods industries were essentially like those in the consumer goods firms before the depression. Only after 1897 the changes came more rapidly, partly because of Wall Street pressures; and the differences that did develop between the two types of industries reflected the basic differences in the nature of their businesses. Like the companies making consumer goods, those manufacturing items for producers set up nation-wide and often world-wide marketing and distributing organizations, consolidated production into a relatively few large plants and fashioned purchasing departments. Because they had fewer customers, their sales departments tended to be smaller than those in firms selling to the mass market. On the other hand, they were more

[16] The story of the shift from rails to industrials as acceptable investments is told in Thomas R. Navin and Marian V. Sears, "The Rise of the Market for Industrial Securities, 1887–1902," *Business History Review*, Vol. XIX (June, 1955), pp. 105–138. Government securities were, of course, important in the years before 1850 and during and after the Civil War, but in the late 1870's and 1880's as in the 1850's, railroads dominated the American security exchanges. As Navin and Sears point out, some coal and mining firms were traded on the New York Exchange, but the only manufacturing securities, outside of those of the Pullman Company, were some textile stocks traded on the local Boston Exchange. The connections between the railroad expansion and the beginnings of modern Wall Street are described in detail in Chandler, *Poor*, chap. 4.

concerned with obtaining control over the sources of their supply than were most of the consumer goods companies.

Here a distinction can be made between the manufacturers who made semi-finished products from raw materials taken from the ground, and those who made finished goods from semi-finished products. The former, producing a uniform product for a few large industrial customers, developed only small sales departments and concentrated on obtaining control of raw materials, and often of the means of transporting such materials from mine to market. The latter, selling a larger variety of products and ones that often required servicing and financing, had much larger marketing and distributing organizations. These makers of finished goods, except for a brief period around 1900, rarely attempted to control their raw materials or their semi-finished steel and other metal supplies. They did, however, in the years after 1900, begin to buy or set up plants making parts and components that went into the construction of their finished products.

Except in steel, integration usually followed combination in the producers' goods industries. And for both makers of semi-finished and finished goods, integration became more of a defensive strategy than it was in the consumers' goods industries processing agricultural products. In the latter the manufacturers had an assured supply of raw materials from the output of the nation's millions of farms. In the former, on the other hand, they had to consider the threatening possibility of an outsider obtaining complete control of raw materials or supplies.

Integration and Combination in the Extractive Industries

By the early twentieth century nearly all the companies making semi-finished product goods controlled the mining of their own raw materials. The industries in which they operated can, therefore, be considered as extractive. This was also true of two consumers' goods industries: oil and fertilizer. The experience of these two provides a good introduction to the motives for integration and the role it played in the coming of "big business" in steel, copper, paper, explosives and other businesses producing semi-finished goods.

In both the oil and fertilizer industries, control over raw materials came well after combination and consolidation of groups of small manufacturing firms. The Standard Oil Trust, after its formation in 1882, consolidated its manufacturing activities and then created a domestic marketing organization. Only in the late 1880's, when the new Indiana field began to be developed and the older Pennsylvania ones began to decline, did the Trust consider going into the production of crude oil. Both Allan Nevins in his biography of John D. Rockefeller and the Hidys in their history of Standard Oil agree that the need to be assured of a steady supply of crude oil was the major reason for the move into production.[17] Other reasons, the Hidys indicate, were a fear that the producers might combine and so control supplies, and the desire of the pipeline subsidiaries to keep their facilities operating at full capacity. Although neither Nevins nor the Hidys suggest that the desire to obtain a more efficient flow of oil from the well to the distributor was a motive for this integration, both describe the committees and staff units that were formed at the central office at 26 Broadway to assure more effective coordination between production, refining, and marketing.

What little evidence there is suggests somewhat the same story in the fertilizer industry. Shortly after its organization in the mid-1890's, the Virginia-Carolina Chemical Company, a merger of many small southern fertilizer firms, began, apparently for the same defensive reasons, to purchase phosphate mines. Quickly its major competitor, the American Agricultural Chemical Company, a similar combination of small northeastern companies formed in 1893, responded by making its own purchases of mines. As the latter company explained in a later annual report: "The growth of the business, as well as the fact that available phosphate properties were being fast taken up, indicated that it was the part of wisdom to make additional provision for the future, and accordingly . . . available phosphate properties were purchased, and the necessary plants were erected and equipped, so the company now has in hand a supply of phosphate rock which will satisfy its growing demand for 60 years and upwards."[18] However, neither of these companies appeared to have set up organizational devices to guide the flow of materials from mine to plant to market; nor did the managers of a third large integrated fertilizer company, the International Agricultural Corporation, formed in 1909.

Defensive motives were certainly significant in the changes in the steel industry. Here the story can be most briefly described by focusing on the history of the industry's leader, the Carnegie Steel Company.[19] That

[17] Ralph W. Hidy and Muriel E. Hidy, *Pioneering in Big Business, 1882–1911* (New York, 1955), pp. 176–188. Allan Nevins, *Study in Power, John D. Rockefeller, Industrialist and Philanthropist* (New York, 1953), Vol. II, pp. 1–3. Nevins adds that another reason for the move into production was "partly to limit the number of active wells and reduce the overproduction of crude oil," Vol. II, p. 2, but he gives no documentation for this statement.

[18] *Annual Report of the American Agricultural Chemical Company, August 14, 1907,* also the same company's *Annual Report* dated August 25, 1902. In addition to the annual reports of the two companies, Clark, *History of Manufactures,* Vol. III, pp. 289–291, provides information. There is a brief summary of the story of the International Agricultural Corporation in Williams Haynes, *American Chemical Industry— A History* (New York, 1945), Vol. III, p. 173.

[19] The information on the Carnegie Steel Company is taken from Burton J. Hendrick, *The Life of Andrew Carnegie,* 2 vols. (New York, 1932), George Harvey, *Henry Clay Frick, the Man* (New York, 1928), James H. Bridge, *The Inside Story of the Carnegie Steel Company* (New York, 1903).

company's chairman, Henry C. Frick, had in the early 1890's consolidated and rationalized the several Carnegie manufacturing properties in and about Pittsburgh into an integrated whole. At the same time, he systematized and departmentalized its purchasing, engineering, and marketing activities. The fashioning of a sales department became more necessary since the shift from rails to structures had enlarged the number of the company's customers.

Then in 1896 the Carnegie company made a massive purchase of ore lands when it joined with Henry W. Oliver to buy out the Rockefeller holdings in the Mesabi Range. As Allan Nevins points out, the depression of the 1890's had worked a rapid transformation in the recently discovered Mesabi region.[20] By 1896, the ore fields had become dominated by three great interests: the Oliver Mining Company, the Minnesota Mining Company, and Rockefeller's Consolidated Iron Mines. A fourth, James J. Hill's Great Northern Railroad, was just entering the field. Frick's purchases, therefore, gave the Carnegie company an assured supply of cheap ore, as well as providing it with a fleet of ore ships. Next, Frick and Carnegie bought and rebuilt a railroad from Lake Erie to Pittsburgh to carry the new supplies to the mills.

Yet the steel company's managers did little to coordinate systematically the mining, shipping, and manufacturing units in their industrial empire. These activities did not become departments controlled from one central office but remained completely separate companies under independent managements, whose contact with one another was through negotiated contracts. This was the same sort of relation that existed between the Frick Coke Company and Carnegie Steel from the time Frick had joined Carnegie in 1889. If the Carnegie company's strategy had been to provide a more effective flow of materials as well as to assure itself of not being caught without a supply of ore and the means to transport it, then Frick and Carnegie would have created some sort of central coordinating office.

The steel industry responded quickly to the Carnegie purchases.[21] In 1898, Chicago's Illinois Steel Company, with capital supplied by J. P.

---

[20] Nevins, *Rockefeller*, Vol. II, p. 252.

[21] The experience of the other steel firms comes primarily from their annual reports and from prospectuses and other reports in the Corporation Records Division of Baker Library. A company publication, *J & L—The Growth of an American Business* (Pittsburgh, 1953) has some additional information on that company. Also, books listed in footnote 26 on the United States Steel Corporation have something on these companies. Two other steel companies listed in Table I made major changes somewhat before and after the period immediately following 1898. One, the Colorado Fuel & Iron Co., established in 1892, quickly became an integrated steel company in the Colorado area. The Bethlehem Steel Corporation was formed in 1904 when Charles F. Schwab, formerly of the Carnegie company and the United States Steel Corporation, reorganized the finances, corporate structure, and administrative organization of the bankrupt United States Shipbuilding Company.

Morgan & Company, joined the Lorain Steel Company (with plants on Lake Erie and in Johnstown, Pennsylvania) to purchase the Minnesota Mining Company, a fleet of ore boats, and railroads in the Mesabi and Chicago areas. Again, little attempt was made to coordinate mining and shipping with manufacturing and marketing. In the same year, many iron and steel firms in Ohio and Pennsylvania merged to form the Republic and National Steel Companies. Shortly thereafter, a similar combination in the Sault Sainte Marie area became the Consolidated Lake Superior Company. These three new mergers began at once to set up their marketing organizations and to obtain control by lease and purchase of raw materials and transportation facilities. In 1900, several small firms making high grade steel did much the same thing by the formation of the Crucible Steel Company of America. In these same years, the larger, established steel companies, like Lackawanna, Cambria, and Jones & Laughlin obtained control of more supplies of ore, coke, and limestone and simultaneously reorganized their manufacturing and marketing organizations. Like Carnegie and Federal, they at first made little effort to bring their mining and coke operations under the direct control of the central office.

In copper, defensive motives for integration appear to have been somewhat less significant. In the 1890's, mining, smelting and refining were combined on a large scale. During the 'eighties the railroad had opened up many western mining areas, particularly in Montana and Arizona; a little later the new electrical and telephone businesses greatly increased the demand for copper. Mining firms like Anaconda, Calumet & Hecla, and Phelps Dodge moved into smelting and refining, while the Guggenheims' Philadelphia Smelting & Refining Company began to buy mining properties.[22] In the copper industry, the high cost of ore shipment meant that smelting and—after the introduction of the electrolytic process in the early 1890's—even refining could be done more cheaply close to the mines. Of the large copper firms, only Calumet & Hecla and the Guggenheims set up refineries in the East before 1898, and both made use of direct water transportation.

After 1898, several large mergers occurred in the nonferrous metals industries. Nearly all were initially promoted by eastern financiers. Of these, the most important were Amalgamated Copper, engineered by H. H. Rogers of Standard Oil and Marcus Daly of Anaconda, the American Smelting and Refining Company which the Guggenheims came to control, and United Copper promoted by F. Augustus Heinze. United Copper remained little more than a holding company. Amalgamated set up a subsidiary to operate a large refinery at Perth Amboy and another, the

[22] Information on the mining companies came from their annual reports and from Isaac P. Marcosson's two books, *Magic Metal—the Story of the American Smelting and Refining Company* (New York, 1949), and *Anaconda* (New York, 1957), also Clark, *History of Manufactures*, Vol. II, pp. 368–369.

United Metals Selling Company, with headquarters in New York City, to market the products of its mining and processing subsidiaries. The holding company's central offices in New York remained small and apparently did comparatively little to coordinate the activities of its several operating companies. The Guggenheims formed a much tighter organization with direct headquarters control of the company's mining, shipping, smelting and marketing departments. On the whole, there appears to have been somewhat closer coordination between mining and processing in the large copper than in the major steel companies.

Lowering of costs through more effective coordination appears to have been a major motive for consolidation and combination in three other businesses whose raw materials came from the ground: explosives, paper, and coal.[23] The mergers that created the Pittsburgh Coal Company in 1899 and greatly enlarged the Consolidation Coal Company in 1903 were followed by a reorganization and consolidation of mining properties and then by the creation of large marketing departments which operated throughout most of the country. The merger of close to 30 paper companies, forming the International Paper Company in 1899, was followed first by consolidation and reorganization of the manufacturing plants, next by the formation of a national marketing organization with headquarters in New York City, and then by the purchase of large tracts of timber in Maine and Canada. These three activities were departmentalized under vice presidents and controlled from the New York office. In all these cases, the central office was responsible for the flow of materials from mine or forest to the customer or retailer.

The explosive industries underwent a comparable sweeping change in 1902 and 1903. Since the 1870's, price and production schedules had been decided by the industry's Gunpowder Trade Association, and almost from its beginning, that Association had been controlled by one firm, the E. I. DuPont de Nemours & Company. However, the member concerns had retained their own corporate identities and managements. In 1902, the DuPonts bought out a large number of these independent companies through exchanges of stock, and then consolidated them into a single centralized organization. In the process, plants were shut down, others enlarged, and new ones built. A nation-wide selling organization was created, and centralized accounting, purchasing, engineering and traffic

---

[23] The story of the leading explosives, paper, salt and coal companies comes from annual reports and also from Charles E. Beachley, *History of the Consolidation Coal Company 1864–1934* (New York, 1934), George H. Love, *An Exciting Century in Coal* (New York, 1955), the company-written, *The International Paper Company, 1898–1948* (n.p., 1948), William S. Dutton, *DuPont—One Hundred and Forty Years* (New York, 1940), and *U. S. v. E. I. DuPont de Nemours & Company et al. in Circuit Court of the United States for the District of Delaware, #280 in Equity (1909), Defendants' Record Testimony*, Vol. I, and for the paper industry, Clark, *History of Manufactures*, Vol. III, pp. 245–252. The American Writing Paper Company, though less successful, had many parallels to International Paper.

departments formed. Once the new organization was completed, then the company's executives obtained control of their raw materials through the purchase of nitrate mines and deposits in Chile.

Except possibly in paper, the control of price and production does not appear to have been a major motive for the initial combinations in the extractive industries making producers' goods. In steel before 1901, and nonferrous metals and coal, there were several combinations, but none acquired as much as 20 per cent of the market. Nor is there any evidence that the creators of the different mergers, while they were forming their organizations, were arranging with one another to set over-all price and production schedules. In explosives, control of competition could not have been a significant reason for the 1902 changes since the DuPont company had enjoyed such control since the 1870's. In coal and explosives, and possibly in copper, the major motive for combination, consolidation, and the integration of supply with the manufacturing and marketing processes seems to have been an expectation of lowered costs through the creation of a national distributing organization, the consolidation of manufacturing activities, and the effective coordination of the different industrial processes by one central office. In steel and possibly copper, the desire for an assured supply of raw materials appears to have been more significant in encouraging combination and integration.

Changes and Integration in the Finished Producers' Goods Industries

Control of price and production was, on the other hand, much more of an obvious motive for combination and resulting consolidation in the industries manufacturing finished products or machinery from the semi-finished materials produced by the extractive firms. Concern over supply, however, was also a cause for change, for after 1898 the users of steel, copper, coal, and other semi-finished materials felt threatened by the growing number of combinations among their suppliers. In any case, between 1898 and 1900 there was a wave of mergers in these industries, largely Wall Street financed, which led to the formation of American Tin Plate, American Wire & Steel, American Steel Hoop, National Tube, American Bridge, American Sheet Metal, Shelby Steel Tube, American Can, National Enameling & Stamping Company and a number of other combinations among steel-fabricating firms.[24] At the same time, there were many amalgamations in the power machinery and implement businesses, such as American Car & Foundry, American Locomotive, Allis-Chalmers, International Steam Pump, and International Harvester. The

[24] The best brief summary of these mergers and the formation of the United States Steel Corporation is in Eliot Jones, *The Trust Problem in the United States* (New York, 1924), pp. 189–200. The companies' annual reports and prospectuses provide additional material.

largest combination among the copper users, the American Brass Company, came in a little later, in 1903, after the Guggenheims, Rogers, and Heinze had completed the major copper mergers.

Nearly all these combinations quickly consolidated their constituent companies into a single operating organization. Manufacturing facilities were unified and systematized, over-all accounting procedures instituted, and national and often world-wide distributing organizations formed. Many set up central traffic and purchasing departments; some even began to assure themselves control over supply by building up their own rolling mills and blast furnaces. As American Wire & Steel and National Tube began to make their own steel, they cancelled contracts with Carnegie and other semi-finished steel producers. This development, in turn, led Carnegie to develop plans for fabricating his own finished products.[25]

The resulting threat of overcapacity and price-cutting led to the formation of the United States Steel Corporation.[26] This giant merger, which included Carnegie, Federal and National Steel, and the first six of the fabricating companies listed above, continued on as a combination. Although the activities of the various subsidiaries were re-formed and redefined, there was no consolidation. United States Steel remained a holding company only, and the central office at 72 Broadway did comparatively little to coordinate the operations of its many subsidiary companies.

After 1901, the fabricators and the machinery manufacturers made little attempt to produce their own steel or copper. Nor did the makers of semi-finished products try, for some years to come, to do their own fabricating. Possibly the metal users realized that even with the formation of United States Steel they were fairly certain of alternative sources of supply. Also they may have found that once they had combined they had enough bargaining power to assure themselves of a supply of steel and other materials more cheaply than they could make it themselves.

While such firms no longer sought to control their basic materials, many, particularly the machinery makers like General Electric, Westinghouse, American Car & Foundry, International Harvester and, a little later, General Motors, began to purchase or set up subsidiaries or departments to make parts and components.[27] Here again the motive was essentially defensive. Since much of their manufacturing had now become mainly assembling, they wanted to be sure to have a supply of parts available at all times. The lack of a vital part could temporarily shut down

[25] Hendrick, *Carnegie*, Vol. II, pp. 116–119.

[26] The beginnings and the operation of the United States Steel Corporation are outlined in Abraham Berglund, *The United States Steel Corporation: A Study of Growth and Combination in the Iron and Steel Industry* (New York, 1907), Arundel Cotter, *The Authentic History of the United States Steel Corporation* (New York, 1916), Ida M. Tarbell, *The Life of Elbert H. Gary, the Story of Steel* (New York, 1925).

[27] This generalization is based on the annual reports of the several companies.

a plant. However, they expected to take only a portion of the output; a major share was sold to outsiders. One outstanding exception to this pattern was Henry Ford. He came to control his raw materials as well as his parts and components, and rarely sold such parts to outside companies. But Ford's insistence on having a completely integrated organization from mine to market, concentrated largely in one huge plant, proved to be one of the most costly mistakes in American business history.

Control of parts and accessory units led to a diversification of the types of products these manufacturing companies made and sold. Such diversification brought, over time, important changes in business organization. Even more significant for stimulating product diversification was the new "full line" strategy adopted by a number of these recently consolidated concerns. Such a policy, initiated largely to help assure the maximum use of the new departments, encouraged technological as well as organizational change.

Pioneers in developing "full lines" in the producers' goods industries were the two great electrical companies: General Electric and Westinghouse. Unlike almost any other of the leading American industrial companies in 1900, these two had begun as research and development rather than manufacturing organizations. Because of their origins, they had the skilled personnel and the necessary equipment to move, in the mid-1890's, from making lighting equipment alone to manufacturing many lines of electric traction and power machinery products.[28] Allis-Chalmers, International Steam Pump, and American Locomotive began, shortly after their formation and subsequent consolidations, to develop new lines using electric and gasoline engines.[29] International Harvester, building up a number of farm implement lines, also started to experiment with the use of the gasoline engine for machinery on the farm. In this same first decade of the twentieth century, rubber, explosive, and chemical companies began to turn to industrial chemistry in their search to develop broader lines of products.

Continuing diversification came, however, largely in industries where science, particularly chemistry and physics, could be most easily applied. And it was in these industries, and in those which were directly affected by the coming of two new sources of power, electricity and the internal combustion engine, that the major innovations in American industry came after 1900. The chemical, automotive, power machinery, rubber, and

[28] As is well described in Harold C. Passer, *The Electrical Manufacturers* (Cambridge, 1953).

[29] The development of new lines by Allis-Chalmers, International Steam Pump, and American Locomotive is mentioned in their annual reports in the first decade of the twentieth century. International Harvester's similar "full line" policies are described in Cyrus McCormick, *The Century of the Reaper* (New York, 1931), chaps. 6–9, and United States Bureau of Corporations, *The International Harvester Co., March 3, 1913* (Washington, 1913), especially pp. 156–158.

petroleum industries led the way to the development of new processes and products, new ways of internal organization and new techniques of external competition as the new century unfolded. The metals industries and those processing agricultural goods have, on the other hand, changed relatively little since the beginning of the century. In these industries, the same firms make much the same products, use much the same processes, and compete in much the same manner in the 1950's as they did in the 1900's. For them the greatest period of change came in the last decade of the nineteenth century.

Conclusion: The Basic Innovations

The middle of the first decade of the new century might be said to mark the end of an era. By 1903, the great merger movement was almost over, and by then the metals industries and those processing agricultural products had developed patterns of internal organization and external competition which were to remain. In those years, too, leading chemical, electrical, rubber, power machinery and implement companies had initiated their "full line" policy, and had instituted the earliest formal research and development departments created in this country. In this decade also, electricity was becoming for the first time a significant source of industrial power, and the automobile was just beginning to revolutionize American transportation. From 1903 on, the new generators of power and the new technologies appear to have become the dominant stimuli to innovation in American industry, and such innovations were primarily those which created new products and processes. Changes in organizational methods and marketing techniques were largely responses to technological advances.

This seems much less true of the changes during the 20 to 25 years before 1903. In that period, the basic innovations were more in the creation of new forms of organization and new ways of marketing. The great modern corporation, carrying on the major industrial processes, namely, purchasing, and often production of materials and parts, manufacturing, marketing, and finance—all within the same organizational structure—had its beginnings in that period. Such organizations hardly existed, outside of the railroads, before the 1880's. By 1900 they had become the basic business unit in American industry.

Each of these major processes became managed by a corporate department, and all were coordinated and supervised from a central office. Of the departments, marketing was the most significant. The creation of nation-wide distributing and selling organizations was the initial step in the growth of many large consumer goods companies. Mergers in both the

The Official Eh & Sally Note Pad

The Official Eli & Sally Note Pad

©GLAZA 1973

aled

consumer and producer goods industries were almost always followed by the formation of a centralized sales department.

The consolidation of plants under a single manufacturing department usually accompanied or followed the formation of a national marketing organization. The creation of such a manufacturing department normally meant the concentration of production in fewer and larger plants, and such consolidation probably lowered unit costs and increased output per worker. The creation of such a department in turn led to the setting up of central traffic, purchasing, and often engineering organizations. Large-scale buying, more rational routing of raw materials and finished products, more systematic plant lay-out, and plant location in relation to materials and markets probably lowered costs still further. Certainly the creators of these organizations believed that it did. In the extractive and machinery industries integration went one step further. Here the motives for controlling raw materials or parts and components were defensive as well as designed to cut costs through providing a more efficient flow of materials from mine to market.

These great national industrial organizations required a large market to provide the volume necessary to support the increased overhead costs. Also, to be profitable, they needed careful coordination between the different functional departments. This coordination required a steady flow of accurate data on costs, sales, and on all purchasing, manufacturing, and marketing activities. As a result, the comptroller's office became an increasingly important department. In fact, one of the first moves after a combination by merger or purchase was to institute more effective and detailed accounting procedures. Also, the leading entrepreneurs of the period, men like Rockefeller, Carnegie, Swift, Duke, Preston, Clark, and the DuPonts, had to become, as had the railroad executives of an earlier generation, experts in reading and interpreting business statistics.

Consolidation and departmentalization meant that the leading industrial corporations became operating rather than holding companies, in the sense that the officers and managers of the companies were directly concerned with operating activities. In fact, of the 50 companies with the largest assets in 1909, only United States Steel, Amalgamated Copper, and one or two other copper companies remained purely holding companies. In most others, the central office included the heads of the major functional departments, usually the president, vice presidents, and sometimes a chairman of the board and one or two representatives of financial interests. These men made major policy and administrative decisions and evaluated the performance of the departments and the corporation as a whole. In the extractive industries a few companies, like Standard Oil (N.J.) and some of the metals companies, were partly holding and partly operating companies. At Standard Oil nearly all important decisions were made in the central headquarters, at 26 Broadway, which housed not only the presidents of the subsidiaries but the powerful policy formulating and coordinating committees.[30] But in some of the metals companies, the subsidiaries producing and transporting raw materials retained a large degree of autonomy.

The coming of the large vertically integrated, centralized, functionally departmentalized industrial organization altered the internal and external situations in which and about which business decisions were made. Information about markets, supplies, and operating performance as well as suggestions for action often had to come up through the several levels of the departmental hierarchies, while decisions and suggestions based on this data had to be transmitted down the same ladder for implementation. Executives on each level became increasingly specialists in one function —in sales, production, purchasing, or finance—and most remained in one department and so handled one function only for the major part of their business careers. Only he who climbed to the very top of the departmental ladder had a chance to see his own company as a single operating unit. Where a company's markets, sources of raw materials, and manufacturing processes remained relatively stable, as was true in the metals industries and in those processing agricultural goods, the nature of the business executive's work became increasingly routine and administrative.

When the internal situation had become bureaucratic, the external one tended to be oligopolistic. Vertical integration by one manufacturer forced others to follow. Thus, in a very short time, many American industries became dominated by a few large firms, with the smaller ones handling local and more specialized aspects of the business. Occasionally industries like oil, tobacco, and sugar, came to be controlled by one company, but in most cases legal action by the federal government in the years after 1900 turned monopolistic industries into oligopolistic ones.

Costs, rather than interfirm competition, began to determine prices. With better information on costs, supplies, and market conditions, the companies were able to determine price quite accurately on the basis of the desired return on investment. The managers of the different major companies had little to gain by cutting prices below an acceptable profit margin. On the other hand, if one firm set its prices excessively high, the other firms could increase their share of the market by selling at a lower price and still maintain a profit. They would, however, rarely cut to the point where this margin was eliminated. As a result, after 1900, price leadership, price umbrellas, and other evidences of oligopolistic competition became common in many American industries. To increase their share of the market and to improve their profit position, the large corporations therefore concerned themselves less with price and concentrated

[30] Hidys, *Pioneering in Big Business,* chap. 3 and pp. 323–388.

more on obtaining new customers by advertising, brand names, and product differentiations; on cutting costs through further improvement and integration of the manufacturing, marketing, and buying processes; and on developing more diversified lines of products.

The coming of the large vertically integrated corporation changed more than just the practices of American industrialists and their industries. The effect on the merchant, particularly the wholesaler, and on the financier, especially the investment banker, has been suggested here. The relation between the growth of these great industrial units and the rise of labor unions has often been pointed out. Certainly the regulation of the large corporation became one of the major political issues of these years, and the devices created to carry out such a regulation were significant innovations in American constitutional, legal, and political institutions. But an examination of such effects is beyond the scope of this paper.

Reasons for the Basic Innovations

One question remains to be reviewed. Why did the vertically integrated corporation come when it did, and in the way it did? The creation by nearly all the large firms of nation-wide selling and distributing organizations indicated the importance of the national market. It was necessary that the market be an increasingly urban one. The city took the largest share of the goods manufactured by the processors of agricultural products. The city, too, with its demands for construction materials, lighting, heating and many other facilities, provided the major market for the metals and other producers' goods industries after railroad construction slowed. Without the rapidly growing urban market there would have been little need and little opportunity for the coming of big business in American industry. And such a market could hardly have existed before the completion of a nation-wide railroad network.

What other reasons might there have been for the swift growth of the great industrial corporation? What about foreign markets? In some industries, particularly oil, the overseas trade may have been an important factor. However, in most businesses the domestic customers took the lion's share of the output, and in nearly all of them the move abroad appears to have come after the creation of the large corporation, and after such corporations had fashioned their domestic marketing organization.

What about the investor looking for profitable investments, and the promoter seeking new promotions? Financiers and promoters certainly had an impact on the changes after 1897, but again they seem primarily to have taken advantage of what had already proved successful. The industrialists themselves, rather than the financiers, initiated most of the major changes in business organization. Availability of capital and cooperation

TABLE I
THE FIFTY LARGEST INDUSTRIALS
(Numbers indicate relative size according to 1909 assets)

Consumers' Goods Companies

Agricultural Processing	*Extractive*	*Manufacturing*
3. Am. Tobacco	2. Standard Oil	4. Int'l. Harvester
8. Armour & Co.	26. Va.-Carolina Chem.	10. U. S. Rubber
9. American Sugar	35. American Agri. Chem.	12. Singer Mfg. Co.
13. Swift & Co.		
30. Nat'l. Biscuit		
33. Distillers' Securities		
50. United Fruit		

Producers' Goods Companies

Agricultural Processing	*Extractive*	*Manufacturing*
6. Central Leather	1. U. S. Steel	7. Pullman
18. Corn Products Co.	5. Amalgamated	15. Gen. Elec.
21. Am. Woolens	(Anaconda) Copper	16. Am. Car & Foundry
	11. Am. Smelting &	19. Am. Can
	Refining	22. Westinghouse
	14. Pittsburgh Coal	24. DuPont
	17. Colo. Fuel & Iron	29. Am. Locomotive
	20. Lackawanna	36. Allis-Chalmers
	23. Consolidation Coal	44. Int. Steam Pump
	25. Republic Steel	46. Western Electric
	27. Int'l. Paper	
	28. Bethlehem Steel	
	31. Cambria Steel	
	33. Associated Oil	
	34. Calumet & Hecla	
	37. Crucible Steel	
	38. Lake Superior Corp.	
	39. U. S. Smelting & Ref.	
	40. United Copper	
	41. National Lead	
	42. Phelps Dodge	
	43. Lehigh Coal	
	45. Jones & Laughlin	
	48. Am. Writing Paper	
	49. Copper Range	

with the financier figured much less prominently in these industrial combinations and consolidations than had been the case with the earlier construction of the railroads and with the financing of the Civil War.

What about technological changes? Actually, except for electricity, the major innovations in the metals industries seem to have come before or after the years under study here. Most of the technological improvements in the agricultural processing industries appear to have been made to meet the demands of the new urban market. The great technological innovations that accompanied the development of electricity, the internal combustion engine, and industrial chemistry did have their beginning in these years, and were, indeed, to have a fundamental impact on the American business economy. Yet this impact was not to be really felt until after 1900.

What about entrepreneurial talent? Certainly the best-known entrepreneurs of this period were those who helped to create the large industrial corporation. If, as Joseph A. Schumpeter suggests, "The defining characteristic [of the entrepreneur and his function] is simply the doing of new things, and doing things that are already done, in a new way (innovation)," Rockefeller, Carnegie, Frick, Swift, Duke, McCormick, the DuPonts, the Guggenheims, Coffin of General Electric, Preston of United Fruit, and Clark of Singer Sewing Machine were all major innovators of their time.[31] And their innovations were not in technology, but rather in organization and in marketing. "Doing a new thing," is, to Schumpeter a "creative response" to a new situation, and the situation to which these innovators responded appears to have been the rise of the national urban market.

There must be an emphasis here on the words "seem" and "appear." The framework used is a preliminary one and the data itself, based on readily available printed material rather than on business records, is hardly as detailed or accurate as could be desired. More data, more precise and explicit questions, and other types and ranges of questions will modify the generalizations suggested here. For the moment, however, I would like to suggest, if only to encourage the raising of questions and the further compilation and analysis of data, that *the* major innovation in the American economy between the 1880's and the turn of the century was the creation of the great corporations in American industry. This innovation, as I have tried to show, was a response to the growth of a national and increasingly urban market that was created by the building of a national railroad network—the dynamic force in the economy in the quarter century before 1880. After 1900 the newly modified methods of interfirm and intrafirm administration remained relatively unchanged (as did the location of major markets and sources of raw materials) except in those industries directly affected by new sources of power and the systematic application of science to industry. In the twentieth century electricity, the internal combustion engine, and systematic, institutionalized

[31] Joseph A. Schumpeter, "The Creative Response in Economic History," *Journal of Economic History*, Vol. VII (May, 1947), p. 151, and also his *Theory of Economic Development*, trans. Redvers Opie (Cambridge, 1934), pp. 74–94.

research and development took the place of the national urban market as the dynamic factor in the American industrial economy.[32]

[32] This point has only been considered briefly here, but has been developed at some length in my "Development, Diversification and Decentralization," to be published in a book of essays tentatively titled *The Postwar American Economy* under the sponsorship of the Department of Economics, Massachusetts Institute of Technology.

Government and Business: Law and Ideology

27. Entrepreneurial Liberty and the Fourteenth Amendment

John P. Roche

In the last quarter of the Nineteenth century and well on into the Twentieth, so the legend runs, the United States was dominated by a "conservative," "individualist," *laissez-faire* elite which succeeded in rewriting the Constitution and notably the Fourteenth Amendment to impose its ideology upon the nation. This notion has a certain superficial persuasiveness, but regrettably it is hardly sustained by a close analysis of the history of the period. There was clearly an elite of businessmen, but it was neither ruggedly individualistic, in terms of classic liberal economic thought, nor "conservative," in any acceptable definition of that much-abused term. On the contrary, this elite lived at the public trough, was nourished by state protection, and devoted most of its time and energies to evading Adam Smith's individualistic injunctions. In ideological terms, it was totally opportunistic: It demanded and applauded vigorous state action in behalf of its key values, and denounced state intervention in behalf of its enemies. The Constitution was not, in short, adapted to the needs of *laissez-faire* "conservatism"—which is a respectable, internally consistent system of political economy—but to the exigent needs of the great private governments. The "Robber Barons" had no ideology, they had interests. They had no theory of the state, but they knew what they wanted from it. Their key value, entrepreneurial liberty, might require a strong state one day (to combat trade unions) and a weak state the next (which would not pass wage and hour legislation), and this inconsistency troubled them not. If some scribe wanted to make them into "industrial

"Entrepreneurial Liberty and the Fourteenth Amendment," by John P. Roche, is reprinted by permission from *Labor History*, IV (Winter, 1963), 3–31.

statesmen," or "pillars of conservatism," that was merely one of the eccentricities of the division of labor.

Nowhere does this opportunism, this absence of theoretical consistency or of any concern for consistency, appear more clearly than in the adaptation of the Fourteenth Amendment, especially the due process clause, to the needs of private government. Central to the power of private governments in the American "Age of Enterprise" was the doctrine that private agreements between parties attained a sacred status, that such contracts were on a higher level of legitimacy than the police power of the state. To put it another way, the sanctity of contract put inter-"personal" (corporations, it should be noted, qualified as "persons") relationships largely beyond the authority of the political sovereign. From a different perspective the question was, to what extent is the authority of the community limited by private arrangements among its citizens; that is, by "liberty of contract"?

The argument began early in the history of the Republic. The framers of the Constitution included, without discussion, a proviso that no state could "impair the obligation of a contract." It is impossible to know what they had in mind, but in all probability the stipulation was aimed at state legal tender laws, such as that in Rhode Island, which had required creditors to accept depreciated paper currency in payment of debts incurred in specie. While on its face the limitation was absolute, it is inconceivable that the authors of the Constitution intended to put private agreements wholly beyond the reach of the state's police power. Like many other provisions of the Constitution, it was agreed to in haste to be interpreted by later generations in leisure.[1]

In the early Supreme Court cases, the Justices established the basic positions which, in differing contexts, have survived to our own time. John Marshall on one side asserted the vested rights view that contracts are made in heaven, that is, they have their roots in the natural law and are superior to the civil law. Marshall was far too shrewd to claim that all interpersonal agreements were inviolable contracts; by employing his favorite device—circular logic—he explained that a law forbidding usury did not impair contractual obligations because an arrangement to pay excessive interest was not, in the first place properly speaking, a "contract." Q.E.D. The opposing view, that contracts are conceived in the womb of the civil law rather than in a natural law Never-Never Land, was vigorously asserted by Justice William Johnson. Contracts, he argued, were always formulated and executed within the jurisdiction of the state police power. True the legislature did not have unlimited authority to modify or abrogate agreements, but it could establish rules and standards

[1] See John P. Roche, "The Founding Fathers," *American Political Science Review*, Vol. 55 (1961), pp 814 ff.

binding on private parties. These rules and regulations could even be applied retrospectively—to contracts made before they were enounced— if it could be shown that the contracting parties *should have known* that the legislature had reserved power in this area.

This is an extremely complex, even metaphysical doctrine. If, for example, X, a brewer, signed a twenty-year contract to supply Y, an innkeeper, with beer and after five years the state instituted prohibition, was the contract voided? From the natural-law viewpoint, the contract cannot be impaired by such a statute, and as the prohibition movement swept across the United States in the mid-Nineteenth century many liquor manufacturers hopefully fortified themselves with long-term contracts with a view to putting their business beyond the reach of the police power. But from the civil-law position, no private arrangements can bind the sovereign; therefore when X and Y made their contract, they did so with the knowledge that it was subject to later legislative modification. To put it another way, all contracts are enacted in a contingent universe, and this contingency is an implicit premise in the private agreement. Once the Taney Court added to this proposition the corollary that all doubts are resolved in favor of the public, the Contract Clause of the Constitution (Art. I, Sec. 10) went into hibernation as a significant limit on public policy.[2]

With this hasty summary in mind, let us direct our attention to the revival of the concept of contract which in the last years of the Nineteenth and first quarter of the Twentieth centuries became the fundamental buttress of private government. This resurgence took place under two main headings. First, the concept of contract was broadened to include the substantive right to pursue a calling, both on an individual and on a corporate level. Second, the right to make contractual arrangements to exercise one's calling became a "property" right protected from state infringement by the due process clause of the Fourteenth Amendment. As Justice Field argued in a classic formulation of this position, his dissent in the *Slaughterhouse Cases* (1873),[3] a butcher has a natural right to exercise his trade—contract for his services—and a state law which deprives him of his freedom to make his own arrangements (contracts) has expropriated his property rights in his enterprise. Field was even prepared to argue that such a statute constituted slavery in violation of the Thirteenth Amendment!

In effect, the old Marshallian interpretation of the contract appeared in a new guise, a far broader and more sophisticated one than the Chief Justice had ever envisioned. Instead of giving a natural law attributes to contracts only, Field and his followers widened the protection to encom-

[2] See generally Benjamin F. Wright, *The Contract Clause in the Constitution* (Cambridge, 1938).
[3] 16 Wall. 36 (1873).

pass the *right to enter into contracts,* that is, to the prerogative of doing business on one's own terms, which I have designated entrepreneurial liberty. And on his own West Coast Circuit, where he was boss, Justice Field implemented his convictions in what was known as "Ninth Circuit Law." Relying on a technicality which prevented Supreme Court review of *habeas corpus* decisions, Field and his judicial associates established as constitutional law in the Ninth Circuit the proposition that the rights to pursue legitimate callings, to make and enforce contracts, and to do business free from extraordinary legislative control were incorporated in the due process and equal protection clauses of the Fourteenth Amendment. In this backdoor fashion, natural entrepreneurial rights entered the Constitution.[4]

While Field never denied the existence of the police power, his whole position was based on the proposition that in any conflict between private *economic* rights and public authority the burden of proof rested on the state. The state, in other words, had to demonstrate to the satisfaction of the Court that its regulations were justified. In the absence of strong historical or contextual proof of legitimacy, Field almost automatically voted "No!," but it was possible on occasion—*e.g., Barbier* v. *Connolly* (1885), *Soon Hing* v. *Crowley* (1885) [5]—to convince him that the police power had been legitimately exercised. Yet in the area of noneconomic rights (rights of Negroes, for example, to equal political treatment) he gave the police power its head.

This is not the place for a discussion of the rapid spread of Justice Field's—and Justice Bradley's—dissenting views in the *Slaughterhouse Cases.* Needless to say, the conception that there was constitutional protection for the right to follow one's calling—and that the contractual arrangements made in pursuing business goals were largely immune to public authority—became the ideological *point d'appui* for the corporations in their struggle against regulation. State judges were particularly susceptible to this line of argument, and in New York, Pennsylvania, West Virginia, and many other states the divine right of contract supplied the rationale for voiding state regulatory legislation.[6] Contracts were the instruments by which men implemented their property rights in their economic capacities; thus legislatively to prohibit paying miners in company script, when they had agreed to this form of remuneration in their employment contracts, was to deprive the *miners* of their "property right" to make their own economic decisions. The average miner never really appreciated this judicial concern for his integrity; from his worm's-eye

[4] See Howard Jay Graham, "Justice Field and the Fourteenth Amendment," *Yale Law Journal,* Vol. 52 (1943), pp. 851–889.

[5] 113 U. S. 27 (1885); 113 U. S. 703 (1885).

[6] See generally Clyde E. Jacobs, *Law Writers and the Courts* (Berkeley, 1954); Benjamin R. Twiss, *Lawyers and the Constitution* (Princeton, 1942).

view a contract with the coal company was hardly the outcome of bargaining between equals. But the judges persisted in protecting him from
his own base instincts, which would have led him to become a "ward of
the state"—a fate worse than death.

This judicial altruism deserves emphasis. There is no necessity to believe that the judges were insincere when they protected the furious
farmers from "serfdom" by striking down legislative enactments designed
to curb railroad shipping practices, or when they rescued the industrial
worker from "slavery" by asserting freedom of contract in his behalf. Just
as in the *Income Tax Cases* (1895) communism was seen as the logical
consequence of a graduated tax, so serfdom and slavery were seen as the
natural end results of dependence on the state. This was the era when,
under the Social Darwinist aegis, that evil abstraction The State was first
loosed in the land. The conflict of the age was seen as one between The
Individual and The State, and the consequences of Statism (the triumph
of the weak over the strong in Spencerian terms) would be decadence
and dictatorship.

The logic of this position was absurd in its own terms. As a contemporary critic like Lester F. Ward pointed out (to an empty house), if the
weak succeeded in beating the strong by ganging up against them,
according to the syllogism of Social Darwinism, they became the "fittest."
In other words, if one argues that Nature awards the prize to the "fittest"
and that the "fittest" are those who emerge on top of the pile, then the
workers or farmers who successfully club down the industrial magnates
with the state as their weapon deserve the Darwinian accolade. The logic
of Social Darwinism was that the winner takes all; no ground rules were
prescribed. What the state, and later the federal judges, did in the name
of impartiality was strip the weak of their capacity for collective action. In
the event that the workers did persuade the state legislature to act in their
behalf, a judge would hastily blow the whistle, cancel the victory, and in
the name of fair play return power to the opposition. Or, to change the
analogy, the courts effectively sent the workers and the farmers into the
boxing ring with the injunction that if they used their best punch on the
corporations, it would be ruled a foul.[7]

Moreover, this judicial posture completely overlooked the extent to
which the great private governments were in point of fact "wards of the
state." Hothouse conditions were established for industrial growth by the
protective tariff which in essence gave these tariff-protected industries the
power to tax the American consumer. On a different level, state and
federal judges were always ready to rush to the aid of a corporation which
was having difficulties with a labor union—even if it was necessary, as in
the *Debs Case*, to improvise a legal foundation for such intervention.

[7] See Richard C. Hofstadter, *Social Darwinism in American Thought* (Philadelphia,
1945), especially Chapter 4.

Indeed, the Debs imprisonment and the Pullman Strike which led to it provide an excellent example of the extent to which the federal government would aid a private government in distress.

In May 1894, trouble broke out in the feudal demesne of George Pullman, the company town of Pullman on the outskirts of Chicago. Workers who protested against wage cuts were thrown out of their "homes"; Pullman refused even to discuss the matter, and his employees *en masse* joined Eugene Debs' American Railway Union (A.R.U.) and struck. Debs, who had led the A.R.U. to a sensational victory over the Great Northern Railroad in 1893, realized that the strike had to be handled with great care—any violence or disorder would provide the federal government with an excuse to intervene as it had in 1877. With great care and tactical brilliance, Debs masterminded a spectacular "functional revolution" against the private government of George Pullman: On June 26 the word went out along the lines to boycott the "Palace Cars" without interrupting other rail transportation. Suddenly, all over the West Pullman cars appeared quietly resting on sidings—the workers simply shunted them out of trains and left them behind.[8]

This tactic unsettled the railroads, who could hardly claim that shunting Pullman cars out of trains was "revolutionary violence," and they hastily devised a counter-tactic: They attached the United States' mail cars to the Pullmans. This hardly deterred the workers, who cut the Palace Cars out of any location in the train, so the managers took the next step: *They* refused to run any trains not made up to *their* specifications, *i.e.*, they declared war on the "public" and tied up the railroads. Knowing the close connection between the General Managers' Association and Attorney General Richard Olney, Debs had been particularly careful not to interrupt mail service; now it was stopped by the Managers themselves, though of course they assigned the blame to the A.R.U.

The national government moved into action on July 2, 1894, when at Olney's instruction an injunction was requested from the United States District Court in Chicago forbidding any interference with rail traffic into that city. Although there was no federal statute governing the matter, the Court took jurisdiction on the grounds that the strike was holding up the mails and was an unlawful restraint on interstate commerce. At this point, violence did break out—aimed at preventing the enforcement of the decree—and the next day, over the objections of the Governor of Illinois, John P. Altgeld, federal troops were moved into Chicago to break the strike. Concurrently Debs and other leaders of the A.R.U. were arrested on a shotgun indictment charging them with violations of the Sherman Anti-Trust Law and contempt of court.[9]

[8] Ray Ginger, *The Bending Cross* (New Brunswick, 1949), p. 121.
[9] *Ibid.*, Chapters 6–7; see generally, Almont Lindsay, *The Pullman Strike* (Chicago, 1942).

We can not linger with the details, which have been chronicled at length by several historians. The important point for our purposes here is the flimsy legal basis on which federal intervention was founded. There simply was no federal law authorizing the Debs injunction, and it supposedly had been determined as far back as 1812 (*United States* v. *Hudson and Goodwin*) [10] that the national government had no common-law jurisdiction; that is, that the federal authorities could not exercise punitive sanctions without statutory authority. But the Supreme Court was equal to the occasion: Justice Brewer for a unanimous Court held that the absence of specific authority was inconsequential since the "obligations which [the federal government] is under to promote the interest of all, and to prevent the wrongdoing of one resulting in injury to the general welfare, is often of itself sufficient to give it standing in court. . . ." *In re Debs* (1895).[11] The implication of this startling and revolutionary holding was that the federal government had an inherent power to protect the "general welfare"—a view which conservatives would later denounce as unconstitutional and communistic, but which they welcomed in 1895 when it justified the imprisonment of "Dictator Debs."

Mr. George Pullman and the General Managers' Association were obviously "wards of the state." Their right to engage in business on their own terms, allegedly founded in higher law, rested in fact on the coercive power of the government: on the injunction, which the Managers' Association significantly called a "gatling gun on paper"; and on the actual gatling guns of United States troops. But while we can, armed with the clarity of hindsight, make this assertion, the fact remains that the myth of rugged individualism dominated the constitutional ethos, seemingly unharmed, even untouched, by the corrosion of contrary data. Let us now turn to an examination of the Supreme Court's application of this dogma of entrepreneurial liberty to three areas of political economy: labor relations, rate regulation, and social legislation.

The trade union movement in both the United States and Great Britain began life with a common-law bar sinister emblazoned on its shield; it was considered as a conspiracy in restraint of trade liable to criminal prosecution, civil suit for damages, or both. While by the end of the Nineteenth century trade unions in the United States were no longer automatically illegal conspiracies, in any attempt to exercise economic power they were subject to an almost infinite number of legal harassments. The long range goal of union organizations has always been job control; that is, the power to require union membership as a condition of employment. With this, of course, goes the right of the union to recognition by management as the bargaining agent (or agents, there can be more than one union involved) for the employees. Few Nineteenth century employers were willing to accept unionization, and when the unions attempted to attain their ends

[10] 7 Cranch 32 (1812).
[11] 158 U. S. 564 (1895).

by striking, they found the weight of legal precedent an almost insuperable barrier to success. I have mentioned above the fiction of equilibrium which was important in trade union litigation; here let us concentrate on a few Supreme Court decisions which exemplified the judicial approach towards industrial relations. These cases, it should be noted, are those which used "liberty of contract" as the rationale of decision—rather than those resting on the commerce power and Sherman Act.

In the wake of the Pullman strike, President Cleveland appointed a special commission to investigate railroad problems. When this body reported to the President in November 1894, it recommended, *inter alia*, that Congress take action to protect the railway workers' right to organize unions, and a bill was subsequently introduced by Congressman Erdman of Pennsylvania which included such a provision. A ferocious legislative battle ensued—the Senate killed two House versions in 1895 and 1897—but finally in 1898 President McKinley signed the Railway Labor Act establishing the Railway Labor Board, mediation machinery, and a provision (Section 10) banning the "yellow dog" contract, the blacklist, and dismissal for union membership.[12] All this enactment accomplished was the legitimatizing of unionism on interstate railroads—essentially it superseded the feudal law of the private railroad government which had made union activity a capital offense in economic terms. In other words, it gave the railroad unions *rights of access*, but no more.

It was one thing to have such a law on the books, quite another to get it enforced. Despite widespread violations, it was not until 1907 that the first test case reached the Supreme Court (two others had aborted *en route*). William Adair, the chief of operations of the Louisville and Nashville Railroad, had been indicted for firing O. B. Coppage on the ground that the latter had, in violation of his contract, joined the Brotherhood of Locomotive Firemen. The railroad claimed that Section 10 of the Erdman Act was unconstitutional: first, it was not properly within Congressional authority under the commerce power to regulate labor relations; and, second, assuming it could be founded on the commerce power, the provision was a violation of the due process clause of the Fifth Amendment as an infringement of "liberty of contract." Our concern here is with the second of these allegations.

In *Adair* v. *United States* (1908),[13] the Supreme Court sustained the railroad view by a vote of six to two. Writing for the majority, Justice Harlan first of all declared Section 10 to be a violation of the Fifth Amendment, and then for good measure he added that the power to regulate labor contracts was *not* encompassed in the commerce power. Section 10, Harlan held, was "an invasion of the personal liberty, as well as of the right of property, guaranteed by" the due process clause of the Fifth Amendment. The Louisville and Nashville Railroad thus had the

[12] See Elias Lieberman, *Unions Before the Bar* (New York, 1950), pp. 44–45.
[13] 208 U. S. 161 (1908).

right "to prescribe the terms upon which the services of Coppage would be accepted, and it was the right of Coppage to become or not, as he chose, an employee of the railroad company upon the terms offered to him." In other words, the Louisville and Nashville Railroad and Coppage "have equality of right, and any legislation that disturbs that equality is an arbitrary interference with the liberty of contract which no government can legally justify in a free land." [14]

Justice Oliver Wendell Holmes, Jr., who as we shall see shortly was himself anything but flexible in his approach to the mythology of the common law, dissented on the ground that the Erdman Act was a legitimate exercise of the commerce power and that "the section (10) is, in substance, a very limited interference with freedom of contract" well within the power of Congress.[15] Justice McKenna also dissented, confining himself almost wholly to the question of the commerce clause.

If the due process clause of the Fifth Amendment could be construed as banning legislative efforts to end the "yellow dog" contract on the national level, it logically followed that the equivalent provision of the Fourteenth Amendment could similarly undermine state efforts to the same end. And so the Court held in 1915 by a six to three division (*Coppage* v. *Kansas*).[16] Justice Pitney, who replaced Harlan in 1912, continued Harlan's views but added to them a pious patina which the bluff old Kentucky Unionist never employed. In some ways the Pitney opinion in *Coppage* v. *Kansas* sounds like a caricature of the "rugged individualist" viewpoint written by an enemy. The right freely to enter into contracts, said the Justice, "is as essential to the laborer as to the capitalist, to the poor as to the rich." Unfortunately perhaps "wherever the right of private property exists, there must and will be inequalities of fortune; and thus it naturally happens that parties negotiating about a contract are not equally hampered by circumstances." [17] Translated into English, Pitney's cloudy legalese amounts to the statement that the poor man's right to negotiate from weakness is as essential to him as the rich man's right to negotiate from strength.

To ensure that his point was appreciated on the appropriate philosophical level, Pitney then turned to cosmology for what might be called the ontological proof of the validity of the "yellow dog" contract:

> And, since *it is self-evident* that, unless all things are held in common, some persons must have more property than others, *it is from the nature of things* impossible to uphold freedom of contract and the right of private property without at the same time recognizing as

[14] *Ibid.* at 172–5.
[15] *Ibid.,* 191. For an example of Holmes at his ritualistic worst see his dissent in the peonage case, *Bailey* v. *Alabama,* 219 U. S. 219 (1911).
[16] 236 U. S. 1 (1915).
[17] *Ibid.,* 14, 17.

legitimate those inequalities of fortune that are the necessary result of the exercise of those rights. (Italics added.) [18]

Holmes dissented tersely; one suspects that he may have been slightly nauseated. The old warrior believed firmly that the first law of life was struggle, but he despised metaphysical efforts to demonstrate that the winners in the battle of life had received some Divine afflatus.[19] Justice Day, joined by Hughes, also dissented, pointing out at some length that the Kansas statute under attack was "intended to promote the same liberty of action for the employee as the employer confessedly [through employer groups such as the General Managers' Association] enjoys. The law should be as zealous to protect the constitutional liberty of the employee as it is to guard that of the employer." [20]

The third, and last, case for discussion here took the principles enounced in *Adair* and *Coppage* to their logical conclusion. The long legal struggle began in 1906 when the United Mine Workers of America (U.M.W.) struck the Hitchman Coal and Coke Company in the West Virginia panhandle. The strike was defeated and in its aftermath the company set up its own "union" which required as a condition of employment that the miners sign a "disloyalty oath" to the U.M.W. in which they promised, under penalty of dismissal, never to affiliate with that Union. In 1907 the U.M.W. began its campaign to recapture the allegiance of the miners, and the company went to court. Without going into the intricate legal details, the company asked for and received an injunction prohibiting the U.M.W. from attempting to organize its workers—such an effort, even though it was peaceful, amounted to a conspiracy to induce breach of contract. Indeed, Judge Dayton forbade the Union from employing "argument, reason and persuasion" with the Hitchman workers; he actually barred union organizers from "talking to" the men.

This "temporary" injunction was in effect until 1912, when Judge Dayton finally got around to a decision on the merits. (In injunctive proceedings, there are various stages: in the first, a preliminary injunction can be issued on an *ex parte* basis—that is, one party threatened by immediate damage, can get a freeze order; in the second, which is an adversary proceeding, both parties present argument and the judge decides whether or not there is an adequate case for continuing the freeze; in the third, if the preliminary injunction has been made temporary at the second state, the judge holds a full trial on the merits and reaches a final determination.) To the surprise of no one, Judge Dayton made the injunction permanent—which meant that any efforts to unionize Hitchman would be punishable as contempt of court. However, the Union was pleased and startled when, two years later (the organizers had not been barred from

[18] *Ibid.*, 17.
[19] *Ibid.*, 26.
[20] *Ibid.*, 40.

the mines for seven years), the Court of Appeals over-ruled Judge Dayton at every point. Hitchman promptly appealed to the Supreme Court.[21]

The Supreme Court, in 1917 (*Hitchman Coal & Coke Co.* v. *Mitchell*),[22] split six to three in favor of the Company. Justice Pitney for the Court had no difficulty fitting the Hitchman situation into his cosmology: If the "yellow dog" contract had Divine sanction, then it was self-evident in the nature of things that the Union's efforts were sacrilegious. The injunction was sustained and the labor movement was effectively barred from ever attempting to organize workers who had signed "yellow dog" contracts—any effort to this end would automatically fall into the category of a conspiracy to achieve an illegal end, breach of contract. The right of union organizers even to freedom of speech was held to be subordinate to the sanctity of contractual obligations.

Justice Brandeis wrote a sharp dissent for himself, Justice Holmes, and Justice Clarke. In essence, Brandeis denied every contention of the majority: The U.M.W. was a legal body employing legal means to achieve a legal end. While he did not question the validity of the "yellow dog" contract, Brandeis pointed out that dismissal was a consequence of joining a union, not of talking about or preparing to join the union. Brandeis' views were warmly greeted by the unions as well as by progressives generally, but the employers had the majority and set to work with it.[23]

In tactical terms, the opinion of the Court enshrined the injunction as the primary weapon against unionization. And it was a devastating weapon. In the first place, as we have seen in *Hitchman,* the procedures were such that, once a temporary injunction had been granted, years might pass before final determination of the issues. Throughout this period the injunction remained in force undermining any sustained organizing campaign. If the union organizers decided to ignore the injunction and go ahead with their drive (even today, with all the conveniences of the National Labor Relations Acts, a unionization campaign calls for sustained, continuous effort), they were promptly arrested for contempt of court. Under the Clayton Act of 1914, they had the right to a jury trial; but jury or no jury, they went out of circulation in the sense that their work for the union ceased. In managerial circles the injunction was rated higher than a regiment of national guardsmen. In psychological terms, the onus for "breaking the law" was always on the unions; a refusal to obey even the most openly bitter anti-labor judge left the unionists under these circumstances in "defiance of the Constitution."

When the Supreme Court incorporated what I have called the dogma of entrepreneurial freedom into the Fourteenth Amendment, it crippled the efforts of the trade unions to organize. In a different sector of the

[21] Lieberman, *op. cit.,* pp. 84–95.
[22] 245 U. S. 229 (1917).
[23] *Ibid.,* 263.

economy this potent concept was at work undermining the efforts of state and local governments to regulate the rates charged by utilities, railroads, and similar corporations. Probably no area of public law is more complex than that concerned with the determination of "reasonable" rates, and we shall not get involved in the substantive problems. Our concern is rather with the antecedent question: Who shall have the power to evaluate the "reasonableness" of rates? What might be called the administrative school of thought, which was on the rise in the years we are discussing, asserted that the determination of rates was a legislative-administrative problem, one which could be handled intelligently only by a body of experts acting under state authority. In this tradition various states established railroad or public utility commissions with rate-fixing powers. The other school of thought asserted that only a judicial body could exercise jurisdiction over "reasonableness," that historically the concept of a "reasonable return" was a common law derivative, that for the legislature to meddle in the area was a violation of the separation of powers, and thus of due process of law.

All utilities are inherently quasi-public in character, and under the old rules of the common law they were subjected to a special degree of control by the sovereign. A railroad, for example, was given a public charter, trolleys operated on the streets by franchise, gas companies ran their pipes with public assent. No one has a natural or civil right to build a railroad any more than he can convert his suburban backyard into a stone quarry or an airport. Throughout the middle years of the Nineteenth century the police power was dominant over the assertion of vested rights, and in 1877 the Supreme Court in the so-called *Granger Cases*,[24] appeared to give the states the green light for vigorous regulation of "businesses affected with a public interest." The *Granger Cases* are fascinating reading; the first, *Munn* v. *Illinois,* is characteristically quoted in case books, but there were eight cases decided *en masse* (with Justice Field in bitter opposition) which effectively undercut every line of attack that corporations could launch against the police power, at least in the constitutional sense. In the leading case, Illinois was permitted to establish maximum storage rates for grain elevators; in the remaining cases a wide range of legislative railroad regulation was approved, including freight and passenger rates. Chief Justice Waite flatly and virtually without discussion rejected the contention that the states could not regulate interstate railroads; he suggested that if various citizens did not like the substance of the regulations, they should go into politics and get the legislature to change its laws. These decisions, barked Field in dissent, "practically destroy all the guarantees of the Constitution and of the common law . . . for the protection of the railroad companies." The nub of the

[24] 94 U. S. 113 (1877).

controversy was the locus of authority to define "reasonable" rates: The corporations asserted that only by a judicial proceeding could this be done—a judge, or a judge and jury, would then decide in a specific case whether the company had overcharged. The states, with the Court's agreement, felt that the evaluation of fair and reasonable rate structures was within the jurisdiction of the legislature—either directly or through delegation to a commission.

From the corporate viewpoint, there were several lines of possible assault on the *Granger* decisions. For the railroads, in particular, the claim could be made that state regulation was an intrusion into Congress' power over interstate commerce. In the absence of any commerce power issue, the corporations could keep chewing away at the police power on several grounds and hope that one or another Justice would be converted, or that new judges coming on the bench would accept their views. There was always hope that the Contract clause could be revived; Justice Field was constantly recommending the useful potentialities of the Fourteenth Amendment; and there were even odd-ball decisions such as Justice Miller's in *Loan Association* v. *Topeka* (1875) [25] which suggested that the Court could find a basis in natural law for frustrating "robbery" carried on under the auspices of the police power. Moreover, the vital statistics of the Court were morbidly reassuring: In the decade following the *Granger Cases* (1877), five new Justices were appointed to the Court, all from legal and professional backgrounds which suggested they would take seriously the threat to property rights.

With this transformation of the Court in mind, let us turn to the famous case of *Chicago, Milwaukee & St. Paul Railway Co.* v. *Minnesota* (1890)[26] in which the Supreme Court began the retreat from the *Granger Cases*. Minnesota had set up a railroad commission charged by the legislature with ensuring that the roads exacted only "equal and reasonable rates," and this commission had ordered the Chicago, Milwaukee & St. Paul to lower its charges for hauling milk. Writing for the six-judge majority, Justice Blatchford neatly side-stepped *Munn* v. *Illinois*, holding that the determination of a "reasonable" rate could not be delegated to a non-judicial body such as a commission. "The question of the reasonableness of a rate of charge for transportation [he asserted] is eminently a question for judicial decision." [27] In essence, Blatchford announced that no administrative (and by implication, legislative—legislatures do not operate "under the forms" supplied "by the wisdom of successive ages for the investigation judicially" of controversial issues) determination of a rate schedule could ever be final. He issued an invitation to any railroad

[25] 20 Wall. 655 (1875). It should be noted that Miller used this improvisation to strike down, not support "privilege."
[26] 134 U. S. 418 (1890).
[27] *Ibid.*, 461.

or utility grieved by legal rate schedules to take the issue of "reasonableness" to court. Perhaps caught up by the spirit of the age, the Justice declared a judicial corner on "reasonableness," and would permit no unsanctified legislative body to infringe the monopoly.

Four years later Justice Brewer—Field's nephew, and if possible a stronger supporter of entrepreneurial freedom than his uncle—filled in the gaps in Blatchford's argument. Under review was a schedule of rates prepared, *after notice and hearings,* by the Texas Railroad Commission which were challenged as "unreasonable" by a railroad bondholder. Conceding that the Court could not itself go into the rate-making business, Brewer made it perfectly clear that the Justices knew "unreasonable" rates when they saw them. A railroad had a constitutional right to charge enough to defray its expenses and make some return to its investors: "justice demands that every one should receive some compensation for the use of his money or property, if it be possible without prejudice to the rights of others." Brewer was a bit vague on the constitutional basis of this right to make a profit, but he seems to have tucked it into the Equal Protection clause of the Fourteenth Amendment: "The equal protection of the laws—the spirit of common justice—forbids that one class [railroad bondholders] should by law be compelled to suffer loss that others [shippers] may make gain." [28]

If one recalls the fantastic financial operations of the railways in the Nineteenth and early Twentieth century, the problem comes into better focus. The common prank of the financiers was overcapitalization—a railroad with a cash value of a million dollars would be capitalized at two million, bonds would be issued calling for 4 or 5 per cent return, and rates would be fixed at a level which would, hopefully, bring this or better. In California in the 1870s, the Southern Pacific Railroad was bitterly contesting its valuation for tax purposes at $16,500 per mile as confiscatory, but was capitalized at $43,500 per mile! [29] Now the question arises: Which figure should be used to compute a "reasonable" rate? If the railroad commission employs the net value of the property, the rates necessary to provide a "fair return" will be considerably below those which would be derived from using the capitalized value of the property. Assuming that a 5 per cent return is considered "reasonable," and we continue the fictitious example above of the one million dollar railroad capitalized at two millions, a fair rate in the first instance would bring in $50,000 a year, in the second, $100,000. In practical terms, freight and passenger charges would have to be doubled to sustain the two million rate-base.

Turn this proposition around and another dimension, basic to the cases under discussion, becomes obvious. A railroad, overcapitalized let us say

[28] *Reagan v. Farmers' Loan & Trust Co.,* 154 U. S. 362, 412, 410 (1894).
[29] Cited in Howard Jay Graham, "An Innocent Abroad: The Constitutional Corporate 'Person'," *U. C. L. A. Law Review,* Vol. 2 (1955), p. 191.

by 50 per cent—a fifteen million dollar indebtedness on a ten million cash
outlay—in order to stay solvent must pay its bondholders a total of
$600,000 a year, assuming a 4 per cent coupon. But a state railroad
commission, after careful assessment of the net value of the actual assets
of the line, fixes a rate schedule which cannot earn more than $450,000 in
profits. Has the commission acted "unreasonably?" The answer to this
question is not founded on legal doctrine, but on economic and political
presuppositions. If a judge adopts the ruthless view of classic *laissez-
faire* economics, he will doubtless hold that the investor has the job of
anticipating future risks and acting accordingly, that it is not the task of
the judiciary to rescue bondholders from the penalties of economic stu-
pidity. If the judge believes that it is the function of the state to protect
the public from extortion, he will unquestionably accept the decision of
the railroad commission as binding on the corporation.

However, to return to the main line of the argument, if the judge
believes that the well-being of the investor and the liberty of action of the
entrepreneur are the key social and economic values, he will defend
the corporation's inflated rate-base against both economic rationality and
the police power. It was this course which the Supreme Court took in the
1890s and early decades of this century. As time went by, the judicial
weapon became more precise: indeed, in 1930 the Court was able to state,
ex cathedra, that a Baltimore trolley company had a constitutional right to
a return of 7.44 per cent on the value of its property! [30] Presumably 7.43
per cent would have been a deprivation of due process.

What is important to note is that the Court assumed, without any
justification, that the restrictions of due process on the state's police power
were identical with the restrictions on its power of eminent domain. [31]
Once this analogy was established, the fight was over—the conclusions
were subsumed in the premises. Now it is quite clear that the state acting
under its power of eminent domain must reimburse the citizen fair value
for his property. If a house is condemned to make room for a superhigh-
way, its owner is entitled to full reimbursement of his investment. *But the
police power does not proceed on the same basis.* One may have paid a
thousand dollars for an ounce of the best heroin, but if it is seized by the
state there will be no compensation. Nor do prohibition laws respect a
man's property right in alcoholic beverages. The only due process a heroin
pusher or a bootlegger can expect is procedural: He has the right to a fair
trial in criminal court. He has no right to a 7.44 per cent return on his
investment.

Thus if one begins with the assumption that the State of Texas, or
Minnesota, in establishing regulations governing railroad rates, was limit-

[30] *United R'ways & Electric Co. of Baltimore* v. *West,* 280 U. S. 234 (1930).
[31] See Robert L. Hale, *Freedom Through Law* (New York, 1952), pp. 461–73.

ing the corrupt endeavors of corporate officials and protecting the public from institutionalized embezzlement and extortion, the Supreme Court's decisions amounted to a protection of criminal behavior. Indeed, this was the way many agrarian radicals and urban progressives interpreted the work of the Court. However, from the viewpoint of Justice Field, Justice Brewer, or the seven other Justices who *unanimously* concurred in the Texas holding discussed above (*Reagan* v. *Farmers' Loan and Trust Co.*, 1894), this criticism was a form of blasphemy. And it should be reiterated that they were honest, dedicated men—dedicated to the proposition that entrepreneurial rights were a mundane manifestation of natural law, and to its Siamese twin which holds that those who would lay profane hands on corporate prerogatives were the harbingers of socialistic serfdom.

Before the Court could with confidence invoke a precise fraction such as 7.44 per cent, there had to be a formula. As Robert L. Hale pointed out many years ago,[32] the process of formulation was rather peculiar. The Court in fact began with the "right" answer, and then had to work backwards to the "right" question. The answer as we have seen was that a utility had the right to a "fair return" or a "reasonable return" on its investment. But what was to be the rate-base, the foundation on which any hypothetical "fair return" would be computed? In 1899 the question for this answer was formulated by Justice Harlan in *Smythe* v. *Ames*.[33]

This is not the place to investigate the chaos which for half a century developed in the wake of the "rule of *Smythe* v. *Ames*"; nor are we here concerned with the circular logic which sustained it (earning power is a key consideration in "value"; thus to diminish the earning power by rate restrictions is automatically to reduce the "value").[34] Its importance lay in the enormous freedom it gave to public utilities and the almost infinite number of roadblocks it put in the way of effective state regulation. No matter how much work a group of utility experts had put into the determination of a rate-scale based on a "fair value," once this schedule had been promulgated by a regulatory commission, an inevitable trip was taken to the federal court. There the whole question was argued *de novo* with the Supreme Court reserving the right to throw out any set of regulations that did not insure a "reasonable" return on "fair value" as violative of the due process clause of the Fourteenth Amendment. And while this argument was, of course, conducted in precise legal terminology, it was in essence an elaborate exercise in constitutional mysticism. As Justice Stone, discussing one component of Harlan's formula, observed many years later: "In assuming the task of determining judicially the present fair replacement value of the vast properties of public utilities,

[32] *Ibid.*, Chapter 15 *passim.*
[33] 169 U. S. 466, 546–7 (1898).
[34] See Hale, *op. cit.*, pp. 416 ff.

courts have been projected into the most speculative undertaking imposed upon them in the entire history of English jurisprudence." [35]

The constitutional dogma of entrepreneurial liberty thus simultaneously crippled the power of the trade unions to achieve recognition and bargaining status and undermined the authority of the state over public utilities. In both instances, the natural right to conduct business on one's own terms was incorporated into the Fourteenth Amendment. Let us now turn to the third dogmatic manifestation: the employment of "liberty of contract" as a weapon against social legislation. It would be wise at this point to re-emphasize a definitional matter which is relevant here, serving to distinguish this category of legislative interference from the one just examined. No public utility could ever, even in the view of a judge as committed to entrepreneurial liberty as Stephen J. Field, justify in legal terms full freedom from special regulation. These "quasi-public" enterprises—railroads, turnpikes, traction companies, gas and water distributors—were designated as businesses "affected with a public interest" and were theoretically far more subordinate to the police power than "private" undertakings. The category of businesses "affected with a public interest" was, however, not simple to define. In the *Granger Cases,* Chief Justice Waite ducked the definitional issue by suggesting that it lay within the jurisdiction of the state legislature; Field retorted that to do so would leave the entire business world at the mercy of meddling legislation, that it would permit legislative interference on a self-validating basis and effectively destroy the line between "quasi-public" and private enterprise.

In his dissent in the *Munn Case,* Field argued that the State of Illinois had no right to regulate the charges of an admittedly monopolistic combine of grain elevator operators. This monopoly, he declared, was an outgrowth of their entrepreneurial talent, not of state action; therefore there was nothing "quasi-public" about their actions. He was infuriated by the Chief Justice's statement that property "becomes clothed with a public interest when it is used in such a manner as to be of public consequence and affect the community at large." Logically Field's argument was sound—Waite's definition was circular—but for the time being he had to bide his time and merely register his protests in choleric dissents. And it should be added, just to maintain the right atmosphere of ambiguity, that the Chief Justice was forced to hedge his bet: in 1886 (*Stone* v. *Farmers' Loan & Trust Co.*) while sustaining the actions of Mississippi's railroad commission, he added by way of dictum that "it is not to be inferred that this [regulatory power] is itself without limit. This power to regulate is not a power to destroy, and limitation is not the

[35] Cited *ibid.,* p. 478 (from *West* v. *Chesapeake & Potomac Tel. Co.*), 295 U. S. 662, 689 (1935).

equivalent of confiscation." [36] In short, Waite too had to admit that there were situations where the legislative power could be checked by judicial application of the Fourteenth Amendment.

While the Court was undergoing the personnel shift discussed earlier, the drums of reform were beating throughout the land. Under pressure from Populists and urban progressives, state legislatures began to enact social legislation designed to ameliorate some of the worst evils of corporate power and industrial squalor. In most instances these statutes had to run the gauntlet of due process in the state courts before they entered the federal forum. While I have not, for reasons of space, devoted coverage to decisions of the inferior federal or state courts, it would be wise at this point to note that the precepts of entrepreneurial liberty gained support on the state judicial level before they did in the federal jurisdiction. The vehicle for this judicial offensive was the due process clause of state constitutions. The courts of Illinois, New York, and Pennsylvania were particularly vigorous in their exposition of the Field-Bradley gloss on due process as set out in the *Slaughter-House Cases* (1873).[37]

Let us examine one extremely significant New York decision, *In re Jacobs* (1885),[38] for the path that it broke, a path which the United States Supreme Court took in several later decisions. The *Tenement House Cigar Case*, as it was called, arose from a New York statute of 1884. Trimmed to the essentials, this law prohibited the manufacture of cigars or other tobacco products on the dwelling floors of tenements (four or more family habitations) in cities of more than 500,000 population (Brooklyn and New York). Like many other pieces of social legislation then and now, it was passed on an *ad hoc* basis, by cigar-smoking legislators, and a cigar-smoking Governor, Grover Cleveland, after a newspaper exposé of the filthy conditions of cigar manufacture. Cigars were then made by hand and the wrapper was sealed by the cigarmaker in a primitive and unhygienic fashion—he licked it with his tongue. As the legislators learned of the squalid environment and the high disease rate of tenement dwellers (tuberculosis was endemic), they rushed to protect the public health from this menace.

An obscure cigarmaker named Peter Jacobs violated the law, was

[36] 116 U. S. 307, 331 (1886). Professor C. Peter Magrath, whose forthcoming biography of Chief Justice Waite will fill a real gap, has been good enough to supply me with material from the Waite Papers which indicate that the Chief Justice inserted this dictum to hold Justice Stanley Matthews in the majority. The decision was 5–3; had Matthews swung the other way, the decision below in favor of the *railroads* would have been sustained by an equally divided Court (4–4). In short, Waite's abstract genuflection to entrepreneurial liberty did not symbolize a change of heart, but rather a tactical compromise, on his part.

[37] Jacobs, *op. cit.*, Ch. 3 *passim.*

[38] 98 N. Y. 98 (N. Y., Ct. of Appeals, 1885).

arrested and convicted, appealed, and then vanished from history.[39] At this point in the process, the poverty-stricken defendant turned the matter over to the highest-priced lawyer in New York, William M. Evarts. Evarts took his responsibilities to the cigarmakers seriously, and presented to the New York Supreme Court a brief arguing that the state law violated the due process clause of the New York Constitution by arbitrarily depriving tenement-house cigarmakers of their livelihood. The Supreme Court agreed with Evarts, and the State appealed to the Court of Appeals (New York's highest tribunal). Here Evarts rang all the changes on entrepreneurial freedom, invoking due process, freedom of contract, and even natural law. He denied that the statute was a health measure; on the contrary, it was a discriminatory piece of class legislation *disguised as a health measure*. Carried away by his compassion for the small entrepreneur, Evarts even saw the evil hand of monopolistic capital behind the bill: it would place "the whole industry under the domination of organized capital and combination on the one hand, and lays it open on the other to unrestrained domination of trade unions." [40]

Not only did the Court of Appeals accept Evarts' contentions, but Judge Earl virtually wrote his decision from Evarts' brief—which in turn plagiarized extensively from the earlier dissents of Justices Field and Bradley. Speaking for a unanimous Court, Earl agreed that the law arbitrarily deprived the cigarmakers of the property rights in their calling and of liberty as well. The Court gave short shrift to the allegation that this was a health measure—there was no evidence that manufacturing cigars was bad for the health—and added:

> Under the mere guise of police regulations, personal rights and private property cannot be arbitrarily invaded, and the determination of the legislature is not final or conclusive. If it passes an act ostensibly for the public health, and thereby destroys or takes away the property of the citizen, or interferes with his personal liberty, then it is for the courts to scrutinize the act and see whether it really relates to and is convenient and appropriate to promote the public health.[41]

To show that it meant business, the same Court six months later uncovered another arbitrary interference with property rights disguised as a health measure—this time an act prohibiting the manufacture of butter substitutes.[42]

Both the late Benjamin R. Twiss and Clyde E. Jacobs have discussed at length the spread of the dogma of entrepreneurial liberty in the state

[39] See Twiss, *op. cit.*, pp. 93–109.
[40] *Ibid.*, p. 103.
[41] 98 N. Y. 98, 110 (1885).
[42] *People v. Marx*, 99 N. Y. 377 (N. Y., Ct. of Appeals, 1885). Cited in Jacobs, *op. cit.*, p. 55. See generally, Roscoe Pound, "Liberty of Contract," *Yale Law Journal*, Vol. 18 (1909), p. 454.

courts and there is no need, or room, here to recapitulate their findings. It is an index of the extent of this phenomenon in the state jurisdiction that when the first important case came before the United States Supreme Court in 1898 (*Holden* v. *Hardy*) those opposing the statute involved pointed out that in fourteen states similar enactments had been declared unconstitutional! *In re Jacobs* became one of the most extensively cited cases in legal history.

In 1897, in a case of little significance here (*Allgeyer* v. *Louisiana*),[43] the Supreme Court squarely affirmed the doctrine of liberty of contract and voided a state insurance regulation which impinged on this "property" right. Then in 1898 came the first big test in the area of "social legislation," *Holden* v. *Hardy*.[44] A Utah statute of 1896 penalized any employer who required more than an eight-hour day of underground miners or smelter workers. Holden violated the law and upon arrest filed a petition for *habeas corpus*. He claimed that since the statute was unconstitutional, he was illegally imprisoned and, getting no succor from the Utah courts, appealed to the Supreme Court. The Utah enactment, he asserted, was a regulation of hours of employment disguised as a health measure; it was an arbitrary infringement on entrepreneurial liberty which hid under the cloak of the police power. But, despite the pressure which had built up in the state and lower federal courts, the Supreme Court sustained the eight-hour law, though on a very narrow basis. Writing for the seven Justice majority, Justice Brown held that traditionally the states had special police jurisdiction over dangerous employments and that the Utah law fell into this category. The problem, Brown suggested, was at root factual; that is, the Court had the task of examining the facts in any specific case and determining whether "there are reasonable grounds for believing that [special health regulation for an industry] is supported by the facts . . . or whether [legislative] action be a mere excuse for an unjust discrimination, or the oppression, or spoilation of a particular class." [45] In short, Justice Brown accepted the premise of *In re Jacobs*, but denied its applicability to the matter *sub judice*.

Justices Rufus Wheeler Peckham and David Brewer dissented without opinion, but it is not difficult to project their views. Brewer we have already identified as Stephen Field's nephew and a fanatical fighter for entrepreneurial freedom of action; Peckham was a graduate of the reactionary New York Court of Appeals. And although the Court's opinion in *Holden* v. *Hardy* had rejected their view of the merits, it had endorsed their presuppositions. Underground miners were a hard test of their principle; they had to accept Holmes' view that hard cases make bad law and await a better opportunity. One was shortly forthcoming.

[43] 165 U. S. 578 (1897).
[44] 169 U. S. 366 (1898).
[45] *Ibid.* at 398.

In 1897, following another series of newspaper articles exposing the foul conditions in bakeries, the New York legislature passed a statute which was designed to deal comprehensively with the problems of the baking industry. Although a health measure in form, in substance it was more; after the success of the Utah eight-hour law (which had been promoted by the Western Federation of Miners), the trade unions decided to press for regulation of working hours as part of the "health" package—similarly the Cigarmakers Union had supported the statute voided in *In re Jacobs*. In addition to requiring bakeries to install sanitary equipment and follow (from our view in the middle of the Twentieth century) minimal health standards—"Every such bakery shall be provided with a proper wash room and water closet . . . apart from the bakeroom" [46]—the enactment stated that "no employee shall be required or permitted to work . . . more than sixty hours in one week, or more than ten hours in any one day."

The New York courts sustained the act as a valid exercise of the state's power and Lochner appealed to the Supreme Court. The decks were cleared and the Court was confronted with the one key issue: Was the New York statute a "health" law? In the light of Justice Brown's remarks in *Holden* v. *Hardy*, both sides presented briefs designed to base their cases on the "facts." Indeed Julius Mayer, for the State, submitted what later became known as a "Brandeis Brief": an elaborate study of the vital statistics of bakers to demonstrate that special measures were justified to protect the health of this category of workers. Bakers, he urged, were like underground miners or smelter operators, engaged in a "dangerous trade"; thus *Holden* v. *Hardy* was binding.

Justice Peckham wrote the opinion of the Court for the five judge majority. Precisely speaking, he held that the New York law was not a "health" measure but an unconstitutional violation of liberty of contract. Broadly construed, and his language was such as to encourage broad construction, he denounced all efforts to limit entrepreneurial freedom in the name of the public health and welfare. His opinion, in fact, was little less than a tirade against "social legislation"; he was determined not to permit the camel's nose under the tent:

> If this statute be valid, and if, therefore, a proper case is made out in which to deny the right of an individual, *sui juris* [legally competent], as employer or employee, to make contracts for the labor of the latter . . . there would seem to be no length to which legislation of this nature might not go.[47]

Disregarding any statistics to the contrary, Peckham then announced that there could be "fair doubt that the trade of the baker" was particu-

[46] The statute is cited in *Lochner* v. *New York*, 198 U. S. 45, 110 (1905).
[47] *Ibid.* at 58.

larly unhealthy—it was healthier than some, and less healthy than others. With some sardonic cruelty he pointed out that "very likely physicians would not recommend the exercise of that or of any other trade as a remedy for ill health," and that "it might safely be affirmed that almost all occupations more or less affect the health . . . labor, even in any department, may possibly carry with it the seeds of unhealthiness." Thus if the state law was upheld, "No trade, no occupation, no mode of earning one's living could escape this all pervading power, and the acts of the legislative in limiting the hours of labor in all employments would be valid, although such limitations might seriously cripple the ability of the laborer to support himself and his family." [48]

It is a great temptation to quote at length from this incredible holding—which in truth reads like a Marxist parody of capitalist principles—but the tone, the temper, and the law have all been conveyed by these excerpts. One final matter deserving notice is Peckham's general bull of excommunication; after listing a number of state court decisions invalidating "social legislation," he concluded: "It is impossible for us to shut our eyes to the fact that many of the laws of this character, while passed under what is claimed to be the police power for the purpose of protecting the public health or welfare, are, in reality, passed from other [and by implication unconstitutional] motives." [49] This was nothing less than an invitation to aggrieved entrepreneurs to bring their legislative woes to the Supreme Court for principal reasons.

Justice Harlan wrote a dissent which was joined by White and Day in which, drawing from the New York brief, he argued that the facts indicated that baking was a dangerous trade and consequently the rule of *Holden* v. *Hardy* should be determining. Separately dissenting, Oliver Wendell Holmes wrote one of his classic little feuilletons in which he seemingly rejected the judicial function as viewed by both Peckham and Harlan. "The Fourteenth Amendment," he noted caustically, "does not enact Mr. Herbert Spencer's Social Statics" and the job of the Court was not to prescribe a political economy for the people, one way or the other: "I strongly believe that my agreement or disagreement [with the principles of "social legislation"] has nothing to do with the right of a majority to embody their opinions in law." Holmes succinctly, with his usual flair for epigrammatic prose, concluded:

> [A Constitution] is made for people of fundamentally differing views, and the accident of our finding certain opinions natural and familiar, or novel, and even shocking, ought not to conclude our judgment upon the question whether statutes embodying them conflict with the Constitution of the United States.
> General propositions [*e.g.*, liberty of contract] do not decide con-

[48] *Ibid.* at 59, 64.
[49] *Ibid.* at 65.

crete cases. The decisions will depend on a judgment or intuition more subtle than any articulate major premise. . . . Every opinion tends to become a law. I think that the word "liberty," in the 14th Amendment, is perverted when it is held to prevent the natural outcome of a dominant opinion, *unless it can be said that a rational and fair man necessarily would admit that the statute proposed would infringe fundamental principles as they have been understood by the traditions of our people and our law.* (Italics added.)[50]

This dissent has been widely hailed as a rejection of the theory that the Court should intervene to substitute its views on economic, or political policy for those of a state legislature, or Congress. Careful reading of the section I have italicized indicates, however, that Holmes too hedged his bet. He did not deny that there might be circumstances when the Court should reject state regulations as violative of due process. In fact, in Holmes' thirty years on the Court, the Justices declared state action to be in violation of the Fourteenth Amendment 174 times, and Holmes only dissented in forty-three.[51] In other words, Holmes was not opposed to judicial oversight *per se*, but he was ready to give the wisdom of the legislature far greater weight than most of his colleagues. To some extent he identified legal theory with autobiography: who is his "rational and fair man" if not a wise and sceptical old historian of the common law who has looked death in the face in battle, and recognizes with the Preacher that "all is Vanity"?

For years Populists, progressives, and Socialists had been demanding that the Supreme Court's authority be circumscribed—William Jennings Bryan had made a campaign issue of the Court's power in 1896 [52]—but the *Lochner Case* also led enlightened conservatives into the ranks of the critics. Even Charles Warren, a constitutional scholar as eminent for his vehement endorsement of judicial review as for his meticulous historical work, was unable to find a good word for Peckham's holding,[53] and the latter was denounced in season and out by the ever-swelling group of distinguished intellectuals, lawyers, and social workers who were spearheading the drive for social legislation.

However, *Lochner* was law and Peckham's views went forth as an authoritative pronouncement on the meaning of due process—even though the shift of one judge could lead to a different determination of similar matters in later litigation. The New York Court of Appeals, in particular, took the words of its alumnus seriously: if *Lochner* was a

[50] *Ibid.* at 75–6.
[51] My computation from data presented in Felix Frankfurter, *Mr. Justice Holmes and the Supreme Court* (Cambridge, 1938), Appendix I.
[52] See Alan F. Westin, "The Supreme Court, the Populist Movement, and the Election of 1896," *Journal of Politics,* Vol. 15 (1953), p. 3.
[53] See his curt observation in *Congress, the Constitution, and the Supreme Court* (Boston, 1925), p. 236, and in "The Progressiveness of the Supreme Court," *Columbia Law Review,* Vol. 13 (1913), p. 294.

John P. Roche

caricature of myopic entrepreneurial principles, the New York decisions in *People* v. *Williams* (1907)[54] and *Ives* v. *South Buffalo Railway Co.* (1911)[55] were caricatures of a caricature. In the former case, a New York law prescribing a ten-hour day and prohibiting night work for women *only* was voided, and in the latter, a very moderate (by later standards) Workmen's Compensation Law was invalidated; both enactments were unconstitutional limitations on entrepreneurial freedom. Whatever may have been the legal niceties (*Holden* v. *Hardy* was, of course, still good law for relevant categories of employment), *Lochner* appeared to be a virtually impregnable barrier to the enactment of effective factory legislation.

There was one hopeful sign, but it was hard to know its portent. In 1908 (*Muller* v. *Oregon*),[56] the Supreme Court unexpectedly sustained an Oregon statute which forbade employers to contract for more than a ten-hour day with women factory workers. The unanimous Court, without in any way undermining or challenging the validity of *Lochner* v. *New York*, revived *Holden* v. *Hardy* and held it applicable. Women, said Justice Brewer, are different—as everyone knows—and the Court takes "judicial cognizance of all matters of general knowledge."[57] In the brief presented for Oregon, Louis D. Brandeis had set forth at elaborate length historical and contemporary evidence that women were entitled to special protection (the first "Brandeis Brief"): since there were two perfectly good precedents, one (*Holden* v. *Hardy*) which would validate the statute, and the other (*Lochner* v. *New York*) which would invalidate it, Brandeis concentrated on a factual presentation to lead the Court into the right category. The extent of his success can be gauged by the unanimity of the Justices and by the fact that Brewer wrote the opinion—though Paul Freund has suggested that Brewer always exhibited "marked sympathy for womenkind," which may have provided a special feature in this case.[58] At any rate, for whatever it may be worth, the Supreme Court did assert as a constitutional principle that women were different, thus providing some foothold for social legislation.

To conclude this analysis, we can summarize by stating that in the period from roughly 1890 to World War I a new principle became entrenched in American constitutional law: the doctrine of entrepreneurial liberty. Essentially this doctrine was a break with the common law and the common law premise of the overriding interest of the community, or police power. The right to use one's property, to exercise one's calling, was given a natural law foundation—in a philosophically vulgar fashion—over and above the authority of the society to enforce the common

[54] 189 N. Y. 131 (N. Y., Ct. of Appeals, 1907).
[55] 201 N. Y. 271 (N. Y., Ct. of Appeals, 1911).
[56] 208 U. S. 412 (1908).
[57] *Ibid.* at 421.
[58] Paul A. Freund, *On Understanding the Supreme Court* (Boston, 1951), p. 126.

weal. The consequence of this doctrine was not a *laissez-faire* universe, but one dominated by private governments which demanded (and to a great extent received) freedom for their activities and restraints on the actions of their competitors, *e.g.*, trade unions, regulatory commissions, or reform legislatures. In historical terms, "free enterprise" thus involved two concomitant propositions: freedom of the entrepreneur to follow his calling, and a governmental, constitutional protection of the entrepreneur from his institutional enemies, public and private. We can get the full flavor of the *Zeitgeist* by concluding with the entrepreneurial benediction pronounced in July, 1902, by George F. Baer, President of the Reading Railroad:

> The rights and interests of the laboring man will be protected and cared for—not by the labor agitators, but by the Christian men to whom God in His infinite wisdom has given the control of the property interests of the country . . .[59]

[59] Cited in Samuel Yellen, *American Labor Struggles* (New York, 1956), p. 160.

Government and Business: Progressive Era

28.   Business Disunity and the Progressive Movement, 1901–1914

Robert H. Wiebe

Histories of post-Civil War America, describing the rise of an industrialized society, stress businessmen's common characteristics at the expense of their differences and seldom uncover any appreciable diversity in their response to broad economic and political issues. In the standard interpretations, the businessmen appear as a united force, determined to protect group interests against all assaults. The only common exception to this treatment is to point out the antagonism between small business and big business, although even here historians tend to reunite many of these businessmen in a community of interests. In some studies the assumption of a single business outlook seems to have served primarily as a convenience to the writer. When entrepreneurs act as a group, furnishing coun-

"Business Disunity and the Progressive Movement, 1901–1914," by Robert H. Wiebe, is reprinted by permission from *Mississippi Valley Historical Review*, XLIV (March, 1958), 664–685.

terpoint for other themes, their unity helps to produce a sharper, more effective narrative.[1] In some other histories a homogeneous community develops naturally from the particular selection of business representatives—either a few prominent and verbal entrepreneurs or certain politicians, lawyers, and theorists—who presumably speak for the mass of less articulate businessmen.[2] However valid this analysis may be for other periods of American history, an examination of businessmen's reactions to the Progressive movement indicates that far from forming a cohesive group they differed widely over the proper solution to America's problems and expended a large portion of their energies in internal conflicts.

The thirteen years between Theodore Roosevelt's ascent to the presidency and the outbreak of a general European war contained an exceptional number of public challenges to the business community's accustomed way of life.[3] Flanked by the relative complacency of the Gilded Age and the 1920's, the Progressive era stood as a period of concentrated reform. Campaigns to make government more responsive to the voters' wishes, to allow the underprivileged a larger share of the nation's benefits, and to regulate the economic system so that it would better serve the public interest were all parts of a general movement, heavy with the accumulation of past discontent, which matured in the Progressives' reform program of the early twentieth century. To integrate the several parts of this program required guidance from the federal government, now more alert to cries for change than it had been in the nineteenth century. Thus the widespread desire for reform gained respectability and momentum during the Roosevelt administrations, grew restive in the interlude of William Howard Taft's presidency, and finally culminated in Woodrow Wilson's New Freedom.

The common denominator for this mixture of campaigns was an attempt to create a more equitable balance of privilege and power in American society. Because the roots for so many Progressive problems lay in the previous half-century's rapid industrialization, businessmen, who

[1] Examples dealing with the Progressive period are George E. Mowry, *Theodore Roosevelt and the Progressive Movement* (Madison, 1946), Chap. I; Russel B. Nye, *Midwestern Progressive Politics: A Historical Study of Its Origins and Development, 1870–1950* (East Lansing, 1951), 258–59. Among the survey treatments in which business unity is assumed are Charles A. and Mary R. Beard, *The Rise of American Civilization* (2 vols., New York, 1927), II, Chaps. XX, XXV, XXVII, and XXIX; Harry J. Carman and Harold C. Syrett, *A History of the American People* (2 vols., New York, 1952), II, Chaps. IV, XI, XII, and XIV.

[2] See Chester McA. Destler, "Opposition of American Businessmen to Social Control during the 'Gilded Age'," *Mississippi Valley Historical Review* (Cedar Rapids), XXXIX (March, 1953), 641–72; Gordon Harrison, *Road to the Right: The Tradition and Hope of American Conservatism* (New York, 1954); Edward C. Kirkland, *Dream and Thought in the Business Community, 1860–1900* (Ithaca, 1956); James W. Prothro, *The Dollar Decade: Business Ideas in the 1920's* (Baton Rouge, 1954).

[3] More accurately, the Progressive period should also include the last two years of Woodrow Wilson's first administration, but the material treated in this article adapts itself to the shorter time-span. The best survey of the full Progressive movement is Harold U. Faulkner, *The Quest for Social Justice* (New York, 1931).

had acted as the overseers of this economic revolution, found their interests involved or their behavior attacked in virtually all aspects of the
reform process. No area caused them deeper concern or elicited a more
complicated response than the attempts to supervise America's economic
system. This issue raised not only the delicate problem of governmental
control but also intricate questions of readjusting privilege among the
entrepreneurs themselves. Three separate parts of this reform goal—the
movement for banking and currency reorganization, the campaign for
railroad rate regulation, and the control of trusts—illustrate how the
business community split into hostile factions over problems which threatened a redistribution of power among its members.

At the turn of the century, businessmen were operating within a banking and currency framework suited to the needs of a departed age. The
national banking laws of 1863, 1864, and 1865 had created a system which
was admirable for its uniformity at the time it passed but which became
dangerously decentralized and inflexible as the economy grew increasingly national and complex.[4] These measures had tied the issuance of
currency to a bank's holdings of government bonds, a regulation which
made the banking structure unrelated to seasonal or exceptional fluctuations in the demand for credit. Combined with the absence of any established method of over-all co-ordination, this regulation meant that banks
could neither expand their note issue to alleviate periodic currency and
credit stringencies nor contract at times of overexpansion. While this
arrangement was especially vulnerable to panics, it also failed annually to
meet the economy's normal credit requirements. Trussed in an archaic
financial system, the bankers themselves led the search for changes which
would offer them greater freedom and security.

In 1902, Representative Charles N. Fowler, an outspoken Republican
from New Jersey, combined two ideas then current among financiers into
the first important reform program of the Progressive era. The heart of his
plan was the replacement of the government-bond currency with one
based upon the amount of a bank's liquid assets, an index to varying
credit needs. Then, in an effort to provide more uniformity in interest
rates, he advocated full legalization of branch banking, which had been
prohibited by the earlier legislation.[5] Urban bankers, especially those
from the Midwest, endorsed the proposal, seeing in it possibilities for
flexibility and expansion.[6] Midwestern country bankers, however, formed
a solid phalanx of opposition. To these smaller entrepreneurs, branch

    [4] For background information, see Paul Studenski and Herman E. Krooss, *Fi-
nancial History of the United States* (New York, 1952), 154–55, 178–80.
    [5] "Address of Hon. Charles N. Fowler of New Jersey," *Proceedings of the American
Bankers' Association* (1902), 99–113. For earlier references to these ideas, see *Proceedings of the American Bankers' Association* (1901), 149–56; *Iron Age* (New
York), LXVIII, No. 24 (December 12, 1901), 30.
    [6] See *Proceedings of the American Bankers' Association* (1902), 132–34, 144, 175–
76; (1906), 142–55, 165–99; (1907), 109–13. See also F. Cyril James, *The Growth
of Chicago Banks* (2 vols., New York, 1938), II. 747.

banking meant an annihilating invasion of their domains from the large urban centers, and the assets scheme, which did not recognize rural credits, promised a continuing city monopoly in currency. During the next few years, the country bankers, headed by Andrew J. Frame, a tireless campaigner from Waukesha, Wisconsin, remained hostile to each variation of the proposal suggested by their city colleagues. They preferred instead an emergency currency which the federal government would authorize local clearing houses to issue in times of crisis and which the government would then retire with a steeply graduated tax as conditions returned to normal.[7] While these forces battled in public, the New York money powers moved more cautiously. They frowned upon the Fowler plan as too revolutoinary, with no safeguards for their dominant role in the nation's finances, and, although they gave a measure of backing to a later assets bill, they gravitated more and more to a banker-controlled central bank as the ideal solution.[8] Through 1907, recognition of a need for reform produced only dissension. With urban financiers divided East and West and their country colleagues suspicious of both, the epigram of a west coast observer summed up these early years: "[The] bankers are still divided, while the public and politicians look on, and smilingly say, 'Who shall decide when doctors disagree?'"[9]

The Panic of 1907 abruptly ended this period of leisurely debate. Warmed by the sun of prosperity, the bankers had not felt pressed to act. The chill of crisis, however, produced a new sense of urgency in their discussions.[10] While city financiers tried to muster strength behind a new

[7] For examples of country banker opposition to the Fowler plan, see *Proceedings of the Minnesota Bankers' Association* (1902), 142–43; *Proceedings of the Iowa Bankers' Association* (1902), 78–84; *Commercial West* (Minneapolis), V, No. 34 (August 22, 1903), 12. Typical alternative programs which they supported are given in *Proceedings of the American Bankers' Association* (1903), 163; *Proceedings of the Kansas Bankers' Association* (1903), 138–42; *Wall Street Journal* (New York), September 29, 1905.

[8] For opposition to the Fowler plan, see James W. Stillman to Theodore Roosevelt, August 14, 1903, Papers of Theodore Roosevelt (Division of Manuscripts, Library of Congress). Their support for a 1906 assets currency bill is described in *Report of the Currency Commission to the American Bankers' Association and Remarks by Hon. A. B. Hepburn* ([New York, 1907]), 1–3; *Proceedings of the American Bankers' Association* (New York, 1907), 107–16. The growth of central bank sentiment is indicated by *Forty-ninth Annual Report of the Corporation of the Chamber of Commerce of the State of New York* (1906–1907), 15–37, 40–57; Charles A. Conant, *A History of Modern Banks of Issue* (6th ed., New York, 1927), 437–40. For further New York–Chicago differences, see James H. Eckles, *The Financial Power of the New West* (n.p., 1905); "Why Chicago Bankers Opposed Aldrich Bill," *Commercial West*, V, No. 10 (March 7, 1903), 15.

[9] Miles C. Moore, "Address of the President [of the Washington State Bankers' Association]," reprinted in *Financial Age* (New York), VIII (August 17, 1903), 265–67.

[10] The Panic also accentuated the city-country split, as smaller financiers accused their city correspondents of freezing rural bank deposits when local currency needs were greatest. George W. Peltier, "President's Address," *Proceedings of the Iowa Bankers' Association* (1908), 18–25; *Transactions of the Arkansas Bankers' Association* (1908), 14.

version of their assets currency program, Congress, in an attempt to assuage public fears, passed a temporary measure, the Aldrich-Vreeland Act.[11] This expedient authorized an emergency currency which regional associations of national banks could distribute in times of special stress. Having favored this type of reform earlier, a respectable number of country bankers, with Andrew Frame again in the forefront, applauded the bill.[12] The urban financiers who demanded a general overhauling could only complain in futile opposition and base their future hopes upon the National Monetary Commission, a congressional body which the Aldrich-Vreeland Act had established to study permanent reorganization.

City bankers emerged from the Panic of 1907 with far greater unity. The crisis of that year, by underlining the constant danger of decentralized reserves, had brought leading urban financiers from East and West into agreement upon the necessity of a central bank.[13] In order to conduct a successful campaign on this principle, they needed the allegiance of businessmen generally, who had tended to favor much milder reforms, and of the country bankers, whose vocal opposition had seriously hampered them in the past.[14] Such a project required tight organization behind a carefully selected plan.

After two years of preliminary propaganda, the city bankers received

[11] City banker efforts to replace the Aldrich-Vreeland bill with an assets plan are described in House Committee on Banking and Currency (60 Cong., 1 Sess.), *Hearings and Arguments on Proposed Currency Legislation* (Washington, 1908), 82–86; James, *Growth of Chicago Banks*, II, 775, 778. Western urban financiers, with some justification, accused big New York bankers of supporting the Aldrich-Vreeland bill despite its weaknesses, because the East monopolized the bonds upon which its currency would be based. "West against Aldrich," *Rand McNally Bankers' Monthly* (Chicago), XXXVI (February, 1908), 78–80.

[12] House Committee on Banking and Currency, *Hearings and Arguments on Proposed Currency Legislation*, 235–58; Charles E. Warren, "President's Annual Address," *Proceedings of the New York State Bankers Association* (1908), 9–17; *Proceedings of the Missouri Bankers Association* (1908), 189–90.

[13] Among the many evidences of the western city bankers' conversion, see George E. Roberts, "A Central Bank of Issue," *Proceedings of the Colorado Bankers' Association* (1908), 42–65; George M. Reynolds, "Annual Address of the President," *Proceedings of the American Bankers' Association* (1909), 69–80; Paul M. Warburg to Nelson W. Aldrich, December 24, 1909, Papers of Nelson W. Aldrich (Division of Manuscripts, Library of Congress); *Commercial West*, XIII, No. 4 (January 25, 1908), 7–8. For different interpretations of this period, see Nathaniel W. Stephenson, *Nelson W. Aldrich: A Leader in American Politics* (New York, 1930), 362–63; James, *Growth of Chicago Banks,* II, 773–74.

[14] Businessmen's suspicions of earlier city bankers' programs are shown in *Proceedings of the National Board of Trade* (1906), 268–69; *Iron Age*, LXX (November 20, 1902), 30–31; New York *Journal of Commerce and Commercial Bulletin*, October 16, 1906. After the Panic, however, these men expressed a far livelier interest in general reform. See, for example, F. B. DeBerard to Buck's Stove and Range Co., August 1, 1908, Papers of Daniel A. Tompkins (Southern Historical Collection, University of North Carolina); also *Eighteenth Annual Report of the Trades League of Philadelphia* (1908), 105–108.

their concrete program early in 1911 from Senator Nelson W. Aldrich, the National Monetary Commission's chairman who had dominated its work under guidance from powerful New York financiers.[15] The Aldrich plan, while camouflaged by general and sometimes deceptive language, called for a central banking institution, with branches, which bankers would own and operate and which would regulate the issuance of assets currency.[16] By prearrangement, a special Business Men's Monetary Conference, sponsored by the National Board of Trade, met the day after the announcement, and, with Aldrich's chief financial mentor, Paul M. Warburg, as floor manager, the Conference gave the plan full endorsement. It also began work toward establishing the National Citizens' League, meant to serve as propaganda headquarters in the coming drive for business support.[17]

Founders of the Citizens' League tried hard to surround it with an aura of nonpartisanship. They chose Chicago as its home in order to avoid the "animosities and jealousies" associated with New York, and then announced as their open-minded goal "an improved banking system for the United States." [18] Beneath this veneer of impartiality, however, the Citizens' League worked diligently for the Aldrich plan, saturating the business community with speeches and literature in an effort to allay suspicions of a centralized banking system. Country bankers and other small businessmen received the most delicate handling, with constant stress placed upon the plan's supposed freedom from Wall Street domination.[19]

[15] Stephenson, *Aldrich*, Chap. XXIV; Thomas W. Lamont, *Henry P. Davison: The Record of a Useful Life* (New York, 1933), 92–102; Frank A. Vanderlip (in collaboration with Boyden Sparkes), *From Farm Boy to Financier* (New York, 1935), 210–19.

[16] "Suggested Plan for Monetary Legislation Submitted to the National Monetary Commission by Hon. Nelson W. Aldrich," *Senate Docs.*, 61 Cong., 3 Sess., No. 784. Newspapers uncritically accepted Aldrich's word that his plan was not centralized. *Washington Post*, January 18, 1911, and *New York Times*, January 18, 1911. Aldrich later made some additional concessions toward banker control, described in Stephenson, *Aldrich*, 389–92, and *Journal of the American Bankers' Association* (New York), III (May, 1911), 643–48, before perfecting his plan. For its final form, see *Publications of the National Monetary Commission* (24 vols., Washington, 1911–1912), XXIV (*Report of National Monetary Commission*).

[17] *Fifty-fourth Annual Report of the Corporation of the Chamber of Commerce of the State of New York* (1911–1912), 146–51; *Proceedings of the National Board of Trade* (1911), 184–207; *New York Times*, January 19, 1911. For details on the establishment of the National Citizens' League, see *The National Citizens' League for the Promotion of a Sound Banking System: The Origins of the League* (Chicago, [1911]); Harry A. Wheeler, "From the President," *Annual Report of the Chicago Association of Commerce* (1911), 11–14.

[18] *The Commercial Club of Chicago Year-Book* (1914–1915), 73; *The National Citizens' League for the Promotion of a Sound Banking System: Constitution and By-Laws* (Chicago, 1911). See also Stephenson, *Aldrich*, 381.

[19] The League's commitment is divulged by its director in "Statement by Prof. J. Laurence Laughlin" (n. d.), Papers of James Laurence Laughlin (Division of Manuscripts, Library of Congress); Laughlin to James B. Forgan, August 13, 1911, quoted in part in Laughlin, *The Federal Reserve Act: Its Origins and Problems* (New York, 1933), 48. After its first important months as propaganda co-ordinator, the League ran

The combination of a definite program and efficient organization achieved remarkable results during a few months of intensive campaigning. Few hazarded open criticism, while a wide assortment of approving resolutions and statements created the semblance of broad business unity behind the plan.[20]

No matter how well city bankers marshaled their business support, they could achieve final victory only by an act of Congress. In early 1912 the nation was poised on the brink of a political upheaval which would sweep reform-minded Democrats into full federal power. Democrats and progressive Republicans, crying out against privileged money powers, already controlled Congress. In such a climate no program associated with Aldrich and New York's great financiers could possibly succeed, and bills based upon the plan died one by one in committee.[21] The façade of business unity which the urban financiers had labored so hard to construct crumbled with the removal of its major prop, the Aldrich plan. Smaller bankers, no longer cowed by organized pressure, now poured forth alternative proposals, most of which recommended thoroughly decentralized systems, with a sprinkling of suggestions for a government-controlled central bank.[22] In this confusion of plans and counterplans, the city financiers suddenly found themselves on the defensive, forced to wait until the Wilson administration had decided upon its choice of reform.

The Democrats' solution, gradually molded by various factions of the party, represented a compromise on the question of centralization, but it rejected banker control over the new system's policy or currency.[23] The Glass-Owen bill, through which the Federal Reserve system originated,

---

afoul of the old Chicago-New York hostilities, which eventually sapped its strength. Laughlin to Wallace D. Simmons, January 15, 1914, Laughlin Papers; Laughlin, *Federal Reserve Act*, 44–47; H. Parker Willis to Carter Glass, November 29, 1912, Papers of Carter Glass (Alderman Library, University of Virginia). Examples of the special treatment accorded smaller bankers and businessmen are *The National Reserve Association: Advantages It Will Give the Smaller Banks and Their Communities* ([Chicago, 1912]); "Address of Mr. Charles A. Conant," *Proceedings of the National Association of Manufacturers* (1911), 206–12; Laughlin, *Federal Reserve Act*, 79; Stephenson, *Aldrich*, 392–94.

[20] Among the rare open dissents are Daniel A. Tompkins, "Disadvantages of the Aldrich Plan," *American Industries* (New York), XI, No. 10 (May, 1911), 17–18; Andrew J. Frame, "Diagnosis of the National Monetary Bill" (Copy), Papers of William Howard Taft (Division of Manuscripts, Library of Congress).

[21] A general description of the Aldrich plan's failure in Congress is given in Stephenson, *Aldrich*, 401–404.

[22] Smaller urban bankers joined in this display of opposition to centralization. The most popular plan came from a minor New York financier, James G. Cannon. See his *Clearing Houses and Currency No. 1* (Syracuse, 1913), copy in Papers of Woodrow Wilson (Division of Manuscripts, Library of Congress). See also House Subcommittee of the Committee on Banking and Currency (62 Cong., 3 Sess.), *Banking and Currency Reform, Hearings* (Washington, 1913), 337–40, 447–51; Leslie Butler, "Address of the President," *Oregon State Bankers Association Proceedings* (1913), 12–14.

[23] The details of this intraparty struggle are described in Arthur S. Link, *Wilson: The New Freedom* (Princeton, 1956), Chap. VII. It is important to point out, how-

authorized twelve regional institutions under loose supervision by a politically appointed Federal Reserve Board. It also provided for the replacement of the government-bond currency with one based upon a bank's asset structure, ultimately backed by the government. Many smaller bankers and businessmen, especially in the West and South, praised this proposal as a wise one which would satisfactorily protect their interests. "We are more willing to take our chances with the Government," explained one Wisconsin country banker.[24] On the other hand, urban financiers who believed in the banker-controlled centralization of the Aldrich plan were naturally unhappy. Yet, despite their common disappointment, the city bankers themselves divided sharply over the proper opposition tactics to follow.

Chicago's two strongest bankers, James B. Forgan and George M. Reynolds, led the two major factions of urban financiers. Forgan, with support from certain big New York financiers and from the officers of the American Bankers' Association, condemned the bill as "unworkable, impracticable and fundamentally unsound," and wanted to scrap it entirely.[25] Reynolds, whose followers decidedly outnumbered Forgan's irreconcilables, countered with a conciliatory plea for moderation, arguing that the bankers faced a practical, not a theoretical, situation and could win concessions only by working within the framework of the administration measure.[26] The two forces met for a test of strength in August, 1913, at a Chicago conference called by the American Bankers' Association's

ever, that Professor Link has ascribed too much unanimity to city banker opinion throughout the Glass-Owen bill's development, ignoring in the process the very real conflicts among those financiers who wanted to alter the measure. To the Wilson administration, these banker differences may have sounded like minor variations on a single theme of total opposition, but to the financiers they represented a clear and significant rift within the banking community, which the hostile forces found extremely difficult to reconcile.

[24] Senate Committee on Banking and Currency (63 Cong., 1 Sess.), *Hearings on H. R. 7837 (S. 2639)* (4 vols., Washington, 1913), II, 1549. See also *ibid.*, II, 2070, 2096; [D. A. Tompkins], "The Glass Currency Bill" (Copy), Papers of Daniel A. Tompkins (Division of Manuscripts, Library of Congress); "Address of W. H. Manly, President," *Proceedings of the Alabama Bankers' Association* (1913), 21–36. Excellent sources for this viewpoint are cited in Link, *Wilson: The New Freedom*, 224.

[25] Quoted in *Financial Age*, XXVIII (August 30, 1913), 344. Other elements of Forgan's intransigeants are described in Senate Committee on Banking and Currency, *Hearings on H. R. 7837*, I, 680–81; Wallace D. Simmons to the Members of the Banking and Currency Committee of the United States Chamber of Commerce, January 10, 1914, Laughlin Papers; Arthur Reynolds, "Annual Address of the First Vice-President," *Proceedings of the American Bankers' Association* (1913), 54–65.

[26] The evolution of the conciliationist group can be seen from A. Barton Hepburn to Carter Glass, December 19, 1912; H. Parker Willis to Glass, December 31, 1912, January 18, 1913; George M. Reynolds to Glass, April 18, 1913; all in Glass Papers; House Subcommittee of the Committee on Banking and Currency (62 Cong., 3 Sess.), *Banking and Currency Reform, Hearings,* 357–62 and *passim;* John V. Farwell to Woodrow Wilson, July 22, 1913, Wilson Papers. Willis and Reynolds, trying to separate those bankers who would co-operate with Congress, warned Glass of the threat from intransigeants such as Forgan and officers of the American Bankers' Association.

Currency Commission, where the conciliationists won a clear victory.[27] Joined by an equally moderate group from the infant United States Chamber of Commerce, a committee from the Chicago conference moved to Washington to negotiate the best adjustment possible with Congress.[28]

In all probability, the banker's mission was a predestined failure. By the time the Wilson administration had mollified the diverse Democratic factions, it was in no mood to grant city financiers any major concessions.[29] But the bankers, as a fitting climax to their Progressive record, exhibited one final show of disunity. At Chicago, the urban leaders had been so involved in reconciling their own differences that they brusquely ignored their sensitive country colleagues, who now followed the conference delegation to Washington and broadcast their grievances. One irate Arkansas financier described the Chicago proceedings to amused congressmen: "That committee was stacked; that was the coldest deal I ever went against in my life. We were invited there simply and solely to set the stage, to have a crowd, to carry a spear and sing a song and dance around, so that the stage would be full while the bigwigs could have the spot lights played on them."[30] While the city financiers scurried to put their house in order, Congress applied the final touches to the Glass-Owen bill.[31] At the end as at the beginning of the Progressive period, the bankers had found their internal conflicts a more powerful force than their desire to reform the financial system.

As in the case of banking reform, the lag of legislation behind America's industrial realities provided the background for the battles of businessmen over railroad regulation. During the latter part of the nineteenth century, entrepreneurs had extended and consolidated the network of existing lines into national transportation systems, forming a skeleton for

[27] Chicago *Tribune*, August 24, 25, 1913. New York *Times*, August 23, 24, 1913. Its conclusions are given in *Report Unanimously Adopted by a Conference Held at Chicago, August 22 and 23, 1913* ([1913]), copy in Wilson Papers.

[28] For the Chamber's moderate approach, see *Nation's Business* (Washington), I, No. 13 (July 15, 1913), 4–6; No. 16 (October 15, 1913), 3; supplemented by the friendly letters of its president, Harry A. Wheeler, to J. Laurence Laughlin, August 19, 1913, Wilson Papers, and to Carter Glass, August 8, 1913, Glass Papers; also reprinted in Henry Parker Willis, *The Federal Reserve System: Legislation, Organization, and Operation* (New York, 1923), 417–21.

[29] Link, *Wilson: The New Freedom*, 226–27, shows that the distinction between intransigeants and conciliationists did not impress the Wilson administration, which viewed the Chicago conference results as proof that no co-operation with the urban bankers was possible. As tactless as they seem to have been, these resolutions were not meant to be an ultimatum, rather a complete list of ideals toward which these men hoped to move Congress.

[30] Senate Committee on Banking and Currency, *Hearings on H. R. 7837*, II, 1566. See also *ibid.*, 1539–65, and McLane Tilton, Jr., to Glass, September 3, 1913, Glass Papers.

[31] These efforts included an extraordinary country bankers' session, as well as some difficult maneuvering among full supporters and adamant opponents of the administration bill, during the regular American Bankers' Association sessions. *Proceedings of the American Bankers' Association* (1913), 75–91, 95–99, 101–16.

the country's remarkable commercial growth. Closely limited by court decisions, state attempts to control these private empires had proved ineffectual. Congress finally made a beginning toward regulation with the Interstate Commerce Act of 1887, but its failure to buttress the law against the weakening effect of judicial interpretations left the Interstate Commerce Commission with little more power than the states to cope with major transportation problems.[32]

Few businessmen were satisfied with the rate structure which had evolved during those years of free interplay between the railroads as carriers and their customers as shippers. For the carriers, the worst abuses lay in an intricate rebate system to which a number of the bigger railroads had resorted as a result of unbridled rail competition and under pressure from giant industries. Business shippers, for their part, felt that the exorbitant transportation rates, which the railroads staunchly defended, constituted the basic evil. During the Progressive era, as the federal government experimented with various techniques of rate control, the carriers and shippers engaged in a continuous struggle, each group maneuvering to protect its special interests.

At the beginning of the century, the shippers, divided occupationally and scattered geographically throughout the nation, had no way of pressing their cause as a group. Their one national spokesman was the Interstate Commerce Law Convention, founded in 1900 by a handful of midwestern grain merchants and millers.[33] Insignificant in size, this organization gained prominence through the incessant activity of its leader, Edward P. Bacon, a politically ambitious grain dealer from Milwaukee, who set himself the task of rallying the country's diversified shippers behind a bill that would give the Interstate Commerce Commission the power to establish reasonable rates. Dubbed a "Peter the Hermit" by his enemies, Bacon began his crusade by taking his bill to Washington in hopes of attracting sufficient attention to launch a broad shippers' movement.[34] With some difficulty, he found sponsors for his measure in 1902, only to lose control of his campaign through bad strategy. Railroad leaders were simultaneously backing anti-rebate legislation, and, in a move to dull the point of Bacon's attack, they lured him into joining his proposal with theirs as the revised Elkins bill. Bacon worked unstintingly for the combination measure, then stood impotently by as the Senate cut

[32] I. L. Sharfman, *The Interstate Commerce Commission: A Study in Administrative Law and Procedure* (4 parts, New York, 1931–1937), Part I, 13–19; William Z. Ripley, *Railroads: Rates and Regulation* (New York, 1912), 456–86.

[33] *Forty-fourth Annual Report of the Chicago Board of Trade* (1901), lxxiv–lxxv; *Railway Age* (Chicago), XL (September 8, 1905), 280–82.

[34] Senate Committee on Interstate Commerce, *Regulation of Railway Rates, Hearings on Bills to Amend the Interstate Commerce Act* (*Senate Docs.*, 59 Cong., 1 Sess., No. 243; 5 vols., Washington, 1906), III, 2503. For early recognition of Bacon's importance, see *Commercial and Financial Chronicle* (New York), LXXIV (February 8, 1902), 291–92.

away his sections of the bill and passed only the Elkins Anti-Rebate Act of 1903. In defeat, Bacon grimly promised "to follow this up by vigorous effort . . . at the next session of Congress." [35]

His prospects brightened considerably as Progressive spokesmen, with the magnetic President Roosevelt prominent among them, made rate regulation a central part of their program. Shippers whom Bacon alone could never have reached now became enthusiastic members of his Interstate Commerce Law Convention.[36] Riding the crest of a Progressive wave, he decided in 1905 to call another meeting of the Convention in preparation for the final thrust. Bacon gambled everything upon the appeal of his richest asset, the Roosevelt name, requiring a pledge from each prospective delegate that he would support the President's rate reforms.[37]

This second strategic error proved fatal. While many shippers willingly responded to his call, an equally strong countermovement arose among businessmen wary of the federal powers connected with Roosevelt and reform. These dissidents had an aggressive and capable leader in David M. Parry, president of the National Association of Manufacturers and a determined opponent of railroad regulation.[38] When the Interstate Commerce Law Convention met in October, 1905, Parry's followers refused to

[35] Edward P. Bacon to John C. Spooner, February 9, 1903, Papers of John C. Spooner (Division of Manuscripts, Library of Congress). For details of Bacon's labors, see Bacon to Spooner, December 2, 23, 1901, June 26, July 3, 1902, January 3, 24, 1903, and Robert Eliot (for the Milwaukee Chamber of Commerce) to Spooner, April 2, 1902, *ibid.* In rare instances a railroad executive agreed that some rate control powers should be given to the Interstate Commerce Commission. The president of the Pennsylvania Railroad, for example, explained that he supported some government control "because we believe that it is better policy to assist in framing and passing a reasonable measure now than to have a more drastic and perhaps a seriously injurious one forced upon us by public clamor." Alexander J. Cassatt to Theodore Roosevelt, April 1, 1902, Roosevelt Papers. See also Destler, "Opposition of American Businessmen to Social Control," *Mississippi Valley Historical Review*, XXXIX (March, 1953), 666–67, for corroboration in an earlier period. Hans Thorelli, *The Federal Antitrust Policy: Origination of an American Tradition* (Baltimore, 1955), 538–49, provides a broader background for the Elkins Act. Sharfman, *Interstate Commerce Commission*, I, 36–37, indicates railroad backing for the rebate portions.

[36] The best general account of this phase of the railroad regulation movement is John M. Blum, *The Republican Roosevelt* (Cambridge, 1954), Chap. VI. *Proceedings of the Interstate Commerce Law Convention* (1904), 27–38, indicates the broadening membership of the Convention while showing that its primary strength still lay in the Midwest. Although Bacon capitalized upon progressive Republican propaganda, he proved totally unable to influence the course of its policy. See Bacon to Spooner, May 4, August 5, 1904, Spooner Papers, for his failure to encourage a stronger Republican stand on regulation during the 1904 campaign; and Bacon to Roosevelt, August 15, 1904; Roosevelt to Bacon, August 19, 1904; Bacon to Roosevelt, August 23, 1904; all in Roosevelt Papers, for Roosevelt's easy mastery over his admirer.

[37] Edward P. Bacon [open letter], September 18, 1905, copy in Roosevelt Papers.

[38] Although Parry, as a carriage and car manufacturer, was ostensibly a shipper, he had considerable railroad investments. Albert K. Steigerwalt, Jr., "The National Association of Manufacturers: Organization and Policies, 1895–1914" (Ph.D. dissertation, University of Michigan, 1952), 175.

sign the necessary pledge, and Bacon, fearing that they would pack his meeting, hastily hired armed guards to bar dissenters from the Convention conference hall.[39] The rebels promptly marched a few blocks away to hold their own sessions, claiming that they were the legitimate voice of business. The farce of two meetings, approximately the same size, allegedly representing the same economic group, yet proclaiming diametrically opposed programs, ruined the effectiveness of Bacon's convention; and thus the victory went to Parry and his associates.[40]

Temporarily the shippers reverted to their earlier state of disorganization. In the final months before Congress acted upon the rate question, shippers, lacking a national representative, had to plead their cause individually or through local groups. The railroads, assisted by their own business allies, redoubled their efforts against rate regulation with a degree of success.[41] Despite the fact that the Hepburn Act of 1906 gave the Interstate Commerce Commission the right to pass judgment upon the carriers' tariffs, the railroads still retained broad use of court review before the Commission's rulings could go into effect. There matters stood until the Panic of 1907 spurred both carriers and shippers to new action. The railroads, trying to capitalize upon a measure of business sympathy for their financial plight, proposed general rate advances in the midst of the crisis. The move backfired. Faced with loud and widespread denunciation from business organizations, the carriers withdrew their plan, and simultaneously the threatened shippers organized once more to defend themselves.[42] This time they built their new association, the National Industrial Traffic League, upon a foundation of powerful midwestern commercial organizations, whose professional traffic managers directed the Traffic League's technical work. Firmly grounded, in contrast to the personalized Interstate Commerce Law Convention, the Traffic League

[39] Chicago *Tribune*, October 25, 26, 1905. New York *Times*, October 27, 1905. Bacon had had ample warning of the rising opposition. See, for example, a widely circulated public letter from David M. Parry to Bacon, January 3, 1905, copy in Papers of Francis G. Newlands (Division of Manuscripts, Yale University Library).

[40] *Proceedings of the Federal Rate Regulation Association* (1905), 3–18, 22–28, 51–52; *Proceedings of the Interstate Commerce Law Convention* (1905), 11–12, 18–19, 60, 66, 99–100. Soon after this fiasco, Bacon disappeared as a factor in the regulation movement, and the Convention disintegrated.

[41] The central railroad argument was presented by railroad presidents Samuel Spencer and David Willcox in House Committee on Interstate and Foreign Commerce, *Hearings on Bills to Amend the Interstate-Commerce Act* (*House Docs.*, 58 Cong., 3 Sess., No. 422; Washington, 1905), 239–63. For other business advocacy of the carriers' arguments, see *ibid.*, 139–44, and Senate Committee on Interstate Commerce, *Regulation of Railway Rates, Hearings* (*Senate Docs.*, 59 Cong., 1 Sess., No. 243), I, 169–71, 486–91.

[42] For examples of the national protest, see *Seventeenth Annual Report of the Trades League of Philadelphia* (1907), 53–56; *Fifty-ninth Annual Report of the Cincinnati Chamber of Commerce and Merchants' Exchange* (1907), 42; *Board of Directors Minutes of the National Association of Manufacturers* (May 18, 1908); *The Members' Annual of the Los Angeles Chamber of Commerce* (1909), 26.

prepared to match railroad arguments before the Interstate Commerce Commission and to encourage new legislation which would strengthen the Commission's powers.[43] The Panic period had accentuated shipper-carrier differences without satisfying either of the antagonists.

In 1910 these strained relations produced a major crisis. The first phase involved the Mann-Elkins Act, which allowed the Interstate Commerce Commission to suspend proposed rate changes and placed its rulings in effect before court review. Since the measure embodied two major planks in the shippers' platform, it received enthusiastic and consistent support from the Traffic League.[44] The railroads, perhaps sensing defeat, repeated their 1908 mistake by trying to slip in over-all rate advances before the bill could pass, but once again they were forced to retreat. Threatened with antitrust prosecution if they did not comply, the carriers agreed in conference with President Taft to postpone the question of increases in return for tacit assurances of an Interstate Commerce Commission hearing as soon as Congress acted on the Mann-Elkins bill.[45] The railroads now centered their primary hopes for relief upon a favorable ruling by the Commission.

Once Congress passed the Mann-Elkins Act, the scene shifted to the Interstate Commerce Commission hearings and the second phase of this shipper-carrier struggle. By then, the shippers had reached their apex of organization. To accompany the midwestern strength of the Traffic League, eastern commercial associations representing shipping interests banded together to hire the brilliant Boston lawyer, Louis D. Brandeis, as their spokesman, and an assortment of local and national business groups contributed what force they could in creating a solid front of shippers to oppose the increases.[46] The railroads were not able to present sufficient evidence to counteract the combined efforts of Brandeis and well-in-

[43] James C. Lincoln, *The National Industrial Traffic League* ([Chicago], 1908); Edward F. Lacey, "The National Industrial Traffic League: Organization and Development" (typed copy in Bureau of Railway Economics Library, Washington, D. C.), 5; House Committee on Interstate and Foreign Commerce (61 Cong., 1 Sess.), *Hearings on Bills Affecting Interstate Commerce* (2 vols., Washington, 1910), I, 395-98.

[44] House Committee on Interstate and Foreign Commerce, *Hearings on Bills Affecting Interstate Commerce, passim.*

[45] For the story of the government's action, see *Bulletin of the American Iron and Steel Association* (Philadelphia), XLIV (July 1, 1910), 59; New York *Times,* June 7, 8, 1910; "Railroad Rate Agreement" (Copy), Taft Papers; Ripley, *Railroads,* 561-62.

[46] The general development and extent of shipper power can be seen from "Resolutions Unanimously Adopted by a Convention of Shippers and Representatives of Shipping and Commercial Organizations Held at Chicago, Ill., May 17, 1910," ICC Docket No. 3400; Louis D. Brandeis, *Brief on Behalf of Traffic Committee of Commercial Organizations of the Atlantic Seaboard* (Washington, 1911), ICC Investigation and Suspension No. 3; "Testimony" (August 29, 1910), 5-48, ICC Investigation and Suspension No. 4; all in Records of the Interstate Commerce Commission (National Archives, Washington).

formed traffic managers, and in February, 1911, the Commission ruled against the rate increases sought by the carriers.[47]

These defeats, as extensive as they were, did not leave the railroads helpless. At the very time shipper unity was approaching its peak of effectiveness, the carriers were in the process of undermining it. In the period of the Panic of 1907 a few alert railroad leaders had initiated a public relations movement which, after 1910, became a concerted campaign to woo the public and divide the hostile shippers. Special agents, friendly industrialists, and railroad executives canvassed the business community, probing the weakest spot in their antagonists' armor, a need for regular, efficient service. Time and again, these men warned that in a period of rising costs unchanged rates would bankrupt the roads and produce transportation chaos.[48] By 1913 the carriers were prepared to try again for rate advances.

In that year, the Interstate Commerce Commission granted the railroads a rehearing of their case for increases. This time the carriers' propaganda had neutralized or converted so many erstwhile shipper foes that there was no chance of re-creating the 1910 battle lines. On the contrary, the railroads dominated the hearings to such an extent that the Commission complained: "There appears to have been a set purpose to convince us that the people were of one mind respecting the very important questions involved in the case, and that, in order to satisfy every public requirement, there remained nothing for the Commission to do but to register this consensus of opinion by immediately entering an order permitting the carriers to make their proposed charges effective." [49] Although it first rejected the carriers' request, the Commission partially reversed itself later in 1914 and allowed the eastern roads their increases.[50] Many shippers, meanwhile, were regretting their temporary moderation. Even during the truce they had emphasized that they re-

[47] Decisions of the Interstate Commerce Commission of the United States (Washington), XX (1911), 243–399. See also Alpheus T. Mason, Brandeis: A Free Man's Life (New York, 1946), 315–51.

[48] For the development of this new diplomacy, see William W. Finley, Addresses and Statements, 1907–1910 (Washington, n. d.), passim; Edward P. Ripley, "The Railroads and Public Approval," First Annual Dinner, Railway Business Association (1909), 30–34; J. Hampton Baumgartner, The Railroads and Public Relations (n. p., 1913); Eric F. Goldman, Two-Way Street: The Emergence of the Public Relations Counsel (Cambridge, 1948), Chap. I.

[49] Decisions of the Interstate Commerce Commission, XXXI (1914), 425–26. For the hard core of continuing shipper opposition, see ibid., 357. Typical examples of the railroad leaders' success in neutralizing their former enemies are given in F. A. Delano to E. E. Clark, May 12, 1913, and H. C. Barlow to John H. Marble, October 22, 1913, ICC Docket No. 5860, Records of the Interstate Commerce Commission; Report of the Boston Chamber of Commerce (1913), 38–39; "National Industrial Traffic League," Railway Age-Gazette (Chicago), LV (November 21, 1913), 962–64.

[50] Decisions of the Interstate Commerce Commission, XXXI (1914), 351–454; XXXII (1914), 325–54.

mained firm defenders of the existing regulatory laws and that they would scrutinize every future railroad request with critical care.[51] The earlier animosity had mellowed but had certainly not disappeared. As difficult as it was for the diversified shipping interests to achieve and maintain a working unity, their common concern over reasonable rates set them apart as the natural business antagonists of the railroads throughout the Progressive period.

The struggle over rate levels had proceeded along obvious lines of economic self-interest. The debate among businessmen over trust control, on the other hand, suffered from hazy definition and from blurred demarcation among opponents. Part of this confusion resulted from the sudden burst of business consolidation, beginning after the election of 1896, which gave the old question of supervising industrial enterprises new dimensions of complexity and public concern.[52] The problem of trust control became a symbol of the Progressive period's general worry over unfamiliar bigness and the decline of competition. Into this stream of unrest flowed the specific enmity of those businessmen who felt oppressed by large enterprises because of direct competition, the price of trust products, or the uncertain future of smaller entrepreneurs in an economy of giants.[53] The exact problem was usually ill-defined, but the business conflicts were nonetheless acrimonious.

Business arguments over trust regulation remained diffuse until the Roosevelt administration dramatically placed itself in the midst of the controversy. In 1902, the government gave its basic regulatory weapon, the Sherman Antitrust Act of 1890, fresh prestige by prosecuting one of the nation's major combinations, the Northern Securities Company.[54] Then, in the wake of this surprise, came the establishment of the Bureau of Corporations as a general investigating agency within the Department of Commerce and Labor. The smaller businessmen whose hostility toward trusts had been frustrated for lack of a satisfactory outlet now flooded the administration with pleas to champion their causes, whether they be battles with the country's great corporations or conflicts with various price-fixing retail leagues.[55] Big-business leaders, on the other hand, con-

[51] *National Industrial Traffic League: Proceedings* (July, 1912), 18; (August, 1914), 29–31; (November, 1914), 3–7. This strictly limited shipper acceptance of railroad requests is also illustrated by their unanimous refusal to allow carriers an increase in spotting charges even during the 1914 truce. See the hundreds of letters in "Protest" Files of ICC Docket No. 5860, Records of the Interstate Commerce Commission.

[52] For general information on this subject, see Harold U. Faulkner, *The Decline of Laissez Faire, 1897–1917* (New York, 1951), 153–63.

[53] For background concerning this sentiment, see Thorelli, *Federal Antitrust Policy,* 149, 350–51. See also *Official Proceedings of the Trans-Mississippi Commercial Congress* (1902), 244.

[54] For the legal status of the Sherman Act in 1902, see Thorelli, *Federal Antitrust Policy,* 592, 599–604.

[55] See, for examples, Sam H. Harris to James R. Garfield (concerning the American Tobacco Co.), January 7, 1905; Kelso and Anglin Correspondence (concerning a

centrated upon coming to terms with this potential enemy, the federal government. Led by Elbert H. Gary, chairman of United States Steel's board of directors, the more discerning of these went directly to the source of their trouble and tried to negotiate private agreements with the administration, by which the corporations would co-operate in investigations in return for undefined but presumably lenient treatment.[56]

These efforts to commit the government to one side or the other in trust prosecution, however, did not actively involve the majority of businessmen. Although the scandals of 1905 and 1906 concerning life insurance companies and food industries shocked many businessmen and quickened their reform impulses, most of them refused to endorse programs which might someday be turned upon them.[57] As a result, the popular solution among mixed business organizations, such as the National Association of Manufacturers and the National Board of Trade, was a national incorporation law, elastic enough to satisfy both those desiring tighter control and those hoping for a relaxation of the Sherman Act's ban on restraint of trade.[58]

Out of the Panic of 1907 emerged a proposal which helped to clear the lines dividing the business community. A group of powerful industrialists decided that their salvation lay in transforming the Sherman Act into an ally instead of a hovering threat. To achieve this, they formulated a plan whereby businessmen would submit their projects for expansion and communities of interest to the Bureau of Corporations which, after a thorough investigation, could immunize them from future prosecution by issuing a protective stamp of approval.[59] With valuable help from President Roosevelt, they were able in early 1908 to bring their proposal before

---

Cleveland lumber dealers' association); E. D. Beebe Correspondence (concerning the National Association of Retail Druggists); Ross E. Parks to Theodore Roosevelt (concerning a grain dealers' organization), July 13, 1906; all in Records of the Federal Trade Commission (National Archives).

[56] The arrangements are described in "Conference at White House, Evening of November 2, 1905"; "Memorandum of Interview In Re *International Harvester Company*, on January 18, 1907"; "Memorandum In Re Second Interview with International Harvester Company on January 19, 1907"; all in Records of Federal Trade Commission. These loose understandings slowly deteriorated until antitrust suits against U. S. Steel and International Harvester officially terminated them. See Edgar A. Bancroft to Luther Conant, Jr., September 10, 1912, *ibid.*

[57] For examples of indignant business reactions to insurance and food scandals, see N. B. Coffman, "Some Unwise Tendencies in Banking as Viewed from the Standpoint of a Country Banker," *Proceedings of the Washington State Bankers' Association* (1905), 75; *Seventy-third Annual Report of the Philadelphia Board of Trade* (1906), 24–25; *Proceedings of the National Board of Trade* (1906), 271; *The Members' Annual of the Los Angeles Chamber of Commerce* (1906), 19.

[58] *Proceedings of the National Association of Manufacturers* (1906), 34–39; *Proceedings of the National Board of Trade* (1904), 80–93.

[59] The background to this proposal is given in *Proceedings of the National Conference on Trusts and Combinations under the Auspices of the National Civic Federation* (1907), 454–55, 465.

Congress as the Hepburn amendments to the Sherman Act.[60] An opposition among lesser businessmen solidified immediately. While speaking most vigorously against certain peripheral labor clauses in the bill, these smaller entrepreneurs made it patently clear to congressmen that they would not tolerate any differentiation between "reasonable" and "unreasonable" restraint of trade, no matter what else the bill might contain. To these dissenters, such a law would invite a few mammoth corporations to dominate the economy with governmental assistance.[61] The Hepburn amendments failed in an election year sensitive to big-business privileges, but its advocates did not abandon their objective.

For a time the debate waned as the nation entered an unstable transition between Roosevelt's Square Deal and Wilson's New Freedom. Businessmen tensely watched the Supreme Court for their next guidepost. In 1911 the Court issued its long-awaited decisions on the Standard Oil and American Tobacco Company antitrust suits, ruling against the legality of each but, in its famous gloss on the Sherman Act, officially separating reasonable from unreasonable restraint of trade. Once announced, these decisions somehow seemed anticlimactic. For smaller businessmen who had opposed this distinction in 1908, the Court's interpretation naturally constituted a defeat, and even for the powerful corporations, who were theoretical victors, the decisions provided little solace.[62] If each large enterprise had to undergo the ordeal of a judicial test in order to survive, who would be next? United States Steel received the unpleasant answer in October, 1911, in the form of an antitrust suit, and International Harvester followed it into court a few months later. These prosecutions underlined the big-business conviction that only a new, liberal law could offer permanent relief.

[60] Roosevelt's role in this process is indicated by Roosevelt to Seth Low, April 1, 1908, in Elting E. Morison (ed.), *The Letters of Theodore Roosevelt* (8 vols., Cambridge, 1951–1954), VI, 986–87; and Low to Roosevelt, April 11, 1908, Records of the Federal Trade Commission. See also Gordon M. Jensen, "The National Civic Federation: American Business in an Age of Social Change and Social Reform, 1900–1910" (Ph.D. dissertation, Princeton University, 1956), 277.

[61] For the core of smaller business opposition, see House Subcommittee of the Committee on the Judiciary (60 Cong., 1 Sess.), *An Act to Regulate Commerce, Etc., Hearings on House Bill 19745* (Washington, 1908), 153–64, 167–68; Senate Subcommittee of the Committee on the Judiciary (60 Cong., 1 Sess.), *Amendment of Sherman Antitrust Law, Hearings on the Bill* (S. 6331) *and the Bill* (S. 6440) (Washington, 1908), 60–62; "New York Board of Trade and Transportation Petition, April 8, 1908" (Copy), Records of the Federal Trade Commission, with an analysis in Roosevelt to Herbert Knox Smith, April 14, 1908, *ibid.*, partially reprinted in Morison (ed.), *Letters of Theodore Roosevelt*, VI, 1007–1008. The industrialists backing the Hepburn amendments would have been happy to drop the labor provisions which superficially aroused the strongest small-business opposition. Jensen, "National Civic Federation," 285–86.

[62] For smaller businessmen's continuing rejection of this viewpoint, see "Report of Mr. P. A. Peterson, President," *Reports of the Illinois Manufacturers' Association* (1911), 3–23; "Address of President Harry H. Pond," *Proceedings of the New Jersey Bankers' Association* (1912), 86–92.

During the Progressive ferment of 1912, industrial leaders reopened the campaign which had stalled with the 1908 defeat of the Hepburn amendments. They altered their advice-and-consent formula to include an interstate trade commission, similar in status to the interstate commerce commission, as well as stricter criminal liability laws, but the goal remained government sanction for business consolidation and co-operation.[63] With this revised edition of their plan in hand, the big businessmen prepared to meet the challenge from the Wilson administration, which had been elected on a platform and in an atmosphere averse to bigness. The Democrats, too, wanted clarification of the Sherman Act, but in the Clayton bill of 1914 they chose a path opposite from the one corporation magnates followed.[64] Instead of liberalizing the antitrust statute, the Clayton omnibus measure promised stiffer governmental control, designating specific corporate practices as destructive of competition and henceforth illegal. Although certain sections, especially those dealing with interlocking directorates and interlacing stock ownership, appealed to many entrepreneurs whose operations were more limited in scope, the measure as a whole seemed to be "a strait-jacket upon American business" which large and small businessmen joined in denouncing.[65]

The companion Democratic proposal for a Federal Trade Commission, however, contained potentially the exact solution big industrialists had sought since the days of the Hepburn amendments. Leading a far larger segment of business than before, these men concentrated their efforts upon constructing a trade commission which would serve as a business guardian. The thrust of their argument, as presented in the Chicago Association of Commerce's "Chicago Plan," by-passed the Clayton bill's approach by rejecting "further detailed definition of 'restraint of trade' or unfair practices," but at the same time embodied the contradictory complaint that "nothing hampers business like uncertainty." The reconciliation lay in a friendly Federal Trade Commission "to which we can submit business practices" and which would then "decide in advance as to the propriety, fairness and benefits of such proposed arrangements, each upon the merits of that particular case." [66]

[63] See proposals offered by the National Civic Federation, Elbert H. Gary, and George W. Perkins, in Senate Committee on Interstate Commerce (62 Cong., 2 Sess.), *Hearings Pursuant to S. Res. 98* (3 vols., Washington, 1912), I, 515–24, 693–95, 1091–92. See also Nelson B. Gaskill, *The Regulation of Competition* (New York, 1936), 37.

[64] The best analysis of the Democrats' evolving trust program is given in Link, *Wilson: The New Freedom*, Chap. XIII.

[65] *The Cleveland Chamber of Commerce* (1915), 155. See also *Fifty-sixth Annual Report of the Corporation of the Chamber of Commerce of the State of New York* (1913–1914), 182–83; *Eighty-second Annual Report of the Philadelphia Board of Trade* (1915), 10–18. For the mixed reaction to interlocking directorates and stock ownership, see the results of a United States Chamber of Commerce referendum reported in *Nation's Business*, II, No. 7 (July 15, 1914), 3.

[66] *The Chicago Plan* ([Chicago, 1914]).

Smaller industrialists who had steadily fought this concept recognized their old enemy in its latest disguise.[67] From their standpoint, none of the measures before Congress could benefit them, and therefore, with the National Association of Manufacturers in the vanguard, they organized a business drive to pressure Congress into immediate adjournment. "The Country Is Suffering from *Too Much Law*," they protested; let us "Free Business from Political Persecution." [68] With these notes of negativism echoing throughout the debates, Congress passed a modified Clayton Act and established the Federal Trade Commission without the advisory or directive powers outlined in the "Chicago Plan." Suspicions which had persistently kept businessmen from uniting on a trust regulation program left them neutralized in 1914 while Congress enacted legislation unsatisfactory to either of the opposing forces.

The business community had split over trust control, as it had over banking and railroad legislation, into factions shaped according to the dictates of particular economic interests. Yet, beyond motives of self-interest, these specific internal contests formed a broader pattern of business conflict. Its first thread was an urban-rural rift, most clearly shown by the battle between city and country bankers over financial reform. Another thread, in some respects similar, involved a division between businessmen of the East and those of the West and South. While the urban-rural split was related to the regional division, due to a concentration of cities in the East, special sectional characteristics separated the second as a unique strand. Thus urban bankers in Chicago and New York competed during this time for financial leadership and prestige; city bankers in the Democratic South more readily accepted Wilsonian reform than did their northern—and largely Republican—counterparts; and urban businessmen in the West, where shippers predominated, fought their eastern colleagues who controlled the railroads. Cleavages according to size provided a third thread, which dominated the debate over trust regulation and which also paralleled the city-country rift among bankers. Finally, functional divisions underlay the contest between shippers and carriers over rate levels and made it difficult for bankers to rally other types of businessmen, who were their customers, behind reform programs

---

[67] This hostility, now diminished because many former opponents supported a commission in order to escape the Clayton Act's controls, is indicated by another U. S. Chamber of Commerce referendum, reported in *Nation's Business*, II, No. 6 (June 18, 1914), 5–6, and analyzed in Senate Committee on Interstate Commerce (63 Cong., 2 Sess.), *Interstate Trade, Hearings on Bills Relating to Trust Legislation* (2 vols., Washington, 1914), II, 688–94.

[68] These are two samples of the stickered slogans which the National Association of Manufacturers offered in unlimited quantities to all applicants. National Association of Manufacturers to Associations, July 30, 1914, Wilson Papers. See also Simmons Hardware Company's widely distributed circular letter of June 9, 1914, *ibid.; Report of the Boston Chamber of Commerce* (1914), 48; John M. Glenn, *Urge Congress to Adjourn* ([Chicago, 1914]).

favorable to the financiers. Interwoven in various ways depending upon the time and the issue, these four strands outlined the quarrels among businessmen over the reform programs of the period. These battles, considered as a group, give consistent testimony that conflict, not co-operation, typified the business community's reaction to crisis during the Progressive era.

PART FOUR

The Managed Economy

Descriptions of the American economy of the 1920's written since 1929 tend to regard the period as a prelude to disaster. Problems are stressed, weaknesses analyzed. William E. Leuchtenburg, while generally critical of American society and political leadership during the 1920's, nevertheless acknowledges in *Selection Twenty-Nine* the remarkable economic achievements of the decade: the rise in real wages, soaring production of consumer goods, new products, sharply increased investment in organized research, and greater leisure for most of the population. Leuchtenburg's essay shows that Americans had good reason at the time to speak euphorically of a "new era."

Of course the boom *did* culminate in 1929 with the stock market crash, and the nation *did* suffer a depression which lasted longer and caused more widespread misery than any in its history.[1] So many mass tragedies crowd the pages of the 1930's that anyone who did not experience them can hardly appreciate their meaning to participants. The graphic description in *Selection Thirty* of the social and economic blows dealt Americans by the Great Depression, is, appropriately, a contemporary account, which appeared originally in *Fortune*. Ironically entitled "No One Has Starved," the essay's thesis is that optimistic statements to that effect by politicians and businessmen were quite unrealistic, for, despite the official

[1] A fine study of the depression's relative severity is Ira O. Scott, "A Comparison of Production During the Depressions of 1873 and 1929," *American Economic Review*, XLII (September, 1952), 569–576.

optimism—and to some extent because of it—millions of Americans were starving by the fall of 1932. The editors of *Fortune* had urged the Republican administration to adopt dramatic new policies of relief for the hungry. Actually, no such policies were forthcoming even in 1932, and President Hoover was branded, probably indelibly, with responsibility for a calamity he neither expected nor caused and seemingly did not fathom.

A brief but cogent analysis of the causes of the debacle is presented in the opening paragraphs of *Selection Thirty-One* by Gilbert Burck and Charles E. Silberman, who assert that the basic reason the Depression lasted so long was the economic ignorance not only of businessmen and the Hoover Administration but of the New Deal leaders as well. Reviewing the economic effects of the various New Deal measures, Burck and Silberman, editors of *Fortune*—a business magazine usually critical of government interference with private enterprise—suggest that the Roosevelt Administration's failure to "stop improvising and choose a sound approach to the nation's problems and stick to it" hindered full recovery. Furthermore, the government's reluctance to continue a high level of deficit spending, in the face of strong criticism from those who feared the inflationary effects of unbalanced budgets, brought on a new collapse in 1937. But Burck and Silberman conclude: "For all its fumbling and faulty signal calling, the New Deal passed on to the postwar generation a heritage of reforms and practices without which today's economy would not be nearly so strong and well-balanced as it is." The illuminating charts created by the *Fortune* staff and reproduced in this selection are, as the *Fortune* editors state, a "portrait of an expensive education."

The Great Depression finally disappeared with the government contracts which accompanied World War II, leaving behind the hope that—like the Black Death—it is a phenomenon gone forever from Western civilization. If symptoms of the malady appear again, there is widespread determination to take immediate counteraction. Not long after the war, however, it became plain that the "farm problem" was still with us—that most of the nation's farm population continued to live in a condition of economic depression despite great increases in farm productivity. As Walter W. Wilcox demonstrates in *Selection Thirty-Two*, the hourly money returns to farm owners and laborers in 1957 were only one-third the hourly wages of workers in manufacturing industries. Wilcox suggests that farmers are in a position analogous to that of groups in other industries mechanizing rapidly. The farm population continues to shrink; farms are being consolidated and made more efficient; and yet, millions of excess farmers, lacking urban employment opportunities, stay on the land in spite of poor yields and low incomes. Although farmers suffer during the transition, society as a whole gains from increased farm production at relatively declining prices. Wilcox concludes that federal farm subsidies and acreage controls—programs that originated during the New Deal period—actually are hastening this mechanization process, while softening somewhat the effect on farmers. Wilcox seems pessimistic about the farmers' future, an attitude reinforced by recent observations that the "farm mess" is a long-standing international problem, not susceptible to easy solutions.[2]

Yet the American economy as a whole continued to thrive during the decades following World War II. John K. Galbraith, seeking to explain this prosperity and to uncover a pattern in the new developments in American capitalism (*Selection Thirty-Three*), put forward the theory of countervailing power. The growth of national labor organizations, the appearance of chain stores, and intrusive government agencies—including those which manage the farm programs—were logical responses to the concentrated power won earlier by giant industrial corporations. Strong sellers served as an incentive to the creation of strong buyers, or strong organizations representing workers or farmers, who wanted their share of the profits. Although he states disarmingly, "There is an old saying, or should be, that it is a wise economist who recognizes the scope of his own generalizations," Galbraith seems to believe that most of the weak spots in our economy could be eliminated if the concept of countervailing power were put to work in the service of those industries and groups of workers and consumers now relatively unorganized. He admits one exception to his generally optimistic view:

[2] For example, Michel A. Heilperin and Robert Lubar, "It's an International 'Farm Mess' Now," *Fortune*, LXVII (May, 1963).

Inflation prevents countervailing power from operating as it theoretically should. Instead the system accelerates the cycle of rising prices and wages. The strong units, which usually neutralize each other in relatively stable times, willingly give in during inflationary periods, confident that increased wage and industrial prices can be passed along to someone else—ultimately the consumer.[3]

There also have been fundamental changes in the management of the manufacturing corporations which produce most of the goods Americans consume. In *Selection Thirty-Four* Alfred D. Chandler, Jr. and Fritz Redlich review the gradual separation of the general policy makers from those who manage the day-to-day operations of large corporations. Tracing present tendencies back to nineteenth-century origins, Chandler and Redlich find that three types of enterprises have succeeded each other, although vestiges of the first two remained long after they ceased to be the dominant form. These were the single-function firm of the early nineteenth century: cloth producer, mercantile house, or canal company, for example; the multi-function but single-product concern of the late nineteenth century, such as the oil, farm machinery and railroad firms; and finally the multi-function, multi-product enterprise of the mid-twentieth century, typified by General Electric and Du Pont. Each type required a different and progressively more complex management structure. Today, Chandler and Redlich point out, a small top-management team, concerned fundamentally with goal determination, long-range planning, coordination of divisions, and budgeting, typically directs the large corporation. Although the authors did not attempt to prophesy the effect on management of increasingly sophisticated electronic computors, this machinery seems likely to intensify even more the specialization within business management, thereby widening further the differences between roles of top and middle management in large firms.[4]

Reviewing several recent studies of the American poor, Dwight MacDonald (*Selection Thirty-Five*) brought some surprising facts to the attention of *The New Yorker* magazine readers: "For a long

[3] For an elaboration of Galbraith's arguments and some effective criticism, see Edward S. Mason, editor, *The Corporation in Modern Society*, Cambridge: Harvard University Press, 1959.

[4] See *Fortune's* series of articles on "The Computor Age," March–October, 1964.

time now almost everyone has assumed that because of the New Deal's social legislation and—more important—the prosperity we have enjoyed since 1940, mass poverty no longer exists in our country." On the edge of an affluent society, however, live forty million or more poor Americans, perhaps as many as one-quarter of the population. MacDonald sees the farm laborer and farm tenant as part of the acute national problem; however, he concentrates upon the urban poor—the aged, the young school drop-outs, and the non-whites who inhabit the city slums. Wages of non-whites average only fifty-eight percent of what white workers receive, and the average per-capita income of our "senior citizens" is about one thousand dollars a year. Not only do these "other Americans" live on incomes inadequate to purchase the necessities of civilized life, but only a small and decreasing proportion of them are able to break out of their cruel situation. Although most of these people may be clothed decently, they are set apart from the rest of the population by location (train commuters, for instance, hardly see the slums over their newspapers) and by educational handicaps, color, or illness; hence MacDonald's title: "Our Invisible Poor." These people are not joiners; they have little or no "countervailing power"; they are not trained for jobs in the expanding sectors of the nation's economy; and their children are not apt to get the education which would enable them to do much better. Despite enormous economic achievements, a quarter of the population has been left behind. It is now recognized that one of the country's most urgent needs is to devise means by which these Americans can share in future development.

Related to the problem of continued poverty is the slow rate of economic growth during the 1950's and early 1960's. Certainly a majority of Americans would like to have access to more goods and services. However, the lagging growth rate (compared to the American past, and to western European countries in the mid-twentieth century) may not be simply an incident of a supposedly mature economy. A warning that the federal government is unlikely to attack these problems systematically was issued by Edward S. Mason, in his presidential address to the American Economic Association in December, 1962 (*Selection Thirty-Six*). Mason pointed out that even the New Deal limited itself largely to social welfare, labor-management relations, and the regulation of capital markets. In the depths of the Great Depression, "the voices raised in favor of expansion of government ownership or a larger role in the direction of resource use were feeble and ineffective." Despite the lessons of the New Deal and World War II, powerful latent hostility between businessmen and government officials still exists and occasionally breaks into open conflict. We cannot expect that American businessmen will readily cooperate with the government in such joint economic planning as apparently is successful in some western European countries. Nor can labor unions be expected to take the initiative in demanding large-scale economic planning. American unions are proud of the fact that their objectives have traditionally been highly practical and non-ideological. Perhaps we will solve the problems of economic growth and stability, Mason concludes, although "the historically determined relationship between government, business, and labor" in the United States may exclude their systematic solution through deliberate national policy.

It should be noted, however, that many studies in American economic history published in the decades since World War II emphasize that government responsibility for economic growth has been at the heart of American development. Some of these works were outgrowths of attempts to trace the antecedents of New Deal programs. But more recently a worldwide interest in the process of economic growth has stimulated a re-evaluation of the American experience. Economic historians have discovered that capitalism and government seldom have been isolated from each other and that private enterprise frequently has been obliged to act as the servant of the public interest. Now the federal government, with its enormous defence and welfare commitments, accounts for about one-quarter of all national expeditures. It seems possible that government policies will be even more effective than in the past in helping to promote economic growth and to ensure a relatively high degree of economic stability.

A Glimpse of the Modern Economy

29.   The Second Industrial Revolution

William E. Leuchtenburg

In the late eighteenth and early nineteenth centuries the industrialization of England accelerated at such a pace that historians have found no term adequate to describe it save one usually reserved for violent political change—revolution. In the late nineteenth century and early twentieth century the productive capacity of the American economy increased at a rate greater than that of the Industrial Revolution. After World War I, the United States, reaping the harvest of half a century of industrial progress, achieved the highest standard of living any people had ever known. National income soared from $480 per capita in 1900 to $681 in 1929. Workers were paid the highest wages of any time in the history of the country; essentially unchanged from 1890 to 1918, the real earnings of workers—what their income actually would buy at the store—shot up at an astonishing rate in the 1920's. At the same time, the number of hours of work was cut: in 1923 United States Steel abandoned the twelve-hour day and put its Gary plant on an eight-hour shift; in 1926 Henry Ford instituted the five-day week, while International Harvester announced the electrifying innovation of a two-week annual vacation with pay for its employees.

In 1922 the country, already enormously productive by comparison with other countries, started a recovery from the postwar depression—a recovery that maintained prosperity, with slight interruptions, until the fall of 1929. The key to the piping prosperity of the decade was the enormous increase in efficiency of production, in part the result of the application of Frederick W. Taylor's theory of scientific management, in part the outgrowth of technological innovations. In 1914 at his Highland Park plant Henry Ford had revolutionized industrial production by installing the first moving assembly line with an endless-chain conveyor; three months later his men assembled an automobile, down to its smallest parts, in 93 minutes. A year before it had taken 14 hours. During these same years, machine power replaced human labor at a startling rate: in 1914, 30 per cent of industry was electrified, in 1929, 70 per cent. The electric motor made the steam engine obsolete; between 1919 and 1927 more than 44 per cent of the steam engines in the United States went to

Reprinted from *The Perils of Prosperity* by William E. Leuchtenburg by permission of The University of Chicago Press. Copyright 1958.

the scrap heap. Since labor came out of the postwar depression with higher real wages—employers feared a new strike wave if they cut wages as sharply as prices fell—business was stimulated to lower production costs. With more efficient management, greater mechanization, intensive research, and ingenious sales methods, industrial production almost doubled during the decade, soaring from an index figure of 58 in the depression year of 1921 to 110 in 1929 (1933–39 = 100). This impressive increase in productivity was achieved without any expansion of the labor force. Manufacturing employed precisely the same number of men in 1929 as it had in 1919. The summit of technological achievement was reached on October 31, 1925, when Ford rolled a completed automobile off his assembly line every ten seconds.

The physical output of American industry increased tremendously. Between 1899 and 1929 the total output of manufacturing jumped 264 per cent. Petroleum products—new oil fields were discovered in Texas, Oklahoma, and California—multiplied more than sixteen times in this period, the basic iron and steel industry five times. The number of telephones installed grew from 1,355,000 in 1900 to 10,525,000 in 1915 to 20,200,000 in 1930. Most impressive was the growth of new industries, some of which did not even exist in 1914. Light metals like aluminum and magnesium experienced a meteoric rise; the output of aluminum more than doubled between 1914 and 1920. American factories turned out a host of new products—cigarette lighters, oil furnaces, wrist watches, antifreeze fluids, reinforced concrete, paint sprayers, book matches, dry ice, Pyrex glass for cooking utensils, and panchromatic motion-picture film.

Many of the new industries were geared to the American home. The American consumed a more varied diet than he ever had before. He thought it commonplace to have fresh fruit and vegetables in midwinter—Louisiana cherries and Arizona melons, Carolina peas and Alabama corn. In 1905, 41 million cases of food were shipped, in 1930, 200 million. Fresh green vegetables, many of them novelties, arrived in northern markets; shipments of lettuce grew from 13,800 carloads in 1920 to 51,500 in 1928, spinach from 2,900 in 1920 to 10,600 in 1927. As people moved into city apartments with kitchenettes, they gave a new spur to the canning industry. Canned fruits and vegetables more than doubled between 1914 and 1929; canned milk almost trebled. In many city homes the family sat down to a meal that started with canned soup, proceeded to canned meat and vegetables, and ended with canned peaches.

The chemicals industry, which started in the 1880's, was enormously stimulated by World War I. The war demonstrated how dependent the country was on foreign supplies of potash, nitrates, and dyes. Potash, essential for fertilizers, had come almost entirely from Germany before the war. When supplies were cut off, prices increased ten times, and this encouraged the creation of a domestic potash industry. When the United

States could not import German indigo, the Dow Chemical Company's infant industry spurted. The government contributed more to the development of the chemicals industry than to any other industry. It confiscated German dye patents during the war and turned them over to American firms; it advanced nitrogen development by constructing a plant at Muscle Shoals in the Tennessee Valley and by operating a Fixed Nitrogen Research Laboratory in the War Department; and it gave high tariff protection to domestic chemicals and dyes.

The war also sparked the development of the new synthetics industry. Thousands of by-product ovens were built to produce coke needed in manufacturing explosives; after the war these ovens were used in the production of synthetic chemicals, especially of plastics. Synthetic plastics had been developed as early as 1869, with the creation of celluloid, but it was not until the postwar years that synthetic fibers and plastics became an important industry. The output of rayon, which transformed the textile business, multiplied sixty-nine times between 1914 and 1931. Bakelite, which was developed before the war, proved of enormous importance in the electrical and radio industries. In 1923, lacquers were introduced; easier to apply than paint, giving better protection and offering a wider range of colors, the quick-drying lacquers reduced the time needed to finish an automobile from twenty-six days to a matter of hours. In 1924, Du Pont established a "cellophane" plant in Buffalo; used to wrap everything from bacon to cigarettes, cellophane at least doubled its sales every year for the rest of the decade. In 1925, a Swiss chemist, who had been invited to America by the government during World War I to build a cellulose nitrate plant, placed "celanese" on the market; an artificial silk superior to rayon, celanese was an important step in the development of synthetic textiles. Scientific geniuses like George Washington Carver found new industrial uses for farm products, many of them surplus crops which were glutting the market. From peanuts, Carver extracted everything from shaving lotion to axle grease; from sweet potatoes, he got shoe-blacking, library paste, and synthetic tapioca.

The most important element in the prosperity of the 1920's was the increase in construction, in part because building had been halted during the war, in part to meet the drift from country to city and from city to suburbs. During the decade, New York got a brand new skyline. European travelers who in 1910 had been awed by 20-story skyscrapers returned in 1930 to find them dwarfed by new giants; some of the old structures had even been demolished to make way for 60-story buildings. The Grand Central section of Manhattan was almost entirely rebuilt; Fifth Avenue resounded with the staccato of riveters and the sharp clash of steel beams. High above the city streets, helmeted workers balanced themselves on girders; beneath them, men operated mammoth cranes or turned huge drums of concrete. Taller and taller the buildings soared;

toward the end of the decade a race to erect the loftiest skyscraper became a fascinating new outdoor sport. On May 1, 1931, the race ended when the Empire State Building climbed past the Bank of Manhattan's 71 stories and the Chrysler Building's 77 stories. Built in less than a year, the 86-story Empire State Building, topped by a graceful mast, was the tallest building in the world.

What New York had, every interior city had to have too, and those on the prairies erected their own towers. Cities the size of Beaumont, Memphis, and Syracuse boasted buildings of at least 21 stories. Tulsa and Oklahoma City, which did not even exist when the first skyscraper was built, had skylines by the end of the decade. Cleveland pointed proudly to its 52-story Terminal Tower, Houston to its Petroleum Building, Chicago to its Tribune Tower. The skyscraper was as certain an expression of the ebullient American spirit as the Gothic cathedral was of medieval Europe. Denounced by many American critics as a vulgar evidence of commercialism and an indiscriminate passion for bigness, the skyline was recognized by European observers for what it was—a radiant, defiant display of American energy and optimism. Too often banal in conception, the skyscraper was at its best—as in Raymond Hood's News Building in New York—a symmetrical rectangle of stark beauty.

Outside the great cities, construction went on at an even faster rate, as people fanned out into the suburbs. The borough of Queens, across the East River from Manhattan, doubled its population in the 1920's. Grosse Point Park near Detroit grew 700 per cent, Shaker Heights outside Cleveland 1,000 per cent, and the movie colony of Beverly Hills 2,500 per cent. Save for California, the greatest real estate boom in the country took place in Florida. Flivvers with northern license plates clogged Miami's Flagler Avenue in the 1920's; not only the man of wealth, who headed for Palm Beach or Boca Raton, but the man of moderate income decided to winter in Florida. "Realtors" converted swamps into Venetian lagoons, and much of the population of Florida was engaged in selling lots. In Coral Gables a real estate man hired William Jennings Bryan to sit on a raft under a beach umbrella and lecture on the beauties of Florida climate; Bryan was followed with dancing by Gilda Gray. The land-speculation mania in Florida reached its high point one day in the summer of 1925 when the Miami *Daily News,* crowded with real estate advertisements, printed an issue of 504 pages, the largest in newspaper history. In 1926, after a hurricane had driven the waters of Biscayne Bay over the cottages of Miami, the land boom collapsed. But still the resorts were strung from Jacksonville to Key West. Miami, once a mangrove swamp, grew 400 per cent in the decade.

The construction of roads and highways poured fresh public funds into the economy. While Secretary Mellon endeavored to cut back federal spending, state and local governments stepped up spending at a rate which more than offset the Mellon program of deflation. Construction programs for highways and buildings employed more men and spent more money than any single private industry. In 1914, there were almost no good roads outside of the East, and crossing the continent was an adventure. Automobiles sank to their hubs in gumbo muds; travelers crossing Iowa were often forced to wait several days until the roads dried before moving on to the next town. Perhaps because cars were viewed as pleasure vehicles, parsimonious state legislatures were reluctant to vote public funds to improve roads.

The Federal Aid Road Act of 1916 offered federal funds to states which would organize highway departments and match federal grants. Spurred by federal initiative, every section of the country launched ambitious road-building programs in the postwar years. In 1906, local governments appropriated 96 per cent of all highway funds; by 1927, they were providing only 53 per cent, while the states spent 37 per cent, and the federal government 10 per cent. Florida built the Tamiami Trail through the swamps of the Everglades; Arizona constructed a road across the desert west of Phoenix; Utah laid a highway over a sea of mud, a relic of ancient Lake Bonneville, near the Nevada line; and in Massachusetts the magnificent Mohawk Trail climbed the Hoosac Range. New York pioneered with the construction of the beautiful Bronx River Parkway which curved its way out of New York City northward through the Westchester countryside. By 1928, the tourist could drive from New York as far west as St. Mary's, Kansas, on paved highways, but it was still not advisable to drive down the Santa Fé Trail southwest of St. Louis in the rainy season, and mountain passes west of Salt Lake City were seldom passable during the winter or early spring.

Without the new automobile industry, the prosperity of the Roaring Twenties would scarcely have been possible; the development of the industry in a single generation was the greatest achievement of modern technology. As recently as 1900, Vermont had enforced a law requiring every motorist to employ "a person of mature age" to walk one-eighth of a mile ahead of him bearing a red flag. That year there was not a single filling station in all the country. In 1902, San Francisco, Cincinnati, and Savannah still maintained speed limits of eight miles an hour. While lawmakers were attempting to keep pace with technology, an enormous change took place within the industry. Ransom Olds started mass production in automobiles; Henry Leland demonstrated that cars could be made with interchangeable parts; and Henry Ford quickly took over both principles and carried them to lengths that left his competitors far behind.

The production of automobiles soared almost at a geometric rate, and the auto industry gave a shot in the arm to the whole economy. In 1900, there had been an annual output of 4,000 cars; by 1929, 4,800,000 automobiles were being produced in a single year, and Americans were driving more than 26 million autos and trucks. In the United States, there was one automobile to each five persons—almost one car per family—as compared to one car to 43 persons in Britain, one to 325 in Italy, one to 7,000 in Russia. In America, the possession of an automobile was not, as in Europe, a class privilege. The auto industry was the most important purchaser of rubber, plate glass, nickel and lead; it bought 15 per cent of the steel output of the nation and spurred the petroleum industry to a tremendous expansion. There was scarcely a corner of the American economy which the automobile industry did not touch; it stimulated public spending for good roads, extended the housing boom into the suburbs, and created dozens of new small enterprises from hotdog stands to billboards.

Detroit became the Mecca of the modern world and Ford its prophet. Russian and German scholars talked reverently of "Fordismus," and industrial missions came from all over the world to study American techniques. "Just as in Rome one goes to the Vatican and endeavours to get audience of the Pope," wrote one British traveler, "so in Detroit one goes to the Ford Works and endeavours to see Henry Ford." "As I caught my first glimpse of Detroit," recorded another Briton, "I felt as I imagine a Seventeenth Century traveller must have felt when he approached Versailles." Ford was worshiped as a miracle-maker: a group of college students voted the Flivver King the third greatest figure of all time, surpassed only by Napoleon and Christ. When Ford announced the Model A early in 1928, 500,000 people made down payments without having seen the car and without knowing the price.

Ford personified the farmboy-mechanic who in a single lifetime reached the top. He fulfilled the dream of an acquisitive society committed to a belief in individual advancement. He brought the automobile to the masses of the world; he was the magical tinkerer who revolutionized human life. He was the high priest of mass production, which people the world over saw as more important than any ideological doctrine as a solution to the curse of poverty. His firm was family-owned; he was hostile to Wall Street; he founded, so it was believed, the doctrine of high wages and low prices, of sharing the benefits of his genius with the world—he was, in short, the Good Businessman. He resolved the moral dilemma of a Puritan-capitalist society. He achieved material success without losing his primal innocence.

"Machinery," declared Ford solemnly, "is the new Messiah." Dazzled by the prosperity of the time and by the endless stream of new gadgets, the American people raised business in the 1920's into a national religion and paid respectful homage to the businessman as the prophet of heaven on earth. As government looked only to the single interest of business, so society gave to the businessman social pre-eminence. There was no social class in America to challenge the business class. To call a scientist or a preacher or a professor or a doctor a good businessman was to pay him the most fulsome of compliments, for the chief index of a man's worth was his income. "Brains," declared Coolidge, "are wealth and wealth is the chief end of man." The opinions of a man like Ford, who believed in reincarnation, hated Jews, doctors, Catholics, and bankers, and abominated tobacco (it was "bad for the bowels"), were listened to with reverent respect, not only when he spoke on business matters but also when he made pronouncements on culture and public morals. "The man who builds a factory builds a temple," observed Coolidge, "the man who works there worships there."

Americans had less interest in a hereafter than in salvation on earth. Material comfort became not a means to an end but the final end of life itself. People continued to go to church, but church rituals were accepted less with reverence than with politeness. The functions of the church were gradually replaced by institutions committed to the ideal of service, to "organized altruism." Forced to accommodate themselves, the churches stressed not the divinity but the humanity of Christ. Churches installed swimming pools, game rooms, and gymnasiums with, as one foreign visitor noticed, "the oxygen of good fellowship" permeating everything. When a British journalist visited one American church, its young preacher invited him to "come and inspect his plant."

The classic statement of the secularization of religion and the religiosity of business was Bruce Barton's *The Man Nobody Knows*, a best seller in 1925 and 1926. Barton praised Jesus handsomely as a topnotch businessman. "He picked up twelve men from the bottom ranks of business and forged them into an organization that conquered the world." Jesus was an A-1 salesman, and the parables were "the most powerful advertisements of all time." No one need doubt that business was the main focus of His concern. Why, Jesus Himself had said: "Wist ye not that I must be about my father's business?"

Religion was valued not as a path to personal salvation or a key to the riddles of the universe but because it paid off in dollars and cents. The dean of the University of Chicago Divinity School told a reporter that a man could make more money if he prayed about his business. Reading the Bible, explained another writer, meant money in your pocket. Insurance men were advised that Exodus offered good tips on risk and liability, while a Chicago bond salesman confided that he had boosted his income by drawing arguments from Ezekiel. "Of all the Plenipotentiaries of Publicity, Ambassadors of Advertising and Bosses of Press Bureaus, none equals Moses," said Elbert Hubbard, for it was Moses who "appointed himself ad-writer for Deity." Taught to write advertising copy for their churches, pastors billed their sermons under captions like "Solomon, a Six-Cylinder Sport." Sermons were entitled after a popular cigarette slogan, "They Satisfy," or after a flour advertisement, "Eventually, Why

Not Now?" (an appeal for conversion), or "Three-in-One Oil" (the Trinity).

Encouraged by the friendly disposition of the federal government, the concentration of industry stepped up sharply in the postwar years. Although the merger movement had reached its apex before the war, it found new areas like the utilities in the 1920's. Most mergers brought together not competitive firms but companies engaged in the same business in different cities. Between 1919 and 1930, 8,000 businesses disappeared. "So long as I am Attorney General," explained Harry Daugherty, "I am not going unnecessarily to harass men who have unwittingly run counter with the statutes." Despite Daugherty's intentions, the Federal Trade Commission occasionally proved obstreperous and interceded to block consolidations and discourage trade associations. When in 1925 Coolidge appointed the lumber attorney William E. Humphrey to the chairmanship of the commission, large-business interests moved into control of the FTC. Humphrey himself denounced the FTC as "an instrument of oppression and disturbance and injury instead of help to business" and a "publicity bureau to spread socialistic propaganda." After Humphrey's accession, the commission approved trade associations and smiled on business agreements to lessen "cutthroat" competition.

Few businesses grew as rapidly as the electric light and power industry—the chief field for mergers in the 1920's. Between 1902 and 1929, the output of electric power multiplied more than 19 times—from 6 billion kilowatt-hours to 117 billion. Almost as much new hydroelectric power was developed between 1920 and 1930 as in all the years before 1920. As local electric light and power companies, which once served a single town, were interconnected in vast regional grids, financiers used the holding-company device to merge small firms into great utility empires. Between 1919 and 1927 over 3,700 utility companies vanished. Promoters organized a group of utility giants starting with the United Light and Power Company and the American Superpower Corporation in 1923 and ending with the Niagara Hudson Company and the Commonwealth and Southern Corporation in 1929. By 1930 ten holding-company groups controlled 72 per cent of the country's electric power.

The most spectacular of the new utility titans was Samuel Insull. Starting as an office boy in London at five shillings a week, Insull rose to the top of a holding-company empire which controlled gas and electric companies in twenty-three states. Operating out of Chicago, he extended his domain over businesses as remote as the Androscoggin Electric Company in Maine and the Tidewater Power Company in North Carolina. Chairman of the board of sixty-five different firms, Insull was involved in business operations in almost every conceivable field, from Mexican irrigation projects to the pathetic attempt to make Port Isabel, Texas, "the Venus of the South." His dairy herd, bathed in ultra-violet rays, was surrounded by electric screens that electrocuted flies. Respected as a philanthropist and a patron of the arts, he built the Chicago Civic Opera, an ornate skyscraper opera house. An intimate of mayors and senators, he was accused of buying political influence and suborning public officials.

The merger movement accelerated rapidly in American banking. The large banks swallowed the little banks or established branch banks which took away their business. In 1920, there were 1,280 branch banks; in 1930, 3,516. The greatest of the branch bankers was a newcomer, Amadeo Peter Giannini, who developed a chain of 500 banks throughout the state of California under a single holding company. His Bank of America National Trust and Savings Association in San Francisco became the fourth largest bank in the country, larger than any bank outside New York. In Manhattan, the National City Bank took over the Farmers Loan & Trust Company; the Guaranty Trust amalgamated with the Bank of Commerce; and the Chase National absorbed the Equitable Trust Company. By 1929, 1 per cent of the banks in the country controlled over 46 per cent of the banking resources of the nation.

Chain stores grew enormously in the postwar years. Chainstore units rose from 29,000 in 1918 to 160,000 in 1929; between 1919 and 1927 their sales jumped 124 per cent in drugstores, 287 per cent in groceries, and 425 per cent in the clothing business. The Great Atlantic and Pacific Tea Company's chain of red-fronted grocery stores grew from 400 in 1912 to 15,500 in 1932. By the end of the period, the A & P was selling a greater volume of goods than Ford at his peak; its billion dollar a year grocery business accounted for one-tenth of all food sold at retail in the United States. In these same years, the Woolworth "five and tens" crowded out many old neighborhood notion stores; for a dime or less, the customer could buy everything from Venetian Night Incense to Mammoth Tulip Sundaes, Hebrew New Year cards to poker chips, gumdrops to French Guiana stamps. A mammoth holding company, Drug, Incorporated, owned 10,000 Rexall drugstores and 706 Liggett stores, as well as the Owl chain on the Pacific Coast, and owned huge drug companies like Vick Chemical, Bayer Aspirin, and Bristol-Myers. By 1932, chain stores accounted for 22 per cent of the retail trade in Baltimore, 31 per cent in Atlanta, 37 per cent in Chicago. In some places the independent grocery store of 1914 had almost disappeared; Philadelphia bought two-thirds of its food in chain stores.

By the end of the decade the consolidation movement in American business reached boom proportions. In 1919, there were 80 bank mergers, in 1927, 259. In 1928, the Chrysler Corporation took over Dodge Brothers, Postum Company amalgamated with Maxwell House Coffee, and Colgate merged with Palmolive-Peet. Two advertising agencies combined to form the wonderfully sonorous firm of Batten, Barton, Durstine & Osborn. By 1929, the 200 largest non-financial corporations in America owned nearly half the corporate wealth of the nation, and they were growing much faster than smaller businesses. From 1924 to 1928, their assets expanded three times as fast as those of smaller corporations. Four meat packers controlled 70 per cent of the production in their industry; four tobacco companies accounted for 94 per cent of the output of cigarettes.

Many industries—textiles, clothing, and bituminous coal, in particular—remained boisterously competitive, however. The growth of oligopoly—domination of an industry by a few firms—often meant more rather than less competition. Although consolidation accelerated in the 1920's, there was not as much actual monopoly—that is, domination of an industry by only one company. No longer did a single firm lord it over the steel or the oil industries. Although the chain-store movement spelled national consolidation, it also destroyed the monopoly of the merchant in the small American town.

The benefits of technological innovation were by no means evenly distributed. While workers' income went up 11 per cent from 1923 to 1929, corporate profits rocketed 62 per cent and dividends 65 per cent. Despite the high productivity of the period, there was a disturbing amount of unemployment. Factory workers in "sick" industries like coal, leather, and textiles saw little of the boom prosperity. The Loray Mill in Gastonia, North Carolina, site of a bloody strike in 1928, paid its workers that year a weekly wage of $18 to men and $9 to women for working a 70-hour week. At the height of Coolidge prosperity, the secretary of the Gastonia Chamber of Commerce boasted that children of fourteen were permitted to work only 11 hours a day. Perhaps as many as two million boys and girls under fifteen continued to work in textile mills, cranberry bogs, and beet fields. In 1929, 71 per cent of American families had incomes under $2,500, generally thought to be the minimum standard for a decent living. The 36,000 wealthiest families in the United States received as much income as the 12,000,000 American families—42 per cent of all those in America—who received under $1,500 a year.

Yet, if one focuses exclusively on farm poverty or on depressed West Virginia coal towns, it is easy to get a distorted picture of life in the 1920's. As Henry May writes, "Sometimes even prosperity—an important fact despite its exceptions—is belittled almost out of existence." If prosperity was by no means as pervasive as Chamber of Commerce publicists claimed, it was still widespread enough to change markedly the life of millions of Americans. The change resulted less from a considerable increase in income for the average American—by later standards the increase does not seem so impressive—than from the fact that Americans could buy things with their paychecks that they had never been able to get before.

People could get into their automobile—almost everyone owned a car—and drive into the country or visit neighbors in the next town. For the first time, they saw America, taking trips to distant campsites or historic shrines and most of all discovering the glories of California and Florida. Electricity—all but farm homes had it by the end of the decade—meant not only electric lights but also a wide range of electric appliances. Women could buy vacuum cleaners and washing machines, toasters and electric sewing machines; in 1921, the production of refrigerators was only 0.6 per cent of what it was to be in 1929. Women of all classes wore clothing luxuries. They discarded cotton stockings and underwear for silk and rayon (in 1900, 12,000 pairs of silk stockings were sold, in 1930, 300 million), and the American woman became known as "America's greatest fur-bearing animal."

On week ends Americans went to the ballpark. Organized sport in America had captivated the country for decades, but it was not until the 1920's that spectator sports took on a central role in American life. In the Cathedral of St. John the Divine in New York, a bay was built with windows depicting various sports. On July 2, 1921, 91,000 fans at Boyles' Thirty Acres in Jersey City paid more than a million dollars to watch Jack Dempsey fight "gorgeous" Georges Carpentier. Dempsey knocked him out in the fourth round, but more important, the country had seen the first "million dollar gate." It was the Golden Age of Sports—of Babe Ruth, Bobby Jones, and Bill Tilden. It was the era of the Dempsey-Tunney fight, the decade when Ruth hit sixty home runs in a season. The biggest change took place in college football. People who had never been near a college crowded the vast new college stadiums to cheer the Four Horsemen of Notre Dame or the Galloping Ghost of Illinois. On one memorable fall afternoon in Urbana, Harold "Red" Grange scored four touchdowns against Michigan in the first twelve minutes of the game. By the end of the 1920's college football had become a major industry, with gate receipts each year of over $21 million.

People could walk down to the neighborhood theater and see the latest movie. Already flourishing before the war, motion pictures after the war became one of the ten great industries of the country, with an invested capital of a billion and a half dollars. In 1922, movie theaters sold 40 million tickets every week; by 1930, the average weekly attendance was 100 million. The faces of Charlie Chaplin and Harold Lloyd were known in every corner of the globe, and "youngsters playing in the back streets of Hull or Newcastle," noted one British writer, "threatened one another with *the works.*" Every respectable American town had its own movie palace. The movie houses became the temples of a secular society. In New York, Roxy's called itself "The Cathedral of the Motion Picture," the Capitol described itself as "The Theater with a Soul," and the Fifty-Fifth Street Theater advertised itself as "The Sanctuary of the Cinema."

Even more intriguing was the new invention of radio. There are many claimants to the honor of being the first station, but radio really arrived on the night of November 2, 1920, when KDKA at East Pittsburgh broadcast the presidential election returns. By 1922 there were radios in three million homes; that year the sale of sets was already a $60 million a year industry. Seven years later $852 million worth of radio sets were sold. Men bought cone-speakers and amplifiers and talked endlessly about how to eliminate static. They introduced a whole new vocabulary and within a few months used the terms—"tune in," "network," "airwaves"—so casually that the words lost their gloss of technological novelty. People clamped on earphones to hear Roxy and His Gang, the Clicquot Club Eskimos, the Ipana Troubadours or the A & P Gypsies. Grantland Rice broadcast the World Series, Floyd Gibbons narrated the news with a machine-gun staccato, and Rudy Vallee warbled the latest songs. From speakers in homes all over America came the sound of the ubiquitous ukelele.

Within a decade the radio and the movie nationalized American popular culture, projecting the same performers and the same stereotypes in every section of the country. In movie theaters everywhere, when olive-skinned Rudolph Valentino carried an impeccably blonde heroine across the burning Sahara and flung her into his tent, women swooned. Men scoffed at the Valentino craze, but barbers reported that men who once had called for bay rum now demanded pomades to make their hair sleek. There was even something of a vogue of sideburns, while dance schools offering the tango did a flourishing business. Endless interviews with Valentino appeared in national periodicals, including one with the inevitable title, "I'm Tired of Being a Sheik."

In the fall of 1929 two former vaudevillians, Freeman Gosden and Charles Correll, began a radio comic strip called "Amos 'n Andy." Within a few months the two blackface comedians, broadcasting over the N.B.C. network, had taken the country by storm. Many people refused to answer their telephone while the program was on the air. Movie theaters in smaller cities were forced to interrupt their show and turn on the broadcast; if they did not, they knew they would lose most of their patrons until the program was over. Millions of Americans followed avidly the affairs of the Fresh Air Taxicab Company, and Madame Queen and the Kingfish became household words. One man inserted an advertisement in a newspaper to ask his friends not to disturb him while the program was being broadcast. Senator Borah referred to Amos and Andy in a debate on the Philippines.

As the country solved the problems of production, greater emphasis was placed on distribution; the old-style manufacturer and tycoon became less important than the salesman and the promoter. In the 1920's the advertising man and the public relations expert came into their own. To staff the agencies of distribution and the "service" industries, a new white-collar class developed in the cities. Together with the civil servant, the salesman, and the salaried manager, these white-collar clerks constituted a "new middle class."

This shift in emphasis produced important changes in the national character. In place of the idea that saving was a virtue, an article of faith as old as the first colonial settlements and the chief conviction of Benjamin Franklin's Poor Richard, a new conviction developed that thrift could be socially harmful and spending a virtue. "We're too poor to economize," wrote Scott Fitzgerald jauntily. "Economy is a luxury." The nineteenth-century man, with a set of personal characteristics adapted to an economy of scarcity, began to give way to the twentieth-century man with the idiosyncrasies of an economy of abundance.

Aggressively optimistic, he was friendlier but had less depth, was more demanding of approval, less certain of himself. He did not knock, he boosted. He had lots of pep, hustle, and zip. He joined the Rotary or Kiwanis, and he believed in "service," a word that was repeated *ad nauseum* during the decade. Sinclair Lewis painted his portrait as George Babbitt, and Babbitt acknowledged that it was a reasonable likeness. "Dare to Be a Babbitt!" urged *Nation's Business*. What the world needed was more Babbitts, "good Rotarians who live orderly lives, and save money, and go to church, and play golf, and send their children to school."

The problem for the twentieth-century man was not the material environment but other people. "Our future," wrote Walter Weyl in 1919, "may depend less on the hours that we work today than on the words or the smile we exchange with some anonymous fellow-passenger in the office-building elevator." Men aimed less at improving their character and more at improving their personality. Neither health nor education nor even one's own "personality" was valued for itself alone, but for what it would do toward making one a "success," success meaning not merely greater income but the social acceptance necessary to stifle self-doubt. The main social knowledge a man had to acquire was how to "sell himself."

The nineteenth-century man coveted individual success; the twentieth-century man sought a place for himself in the bureaucracy. Probably the most important development within corporations during these years was the divorce of ownership from control. In 1900, there were four million owners of stocks; by 1930, twenty million. Control of business policy passed from the hands of owners, many of whom had not the remotest curiosity about or knowledge of the firm in which they held stock, and into the hands of a salaried bureaucracy. By the end of the decade a "managerial revolution" had occurred: plant managers and corporation executives, rather than owners, made the chief decisions. Young men no longer aimed to found their own businesses, to be Carnegies or Vanderbilts; they wanted to rise to a high position as a hired manager or a salaried executive. The businessman was less interested in risk and more in stabilizing his business. Unlike the nineteenth-century tycoon with the attitude of "the public be damned," the postwar businessman was extremely self-conscious about how he appeared to others.

Business developed ingenious methods to transform anxiety about scarcity into a desire for "luxury consumption of leisure and the surplus product." The advertising man and the salesman assaulted the older virtues of thrift and prudence. Behaviorist psychology, with its manipulative view of man, was perfectly adapted to mass advertising; Watson himself left the Johns Hopkins University under fire to become vice-president of an advertising agency. Advertisers sold not products but qualities like social prestige, which the possession of the products would allegedly secure. With debt no longer regarded as shameful, people bought on installment. Three out of every four radios were purchased on the installment plan, 60 per cent of all automobiles and furniture. "You furnish the girl; we furnish the home," advertised one furniture factory. Ten years after the war, conspicuous consumption had become a national mania. When a French perfume would not sell at ordinary rates, the manufacturer raised its price and made a fortune.

Henry Ford had built the Model-T flivver, a sturdy, simply constructed car without grace or beauty, and he had sold millions of them. When he started to lose sales in the 1920's to the more modern General Motors car, he refused to admit that the Model T was no longer marketable. "The customer," he snapped, "can have a Ford any color he wants—so long as it's black." But by the mid-1920's the country had less interest in price than in style and comfort. The purchase of an automobile had been a male prerogative—only men knew what lay under the hood—and men mostly bought cars that offered the soundest mechanical features. As women increasingly decided which car the family would buy, carburetors and gaskets became less important than the color of an automobile and the texture of its upholstery. In May, 1927, Ford surrendered; he halted production on the Model T, and when the Model A came out, it had modern design and construction and could be bought in a choice of colors from Dawn Gray to Arabian Sand.

The Coolidge era is usually viewed as a period of extreme conservatism, but it was thought of at the time as representing a great stride forward in social policy, a New Era in American life. During these years employers embarked on a program of welfare capitalism. They built clean, trim, well-lighted factories, with safety devices to forestall injury. They installed cafeterias, complete with trained dieticians, and formed glee clubs and baseball teams. The Hammermill Paper Company sold its employees cut-rate gasoline; L. Bamberger and Company provided free legal service; and Bausch and Lomb set up eye and dental clinics for its workers. In part to avert unionization, employers replaced tyrannical foremen with trained personnel men and organized company unions. They instituted group insurance plans and introduced profit-sharing; probably more than a million workers owned stock by 1929, an innovation which proved of dubious value by the end of the year. "If every family owned even a $100 bond of the United States or a legitimate corporation," declared Franklin

D. Roosevelt, "there would be no talk of bolshevism, and we would incidentally solve all national problems in a more democratic way."

Although the new prosperity favored an exceptionally materialistic view of life, it resulted in more than just increased sales of cigarette lighters and kitchen gadgets. The country spent more than twice as much as it had before the war on libraries, almost three times as much for hospitals. The United States in 1928 paid out as much for education as all the rest of the world. In 1900 a child had only one chance in ten of going to high school; by 1931 he had one chance in two. In 1900 he had only one chance in thirty-three of going to college; by 1931 he had better than one in seven. In part the result of increased wealth—which financed research, improved sanitation, and made possible better nutrition—science in the first third of the twentieth century increased American life expectancy from 49 to 59 years, cut infant mortality two-thirds, and slashed the death rate of typhoid from 36 to 2 per 100,000, of diphtheria from 43 to 2, of measles from 12 to 1.

In December, 1928, President Coolidge declared: "No Congress of the United States ever assembled, on surveying the state of the Union, has met with a more pleasing prospect than that which appears at the present time." By 1928, Coolidge had the assent of many of the New Era's former critics. "The more or less unconscious and unplanned activities of business men," noted Walter Lippmann, "are for once more novel, more daring, and in general more revolutionary than the theories of the progressives." "Big business in America," wrote Lincoln Steffens, who had long been a fierce critic of American capitalism, "is producing what the Socialists held up as their goal; food, shelter and clothing for all. You will see it during the Hoover administration."

New Era publicists argued that a new kind of "economic democracy" had been established. The businessman, enjoying high profits, shared them in "high wages" with his worker. The worker himself, by investing in the stock market, open to all, could own a share of industry. "We are reaching and maintaining the position," declared Coolidge as early as 1919, "where the property class and the employed class are not separate, but identical." The consumer, spending his dollars, it was said, cast votes to determine what should be produced. Soundly based on technological innovations, its gains dispersed through high wages, administered by enlightened businessmen, a new civilization appeared to be emerging. Without the class hatred or bureaucratic despotism of communism, the United States, it seemed, was on its way toward the final abolition of poverty.

The Great Depression

30.   "No One Has Starved"

The Editors of Fortune Magazine

Dull mornings last winter the sheriff of Miami, Florida, used to fill a truck with homeless men and run them up to the county line. Where the sheriff of Fort Lauderdale used to meet them and load them into a second truck and run them up to *his* county line. Where the sheriff of Saint Lucie's would meet them and load them into a third truck and run them up to *his* county line. Where the sheriff of Brevard County would *not* meet them. And whence they would trickle back down the roads to Miami. To repeat.

It was a system. And it worked. The only trouble was that it worked too well. It kept the transients transient and it even increased the transient population in the process. But it got to be pretty expensive, one way or another, if you sat down and figured it all out—trucks and gas and time and a little coffee . . .

That was last winter.

Next winter there will be no truck. And there will be no truck, not because the transients will have disappeared from Miami: if anything, there will be more blistered Fords with North Dakota licenses and more heel-worn shoes with the Boston trade-mark rubbed out next winter than there were last. But because the sheriff of Miami, like the President of the U. S., will next winter think of transients and unemployed miners and jobless mill workers in completely different terms.

The difference will be made by the Emergency Relief Act. Or rather by the fact that the Emergency Relief Act exists. For the Act itself with its $300,000,000 for direct relief loans to the states is neither an adequate nor an impressive piece of legislation. But the passage of the Act, like the green branch which young Mr. Ringling used to lay across the forks of the Wisconsin roads for his circus to follow, marks a turning in American political history. And the beginning of a new chapter in American unemployment relief. It constitutes an open and legible acknowledgment of governmental responsibility for the welfare of the victims of industrial unemployment. And its ultimate effect must be the substitution of an ordered, realistic, and intelligent relief program for the wasteful and uneconomic methods (of which the Miami truck is an adequate symbol) employed during the first three years of the depression.

WHAT DO YOU DO?

You are a carpenter. Your last cent is gone. They have cut off the gas. The kid is white and stupid looking. You have always earned your own way before but you can't get a job now for love or money. What do you do?

In some, but by no means all, cities you can get a meal at the Salvation Army or the Municipal Lodging House merely by waiting a few hours in a breadline. But that's no use now. So you go to the cop. He pulls out his directory and sends you to one of the listed charitable societies. The society takes your name and gives you emergency aid if you need it. It then asks you a list of questions about your age, your nationality, your religion, and your need. Your answers to these questions will determine to which of the charities specializing in Jews, Catholics, Protestants, abandoned babies, homeless boys, sickly children, pregnant women, disabled veterans, and the like you should be sent. You draw the Episcopal Family Relief Society. The Relief Society clears your name through the central agency to see that you are not receiving help elsewhere and sends around within the next few days to visit your family, prepare a budget, detail a nurse (if there is one), and eventually to allot you $2 to $8 a week, depending on the locality and funds available. If its funds are exhausted it asks you to wait. Meanwhile you register for work. You wait anyway.

❋   ❋   ❋

You are a white collar man. You have a wife and two children. What do you do?

You do as the carpenter did . . .

There can be no serious question of the failure of those methods. For the methods were never seriously capable of success. They were diffuse, unrelated, and unplanned. The theory was that private charitable organizations and semi-public welfare groups, established to care for the old and the sick and the indigent, were capable of caring for the casuals of a world-wide economic disaster. And the theory in application meant that social agencies manned for the service of a few hundred families, and city shelters set up to house and feed a handful of homeless men, were compelled by the brutal necessities of hunger to care for hundreds of thousands of families and whole armies of the displaced and the jobless. And to depend for their resources upon the contributions of communities no longer able to contribute, and upon the irresolution and vacillation of state Legislatures and municipal assemblies long since in the red on their annual budgets. The result was the picture now presented in city after city and state after state—heterogeneous groups of official and semi-official and unofficial relief agencies struggling under the earnest and untrained leadership of the local men of affairs against an inertia of misery and suffering and want they are powerless to overcome.

But the psychological consequence was even worse. Since the problem was never honestly attacked as a national problem, and since the facts were never frankly faced as facts, people came to believe that American unemployment was relatively unimportant. They saw little idleness and they therefore believed there was little idleness. It is possible to drive for blocks in the usual shopping and residential districts of New York and Chicago without seeing a breadline or a food station or a hungry mob or indeed anything else much more exciting than a few casuals asleep on a park bench. And for that reason, and because their newspapers played down the subject as an additional depressant in depressing times, and because they were bored with relief measures anyway, the great American public simply ignored the whole thing. They would still ignore it today were it not that the committee hearings and the Congressional debate and the Presidential veto of relief bills this last June attracted their attention. And that the final passage of the Emergency Relief and Construction Act of 1932 has committed their government and themselves to a policy of affirmative action which compels both it and them to know definitely and precisely what the existing situation is.

It should be remarked at this point that nothing the federal government has yet done or is likely to do in the near future constitutes a policy of *constructive* action. Unemployment basically is not a social disease but an industrial phenomenon. The natural and inevitable consequence of a machine civilization is a lessened demand for human labor. (An almost total elimination of human labor in plowing, for example, is now foreseeable.) And the natural and inevitable consequence of a lessened demand for human labor is an increase of idleness. Indeed the prophets of the machine age have always promised an increase of idleness, under the name of leisure, as one of the goals of industry. A constructive solution of unemployment therefore means an industrial solution—a restatement of industrialism which will treat technological displacement not as an illness to be cured but as a goal to be achieved—and achieved with the widest dispensation of benefits and the least incidental misery.

But the present relief problem as focused by the federal Act is not a problem of ultimate solutions but of immediate palliatives. One does not talk architecture while the house is on fire and the tenants are still inside.

The question at this moment is the pure question of fact. Having decided at last to face reality and do something about it, what is reality? How many men are unemployed in the U. S.? How many are in want? *What are the facts?*

TWENTY-FIVE MILLIONS

The following minimal statements may be accepted as true—with the certainty that they underestimate the real situation:

(1) Unemployment has steadily increased in the U. S. since the beginning of the depression and the rate of increase during the first part of 1932 was more rapid than in any other depression year.

(2) The number of persons totally unemployed is now at least 10,000,000.*

(3) The number of persons totally unemployed next winter will, at the present rate of increase, be 11,000,000.

(4) Eleven millions unemployed means better than one man out of every four employable workers.

(5) This percentage is higher than the percentage of unemployed British workers registered under the compulsory insurance laws (17.1 per cent in May, 1932, as against 17.3 per cent in April and 18.4 per cent in January) and higher than the French, the Italian, and the Canadian percentages, but lower than the German (43.9 per cent of trade unionists in April, 1932) and the Norwegian.

(6) Eleven millions unemployed means 27,500,000 whose regular source of livelihood has been cut off.

(7) Twenty-seven and a half millions without regular income includes the families of totally unemployed workers alone. Taking account of the numbers of workers on part time, the total of those without adequate income becomes 34,000,000 or better than a quarter of the entire population of the country.

(8) Thirty-four million persons without adequate income does not mean 34,000,000 in present want. Many families have savings. But savings are eventually dissipated and the number in actual want tends to approximate the number without adequate income. How nearly it approximates it now or will next winter no man can say. But it is conservative to estimate that the problem of next winter's relief is a problem of caring for approximately 25,000,000 souls.

* *I.e., persons "usually employed but now unemployed and seeking work" as defined in the census schedule. Criticisms of authoritative unemployment figures on the ground that they include a large percentage of "unemployables" are unfounded. "All census enumerations," says Commissioner Stewart, "have excluded the unemployables . . . the ne'er-do-wells were not counted . . ."*

An Appendix (B) on page 88 explains the computation of these figures.*
But it should be stated at once that they are based upon estimates. For
nothing but estimates exists. No heritage from the fumbling of the last
three years is more discouraging than the complete lack of statistics. The
Director of the President's Organization on Unemployment Relief, Mr.
Walter S. Gifford of the American Telephone & Telegraph Co., was forced
to acknowledge before a subcommittee of the Senate in January, 1932,
that he did not know, nor did his Organization know, how many persons
were out of work and in need of assistance in the U. S. nor even how many
persons were actually receiving aid at the time of his testimony. And more
recently the Commissioner of Labor Statistics, Mr. Ethelbert Stewart,
generally recognized as the government's foremost authority on unemployment, has been allowed to lose his office at the most critical period in
American unemployment history because, according to press accounts,
the Secretary of Labor, Mr. Doak, was irritated by the Commissioner's
correction of one of his over-optimistic statements.

Fortunately, however, the more important estimators agree among
themselves and the total of 25,000,000 may fairly be accepted.

But it is impossible to think or to act in units of 25,000,000 human
beings. Like the casualty lists of the British War Office during the Battle
of the Somme, they mean nothing. They are at once too large and to
small. A handful of men and women and children digging for their rotten
food in the St. Louis dumps are more numerous, humanly speaking, than
all the millions that ever found themselves in an actuary's column. The
25,000,000 only become human in their cities and their mill towns and
their mining villages. And their situation only becomes comprehensible in
terms of the relief they have already received.

That is to say that the general situation can only be judged by the
situation in the particular localities. But certain generalizations are possible. Of which the chief is the broad conclusion that few if any of the
industrial areas have been able to maintain a minimum decency level of
life for their unemployed. Budgetary standards as set up by welfare
organizations, public and private, after years of experiment have been
discarded. Food only, in most cases, is provided and little enough of that.
Rents are seldom paid. Shoes and clothing are given in rare instances only.
Money for doctors and dentists is not to be had. And free clinics are filled
to overflowing. Weekly allowances per family have fallen as low as $2.39
in New York with $3 and $4 the rule in most cities and $5 a high figure.
And even on these terms funds budgeted for a twelve-month period have
been exhausted in three or four. City after city has been compelled to
abandon a part of its dependent population. "We are merely trying to

* Editors' note: See page 88 of September, 1932 issue of *Fortune Magazine* for
Appendix B.

prevent hunger and exposure," reported a St. Paul welfare head last May. And the same sentence would be echoed by workers in other cities with such additions as were reported at the same time from Pittsburgh where a cut of 50 per cent was regarded as "inevitable," from Dallas where Mexicans and Negroes were not given relief, from Alabama where discontinuance of relief in mining and agricultural sections was foreseen, from New Orleans where no new applicants were being received and 2,500 families in need of relief were receiving none, from Omaha where two-thirds of the cases receiving relief were to be discontinued, from Colorado where the counties had suspended relief for lack of funds . . . from Scranton . . . from Cleveland . . . from Syracuse . . . But the individual localities present their own picture:

New York City

About 1,000,000 out of the city's 3,200,000 working population are unemployed. Last April 410,000 were estimated to be in dire want. Seven hundred and fifty thousand in 150,000 families were receiving emergency aid while 160,000 more in 32,000 families were waiting to receive aid not then available. Of these latter families—families which normally earn an average of $141.50 a month—the average income from all sources was $8.20. Of families receiving relief, the allowance has been anything from a box of groceries up to $60 a month. In general, New York relief, in the phrase of Mr. William Hodson, executive director of the New York Welfare Council, has been on "a disaster basis." And the effects have been disaster effects. It is impossible to estimate the number of deaths in the last year in which starvation was a contributing cause. But ninety-five persons suffering directly from starvation were admitted to the city hospitals in 1931, of whom twenty died; and 143 suffering from malnutrition, of whom twenty-five died. While visiting nurses and welfare workers report a general increase in malnutrition, and the clinics and medical relief agencies are so overcrowded they can give adequate relief to no one, although 75 per cent of persons applying to one relief agency had some form of illness. Housing is, of course, with the general lowering of standards and the doubling-up of families, worse even than it was during the boom. Relief expenditures for 1930 were something over $6,000,000; for 1931, more than $25,000,000; and for the first four months of 1932 over $20,000,000, or $5,000,000 per month. But large as this latter figure is it must be compared with the wage and salary loss by reason of unemployment, which is at least $100,000,000 per month. The need, even with static unemployment figures, is cumulative, and $75,000,000 for the next twelve months is a low estimate.

PHILADELPHIA

The situation in Philadelphia was described by its Community Council in July, 1932, as one of "slow starvation and progressive disintegration of family life . . ." "Normal" unemployment in Philadelphia is 40,000 to 50,000. In April, 1931, 228,000 or 25.6 per cent of the city's normally employed were unemployed, and 122,000 or 13.7 per cent were on part time. Of the city's 445,000 families with employable workers, 210,000 had workers unemployed or on part time, about one in four had no worker employed on full time, and 12 per cent had *no* worker employed. Even the average person unemployed had been out of work for thirty-seven weeks and had had only a little over one week of casual or relief work during the period. By December, 1931, the number of unemployed had reached 238,000 with 43,000 families receiving relief and 56,000 families in which no one was at work. And by May, 1932, the total of unemployed was 298,000. In the following month the Governor of the state estimated that 250,000 persons in Philadelphia "faced actual starvation." Over the state at large the same conditions held. In June, 1931, 919,000 or 25 per cent of the normally employed in the state were unemployed, according to the "secret" report then submitted to the Governor, and the number had risen to 1,000,000 by December and to 1,250,000 in August, 1932. One hundred and fifty thousand children were in need of charity. Malnutrition had increased in forty-eight counties—27 per cent of school children being undernourished (216,000 out of a school population of 800,000). New patients in the tuberculosis clinics had doubled. And the general death rate and disease rate had risen. Only nine counties were well organized. Fifty-five gave cause for grave concern and nineteen were listed as distressed counties in dire need. Moreover, relief allowances have steadily dropped. Last December 43,000 of the 56,000 families in Philadelphia where no one was employed were receiving relief at the rate of $4.39 per week for families averaging 4.8 persons. By May the number of families receiving relief had risen to 55,000 and the amount of relief had dropped to $4.23, of which $3.93 was for food, being two-thirds of the minimum required for health. No provision is made for rents and the result is that the landlords of Philadelphia, like the landlords of the country at large, are compelled to choose between throwing their tenants into the streets or providing from their own pockets the shelter required. Outside of Philadelphia the weekly grant to a family is $3 or less in thirteen counties, and $3 to $4 in six more, while in some of the small steel towns it may be even lower. Funds in the counties are either exhausted or will be exhausted before November.

Detroit

Relief in Detroit was originally upon a boom-time, boom-extravagance basis with gross incompetence in the administration of funds, an embezzlement of $207,000, and doles of silk stockings and cosmetics. The resultant imminent barkruptcy forced a contraction of expenditures, and relief in May, 1932, with a greatly increased need, was only $859,925 as against $2,088,850 in January, 1931. There were 223,000 unemployed last November in the city and 410,000 in the state. In January the city was caring for 48,000 distressed families. This number was cut to 22,000 in April and relief was given at the rate of fifteen cents per day per person. In July under pressure of further shortage a further cut of 5,000 families totaling 20,000 persons was determined. Aid was to be denied to able-bodied persons who had been public charges for a year or more whether work was available for them or not, and childless couples and small families with no definite ties in Detroit were to be forced to leave the city. The resultant relief roll was expected to be 17,757 families, of whom 7,000 were dependent because of age or illness. The great majority on relief are laborers but Detroit also carries or has carried forty-five ministers, thirty bank tellers, lawyers, dentists, musicians, and "two families after whom streets are named." Riots, chiefly employment riots, have been fairly common with bloodshed in at least one. And enormous breadlines and the like are daily sights. No adequate statistics on public health in Detroit exist but it may safely be assumed to be at least as low as New York's.

Chicago

Unemployed in Chicago number somewhere between 660,000 and 700,000 or 40 per cent of its employable workers while the number for the state at large is about one in three of the gainfully employed. About 100,000 families have applied down to July for relief in Cook County. The minimum relief budget has been $2.40 per week for an adult and $1.50 per week for a child for food, with $22 to $23 per month to a family. But these figures have since been cut to $2.15 weekly for a man, $1.10 for a child. And persons demanding relief must be completely destitute to receive it. Rents are not paid by the relief agencies and housing is, in certain sections, unspeakably bad. The situation of city employees is tragic. Teachers in May, 1932, had had only five months cash for the last thirteen months, 3,177 of them had lost $2,367,000 in bank failures, 2,278 of them had lost $7,800,000 in lapsed policies, 805 had borrowed $232,000 from loan sharks at rates adding up to 42 per cent a year, and 759 had lost their homes. (The city at one time undertook to sell for tax default the houses of its employees unable to pay taxes because of its own default in wages.) The vicissitudes of Chicago's relief funds are noticed in Appendix A.* It is estimated that $35,000,000 will be spent in 1932 for an inadequate job and that an adequate job would cost $50,000,000.

OTHER URBAN CENTERS

In *St. Louis* 125,000 of the city's 330,000 employable persons were unemployed last December, one-eighth of the population was estimated to face eviction and starvation, three-fourths of the families under care presented one or more medical problems each, and relief campaigners published full-page advertisements pointing to the number of hungry men and women rifling garbage buckets for their food. Starvation is reported as a contributory cause in several deaths. And even so the relief agencies were forced by lack of funds to drop 8,000 families on July 1 and 5,000 more on July 15. Since these cuts were made, large numbers of the destitute have been living in refuse dumps along the river where they build shacks and dig in the dump for food. The city's Board of Estimate and Apportionment has petitioned the Governor to apply for a $2,000,000 loan from the federal government but the amount will not suffice to carry the city through the winter.

Across the river in *East St. Louis* 60 per cent of the workers are jobless and the mayor has forbidden all meetings of the unemployed even in halls. In *Kansas City* 12,000 family heads and 28,000 single persons were unemployed last December and by April private funds were exhausted with no public funds in sight.

In the Ohio cities unemployment as of July runs 80 per cent of 1928 employment in *Toledo*, 60 per cent in *Akron*, 50 per cent in *Cleveland*, 45 per cent in *Youngstown*, 45 per cent in *Dayton*, 40 per cent in *Columbus*, and 40 per cent in *Cincinnati*. Toledo has been feeding 9,000 families or 40,000 individuals. The food lists have been approved by doctors but the "quantities given," according to the Social Service Federation, "are certainly at the very minimum subsistence level and are scarcely adequate." Clothing and shelter are not provided. And the number of families needing relief will be 15,000 by next winter. In Cleveland the average of direct relief to families is $17.09 monthly. A total of 31,000 families is expected in December, rising to 38,000 next March. Income for 1932 will be about $2,000,000 short of expenditures. In Youngstown, due to the local optimism, no united relief was undertaken until January, 1931. Meantime homeless men slept in the garbage in the municipal incinerator to keep

* Editors' note: See page 88 of September, 1932 issue of *Fortune Magazine* for Appendix A.

warm. In January an abandoned police station was made into a flophouse. Attempts of Communists to organize the flophouseholders failed and a bond issue was eventually floated. Men in desperate need get two days work a week. As ex-Mayor Heffernan puts it: "If a man owned a small home, if a young couple possessed furniture, if a woman had a good coat or her husband a presentable suit, these things had to be sacrificed first. Not until they had drained every other resource was official charity able to do anything for them." Average relief in Akron has run at $14 per month with few rents being paid by the relief agencies. In Canton relief is down to $13.97 per family per month but there has been a slight decline in the number aided. Landlords have carried many families a year or more here as elsewhere. The Canton Community Fund Drive fell short about $102,000 of its $345,000 goal. In Cincinnati, of the 50,000 unemployed, at least half have not yet asked relief. About 21,000 families are now carried at an average per family of $5 per week. In Dayton, with 6,000 families in need, much despondency and illness due to inadequate relief is reported.

Upstate New York cities present a similar picture with relief somewhat better organized. *Pittsburgh* has 178,000 unemployed and 30,000 families on relief with expenditures for 1932 about four times 1931. Father Cox, head of the Pittsburgh hunger marchers, has purchased thirty-six acres on the outskirts of the city where a town for the unemployed will be built. In May it had shelter for 100 families. *Los Angeles* had last winter 151,000 unemployed, of whom 60,000 were heads of families, but now reports 118,000. Relief is about $23.58 per family per month, with the 1931 county poor appropriation for the 225,000 unemployed in the county smaller than the 1930 appropriation. *San Francisco* now reports 40,000 unemployed and 12,000 families on relief with an allowance for food and housing of twenty-eight cents per person a day. California has been able to give a considerable amount of work through labor camps and work relief financed from county funds and supplying in one section $24 worth of work per man every six weeks. *Birmingham* had an unemployed total of 25,000 out of its working population of 115,000 at the beginning of the year and provides an allowance of $2.50 to $4 per week for families averaging 4.3 persons. There were 12,000 tax delinquencies and had been 6,000 tax sales and neither county nor state aid was probable. *Portland, Oregon,* has 37,500 unemployed and 13,445 families on relief. *New Orleans* has 20,000 unemployed and 2,500 families receiving aid with no more private funds in sight and completely inadequate relief. *Boston* has 103,600 unemployed with a daily food relief expenditure of seventeen cents to thirty cents and an enforced contribution system for city employees. And *Minneapolis, St. Paul,* and *Duluth* registered respectively last winter 44,000, 20,000, and 10,000 unemployed with relief in Minneapolis, at least, on a minimal basis.

Textiles and Mines

Obviously, however, urban figures give an incomplete picture of the whole industrial situation, for they do not include such areas as the industrial area of New Jersey. In Passaic County, for example, 23,749 persons, heads of families, representing 90,699 of the county's 300,000 population, have applied for relief. The authorities have been forced to pick 12,171 families, about half, and give them relief amounting to about $9 a month per family. And in Paterson 8,500 of the registered 12,000 unemployed are without relief of any kind. Moreover, the situation in the textile areas of the state is complicated by the fact that certain employers have taken advantage of the necessity of their employees to reëstablish sweatshop conditions. Under such circumstances the employed as well as the unemployed become a burden upon the community. But elsewhere in the textile mill towns even the pretense of a living wage has been dropped. North Carolina has 100,000 unemployed textile workers with another 100,000 on the payrolls of closed plants, most of whom are begging on the roads, having long ago exhausted their savings from the low wage paid them before the depression. And those employed on part time are hardly better off since the full-time wage now averages about $6.50. In Georgia, in the Piedmont Mill Village of Egan Park, fifteen families have banded together to keep alive on a total weekly income of $10. And similar stories come from other towns in the region. While some of the small steel towns are almost as badly off. At Donora, Pennsylvania, there were in March 277 regular workers out of a population of 13,900 while 2,500 others performed "made work" at $3.50 per week and 2,000 others "seem to have disappeared." It is hardly necessary to add that malnutrition, undernourishment, rickets, tuberculosis, and other diseases increase under such conditions. And that relief in these areas is badly organized or nonexistent.

The story of factory unemployment is, however, only part of the story. In *agriculture* and in *mining*, particularly soft-coal mining, the depression is not in its fourth year but in its eighth or tenth or twelfth. It is estimated that there is a destitute coal-mining population of 1,200,000 souls dependent upon some 240,000 unemployed and distressed bituminous miners, most of whom live in six states in regions where coal mining is the only important enterprise, where merchants are bankrupt, banks closed, schools without funds, and once wealthy residents in actual want. And this situation is of many years' standing for even in the boom years of 1928 and 1929 the industry as a whole lost a total of $41,000,000. The American Friends Service Committee, which has worked with children in Kentucky,

West Virginia, and Williamson and Franklin counties, Illinois, estimates that of the 500,000 soft-coal workers making a living in 1928 only 300,000 are now employed and on wages often as low as $8 a week. Over the entire area from 20 per cent to 99 per cent of the children are found to be underweight and the probability is that 20,000 children and 20,000 adults will shortly be in actual and pressing want.

Kentucky conditions have been well aired as a result of the Fascist policy pursued by the local authorities, particularly in Harlan County. Miners in that county who work at all work one to one and a half days a week with payment in scrip from which the company deducts an average of $11.80 monthly for rent, medical attention, powder and caps, and insurance. To pay this deduction, a man must mine forty-five tons a month, which means that he must work nine days. Most of them work a total of six days and the result is a load of debt with no balance for food. As a consequence, pellagra—a deficiency disease of the nerve centers finally causing insanity—is common. In Pineville, Kentucky, 157 children are fed one meal a day at a soup kitchen—the meal consisting of boiled potatoes, boiled beans, and cornbread, an ideal pellagra-breeding diet. Most of the miners attempt to farm but the land is poor and jars for canning are too expensive for a community in which cash is practically nonexistent. Moreover, there was last year a severe drought in this district, and a great many miners' crops were destroyed by sun and pests—a fact which must be compared with the September, 1931, statement of Executive-Director Croxton of the President's Organization on Unemployment Relief to the effect that the unemployment situation in West Virginia and Kentucky would be alleviated by the "bountiful crops."

The state of Franklin and Williamson counties in Illinois is, if anything, worse. All mines in the counties were closed by April, 1932. A cross section of twelve homes in the town of Benton showed no money, worn-out clothing, houses bare of "unnecessary" furniture, dishes made of flour, emaciated parents, undernourished children, unpaid rentals, and an average family indebtedness for groceries and doctors' bills of $300. Twenty-five thousand persons in the two counties were either in want last spring or rapidly approaching it.

Other coal-mining states are in the same condition. There were 20,000 distressed miners in Ohio in February, 1932. In Pennsylvania last winter there were 60,000 in distress, many small communities were half deserted, one day's work a month was the frequent rule, undernourishment and malnutrition were common, and school children were stupid and sleepy with hunger. In West Virginia the number of distressed miners was about 30,000, thousands of men and women lived in tents, many children were eating every other day, prostitution among young girls was increasing, dysentery and pellagra were common diseases, and 15,000 men in Logan County alone were working twelve to eighteen hours a day without extra pay. In Arizona 200 miners' families in utter destitution were living under one of the bridges of the Salt River.

So it goes from one city to another and out into the mill towns and the mine villages and on beyond into the farms where the hides of a carload of cattle will hardly buy a pair of shoes and alfalfa costing $12 a ton to raise sells at $2.50 and the tractors rust in the fields. The difficulty with such facts is that in mass they cease to have meaning. And the reiteration of the statement that hundreds of thousands of people have faced or are facing starvation with inadequate doles to support them merely produces skepticism. "They haven't starved yet," remarks the reader. "They get along somehow."

It is true they get along somehow. But just how they get along is another matter. There were eleven days in Philadelphia last April when private funds had run out and public funds were not yet available. During that period, the relief organizations studied ninety-one families to see just how people get along under those circumstances. They found out. One woman borrowed fifty cents, bought stale bread at three and one-half cents a loaf, and the family lived on it for eleven days. Another put the last food order into soup stock and vegetables and made a soup. When a member of the family was hungry, he ate as little as he could. Another picked up spoiled vegetables along the docks and except for three foodless days, the family ate them. Another made a stew with her last food order, which she cooked over and over daily to keep it from spoiling. Another family lived on dandelions. Another on potatoes. Another had no food for two and one-half days. And one in ten of the women were pregnant and one in three of the children of nursing age. And they "got along."

TREK

Such is the problem created by three years of increasing unemployment and two years of hand-to-mouth relief: city after city attempting to feed a half or a third or a quarter of its citizens upon gifts made from the reduced earnings, or from taxes levied on the over-appraised homes of the other half or the other two-thirds or the other three-quarters; city after city maintaining the lives but not the health of its unemployed on a survival ration; city after city where the whole mechanism of relief has failed or is about to fail or has survived only by abandoning a major part of its task; and beyond the cities the mill towns and the coal mines and the cropper farms where relief is merely a name.

But the depression, along with its misery, has produced its social curiosities, not the least of which is the wandering population it has spilled upon the roads. Means of locomotion vary but the objective is always the same—somewhere else. No one has yet undertaken to estimate the number of hitchhikers whose thumbs jerk onward along the American pike, nor the number of spavined Fords dragging destitute families from town to town in search of a solvent relative or a generous friend. But the total migratory population of the country has been put at 600,000 to 1,000,000. The Pacific Coast, the Southwest, and the Atlantic South are the habitat of the larger groups. Los Angeles once had over 70,000 with a daily influx of 1,500 more while the state of California reported an increase of 311.8 per cent in the monthly average of meals served to homeless men in early 1931 as compared with early 1929. And 365 vagrant boys running from fourteen to twenty and including college students, high school students, and eighth-graders applied to the Salt Lake Salvation Army and the Salt Lake County Jail for shelter between May 15 and June 15, 1932. Many of them were homeless, destitute children of families broken up by unemployment. And save for the fact that almost all of them were traveling alone or with one companion, and that most of them wanted work, they suggested with an uncomfortable accuracy the vagrant children who haunted the Russian railway stations after the October Revolution.

The presence of these wandering groups is curious and significant. It has long been recognized that the population of the U. S. was becoming increasingly migratory in character. But it was not until the depression that the meaning of the phenomenon was made clear. When millions of people have no relation to the land and are able at the same time to find cheap transportation, the effect of an economic crisis is not to fix them in one place but to drive them elsewhere. And the consequence, as regards these groups, is a complete failure of local relief. The destitute families of the Fords and the homeless men of the flat cars are entitled to relief in no city. As the history of the Bonus Expeditionary Force after its ouster from Washington makes clear.

BUGABOOS AND REDS

So far at least the phenomenon of migration is the only important social consequence of the depression, and the Communistic outbreaks foreseen by extremists in both directions have not taken place. The unemployed of Passaic County, New Jersey, may be and doubtless are in ugly temper. And the state of mind of the idle miners in Harlan County, Kentucky, may have been such as to justify, through fear, the otherwise unjustifiable repressive measures adopted by the local authorities. But by and large there has been extraordinarily little unrest. The two major manifestations of the year, the January hunger march of Father Cox's army to Washington and the later Bonus Expeditionary Force, were notoriously and avowedly anti-revolutionary, and contrasted remarkably in number with the feeble 1,500 produced for the Communist hunger march of last December. And most of the food riots reported from various cities—or not reported—have so far been bloodless, the only fatalities having occurred in the mismanaged resistance to a job march upon the Ford factories in Dearborn in March, when four were killed and fifty wounded, the July attempt of St. Louis police to prevent a mob of 300 from rushing the City Hall where the Board of Aldermen was considering (and thereupon promptly passing) special tax bills for relief, the demonstration of 400 against the employment of non-union men on public works in Marseilles, Illinois, in the same month in which one man was killed and twenty-two wounded, and the Battle of Pennsylvania Avenue. Other and milder disturbances occurred in New York in January (a riot before the Home Relief Bureau Office), in Chicago in February (a demonstration of 20,000 said to have been led by Communists), in Boston in May (a hunger march of 500), in Philadelphia in May (a demonstration before the City Hall in which twenty people were beaten), in Charleston, West Virginia, in June (a hunger siege of 500 around the State House), in Clinton, Massachusetts, in July (a demonstration for food by 300 men, women, and crying children), in Sioux City, Iowa, in July (a demonstration of 500 unemployed against the use of a steam shovel on a post-office site), in North Carolina in July (a demonstration of 5,000 textile workers against a wage cut, resulting in the forced closing of the mills of five towns), and in Olympia, Washington, in July (a concentration of jobless upon the State Capitol demanding relief). But the tension has naturally increased in the industrial communities as time has passed. Indiana has recently offered the spectacle of striking miners besieging strike breakers in violation of an anti-picketing injunction with the purpose of either inviting their own arrest so that they might be fed in jail, or starving out their enemies. And it is not necessary to appeal, as Mayor Cermak did last winter, to class fear in order to point out that there is a limit beyond which hunger and misery become violent.

EXPERIMENTS AND DEDUCTIONS

It remains to inquire what part of the experience of the first three years of relief is useful for the future development of a planned unemployment program.

In general the lessons are negative. For example, it has been the experience of most of the large centers that "work relief"—i. e., relief by wages paid for made-work performed by the unemployed—is too expensive. Philadelphia, Cleveland, Toledo, Chicago, Kansas City, Missouri, St. Louis, and Memphis, cities which gave considerable sums for work relief in March, 1931, had abandoned work relief in March, 1932. New Jersey, through its Director of Emergency Relief, Chester I. Barnard, characterized municipal work relief as "wasteful and inefficient" and suggested instead direct and dependency relief. And in Wisconsin where an emergency tax on incomes was levied to pay for the elimination of railroad grade crossings by unemployed laborers, it became necessary to discontinue collections because of the rise in state and local taxation. It was found that instead of the 10,000 anticipated only about 2,500 unemployed had been put to work in any one day.

There are, however, a few constructive suggestions to be harvested. One or two cities have attacked the feeding of their unemployed from a scientific point of view and have worked out a diet and a technique of purchase and distribution which may simplify the task in the future. Tulsa, Oklahoma, is the leading example. Under the Tulsa Commissary plan, food is bought in large quantities (from the local dealers when possible) at wholesale prices, collected in a central storehouse, and there divided into three types of rations, for children, adolescents, and adults, each ration being put up in a distinctive paper bag. Ration No. I for children contains a minimum of 1,400 calories daily (not less than 30 per cent fats and 18 per cent proteins and not more than 52 per cent carbohydrates); ration No. II for adolescents, eight to fifteen, contains a minimum of 2,000 calories daily, divided 33 per cent, 15 per cent, and 52 per cent; and ration No. III for adults contains at least 2,100 calories daily, divided 20 per cent, 12 per cent, and 67 per cent. All rations have in addition 120 calories of animal protein daily and No. I and No. II have at least one pint of skimmed milk, two tablespoons of tomato juice (or equivalent), and at least one liberal serving of one green vegetable daily. Altogether, the weekly ration for a family would contain whole wheat, cornmeal, oatmeal, beans, white potatoes, sweet potatoes, lean, boneless ground meat, "compound," sugar, carrots or cabbage or onions or spinach, turnips, peanut butter, powdered milk, salt pork, cocoa, salt, tomatoes, baking powder, soap, and cod-liver oil. When the price permits, other foods meeting the requirements are substituted for variety: for example, antiscorbutics such as grapefruit, pears, apples, etc., are used to supplement the tomato juice. Fresh vegetables vary daily. Prunes and other dried fruits are substituted from time to time, etc. For meat, whole fat bulls are bought, boned, and ground as needed. Bread is not issued but flour plus yeast, thus saving one cent per ration daily. Powdered milk is given instead of fresh to save expense in delivery, and the fat deficiency is made up with cod-liver oil. And to insure proper preparation, etc., demonstrations on good stoves and on frying pans plus gallon pails are given in front of the commissary.

Tulsa issues 2,000 such weekly rations daily to 12,000 people per week who know that if their children do not show an immediate gain in weight it is because the child is sick, the food badly prepared, or the parents are eating the child's portion. And the cost per day per person to the city of Tulsa is six cents!

Just how low that figure is may be seen by comparing it with the U. S. Army cost per person per day of thirty-four cents, the Navy average of 44.3 cents, the Marine figure of 36.8 and the U. S. Children's Bureau estimate (which concludes that the weekly cost of a market order to provide minimum adequate sustenance for a family of five is $7.65 to $10.25 or a minimum of almost twenty-two cents per day per person). And with the averages of other cities—Fort Worth thirty-six cents for adults and thirty cents for children, Boston thirty cents for adults and seventeen cents for children, and Denver fifty cents. Certain cities, however, are low: Chicago nine to ten cents, Syracuse nine cents, Toledo six and one-half cents, and Niles, Ohio, three cents. But none of these supplies a balanced diet as successful as that provided in Tulsa. Under the Toledo plan, followed by Syracuse and many of the other cities, a family ration of evaporated milk, salt pork, soup beef, canned salmon, cheese, one egg, navy beans, dried peas, cabbage, carrots, onions, potatoes, prunes, apples, macaroni, tomatoes, peanut butter, butter substitute, lard, molasses, sugar, bread, flour, baking powder, rice, wheat grits, cocoa, coffee, computed to contain a total of 18,900 calories, is provided for six and one-half cents in Toledo, and nine cents in Syracuse, by carload buying and central distribution. Toledo feeds about 50,000 on this basis.

Prices, of course, vary in different sections of the country. Massachusetts works out its calories at ten cents per 1,000 calories resulting in a weekly grant, for the ration recommended by the Connecticut Valley Branch of the Joint Committee on Unemployment, of $2.29 for an adult male or about thirty-three cents a day. That ration, however, amounts to 3,265 calories as against the 2,100 provided in Tulsa.

One of the immediate problems of planned and intelligent relief will be to extend the scope of such experiments and reduce the number of localities like Benton, Illinois, where the weekly handout for a family of seven consists of flour, beans, lard, salt, and sugar worth at retail $1.50 and containing neither meat, bread, butter, coffee, eggs, vegetables, fruit, or milk, and the number of grocery order-blank stations where housewives are able to concentrate upon heavy "filling" foods without regard to the balance of proteins and carbohydrates. Grocers in the Pennsylvania coal fields report they have little call for meats or green vegetables or for much of anything beyond oatmeal, beans, flour, and potatoes.

Experiments with mass diet, however, go to only a part of the problem. Real relief must encompass the whole. And so far experiments in that direction are few.

SEATTLE

The Unemployed Citizens League of Seattle is an application of the relief principle that the unemployed should be put to work for the unemployed. It originated last fall under the leadership of a group of teachers and students in the Seattle Labor College and now feeds 13,000 families (about 50,000 individuals) through twenty-two commissaries established in various districts of the city, while also providing such services as tailoring, barbering, cobbling, etc. run by the unemployed for the benefit of their fellows. The League is made up of locals, each of which is responsible to the Central Foundation for the proper operation of its commissary. Food and wood for the commissaries are secured by the unemployed by their own labor or through funds of the County Commissioners and the Mayor's Unemployment Commission, and distributed on a communistic basis to each family on the basis of its size. Members of the League who are able-bodied are expected to be available for six hours work per day two days per week. Labor is allocated (by the committees of the Central Federation on relief, housing, transportation, fuel, investigation, child welfare, garden, health, etc.) to necessary projects. Thus the housing committee will have minor repairs made on houses donated rent free for the use of evicted families, the work of repair constituting the pay for a certain period of occupancy. And plans are on foot to take over closed factories, bakeries, etc., where commodities may be manufactured by the members of the League for their own consumption. No member of the League receives pay and no money is in use for exchange.

Recently the League has entered politics, electing three candidates in the municipal elections and threatening to run an independent ticket in the state election. A state-wide convention has been held to spread the idea in the Northwest. It has already taken hold in Tacoma, where half the estimated unemployed were signed up in May in fourteen locals. And the Chicago Workers Committee on Unemployment with a membership of 15,000 announces that it will shortly put an adaptation of the Seattle plan into effect in Chicago. A start has also been made in New Jersey.

The political program of the League calls for unemployment relief at city, county, and federal expense; unemployment insurance; no evictions or gas stoppage for failure to pay rent; lowering of legal interest rate; relief work on state and county jobs at $4.50 per day with a program of public improvements; moratoriums on taxes, mortgages, and bank loans for the distressed; free medical, dental, burial, and hospital service; the five-day week and six-hour day in all public employment; and a tax on employers for each hour worked in excess of six per day or thirty per week—the proceeds to go for unemployment relief.

THE TECHNOLOGIST

The weakness of the Seattle project is that it mixes such a political program or indeed any political program with the more realistic and more technical aspects of the plan. For the two do not coincide. Political relief measures have been attempted and have failed. The future now belongs to the technician. The paradox of the unemployment situation, as its critics have frequently pointed out, is that there exist side by side in the same society a huge, inert productive apparatus and a vast and daily increasing human demand. There is as much hunger as there is unsold food. There are as many unclothed bodies as there are unprocessed cloths. Only the machinery of exchange has stalled. And since the masters and experts of exchange have been unable to set that machinery in motion again the problem falls into the hands of the industrialist himself—the technician.

Attacks upon a purely technical solution have already been made. They proceed upon the theory that unemployed men must be put to work in unemployed factories under unemployed management producing goods for unemployed consumption. As a theory the proposition is sound enough. Its defect lies in the fact that profit-making industry, and particularly the retail food trade, may be found in opposition. For though the retail food trade cannot sell to the destitute unemployed it can sell to relief organizations feeding the destitute unemployed. The answer is of course that industry as a whole cannot afford to keep the present enormously costly relief mechanism alive simply to enable certain retailers to profit by its necessities. And the further and more specific answer is that some of the great chain-store organizations have recognized that fact and have offered to put their purchasing and warehousing organizations at the disposal of an unemployed coöperative organization if and when it is set up. There remains the more far-reaching criticism that if such a plan were successful on a large scale a situation might be created, with the return of prosperity, which would conceivably present social difficulties. To which the technicians make two answers: that the present relief burden cannot be borne by industry and that no other alternative offers itself; and, secondly, that a closer coöperation between labor and management is desirable and in any case inevitable. The success of the program will depend upon the success of its sponsors in establishing this point of view.

The two principal difficulties encountered are to secure the necessary coöperation and the necessary raw materials and power, and to establish a basis for distribution to "buyers" without money. The first will be met, at the beginning at least, by credits provided by public or charitable agencies. And studies by one group indicate that, on the basis of March, 1932, figures, food for the unemployed population of the state of New York could be supplied by coöperative exchanges at a saving of 40 per cent, and food and clothing at a saving of 50 per cent, under the costs of present relief methods.

The second difficulty, the distribution problem, can be solved by the use of "barter cards" or similar devices based, for example, on the man-hour unit. A swap of services between members of the association would be easily arranged. A swap of services by a man within the association for goods offered by a man without would be cared for merely by providing a clearing house. The difficulty arises when the labor of a member of the association is used to secure goods which will be consumed by the whole association on a coöperative basis. But that difficulty is certainly not insurmountable.

Such a program obviously necessitates a close organization of the unemployed for their common advantage, and one of the schemes recently worked out calls for county, regional, and state units to handle both the primary industrial matters and the scarcely less important secondary heads of cultural and recreational activity. Employment will, of course, be spread as broadly as possible and hours will be reduced to the lowest point compatible with successful production. It is therefore scarcely necessary to stress the point that such schemes will constitute experiments in industry of a great possible importance.

And the Philosophers

But even if such schemes are developed within the next few months, and even though federal contributions under the Relief Act should be largely increased this winter, the immediate burden will still lie where it has lain so long—upon the shoulders of private charity. And for two reasons. First because the present federal relief appropriation is inadequate. And second because federal relief will not in any case relieve the established charities of their old, established work among the young and the sick and the unfortunate—work which increases in times of depression and which the needs of unemployment relief have, in many cities, swamped. A National Citizens Committee for the Welfare and Relief Mobilization of 1932 under the chairmanship of Mr. Newton D. Baker has already been formed by the Association of Community Chests and Councils to prepare the ground for the difficult Community Chest drive of this fall. And there is considerable hope that the result may be the coördination of charitable activities which has so far failed to materialize.

Such, broadly speaking, are the facts of unemployment relief in the late summer of 1932. Ahead, whether the depression "ends" this fall or not, is the problem of caring for some 25,000,000 souls through what may prove to be one of the most difficult winters of the Republic's history. Behind are three years of muddled purpose, insufficient funds, and unscientific direction. Across the threshold lies a new federal policy and a formal acceptance of the issue. The immediate consequences, to be counted next spring, will depend upon the intelligence with which the adequate forces of the country are administered. The ultimate consequences and the final solution will depend upon American industry. And for that reason the present agitation for the thirty-hour week which began in industry and which is backed by industry is perhaps the most important single development of the depression.

Causes of Economic Disaster

31. Why the Depression Lasted So Long

Gilbert Burck and Charles Silberman

The basic reason the depression lasted so long was, of course, the economic ignorance of the times. Economics is one of the most elusive subjects that has ever engaged the intelligence of man, and economics has never been more baffling or elusive than it was in the 1930's. Venerable economic principles, the principles on which industrial civilization was erected, were suddenly powerless to account and prescribe for what was happening. All that most experts understood was that something new was happening, and it was years before they knew just what to make of it.

Neither Herbert Hoover nor Franklin Roosevelt, alas, knew what to make of it. Herbert Hoover, the very symbol of laissez faire, switched from laissez faire to a modified interventionism. But he would not desert his convictions on the inviolability of the gold standard and the balanced budget, and he ended up by prolonging the deflation without mitigating it very much. Roosevelt, on the other hand, unhesitatingly and even gaily threw over laissez faire and embraced a managed economy. But he, too, was haunted by the ideal of a balanced budget, and his deficits were too small to counteract the decline in private spending. And in 1936 he lost his nerve and practically balanced the 1937 budget—with disastrous results.

Reprinted from the March, 1955 issue of *Fortune Magazine* by special permission; © 1955, Time Inc.

THE SPIRAL BEGINS

The depression had begun, as *Fortune* related last month, because of several basic weaknesses in the outwardly strong "New Era" economy of the 1920's. Among them were an increasingly lopsided distribution of the benefits of rising productivity, declining population growth, and relatively ineffective marketing techniques; because of these weaknesses, expenditures on consumer durables began to slide off in the mid-Twenties, and expenditures on home building fell sharply. Farm prices and income also fell. These declines made a correction practically inevitable.

But the correction, which might have been moderate had it occurred in 1928, was temporarily forfended by the stock-market boom, which erected false props of prosperity under the economy. It artificially stimulated certain forms of consumption as well as capital spending. Stocks kept soaring up even after business had turned down. Thus the boom in stocks, by postponing the correction and creating over-capacity, made a moderate correction impossible. The patient was in a bad way, but the heady philter of speculation deluded him into thinking he had never felt better. His first reaction, after his fortune changed for the worse, was that he would get better soon. But it was not long before his basic weaknesses exacerbated his illness and all but ruined him.

At first, many observers argued that the stock-market crash would affect only those who had lost money in it. Even these were a considerable deflationary force. Millions of people, rich and poor, even those who did not have to pay off margin accounts out of income, were forced to economize. The luxury market began to soften rapidly. And the great soft spots in the economy—consumer durables, housebuilding, and farm prices—grew softer still.

What is more important, the whole nation was heavily and precariously in hock to itself, and falling prices and the liquidation of security and real-estate values made the burden intolerable. In 1929 the interest on corporate debt took 40 per cent of all corporate profit before taxes, against about 10 per cent today. Nonfarm mortgage debt—most of it callable in five years—was equal to 50 per cent of disposable income, against only 36 per cent now, and interest rates in 1929 were 50 to 100 per cent higher than they are now. Farm mortgage debt came to more than 150 per cent of farm income, compared to 63 per cent now.

The banking system, despite the creation of the Federal Reserve in 1913, was not half so strong as most people thought it was. It was still a frontier system, hospitable to boom and vulnerable to bust. It contained too many small and weak banks, and only a third of all banks were members of the Federal Reserve. There was no deposit insurance. Too many bankers had acquired the habit of manipulating and promoting "securities." Even in the prosperous 1920's about one out of every five commercial banks failed. Now the banking system was up against challenges that would have strained the strongest one.

When the stock and real-estate markets cracked, the banks already had nearly 25 per cent of their assets in security loans and 10 per cent in real-estate loans. The colossal decline in value of securities—$45 *billion*, or more than 50 per cent, by 1931, for those on the New York Stock Exchange alone—weakened the banks immeasurably. So did the real-estate decline. Farm prices and incomes collapsed and the defaults on farm mortgages brought down many farm banks with them. Inflated urban real-estate values, on which mortgage debt was based, also collapsed. As Secretary of the Treasury Andrew Mellon told Herbert Hoover in the early stages of the depression, "There is a mighty lot of real-estate lying around the United States which does not know who owns it."

In the meantime, every intelligent businessman, watching inventory accumulate and sales and profits drop sharply, knew he had to retrench. So business cut back purchases of inventory and capital goods, and industrial production declined 20 per cent within a year after the crash. Although business responded to President Hoover's pleas and for a while maintained wage rates, it laid off workers across the board. Not only did all these cutbacks contract the consumer market, the consumers who still had high incomes worried increasingly about their jobs, and began to cut their own spending. Few seemed willing to mortgage an uncertain future to buy durables like cars and appliances. And so business was forced to retrench still more.

Flight of Gold

Thus, for a full year and a half, the whole economy slid downward. But in the spring of 1931 there seemed to be signs that the worst was over. Industrial production and gross national product, which had declined 30 per cent and 15 per cent respectively, actually turned up slightly. Stock prices rose, and President Hoover was quoted as saying that prosperity was just around the corner.

Even as he spoke, however, ominous tidings were coming from overseas. Europe's economies, which had been buoyed up during much of the 1920's by U. S. loans and large U. S. imports, were confronted with a virtual cessation of both. The big problem of these economies, too, was debt—not only to one another, but to the U. S. Their ability to pay those debts was not helped by the passage of the ill-famed Hawley-Smoot Tariff of 1930, which, signed reluctantly by Hoover, gave the rest of the world notice that it would have a difficult time earning the dollars to pay the U. S. As the situation worsened, gold and foreign exchange—"hot money" —moved frantically from country to country, looking for a refuge and wrecking credit systems in the process. The Kredit Anstalt, the largest bank in Austria, suddenly closed its doors in May, 1931, and every bank in Europe trembled. Business declined sharply, and even the cartel-dictated price structures began to crack.

Although Hoover met this challenge with imagination and resolution— he personally drafted and sold to key members of Congress an international moratorium on debts, described by the London *Economist* as the gesture of a great man—the gesture availed little. By September, 1931, Britain was forced off the gold standard. Fears that the U. S. would follow, plus the fact that U. S. production had turned down again, led to panic flights of foreign capital from the U. S., and of U. S. gold into foreign coffers and hoards at home. In slightly more than a month, beginning in mid-September, the U. S. lost $725 million worth of gold.

The Federal Reserve, which had previously adopted an easy-money policy to stimulate business, found its gold reserves threatened, and elected to protect the gold standard in the traditional way. On October 9, 1931, as though fighting inflation, it raised its rediscount rate from 1.5 to 2.5 per cent, and a week later to no less than 3.5 per cent. This served to check gold movements, but at the sacrifice of any chance of domestic recovery. Interest rates rose, stock prices dropped abruptly, production declined, and banks tightened credit—and the credit-tightening process started liquidation all over again. And, of course, the banks' attempts to "get liquid" made it steadily harder for everybody to "get liquid."

Bank failures, which had numbered 158 in August, rose to 522 in October—the largest number in any month before or since. It was at this point that fear, Roosevelt's "nameless, terrifying fear," gripped the country. Hoarding rose $500 million in two months. Unemployment rose still higher while industrial production fell still lower—12 per cent in three months. What had capped the crisis, what had turned it into the most serious financial panic in U. S. history, seemed to be Herbert Hoover's determination to remain on the gold standard in the face of the world financial crisis.

IN THE DEPTHS

This is not to say that Hoover's policy, as so many believe, was one of doing nothing. Contrary, too, to popular myth, Hoover's economics were not incorrigibly laissez faire. Many of his associates, particularly Andrew Mellon, urged him to let things alone, arguing that the liquidation would end quickly, as previous liquidations had ended, if only left alone. But

Hoover pointed out that the vast majority of Americans no longer lived and worked on the land, and no longer could sit out a depression on the farm; the depression meant heavy unemployment in the cities, and untold and unprecedented suffering. So he had announced late in 1929 that recovery was the government's responsibility. In 1930–32 he actually introduced many of the important measures that later became the bases of Roosevelt's recovery program. Through RFC he supplemented private credit for business with government credit. He created a little employment through public works. He plugged for high wage rates. He tried to cope with farm surpluses by withholding them from the market. And he tried to expand credit.

Having done all this, however, Hoover stuck doggedly not only to the gold standard but also to the balanced budget, which remained for him the categorical imperatives of the free-enterprise system. Their abandonment under any circumstances was something that could be seriously considered only by knaves, collectivists, or crackpots. It was primarily to save the gold standard that he pushed through the Glass-Steagall Act of February, 1932, which allowed the Federal Reserve to use government bonds to back the currency, and so released $1 billion in gold for possible export. Although Hoover ran deficits in 1931 and 1932, these were largely involuntary. And it was to balance the budget that he persuaded the American Legion to forgo demanding a bonus, vetoed a direct relief bill, and took a resolute stand against "squandering the nation into prosperity."

To be sure, practically everybody in 1931 and 1932 thought as Hoover did—including Franklin Roosevelt. Practically nobody understood what today is commonly understood—that a deficit, if it occurs when a nation's resources and labor force are only partly utilized, need not be inflationary. Although John Maynard Keynes was already arguing in the press that deficit financing could cure the depression, it was not till 1936 that he launched the "Keynesian Revolution" with his *General Theory of Employment, Interest, and Money*, which, among other things, popularized the notion that a government's finances should be managed primarily in terms of their effect on the economy's stability.

Another and less academic partisan of deficit spending was a then obscure Utah banker named Marriner Eccles, who had never read Keynes. What the government should do, he told his scandalized banker friends, was not merely to loosen credit, not merely to devalue, but to spend more than it took in, in order to increase the nation's buying power.* The government of 1930–32, he argued was like the stewards on the doomed *Titanic*, who locked all the staterooms so that nothing could be stolen as the ship sank.

* *Later on, as Federal Reserve governor, Eccles also argued consistently enough that in inflationary time the government should reduce the nation's buying power by running a surplus.*

CROSS OF GOLD

Taking everything together, history may well agree with the verdicts of Walter Lippmann and the late A. D. Gayer, the Columbia University monetary economist. Professor Gayer argued that Hoover's inconsistency was disastrous in that either he should have followed Andrew Mellon's formula and let deflation take its natural, brutal course, which might well have been a swifter course, or he should have supported employment and personal income directly besides shoring up banks, insurance companies and railroads. He succeeded only in prolonging the decline without mitigating it very much. As for Lippmann, he argued in the 1930's that the one real difference between the Hoover and Roosevelt administrations was the former's refusal to abandon the gold standard, and that the Hoover Administration crucified itself on a cross of gold.

By the close of 1932 the whole nation had been pretty well crucified on the same cross. Industrial production stood at only 50 per cent of its mid-1929 level, and gross national product had fallen 40 per cent, to $67 billion (1929 dollars). Nearly 13 million men—some estimates ran to 15 million or 16 million—were out of work, not counting several million more on short weeks. Wages and salaries had fallen 40 per cent.

Since people always stop buying postponable things first, the worst decline was suffered by the durable-goods business, which had boomed early in the 1920's. Unlike the volume of non-durables and services, which in real terms declined no more than 15 per cent, that of durable consumer goods dropped 50 per cent (see chart on page 502). Auto production fell from 4,600,000 in 1929 to 1,100,000 in 1932. Residential construction withered away to less than 25 per cent of its 1929 volume; only 134,000 new nonfarm units were started in 1932, compared to 509,000 in 1929, and 937,000 in 1925, at the peak of the residential boom. Because corporations (taken together) lost $2 billion in 1932 and again in 1933, and because excess capacity was depressing prices in almost every industry, business cut its purchases of capital equipment (producer durables) by 50 per cent, and cut industrial and commercial construction 70 per cent.

Meantime, the financial crisis grew more acute. The Dow-Jones average dropped to 40, mortgage foreclosures rose sharply, and bank failures mounted. In the first two months of 1933 hoarding increased by $900 million, and the merest rumor was enough to start a run on a bank. Farm-mortgage riots spread all over the Midwest as farmers took over foreclosure sales and forced the resale of foreclosed properties to mortgagees for a few dollars.

The great mass of people, including most businessmen, were not only bewildered and panicky, but angry and frustrated, ready to try almost

And Durables Never Did Recover

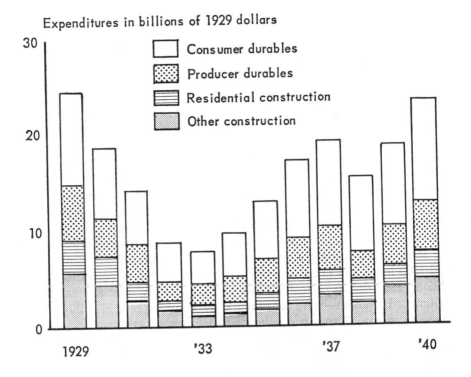

Expenditures in billions of 1929 dollars

Consumer durables
Producer durables
Residential construction
Other construction

anything that plausibly offered relief. Some of them fell for demagogues like Huey Long, with his "Share Our Wealth" platform, and Dr. Townsend and his old-age pensions, and Father Coughlin and his "Social Justice" campaign. Some of the more intellectual were much affected by books like Stuart Chase's *A New Deal*, a large part of which was devoted to expounding the "loathsomeness" of laissez faire—not the laissez faire of Adam Smith, who elevated the consumers' interests above all others, but a horrendous straw man embodying the worst traits of Jesse James, Daniel Drew, and Charles Ponzi. The book's title, significantly, was later appropriated by Franklin Roosevelt's Brain Trust to describe the Administration's aims.

A few of the nation's leading intellectuals went Communist or near-Communist. But actually the heyday of party-lining came later, and was more a response to Hitlerism and the Spanish Civil War than to events in the U. S. Such "leftism" as manifested itself at the depths of the depression was mainly in the pragmatic, idealistic American tradition of acting violently against injustice and oppression. And the wonder is not that so many Americans went left but that so few did. In November, 1932, the

Communist party polled only 103,000 votes, and the Socialist party 885,000, vs. 15,800,000 for the Republicans and 22,800,000 for the Democrats.

ENTER F.D.R.

The election of Franklin Roosevelt, and his refusal to join Hoover in committing himself to a "sound dollar" before his inauguration, may have accelerated the flight of gold and cash from the banks. Hoover still insists that the bank crisis could have been averted if only Roosevelt had committed himself to maintain the gold standard. But the second flight of gold had occurred in the spring of 1932, before the election, and the financial crisis that followed probably rendered inevitable the bank holiday of 1933.

By inauguration day, at any rate, the holiday *was* inevitable—most states had already closed their banks. Roosevelt acted promptly, proclaimed a bank holiday on March 6, and on March 9 he jammed through Congress the Emergency Banking Act, which validated the holiday, furnished capital to distressed banks, and provided a plan for reopening all banks save the hopeless ones. Within three days 75 per cent of the Federal Reserve member banks were reopened and currency was flowing back to them.

THE ROVING QUARTERBACK

When Roosevelt took office his advisers were full of ideas, many conflicting, about what had gone wrong—the nation's capital stock had been overexpanded, prices had been "managed," labor hadn't got a fair share of income, public utilities had been antisocial, and so on. But at first Roosevelt and his Administration had one important broad, fixed objective: to raise production by stimulating purchasing power, and to achieve this objective they were willing to try anything plausible. In a press conference Roosevelt compared himself to a football quarterback who can call only one play at a time, and must decide each play on the basis of how the previous one worked.

This pragmatic, experimental approach was perhaps the only intelligent one in those early days of the New Deal, and for a time it worked very well. Roosevelt's cheerful ignorance of economics, far from being a handicap, was if anything an advantage, for it made him receptive to the new and unorthodox. The trouble came later on, when it became neces-

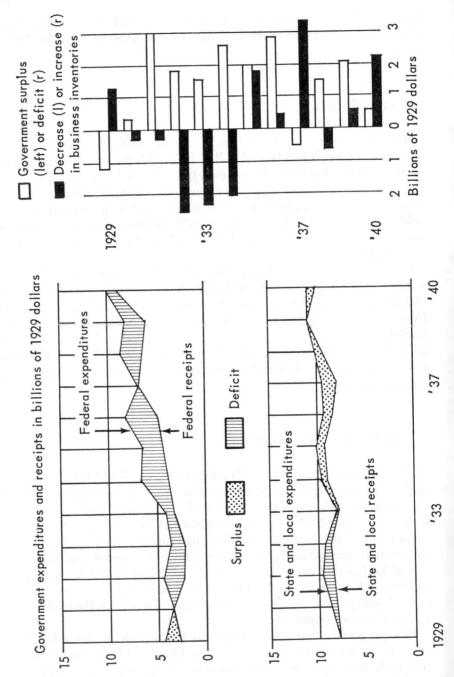

Government Deficits

Government surplus (left) or deficit (r)

Decrease (l) or increase (r) in business inventories

Billions of 1929 dollars

1929   '33   '37   '40

Government expenditures and receipts in billions of 1929 dollars

Federal expenditures

Federal receipts

Deficit

Surplus

State and local expenditures

State and local receipts

1929   '33   '37   '40

sary to stop improvising and choose a sound approach to the nation's problems and stick to it.

But the earliest measures of the new Administration, in March, 1933, were consistent enough. In his 1932 campaign Roosevelt had, much to his later embarrassment, argued eloquently against an unbalanced budget. "Stop the deficits," he had implored. "I accuse the Administration of being the biggest spending Administration in peacetimes in all our history." And the first thing the New Deal had to do, after reopening the solvent banks, was to "restore confidence" by demonstrating that it could cut expenditures and balance the budget. An economy act was passed, and federal salaries and other costs were cut. What would have happened if this deflationary course had been followed to the bitter end is hard to say, but even most businessmen by this time were afraid to let it happen.

THE MULTIPLE ATTACK

At all events, the Administration reversed itself and moved rapidly toward credit expansion, monetary inflation, price and wage rises, relief payments, and public works. The most important decision was to go off gold, and the decision was in effect forced on Roosevelt by an inflation-minded Congress. On April 20, 1933, Roosevelt placed an embargo on gold, and thus in effect took the country off the gold standard.

There followed, between 1933 and 1937, a continuous avalanche of congressional acts and executive orders dealing with recovery. There were steps primarily designed to raise prices and boost purchasing power —though some of them involved various reforms. There was, of course, pump priming by means of a bewildering succession of public works and relief measures. There was the Federal Emergency Relief Administration, the Civilian Conservation Corps, the Civil Works Administration, and PWA, which under "Honest" Harold Ickes spent so little money that WPA had to be formed under Harry Hopkins. Partly as a result of these measures, as the chart on page 504 shows, federal expenditures rose from $3.7 billion in 1932 to $8.2 billion in 1936 (in 1929 dollars).

There was TVA, which got the government into the power business in a colossal way. There were aids to agriculture like "parity" prices and the AAA, which raised prices by paying farmers to restrict production. There were several labor measures, discussed later, which raised union membership from about two million in 1932 to over 11 million in 1941. There were a variety of measures easing home and farm mortgages. And there was the social-security system, founded in 1936.

Among the solidest early achievements of the New Deal were the laws reforming and strengthening the banking system, such as the Banking Act of 1933, which provided for deposit insurance and for the divorce of investment and commercial banking; the Banking Act of 1935, which centralized Federal Reserve power, particularly over open-market operations; and the Securities and Exchange Acts of 1934–35, which reformed the issuing and buying and selling of securities. Sidney Weinberg, who fought hard against the Securities and Exchange Acts, now says he would go on a crusade against any move to repeal them. And Professor Milton Friedman of the University of Chicago, one of the leading orthodox economists, argues that the Federal Deposit Insurance Corporation is by all odds the most important of the changes affecting the cyclical characteristics of the American economy, perhaps even more important than the establishment of the Federal Reserve.

THE BRIGHT BLUE EAGLE

The most inconsistent New Deal creation, the one that remains the supreme example of the Administration's let's-give-it-a-try, all-things-to-all-men approach, was NRA, or the National Recovery Administration, created in 1933. NRA was a kind of state-run supercartel, with a genially ferocious dictator in the person of General Hugh ("Ironpants") Johnson in charge and a new national flag in the form of the "bright badge" of the Blue Eagle. Had NRA survived and succeeded, it would have accomplished publicly all that any group of European cartelists, meeting behind closed doors and puffing big cigars, has ever been able to accomplish. It would have wiped out the antitrust acts and committed the whole nation to planned restrictionism, with government, capital, management, and labor restricting together.

NRA's immediate genesis seems to have been a 1933 memo by Gerard Swope, president of General Electric, who advanced industry's plausible argument that cut-throat competition in a depression would make things worse rather than better. NRA put a floor under wages and hours, and through Section 7a guaranteed labor the right to organize and bargain collectively. Since productivity had been rising, this was long overdue. But NRA also allowed business to get together and adopt codes that incorporated price-fixing and production-restriction agreements, which might well have hamstrung the increase of American productivity. Hundreds of businessmen took their codes before the redfaced, wisecracking Johnson, who assured them he would crack down unmercifully on the chiselers. "May God Almighty," he roared, "have mercy on anyone who attempts to trifle with that bird [the Blue Eagle]." Fortunately for the U. S., there were too many chiselers in business even for General Johnson. Long before May, 1935, when the Supreme Court declared the NRA unconstitutional, the codes were being violated all across the nation.

The labor provisions of the act started a wave of unionization, and they,

Output Came Back But Then Collapsed Again

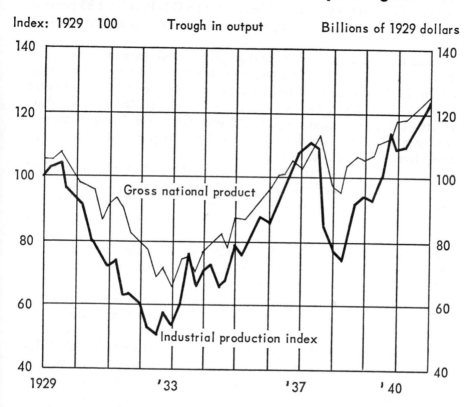

Index: 1929   100   Trough in output   Billions of 1929 dollars

too, encountered employer resistance. Section 7a of the dead NRA, however, was quickly replaced by the National Labor Relations Act (the Wagner Act), which specifically authorized collective bargaining, defined unfair employer practices, and set up the National Labor Relations Board to help enforce the act.

THE CONTROVERSIAL LAG

For all their inconsistencies, the New Deal's early measures did achieve their major aim: they raised farm and industrial prices and wages, and so stimulated consumption and industrial production. Gross national product, as the chart on this page shows, rose just about as fast as it had declined, and by the third quarter of 1937 stood 5 per cent above its mid-1929 level. Industrial production had also passed the 1929 peak, and volume of consumer non-durables was 10 per cent above 1929. This, however, was not full recovery. Because the national working force had increased 10 per cent and its productivity 15 per cent, true recovery, that is, fairly full employment, would have meant a G.N.P. at least 25 per cent higher than in 1929. As it was, there were still more than seven million unemployed early in 1937.

What blocked full recovery, and so perpetuated mass unemployment, was the fact that the durables sector of the economy hardly recovered at all. By 1937 the volume of residential construction was still 40 per cent below its 1929 level, industrial and commercial construction ("other" construction on the chart on page 502 was 50 per cent below 1929, and producer and consumer durables were 5 and 6 per cent below 1929, respectively. Why did they lag?

The story of residential construction may be told simply. There had been considerable overbuilding in the 1920's, and the low incomes and low household formation of the Thirties created little additional demand. The birth rate fell 19 per cent, and people doubled up. And so long as lenders feared that new houses would have to compete with houses on which they had foreclosed, or held shaky mortgages, they were reluctant to give mortgages for new construction. Then, too, building costs did not fall so much as costs in general.

The stagnation in capital spending—on industrial and commercial construction and producers' goods—is not so simple a story. The volume of commercial construction was so great in 1929 that it was not equaled again until 1954; thus the overbuilding and speculative real-estate inflation of the 1920's were among the main reasons why 1937's volume remained only half of 1929's volume. Then, too, commercial construction is closely related to the rate of home building, which was low.

Even the fact that the 1937 volume of producers' goods was only 5 per cent below its 1929 volume was disappointing. For there was (and is) occurring a long-term shift in capital spending from plant to equipment, and thus the volume of producers' equipment relative to the trend was actually low. And why did not this capital spending on equipment and plant recover?

Too Many Adjustments

One answer popular in the late 1930's was Alvin Hansen's theory of secular stagnation, which blamed oversaving at a time when investment opportunities were declining, thanks to the economy's "maturity." What seems today a more plausible reason is that business probably was not able to adjust to all the changes that confronted it in a few short years:

▶ The reform of the credit system, as well as SEC regulations, were badly needed, but probably discouraged new-issue flotation.

▶ Legalized unionization elevated wage rates 41 per cent in 1933–37.

Even harder to accept, for many businessmen, was that unions had to be recognized and bargained with.

► Increasingly higher taxes altered the calculations on which investments had been based. In his attempts to balance the budget, Hoover had raised tax *rates* drastically in 1932. The New Deal raised them further, and added new taxes—e.g., excess-profits taxes, social-security taxes, and the undistributed-profits tax. It had also closed many loopholes, such as personal holding companies. As business and income picked up, therefore, tax payments rose even more. Federal receipts more than tripled between 1932 and 1937, rising (in 1929 dollars) from $2 billion to $6.8 billion, or nearly double the 1929 figure of $3.8 billion.

Banking regulations, unionization, and higher taxes, of course, are commonplace enough today. But the speed with which business had to adjust to them had a lot to do with its reluctance to make capital investment. Its adjustment problems were not eased by the increasingly uncompromising attitude of President Roosevelt. He had provocation, it is true. Some businessmen were venting a virtually psychopathic hatred of "that man." Roosevelt went on to assume that all businessmen, save a few New Deal "captives," were enemies of the people. His 1936 message to Congress was studded with such fighting phrases as "entrenched greed" and "resplendent economic autocracy," and his campaign speeches were even less conciliatory. "They are unanimous in their hate of me," he boasted with a certain accuracy of those who opposed him. But then he added childishly: "I welcome their hate."

Not Enough Spending?

Yet there remains one other important circumstance that probably contributed greatly to the lag in capital goods. What really shapes business decisions to buy capital goods is not a vague sense of confidence or doubt, not necessarily even an inflationary or deflationary government policy, but the outlook for sales and profits. Partly because of rising wages, partly because of rising taxes (and partly because 1929 profits were unusually high), profits in the 1930's did not recover so fast as wages and production. Corporate profits in 1937, after taxes, were 43 per cent below their 1929 level, and the sales outlook for the durable industries was still bad. But could anything have been done about *that?* The government could have kept taxes down by running somewhat bigger deficits. And why didn't this high-spending government run bigger deficits? Simply because Roosevelt was constantly plagued by the ideal of a balanced budget and by congressional advocates of sound money, and never seemed to understand quite how an unbalanced budget need not be inflationary (though he actually needed some inflation). Thus is irony defined.

Here We Go Again, Boys

And it was the lack of a consistent New Deal fiscal policy that was partly if not largely responsible for the disheartening recession of 1937–38, the steepest economic descent on record. In a few months the nation lost half the ground it had gained since 1932; industrial production fell 30 per cent, unemployment passed ten million. Stocks plummeted; e.g., New York Central declined from 41½ to 10 in about six months.

The reasons for the recession seem clear enough today. The 1936–37 boom, fed by the 1936 soldier's bonus, pushed up industrial production, commercial loans, and stock prices. Settlement of the automobile sitdown and other strikes led to a rash of wage increases. Businessmen, fearing that rising wages would mean higher prices, and expecting the government to continue to run a deficit, put their money into goods, speculatively placing orders for both current and future needs, and touching off an inventory boom. Yet rising wages did not increase consumption enough to stabilize the economy, and they did not because the government's irresolute fiscal policy in 1937 reduced its contribution to the nation's buying power by $3.2 billion, or more than the inventory accumulation and more than the aggregate wage increase.

How did this happen? It happened because in 1936 Roosevelt had begun to worry about inflation and the mounting pressures of business and the press, and had tried to balance the budget. He had even vetoed the 1936 soldier's bonus. But Congress had passed a $1.7-billion bonus over his veto, so in 1936 the government ran a deficit of $3.4 billion (1929 dollars).

In 1937, however, the government had no bonus to pay, and so spent $1.2 billion less than it did in 1936. At the same time, moreover, it collected $1.5 billion in new social-security taxes, practically none of which it disbursed. So for all practical purposes Roosevelt and Secretary of the Treasury Morgenthau balanced the budget. And thus it was that they reduced the government's contribution to the nation's buying power by more than $3 billion. Businessmen, seeing their inventories mount while sales (especially of durables) fell, curtailed orders. By the late summer of 1937, the landslide began to gather way.

Franklin Roosevelt, who had been so hospitable to the new economics (up to a point), now found himself in the same frustrating, discouraging position that Herbert Hoover had been in five and six years before. For the first time in his associates' memory, Roosevelt was unable to make up his mind quickly on an important issue. Even while Secretary Morgenthau was promising another balanced budget, Roosevelt was conferring and discussing and mulling over the problem. Finally, on April 14, 1938, a full seven months after the recession began, he countermanded Morgenthau and asked Congress to appropriate $3 billion for relief, public works, housing, and flood control. The economy revived quickly as inventories were rebuilt, and by late 1939 most of the lost ground was recovered. But full employment was not restored until 1942, when World War II was in full swing.

THE HERITAGE OF REFORM

For all its fumbling and faulty signal calling, the New Deal passed on to the postwar generation a heritage of reforms and practices without which today's economy would not be nearly so strong and well balanced as it is. Aside from social security and financial reforms, the most important features of the heritage are the practices that enable our economy to remain a market economy despite big business, big unions, and big government, which have no place in a classic market economy of many small suppliers, each without significant control over the market.

Labor's right to organize its own unions and bargain collectively, for example, may give labor what sometimes amounts to monopoly power, but a vigorous labor movement helps solve the major problem of an economy whose output is increasing much faster than its population: how to distribute the benefits of rising productivity as fast as they are created.

Another important legacy of the great depression is an expanded understanding of how delicately a big economy is balanced, and the extent to which the government can or cannot effectively check imbalances before they grow serious. What with the growth in the government's fact-finding activities, the imbalances of the kind that eventually ruined the economy of the 1920's could not today go unnoticed, and it is unlikely that they could go uncorrected.

Today, at all events, we have the spectacle of a Republican Administration talking in a way that not merely would have astonished Calvin Coolidge, but in its calm assertion of responsibility in a relatively minor swing of the business cycle might have given pause even to Franklin Roosevelt. "Definite and deliberate steps were taken to promote a stable prosperity," Dwight Eisenhower told Congress . . . in discussing the 1953–54 recession (in his annual Economic Report). The steps included a reversal of the Administration's hard-money policy and an unhesitating if temporary abandonment of its attempts to balance the budget. Together with "automatic" stabilizers like unemployment insurance and reduced tax payments, these steps more than offset a $4.4-billion decline in income derived from manufacturing, and gave people $1 billion more to spend than the year before. Says the report: "This remarkable result—namely, a rise in disposable personal income accompanying a 10 per cent decline in industrial production—has no parallel in our recorded economic history."

The Price

But all the depression-generated reforms and practices were not real-ized without a price. They encouraged a general idea that if a little government is a good thing, a lot of government is that much better. Specifically, they encouraged a belief that only continually *expanding* government expenditures and deficits can sustain prosperity. They en-couraged those thinkers who solemnly proposed to cure the abuses of private monopolies by replacing them with government monopolies. They were, of course, a godsend to many politicians and bureaucrats. And the trend toward bigger government was strengthened by World War II, when the government had to control prices, allocate materials, and ration goods and manpower.

The inevitable reaction, both at home and abroad, set in shortly after World War II, when the much-heralded postwar crash never came, when in fact inflation turned out to be the great problem. There was a general realization that a market that is imperfect by strict classical standards is vastly better than none at all, that competition does work, that inflation in prosperous times is an evil less reprehensible only than dogmatic liquida-tion when millions are unemployed, that business and the businessman are worth a new vote of confidence.

This reaction, however, is not merely a pendulum's swing back to the 1920's and the decadent laissez faire Stuart Chase described so indig-nantly. The reaction may be best described in terms of Hegel's opposing thesis and antithesis, out of which a new synthesis is born. In his last Economic Report, President Eisenhower tried to indicate its direction. Discussing the doctrinaire manifestations of the old and the new posi-tions, he described one as insensitive to the misfortunes of depression, the other to the inequities of inflation. "Each carries the danger of undermin-ing, sooner or later, our system of free competitive enterprise. . . . The need of our times is for economic policies that recognize the proven success of sustained economic growth and betterment . . . and respect the need of people for a sense of security as well as opportunity." Such is the tendency of the New Economy, which if wisely guided can accelerate the astonishing progress that has enabled the material well-being of Americans to advance more in the past fifty years than the material well-being of the human race has advanced in all the previous centuries of Western history.

The Eternal Farm Problem

32. The Farm Policy Dilemma

Walter W. Wilcox

Farm income is low today—using any modern yardstick one may choose.

Farm operator families on the 2,213,000 commercial (high production) farms received an average income of $5,415 in 1956 while all nonfarm families, including those living on skid row and public relief programs, received an average income of $6,900. The realized returns to all farm labor and management was only 69 cents an hour in 1957 while workers in manufacturing industries received $2.07 an hour.[1]

Farm income would be even lower except for the price-supporting activities of the federal government.

A rough and incomplete appraisal indicates government price-support and related programs, on a year-by-year basis, must have raised total net farm income substantially above what it otherwise would have been each year in the late 1930's and early 1940's, in 1948 and 1949, and from 1952 to date.

This rough approximation of the income effects of price supports takes account of the direct government payments and the removal of supplies from commercial markets by the price supporting programs. Supplies were removed from commercial markets by surplus removal purchases using Section 32 funds, and by the net annual increases in CCC loans and inventories in these years. It is assumed that each $1 of aggregate farm output removed from commercial markets by these programs increased farm income $2.50—or that the price elasticity of aggregate output was approximately −0.4.[2]

This estimate fails to take account of the income effects of acreage

[1] Interest at a rate of 4¾ per cent was allowed on the current value of farm real estate, machinery, equipment and farm working capital by the AMS in estimating the returns per hour to farm labor. See the statements on farm income comparisons by Koffsky, Grove and Johnson in *Policy for Commercial Agriculture;* Papers submitted by Panelists, Joint Committee Print, Joint Economic Committee, U. S. Congress, November 1957, pp. 79–90 and 453.

[2] Wheat, cotton, corn and dairy products made up most of the farm output removed from commercial channels. The short run price elasticities of these products are about as follows: wheat—0.3, cotton—0.5, corn—0.5, milk used for manufacturing—0.4.

"The Farm Policy Dilemma," by Walter W. Wilcox, is reprinted by permission from *Journal of Farm Economics*, XL (August, 1958), 563–571.

allotments in holding down aggregate output on a year-by-year basis of cotton, wheat, tobacco and several other crops. It fails to include the income gains which resulted from a shift in productive resources from crops having a highly inelastic demand such as wheat and tobacco to other products having a less inelastic demand such as soybeans, feed grains and livestock. It also fails to take account of the dynamic effects of the higher and more stable farm income in the earlier years on the level of farm output and prices in later years.

This rough, incomplete measurement indicates that in the absence of price supporting programs realized net farm income on a year-by-year basis would have been 20 to 55 per cent lower in the years 1937–39, 14 to 43 per cent lower in 1940–42, 24 to 34 per cent lower in 1948–49, and 28 per cent or more lower 1952 to date (Table 1).[3]

In the longer run, the public as well as farmers appear to have reaped net benefits from farm price programs—benefits which are substantially the same as those realized from research and educational programs. Consider these facts, for example: In the 19 years preceding the adoption of farm price support and related adjustment programs, farm output increased 6 per cent. In the 20 years of farm price support programs (excluding the war years 1941–45), farm output increased 40 per cent. As a specific example of the influence of farm price support programs, Gray, Sorenson and Cochrane found that potato production was higher and prices were lower when price supports were in effect in the late 1940's than would have been expected under free market conditions.[4]

Many factors have contributed to the rapid increase in output in recent years. One of the factors has been the increased stability and higher level of farm income resulting from farm price support programs in the past 25 years.

Largely because farmers have been unable or unwilling to balance output with available markets, their income gains from price support programs have resulted in gains for other sectors of the economy. These gains are of two types—additional workers released by investment in labor saving machinery and increased output of food and fiber in subsequent years.

It is highly probable that the aggregate influence of increased stability, and the higher level of farm income resulting from price support programs has accelerated technological progress and increased efficiency in agriculture, more than offsetting the inefficiencies in resource use caused by specific commodity programs. As evidence in support of this, Dr.

[3] A more accurate evaluation of the economic effects of these programs is highly desirable. Plans are under way to have the U.S.D.A. regularly report the relevant data on net physical quantities of each commodity removed from commercial markets by price support operations. With such data a more precise evaluation of the impact of farm price support programs on farm income should be possible.

[4] Minnesota Agricultural Experiment Station Bulletin 424, 1954.

TABLE 1. SELECTED PRICE SUPPORT ACTIVITIES AND
REALIZED NET FARM INCOME, 1937–56 [1]

Calendar year	Section 32 purchases Millions	Increase in C.C.C. loans and inventories Millions	Columns 1 & 2 ×2.5[2] Millions	Government payments Millions	Rough estimate: Contribution of price support activities (Total columns 3 & 4) Millions	Realized net farm income Millions	Contribution of price support activities as percentage of net farm income (Column 5 ÷ 6)
1937	$ 35.2	$ 241.1	$ 690.7	$367	$1,057.7	$ 5,232	20
1938	211.6	523.5	1,837.7	482	2,319.7	4,273	55
1939	143.9	105.4	623.2	763	1,386.2	4,394	32
1940	226.1	215.9	1,105.0	723	1,828.0	4,289	43
1941	196.3	−71.6	311.7	544	855.7	6,153	14
1942	112.0	261.	932.5	650	1,582.5	8,825	18
1943	63.4	−77.8	−36.0	645	609.0	11,875	5
1944	24.9	−88.1	−158.0	776	618.0	12,217	5
1945	19.2	−692.3	−1,682.7	742	940.7	12,850	−7
1946	78.4	−38.9	98.7	772	870.7	15,000	6
1947	51.2	−120.5	−173.2	314	140.8	17,191	1
1948	75.6	2,013.1	5,221.7	257	5,478.7	15,943	34
1949	96.6	1,161.6	3,145.5	186	3,331.5	13,673	24
1950	46.0	−1,718.6	−4,181.5	283	−3,898.5	12,857	−30
1951	37.5	−339.9	−756.0	285	−471.8	14,802	−3
1952	82.3	1,674.1[3]	4,391.0	275	4,666.0	14,256	33
1953	177.6	2,505.6[3]	6,708.0	213	6,921.0	13,880	50
1954	58.9	1,205.0[3]	3,159.7	257	3,416.7	12,190	28
1955	179.1	1,763.7[3]	4,857.0	229	5,086.0	11,581	44
1956	171.1	1,125.7[3]	3,242.0	554	3,796.0	12,070	31

[1] See preceding text and footnote [2] with respect to limitations of these data as an accurate measure of the economic effect of price support activities. Section 32 purchases and increase in CCC loans and inventories on fiscal year basis lagged six months in relation to farm income and Government payments. Section 32 purchases taken from U.S.D.A. *Realized Cost of Programs Primarily for Stabilization of Farm Prices and Income*, In 83d Congress, 2d session, Senate. Farm Program. Hearings before Committee on Agriculture & Forestry. Part 1, January 17 and 22, 1958. Washington, U. S. Government Printing Office, 1958, p. 42. Net increase in CCC loans and purchases computed from U.S.D.A. *Commodity Credit Corporation Charts*. Washington, D. C., November 1957. Tables 5A, 6A and 6B. Government payments and realized net farm income taken from U.S.D.A. *Agricultural Statistics 1956*, and *Agricultural Statistics, 1942*. Washington, U. S. Government Printing Office, 1957 & 1943, pp. 470 and 660.

[2] The sum of columns 1 and 2 are multiplied by 2.5 since statistical analyses indicate that farm income is increased about $2.50 for each $1 reduction in farm products supplied to commercial markets when farm products are in ample supply. (See previous footnote [2].)

[3] Net removal of farm commodities from commercial markets by CCC operations. (Source: computed from U.S.D.A. data.)

Barton's studies indicate that farm output per unit of total resources used *has been increasing twice as rapidly in the past 25 years as in the 20 years 1910 to 1930.*[5] Surely the inefficiencies in resource use introduced by acreage allotment programs must have been more than offset by the income effects of the price support programs to permit such a record.

Agricultural economists have sometimes assumed that the improved income position of agriculture has slowed down desirable migration out of farming. However, Professor Bishop has found that this is not true. Price support programs have not retarded the migration of workers out of agriculture.[6] This is not surprising since the income position of farm people has continued to be less satisfactory than that of nonfarm people in spite of the improvement resulting from price support activities.

[5] See Joint Committee Print (footnote 1), p. 22.
[6] *Ibid.*, pp. 437–447.

Probably somewhat the reverse influence has prevailed. Farm enlargement and farm consolidation must have been facilitated by the increased stability and higher short-run level of farm income resulting from price support programs. Also, stable or rising land prices, in part the result of these programs, have permitted farmers to leave farming without capital losses. This is an important aid to outmigration.

This brief summary of the effect of past price support programs is in no sense intended to be a defense of the status quo. Existing price support activities have been in urgent need of modernization for the past 10 years. Yet in view of these past accomplishments, it is surprising that agriculture's spokesman in the cabinet, his research staff, and agricultural economists generally have been silent with respect to these facts while publicizing the government costs of farm price support programs. Intelligent plans cannot be made for the future by those who only see the past through jaundiced eyes.

PRODUCTION TRENDS

Although realized net farm income dropped 19 per cent in the five-year period 1952–57, total inputs used in agricultural production have increased slightly. A 12 per cent decline in number of farm workers [7] was fully offset by increases in other inputs.

It is of interest to observe that since World War II, the dynamic effect of labor leaving agriculture probably has been output-increasing. Labor leaving a continuing commercial farm enterprise often is replaced by modern mechanical equipment which results in improved technical production practices and always requires amortization, hence puts pressure on the family to increase output. If it is a son or daughter of the farm family itself who leaves, the young migrant may require financing for a period until he finishes an educational or training program. This additional financial burden also stimulates efforts to increase output and income on the home farm. When land is released by established farm operators leaving agriculture, on balance it probably goes to more efficient producers. Given the present labor supply and improved technology available for use in agriculture, similar influences are expected to continue dominant for at least another five or 10 years.

On the basis of these facts and others which are commonly known, it seems probable that farm output in the next 10 years or so will continue to increase as fast or faster than population increases.[8] This of course will be

[7] Based on the U.S.D.A. farm labor series. The decline was only 8 per cent in the commerce farm labor series.

[8] See, for example, *American Agriculture in 1965*, by James T. Bonnen, Joint Economic Committee Print (footnote 1), pp. 145–156.

merely a continuation of the situation which has existed in the recent past. Furthermore, it seems probable that output will continue to be excessive in relation to market outlets even though farm prices drop further. (It is highly probable that additional capital will be channeled into agriculture by processors and production supply companies as vertical integration in agriculture increases.)

MARKET EXPANSION POTENTIALS

"Market expansion" at lower price levels and "learning to live with abundance" are phrases or slogans which have appeared with increasing frequency in recent months in public statements relating to agriculture. The probable economic results of such policies have been made to appear highly attractive. Yet data published in the *Marketing and Transportation Situation,* an official publication of the Department of Agriculture, testify to the ineffectiveness of such policies in the past five years.

Consider these facts with respect to the recent past:

Nine per cent more American consumers, with 10 per cent higher per capita real incomes in 1957, bought 11 per cent more food from farmers on a value weighted basis, including more high-cost animal products relative to cereals and potatoes than in 1952. Yet in 1957 farmers were paid only $19.5 billion for this food—$600 million less than they were paid for the smaller quantity containing fewer livestock products in 1952. This is an indication of the lack of effectiveness of market expansion in recent years in conjunction with "living with abundance" in commercial markets.

This experience may be stated in another way. Although farmers' production expenses were $416 million higher in 1957 than in 1952, and consumers' disposable income was $63.2 billion higher, farmers received fewer dollars for their 11 per cent larger food deliveries last year because of the abundance of farm products in the market places. These are the economic consequences of "abundance" even though the advertising and promotional efforts of both the producers and food trade were at record levels in 1957.

In view of this record, how can so many people in such important positions place such great confidence in market expansion as a method of increasing farm income at this time? Market expansion is a long-run, not a short-run solution to the farm problem. And farm output or market supplies must be brought more nearly into balance with market outlets at current prices before the modest accomplishments of our greatest market expansion efforts will show satisfactory results.

Rising Land Values No Indication of Economic Health

Farm real estate values have risen sharply since 1947–49. A part of this increase was a return to more normal, long-run relationships between farm land values and farm income. Increases in land values since 1952, however, in an important respect are an indication of maladjustments in agriculture. They cannot be considered a sign of economic health as has been suggested in recent months. Rather, in large areas they reflect economic pressure for farm enlargement and the difficulty people have in finding a satisfactory substitute for farming as an occupation.

Farmers buy about two-thirds of the farm land that is sold each year. The competition for additional land for farm enlargement together with the other demands for agricultural land has resulted in farm operators receiving very low returns for their management and labor (Table 2).

Although recent increases in farm land values are the result of many factors, it is not a healthy situation to find land values and wages of industrial workers rising while returns to farm labor are falling. This is especially true when the returns to farm labor were already less than half the wages received by industrial workers. As indicated in the opening paragraph, returns to all farm labor and management in 1957 fell to 69 cents an hour. This was only one-third the hourly earnings of manufacturing employees.

Income Losses Not Offset by Fewer Farmers

Although livestock producers are enjoying satisfactory incomes in 1958, it appears probable that feed grain and livestock producers will suffer the greatest income losses in the next few years. There are several reasons for this: Feed grain stocks have been accumulating for five years under the price support program which has indirectly supported livestock prices and incomes. These stocks cannot be diverted to foreign countries to the same extent that it is possible to divert wheat and cotton stocks. Increased quantities of wheat will be offered for feed under freer market conditions largely offsetting such reductions in feed production as may occur as the result of increasing cotton and wheat acreage allotments. Further, substantial increases in the output of livestock products per unit of feed consumption are probable, especially in hog production.

Movement of people out of agriculture and farm consolidation has been advocated as a means of maintaining farm family incomes at a satisfactory level even though total net farm income falls. Between 1947 and 1956 the number of farms in the United States declined 1.7 per cent per year. The

TABLE 2. INDEXES OF FARM REAL ESTATE VALUES, RETURNS PER HOUR OF FARM
LABOR AND HOURLY EARNINGS OF MANUFACTURING EMPLOYEES,
1952–57 [1947–49 = 100]

Year	Farm real estate values per acre	Realized return per hour to all farm labor and management [1]	Hourly earnings of mfg. employees
1952	132	92	126
1953	132	90	133
1954	128	81	136
1955	133	75	141
1956	138	82	149
1957	147	77	156

[1] After allowance for interest at 4¾ per cent on capital investment. Agricultural Marketing Service, U.S.D.A.

total farm population also has been declining at the rate of 1.5 to 2 per cent a year in recent years. Much of this movement of people to nonfarm jobs has been people leaving low-income farms which produce very few products for sale as well as people leaving commercial farms.

Some people suggest that public programs should be undertaken to speed up these trends. Even though the current recession were short-lived, it is doubtful that measures to speed up these movements will receive public support in view of the community adjustment problems growing out of the current rate of farm consolidation and migration of people from farms. The rate of movement of people out of agriculture in the next five to 10 years will depend primarily on the rate at which new job opportunities open up.

If one can depend on a continuation of production trends and the results of recent statistical analyses of supplies and prices, there is little likelihood of sufficient farm consolidation or movement of people off commercial farms to maintain current income levels on a per family or per capita basis if free market conditions prevail in the next five to 10 years.

As will be elaborated in subsequent paragraphs, a decline in net farm income of 25 to 40 per cent is in prospect under free market conditions in the years immediately ahead. Farm people may either consciously choose to return to free markets, or because of a failure to agree on other courses of action, they may allow free market forces to operate again. If this occurs, the expected fall in total income, because of farmers' lack of bargaining power, will be softened somewhat by increased off-farm work of family members. The drop in income also will be mitigated by an annual reduction of perhaps 2 per cent a year in the number of farms and the number of farm people sharing the income. But the expected drop in income is not likely to be fully offset by the fewer people in agriculture within the next five to 10 years.

THE ALTERNATIVES

It is against this background that one must consider agriculture's possible courses of action in the next five or 10 years. Agriculture has a choice among three relatively unattractive courses of action, or some combination of them.

(1) It may continue the current supplementary distribution programs at home and abroad at the same or at a somewhat higher level than they have been operating during the past three years. This is roughly $1 to $2 billion a year in terms of values at the farm. These programs have made little progress in reducing aggregate stocks. Reductions in dairy products, cotton and wheat have been largely offset by increased stocks of feed grains. A continuation of these distribution programs at recent or at a somewhat higher level at best would merely maintain farm income at current levels in an otherwise rapidly expanding economy. However, it is doubtful that current acreage allotments have a significant effect on total farm output other than changing its content somewhat, hence are not essential to the success of this course of action. Their continuation, however, may be essential for the maintenance of the incomes of the producers of the restricted crops which have a highly inelastic demand.

(2) A second course would be to develop effective aggregate production controls which hold production 4 to 6 per cent below what it otherwise would be year after year for at least five to 10 years, again merely to maintain farm income at current levels, or

(3) Allow all production to move through commercial markets and accept a drop of $2 to $5 billion or 25 to 40 per cent in net farm income as compared with 1956–57.[9]

If net farm income falls only 25 to 40 per cent from current levels, it is doubtful that the adverse effects on the supply function would be sufficient to bring output into balance with market outlets except at prices 10 per cent or more below 1956–57 levels. Under free market conditions, output might well continue to be 2 to 4 per cent in excess of the amount needed to supply available markets at stable prices, forcing farm prices down 10 per cent or more. Production costs now take about 65 per cent of the gross farm income. Under these conditions, a 10.5 per cent

---

[9] A fourth course would be to make up the difference by direct government payments between family incomes received from prices in the market place and some agreed desirable level of family income.

This course of action appears to be sufficiently improbable to warrant placing it in a footnote. However, proposals for individual commodity programs involving a combination of government payments making up the difference between market prices and an announced support level on domestic allotments, with free market prices on the balance of the production already has substantial legislative support.

reduction in farm prices would result in a 30 per cent reduction in net farm income.

CONCLUDING OBSERVATIONS

Adequate income is one of the prerequisites for a good farm life. However, farm families have many goals in addition to monetary income. They desire freedom to make their own decisions. They desire the respect and approval of their urban acquaintances.

In our democracy farm families themselves have the opportunity to choose among many conflicting goals. The role of the expert (social scientist) and an important part of the complex role of the farm leader is that of supplying farm people with relevant facts and analyses as a basis for intelligent policy choices in line with their value systems.

It is inevitable that there is much confusion in this field. But the confusion has been confounded in recent years by a failure on the part of many in leadership positions (including some with advanced degrees) to distinguish between facts and values. Consciously or unconsciously they have ignored facts which did not fit in with their value systems. Consciously or unconsciously they have discouraged research which might develop findings not in accord with their value systems. In the arena of public discussion there has been no distinction on the part of many leaders between an intelligent interpretation of social scientists' findings and statements calculated to mold the value systems of farm people into particular patterns.

It is easy to understand the failure of farm leaders to distinguish between educational activities based on research results and an attempt to mold the value systems of farm people in patterns similar to theirs. It is more difficult to understand the great dearth of comprehensive analyses on which to base intelligent policy decisions. Surely the scarcity of relevant comprehensive analyses is not due to a lack of social scientists with advanced degrees in high administrative and advisory posts, or to a shortage of well-trained social scientists.

In any event this analysis is designed to add to the body of relevant facts which are so urgently needed and it is hoped that it will move the "great debate" forward to a higher, at least to a more factual level.

The New Capitalism

33.   The Theory of Countervailing Power

John K. Galbraith

On the night of November 2, 1907, the elder Morgan played solitaire in his library while the panic gripped Wall Street. Then, when the other bankers had divided up the cost of saving the tottering Trust Company of America, he presided at the signing of the agreement, authorized the purchase of the Tennessee Coal & Iron Company by the Steel Corporation to encourage the market, cleared the transaction with President Roosevelt and the panic was over. There, as legend has preserved and doubtless improved the story, was a man with power a self-respecting man could fear.

A mere two decades later, in the crash of 1929, it was evident that the Wall Street bankers were as helpless as everyone else. Their effort in the autumn of that year to check the collapse in the market is now recalled as an amusing anecdote; the heads of the New York Stock Exchange and the National City Bank fell into the toils of the law and the first went to prison; the son of the Great Morgan went to a Congressional hearing in Washington and acquired fame, not for his authority, but for his embarrassment when a circus midget was placed on his knee.

As the banker, as a symbol of economic power, passed into the shadows his place was taken by the giant industrial corporation. The substitute was much more plausible. The association of power with the banker had always depended on the somewhat tenuous belief in a "money trust"—on the notion that the means for financing the initiation and expansion of business enterprises was concentrated in the hands of a few men. The ancestry of this idea was in Marx's doctrine of finance capital; it was not susceptible to statistical or other empirical verification at least in the United States.

By contrast, the fact that a substantial proportion of all production was concentrated in the hands of a relatively small number of huge firms was readily verified. That three or four giant firms in an industry might exercise power analogous to that of a monopoly, and not different in consequences, was an idea that had come to have the most respectable of ancestry in classical economics. So as the J. P. Morgan Company left the stage, it was replaced by the two hundred largest corporations—giant devils in company strength. Here was economic power identified by the greatest and most conservative tradition in economic theory. Here was power to control the prices the citizen paid, the wages he received, and which interposed the most formidable of obstacles of size and experience to the aspiring new firm. What more might it accomplish were it to turn its vast resources to corrupting politics and controlling access to public opinion?

Yet, as was so dramatically revealed to be the case with the omnipotence of the banker in 1929, there are considerable gaps between the myth and the fact. The comparative importance of a small number of great corporations in the American economy cannot be denied except by those who have a singular immunity to statistical evidence or striking capacity to manipulate it. In principle the American is controlled, livelihood and soul, by the large corporation; in practice he seems not to be completely enslaved. Once again the danger is in the future; the present seems still tolerable. Once again there may be lessons from the present which, if learned, will save us in the future.

II

As with social efficiency, and its neglect of technical dynamics, the paradox of the unexercised power of the large corporation begins with an important oversight in the underlying economic theory. In the competitive model—the economy of many sellers each with a small share of the total market—the restraint on the private exercise of economic power was provided by other firms on the same side of the market. It was the eagerness of competitors to sell, not the complaints of buyers, that saved the latter from spoliation. It was assumed, no doubt accurately, that the nineteenth-century textile manufacturer who overcharged for his product would promptly lose his market to another manufacturer who did not. If all manufacturers found themselves in a position where they could exploit a strong demand, and mark up their prices accordingly, there would soon be an inflow of new competitors. The resulting increase in supply would bring prices and profits back to normal.

As with the seller who was tempted to use his economic power against the customer, so with the buyer who was tempted to use it against his labor or suppliers. The man who paid less than prevailing wage would lose his labor force to those who paid the worker his full (marginal) contribution to the earnings of the firm. In all cases the incentive to socially desirable behavior was provided by the competitor. It was to the same side of the market—the restraint of sellers by other sellers and of buyers by other buyers, in other words to competition—that economists came to look for the self-regulatory mechanism of the economy.

They also came to look to competition exclusively and in formal theory still do. The notion that there might be another regulatory mechanism in the economy has been almost completely excluded from economic thought. Thus, with the widespread disappearance of competition in its classical form and its replacement by the small group of firms if not in overt, at least in conventional or tacit collusion, it was easy to suppose that since competition had disappeared, all effective restraint on private power had disappeared. Indeed this conclusion was all but inevitable if no search was made for other restraints and so complete was the preoccupation with competition that none was made.

In fact, new restraints on private power did appear to replace competition. They were nurtured by the same process of concentration which impaired or destroyed competition. But they appeared not on the same side of the market but on the opposite side, not with competitors but with customers or suppliers. It will be convenient to have a name for this counterpart of competition and I shall call it *countervailing power*.[1]

To begin with a broad and somewhat too dogmatically stated proposition, private economic power is held in check by the countervailing power of those who are subject to it. The first begets the second. The long trend toward concentration of industrial enterprise in the hands of a relatively few firms has brought into existence not only strong sellers, as economists have supposed, but also strong buyers as they have failed to see. The two develop together, not in precise step but in such manner that there can be no doubt that the one is in response to the other.

The fact that a seller enjoys a measure of monopoly power, and is reaping a measure of monopoly return as a result, means that there is an inducement to those firms from whom he buys or those to whom he sells to develop the power with which they can defend themselves against exploitation. It means also that there is a reward to them, in the form of a share of the gains of their opponents' market power, if they are able to do so. In this way the existence of market power creates an incentive to the organization of another position of power that neutralizes it.

The contention I am here making is a formidable one. It comes to this: Competition which, at least since the time of Adam Smith, has been viewed as the autonomous regulator of economic activity and as the only available regulatory mechanism apart from the state, has, in fact, been superseded. Not entirely, to be sure. I should like to be explicit on this point. Competition still plays a role. There are still important markets where the power of the firm as (say) a seller is checked or circumscribed by those who provide a similar or a substitute product or service. This, in the broadest sense that can be meaningful, is the meaning of competition. The role of the buyer on the other side of such markets is essentially a

---

[1] I have been tempted to coin a new word for this which would have the same convenience as the term competition and had I done so my choice would have been "countervailence." However, the phrase "countervailing power" is more descriptive and does not have the raw sound of any newly fabricated word.

passive one. It consists in looking for, perhaps asking for, and responding to the best bargain. The active restraint is provided by the competitor who offers, or threatens to offer, a better bargain. However, this is not the only or even the typical restraint on the exercise of economic power. In the typical modern market of few sellers, the active restraint is provided not by competitors but from the other side of the market by strong buyers. Given the convention against price competition, it is the role of the competitor that becomes passive in these markets.

It was always one of the basic presuppositions of competition that market power exercised in its absence would invite the competitors who would eliminate such exercise of power. The profits of a monopoly position inspired competitors to try for a share. In other words competition was regarded as a *self-generating* regulatory force. The doubt whether this was in fact so after a market had been pre-empted by a few large sellers, after entry of new firms had become difficult and after existing firms had accepted a convention against price competition, was what destroyed the faith in competition as a regulatory mechanism. Countervailing power is also a self-generating force and this is a matter of great importance. Something, although not very much, could be claimed for the regulatory role of the strong buyer in relation to the market power of sellers, did it happen that, as an accident of economic development, such strong buyers were frequently juxtaposed to strong sellers. However the tendency of power to be organized in response to a given position of power is the vital characteristic of the phenomenon I am here identifying. As noted, power on one side of a market creates both the need for, and the prospect of reward to, the exercise of countervailing power from the other side.[2] This means that, as a common rule, we can rely on countervailing power to appear as a curb on economic power. There are also, it should be added, circumstances in which it does not appear or is effectively prevented from appearing. To these I shall return. For some reason, critics of the theory have seized with particular avidity on these exceptions to deny the existence of the phenomenon itself. It is plain that by a similar line of argument one could deny the existence of competition by finding one monopoly.

[2] This has been one of the reasons I have rejected the terminology of bilateral monopoly in characterizing this phenomenon. As bilateral monopoly is treated in economic literature, it is an adventitious occurrence. This, obviously, misses the point and it is one of the reasons that the investigations of bilateral monopoly, which one would have thought might have been an avenue to the regulatory mechanisms here isolated, have in fact been a blind alley. However, this line of investigation has also been sterilized by the confining formality of the assumptions of monopolistic and (more rarely) oligopolistic motivation and behavior with which it has been approached. (Cf. for example, William H. Nicholls, *Imperfect Competition within Agricultural Industries*, Ames, Iowa: 1941, pp. 58 ff.) As noted later, oligopoly facilitates the exercise of countervailing market power by enabling the strong buyer to play one seller off against another.

In the market of small numbers or oligopoly, the practical barriers to entry and the convention against price competition have eliminated the self-generating capacity of competition. The self-generating tendency of countervailing power, by contrast, is readily assimilated to the common sense of the situation and its existence, once we have learned to look for it, is readily subject to empirical observation.

Market power can be exercised by strong buyers against weak sellers as well as by strong sellers against weak buyers. In the competitive model, competition acted as a restraint on both kinds of exercise of power. This is also the case with countervailing power. In turning to its practical manifestations, it will be convenient, in fact, to begin with a case where it is exercised by weak sellers against strong buyers.

III

The operation of countervailing power is to be seen with the greatest clarity in the labor market where it is also most fully developed. Because of his comparative immobility, the individual worker has long been highly vulnerable to private economic power. The customer of any particular steel mill, at the turn of the century, could always take himself elsewhere if he felt he was being overcharged. Or he could exercise his sovereign privilege of not buying steel at all. The worker had no comparable freedom if he felt he was being underpaid. Normally he could not move and he had to have work. Not often has the power of one man over another been used more callously than in the American labor market after the rise of the large corporation. As late as the early twenties, the steel industry worked a twelve-hour day and seventy-two-hour week with an incredible twenty-four-hour stint every fortnight when the shift changed.

No such power is exercised today and for the reason that its earlier exercise stimulated the counteraction that brought it to an end. In the ultimate sense it was the power of the steel industry, not the organizing abilities of John L. Lewis and Philip Murray, that brought the United Steel Workers into being. The economic power that the worker faced in the sale of his labor—the competition of many sellers dealing with few buyers—made it necessary that he organize for his own protection. There were rewards to the power of the steel companies in which, when he had successfully developed countervailing power, he could share.

As a general though not invariable rule one finds the strongest unions in the United States where markets are served by strong corporations. And it is not an accident that the large automobile, steel, electrical, rubber, farm-machinery and non-ferrous metal-mining and smelting companies all bargain with powerful unions. Not only has the strength of the corporations in these industries made it necessary for workers to develop the protection of countervailing power; it has provided unions with the opportunity for getting something more as well. If successful they could share in the fruits of the corporation's market power. By contrast there is not a single union of any consequence in American agriculture, the country's closest approach to the competitive model. The reason lies not in the difficulties in organization; these are considerable, but greater difficulties in organization have been overcome. The reason is that the farmer has not possessed any power over his labor force, and at least until recent times has not had any rewards from market power which it was worth the while of a union to seek. As an interesting verification of the point, in the Great Valley of California, the large farmers of that area have had considerable power vis-à-vis their labor force. Almost uniquely in the United States, that region has been marked by persistent attempts at organization by farm workers.

Elsewhere in industries which approach the competition of the model one typically finds weaker or less comprehensive unions. The textile industry,[3] boot and shoe manufacture, lumbering and other forest industries in most parts of the country, and smaller wholesale and retail enterprises, are all cases in point. I do not, of course, advance the theory of countervailing power as a monolithic explanation of trade-union organization. No such complex social phenomenon is likely to have any single, simple explanation. American trade unions developed in the face of the implacable hostility, not alone of employers, but often of the community as well. In this environment organization of the skilled crafts was much easier than the average, which undoubtedly explains the earlier appearance of durable unions here. In the modern bituminous coal-mining and more clearly in the clothing industry, unions have another explanation. They have emerged as a supplement to the weak market position of the operators and manufacturers. They have assumed price- and market-regulating functions that are the normal functions of managements, and on which the latter, because of the competitive character of the industry, have been forced to default. Nevertheless, as an explanation of the incidence of trade-union strength in the American economy, the theory of countervailing power clearly fits the broad contours of experience. There is, I venture, no other so satisfactory explanation of the great dynamic of labor organization in the modern capitalist community and none which so sensibly integrates the union into the theory of that society.

IV

The labor market serves admirably to illustrate the incentives to the development of countervailing power and it is of great importance in this

[3] It is important, as I have been reminded by the objections of English friends, to bear in mind that market power must always be viewed in relative terms. In the last century unions developed in the British textile industry and this industry in turn conformed broadly to the competition of the model. However, as buyers of labor the mill proprietors enjoyed a far stronger market position, the result of their greater resources and respect for their group interest, than did the individual workers.

market. However, its development, in response to positions of market power, is pervasive in the economy. As a regulatory device one of its most important manifestations is in the relation of the large retailer to the firms from which it buys. The way in which countervailing power operates in these markets is worth examining in some detail.

One of the seemingly harmless simplifications of formal economic theory has been the assumption that producers of consumers' goods sell their products directly to consumers. All business units are held, for this reason, to have broadly parallel interests. Each buys labor and materials, combines them and passes them along to the public at prices that, over some period of time, maximize returns. It is recognized that this is, indeed, a simplification; courses in marketing in the universities deal with what is excluded by this assumption. Yet it has long been supposed that the assumption does no appreciable violence to reality.

Did the real world correspond to the assumed one, the lot of the consumer would be an unhappy one. In fact goods pass to consumers by way of retailers and other intermediaries and this is a circumstance of first importance. Retailers are required by their situation to develop countervailing power on the consumer's behalf.

As I have previously observed, retailing remains one of the industries to which entry is characteristically free. It takes small capital and no very rare talent to set up as a seller of goods. Through history there have always been an ample supply of men with both and with access to something to sell. The small man can provide convenience and intimacy of service and can give an attention to detail, all of which allow him to co-exist with larger competitors.

The advantage of the larger competitor ordinarily lies in its lower prices. It lives constantly under the threat of an erosion of its business by the more rapid growth of rivals and by the appearance of new firms. This loss of volume, in turn, destroys the chance for the lower costs and lower prices on which the firm depends. This means that the larger retailer is extraordinarily sensitive to higher prices by its suppliers. It means also that it is strongly rewarded if it can develop the market power which permits it to force lower prices.

The opportunity to exercise such power exists only when the suppliers are enjoying something that can be taken away; i.e., when they are enjoying the fruits of market power from which they can be separated. Thus, as in the labor market, we find the mass retailer, from a position across the market, with both a protective and a profit incentive to develop countervailing power when the firm with which it is doing business is in possession of market power. Critics have suggested that these are possibly important but certainly disparate phenomena. This may be so, but only if all similarity between social phenomena be denied. In the present instance the market context is the same. The motivating incentives are identical. The fact that it has characteristics in common has been what has caused people to call competition competition when they encountered it, say, in agriculture and then again in the laundry business.

Countervailing power in the retail business is identified with the large and powerful retail enterprises. Its practical manifestation, over the last half-century, has been the rise of the food chains, the variety chains, the mail-order houses (now graduated into chain stores), the department-store chains, and the co-operative buying organizations of the surviving independent department and food stores.

This development was the countervailing response to previously established positions of power. The gains from invading these positions have been considerable and in some instances even spectacular. The rubber tire industry is a fairly commonplace example of oligopoly. Four large firms are dominant in the market. In the thirties, Sears, Roebuck & Co. was able, by exploiting its role as a large and indispensable customer, to procure tires from Goodyear Tire & Rubber Company at a price from twenty-nine to forty per cent lower than the going market. These it resold to thrifty motorists for from a fifth to a quarter less than the same tires carrying the regular Goodyear brand.

As a partial consequence of the failure of the government to recognize the role of countervailing power many hundreds of pages of court records have detailed the exercise of this power by the Great Atlantic & Pacific Tea Company. There is little doubt that this firm, at least in its uninhibited days, used the countervailing power it had developed with considerable artistry. In 1937, a survey by the company indicated that, for an investment of $175,000, it could supply itself with corn flakes. Assuming that it charged itself the price it was then paying to one of the three companies manufacturing this delicacy, it could earn a modest sixty-eight per cent on the outlay. Armed with this information, and the threat to go into the business which its power could readily make effective, it had no difficulty in bringing down the price by approximately ten per cent.[4] Such gains from the exercise of countervailing power, it will be clear, could only occur where there is an exercise of original market power with which to contend. The A & P could have reaped no comparable gains in buying staple products from the farmer. Committed as he is to the competition of the competitive model, the farmer has no gains to surrender. Provided, as he is, with the opportunity of selling all he produces at the impersonally determined market price, he has not the slightest incentive to make a special price to A & P at least beyond that which might in some circumstances be associated with the simple economies of bulk sale.

The examples of the exercise of countervailing power by Sears, Roe-

[4] I am indebted to my friend Professor M. A. Adelman of the Massachusetts Institute of Technology for these details.

buck and A & P just cited show how this power is deployed in its most dramatic form. The day-to-day exercise of the buyer's power is a good deal less spectacular but also a good deal more significant. At the end of virtually every channel by which consumers' goods reach the public there is, in practice, a layer of powerful buyers. In the food market there are the great food chains; in clothing there are the department stores, the chain department stores and the department store buying organizations; in appliances there are Sears, Roebuck and Montgomery Ward and the department stores; these latter firms are also important outlets for furniture and other house furnishings; the drug and cosmetic manufacturer has to seek part of his market through the large drug chains and the department stores; a vast miscellany of consumers' goods pass to the public through Woolworth's, Kresge's and other variety chains.

The buyers of all these firms deal directly with the manufacturer and there are few of the latter who, in setting prices, do not have to reckon with the attitude and reaction of their powerful customers. The retail buyers have a variety of weapons at their disposal to use against the market power of their suppliers. Their ultimate sanction is to develop their own source of supply as the food chains, Sears, Roebuck and Montgomery Ward have extensively done. They can also concentrate their entire patronage on a single supplier and, in return for a lower price, give him security in his volume and relieve him of selling and advertising costs. This policy has been widely followed and there have also been numerous complaints of the leverage it gives the retailer on his source of supply.

The more commonplace but more important tactic in the exercise of countervailing power consists, merely, in keeping the seller in a state of uncertainty as to the intentions of a buyer who is indispensable to him. The larger of the retail buying organizations place orders around which the production schedules and occasionally the investment of even the largest manufacturers become organized. A shift in this custom imposes prompt and heavy loss. The threat or even the fear of this sanction is enough to cause the supplier to surrender some or all of the rewards of his market power. He must frequently, in addition, make a partial surrender to less potent buyers if he is not to be more than ever in the power of his large customers. It will be clear that in this operation there are rare opportunities for playing one supplier off against another.

A measure of the importance which large retailing organizations attach to the deployment of their countervailing power is the prestige they accord to their buyers. These men (and women) are the key employees of the modern large retail organizations; they are highly paid and they are among the most intelligent and resourceful people to be found anywhere in business. In the everyday course of business, they may be considerably better known and command rather more respect than the salesmen from whom they buy. This is a not unimportant index of the power they wield.

There are producers of consumers' goods who have protected themselves from exercise of countervailing power. Some, like the automobile and the oil industry, have done so by integrating their distribution through to the consumer—a strategy which attests the importance of the use of countervailing power by retailers. Others have found it possible to maintain dominance over an organization of small and dependent and therefore fairly powerless dealers. It seems probable that in a few industries, tobacco manufacture for example, the members are ordinarily strong enough and have sufficient solidarity to withstand any pressure applied to them by the most powerful buyer. However, even the tobacco manufacturers, under conditions that were especially favorable to the exercise of countervailing power in the thirtes, were forced to make liberal price concessions, in the form of advertising allowances, to the A & P [5] and possibly also to other large customers. When the comprehensive representation of large retailers in the various fields of consumers' goods distribution is considered, it is reasonable to conclude—the reader is warned that this is an important generalization—that most positions of market power in the production of consumers' goods are covered by positions of countervailing power. As noted, there are exceptions and, as between markets, countervailing power is exercised with varying strength and effectiveness. The existence of exceptions does not impair the significance of the regulatory phenomenon here described. To its devotees the virtues of competition were great but few if any ever held its reign to be universal.

Countervailing power also manifests itself, although less visibly, in producers' goods markets. For many years the power of the automobile companies, as purchasers of steel, has sharply curbed the power of the steel mills as sellers. Detroit is the only city where the historic basing-point system was not used to price steel. Under the basing-point system, all producers regardless of location quoted the same price at any particular point of delivery. This obviously minimized the opportunity of a strong buyer to play one seller off against the other. The large firms in the automobile industry had developed the countervailing power which enabled them to do precisely this. They were not disposed to tolerate any limitations on their exercise of such power. In explaining the quotation of "arbitrary prices" on Detroit steel, a leading student of the basing-point system some years ago recognized, implicitly but accurately, the role of countervailing power by observing that "it is difficult to apply high cartel

[5] Richard B. Tennant, *The American Cigarette Industry* (New Haven: Yale University Press, 1950), p. 312.

prices to particularly large and strong customers such as the automobile manufacturers in Detroit." [6]

The more normal operation of countervailing power in producers' goods markets has, as its point of departure, the relatively small number of customers which firms in these industries typically have. Where the cigarette or soap manufacturer numbers his retail outlets by the hundreds of thousands and his final consumers by the millions, the machinery or equipment manufacturer counts his customers by the hundreds or thousands and, very often, his important ones by the dozen. But here, as elsewhere, the market pays a premium to those who develop power as buyers that is equivalent to the market power of those from whom they buy. The reverse is true where weak sellers do business with strong buyers.

v

There is an old saying, or should be, that it is a wise economist who recognizes the scope of his own generalizations. It is now time to consider the limits in place and time on the operations of countervailing power. A study of the instances where countervailing power fails to function is not without advantage in showing its achievements in the decisively important areas where it does operate. As noted, some industries, because they are integrated through to the consumer or because their product passes through a dependent dealer organization have not been faced with countervailing power. There are a few cases where a very strong market position has proven impregnable even against the attacks of strong buyers. And there are cases where the dangers from countervailing power have, apparently, been recognized and where it has been successfully resisted.

An example of successful resistance to countervailing power is the residential-building industry. No segment of American capitalism evokes less pride. Yet anyone approaching the industry with the preconceptions of competition in mind is unlikely to see, very accurately, the reasons for its shortcomings. There are many thousands of individual firms in the business of building houses. Nearly all are small; the capital of the typical housebuilder runs from a few hundred to a few thousand dollars. The members of the industry oppose little market power to the would-be house owner. Except in times of extremely high building activity there is aggressive competition for business.

The industry does show many detailed manifestations of guild restraint. Builders are frequently in alliance with each other, unions, and local politicians to protect prices and wages and to maintain established

[6] Fritz Machlup, *The Basing Point System* (Philadelphia: Blakiston Co., 1949), p. 115.

building techniques. These derelictions have been seized upon avidly by the critics of the industry. Since they represent its major departure from the competitive model, they have been assumed to be the cause of the poor performance of the housing industry. It has long been an article of faith with liberals that if competition could be brought to the housing business all would be well.

In fact were all restraint and collusion swept away—were there full and free competition in bidding, no restrictive building codes, no collusion with union leaders or local politicians to enhance prices—it seems improbable that the price of new houses would be much changed and the satisfaction of customers with what they get for what they pay much enhanced. The reason is that the typical builder would still be a small and powerless figure buying his building materials in small quantities at high cost from suppliers with effective market power and facing in this case essentially the same problem vis-à-vis the unions as sellers of labor. It is these factors which, very largely, determine the cost of the house.

The builder is more or less deliberately kept without power. With few exceptions, the manufacturers of building supplies decline to sell to him direct. This prevents any builder from bringing pressure to bear on his source of supply; at the same time it helps keep all builders relatively small and powerless by uniformly denying them the economies of direct purchase. All must pay jobbers' and retailers' margins. A few builders—a spectacular case is Levitt & Sons of Long Island—have managed to circumvent this ban.[7] As the result of more effective buying, a much stronger position in dealing with labor, and the savings from large-scale production of houses, they have notably increased the satisfaction of customers with what they receive for their money. Few can doubt that the future of the industry, if its future is to improve on its past, lies with such firms.

Thus it is the notion of countervailing power, not of competition, which points the way to progress in the housing industry. What is needed is fewer firms of far greater scale with resulting capacity to bring power to bear upon unions and suppliers. It is the absence of such firms, and of the resulting economies, which helps explain why one sector of this industry—low-cost housing where cost is especially important in relation to ability-to-pay—has passed under government management. In the absence of an effective regulating mechanism within the industry in the form of countervailing power, private entrepreneurship has been superseded. In accordance with classical expectations the state has had to intervene. Only the failure was not of competition but of countervailing power.

[7] Levitt has established a wholly owned building-supply company to buy materials for its projects. *Fortune*, August 1947, p. 168. He also, most significantly, grew to importance as a non-union employer.

VI

The development of countervailing power requires a certain minimum opportunity and capacity for organization, corporate or otherwise. If the large retail buying organizations had not developed the countervailing power which they have used, by proxy, on behalf of the individual consumer, consumers would have been faced with the need to organize the equivalent of the retailer's power. This would have been a formidable task but it has been accomplished in Scandinavia where the consumer's co-operative, instead of the chain store, is the dominant instrument of countervailing power in consumers' goods markets. There has been a similar though less comprehensive development in England and Scotland. In the Scandinavian countries the co-operatives have long been regarded explicitly as instruments for bringing power to bear on the cartels; i.e., for exercise of countervailing power. This is readily conceded by many who have the greatest difficulty in seeing private mass buyers in the same role. But the fact that consumer co-operatives are not of any great importance in the United States is to be explained, not by any inherent incapacity of the American for such organization, but because the chain stores pre-empted the gains of countervailing power first. The counterpart of the Swedish Kooperative Forbundet or the British Co-operative Wholesale Societies has not appeared in the United States simply because it could not compete with the A & P and other large food chains. The meaning of this, which incidentally has been lost on devotees of the theology of co-operation, is that the chain stores are approximately as efficient in the exercise of countervailing power as a co-operative would be. In parts of the American economy where proprietary mass buyers have not made their appearance, notably in the purchase of farm supplies, individuals (who are also individualists) have shown as much capacity to organize as the Scandinavians and the British and have similarly obtained the protection and rewards of countervailing power. The Grange League Federation, the Eastern States Farmers' Exchange and the Illinois Farm Supply Company, co-operatives with annual sales running to multi-million-dollar figures, are among the illustrations of the point.

However, it must not be assumed that it is easy for great numbers of individuals to coalesce and organize countervailing power. In less developed communities, Puerto Rico for example, one finds people fully exposed to the exactions of strategically situated importers, merchants and wholesalers and without the apparent capacity to develop countervailing power in their own behalf. Anyone, incidentally, who doubts the force of the countervailing power exercised by large retailer-buying organizations would do well to consider the revolution which the entry of the large chain stores would work in an economy like that of Puerto Rico and also how such an intrusion would be resented and perhaps resisted by importers and merchants now able to exercise their market power with impunity against the thousands of small, independent and inefficient retailers who are their present outlets.[8]

In the light of the difficulty in organizing countervailing power, it is not surprising that the assistance of government has repeatedly been sought in this task. Without the phenomenon itself being fully recognized, the provision of state assistance to the development of countervailing power has become a major function of government—perhaps *the* major domestic function of government. Much of the domestic legislation of the last twenty years, that of the New Deal episode in particular, only becomes fully comprehensible when it is viewed in this light. To this I shall return in the next chapter.

VII

I come now to the major limitation on the operation of countervailing power—a matter of much importance in our time. Countervailing power is not exercised uniformly under all conditions of demand. It does not function at all as a restraint on market power when there is inflation or inflationary pressure on markets.

Because the competitive model, in association with Say's Law, was assumed to find its equilibrium at or near full employment levels, economists for a long time were little inclined to inquire whether markets in general, or competition in particular, might behave differently at different levels of economic activity, i.e., whether they might behave differently in prosperity and depression. In any case the conventional division of labor in economics has assigned to one group of scholars the task of examining markets and competitive behavior, to another a consideration of the causes of fluctuations in the economy. The two fields of exploration are even today separated by watertight bulkheads, or less metaphorically, by professorial division of labor and course requirements. Those who have taught and written on market behavior have assumed a condition of general stability in the economy in which sellers were eager for buyers. To the extent, as on occasion in recent years, that they have had to do their teaching or thinking in a time of inflation—in a time when, as the result of strong demand, eager buyers were besieging reluctant sellers—they have dismissed the circumstance as abnormal. They have drawn their classroom and textbook illustrations from the last period of deflation, severe or mild.

So long as competition was assumed to be the basic regulatory force in the economy these simplifications, although they led to some error, were not too serious. There is a broad continuity in competitive behavior from

---

[8] This is the subject of a detailed study recently published by the Harvard University Press. (*Marketing Efficiency in Puerto Rico* by John Kenneth Galbraith, Richard H. Holton and colleagues.)

conditions of weak to conditions of strong demand. At any given moment there is a going price in competitive markets that reflects the current equilibrium of supply-and-demand relationships. Even though demand is strong and prices are high and rising, the seller who prices above the going or equilibrium level is punished by the loss of his customers. The buyer still has an incentive to look for the lowest price he can find. Thus market behavior is not fundamentally different from what it is when demand is low and prices are falling.

There are, by contrast, differences of considerable importance in market behavior between conditions of insufficient and excessive demand when there is oligopoly, i.e., when the market has only a small number of sellers. The convention against price competition, when small numbers of sellers share a market, is obviously not very difficult to maintain if all can sell all they produce and none is subject to the temptation to cut prices. Devices like price leadership, open book pricing and the basing-point system which facilitate observance of the convention all work well because they are under little strain. Thus the basing-point system by making known, or easily calculable, the approved prices at every possible point of delivery in the country provided protection against accidental or surreptitious price-cutting. Such protection is not necessary when there is no temptation to cut prices. By an interesting paradox when the basing-point system was attacked by the government in the late depression years it was of great consequence to the steel, cement and other industries that employed it. When, after the deliberate processes of the law, the system was finally abolished by the courts in April 1948, the consequences for the industries in question were rather slight. The steel and cement companies were then straining to meet demand that was in excess of their capacity. They were under no temptation to cut prices and thus had no current reason to regret the passing of the basing-point system.

These differences in market behavior under conditions of strong and of weak demand are important and there are serious grounds for criticizing their neglect—or rather the assumption that there is normally a shortage of buyers—in the conventional market analysis. However, the effect of changes in demand on market behavior becomes of really profound significance only when the role of countervailing power is recognized.

Countervailing power, as fully noted in the earlier parts of this chapter, is organized either by buyers or by sellers in response to a stronger position across the market. But strength, i.e., relative strength, obviously depends on the state of aggregate demand. When demand is strong, especially when it is at inflationary levels, the bargaining position of poorly organized or even of unorganized workers is favorable. When demand is weak the bargaining position of the strongest union deteriorates to some extent. The situation is similar where countervailing power is exercised by a buyer. A scarcity of demand is a prerequisite to his bringing power to bear on suppliers. If buyers are plentiful—if supply is small in relation to current demand—sellers are under no compulsion to surrender to the bargaining power of any particular customer. They have alternatives.[9]

Broadly speaking, positions of countervailing power have been developed in a context of limited—or, more accurately, of not unlimited demand. This is partly because such periods have had a much higher incidence in history than the episodes of unlimited or inflationary demand. It is partly because periods of drastically restricted demand, by providing exceptional opportunity for aggression by the strong against the weak, have also provided an exceptional incentive to building countervailing power. Much of the structure of organization on which countervailing power depends traces its origins to such periods.

The depression years of the thirties, needless to say, were a particularly fruitful period in this respect. Accordingly, and in sharp contrast with most other types of business, these years were very favorable to the development of the chain stores and also of various group buying enterprises. The intensity of the trade agitation against the mass retailers, culminating in 1936 in the passage of the Robinson-Patman Act (designed as we shall see presently to limit their exercise of this power), was itself a measure of the chain's advantage in this period. By contrast, during the years of strong demand and short supply of World War II, the chain stores lost ground, relatively, to independents. As this strong demand in relation to supply destroyed their capacity to exercise countervailing power, their advantage disappeared. It is likewise interesting to note that the trade agitation and resentment against the chains almost completely disappeared during the war and postwar years.

The depression years also provided a notable inducement to the trade union movement. With prosperity in the forties and fifties labor organization too lost its momentum. Finally, to the depression years we owe nearly all of the modern arrangements for exercise of countervailing power by and on behalf of the farmers.

Given this structural accommodation by the economy to limited demand, the appearance of unlimited demand is somewhat devastating. There is everywhere a shift of bargaining power to sellers. The balance of force appropriate to limited demand is everywhere upset. The market

---

[9] The everyday business distinction between a "buyers" and a "sellers" market and the frequency of its use reflect the importance which participants in actual markets attach to the ebb and flow of countervailing power. That this distinction has no standing in formal economics follows from the fact that countervailing power has not been recognized by economists. As frequently happens, practical men have devised a terminology to denote a phenomenon of great significance to themselves but which, since it has not been assimilated to economic theory, has never appeared in the textbooks. The concept of the "break-even point," generally employed by businessmen but largely ignored in economic theory, is another case in point.

power of strong sellers, until now offset by that of strong buyers, is enhanced. The countervailing power of weak sellers is suddenly and adventitiously reinforced.

These effects can again be seen with greatest clarity in the labor market. Here they also have their most portentous consequences. In industries where strong firms bargain with strong unions, the management of the former has what has come to be considered a normal resistance to wage increases when demand is not pressing upon capacity. To yield is to increase unit costs. The firm cannot with impunity pass along these higher costs to its customers. There may be a question as to whether other firms in the industry will follow suit; there will always be a question of the effect of the higher prices on sales. If the demand for the products is in any measure elastic the consequence of the higher prices will be a loss of volume. This, with its effect on employment in the industry, is something of which modern union leadership, as well as management, is usually conscious. Thus the trial of strength between union and management associated with collective bargaining is, essentially although not exclusively, over the division of profits. When demand is limited, we have, in other words, an essentially healthy manifestation of countervailing power. The union opposes its power as a seller of labor to that of management as a buyer: principally at stake is the division of the returns. An occasional strike is an indication that countervailing power is being employed in a sound context where the costs of any wage increase cannot readily be passed along to someone else. It should be an occasion for mild rejoicing in the conservative press. The *Daily Worker,* eagerly contemplating the downfall of capitalism, should regret this manifestation of the continued health of the system.

Under conditions of strong demand, however, collective bargaining takes on a radically different form. Then management is no longer constrained to resist union demands on the grounds that higher prices will be reflected in shrinking volume. There is now an adequate supply of eager buyers. The firm that first surrenders to the union need not worry lest it be either the first or the only one to increase prices. There are buyers for all. No one has occasion, as the result of price increases, to worry about a general shrinkage in volume. A strong demand means an inelastic demand. On the other hand, there are grave disadvantages for management in resisting the union. Since profits are not at stake, any time lost as the result of a strike is a dead loss. Worker morale and the actual loss of part of the working force to employers who offer better wages must be reckoned with. Thus when demand is sufficiently strong to press upon the capacity of industry generally to supply it, there is no real conflict of interest between union and employer. Or to put it differently, all bargaining strength shifts to the side of the union. The latter becomes simply an engine for increasing prices, for it is to the mutual advantage of union and employer to effect a coalition and to pass the costs of their agreement on in higher prices. Other buyers along the line, who under other circumstances might have exercised their countervailing power against the price increases, are similarly inhibited. Thus under inflationary pressure of demand, the whole structure of countervailing power in the economy is dissolved.

We were able to witness one fairly good example of this dissolution of countervailing power in the continuing rounds of wage and price increases following World War II. The full coalition between management and labor, under the conditions of inflationary demand of these years, was partly disguised by the conventional expressions of animosity and by the uncertainty of management as to how long the inflation would last. However, by 1950–51 the "Fifth Round" was negotiated with scarcely an important strike. The President of the United States Steel Corporation, in yielding to the union in November 1950, indicated a *de facto* coalition when he pointed out that the "half-cent" inflation in steel prices, which would be passed along to customers, was a small price to pay for "uninterrupted and expanded" production. The consequences of this failure of countervailing power in times of inflation are considerable. They take on added importance with the easing of the depression psychosis with the passage of years. I shall return to these problems in the final chapter. First, however, it is necessary to examine the role of the state in the development of countervailing power.

Management of Large Corporations

34. Recent Developments in American Business Administration and Their Conceptualization *

Alfred D. Chandler, Jr., and Fritz Redlich

I

The evolution of large-scale, twentieth-century-style business organization raises certain problems for the economic theorist who deals with the personal element in business and economic development. This is because in the all-important process of decision-making for business enterprise

* This study was partially supported by the Sloan Research Fund of the School of Industrial Management at Massachusetts Institute of Technology.

change was reflected in two different ways. Or to put it in other words, two trends have appeared simultaneously in this connection, trends which all but contradict each other.

On the one hand, the decision-making process in large-scale corporations has become increasingly complicated as more and more persons participate in it, while at the same time the *preparation* of decisions has turned into a more pressing and critical function to be carried out by the officers and employees plus outside advisers. When their work is completed these men report facts and figures, analyzing and submitting them in such a form that conclusions can easily be drawn by the "top management" actually making the decisions. Those preparing them select what they consider important information and drop what they consider of no immediate interest and concern. By molding the result into a digestible form, they gain, often unbeknown to themselves as well as to the top personnel, an extraordinary influence on decision-making.

If the theorist then starts from the inherited concept of the entrepreneur as the decision-making man or team of men, he runs into difficulties. More and more unidentifiable employees below the top level participate in the process just described, or at least prejudice it by actions of their own. If we consider them part of the entrepreneurial team, the latter term loses its significance, for one can speak of a team only where there is personal contact among the members. If, on the other hand, we use the word "team" so loosely as to exclude that criterion, the concept of the "entrepreneur" becomes a mere symbol for human interplay within the large-scale corporation.

As a matter of fact, this solution was the one preferred by Professor Frederick Harbison, partly because of his loose interpretation of what the entrepreneurial function is.[1] As a result, he considers the "entrepreneur" as essentially an *"organization* which comprises all of the people required to perform"[2] that function. Even one of us, the writers, veered at one time towards this answer to the undeniable problem.[3]

If this were the only answer possible, the consequences would be serious. Those interested in pertinent empirical studies and historians who use the theoretical terms of entrepreneur and entrepreneurship are usually interested in the personal element in business and economic development. By that concept, they hope to identify the men who are or were the leaders within enterprises, the men molding them and fitting them into the market and the national economy; at the same time, if

---

[1] Frederick Harbison, "Entrepreneurial Organization as a Factor in Economic Development," *The Quarterly Journal of Economics,* vol. LXX (Cambridge, Mass., 1956), pp. 364 ff.

[2] *Ibid.,* p. 365.

[3] Fritz Redlich, "Unternehmungs- und Unternehmergeschichte," in: *Handwörterbuch der Sozialwissenschaften,* Lfg. 26 (Stuttgart, Tübingen and Göttingen, 1959), p. 540.

creative individuals, they are or were also the leaders in economic development. Consequently, in using the term of "entrepreneur" to stand for human cooperation in business enterprise, an important topic indeed, we lose the very tool which many of us most need in our research. Such a road cannot be followed.

Fortunately, there is a second possible approach. While on the one hand, more and more persons are drawn openly or tacitly into the decision-making process, those who have the ultimate authority and actually make the final and strategic decisions have become increasingly remote from the daily operations of their enterprise. This alienation from daily operations has proceeded to the point that some authors have seen these leading figures in enterprises as having risen beyond the decision-making process. This is certainly incorrect, as will be shown, but one of us himself temporarily adopted this false way of reasoning.

The second avenue to the solution of our problem lies in resolutely taking a step further in an ideological process by which the "entrepreneur" was developed out of Adam Smith's "capitalist." Adam Smith's "capitalist," as will be remembered, was the conceptual counterpart of the eighteenth-century merchant. He was the individual who provided the capital for his enterprise and, therefore, bore the financial risk, made any necessary strategic decisions, and functioned all the while as the day-to-day manager of his concern. The term "capitalist" stood for an undeveloped, unanalyzed genus.

With the coming of the business corporation, the providing of capital split off from that of running the enterprise, and Jean Baptiste Say was the first to recognize what he called the "entrepreneur" as separate from the capitalist. In Say's days, the "entrepreneur" was the counterpart of a man doing a fairly extensive business by using other people's capital. As we would say today, he was a manager-entrepreneur who, like the eighteenth-century merchant, had occasionally to make a strategic decision and for the rest managed his plant, industrial, commercial or what have you. Many decades passed before this figure was scrutinized closely, although some mid-nineteenth-century economists sensed intuitively that the type needed further analysis. The latter became urgent with the development of a new kind of large-scale enterprise in the late nineteenth and early twentieth centuries. In such enterprises, men were needed to spend time preparing and making an increasing number of strategic decisions for the solution of major problems arising in their concerns, while they left their daily round of work to another set of men. For the latter, the term "managers" came to be used to distinguish them from the former, the "entrepreneurs." To the "entrepreneurs" an enterprise appeared as an organism to be kept alive, to the "managers" as a mechanism to be kept in working order. Here, of course, we deal with an analysis of two functions which in reality overlap.

By 1960, however, new steps in economic development had come to be reflected in new forms of business organization. "Progress," if you please, demands a parallel step in economic analysis. More concretely, the early twentieth-century concept of "entrepreneur" needs further splitting up, so that new tools may emerge with which to handle mid-twentieth-century reality. However, before we can start our theoretical reasoning, we must present in the next two sections of the paper a description of the development of mid-twentieth-century large-scale business organization and business administration in the United States out of earlier nineteenth-century forms.

II

An historical survey of American business points to the development in this country of three types of enterprise.[4] The oldest one prevailing a hundred years ago was what one might call the single-function firm, i.e., a firm fulfilling one function only. The mercantile house only bought and sold goods. The shipping company as well as the canal and turnpike companies were interested in the single activity of transportation; while the mining concerns specialized in extracting raw material from the ground. Finally, the manufacturing firm only produced goods and, at the same time, produced only a single line of goods. Like the plantation owner, the mid-nineteenth-century manufacturer purchased the necessary materials from and sold his output to commission agents or a few wholesalers. Thus we can characterize a manufacturing firm of that period as a single-product, single-function concern. To be sure, the phrase used above, "fulfilling one function only," should not be taken literally. It means only that one function dominated or dominates a certain kind of enterprise; all others were or are subordinated to the main one and, as far as possible, left to other independent enterprises. Thereby these became or become auxiliary to the enterprise concerned which could not have existed or cannot exist without their contribution.

The years between the Civil War and the turn of the century witnessed the evolution and rapid growth in manufacturing of what can be characterized as multi-function enterprises. Under the stimulus of the devel-

---

[4] The following section is based on a historical analysis of the changing corporate structure and strategy in the United States. It includes case studies of organizational innovations made by du Pont, General Motors, Jersey Standard, and Sears, Roebuck; and also a broader investigation of the experience of more than seventy of the largest industrial and transportation companies in the United States. Preliminary results of this investigation can be found in Alfred D. Chandler, Jr., "Management Decentralization: An Historical Analysis," *Business History Review*, vol. XXX (Boston, Mass., 1956), pp. 111 ff. Chandler, "The Beginnings of 'Big Business' in American Industry," *ibid.*, vol. XXXIII (1959), pp. 1 ff. Chandler, "Development, Diversification and Decentralization," in: *Postwar Economic Trends in the United States*, ed. by Ralph E. Freeman, American Project Series, Center of International Studies, Massachusetts Institute of Technology (New York, 1960), pp. 235 ff.

opment of a national market, created with the help of the railroads and becoming quickly and increasingly a predominantly urban market, manufacturing firms not only came to have plants in different parts of the country but also took upon themselves the simultaneous handling of different activities. Many industrial enterprises developed an elaborate marketing organization dealing directly with consumers. They thereby freed themselves from the dependence on the wholesaler. Simultaneously they started producing one, several, or all of the raw materials needed in the process of manufacturing. In taking over what can be called the procurement function, they again freed themselves from the dependence on wholesalers and at the same time from that on the producers of raw material. Some manufacturing firms even took over the control of the transportation of their raw materials and finished goods. To a lesser extent, mining and marketing firms moved into manufacturing. Yet, as should be stressed, nearly all such multi-functional manufacturing concerns operated within the confines of one industry: they produced one major line of products and a few by-products. Thus they must be characterized as single-product, yet multi-function industrial concerns.

During the first half of the twentieth century, a new stage in the development was being reached. Many single-product, multi-function industrial enterprises in meeting the needs and opportunities created by a highly dynamic technology developed different lines of products, each with its own set of by-products. From single-product, multi-function manufacturing enterprises, they now grew into multi-product and multi-function industrial concerns, the maintenance and expansion of which required the tackling of more complicated tasks and the solving of more difficult problems than those involved in operating the older types.[5] The different ranges of decisions in these three types of enterprises—single product and single-function, single-product yet multi-function, and multi-product and multi-function—led to three different types of industrial administration. (*Mutatis mutandis* this was the case also in other lines of business besides manufacturing.)

Modern structure and administration of industrial enterprise began in the United States with the geographical dispersion of such firms. That is, it began when manufacturing enterprises came to possess a number of factories by building or buying new units or by combining with other firms. Geographical dispersion was the initial step in making modern industrial enterprise, because it made necessary the distinction between headquarters and field. This distinction implies that the executives re-

[5] The term multi-product firm will be used in this paper to refer to one making quite different product lines, each with its own set of by-products, for quite different markets. An example of such a multi-product firm would be a large chemical company which has such different lines as plastics, film, textile fibers, polychemicals, explosives, paints, pigments, rubber products, electro-chemicals, and photographic products.

sponsible for a firm's affairs had, for the first time, to supervise the work of other executives, those charged with managing the factories or branch offices in the field. The leading men at headquarters also had to coordinate the activities of the several field-units, that is to say, they had to standardize the procedures for these various units. The development of such procedures as well as the planning for expansion, maintenance, or contraction of the activities in the field became part and parcel of setting the goals and objectives of the firm in question.

The new trend gained momentum after the Civil War as the expanding market permitted an increased volume of manufacturing and marketing. In this period, evolving modern industrial enterprise was fortunate in that it could draw on the administrative experience gained in another type of dispersed and single-function enterprise, railroading. In this area the development had started as early as the 1850's, when the rapidly growing railroads demanded far more capital, equipment, and professionally trained personnel than did enterprises typical of the time. They were more complex than other contemporary geographically dispersed single-function firms because of their need for careful, minute to minute, coordination and supervision of the operating sub-divisions. Such control was necessary to assure not only effective use of existing operating equipment, but also the efficient movement of goods and the safety of the passengers.

In the early railroads, the key decisions were usually made by the so-called general manager, a full time specialist, acting in close consultation with the representatives of the large investors. Like the manager of a contemporary textile mill, he made the major operational decisions, but was also responsible for the basic strategic ones, such as those on expansion, rates, and so forth. Moreover, he was one of the very first American businessmen to work out an explicit operating structure, that is, to establish clearly the channels of authority and communication within the organization. Naturally the executives of a railroad, sprawled out over a large geographical area and employing, as early as the 1850's, as many as five or six thousand men, could hardly supervise personally all of their company's activities.[6]

To deal with their new problems, the basic structure of American railroad corporations was worked out during the 1850's. In running a railroad its executive had to supervise three sets of activities—the moving of the trains, getting freight and passengers, and handling the financial transactions involved. Therefore, the organization of most railroads consisted of three major departments, transportation, traffic, and finance.[7]

    [6] Thomas C. Cochran, *The Railroad Leaders, 1845–1890: the Business Mind in Action* (Cambridge, Mass., 1953), chaps. 5–9. Alfred D. Chandler, Jr., *Henry Varnum Poor—Business Editor, Analyst, and Reformer* (Cambridge, Mass., 1956), chap. 7.
    [7] Ray Morris, *Railroad Administration*, Appleton's Railway Series (New York and London, 1910), chaps. 2–3.

The most important department, transportation, in turn, was divided into three functional sections—transportation, maintenance of way, and maintenance of motor power. Because the moving of trains was the critical task, the officials in charge of transportation had to assume the authority and responsibility for all operating decisions. They became communication centers both on the local and central levels. On the former, namely, the level of the so-called division, which covered usually two to four hundred miles and was the smallest operating unit, headed by a "division manager," those who handled motor power and maintenance of way, as well as the conductors and freight agents, were made responsible to the division's transportation manager. On the central level, the manager in charge of transportation was senior to the heads of the other two departments. He and the division managers, reporting to and receiving orders from the general manager, came to be called line officers and the others to be considered as staff men.

After the Civil War and the great expansion of the railroad networks, the railroad system rather than the individual road became the dominating operating organization. The more complex became operations, the more an explicit over-all structure was needed. On such great systems as the Pennsylvania, the Vanderbilt roads, the Illinois Central, the Chicago and Northwestern, the Louisville and Nashville, the Rock Island, the problems of coordination, appraisal, and over-all policy planning became too complex to be handled by two or three men who had operational and other duties as well. Thus it became necessary to devise new organizational structures. These, formed at the time when the great systems emerged in the 1870's, and 1880's, had characteristic features in common and consisted of a central office and several operating units, each of which was comparable to a single large railroad company.[8] The Pennsylvania had three such units—the lines east of Pittsburgh, west of Pittsburgh, and those to St. Louis.

The comparable units of the Vanderbilt system were essentially the roads that had existed prior to their absorption, such as the Lake Shore, the Michigan Central, and, after 1889, the Cleveland, Cincinnati, Chicago and St. Louis, and the New York Central. The general managers of these operating units now became primarily concerned with the mechanics of day-to-day activities, while the central office team took over the responsibility for those over-all decisions which we have come to call entrepreneurial. The central office became responsible for assuring effective coordination or traffic flow between the different major operating units. It appraised operating performance and took executive action on such appraisals. The most vital task of the general officers, however, was to

---

[8] *Ibid.*, chap. 4. The following is based on a survey of the annual and other reports of the Pennsylvania Railroad and the New York Central system.

consider the major strategies of new construction and of purchases and sales of lines.

Nevertheless as time passed, these senior officers did not stay clear from, but became again increasingly involved in operational duties. There were several reasons for this relapse. First and foremost, as the systems were rounded out and completed, the need to buy and build lessened and strategic problems became fewer. They decreased further as the Interstate Commerce Commission took over rate setting. In addition, systems of appraisal and coordination worked out in minute detail became more and more routinized. Thus by the early twentieth century, the duties of the railroad central offices assumed more of a routine character and the men occupying these positions handled anew operating functions.

We shall return to this subject in the fourth section of this paper after we have developed theoretical concepts by which we can better explain administrative progress in one period of railroading and administrative relapse in a later one. Suffice it here to sum up in empirical language what is essential from the point of view of this paper. While modern business administration evolved in the field of railroading, the character of that business forbade carrying the achievement to its logical conclusions. For a time, separation of operational functions from strategy determination was attempted. It did not become permanent. Major decisions in either area remained unseparated in the hands of the same top personnel.

We are now ready to turn to the single-product yet multi-function *industrial* enterprise that developed out of the single-product and single-function organization which dominated the American industrial scene until about 1860. A typical industrial enterprise such as a textile works, rolling mill, or shipyard of the ante-bellum days manufactured only one product or a single line of products and sold, usually in bulk, to one sales agent or a very few wholesalers. Even after such an enterprise expanded its operations in the 1870's and 1880's to include a number of geographically dispersed plants, it remained a single-function activity. Twenty years later, however, major sectors of American industry were dominated by single-product yet multi-function firms. As these consolidated enterprises, the result of vertical integration, came to do their own marketing, their own purchasing from the primary sources and often their own producing of raw materials, *the different functional activities soon became organized into different departments.*

In a typical single-product yet multi-function firm, each functional department was as important as the others. The line and staff set-up of the railroads had little relevance for the over-all structure here. The major departments might have their own auxiliaries like engineering in manufacturing and advertising in sales. But each department head was a specialist and supreme in his own sphere. Usually a vice-president, he had his managing director for dealing with the routine activities of his department. The vice-presidents, as individuals, planned the broader development within their functionally determined departments. Collectively, together with the president and chairman of the board, they guided the destinies of their vast business empires. For this purpose, the men concerned usually cooperated in so-called executive committees. In making the distinction between vice-president and manager or managing director, the corporations in question were defining the difference between policy-making and operations.

The executive committees of the single-product yet multi-function enterprises had the same underlying duties as the "general managers" of the railroad systems. But as the nature of their business was different, so was the nature of the appraising, coordinating, and policy-making duties. Appraisal was the least different from that of the railroads. It meant constant concern for the development of increasingly meaningful profit and loss figures. But because more basic and quite different functions were involved, the over-all determination of profit and loss proved more difficult. So, too, the senior officers in those enterprises had to assess performance, not just in one, but in nearly all major parts of the over-all industrial process.

Coordination of the enterprise's various activities was more complex than in a geographically dispersed single-function firm, including even the large railroads. A steady flow of product through the different departments—from the raw materials to the ultimate consumer—had to be assured. The rate of flow depended on market demand. Thus coordination of interdepartmental activity with market demand was necessary if for no other purpose than for making effective use of the company's total facilities and resources. Therefore, coordination became a critical central office function. Yet where the markets and sources of supply remained fairly unchanged, as was true after 1900 in many of the agricultural processing and metal industries, it became increasingly a routine task.

Even more critical was planning for the maintenance and expansion of the enterprise as a whole. This meant that the senior officers had to make basic decisions with respect to the several very different functional activities. The executive committee had to allocate funds among departments and thus decided whether to expand or contract in sales, manufacturing, the control of raw materials, engineering, etc. In so doing, it had to face a new specific difficulty. Since this top committee was made up of department heads, i.e., of functional specialists, the final policy tended to be the result of negotiations and compromise between the different departments. In addition, the top level team, so composed, had neither enough time, nor enough impartial information to handle over-all problems satisfactorily. Its members spent most of their working day on departmental matters, and the information on which the executive committee acted was biased just because it was framed by these executives in their capacities as functional operating officers. Factual and analytical reports were usually presented so as to favor one of the alternatives under discussion, although this was not always done consciously.

In some single-product yet multi-function industries, just as in railroading, the administrative pattern froze once it had been elaborated. As long as the enterprise in question sold one major line of goods manufactured from one group of raw materials by means of one relatively simple marketing technique and in a comparatively unchanging and steady market, the questions and problems decided by the top team became relatively simple as time went on. This held true of the steel, copper, nickel, and some other metal industries, of meat packing, tobacco processing, distilling, flour milling, and other agricultural processing industries. But resting on one's oars was not possible where the decision-making remained difficult, because markets, production techniques, or sources of supply were changing continuously or rapidly.

Let us sum up what is essential from the point of view of this article: the administration of single-product yet multi-function industrial enterprises pivoted and pivots around functional departments whose heads—specialists—together with the corporation president and chairman of the board formed and form an executive committee. That is to say, the committee, set up to make strategic decisions, consisted and consists of men who were and are themselves rooted in the fulfillment of certain functions. Once more, major decisions in two fields, operations and strategy, rested or rest in identical hands.

By 1910, the *threshold* of a new administrative development was being raised in those industries which came into the orbit of the two new generators of power, the internal combustion engine and the electric motor. The development gained momentum with the rapid growth of the science-based industries. By 1940, however, it was still concentrated in five major industries: electrical and electronics, power machinery including the automobile, rubber, petroleum, and chemicals. It resulted primarily from product diversification, based on new and expanding technologies. After 1900, Allis Chalmers, for example, moved from building steam machinery to making electrical apparatus and equipment, to developing trucks and other commercial vehicles, and finally into the producing and selling of tractors and farm machinery. International Harvester, after applying the internal combustion engine to farm implements, moved to making tractors and then trucks and commercial vehicles. As new lines were developed in individual enterprises, it became increasingly hard to handle the purchasing, manufacturing, and marketing of each within the same centralized, functionally departmentalized operating organization. Marketing was particularly difficult since the new products went to quite different types of customers.

In the electrical and chemical industries, the continuous development of new products raised even more intense difficulties, for their markets were still more varied. By the mid-1920's, companies like General Electric, du Pont, and Union Carbide had not only moved into the making of quite different producers' goods, ranging from metal products to plastics, but also had begun to sell consumers' goods. The chemical enterprises sold paints, batteries, and antifreeze directly to consumers, and the great electrical firms began to move into the same broad market by making appliances such as refrigerators, washing machines, vacuum cleaners, and stoves. In the rubber and oil industries, there was less strain on the existing functionally departmentalized organizations. Although revolutionized by the coming of the automobile, some leading companies tended to stay within the bounds of a single industry. On the other hand, firms like Goodrich and United States Rubber, when taking up the production of a broad variety of rubber products, including rubber chemicals, and the oil companies developing petro-chemicals, faced structural problems initially comparable to those met by the electrical and chemical firms.

The strategy of diversification and concomitantly the development of the multi-product and multi-function industrial enterprise quickly demanded a new form of organization. The old functional departments were wholly unable to handle the problems arising from the engineering, producing, and marketing of entirely different goods, to say nothing of those of supplying materials for the manufacture of each. *Consequently, as the enterprises moved into the new lines, the administration of each major line was organized on a multi-function basis.*[9] In other words, the major operating unit within the enterprise came to be based on a product line, not a function. Each head of a product division had under his control a full set of functional departments—manufacturing, sales, finance, purchasing, engineering, and research and development. Within the bounds and limits, i.e., the policy established by the central office, the chief officers of those product units made major decisions. These, however, must be distinguished from those emanating from headquarters.

Within the framework of central policy, the duties of a division head were quite comparable to those of a senior executive of a single-product yet multi-function enterprise. Divisional performance was appraised by the financial success (return on investment) and to a lesser extent by the share in the market which the division chiefs could conquer or maintain. From these units, data flowed continuously to the headquarters in the form of statistics, charts, reports, etc., supplemented by oral communica-

[9] This same type of organization was developed by the single-line firm, particularly large oil companies, whose activities had become world-wide—or multi-regional—in scope. The head of each regional unit usually managed the several functions of the business and operated quite autonomously within the framework set by the central office.

tions during visits, both of unit heads to headquarters and of the central office executives to the operating units.

A relatively small team of four to a dozen men, located in adjoining offices in the central headquarters, now became responsible for the enterprise as a whole. The team's functions were appraisal, coordination, and the determination of policy both for the enterprise as a whole and for its multi-function, product-based operating units. In carrying out these duties, the general officers at central headquarters had the assistance of a staff of specialists. Normally, the new advisory staff had offices pertaining to one or several of the major functions to be performed, such as advertising, marketing, production, purchasing, engineering, labor relations, public relations, research and development, and so forth.

In such a structure, then, the top team is an easily identifiable group, and it is recognizable by what it does—by its functions and activities—rather than by the personality traits of its members. It cannot be stressed strongly enough, as did Sombart and other researchers, that such business executives are not necessarily possessed of *charisma*. Personally unknown to the possibly tens of thousands of workers and employees, they need no *charisma* and usually have none. If one of them has this quality, it may show up in his relations to the other members of the team, in his political influence, and in his role in trade associations and the like.

This team communicates directly and interacts only with the men responsible for operations, but is in no way the latters' captive. In making *critical* decisions as to the maintenance and expansion of the enterprise, its alternatives are *sui generis* and not forced on it by the operators. Its decisions are concerned with balancing conflicting interests between the operators whose demands are determined by the products and/or functions for which they are responsible. In making those decisions, the top team has data and opinions presented by the functional staff specialists at headquarters who have little or no divisional connections or biases.

This new type of organization started immediately after World War I at General Motors and du Pont. A few others followed in the 1920's and 1930's. But it was only with the great economic expansion during and after World War II, with the rapid increase of systematic research and development, and with the demands of the present-day economy and technology, that this modernized, decentralized type of structure became widespread. Increasingly used by multi-product and multi-function firms in the five industries already listed, it was taken over also by some of the older agricultural processing companies, such as Armour or Procter and Gamble, to the extent that they too moved into chemicals and built highly diversified product lines.

We can consider as the characteristic feature of the newest kind of business administration that not only are operations (management) and policy-making separated but that also a middle level which has essentially administrative functions has been inserted. We will return to this matter in the fourth and analytical section of this paper. Suffice it to stress here what should be evident from our presentation that the delegation of functions by the top team has not left it without tasks. New ones had to be and were added to the traditional functions. While, for example, in a single-product enterprise, the question of what to produce is solved once for all with the establishment of the works and reappears only in cases of critical reorganization, the current determination of what to produce becomes a major type of strategic decision in the modern multi-product and multi-function industries.

Goal determination takes the time and energy of the top team. And since its members are no longer responsible for operations and administration, they are psychologically more committed to seeing the concern as a whole. They have the time for planning and, last but not least, they have excellent information. The steady flow of relevant data assembled by the central staff, supplemented by those on the performance of the divisions and by regular visits with the administrators, provides such information as is necessary for policy-making.

A General Motors report of 1937 is of the greatest interest in this context. It stated that the administration was being left to the divisions and the formulation of policy to the central headquarters, and it defined the distinction in this way [10] : "By 'administration' is meant the daily conduct of the Corporation's affairs. By 'formation of policies' is meant both the establishment of the broad principles by which administration is to be guided and the determination of the fundamental concepts of the business. The prime objectives of the business; the scope of its operations, both as to products and markets; the desirability of expansion, horizontally or vertically or both; the provision of the essential capital for its operations, and the question of distribution of its profits as between the amount paid in dividends and the amount retained in the business—all are problems involving 'formation of policies' and illustrate the principle involved."

III

We have painted with broad strokes of the brush the development of American business organization between about 1850 and 1950. From our point of view, the significant finding can be characterized as the evolution of a three-level out of a two-level organization. We have now to look for the tools which were developed parallel with the organizational evolution, for the tools which made the latter possible. Critical and crucial was progress in the field of communication, the more so the closer we come

[10] *Twenty-ninth Annual Report of General Motors Corporation, Year Ended December 31, 1937*, Prepared for Presentation to the Stockholders at the Annual Meeting to Be Held in Wilmington, Delaware, Tuesday, April 26, 1938, p. 37.

down to our own time. As the top team of our day became increasingly concerned with over-all policy and strategy and less involved in the day-to-day conduct of the business and as both the operating and administrative structures of the firms concerned became larger and more intricate, the need grew for free flowing and efficient channels of communication between the top team and the various levels of the organization. At the same time and on all levels, more and more precise data were also needed concerning the all but bewildering external situation, particularly in the markets. And naturally, as the business units grew in size and the activities in complexity parallel with the spreading industrialization and urbanization of the nation and as the industrial technique and its scientific basis became more and more involved, effective communication became harder and harder.

Two methods could be used for improving communication lines between the top team and the lower levels or for guaranteeing at least a steady flow of communication. One was to define more clearly the *channels* of communication and authority; the other was to develop more useful *kinds* of information to move through the channels. Thus began systematic, periodic reports, operating statistics, forecasts, and so forth. In this country, the creation of the first precise internal channels of communication and of detailed operating statistics was again the work of the railroads. Contemporary mercantile houses or textile or iron mills had as little need for a detailed reporting system as for formal operating structures, as has been described. Nor would they have been able to get much information on the external situation other than prices current or shipping news.

In the early years of railroad expansion, particularly in the decade of the 1850's, much thought was given not only to formal organization, but also to the development of operating statistics. While many companies defined their lines of communication and authority, in an *ad hoc* way, i.e., as particular problems had to be worked out, some attacked them more systematically. The Erie had a detailed organization chart by 1854; the Pennsylvania a printed organization manual by 1858.[11] In 1889 when the Illinois Central, planning a reorganization, made a survey of twenty-two major railroads, it found that one third of these had printed codes or rules "defining the power and duties of (their) officers." [12] Some others had carefully regulated their organizations, although the result had not been published and was not available for distribution. The rest still

---

[11] Chandler, *Henry Varnum Poor*, pp. 147 ff. *Pennsylvania Railroad Company, Organization for Conducting the Business of the Road, Adopted December 26, 1857* (Philadelphia, 1858).

[12] "Minutes of the Meeting of the 'Board', Appointed by the Resolution of the Illinois Central Board of Directors, May 15, 1889, Held at the General Offices in Chicago, Friday, June 21, 1889, 11 A.M.," from the Illinois Central Railroad Company's files.

operated under informal codes of "usages and procedures," built up over time.

Statistics as first developed by the railroads reflected, like their organizational structure, the basic need of assuring the safe and efficient running of the trains. Hence the roads assembled a wealth of satisfactory *operating* data. Reporting and statistical procedures worked out as early as the 1850's came into common use after the Civil War.[13] Railroad officers were soon to learn the value of these data for determining cost and with it profits, an extremely difficult problem. By the early 1870's, Albert Fink and other railroad men had worked out quite sophisticated techniques for establishing cost per ton mile operated.[14] By the end of the century, the term "control through statistics" was regularly used in railroading.[15]

But this control remained operational rather than anything else. The railroads developed satisfactory data for appraising past performance, but they did almost nothing to work out forecasts, budgets, or such statistical procedures as might be used to plan ahead. This lack can undoubtedly be explained by the fact that after 1900 strategy and planning became less important in railroading, as described earlier in this paper. The existing data and procedures were sufficient to carry out the major central office functions of appraising the performance of the different operating units and of coordinating traffic flow between the units.

Little of what the railroads had achieved in this field was carried over into the single-product yet multi-function manufacturing enterprise because of the different character of its business. However, by the turn of the century, in working out a specific structure of its own, it also had to develop lines of communication and authority that suited its own needs. In so doing, some of the big enterprises proceeded quite systematically.[16] Questions relating to structure and the means of sustaining it came to be discussed by the end of World War I in the business and industrial literature of the day, such as trade journals and other periodicals and even in textbooks.[17] At the same time, the data flowing through the more clearly

[13] Chandler, *Henry Varnum Poor*, pp. 137 ff., 145 ff.

[14] Particularly valuable in this connection is the *Annual Report of the Louisville and Nashville Railroad for the Year Ending June 30, 1874*, written by Albert Fink.

[15] Ray Morris, *Railroad Administration*, has a chapter entitled "Control Through Statistics."

[16] Some of the large companies which had systematically worked out their structures before World War I included United States Rubber Company, International Harvester, American Smelting and Refining, Westinghouse, Allis Chalmers, General Electric, and Bethlehem Steel.

[17] A brief examination of the first volumes of the journal, *Management and Administration* (New York), which began publication in 1921 is useful in this connection. So also is Leon Carroll Marshall, *Business Administration* (Chicago, Ill., 1921), one of the best anthologies of business literature. Two of the best early books on structure are Russell Robb, *Lectures on Organization* (privately printed [Boston?], 1911), and Dexter S. Kimball, *Principles of Industrial Organization* (New York, 1913), p. 22.

defined channels were being greatly improved. In industrial enterprises, unlike the railroads, internal statistics grew out of the need for cost analysis rather than for detailed day-to-day operating information. Effective means for allocating overhead and for determining variable costs led, in turn, to the recognition that variable costs are closely related to volume and that realistic cost analysis called for the determination of expected future as well as past performance.

The needs of interdepartmental coordination also brought pressure on the large-scale enterprise to predict its future in addition to gauging its past performance. Ultimately the total of product flow through various departments depended on demand. The more accurately demand could be forecast, the more evenly the flow could be channelled and thus the over-all organization could be operated closer to maximum capacity. The importance of forecasting demand for the purpose of determining quantities to be produced, of coordinating product flow, and of finding variable costs was greater for firms operating in the mass-consumer market than it was for those making producers' goods, and greater also in the production of consumer durables than in that of consumer perishables. The great meat packers like Armour and Swift could maintain flow by keeping a constant telegraphic communication between the sales managers of the branch houses in the great eastern metropolises and the buyers of cattle and other livestock in the stockyards of western cities.[18] On the other hand, General Motors discovered, right after World War I, that the maintenance of any kind of steady flow and with it the steady use of plant and personnel called first of all for careful forecasts of annual demand and the development of detailed production schedules based on these estimates.[19] Then came the need to work out procedures to make possible the *adjustment* of the forecasts and production schedule to the *actual conditions* of the changing market. This was done at General Motors by obtaining reports every ten days from the dealers as to the actual number of cars sold and also frequent reports on new car registrations. After 1925, the year in which General Motors started basing nearly all its activities on expected market demand, the use of forecasts and of statistics for anticipating market behavior was becoming a fairly widespread practice in American industry.

The needs of planning, like those of coordination and appraisal, equally turned American industrialists to acting on the basis of anticipated rather

[18] *Report of the Commissioner of Corporations on the Beef Industry* (Washington, D. C., 1905), p. 21.

[19] Donaldson Brown, "Pricing Policy in Relation to Financial Control," a series of articles appearing in *Management and Administration* in the spring of 1924. Also C. S. Mott, "Organizing a Great Industrial," *ibid.*, pp. 527 ff.; Albert Bradley, "Setting Up a Forecasting Program," American Management Association, *Annual Convention Series No. 41* (March, 1926); and Donaldson Brown, "Decentralized Responsibilities With Centralized Coordination," *ibid.*, No. 57 (Feb., 1927).

than past performance. The development and expansion of the different functional activities and the resulting problems of allocating funds among departments and within departments led in many enterprises to the systematizing of appropriation procedures. Senior officers asked that each request for capital expenditure include carefully worked out cost information, indicate an estimated return on investment on the proposed project and the project's relation to the over-all program of the operating unit involved and of the company itself. Soon comparable reports were requested for estimated operating as well as capital expenditures.

Both came to be combined into regular—semiannual or annual—budgets. The budget became both a means of supervision and an expression of policy. As to the former, operating performance could be checked against the estimates and proposals in the budget. As to the latter, the budget by its allocation of available funds set the limits on the departmental or divisional activities, and at the same time it indicated the areas where the senior officers believed the company should expand or contract its activities. The budget was and is considered more as a guide than as an unadjustable schedule to be followed without questioning. Budget-making forced firms, as early as World War I, into forecasting the financial and economic conditions outside of the companies concerned, so that financial planning and the allocation of funds might be put on a rational basis. In those same years—those immediately following World War I—periodicals and books on business came to take an increasing interest in the discussion of forecasting, budgeting, techniques of inventory, production, and marketing control.[20]

The coming of the multi-product and multi-function enterprise brought, besides increasing stress on formal structure, a further refinement of existing statistical and other communication techniques. The problem of structure in this new type of enterprise was essentially one of redefining channels of authority and communication to meet the new complexities. In addition, statistical procedures were refined in two new ways. There was the need of getting *precise* information in as *compact* a form as possible. Otherwise the general officers at headquarters would not have found the time to make effective use of it in appraising performance, coordinating the units, and making over-all policy. Secondly, statistical techniques had to be *perfected* so that the *rapidly increasing* amount of all kinds of information on production, purchasing and marketing could be used more effectively on all levels, particularly in the administrative divisions. Also the reports and personal visits between the policy-makers at the center and the administrators on a lower level became more and more important in assuring communication between central headquarters and the administrative divisions. In the development of those new statisti-

[20] Again the articles in the early numbers of *Management and Administration* are particularly revealing.

cal techniques and procedures, the central staff played a more significant role than did the operating units.

These practices then provided the executives with data essential to supervising and maintaining control over their increasingly intricate enterprises in an external situation growing always more complex. Statistical and financial controls made possible the delegation of major decisions to the men in charge of the multi-functional product divisions. Through constant objective checks on divisional performance, errors and mistakes of these subordinates could usually be caught before major harm was done to the over-all enterprise. The senior men could take action because they controlled the selection of executive personnel and because, through budgeting, they allocated the funds to the operating divisions. In the way they allocated their resources—capital and personnel—and in the promotion, transferral and retirement of operating executives, they determined the framework in which the operating units worked and thus put into effect their concept of the long-term goals and objectives of the enterprise.

IV

The material presented in the two preceding sections of this paper is of great significance. Focusing his attention on the development of large-scale industry in the last hundred years, the writer of those sections discovered three types of enterprise, designated here as single-function or, in manufacturing, as single-product and single-function, single-product yet multi-function, and multi-product and multi-function. In the course of his investigations, he found that to each type of enterprise there belongs a specific type of business administration functionally related to the tasks to be fulfilled in that type. The three kinds of enterprise and the concomitant kinds of business administration appeared in historical sequence and can, if you please, be considered as stages in the development of large-scale business enterprise and of business administration. Yet, if we do so, we must see them as what they are, namely, ideal types, and so we must heed Sombart's warning. He taught us that any generic type including those of formal organization, once brought into existence in the historic process, does not disappear with the evolution of new ones. Old and new come to stand side by side for decades if not centuries. The forces which brought them into existence and the needs to which they cater are liable to persist for shorter or longer periods as do the forms to which these gave rise. It is doubtful whether the American graduate schools of business administration are aware of this fact in planning their teaching in that field.

When we examine our material from another point of view, it becomes evident that the two kinds of business administration which were developed to fit the needs of the older forms of enterprise are two-level affairs, while that corresponding to the most modern types of enterprise takes place on three levels. The first two levels are operations (management) on the one hand, and coordination of operations, goal determination, and planning on the other. In the multi-product and multi-function enterprise, however, the top level was split up by the delegation of one of its activities, the coordination of operations of the various functional departments within the major lines of products. The coordination of these functional units, working possibly in the most disparate fields, demanded such special care that it became necessary to give full time attention to administering the operators (managers) of these units. This then became the task of a new, middle level of business administration. For want of a better word, we will characterize it as the "locum-tenential" level, because certain officers other than the top team, but *in lieu* of it, undertake to administer on their own responsibility particular lines of products, a situation which implies supervision and coordination of the functional operators concerned. Thereafter, the top team could specialize on goal determination and planning. Since typically we deal, in this area, with what Arthur Spiethoff has called "historical theory," the theorist of today must take notice of these changes, replacing the distinction between manager and entrepreneur with that between operator (manager), "locum tenens," and enterpreneur, reserving this latter term for those who determine the goal of and plan for the enterprise in question.

One cannot emphasize too strongly that operator (manager), "locum tenens," and entrepreneur are ideal types with which the generic figures of reality must be compared, if analysis of reality is desired. Of course, while a theoretical model must be clear-cut to serve as a useful tool for the analysis of reality, reality itself never is precise. The performers of any one of those critical functions fulfill other, i.e., noncritical ones also. Moreover, those working on the higher levels may also have a hand temporarily or permanently in the performance of the typical functions of the one just below. Vice versa, an able man serving on a lower level may, because of his ability or insight, be called to advise the next higher level. Yet the larger the enterprise tends to be and the nearer to the present time, the clearer becomes the separation of functions.

In any enterprise, including one active on a small scale, two functions *must* be fulfilled: namely, operation and goal determination; or from another point of view, running the whole or some departments, on the one hand, and keeping the enterprise alive on the other. But the functions may remain cojoined. The need for separation appears only gradually as the enterprise grows and/or becomes more geographically decentralized, i.e., with plants dispersed over a wider area. Under such conditions, the "headquarters" and the "field" part company, the former cutting loose from the actual operations (management). Nevertheless, and absurdly, the top level is still today called "top management" in business and by many business historians as *lucus a non lucendo*.[21] A French adage can also be adapted to our purpose: *"l'entrepreneur* (i.e., the theoretical figure standing for the top-level team) *règne mais il ne gouverne pas."* On the other hand, the coordination of operations appears only with and is incumbent on large-scale and geographically decentralized enterprises but, under such circumstances, the need appears automatically. Originally, it was included among the functions of the top team, until in the latest type of business administration it was divorced and emancipated on the middle, "locum-tenential" level.

Once the conceptual frame here proposed is adopted, new light can be thrown on several phenomena, two of which are of interest here.[22] First, we can see that the initial steps towards a three-stage business administration was taken in railroading, and in stressing this fact we take up an earlier thread. As early as the 1870's we find the planning entrepreneur at headquarters in railroad enterprises. The heads of the regional units stood for the "locum tenens" of theory, while the heads of the various departments corresponded to the operators (managers) of theory. The relapse into a simpler and, from the point of view of the historian, older type of administration, described earlier, can then be explained by the need for fewer decisions once the railroad net was practically completed with the concomitant and continuous systematization of day-to-day operations. Railroads could return to the simpler two-stage administration with only headquarters and field organized in functional departments.

Secondly, the phenomenon of decentralization comes up for a new interpretation. The term of "decentralization" has been used to denote geographical as well as administrative decentralization. Of these, only the latter type is of interest to us. Within our conceptual frame, administrative decentralization, predicated on the delegation of functions, i.e., the power to make decisions in the delegated field, appears on two levels, the operational (managerial) and the "locum-tenential." The former is historically the older one. In large-scale nineteenth-century enterprise, certain decisions were made at headquarters, others in the "field." A historically later and different kind of decentralization appeared first in the 1920's when the middle level of business administration, the "locum-tenential," became semi-independent. Consequently, today we find in some enterprises two levels of decentralization, a fact which has only begun to be recognized by researches. Operators and "locum tenentes" have in common a concern with day-to-day activities, while the top team, being rather remote from these, acts, one might say, from year-to-year and intermittently. But in this connection, one needs to guard against a misunderstanding. Day-to-day actions are by no means synonymous with routine.

[21] For the origin and history of this phrase see Henry T. Thomas, *Dictionary of Latin Quotations* (London, 1859), p. 209.
[22] The following is a schematic somewhat oversimplified sketch.

The fact that many modern economists are inclined to overlook this difference is an evil by-product of Schumpeter's magnificent vision. Schumpeter is not to blame, but rather those economists who use a figure designed for a model of economic development when they study the theory of business enterprise and of business leadership. To be sure, this does not exonerate Schumpeter from the blame of having used an unnecessarily confusing and impractical terminology. Once he had reached the pinnacle of his prestige, his theory and terminology all but blocked the road to satisfactory insight. Day-to-day actions can, but should not be, taken in the spirit of routine. They can also be tackled in the spirit of innovation and it is high time that the creative operator (manager) and creative "locum tenens" should be studied from this point of view. But again, the term of "innovation," as defined by Schumpeter, is too narrow and untenable even in his own model. There are primary and derivative innovations; there are subjective and objective ones.[23] There are some business innovations which imply new combinations of the factors of production, i.e., change in the production function, and there are very important ones, especially in the field of business organization, which do not. In our scheme, the former are typical of the entrepreneurial, but are possible also on a "locum-tenential" level; the latter can be introduced on any level. As a matter of fact, an enterprise whose day-to-day operations have become mere routine is doomed, while there is also an unavoidable and safe routine element in planning.

To repeat, in the study of business enterprise the difference between entrepreneur, "locum tenens," and operator (manager) is one between tasks to be performd by these various cooperating and complementary figures. This holds true even though it would appear at first glance that they have one task in common, namely, coordination. But a mere word should not deceive us. On every level of the hierarchy, different kinds of coordination take place. On the operational (managerial) level, executives—plant managers, heads of branch offices or groups of product salesmen, purchasing agents, or scientists—are coordinated to carry out a single basic function—manufacturing, sales, purchasing, or research. On the "locum-tenential" level, functions relating to the processing of a major line of products, all the way from the raw material to the consumer, are coordinated. Finally, the top team (the entrepreneur) coordinates the various lines of products in the best interest of the enterprise.

The performance of the various tasks is reflected in the different horizons of the officers in question. The operator (manager) thinks in terms of a single function, the "locum tenens" in terms of a line of products or an industry, while the enterpreneur has the national economy and even the whole world in his mind in making his decisions.

[23] Fritz Redlich, "Innovation in Business," *The American Journal of Economics and Sociology*, vol. X (New York, 1950/51), pp. 285 ff.

Administrative problems of course are solved by decisions. Consequently, to our three kinds of business administration, there correspond three levels of business decisions: operational (managerial), "locum-tenential," and entrepreneurial, the last term to be used if we stick to the tradition and call the top team "the entrepreneur" whenever we speak in theoretical terms. Correspondingly, as there are three levels of business administration, three horizons, three levels of tasks, and three levels of decision-making, so there are three levels of policy. There is the operational (managerial), "locum-tenential," and entrepreneurial policy. Only in the past could one define and describe the entrepreneur as a policy-maker pure and simple in a business enterprise. We shall return to this matter of policy shortly.

Taking a cue from military language, we can designate operational (managerial) and "locum-tenential" decisions as tactical in contrast to entrepreneurial as strategic decisions. In military science, specifically in Clausewitz's language, tactics implies the leading of forces for the purpose of a battle, while strategy connotes the conducting of battles for the purpose of war. Or, as was taught in German military schools, tactics implies leading forces *in* battle, strategy leading forces *into* battle. If we adapt this terminology to the study of business administration, we could say: strategic decisions are those that allocate the means of production, including available liquid funds and available manpower, particularly skilled personnel, according to the purpose of the enterprise; while tactical decisions apply allocated means and manpower for the purpose of administrating those units which are under the care of the "locum tenentes" and managers. Or to put it more pointedly, the difference is one between the allocation as against the application of means of production.

This then is the place to show how reality, i.e., what the businessman calls "top management," deviates from the ideal type, the model of "the entrepreneur." When a businessman reaches a certain place in the administrative hierarchy of enterprise, he becomes a member of "top management" and remains so until he retires. In theory, however, entrepreneurship, i.e., the participation in the goal-determining and planning team, is actualized only in making a *particular* decision. Outside of the intermittent process of making strategic decisions, any given person is a member of the entrepreneurial team only potentially while the specific entrepreneurial decisions in large-scale business enterprise are made by an ever slightly varying team.

The discussion of decisions has brought us to that of business policy. Here again the development of large-scale industry and of appropriate forms of business administration has been accompanied by historical change. Leland Jenks has shown in another context that in the nineteenth century, problems of business administration were solved *ad hoc*.[24] In such

---

[24] Leland Jenks, "Some Early Phases of the Management Movement," *Administrative Management Quarterly*, vol. V (Ithaca, New York, 1960/61), p. 424.

a situation, business policy could develop only slowly; and by business policy we mean a consistent sequence of decisions, even if not recognized as such by the men concerned. The fact of *conscious* policy determination is established in railroading for the 1850's and in industry for the 1880's.[25] Actually business policy seems to be the natural concomitant of geographically dispersed enterprise. In no other way can widely scattered operating decisions be coordinated and supervised. Ultimately, in the course of a hundred years of administrative development, the more or less conscious consistency of decisions has emerged until, at least on the entrepreneurial level, business policy has become equivalent to a master plan. To this master plan, i.e., entrepreneurial policy, "locum tenentes" as well as operators (managers) must adhere, and adherence is enforced by budgetary procedures.

At this point then, we meet a crucial problem. We have designated the functions of the top team as goal determination and planning. These functions can be performed only by men who are in control of the concern's capital, allotted and unallotted alike. Thus the function of goal determination and planning is underpinned by that of fund allocation or budgeting (synonymous terms in modern enterprise). As a matter of fact, the first appearance of a budget in business enterprise cannot be overestimated in its historical importance. It is an indicator of emerging bureaucratization of business, the correlative to modern large-scale enterprise. The budget sets a goal, while traditionally business enterprise was satisfied with gauging the result once a year by a profit and loss statment. The function of fund allocation (budgeting) which goes with that of goal determination and planning is the factor which determines the locus of ultimate authority in enterprise.

Not only the authors of this paper, but also other scholars seem to have felt that the concept of "entrepreneur" demands rethinking. G. Heberton Evans has recently made a pertinent suggestion; [26] and Heinz Hartmann has attempted to give the discussion a new bent.[27] With regard to the latter's interesting paper, we find ourselves sitting on the horns of a curious dilemma. We entirely agree with his findings, namely, that it is useful to distinguish between top level and operators both in theoretical and empirical investigations, although we also take cognizance of the new middle level in the administrative hierarchy. We agree that one can and should characterize the top team as the locus of the ultimate authority in enterprise. But we disagree with his starting point and his reasoning. Ultimate authority in business enterprise, as we see it, rests with those

[25] Ralph W. and Muriel E. Hidy, *History of Standard Oil Company* (*New Jersey*), vol. I, *Pioneering in Big Business 1882–1911* (New York, 1955), p. 62.

[26] G. Heberton Evans, Jr., "Business Entrepreneurs, Their Major Functions and Related Tenets," *The Journal of Economic History*, vol. XIX (New York, 1959), pp. 250 ff.

[27] Heinz Hartman, "Managers and Enterpreneurs: A Useful Distinction?," *Administrative Science Quarterly*, vol. III (Ithaca, New York, 1958/59), pp. 429 ff.

who hold the purse strings, and in modern large-scale enterprise, those persons hold the purse strings who perform the function of goal setting and planning. The difference of opinion then is that we explain ultimate authority within business enterprise by reference to a function which implies control over a concern's capital, while Hartmann thinks he can explain it without such a reference, and so is led into metaphysics. Metaphysics, however, is not needed when the problem is how to explain, not the acceptance of business enterprise in capitalistic society, but the acceptance of ultimate authority within socially accepted business enterprise. Only in the former case is a sanctioning reference to property rights demanded.

Whoever joins an enterprise in capitalistic society does not question that he must obey; but to make him obey more willingly, i.e., cooperate, a specific department, that of personnel relations, has been established in modern large-scale concerns. It uses propaganda methods and among its other tasks builds up the participants in "top management" just as an office-seeking politician is built up in the minds of the voters. But if the top team actually needed to be legitimized *within* the enterprise by referring to the stockholders for authorization, the latter would be the real locus of ultimate authority. This they are not, as Hartmann himself pointed out. Stockholders have only a negative (veto) power, not a positive one. They can direct the top team not to do certain things, but they cannot force it to do others. Only in very special cases can they overturn a particular "top management." Therefore, we go along with and, so we think, fortify Hartmann in what seems to be his purpose, namely, in seeing the ultimate authority in enterprise, as far as administration goes, as resting in the top management team, which is in fact self-perpetuating.

Our findings can be summed up thus: if in theoretical contexts we wish to conceptualize the top team which keeps modern large-scale business alive, we cannot start from the difference between innovation and routine. Nor can we see as essential characteristics of the top team the making of decisions or the determining of policy. Like some earlier theorists, we can see as the criterion the making of *strategic* decisions, provided it is well understood what we mean by "strategic." We can and should start from the specific functions which the top team performs—goal determination, planning, and budgeting. We can and should stress that the team holds the ultimate authority in the enterprise concerned. If then, in line with tradition, we wish to use the term "entrepreneur" to designate that top team, here are the elements to define it.

How the Other Quarter Lives

35.   Our Invisible Poor

Dwight MacDonald

In his significantly titled "The Affluent Society" (1958) Professor J. K. Galbraith states that poverty in this country is no longer "a massive affliction [but] more nearly an afterthought." Dr. Galbraith is a humane critic of the American capitalist system, and he is generously indignant about the continued existence of even this nonmassive and afterthought-ish poverty. But the interesting thing about his pronouncement, aside from the fact that it is inaccurate, is that it was generally accepted as obvious. For a long time now, almost everybody has assumed that, because of the New Deal's social legislation and—more important—the prosperity we have enjoyed since 1940, mass poverty no longer exists in this country.

Dr. Galbraith states that our poor have dwindled to two hard-core categories. One is the "insular poverty" of those who live in the rural South or in depressed areas like West Virginia. The other category is "case poverty," which he says is "commonly and properly related to [such]characteristics of the individuals so afflicted [as] mental deficiency, bad health, inability to adapt to the discipline of modern economic life, excessive procreation, alcohol, insufficient education." He reasons that such poverty must be due to individual defects, since "nearly everyone else has mastered his environment; this proves that it is not intractable." Without pressing the similarity of this concept to the "Social Darwinism" whose fallacies Dr. Galbraith easily disposes of elsewhere in his book, one may observe that most of these characteristics are as much the result of poverty as its cause.

Dr. Galbraith's error is understandable, and common. Last April the newspapers reported some exhilarating statistics in a Department of Commerce study: the average family income increased from $2,340 in 1929 to $7,020 in 1961. (These figures are calculated in current dollars, as are all the others I shall cite.) But the papers did not report the fine type, so to speak, which showed that almost all the recent gain was made by families with incomes of over $7,500, and that the rate at which poverty is being eliminated has slowed down alarmingly since 1953. Only the spe-

"Our Invisible Poor," by Dwight MacDonald, is reprinted by permission from *The New Yorker,* January 19, 1963.

cialists and the statisticians read the fine type, which is why illusions continue to exist about American poverty.

Now Michael Harrington, an alumnus of the *Catholic Worker* and the Fund for the Republic who is at present a contributing editor of *Dissent* and the chief editor of the Socialist Party biweekly, *New America*, has written "The Other America: Poverty in the United States" (Macmillan). In the admirably short space of under two hundred pages, he outlines the problem, describes in imaginative detail what it means to be poor in this country today, summarizes the findings of recent studies by economists and sociologists, and analyzes the reasons for the persistence of mass poverty in the midst of general prosperity. It is an excellent book—and a most important one.

My only serious criticism is that Mr. Harrington has popularized the treatment a bit too much. Not in the writing, which is on a decent level, but in a certain vagueness. There are no index, no bibliography, no reference footnotes. In our overspecialized culture, books like this tend to fall into two categories: Popular (no scholarly "apparatus") and Academic (too much). I favor something intermediate—why should the academics have *all* the footnotes? The lack of references means that the book is of limited use to future researchers and writers. A pity, since the author has brought together a great range of material.

I must also object that Mr. Harrington's treatment of statistics is more than a little impressionistic. His appendix, which he calls a coming to grips with the professional material, doesn't live up to its billing. "If my interpretation is bleak and grim," he writes, "and even if it overstates the case slightly, that is intentional. My moral point of departure is a sense of outrage. . . . In such a discussion it is inevitable that one gets mixed up with dry, graceless, technical matters. That should not conceal the crucial fact that these numbers represent people and that any tendency toward understatement is an intellectual way of acquiescing in suffering." But a fact is a fact, and Mr. Harrington confuses the issue when he writes that "these numbers represent people." They do—and one virtue of his book is that he never forgets it—but in dealing with statistics, this truism must be firmly repressed lest one begin to think from the heart rather than from the head, as he seems to do when he charges those statisticians who "understate" the numbers of the poor with having found "an intellectual way of acquiescing in suffering." This is moral bullying, and it reminds me, *toutes proportions gardées*, of the habitual confusion in Communist thinking between facts and political inferences from them. "A sense of outrage" is proper for a "moral point of departure," but statistics are the appropriate *factual* point of departure, as in the writings of Marx and Engels on the agony of the nineteenth-century English working class—writings that are by no means lacking in a sense of moral outrage, either.

These objections, however, do not affect Mr. Harrington's two main contentions: that mass poverty still exists in the United States, and that it is disappearing more slowly than is commonly thought. Two recent dry, graceless, and technical reports bear him out. One is that Commerce Department study, already mentioned. More important is "Poverty and Deprivation in the U. S.," a bulky pamphlet issued by the Conference on Economic Progress, in Washington, whose national committee includes Thurman Arnold, Leon H. Keyserling (said to be the principal author of the pamphlet), and Walter P. Reuther.

In the last year we seem to have suddenly awakened, rubbing our eyes like Rip van Winkle, to the fact that mass poverty persists, and that it is one of our two gravest social problems. (The other is related: While only eleven per cent of our population is non-white, twenty-five per cent of our poor are.) Two other current books confirm Mr. Harrington's thesis: "Wealth and Power in America" (Praeger), by Dr. Gabriel Kolko, a social historian who has recently been at Harvard and the University of Melbourne, Australia, and "Income and Welfare in the United States" (McGraw-Hill), compiled by an imposing battery of four socio-economists headed by Dr. James N. Morgan, who rejoices in the title of Program Director of the Survey Research Center of the Institute for Social Research at the University of Michigan.

Dr. Kolko's book resembles Mr. Harrington's in several ways: It is short, it is based on earlier studies, and it is liberally inclined. It is less readable, because it is written in an academic jargon that is merely a vehicle for the clinching Statistic. Although it is impossible to write seriously about poverty without a copious use of statistics—as this review will demonstrate—it *is* possible to bring thought and feeling to bear on such raw material. Mr. Harrington does this more successfully than Dr. Kolko, whose prose is afflicted not only with academic blight but also with creeping ideology. Dr. Kolko leans so far to the socialist side that he sometimes falls on his nose, as when he clinches in inequality of wealth in the United States with a statistic: "In 1959, 23% of those earning less than $1,000 [a year] owned a car, compared to 95% of those earning more than $10,000." The real point is just the opposite, as any citizen of Iran, Ghana, Yemen, or the U.S.S.R. would appreciate—not that the rich have cars but that almost a quarter of the extremely poor do. Similarly, although Dr. Kolko has two chapters on poverty that confirm Mr. Harrington's argument, his main point is a different and more vulnerable one: "The basic distribution of income and wealth in the United States is essentially the same now as it was in 1939, or even 1910." This is a half fact. The rich are almost as rich as ever and the poor are even poorer, in the percentage of the national income they receive. Yet, as will become apparent later, there have been major changes in the distribution of wealth, and there has been a general improvement in living standards, so that the poor are much fewer today than they were in 1939. "Most low-income groups live substantially better today," Dr. Kolko admits. "But even though their real wages have mounted, their percentage of the national income has not changed." That in the last half century the rich have kept their riches and the poor their poverty is indeed a scandal. But it is theoretically possible, assuming enough general increase in wealth, that the relatively poor might by now have achieved a decent standard of living, no matter how inferior to that of the rich. As the books under consideration show, however, this theoretical possibility has not been realized.

Inequality of wealth is not necessarily a major social problem per se. Poverty is. The late French philosopher Charles Péguy remarks, in his classic essay on poverty, "The duty of tearing the destitutes from their destitution and the duty of distributing goods equitably are not of the same order. The first is an urgent duty, the second is a duty of convenience. . . . When all men are provided with the necessities . . . what do we care about the distribution of luxury?" What indeed? Envy and emulation are the motives—and not very good ones—for the equalization of wealth. The problem of poverty goes much deeper.

Income and Welfare in the United States differs from the other works reviewed here in length (531 big pages) and in being the result of original research; 2,800 families were interviewed "in depth." I must confess that, aside from a few interesting bits of data, I got almost nothing out of it. I assume the authors think poverty is still an important social problem, else why would they have gone to all this labor, but I'm not at all sure what their general conclusions are; maybe there aren't supposed to be any, in the best tradition of American scholarship. Their book is one of those behemoths of collective research financed by a foundation (in this case, largely by Ford) that daunt the stoutest-hearted lay reader (in this case, me). Based on "a multi-stage area probability sample that gives equal chance of selection to all non-institutional dwelling units in the conterminous United States [and that] was clustered geographically at each stage and stratified with interlaced controls," it is a specimen of what Charles Lamb called *biblia abiblia*—things that have the outward appearance of books but are not books, since they cannot be read. Methodologically, it employs something called the "multivariate analysis," which is explained in Appendix E. Typographically, Appendix E looks like language, but it turns out to be strewn with booby traps, all doubtless well known in the trade, like "dummy variables," "F ratios," "regression coefficients," "beta coefficients" (and "partial beta coefficients"), and two kinds of "standard deviations"—"of explanatory variable A" and "of the dependent variable."

My experience with such works may be summarized as follows: (alpha) the coefficient of comprehensibility decreases in direct ratio to the increase in length, or the longer the incomprehensible, a notion that is

illustrated here by the fact that Dr. Kolko's short work is more understandable than Dr. Morgan et al.'s long one; (beta) the standard deviation from truism is inversely related to the magnitude of the generalization, or the bigger the statement the more obvious. (Beta) is illustrated by
the authors' five general proposals for action ("Implications for Public
Policy"). The second of these is: "Fuller employment and the elimination
of discrimination based on prejudice would contribute greatly to the
independence of non-white persons, women, teenagers, and some of the
aged." That is, if Negroes and the rest had jobs and were not discrimi-
nated against, they would be better off—a point that doesn't need to be
argued or, for that matter, stated. The authors have achieved such a
mastery of truism that they sometimes achieve the same monumental
effect even in non-magnitudinous statements, as: "Table 28–1 shows that
the proportion of parents who indicated that their children will attend
private colleges is approximately twice as large for those with incomes
over $10,000 as for those with incomes under $3,000." Could be.

What is "poverty"? It is a historically relative concept, first of all. "There
are new definitions [in America] of what man can achieve, of what a
human standard of life should be," Mr. Harrington writes. "Those who
suffer levels of life well below those that are possible, even though they
live better than medieval knights or Asian peasants, or poor. . . . Poverty
should be defined in terms of those who are denied the minimal levels of
health, housing, food, and education that our present stage of scientific
knowledge specifies as necessary for life as it is now lived in the United
States." His dividing line follows that proposed in recent studies by the
United States Bureau of Labor Statistics: $4,000 a year for a family of four
and $2,000 for an individual living alone. (All kinds of income are
included, such as food grown and consumed on farms.) This is the cutoff
line generally drawn today.

Mr. Harrington estimates that between forty and fifty million Americans, or about a fourth of the population, are now living in poverty. Not
just below the level of comfortable living, but real poverty, in the old-
fashioned sense of the word—that they are hard put to it to get the mere
necessities, beginning with enough to eat. This is difficult to believe in the
United States of 1963, but one has to make the effort, and it is now being
made. The extent of our poverty has suddenly become visible. The same
thing has happened in England, where working-class gains as a result of
the Labour Party's post-1945 welfare state blinded almost everybody to
the continued existence of mass poverty. It was not until Professor Richard M. Titmuss, of the London School of Economics, published a series of
articles in the *New Statesman* last fall, based on his new book, "Income
Distribution and Social Change" (Allen & Unwin), that even the liberal
public in England became aware that the problem still persists on a scale
that is "statistically significant," as the economists put it.

Statistics on poverty are even trickier than most. For example, age and geography make a difference. There is a distinction, which cannot be rendered arithmetically, between poverty and low income. A childless young couple with $3,000 a year is not poor in the way an elderly couple might be with the same income. The young couple's statistical poverty may be a temporary inconvenience; if the husband is a graduate student or a skilled worker, there are prospects of later affluence or at least comfort. But the old couple can look forward only to diminishing earnings and increasing medical expenses. So also geographically: A family of four in a small town with $4,000 a year may be better off than a like family in a city—lower rent, no bus fares to get to work, fewer occasions (or temptations) to spend money. Even more so with a rural family. Although allowance is made for the value of the vegetables they may raise to feed themselves, it is impossible to calculate how much money they *don't* spend on clothes, say, or furniture, because they don't have to keep up with the Joneses. Lurking in the crevices of a city, like piranha fish in a Brazilian stream, are numerous tempting opportunities for expenditure, small but voracious, which can strip a budget to its bones in a surprisingly short time. The subtlety and complexity of poverty statistics may be discovered by a look at Dr. Kolko's statement that in 1959 "23% of those earning less than $1,000 owned a car." Does this include college students, or are they included in their families' statistics? If the first is true, then Dr. Kolko's figure loses much of its meaning. If the second is, then it is almost *too* meaningful, since it says that one-fourth of those earning less than twenty dollars a week are able to afford a car. Which it is, deponent sayeth not.

It is not, therefore, surprising to find that there is some disagreement about just how many millions of Americans are poor. The point is that all these recent studies agree that American poverty is still a mass phenomenon. One of the lowest estimates appears in the University of Michigan's "Income and Welfare," which states, "Poor families comprise one-fifth of the nation's families." The authors do not develop this large and crucial statement, or even give sources for it, despite their meticulous pedantry in all unimportant matters. So one can only murmur that the other experts put the number of poor much higher. (Though even a fifth is still over 35,000,000 people.) The lowness of the Michigan estimate is especially puzzling since its cutoff figure for poverty is $4,330, which is slightly higher than the commonly accepted one. The tendentious Dr. Kolko is also unconvincing, in the opposite direction. "Since 1947," he writes, "one-half of the nation's families and unattached individuals have had an income too small to provide them with a maintenance standard of living," which he sets at $4,500 a year for a family. He does give a table, with a long supporting footnote that failed to make clear to me how he could have possibly decided that 90,000,000 Americans are now living on less than $4,500 a year; I suspect some confusion between a "maintenance" and a "minimum-comfort" budget.

More persuasive estimates appear in the Conference on Economic Progress pamphlet, "Poverty and Deprivation." Using the $4,000 cutoff, the authors conclude that 38,000,000 persons are now living in poverty, which is slightly less than Mr. Harrington's lowest estimate. One reason may be that the pamphlet discriminates, as most studies don't, between "multiple-person families" and "unattached individuals," rating the latter as poor only if they have less than $2,000 a year. But there is more to it than that, including a few things I don't feel competent to judge. Income statistics are never compiled on exactly the same bases and there are all kinds of refinements, which vary from one study to another. Thus the Commerce Department's April report estimates there are 17,500,000 families *and* "unattached individuals" with incomes of less than $4,000. How many of the latter are there? "Poverty and Deprivation" puts the number of single persons with under $2,000 at 4,000,000. Let us say that in the 17,500,000 under $4,000 there are 6,500,000 single persons—the proportion of unattached individuals tends to go down as income rises. This homemade estimate gives us 11,000,000 families with incomes of under $4,000. Figuring the average American family at three and a half persons—which it is—this makes 38,500,000 individuals in families, or a grand total, if we add in the 4,000,000 "unattached individuals" with under $2,000 a year, of 42,500,000 Americans now living in poverty, which is close to a fourth of the total population.

The reason Dr. Galbraith was able to see poverty as no longer "a massive affliction" is that he used a cutoff of $1,000, which even in 1949, when it was adopted in a Congressional study, was probably too low (the C.I.O. argued for $2,000) and in 1958, when "The Affluent Society" appeared, was simply fantastic.

The model postwar budgets drawn up in 1951 by the Bureau of Labor Statistics to "maintain a level of adequate living" give a concrete idea of what poverty means in this country—or would mean if poor families lived within their income and spent it wisely, which they don't. Dr. Kolko summarizes the kind of living these budgets provide:

> Three members of the family see a movie once every three weeks, and one member sees a movie once every two weeks. There is no telephone in the house, but the family makes three pay calls a week. They buy one book a year and write one letter a week.
> The father buys one heavy wool suit every two years and a light wool suit every three years; the wife, one suit every ten years or one skirt every five years. Every three or four years, depending on the distance and time involved, the family takes a vacation outside their own city. In 1950, the family spent a total of $80 to $90 on all types of home furnishings, electrical appliances, and laundry equipment.

. . . The family eats cheaper cuts of meat several times a week, but has more expensive cuts on holidays. The entire family consumes a total of two five-cent ice cream cones, one five-cent candy bar, two bottles of soda, and one bottle of beer a week. The family owes no money, but has no savings except for a small insurance policy.

One other item is included in the B.L.S. "maintenance" budget: a new car every twelve to eighteen years.

This is an ideal picture, drawn up by social workers, of how a poor family *should* spend its money. But the poor are much less provident—installment debts take up a lot of their cash, and only a statistician could expect an actual live woman, however poor, to buy new clothes at intervals of five or ten years. Also, one suspects that a lot more movies are seen and ice-cream cones and bottles of beer are consumed than in the Spartan ideal. But these necessary luxuries are had only at the cost of displacing other items—necessary necessities, so to speak—in the B.L.S. budget.

The Conference on Economic Progress's "Poverty and Deprivation" deals not only with the poor but also with another large section of the "underprivileged," which is an American euphemism almost as good as "senior citizen"; namely, the 37,000,000 persons whose family income is between $4,000 and $5,999 and the 2,000,000 singles who have from $2,000 to $2,999. The authors define "deprivation" as "above poverty but short of minimum requirements for a modestly comfortable level of living." They claim that 77,000,000 Americans, or *almost half the population,* live in poverty or deprivation. One recalls the furor Roosevelt around with his "one-third of a nation—ill-housed, ill-clad, ill-nourished." But the political climate was different then.

The distinction between a family income of $3,500 ("poverty") and $4,500 ("deprivation") is not vivid to those who run things—the 31 per cent whose incomes are between $7,500 and $14,999 and the 7 per cent of the topmost top dogs, who get $15,000 or more. These two minorities, sizable enough to feel they *are* the nation, have been as unaware of the continued existence of mass poverty as this reviewer was until he read Mr. Harrington's book. They are businessmen, congressmen, judges, government officials, politicians, lawyers, doctors, engineers, scientists, editors, journalists, and administrators in colleges, churches, and foundations. Since their education, income, and social status are superior, they, if anybody, might be expected to accept responsibility for what the Constitution calls "the general welfare." They have not done so in the case of the poor. And they have a good excuse. It is becoming harder and harder simply to *see* the one-fourth of our fellow-citizens who live below the poverty line.

The poor are increasingly slipping out of the very experience and consciousness of the nation [Mr. Harrington writes]. If the middle class never did like ugliness and poverty, it was at least aware of them. "Across the tracks" was not a very long way to go. . . . Now the American city has been transformed. The poor still inhabit the miserable housing in the central area, but they are increasingly isolated from contact with, or sight of, anybody else. . . . Living out in the suburbs, it is easy to assume that ours is, indeed, an affluent society. . . .

Clothes make the poor invisible too: America has the best-dressed poverty the world has ever known. . . . It is much easier in the United States to be decently dressed than it is to be decently housed, fed, or doctored. . . .

Many of the poor are the wrong age to be seen. A good number of them are sixty-five years of age or better; an even larger number are under eighteen. . . .

And finally, the poor are politically invisible. . . . They are without lobbies of their own; they put forward no legislative program. As a group, they are atomized. They have no face; they have no voice. . . . Only the social agencies have a really direct involvement with the other America, and they are without any great political power. . . .

Forty to fifty million people are becoming increasingly invisible.

These invisible people fall mostly into the following categories, some of them overlapping: poor farmers, who operate 40 per cent of the farms and get 7 per cent of the farm cash income; migratory farm workers; unskilled, unorganized workers in offices, hotels, restaurants, hospitals, laundries, and other service jobs; inhabitants of areas where poverty is either endemic ("peculiar to a people or district"), as in the rural South, or epidemic ("prevalent among a community at a special time and produced by some special causes"), as in West Virginia, where the special cause was the closing of coal mines and steel plants; Negroes and Puerto Ricans, who are a fourth of the total poor; the alcoholic derelicts in the big-city skid rows; the hillbillies from Kentucky, Tennessee, and Oklahoma who have migrated to Midwestern cities in search of better jobs. And, finally, almost half our "senior citizens."

The only pages in "Poverty and Deprivation" that can be read are the statistical tables. The rest is a jungle of inchoate data that seems deliberately to eschew, like other collective research projects, such human qualities as reason (the reader has to do most of the work of ordering the material) and feeling (if Mr. Harrington sometimes has too much, it is a venial sin compared to the bleakness of this prose). My hypothesis is that "Poverty and Deprivation" was composed on that X-0 "electronic brain" at M.I.T. This would account both for the vitality of the tables and for the deadness of the text.

And what shall one say about the University of Michigan's "Income and Welfare in the United States"? Even its *tables* are not readable. And its text makes "Poverty and Deprivation" look like the Federalist Papers. On the first page, the authors unloose a generalization of stupefying generality: "The United States has arrived at the point where poverty could be abolished easily and simply by a stroke of the pen. [Where have we heard *that* before?] To raise every individual and family in the nation now below a subsistence income to the subsistence level would cost about $10 billion a year. This is less than 2 per cent of the gross national product. It is less than 10 per cent of tax revenues. [They mean, but forgot to say so, *federal* taxes, since if state and local taxes were added, the total would be much higher than $100 billion.] It is about one-fifth of the cost of national defense." (They might have added that it is slightly more than three times the $3 billion Americans spend on their dogs and cats and canaries every year.) This got big headlines in the press, as must have been expected: " 'STROKE OF PEN' COULD ELIMINATE POVERTY IN U. S., 4 SCIENTISTS SAY." But the authors, having dropped the $10 billion figure on the first page, never explain its meaning—is it a seedbed operation or a permanent dole? They are not clear even on how they arrived at it. At their own estimate of 35,000,000 poor, $10 billion would work out to slightly less than $300 per person. This seems too little to abolish poverty "easily and simply by a stroke of the pen."

There are other vaguenesses: "A careful analysis of the characteristics of families whose incomes are inadequate reveals that they should earn considerably more than they do on the basis of their education and other characteristics. The multivariate analysis . . . indicates that heads of poor families should average $2,204 in earnings. In fact heads of poor families earned an average of only $932 in 1959." I have already confessed my inability to understand the multivariate analysis, but the compilers seem to be saying that according to the variables in their study (race, age, sex, education, physical disabilities, and locale), heads of poor families should now be making twice as much as they are. And why don't they? "The discrepancy may arise from psychological dependency, lack of motivation, lack of intelligence, and a variety of other factors that were not studied—and what those "other factors" were, exactly. Also, whether such a discrepancy—the earnings the researchers expected to find were actually more than twice those they *did* find—may not indicate some ghastly flaw in that "multivariate analysis." There is, of course, no suggestion in the book that Dr. Morgan and his team are in any way worried.

The most obvious citizens of the Other America are those whose skins are the wrong color. The folk slogans are realistic: "Last to be hired, first to be fired" and "If you're black, stay back." There has been some progress. In 1939, the non-white worker's wage averaged 41.4 per cent of the white worker's; by 1958 it had climbed to 58 per cent. A famous victory, but the non-whites still average only slightly more than half as much as the whites. Even this modest gain was due not to any Rooseveltian or

Trumanian social reform but merely to the fact that for some years there was a war on and workers were in demand, whether black, white, or violet. By 1947, the non-whites had achieved most of their advance—to 54 per cent of white earnings, which means they have gained, in the last fifteen years, just 4 per cent.

The least obvious poverty affects our "senior citizens"—those over sixty-five. Mr. Harrington estimates that half of them—8,000,000—live in poverty, and he thinks they are even more atomized and politically helpless than the rest of the Other America. He estimates that one-fourth of the "unrelated individuals" among them, or a million persons, have less than $580 a year, which is about what is allotted *for food alone* in the Department of Agriculture's minimum-subsistence budget. (The average American family now spends only 20 per cent of its income for food—an indication of the remarkable prosperity we are all enjoying, except for one-quarter of us.) One can imagine, or perhaps one can't, what it would be like to live on $580 a year, or $11 a week. It is only fair to note that most of our senior citizens do better: The average per-capita income of those over sixty-five is now estimated to be slightly over $20 a week. That is, about $1,000 a year.

The aged poor have two sources of income besides their earnings or savings. One is contributions by relatives. A 1961 White House Conference Report put this at 10 per cent of income, which works out to $8 a week for an income of $4,000—and the 8,000,000 aged poor all have less than that. The other is Social Security, whose benefits in 1959 averaged $18 a week. Even this modest sum is more than any of the under-$4,000 got, since payments are proportionate to earnings and the poor, of course, earned less than the rest. A quarter of them, and those in general the neediest, are not covered by Social Security. The last resort is relief, and Mr. Harrington describes most vividly the humiliations the poor often have to put up with to get that.

The problem of the aged poor is aggravated by the fact that, unlike the Italians or the English, we seem to have little respect for or interest in our "senior citizens," beyond giving them that honorific title, and we don't include them in family life. If we can afford it, we are likely to send them to nursing homes—"a storage-bin philosophy," a Senate report calls it—and if we can't, which is the case with the poor, they must make do with the resources noted above. The Michigan study has a depressing chapter on "The Economics of Living with Relatives." Nearly two-thirds of the heads of families queried were opposed to having their aged parents live with their children. "The old do not understand the young, and the young do not understand the old or the young," observed one respondent, who must have had a sense of humor. Other replies were "Old people are pretty hard to get along with" and "The parents and the children try to boss each other and when they live with you there's always fighting." The minority in favor gave practical reasons, like "It's a good thing to have them with you so you can see after them" and "The old folks might get a pension or something, so they could help you out." Hardly anyone expressed any particular respect for the old, or a feeling that their experience might enrich family life. The most depressing finding was "People most able to provide support for relatives are most opposed to it. Older people with some college education are eleven to one against it." The most favorable toward including older people in the home were Negroes, and even they were mostly against it.

The whole problem of poverty and the aged is especially serious today because Americans are living longer. In the first half of this century, life expectancy increased 17.6 years for men and 20.3 years for women. And between 1950 and 1960 the over-sixty-five group increased twice as fast as the population as a whole.

The worst part of being old and poor in this country is the loneliness. Mr. Harrington notes that we have not only racial ghettos but geriatric ones, in the cheap rooming-house districts of large cities. He gives one peculiarly disturbing statistic: "One-third of the aged in the United States, some 5,000,000 or more human beings, have no phone in their place of residence. They are literally cut off from the rest of America."

Ernest Hemingway's celebrated deflation of Scott Fitzgerald's romantic notion that the rich are "different" somehow—"Yes, they have money" —doesn't apply to the poor. They are different in more important ways than their lack of money, as Mr. Harrington demonstrates:

> Emotional upset is one of the main forms of the vicious circle of impoverishment. The structure of the society is hostile to these people. The poor tend to become pessimistic and depressed; they seek immediate gratification instead of saving; they act out.
>
> Once this mood, this unarticulated philosophy becomes a fact, society can change, the recession can end, and yet there is no motive for movement. The depression has become internalized. The middle class looks upon this process and sees "lazy" people who "just don't want to get ahead." People who are much too sensitive to demand of cripples that they run races ask of the poor that they get up and act just like everyone else in the society.
>
> The poor are not like everyone else. . . . They think and feel differently; they look upon a different America than the middle class looks upon.

The poor are also different in a physical sense: they are much less healthy. According to "Poverty and Deprivation," the proportion of those "disabled or limited in their major activity by chronic ill health" rises sharply as income sinks. In reasonably well-off families ($7,000 and up), 4.3 per cent are so disabled; in reasonably poor families ($2,000 to $3,999), the proportion doubles, to 8 per cent; and in unreasonably poor families (under $2,000), it doubles again, to 16.5 per cent. An obvious cause, among others, for the very poor being four times as much disabled by "chronic ill health" as the well-to-do is that they have much less money to spend for medical care—in fact, almost nothing. This weighs with special heaviness on the aged poor. During the fifties, Mr. Harrington notes, "all costs on the Consumer Price Index went up by 12 per cent. But medical costs, that terrible staple of the aged, went up by 36 per cent, hospitalization rose by 65 per cent, and group hospitalization costs (Blue Cross premiums) were up by 83 per cent."

This last figure is particularly interesting, since Blue Cross and such plans are the A.M.A.'s alternative to socialized medicine, or, rather, to the timid fumblings toward it that even our most liberal politicians have dared to propose. Such figures throw an unpleasant light on the Senate's rejection of Medicare. The defeat was all the more bitter because, in the usual effort to appease the conservatives (with the usual lack of success—only five Republicans and only four Southern Democrats voted pro), the bill was watered down in advance. Not until he had spent $90 of his own money—which is 10 per cent of the annual income of some 3,000,000 aged poor—would a patient have been eligible. And the original program included only people already covered by Social Security or Railroad Retirement pensions and excluded the neediest of all—the 2,500,000 aged poor who are left out of both these systems. These untouchables were finally included in order to placate five liberal Republican senators, led by Javits of New York. They did vote for Medicare, but they were the only Republicans who did.

Mental as well as physical illness is much greater among the poor, even though our complacent cliché is that nervous breakdowns are a prerogative of the rich because the poor "can't afford" them. (They can't, but they have them anyway.) This bit of middle-class folklore should be laid to rest by a study made in New Haven: "Social Class and Mental Illness," by August B. Hollingshead and Frederick C. Redlich (Wiley). They found that the rate of "treated psychiatric illness" is about the same from the rich down through decently paid workers—an average of 573 per 100,000. But in the bottom fifth it shoots up to 1,659 per 100,000. There is an even more striking difference in the *kind* of mental illness. Of those in the four top income groups who had undergone psychiatric treatment, 65 per cent had been treated for neurotic problems and 35 per cent for psychotic disturbances. In the bottom fifth, the treated illnesses were almost all psychotic (90 per cent). This shows there is something to the notion that the poor "can't afford" nervous breakdowns—the milder kind, that is—since the reason the proportion of *treated* neuroses among the poor is only 10 per cent is that a neurotic can keep going, after a fashion. But the argument cuts deeper the other way. The poor go to a psychiatrist (or, more commonly, are committed to a mental institution) only when they are completely unable to function because of psychotic symptoms. Therefore, even that nearly threefold increase in mental disorders among the poor is probably an underestimate.

The poor are different, then, both physically and psychologically. During the fifties, a team of psychiatrists from Cornell studied "Midtown," a residential area in this city that contained 170,000 people, of all social classes. The area was 99 per cent white, so the findings may be presumed to understate the problem of poverty. The description of the poor—the "low social economic status individual"—is blunt: "[They are] rigid, suspicious, and have a fatalistic outlook on life. They do not plan ahead. . . . They are prone to depression, have feelings of futility, lack of belongingness, friendliness, and a lack of trust in others." Only a Dr. Pangloss would expect anything else. As Mr. Harrington points out, such characteristics are "a realistic adaptation to a socially perverse situation."

As for the isolation that is the lot of the American poor, that is a point on which Mr. Harrington is very good:

> America has a self-image of itself as a nation of joiners and doers. There are social clubs, charities, community drives, and the like. [One might add organizations like the Elks and Masons, Rotary and Kiwanis, cultural groups like our women's clubs, also alumni associations and professional organizations.] And yet this entire structure is a phenomenon of the middle class. Some time ago, a study in Franklin, Indiana [this vagueness of reference is all too typical of "The Other America"], reported that the percentage of people in the bottom class who were without affiliations of any kind was eight times as great as the percentage in the high-income class.
>
> Paradoxically, one of the factors that intensifies the social isolation of the poor is that America thinks of itself as a nation without social classes. As a result, there are few social or civic organizations that are separated on the basis of income and class. The "working-class culture" that sociologists have described in a country like England does not exist here. . . . The poor person who might want to join an organization is afraid. Because he or she will have less education, less money, less competence to articulate ideas than anyone else in the group, they stay away.

One reason our society is a comparatively violent one is that the French and Italian and British poor have a communal life and culture that the American poor lack. As one reads "The Other America," one wonders why there is not even more violence than there is.

The richest city of all, New York, has been steadily growing poorer, if one looks beyond Park Avenue and Wall Street. Of its 2,080,000 families, just under half (49 per cent) had incomes in 1959 of less than $6,000; for the city's non-white families, the percentage was 71. And a fourth of all New York families in 1959 were below the poverty line of $4,000. These percentages are at present slightly higher than the national average—an ominous reversal of the city's earlier position. In 1932, the average national weekly wage was only 67 per cent of the New York City average. In 1960, it was 108 per cent. The city's manufacturing workers in 1946 earned $11 more a week than the national average; in 1960 they earned $6.55 a week less. The two chief reasons are probably the postwar influx of Puerto Ricans and the exodus to the suburbs of the well-to-do. But whatever the reasons, the city seems to be turning into an economically backward area, like Arkansas or New Hampshire. Even the bankers—the "non-supervisory" ones, that is—are modestly paid: 54 per cent of the males and 78 per cent of the females make less than $80 a week. All these statistics come from John O'Rourke, president of Joint Council 16, International Brotherhood of Teamsters, which has 168,000 members in the area. Mr. O'Rourke has been campaigning to persuade Mayor Wagner to raise the city's minimum hourly wage to $1.50. (The Mayor had gone as far as $1.25.) The New York teamsters are motivated by enlightened self-interest: the more other wages stagnate, the harder it will be to maintain their own comparatively high level of pay. They complain especially about the low wages in the highly organized garment trade, to which Mr. Dubinsky's International Ladies' Garment Workers' Union replies that if it presses for higher wages the manufactures will simply move to low-wage, non-union areas, mostly in the South, as the New England textile manufacturers did many years ago—a riposte that is as realistic as it is uncheering. However, Mr. O'Rourke has an enterprising research staff, plenty of persistence, and a sharp tongue. "New Yorkers," he says, "are accustomed to thinking of themselves as pacesetters in an allegedly affluent society [but] at the rate we are going, we will soon qualify for the title 'Sweatshop Capital of the Nation.'"

The main reason the American poor have become invisible is that since 1936 their numbers have been reduced by two-thirds. Astounding as it may seem, the fact is that President Roosevelt's "one-third of a nation" was a considerable understatement; over two-thirds of us then lived below the poverty line, as is shown by the tables that follow. But today the poor are a minority, and minorities can be ignored if they are so heterogeneous that they cannot be organized. When the poor were a majority, they simply could not be overlooked. Poverty is also hard to see today because the middle class ($6,000 to $14,999) has vastly increased —from 13 per cent of all families in 1936 to a near-majority (47 per cent) today. That mass poverty can persist despite this rise to affluence is hard to believe, or see, especially if one is among those who have risen.

Two tables in "Poverty and Deprivation" summarize what has been happening in the last thirty years. They cover only multiple-person families; all figures are converted to 1960 dollars; and the income is before taxes. I have omitted, for clarity, all fractions.

The first table is the percentage of families with a given income:

	1935–6	1947	1953	1960
Under $ 4,000	68%	37%	28%	23%
$4,000 to $ 5,999	17	29	28	23
$6,000 to $ 7,499	6	12	17	16
$7,500 to $14,999	7	17	23	31
Over $15,000	2	4	5	7

The second table is the share each group had in the family income of the nation:

	1935–6	1947	1953	1960
Under $ 4,000	35%	16%	11%	7%
$4,000 to $ 5,999	21	24	21	15
$6,000 to $ 7,499	10	14	17	14
$7,500 to $14,999	16	28	33	40
Over $15,000	18	18	19	24

Several interesting conclusions can be drawn from these tables:

(1) The New Deal didn't do anything about poverty: The under-$4,000 families in 1936 were 68 per cent of the total population, which was slightly *more* than the 1929 figure of 65 per cent.

(2) The war economy (hot and cold) did do something about poverty: Between 1936 and 1960 the proportion of all families who were poor was reduced from 68 per cent to 23 per cent.

(3) If the percentage of under-$4,000 families decreased by two-thirds between 1936 and 1960, their share of the national income dropped a great deal more—from 35 per cent to 7 per cent.

(4) The well-to-do ($7,500 to $14,999) have enormously increased, from 7 per cent of all families in 1936 to 31 per cent today. The rich ($15,000 and over) have also multiplied—from 2 to 7 per cent. But it should be noted that the very rich, according to another new study, "The Share of Top Wealth-Holders in National Wealth, 1922–1956," by Robert J. Lampman (Princeton), have experienced a decline. He finds that the top 1 per cent of wealth-holders owned 38 per cent of the national wealth in 1929 and own only 28 per cent today. (Though let's not get sentimental over that "only.") Thus, *pace* Dr. Kolko, there has in fact been a redistribution of wealth—in favor of the well-to-do and the rich at the expense of the poor and the very rich.

(5) The reduction of poverty has slowed down. In the six years 1947–53, the number of poor families declined 9 per cent, but in the following seven years only 5 per cent. The economic stasis that set in with Eisenhower and that still persisted under Kennedy was responsible. (This stagnation, however, did not affect the over-$7,500 families, who increased from 28 per cent to 38 per cent between 1953 and 1960.) In the New York

Times Magazine for last November 11th, Herman P. Miller, of the Bureau of the Census, wrote, "During the forties, lower-paid occupations made the greatest relative gains in average income. Laborers and service workers . . . had increases of about 180% . . . and professional and managerial workers, the highest paid workers of all, had the lowest relative gains—96%." But in the last decade the trend has been reversed; laborers and service workers have gained 39% while professional-managerial workers have gained 68%. This is because in the war-time forties the unskilled were in great demand, while now they are being replaced by machines. Automation is today the same kind of menace to the unskilled—that is, the poor—that the enclosure movement was to the British agricultural population centuries ago. "The facts show that our 'social revolution' ended nearly twenty years ago," Mr. Miller concludes, "yet important segments of the American public, many of them highly placed Government officials and prominent educators, think and act as though it were a continuing process."

"A reduction of about 19% [in the under-$6,000 families] in more than thirty years, or at a rate of about 0.7% per year, is no ground for complacency," the authors of "Poverty and Deprivation" justly observe. There is even less ground for complacency in the recent figures on *extreme* poverty. The authors estimate the number of families in 1929 with incomes of under $2,000 (in current dollars) at 7,500,000. By 1947 there were less than 4,000,000, not because of any philanthropic effort by their more prosperous fellow-citizens but entirely because of those first glorious years of a war economy. Six years later, in 1953, when the economy had begun to slow down, there were still 3,300,000 of the families with incomes of less than $2,000, and seven years later, in 1960, "there had been no further reduction." Thus in the last fifteen years the bottom dogs have remained on the bottom, sharing hardly at all in the advances that the income groups above them have made in an ascending scale that is exquisitely adjusted, by the automatic workings of capitalism, so that it is inversely proportionate to need.

There are, finally, the bottomest bottom dogs; i.e., *families* with incomes of *under $1,000*. I apologize for the italics, but some facts insist on them. According to "Poverty and Deprivation," the numbers of these families "appear to have risen slightly" of late (1953–60), from 800,000 to about 1,000,000. It is only fair, and patriotic, to add that according to the Commerce Department study, about 10,000,000 of our families and unattached individuals now enjoy incomes of $10,000 a year and up. So while some 3,500,000 Americans are in under-$1,000 families, ten times as many are in over-$10,000 families. Not bad at all—in a way.

The post-1940 decrease in poverty was not due to the policies or actions of those who are not poor, those in positions of power and responsibility. The war economy needed workers, wages went up, and the poor became less poor. When economic stasis set in, the rate of decrease in poverty slowed down proportionately, and it is still slow. Kennedy's efforts to "get the country moving again" have been unsuccessful, possibly because he has, despite the suggestions of many of his economic advisers, not yet advocated the one big step that might push the economy off dead center: a massive increase in government spending. This would be politically courageous, perhaps even dangerous, because of the superstitious fear of "deficit spending" and an "unbalanced" federal budget. American folklore insists that a government's budget must be arranged like a private family's. Walter Lippmann wrote, after the collapse of the stock market last spring:

> There is mounting evidence that those economists were right who told the Administration last winter that it was making the mistake of trying to balance the budget too soon. It will be said that the budget is not balanced: it shows a deficit in fiscal 1962 of $7 billion. . . . But . . . the budget that matters is the Department of Commerce's income and product accounts budget. Nobody looks at it except the economists [but] while the Administrative budget is necessary for administration and is like a man's checkbook, the income budget tells the real story. . . .
>
> [It] shows that at the end of 1962 the outgo and ingo accounts will be virtually in balance, with a deficit of only about half a billion dollars. Thus, in reality, the Kennedy administration is no longer stimulating the economy, and the economy is stagnating for lack of stimulation. We have one of the lowest rates of growth among the advanced industrial nations of the world.

One shouldn't be hard on the President. Franklin Roosevelt, a more daring and experimental politician, at least in his domestic policy, listened to the American disciples of J. M. Keynes in the early New Deal years and unbalanced his budgets, with splendid results. But by 1936 he had lost his nerve. He cut back government spending and there ensued the 1937 recession, from which the economy recovered only when war orders began to make up for the deficiency in domestic buying power. "Poverty and Deprivation" estimates that between 1953 and 1961 the annual growth rate of our economy was "only 2.5 per cent per annum contrasted with an estimated 4.2 per cent required to maintain utilization of manpower and other productive resources." The poor, who always experience the worst the first, understand quite personally the meaning of that dry statistic, as they understand Kipling's "The toad beneath the harrow knows/Exactly where each tooth-point goes." They are also most intimately acquainted with another set of statistics: the steady postwar rise in the unemployment rate, from 3.1 per cent in 1949 to 4.3 per cent in 1954 to 5.1 per cent in 1958 to over 7 per cent in 1961. (The Tory Government is worried because British unemployment is now at its highest point for the last three years. This point is 2.1 per cent, which is less than our lowest rate in the last fifteen years.)

Some of the post-1940 gains of the poor have been their own doing. "Moonlighting"—or holding two or more jobs at once—was practiced by about 3 per cent of the employed in 1950; today this percentage has almost doubled. Far more important is what might be called "wife-flitting": Between 1940 and 1957, the percentage of wives with jobs outside the home doubled, from 15 per cent to 30 per cent. The head of the United States Children's Bureau, Mrs. Katherine B. Oettinger, announced last summer, not at all triumphantly, that there are now two-thirds more working mothers than there were ten years ago and that these mothers have about 15,000,000 children under eighteen—of whom 4,000,000 are under six. This kind of economic enterprise ought to impress Senator Goldwater and the ideologues of the *National Review,* whose reaction to the poor, when they think about such an uninspiring subject, is "Why don't they *do* something about it?" The poor have done something about it and the family pay check is bigger and the statistics on poverty look better. But the effects on family life and on those 4,000,000 pre-school children is something else. Mrs. Oettinger quoted a roadside sign, "IRONING, DAY CARE AND WORMS FOR FISHING BAIT," and mentioned a baby-sitter who pacified her charge with sleeping pills and another who met the problem of a cold apartment by putting the baby in the oven. "The situation has become a 'national disgrace,' with many unfortunate conditions that do not come to public attention until a crisis arises," the *Times* summed up her conclusion. This crisis has finally penetrated to public attention. The President recently signed a law that might be called Day-care. It provides $5,000,000 for such facilities this fiscal year, which works out to $1.25 for each of the 4,000,000 under-six children with working mothers. Next year, the program will provide all of $2.50 per child. This is a free, democratic society's notion of an adequate response. Almost a century ago, Bismarck instituted in Germany state-financed social benefits far beyond anything we have yet ventured. Granted that he did it merely to take the play away from the Social Democratic Party founded by Marx and Engels. Still, one imagines that Count Bismarck must be amused—in the circle of Hell reserved for reactionaries—by that $2.50 a child.

It's not that Public Opinion doesn't become Aroused every now and then. But the arousement never leads to much. It was aroused twenty-four years ago when John Steinbeck published "The Grapes of Wrath," but Mr. Harrington reports that things in the Imperial Valley are still much the same: low wages, bad housing, no effective union. Public Opinion is too public—that is, too general; of its very nature, it can have no sustained interest in California agriculture. The only groups with such a continuing interest are the workers and the farmers who hire them.

Once Public Opinion ceased to be Aroused, the battle was again between the two antagonists with a real, personal stake in the outcome, and there was no question about which was stronger. So with the rural poor in general. In the late fifties, the average annual wage for white male American farm workers was slightly over $1,000; women, children, Negroes, and Mexicans got less. One recalls Edward R. Murrow's celebrated television program about these people, "Harvest of Shame." Once more everybody was shocked, but the harvest is still shameful. One also recalls that Mr. Murrow, after President Kennedy had appointed him head of the United States Information Agency, tried to persuade the B.B.C. not to show "Harvest of Shame." His argument was that it would give an undesirable "image" of America to foreign audiences.

There is a monotony about the injustices suffered by the poor that perhaps accounts for the lack of interest the rest of society shows in them. Everything seems to go wrong with them. They never win. It's just boring.

Public housing turns out not to be for them. The 1949 Housing Act authorized 810,000 new units of low-cost housing in the following four years. Twelve years later, in 1961, the A.F.L.-C.I.O. proposed 400,000 units to complete the lagging 1949 program. The Kennedy administration ventured to recommend 100,000 to Congress. Thus, instead of 810,000 low-cost units by 1953, the poor will get, if they are lucky, 500,000 by 1963. And they are more likely to be injured than helped by slum clearance, since the new projects usually have higher rents than the displaced slum-dwellers can afford. (There has been no dearth of government-financed *middle*-income housing since 1949.) These refugees from the bulldozers for the most part simply emigrate to other slums. They also become invisible; Mr. Harrington notes that half of them are recorded as "address unknown." Several years ago, Charles Abrams, who was New York State Rent Administrator under Harriman and who is now president of the National Committee Against Discrimination in Housing, summed up what he had learned in two decades in public housing: "Once social reforms have won total appeal in the public mind, their slogans and goal-symbols may degenerate into tools of the dominant class for beleaguering the minority and often for defeating the very aims which the original sponsors had intended for their reforms." Mr. Abrams was probably thinking, in part, of the Title I adventures of Robert Moses in dealing with New York housing. There is a Moses or two in every American city, determined to lead us away from the promised land.

And this is not the end of tribulation. The poor, who can least afford to lose pay because of ill health, lose the most. A National Health Survey, made a few years ago, found that workers earning under $2,000 a year had twice as many "restricted-activity days" as those earning over $4,000.

The poor are even fatter than the rich. (The cartoonists will have to revise their clichés.) "Obesity is seven times more frequent among women of the lowest socio-economic level than it is among those of the highest level," state Drs. Moore, Stunkard, and Srole in a recent issue of the *Journal of the American Medical Association*. (The proportion is almost the same for men.) They also found that overweight associated with poverty is related to mental disease. Fatness used to be a sign of wealth, as it still is in some parts of Africa, but in more advanced societies it is now a stigma of poverty, since it means too many cheap carbohydrates and too little exercise—which has changed from a necessity for the poor into a luxury for the rich, as may be confirmed by a glance at the models in any fashion magazine.

Although they are the most in need of hospital insurance, the poor have the least, since they can't afford the premiums; only 40 per cent of poor families have it, as against 63 per cent of all families. (It should be noted, however, that the poor who are war veterans can get free treatment, at government expense, in Veterans Administration Hospitals.)

The poor actually pay more taxes, in proportion to their income, than the rich. A recent study by the Tax Foundation estimates that 28 per cent of incomes under $2,000 goes for taxes, as against 24 per cent of the incomes of families earning five to seven times as much. Sales and other excise taxes are largely responsible for this curious statistic. It is true that such taxes fall impartially on all, like the blessed rain from heaven, but it is a form of egalitarianism that perhaps only Senator Goldwater can fully appreciate.

The final irony is that the Welfare State, which Roosevelt erected and which Eisenhower, no matter how strongly he felt about it, didn't attempt to pull down, is not for the poor, either. Agricultural workers are not covered by Social Security, nor are many of the desperately poor among the aged, such as "unrelated individuals" with incomes of less than $1,000, of whom only 37 per cent are covered, which is just half the percentage of coverage among the aged in general. Of the Welfare State, Mr. Harrington says, "Its creation had been stimulated by mass impoverishment and misery, yet it helped the poor least of all. Laws like unemployment compensation, the Wagner Act, the various farm programs, all these were designed for the middle third in the cities, for the organized workers, and for the . . . big market farmers. . . . [It] benefits those least who need help most." The industrial workers, led by John L. Lewis, mobilized enough political force to put through Section 7(a) of the National Industrial Recovery Act, which, with the Wagner Act, made the C.I.O. possible. The big farmers put enough pressure on Henry Wallace, Roosevelt's first Secretary of Agriculture—who talked a good fight for liberal principles but was a Hamlet when it came to action—to establish the two basic propositions of Welfare State agriculture: subsidies that now cost $3 billion a year and that chiefly benefit the big farmers; and the exclusion of sharecroppers, tenant farmers, and migratory workers from the protection of minimum-wage and Social Security laws.

No doubt the Kennedy administration would like to do more for the poor than it has, but it is hampered by the cabal of Republicans and Southern Democrats in Congress. The 1961 revision of the Fair Labor Standards Act, which raised the national minimum wage to the not exorbitant figure of $1.15 an hour, was a slight improvement over the previous act. For instance, it increased coverage of retail-trade workers from 3 per cent to 33 per cent. (But one-fourth of the retail workers still excluded earn less than $1 an hour.) There was also a considerable amount of shadowboxing involved: Of the 3,600,000 workers newly covered, only 663,000 were making less than $1 an hour. And there was the exclusion of a particularly ill-paid group of workers. Nobody had anything against the laundry workers *personally*. It was just that they were weak, unorganized, and politically expendable. To appease the conservatives in Congress, whose votes were needed to get the revision through, they were therefore expended. The result is that of the 500,000 workers in the laundry, dry-cleaning, and dyeing industries, just 17,000 are now protected by the Fair Labor Standards Act.

In short, one reaches the unstartling conclusion that rewards in class societies, including Communist ones, are according to power rather than need. A recent illustration is the campaign of an obscure organization called Veterans of World War I of the U. S. A. to get a bill through Congress for pensions of about $25 a week. It was formed by older men who think other veterans' organizations (such as the American Legion, which claims 2,500,000 members to their 200,000) are dominated by the relatively young. It asks for pensions for veterans of the First World War with incomes of under $2,400 (if single) or $3,600 (if married)—that is, only for *poor* veterans. The editorials have been violent: "STOP THIS VETERANS' GRAB," implored the *Herald Tribune;* "WORLD WAR I PENSION GRAB," echoed the *Saturday Evening Post*. Their objection was, in part, that many of the beneficiaries would not be bonafide poor, since pensions, annuities, and Social Security benefits were excluded from the maximum income needed to qualify. Considering that the average Social Security payment is about $1,000 a year, this would not put any potential beneficiary into the rich or even the comfortably-off class, even if one assumes another $1,000, which is surely too high, from annuities and pensions. It's all very confusing. The one clear aspect is that the minuscule Veterans of World War I of the U. S. A. came very near to bringing it off. Although their bill was opposed by both the White House and by the chairman of the House Committee on Veterans' Affairs, two hundred and one members of the House signed a petition to bring the measure to a vote, only eighteen less than needed "to accomplish this unusual parliamentary strategy," as the *Times* put it. These congressmen were motivated by politics rather than charity, one may assume. Many were up for reëlection last November, and the two hundred thousand Veterans of World War I had two advantages over the fifty million poor: They were organized, and they had a patriotic appeal only a wink away from the demagogic. Their "unusual parliamentary strategy" failed by eighteen votes in the Congress. But there will be another Congress.

It seems likely that mass poverty will continue in this country for a long time. The more it is reduced, the harder it is to keep on reducing it. The poor, having dwindled from two-thirds of the population in 1936 to one-quarter today, no longer are a significant political force, as is shown by the Senate's rejection of Medicare and by the Democrats' dropping it as an issue in the elections last year. Also, as poverty decreases, those left behind tend more and more to be the ones who have for so long accepted poverty as their destiny that they need outside help to climb out of it. This new minority mass poverty, so much more isolated and hopeless than the old majority poverty, shows signs of becoming chronic. "The permanence of low incomes is inferred from a variety of findings," write the authors of the Michigan survey. "In many poor families the head has never earned enough to cover the family's present needs." They give a vignette of what the statistics mean in human terms:

> For most families, however, the problem of chronic poverty is seri-
> ous. One such family is headed by a thirty-two-year-old man who
> is employed as a dishwasher. Though he works steadily and more
> than full time, he earned slightly over $2,000 in 1959. His wife earned
> $300 more, but their combined incomes are not enough to support
> themselves and their three children. Although the head of the family
> is only thirty-two, he feels that he has no chance of advancement
> partly because he finished only seven grades of school. . . . The
> possibility of such families leaving the ranks of the poor is not high.

Children born into poor families today have less chance of "improving themselves" than the children of the pre-1940 poor. Rags to riches is now more likely to be rags to rags. "Indeed," the Michigan surveyors conclude, "it appears that a number of the heads of poor families have moved into less skilled jobs than their fathers had." Over a third of the children of the poor, according to the survey, don't go beyond the eighth grade and "will probably perpetuate the poverty of their parents." There are a great many of these children. In an important study of poverty, made for a Congressional committee in 1959, Dr. Robert J. Lampman estimated that eleven million of the poor were under eighteen. "A considerable number of younger persons are starting life in a condition of 'inherited poverty,'" he observed. To which Mr. Harrington adds, "The character of poverty has changed, and it has become more deadly for the young. It is no longer associated with immigrant groups with high aspirations; it is now identified with those whose social existence makes it more and more difficult to break out into the larger society." Even when children from poor families show intellectual promise, there is nothing in the values of their friends or families to encourage them to make use of it. Dr. Kolko, citing impressive sources, states that of the top 16 per cent of high-school students—those scoring 120 and over in I.Q. tests—only half go on to college. The explanation for this amazing—and alarming—situation is as much cultural as economic. The children of the poor now tend to lack what the sociologists call "motivation." At least one foundation is working on the problem of why so many bright children from poor families don't ever try to go beyond high school.

Mr. Raymond M. Hilliard, at present director of the Cook County (i.e., Chicago) Department of Public Aid and formerly Commissioner of Welfare for New York City, recently directed a "representative-sample" investigation, which showed that more than half of the 225,000 able-bodied Cook County residents who were on relief were "functionally illiterate." One reason Cook County has to spend $16,500,000 a month on relief is "the lack of basic educational skills of relief recipients which are essential to compete in our modern society." An interesting footnote, apropos of recent happenings at "Ole Miss," is that the illiteracy rate of the relief recipients who were educated in Chicago is 33 per cent, while among those who were educated in Mississippi and later moved to Chicago it is 77 per cent.

The problem of educating the poor has changed since 1900. Then it was the language and cultural difficulties of immigrants from foreign countries; now it is the subtler but more intractable problems of internal migration from backward regions, mostly in the South. The old immigrants wanted to Better Themselves and to Get Ahead. The new migrants are less ambitious, and they come into a less ambitious atmosphere. "When they arrive in the city," wrote Christopher Jencks in an excellent two-part survey, "Slums and Schools," in the *New Republic* last fall, "they join others equally unprepared for urban life in the slums—a milieu which is in many ways utterly dissociated from the rest of America. Often this milieu is self-perpetuating. I have been unable to find any statistics on how many of these migrants' children and grandchildren have become middle-class, but it is probably not too inaccurate to estimate that about 30,000,000 people live in urban slums, and that about half are second-generation residents." The immigrants of 1890–1910 also arrived in a milieu that was "in many ways utterly dissociated from the rest of America," yet they had a vision—a rather materialistic one, but still a vision—of what life in America could be if they worked hard enough; and they did work, and they did aspire to something more than they had; and they did get out of the slums. The disturbing thing about the poor today is that so many of them seem to lack any such vision. Mr. Jencks remarks:

> While the economy is changing in a way which makes the eventual liquidation of the slums at least conceivable, young people are not seizing the opportunities this change presents. Too many are dropping

out of school before graduation (more than half in many slums); too few are going to college. . . . As a result there are serious shortages of teachers, nurses, doctors, technicians, and scientifically trained executives, but 4,500,000 unemployables.

"Poverty is the parent of revolution and crime," Aristotle wrote. This is now a half truth—the last half. Our poor are alienated; they don't consider themselves part of society. But precisely because they don't they are not politically dangerous. It is people with "a stake in the country" who make revolutions. The best—though by no means the only—reason for worrying about the Other America is that its existence should make us feel uncomfortable.

The federal government is the only purposeful force—I assume wars are not purposeful—that can reduce the numbers of the poor and make their lives more bearable. The authors of "Poverty and Deprivation" take a dim view of the Kennedy administration's efforts to date:

> The Federal Budget is the most important single instrument available to us as a free people to induce satisfactory economic performance, and to reduce poverty and deprivation. . . .
> Projected Federal outlays in the fiscal 1963 Budget are too small. The items in this Budget covering programs directly related to human improvement and the reduction of mass poverty and deprivation allocate far too small a portion of our total national production to these great purposes.

The effect of government policy on poverty has two quite distinct aspects. One is the indirect effect of the stimulation of the economy by federal spending. Such stimulation—though by wartime demands rather than government policy—has in the past produced a prosperity that did cut down American poverty by almost two-thirds. But I am inclined to agree with Dr. Galbraith that it would not have a comparable effect on present-day poverty:

> It is assumed that with increasing output poverty must disappear [he writes]. Increased output eliminated the general poverty of all who worked. Accordingly it must, sooner or later, eliminate the special poverty that still remains. . . . Yet just as the arithmetic of modern politics makes it tempting to overlook the very poor, so the supposition that increasing output will remedy their case has made it easy to do so too.

He underestimates the massiveness of American poverty, but he is right when he says there is now a hard core of the specially disadvantaged— because of age, race, environment, physical or mental defects, etc.—that would not be significantly reduced by general prosperity. (Although I think the majority of our present poor *would* benefit, if only by a reduction in the present high rate of unemployment.)

To do something about this hard core, a second line of government policy would be required; namely, direct intervention to help the poor. We have had this since the New Deal, but it has always been grudging and miserly, and we have never accepted the principle that every citizen should be provided, at state expense, with a reasonable minimum standard of living regardless of any other considerations. It should not depend on earnings, as does Social Security, which continues the inequalities and inequities and so tends to keep the poor forever poor. Nor should it exclude millions of our poorest citizens because they lack the political pressure to force their way into the Welfare State. The governmental obligation to provide, out of taxes, such a minimum living standard for all who need it should be taken as much for granted as free public schools have always been in our history.

It may be objected that the economy cannot bear the cost, and certainly costs must be calculated. But the point is not the calculation but the principle. Statistics—and especially statistical forecasts—can be pushed one way or the other. Who can determine in advance to what extent the extra expense of giving our 40,000,000 poor enough income to rise above the poverty line would be offset by the lift to the economy from their increased purchasing power? We really don't know. Nor did we know what the budgetary effects would be when we established the principle of free public education. The rationale then was that all citizens should have an equal chance of competing for a better status. The rationale now is different: that every citizen has a right to become or remain part of our society because if this right is denied, as it is in the case of at least one-fourth of our citizens, it impoverishes us all. Since 1932, "the goverment"—local, state, and federal—has recognized a responsibility to provide its citizens with a subsistence living. Apples will never again be sold on the street by jobless accountants, it seems safe to predict, nor will any serious political leader ever again suggest that share-the-work and local charity can solve the problem of unemployment. "Nobody starves" in this country any more, but, like every social statistic, this is a tricky business. Nobody starves, but who can measure the starvation, not to be calculated by daily intake of proteins and calories, that reduces life for many of our poor to a long vestibule to death? Nobody starves, but every fourth citizen rubs along on a standard of living that is below what Mr. Harrington defines as "the minimal levels of health, housing, food, and education that our present stage of scientific knowledge specifies as necessary for life as it is now lived in the United States." Nobody starves, but a fourth of us are excluded from the common social existence. Not to be able to afford a movie or a glass of beer is a kind of starvation—if everybody else can.

The problem is obvious: the persistence of mass poverty in a prosperous country. The solution is also obvious: to provide, out of taxes, the kind of subsidies that have always been given to the public schools (not to mention the police and fire departments and the post office)—subsidies that would raise incomes above the poverty level, so that every citizen could feel he is indeed such. *"Civis Romanus sum!"* cried St. Paul when he was threatened with flogging—and he was not flogged. Until our poor can be proud to say *"Civis Americanus sum!,"* until the act of justice that would make this possible has been performed by the three-quarters of Americans who are not poor—until then the shame of the Other America will continue.

Contemporary Economic Problems

36. Interests, Ideologies, and the Problem of Stability and Growth *

Edward S. Mason

The question I propose to consider is whether or to what extent the current relations between government and various interest groups in the United States prevent, or at least handicap, the attainment of stability and growth. That this question is both serious and difficult requires no argument. It is now six years since we have experienced a level of unemployment as low as 4 per cent of the labor force. During this period the growth of national income has been substantially below the long-term trend. During this same period nearly all of the advanced countries of Western Europe have established an employment record much better than ours and most of them have attained a growth rate which, though it may not persist, is currently at least double the U. S. rate. Are the relations between government, business, and labor in these countries more conducive to stability and growth and, if so, is there something we could learn from them?

Stabilization, of course, must be interpreted within the context of a continuous increase in the labor force and the employment of capital. It is a necessary but not sufficient condition to the attainment of whatever is considered to be a feasible and adequate growth rate. The movement

* Presidential address delivered at the Seventy-Fifth Annual Meeting of the American Economic Association, Pittsburgh, December 27, 1962.

"Interests, Ideologies, and the Problem of Stability and Growth," by Edward S. Mason, is reprinted by permission from the *American Economic Review*, LIII (March, 1963), 1–18.

from a relatively high to a relatively satisfactory level of unemployment is not a once-and-for-all step towards higher national income but a preliminary condition to a growth rate that is probably somewhat higher than is possible with substantial slack in the economy. Obviously stabilization policy does not encompass the whole of the growth problem. Denison has made us familiar with some of the steps that would need to be taken if we seek to raise the full employment growth rate [2]. The prospects for growth can also be affected by the choice of routes toward full employment. I am not, however, concerned here with an examination of the full range of growth considerations. I link stabilization with growth policy because there is in fact a connection. The investment, pricing, and innovation practices of firms operating at high levels of capacity would appear to be more conducive to growth in the economy as a whole than policies adapted to substantial slack. But it is only in this sense that I am here concerned with growth problems.

The relations of special groups to government as they affect stabilization and growth policies are usually discussed under the headings of "interests" and "ideologies." Are there objective economic interests represented by particular groups having sufficient political power to influence public action which impede or prevent effective stabilization or growth policies? Are there casts of thought or opinion motivated (subconsciously) by interests, and permitted to survive by ignorance, that effectively handicap sensible action? Keynes held firm views on these questions and in a famous phrase asserted that "it is ideas, not vested interests, which are dangerous for good and evil." On the other hand he painted a picture of the role of government in a mature society together with the "euthanasia of the rentier" that was not calculated to appeal to their interests as conceived by all groups. My colleague, J. K. Galbraith, has written in the same vein and has succeeded in antagonizing a good part of the profession by describing as "conventional wisdom" the orthodox ideas he conceived as impediments to progress. I suppose that the opposite of conventional wisdom is enlightened wisdom which, if we possessed it, would certainly help in the solution of the problems before us. But, in addition to interests and ideologies, I should like to introduce another range of considerations that needs to be taken into account. I refer to sheer ignorance.

When one considers the outcome, during the last year or two, of short-term forecasts undertaken by some of the most respected of our colleagues both in and out of government it is difficult to resist the conclusion that there are some things about the functioning of the economy that we do not yet know. Let me illustrate this point with another example. What would be the probable effect on the U. S. balance of payments if we attemped by appropriate fiscal and monetary measures to attain a 4 per cent unemployment rate by, say, July 1, 1964? It is certainly possible to say something about what would be involved in sectoral growth rates and to proceed from this to a reasonable estimate of the effect on commodity imports. One view, held in respectable quarters, is that such a development would bring with it an increase in gross national product of about $30 billion (over and above the growth that would be expected if the percentage of unemployment did not change) and an increase in commodity imports perhaps $1 billion. This adverse effect on the balance of payments would certainly be offset to some extent by a decrease in the flow of long-term investment capital abroad though this is much more difficult to estimate.

The difficulties are compounded when one attempts to estimate the effect of the proposed action on export earnings and on the flow of short-term funds. How will expansion of output affect the competitive position of U. S. exporters? Clearly much depends on what happens to wage rates, wage costs, and wage-price relationships. During the period 1955–57 when unemployment averaged 4.3 per cent the price level increased by 2½ per cent a year. On the other hand there were special influences at work, particularly in the durable goods area, that may make this period an inappropriate guide to future prospects. If some significant general rise in wage rates does take place and if prices are adjusted to this increase, the extent of the adverse effects on export earnings will depend, among other things, on what, in the meantime, happens to prices in the principal export markets. Clearly this is an area in which estimates will be subject to a sizeable margin of error. Finally, how will the Swiss bankers and their friends in Wall Street react to the particular combination of fiscal and monetary policies deemed necessary to attain a 4 per cent level of unemployment? Will short-term funds move out of the United States and will there be a large conversion of dollars into gold?

These difficulties and uncertainties are mentioned not to convey the impression that there is no solution to the problem but to suggest that there are several solutions, each one of which may be supported by intelligent and honorable men not obviously influenced either by interest or by dogma. It is certainly possible to support with strong arguments the position that the balance of payments comes first and that until confidence in the dollar has been restored it would be unwise to undertake any very significantly expansionary monetary or fiscal policy. It is also possible for sensible men to espouse the opposite position; that we can, by a proper combination of fiscal and monetary measures, move within a reasonable period of time to a position of full employment without inflicting on our balance of payments a strain that no practical expansion of international liquidity can manage.

This matter of ignorance is introduced into the discussion because it modifies quite substantially the significance to be attached to "interests" and "ideologies" in relation to stabilization and growth policies and because it has a bearing, I believe, on the questions whether and how a more satisfactory relationship between government and special groups may be established. It is possible to argue convincingly that vested interests of one sort or another prevent a solution of a problem only if it can be shown that in the absence of these interests the problem would in fact be solved. Certain modern Marxists, for example, with a Keynesian slant, hold that persistent stagnation must be our fate because, although government spending could fill the gap supposedly caused by an inadequacy of investment opportunities, private interests in the perpetuation of traditional government-business relations will not permit it to play this role. But to make a case for this view, it would be necessary to demonstrate that, (a) in the absence of a large increase in public spending, investment opportunities will in fact fall short of absorbing the intended volume of savings; (b) under these circumstances business interests will be better served by persistent stagnation than by any practical change in the role of government that could overcome stagnation; and (c) business has sufficient political power to impose its interests on the public. To the extent, however, that each of the propositions is shrouded in doubt, the significance to be attached to the role of vested or special interests becomes far from clear.

Parenthetically, it is a matter of some interest that the Marxian analysis of capitalism seems to have subtly shifted from an emphasis on the economic "laws" of capitalist development which must inevitably bring to a close this stage of history to an emphasis on the socio-economic structure of political power which will inhibit the use of any governmental measures that might be expected to make capitalism work.

To say, however, that the recognition of a substantial area of ignorance somewhat modifies our interpretation of the role of interests and ideologies is not to deny that interests and ideologies significantly limit and influence the choice of stabilization policies. As any reader of the public prints or of testimony before the Joint Economic Committee knows, quite different analyses of the reasons for the current stagnation and quite different recommendations for action emanate from business and labor groups. And quite different explanations of the "secret" of Western European growth rates are advanced.

It is difficult to characterize what is after all a fairly wide spectrum of business opinion, but typically two considerations dominate the business arguments: the burden of taxation on savings and investment and the power of trade unions to push up wage rates. It follows that any significant revamping of the tax structure should reduce the corporate income tax and the upper brackets of the personal income tax and if possible shift some of the burden from direct to indirect taxes. Even with this additional inducement to invest the economy will quickly tend to run into inflation unless something is done to curb the power of trade unions to push up wage rates. Since investment rather than consumption is the crux of the difficulty, monetary policy is to be preferred to fiscal measures designed to increase aggregate demand. If fiscal measures are nevertheless used they should clearly emphasize tax reduction rather than increase of government expenditures. And in no case should fiscal measures prevent a balancing of the budget over the business cycle. The business case tends to emphasize growth, mainly through increase in plant-and-equipment expenditures, rather than stabilization. Indeed, there is some tendency to deny the existence of a stabilization problem in any other sense than that which relates to the price level and balance of payments. The high unemployment figures tend to be attributed to the vagaries of U. S. employment statistics or to the unwillingness of labor to accept employment in the areas in which it is offered. Higher growth rates in various European countries are attributed to tax and monetary policies that are more adapted to a "capitalistic" environment than those of the United States.

The analysis of the problem as presented by labor spokesmen tends to rely heavily on the purchasing power argument. Increasing purchasing power by increasing wage rates is now, perhaps, somewhat passé because of the rather too obvious connection with wage costs and prices. Fiscal policy is currently the preferred route and increase in government expenditures has much to recommend it in view of deficiencies in services that only government can provide. If, however, tax reduction is preferred, cuts should be limited to the lower end of the scale where tax relief will increase consumption rather than savings. Investment is considered to be a function of output and profits will be fully adequate both as a source of savings and as an incentive to invest when the economy is operating at close to capacity. Collective bargaining as it presently functions is essentially satisfactory and there is no case either for reducing the bargaining power of unions or for administrative control of wages and prices. The balance-of-payments problem tends to be somewhat neglected in labor pronouncement, except as it is affected by the investment abroad of U. S. capital.

It is not my purpose here to evaluate either the business or the labor argument. It would be difficult, however, for such different analyses and recommendations to continue to exist side by side were it not for a substantial area of ignorance concerning the relation of magnitudes relevant to stabilization policy. Furthermore, the presence of ignorance seems, in a perverse sort of way, to harden conflicts and to exacerbate group relationships. It might be thought that the existence of considerable uncertainty concerning the effects of a proposed course of action might lead to a more cautious statement of claims and counterclaims. In fact, it seems to produce the reverse behavior. Since each group can rightfully claim that the opposition's case is not demonstrably correct or in certain respects is incomplete, the weakness of the case is attributed to the influence of special interests or willful misunderstanding. And under attack conceptions of interest tend to narrow and ideological positions to harden.

It must, of course, be recognized that institutional relations and ideologies do change under the pressures of circumstance. The 1930's witnessed a quasi-revolutionary shift in the relationship of government, business, and labor in the United States and this shift was accompanied by the public acceptance of substantial changes in ideas concerning the functioning of the economy and the role of government therein. A sobering question that now confronts us is whether it will require a longer period of stagnation and deeper depression than we have experienced over the last six years to force changes in institutional relationships and ideologies and, if so, what shape are those changes likely to take? Or is it possible through some process of social invention and adaptation to accomplish necessary changes without waiting for the build-up of irresistible pressures?

One of the difficulties in the current situation is that 5½ to 6 per cent unemployment and an annual growth rate of a little more than 2½ per cent do not seem too serious. Before the advent of unemployment insurance, unemployment meant misery. Now it is interpreted to mean lost output, a concept that presumably has some significance for statisticians, economists and such ilk but does not impinge heavily on the consciousness of most people. With per capita incomes at $2,800 and average family incomes between $6,000 and $7,000 it is also somewhat difficult to get excited about the lagging U. S. growth rate. Furthermore, it is easy for apologists of the *status quo* to point at any given time to the fact that output, employment or almost any figure you care to name is, in a favorite phrase, "the highest in our history." One is inclined to sympathize with the plaintive enquiry of Senator Javits who, after listening to testimony of this sort, was moved to ask "Why, if all of our indexes are up, are we very worried?" [12, p. 13].

It is, however, becoming increasingly difficult to deny that U. S. unemployment figures mean what they purport to mean. Even after adjustment to U. S. reporting techniques the unemployment rate in 1960 in France was 1.9 per cent, Great Britain 2.4 per cent, Germany 1 per cent, Sweden 1.5 per cent, while ours was 5.6 per cent [11, p. 220]. The divergence of our growth rate from those of the principal Western European growth rates, and indeed from our own long-term trend, has been too persistent and too glaring to be ignored. Moreover, though the record of the last five years may be brushed off as atypical, it is difficult to brush off the longer-term implications. If stagnation persists the labor pressure for a thirty-five hour week is going to assume dangerous proportions and what this would do to our balance of payments problem is not pleasant to contemplate. Furthermore, as firms operate at relatively low levels of capacity, the expectations on which price and investment policies are based are bound to be affected. There is some evidence of this already, and there is enough in the administered price doctrine to justify a fear that in many markets adjustment of price policies to lower use of capacity is a relatively easy matter. A real danger of stagnation is that in an economy in which economic units are large enough to resist the pressure of market forces it will induce policies and practices that insure the persistence of stagnation.

But, having recognized that no one of the numerous protagonists is likely to have a monopoly of the truth, how is the relationship of the various interest groups to each other and to government in the United States likely to affect the choice among various possible stabilization and growth policies? To deal with this question it is necessary to say something about these relationships, to consider what limitations, if any, they impose on policy choices, and to offer an opinion on the question whether, in view of these limitations, the possibilities that seem to be open are adequate to the problems that confront us.

There is an old saying to the effect that every country gets the socialists it deserves. It is equally true that every country gets the government, the type of business leaders, and the forms of labor organization it deserves. This is no more than to observe that institutions and group relations are shaped in an historical context that differs substantially from country to country. It is clear to the most obtuse observer that there is a much more distant relationship between business and government leadership in the United States, than, say, in Britain, France, or the Netherlands. The Federation of British Industries has an entree to government, whether Conservative or Labour, that neither the National Association of Manufacturers nor the Chamber of Commerce has or, for that matter, would desire. A British businessman can say, "Some of my best friends are civil servants," and really mean it. This would be rare in the United States.

In France the relationship, at least since the war, has been even closer. The type of planning favored in France brings together government and business decision-makers, with their technicians, on a long series of critical economic issues. I shall want to say something later about the relevance of French practice to the United States but it is obvious that what is called indicative planning in France demands intimate government-business collaboration. In the Netherlands, government, business, and labor collaborate on a national wage policy and government and business participate jointly in other aspects of aggregative planning.

The relationship between government and business in the United States can only be described as one of latent hostility which occasionally, as in the past year, breaks out into rather more open hostility. The traditional visitor from Mars becoming privy to significant domestic events of the last twelve months including the steel decision, the behavior of the stock market, antitrust actions, and speeches of various high government officials, would be hard put to it to explain the bitterness expressed in many quarters. He could only conclude, I believe, that these expressions arose from frustrations and resentments lying deeper in the environment than the surface mirrored by these events. A search for the source of these deeper manifestations leads one, I would suppose, to consideration of certain obvious facts of geography and physical environment, of the still undigested consequences of the revolutionary change in the role of government brought about by the events of the 1930's and the war, and going further back, to consideration of the unique position attained by business in the United States in the period after the Civil War.

What significance is to be attached to the fact that Washington is a purely governmental city without industry and that the industrial centers in the United States are generally far removed from this political focus, I do not know. The fact that London and Paris are both political and business centers no doubt helps to give the old school tie greater scope than it would otherwise have. But the size and geographical dispersion of our population would in any case prevent this kind of concentration even if our business and political centers were one. The dispersion, however, does not adequately explain what seems to me a much sharper separation of elite groups, government, business, professional, artistic, academic, etc. than one encounters in most Western European countries. Despite the continuing rapid vertical social mobility in the United States horizontal penetration appears to encounter greater difficulties. Recently two outstanding businessmen have commented on certain aspects of this phenomenon. Clarence Randall has alleged that as business executives move up in the hierarchy their circle of contacts narrows and that they tend to reach a stage at the top where they talk only to themselves. A Bostonian might be entitled to feel that this is even worse than talking only to God. Ralph Lazarus has taken note of the suburban golden ghettos in which well-to-do business and professional men preserve their families from any contact with more sordid, but perhaps livelier, elements of American civilization. However this may be, it seems probable that the size, geographical dispersion, and racial heterogeneity of population have some part to play in explaining the relative distance between government and business in the United States.

Much more important, in my opinion, is the fact that the really revolutionary changes in the role of government and in the relation of various groups to government produced by the great depression and the war have not yet been fully accepted in this country. Where counterrevolution is still considered to be a possibility no one is quite prepared to lay down his arms. This, of course, puts the matter too strongly, but there continues to be a conflict between what in fact—and quite demonstrably—has happened and the views that are held in various quarters concerning the possibilities of action in the light of these facts. Characterizing the situation in the broadest possible terms I am inclined to emphasize the following developments: Government expenditures as a percentage of gross national product have, of course, increased enormously since the 1920's. If one lumps federal, state, and local expenditures together they are currently running at twice the volume of gross private capital formation in the United States. It is obvious, therefore, that variations in these expenditures and in the relation between tax revenues and expenditures can have an effect on aggregate demand, output, and employment that was out of the question in the 1920's. At the same time the role of government in the process of economic decision-making, its "weight," if I may use the term, has in many ways not increased commensurately with its share in total outlays.

Although the relative growth of the public sector has necessarily meant a relative decline in the position of the private sector there has been no significant change in the predominant role assigned to business in the process of capital formation and the direction of investment. Even at the depth of the depression in the United States when business leadership was in nearly total eclipse the voices raised in favor of expansion of government ownership or a larger role in the direction of resource use were feeble and ineffective. The Tennessee Valley Authority was about the only "socialistic" action that can be attributed to the New Deal. The lasting changes of the 1930's were mainly in the fields of social welfare, labor-management relations, and the regulation of capital markets. The great increases in government expenditures came, of course, during and after the war. An observer of the current scene can hardly fail to be impressed by the absence of doctrinal dispute on the proper role of business. Government ownership is a dead issue if, indeed, it ever was a live one. Government regulation of public utilities on which much hope was placed at the turn of the century is in at least partial eclipse. The demand, particularly in the field of transportation, is for less rather than for more. Government has gone very far in turning over to, or permitting business participation in, decisions which elsewhere are made only by government. This tendency has been most pronounced in the field of research and development but it extends also to the loan insurance and loan guarantee schemes of the Federal Housing Authority and is part of a more general trend toward "contracting out" functions that government proposes to support. This is one reason why federal employment has not increased as rapidly as federal expenditures. But it also suggests that there is very little disposition in this country for government encroachment on traditional areas of business responsibility.

Part of the reason for a failure of both government and business to adjust adequately to the change in this relative command over resources is the rapidity with which the change was accomplished. If one examines the history of federal expenditures as a percentage of gross national product there was a continuous decline from about 5 per cent in 1870 (when federal finances still bore some of the Civil War Impact) to roughly 2 per cent in 1912, 1913, and 1914.[1] The First World War, of course, greatly increased this percentage but it is remarkable how rapidly and completely the share of the federal government expenditures in GNP declined after the war. Despite a sizeable increase in interest payments on the public debt the share of total federal expenditures in GNP was only 4.6 per cent in 1922 and declined to 3 per cent in 1929. In that year federal expenditures were less than half of state and local expenditures but all government expenditures as a percentage of national income were distinctly lower than in most Western European countries. The rise in government expenditures began much earlier in Western Europe, and this longer period of growth, it may be conjectured, has had something to do with an obviously more complete assimilation of the changed role of government by the community as a whole.

The great increase in federal expenditures both as a percentage of GNP and in relation to state and local expenditures began only in the 1930's. The share of federal expenditures in GNP increased from 4.1 per cent in 1930 to around 10 per cent by the end of the decade. This high percentage reflected, of course, both the large public expenditure for newly introduced social services, and the low level of GNP still laboring under massive unemployment. Federal civilian expenditures as a percentage of state and local expenditures reached a high point of 52 per cent in 1948 and have declined somewhat since then. It is interesting to note that federal civilian expenditures as a percentage of GNP have not increased since 1938 [5, p. 50]. After a very rapid reduction in military expenditures following the war the disturbed international situation has produced a level of federal outlays that shows little tendency to decline. National defense expenditures accounted for 85 per cent of federal purchases of goods and services in 1961 and total federal expenditures amounted to over 19 per cent of GNP. This is to be compared with the 3 per cent figure in 1929. Big Government in the sense of a big sector of the economy is a comparatively recent phenomenon in the United States and there is evidence that we have not yet completely accommodated ourselves to this fact.

If one wishes to push the analysis of government-business relations farther back in time he would need to take account of the extraordinary position acquired by business in the society after the Civil War. It is probably not too much to say that its supremacy was contested by no other elite. The Civil War in destroying the plantation aristocracy had eliminated one potential rival. And, as Schumpeter has emphasized, U. S.

[1] The figures in this paragraph are taken from Kendrick [5, pp. 10–11].

business developed in an environment in which it did not have to contend
with an aristocracy by birth from whose numbers have come so many
members of the ruling class in Western Europe. As late as the 1920's
Calvin Coolidge could say with conviction and pride that "The business
of America is business," and be understood by his fellow citizens.

So far as labor organizations are concerned, the growth of trade unions
with government encouragement and assistance has, of course, had a
profound effect on labor-management relations not only in the area of
unionization but outside. Furthermore, I think it can safely be said that
unions are here to stay. Concerning the relation of American unionism to
stabilization and growth policy two observations seem pertinent. It is
clear by now that one cannot look to American labor for anything in the
way of social or political initiative. As one observer puts it, "The labor
movement in the United States has taken pride in the fact that it is
non-ideological. It has revelled in its bread-and-butter or pork chop
personality [1, p. 124]." Higher wages, more job security and, if substantial unemployment persists, a demand for a shorter work week, pretty
much define the area of union initiative. Secondly, the development of
U. S. unionism has been such as to make the formulation or implementation of anything like a national wage policy extraordinarily difficult. Power
is more decentralized than in almost any Western European labor movement and all informed students agree that a nationally organized and
nationally effective trade union organization is a necessary, though not
sufficient, condition to a successful national wage policy. It may be
expected that labor leadership will pronounce in favor of increased government expenditures and of tax reduction concentrating on the lower
income brackets, though how much effect this has on the voting tendencies of the rank and file it is difficult to say. Bearing these considerations in
mind it is perhaps fair to say that organized labor's role with respect to
stabilization and growth policy is apt to be passive rather than active. It
can obstruct certain courses of action; it can support others; but it is
unlikely to initiate.

How does this melange of special interests, conflicting ideologies, and
ignorance affect the prospects for stabilization and growth in the United
States and the choice of means thereto? The influence of what, for want of
a better word, I shall call institutional considerations seems to me large;
larger than is sometimes assumed by our "aggregative" colleagues. They
not only help to explain differences in the response in different economies
to objectively similar stimuli but in a particular economy bring about
changes over time in the relationship of various magnitudes that make the
life of forecasters and policy planners difficult. More important, these
considerations tend, at any particular time, to set definite limits to what it
is desirable or feasible to attempt in the direction of stabilization policy.

The French approach to stabilization and growth, or even the Dutch, both of which, at least superficially, seem eminently successful in their own environment, have very little relevance for U. S. conditions. To begin with, it would have to be recognized that it is impossible to determine to what extent the recent growth rate in France is to be attributed to so-called "indicative" planning. Growth rates in Germany and Italy have been at least as striking without the benefit of anything that could properly be called planning. Indeed the German economy seems, in some respects, to be less "directed" than our own. The projections of various economic magnitudes with which we are so liberally supplied by the Council of Economic Advisers and other agencies are almost completely lacking there. In France numerous other influences, in addition to planning, may have a bearing on stabilization and growth. One could mention the monetary reforms of 1958; the current and anticipatory effects of the Common Market; the opportunities for technological advance offered by postwar reconstruction and capital replacement; the development, with higher per capita incomes, of economic activities in which scale economies are important; the continued existence of bottlenecks providing lucrative investment opportunities; and, no doubt, many others. Indeed, as one regards the metamorphosis of the French entrepreneur, within a relatively few years, from the traditional "lazy man of Europe" into his present bustling, expansive incarnation one wonders whether economic analysis can provide all the answers.

Insofar, however, as French planning has made a significant contribution to stability and growth its main impact, it appears to me, has been on the degree of uncertainty surrounding both public and private investment decisions. French planning does seem to have been able to make growth targets credible to the people who make investment decisions. This appears to have been made possible by an extraordinarily close association of business men and public officials assisted by competent technical advice. The tentative investment decisions are binding neither on the government nor on business but since representatives of both have participated actively in the planning process there are reciprocal expectations that become difficult to ignore. And as expectations have tended, by and large, to be fulfilled, uncertainties surrounding new decisions diminish.

Reflection, however, on the institutional arrangements that make such an enterprise possible and fruitful in France serves only to suggest how unpracticable this model is for the United States, even if it were considered to be desirable. Government accounts for from 35 to 40 per cent of capital formation in France and consequently public investment decisions are matters of moment to business. A long cartel tradition has accustomed French business to industry planning. The postwar necessities of reconstruction and replacement required government-business cooperation, and relationships useful to present planning activities were developed.

Inadequacies of capital markets in France have encouraged government financing of private enterprise and close control of security issues. French labor has either not been strong enough to inject itself effectively into the planning process or has been willing to leave these matters to government and business. Possibly the softening of partisan activities and the downgrading of parliamentary procedures under a quasi-dictatorial regime have encouraged a certain degree of *dirigisme* in the economy. In any case it should be obvious that there is little in the French situation that is directly relevant to U. S. practice.

The same thing must be said of the Netherlands, though the Dutch do not attempt anything as ambitious as the direction of investment among sectors. The so-called aggregative planning of the Netherlands is scarcely more than effective stabilization policy with growth left to take care of itself. Even so, the institutional relationships that make this policy effective are largely lacking in the United States. Although there has been no great pressure for public ownership in the Netherlands, government operation of railways, public utilities, and mines and extensive participation in land reclamation schemes assures a large share for government in total capital formation. Wages have been subject to comprehensive control since 1945 and the advisory Labor Foundation, representing centrally organized management and labor groups has played a dominant role in the formulation of wage policy [6, pp. 41–42]. The very great dependence of the Netherlands on foreign trade makes the balance of payments a critical element in stabilization policy and helps to assure that fiscal and monetary measures designed to promote stability are not undermined by conflicting wage and price policies. Dutch planning, moreover, is assisted by highly competent technical advice which tends to be heeded by policy-making authorities.

When one considers these and other examples of successful stabilization and growth policies in Western Europe it becomes clear that their transfer to the United States would be impractical without very large changes in institutional relationships. This does not mean that successful stabilization policy is impossible in the United States but it does mean that certain policy instruments are not available. Undoubtedly the lack is most striking in the wage-price field which Samuelson has called "the biggest unsolved economic problem of our time [8, p. 360]." That this problem is not limited to the United States is indicated by the plea of the OEEC experts on "The Problem of Rising Prices" for a national wage policy.[2] Nevertheless, both the difficulties and our lack of progress in this area seem more striking than elsewhere. In Norway and the Netherlands government participates with centrally organized labor and management

---

[2] "In the view of the majority of the group, the essential element, to be stressed first of all, is that the stabilization authorities must have a wages policy for dealing with the problem of wages—just as they must have monetary and fiscal policies for dealing with the problem of demand" [10, p. 56].

groups in the formulation of a relatively successful national wage policy. In Sweden, although wage rates are nationally negotiated without government participation, much attention is given to a wage policy designed to stabilize prices at full employment [7, p. 93]. None of the countries of Western Europe has been able wholly to avoid "wage-drift" or an upward price creep but this has tended to take place at 1.5 or 2 per cent unemployment rather than at 4 to 5 per cent.

Certainly the difficulties confronting anything like a national wage policy in this country are formidable. We lack the nationally organized management and labor groups which are a necessary though not sufficient condition. The significance of relative balance in international payments which has made wage-price stability of critical importance in a number of Western European countries has only recently become apparent in the United States. Opposition in this country both in management and labor circles to government intervention in the wage-price field is stronger than elsewhere. And in general it would have to be said that there is a distrust of governmental initiative in the whole area of stabilization policy that is lacking in Western Europe [4, p. 108].

How significant the absence of a wage-price policy is likely to be for effective stabilization measures appears to me to depend principally on two relatively unknown considerations. The first has to do with the question whether the forces that in the period 1953–58 produced an annual 3 per cent per man-hour increase in output, a 4½ per cent increase per hour in total compensation, and a 2.1 per cent increase in wholesale prices have significantly changed [3, p. 137]. That there have been important changes bearing on this problem there can be no doubt. The attitudes and expectation suggested by the phrase "inflation as a way of life" have certainly suffered a severe blow. In a number of basic industries which have hitherto been leaders in the wage push a combination of relatively slow secular increase in output with massive technological change having serious employment effects will inevitably moderate wage demands. In the very important field of national defense industries national security considerations tend inevitably to damp both wage and price initiatives. Finally, persistence of a serious balance-of-payments problem will force government intervention in certain wage or price decisions regardless of labor or business attitudes.

The second consideration has to do with whether an approach toward fuller use of capacity will release, with increased investment, that flood of technical improvements the expansionists foresee. It is certainly quite possible, if the wage-price creep can be held to modest proportions, that the competitive position of U. S. exports would be improved rather than lessened by a closer approach to full employment.

However that may be, it is probably correct to say that the absence of a national wage policy does and will continue significantly to affect our stabilization policy. The effect is already clearly visible in the current definition of full employment as 4 per cent unemployment. The expectation of a wage-price creep helps to explain why full employment does not enjoy the high priority in the stabilization trinity of employment, price level, and balance of payments it appears to enjoy in Western Europe. And it probably means that monetary and fiscal measures will tend to be employed tentatively and step by step pending a testing of wage and price effects.

The second major policy instrument that tends to be blunted by the group interests and ideologies here under consideration is fiscal policy. I neglect the question of monetary policy for what seem to me the adequate reasons that neither the quasi-independence of monetary authority nor the interests and ideas of special groups offer a serious obstacle to a monetary policy oriented toward stability and growth.[3] The same thing cannot be said of fiscal policy. Minor reasons for a lack of flexibility in this instrument are such restraints as debt ceilings and interest limitations on government securities. The major difficulties, however, are deeply held views on the desirability of budgetary balance, suspicion of almost any increase in government spending, conflicting views of interest groups on proper changes in the tax structure, and, above all, a general distrust of government as a manager of the economic environment. As one observer has noted, "Counter-cyclical finance is attacked by conservatives in the United States because of fear of irresponsible extension of government power while in Europe it has been recognized as a conservative alternative to more extreme government intervention [9, p. 605]."

It is somewhat difficult to understand the conservative American view since there is no discernible support in the United States for government ownership or control of activities now in the private sector. Indeed, as I have pointed out, there is a strong disposition to "contract out" to private enterprise services that tend elsewhere to be performed by government. It seems possible that, over the longer run, this absence of ideological conflict in the traditional sphere of government versus private ownership may facilitate the development of a flexible fiscal policy. In the shorter run, however, the obstacles are formidable. Perhaps the critical questions are these: Will predilections for a budget that is balanced, at least over the business cycle, prevent a shift in fiscal policy toward a budget that is balanced only at full employment? And will the tax reduction that may be involved in this process strike some kind of an acceptable balance between the incentives to investment demanded by the business group and the stimulus to consumption demanded by labor? If not, the prospects for successful stabilization policy are much darker than they need be.

In any case, the relative weakness of policy instruments in the United

---

[3] Although the monetary authority is certainly subject to strong pressures, its quasi-independent status appears to provide enough insulation to permit effective resistance.

States and the latent hostility apparent in government-business relations tends to deprive growth targets of any operational significance. It may be useful to project a 4 per cent growth rate at full employment as a rough indication of the extent to which actual performance falls short of potential but it cannot be assumed that any one is going to do anything about it. The limitations that our institutional structure plus current balance-of-payments considerations place upon the relevant possibilities of action tend to deprive such targets of the credibility they would need to possess in order significantly to affect business decision-making.

It seems probable that any one of the "radical" plans for handling the balance-of-payments problem such as increasing the price of gold, devaluation, or expanding the reserve functions of the International Monetary Fund, might open up new opportunities for stabilization policy. It seems probable that none of these courses of action will be followed. It is more likely that, if relief is provided, it will take the form of a reduction of foreign, particularly economic, aid programs. But whether this happens or not the balance of payments as an essential part of the stabilization problem promises to be with us for a long time.

In spite of the obstacles to effective stabilization and growth policies stressed in this paper, the United States may nevertheless move toward a satisfactory growth rate within a context of relative stability. The acceleration of family formation foreseen for the mid-'60's, an unexpectedly rapid exploitation of new technological possibilities, or even unplanned changes in labor-management or other group relationships, might make such a development possible. I have too little confidence in economic forecasts including my own to deny this possibility. But it does seem clear that any approach to a satisfactory situation with respect to stability and growth will owe much less to deliberate policy and much more to autonomous developments in the economy than has been true in recent years in Western Europe. And for this the historically determined relationships between government, business, and labor are largely responsible.

REFERENCES

1. NEIL CHAMBERLAIN, "The Corporation and the Trade Union," in E. S. Mason, ed., *The Corporation and Modern Society*. Cambridge 1959.
2. E. F. DENISON, *The Sources of Economic Growth in the United States and the Alternatives Before Us*, Committee for Economic Development Supplementary Paper 13. New York 1962.
3. J. T. DUNLOP, "Policy Problems" in American Assembly, *Wages, Prices, Profits and Productivity*. New York 1959.
4. MILTON GILBERT, "The Postwar Business Cycle in Western Europe," *Am. Econ. Rev., Proc.*, May 1962, 52, 93–109.

5. M. SLADE KENDRICK, *A Century and a Half of Federal Expenditures,* Nat. Bur. Econ. Research Occas. Paper 48. New York 1955.
6. M. W. LEISERSON, "A Brief Interpretive Survey of Wage-Price Problems in Europe," Study Paper 11, Joint Economic Committee. Washington 1959.
7. B. C. ROBERTS, *National Wages Policy in War and Peace.* London 1958.
8. P. A. SAMUELSON, *Economics,* 4th ed. New York 1958.
9. P. B. TRESCOTT, Review of *United States Fiscal Policy 1945–1949* by A. E. Holmans in *Am. Econ. Rev.,* June 1962, *52,* 605–6.
10. Organization for European Economic Cooperation, *The Problem of Rising Prices.* Paris 1961.
11. President's Committee to Appraise Employment and Unemployment Statistics, *Measuring Employment and Unemployment.* Washington 1962.
12. U. S. Congress, Joint Economic Committee, *State of the Economy and Policies for Full Employment.* Washington 1962.

Index

Abramovitz, Moses, 247
Abrams, Charles, 582
Adair, William, 417
Adams, Charles Francis, Jr., 367
Adams, Henry, 226, 231
Adams, John Quincy, 243
Adams, J. T., 9
Administration of the Colonies, 115
Affluent Society, The, 563, 569
Agricultural Workers Organization (A.W.O.), 347 ff.
agriculture, 128, 328 ff., 486
  vs. economic growth, 258 ff.
  in Northwest, 330
  financing of, 332 f.
  Federal aid to, 337, 514 ff.
  market expansion, 517
  future of, 520
Albion, Robert G., 269, 270
Aldrich, Nelson W., 439
Aldrich-Vreeland Act, 438
Allen, Francis O., 41, 46
Allen, Frederick Lewis, 372, 378
Allen, James S., 309
American Agricultural Chemical Company, 397
American Democracy, The, 355
American Federation of Labor (A.F.L.), 303, 353, 357, 359
American Railroad Journal, 201, 204, 326
American Railway Union (A.R.U.), 415
American system, 190, 196
  historians of, 179 f.
American Tobacco Co., 388
Anderson, John, 297
Andrews, Charles M., 23, 51, 53, 105
Annapolis, Md., 68
Appleton, Nathan, 148
Aptheker, Herbert, 377
Arber, Edward, 48
Ashleigh, Charles, 352
Ashton, Thomas S., 13, 74, 77, 79, 81, 86
Astor, John Jacob, 129

Astor, William B., 325
Atkinson, Edward, 311, 316, 317, 321, 366
Atlantic Monthly, 364
automobile industry, 465 ff.

Bacon, Edward P., 443
Bacon, Thomas, 61
Baer, George F., 368
Bailyn, Bernard, 2
Baker, O. E., 337, 340
baking industry, 430
balance of payments, 591, 602
balance of trade, 246 ff.
Baldwin, F. E., 31
Baldwin, R. E., 261
Baltimore, Md., 133
Baltimore and Ohio Railroad, 191, 192, 204
Baltimore Company, 3, 65–67, 72–73, 77
  trade with England, 78 ff.
Banister, John, 80
banking, 230 f., 436 ff., 469, 497 f., 503, 522
Banks, 228, 230
  of North America, 132, 136
  of Massachusetts, 136
  First United States, 138, 174, 229
  Second United States, 174, 224 ff.
  Indiana State Bank, 232
  of Missouri, 232
  of Iowa, 232
Barker, Charles A., 73
Barnard, J. G., 212
Bassett, John S., 225, 227, 228, 234
Baumgartner, J. Hampton, 447
Baxter, William T., 100, 105
Beachley, Charles E., 400
Beale, Howard K., 308, 309
Bean, Louis H., 338
Beard, Charles, 308, 364, 368, 377, 435
Beard, Earl S., 178, 205
Beard, Mary R., 308, 364, 435

1D23498